Executive Compensation

EXECUTIVE COMPENSATION

The Professional's Guide

to

Current Issues & Practices

Series Editors

Michael L. Davis · Jerry T. Edge

Windsor Professional Information

San Diego

Requests for permission or further information should be addressed to:
Permissions Department
Windsor Professional Information
11835 Carmel Mountain Road, Suite 1304
San Diego, CA 92128
or
info@windsorpub.com

This publication is designed to provide accurate and authoritative information
in regard to the subject matter covered. It is sold with the understanding the publisher
is not engaged in rendering legal, accounting, or other professional services.
If legal advice or other expert assistance is required, the services of a
competent professional should be sought.

−From a Declaration of Principles jointly adopted by a
Committee of the American Bar Association and a Committee of Publishers

Library of Congress Cataloging-in-Publication Data
Windsor Professional Information.
Executive Compensation
p. cm.
Includes index
1. Executives−Salaries, etc. I. Title
ISBN 1-893190-25-0

Printed in the United States of America

First Edition

The paper used in this publication meets the minimum requirements of the
American National Standard for Information Sciences−
Permanence of Paper for Printed Library Materials

TABLE OF CONTENTS

PART I

Framework for Executive Compensation/Total Rewards

1. A Strategic View of Executive Compensation

2. Linking Executive Compensation Strategy to Business Strategy

3. Developing an Executive Total Rewards Strategic Plan

PART II

Key Elements of Executive Compensation and Benefits

4. The Design and Use of Short Term Variable Pay Plans

5. Executive Stock Options

6. Executive Benefits and Perquisites: An Overview of Current Trends and Programs

7. Deferred Compensation Plans

PART III

Advanced Topics in Executive Total Remuneration

PART IV

Special Topics in Executive Total Remuneration

FOREWORD

by Frederic W. Cook

THE CURRENT TIMES IN EXECUTIVE COMPENSATION are not only dynamic and challenging, but also propitious for those in the profession; for this is a time when their knowledge and expertise is both needed and valued most highly. In every profession, there will always be those who provide leadership, whether in thought or action. This publication, by seeking to sponsor and facilitate the availability of such information, serves the interests of the individual professional and the profession as a whole.

This book is created for compensation professionals at work either within or as consultants to business organizations. Specifically, the book is aimed at those who practice, or aspire to practice, at the most demanding and highest profile level in the compensation field: executive compensation. An executive compensation professional is one who brings the knowledge, skill and practices of compensation planning to assist organizations in attracting, retaining and motivating their top management and other key employees in pursuit of the organization's mission. He or she may work inside the company–in essence having one client, or may work within a consulting firm advising many clients.

The top of the executive compensation profession on the corporate side is the senior compensation professional of a large multi-business global corporation with direct access to senior management, the CEO and the independent compensation committee of the board of directors. On the consulting side, the top of the profession is the executive compensation consultant who leads his or her firm's work in advising top management and the independent compensation committee of the board on top-level compensation issues.

This new publication, with its available updates and links to web-based resources, can give the aspiring and the experienced executive compensation professional an "advanced degree" in the practice of executive compensation. The consummate professional, however, will know that complete guidance will not come from the page, but rather from "between the lines," as only you can provide the integrity and resolve to use these skills in pursuit of worthy aims.

Once the executive compensation professional has the requisite skills to practice at the highest level, it is necessary that he or she do so with good judgment and integrity. This requires a sure sense of self and the ability to discern the right course of action from wrong. Powerful people in business are often motivated by money and may seek to use the staff resources of the company, or its outside consultants, to achieve their own financial ends rather than the good of the company as a whole. It is easy to become drawn into this powerful vortex. To prevent this, it is essential that you practice your skills with independence and to refuse to have your skills be manipulated or prostituted in the course of others' pursuit of wrongful ends.

Among its other definitions, independence is the ability to speak truth to power, to say no when something is being proposed or pursued that is wrong. It is not always easy, but is always rewarding. To do the right thing means having your self-respect as well as that of your peers. The reputation of our shared profession as a whole is—and will be—comprised of our actions as individuals.

Everyone works for someone else, whether as a staff executive or outside advisor. And that "someone else" often controls your pay or fees. Yet that person does not own you or your work. Only you do. Your loyalty belongs not to the person approving your pay or fees, but to the total organization whose interests you serve and to the compensation profession of which we are members. Those who are confused as to where their loyalties lie are destined to pay a price in terms of both their careers and self-respect that will not be off-set by any level of "success."

Look beneath any corporate scandal and you will find a complicit corporate staff or outside advisors who became co-opted by immoral leadership and who became vested in protecting wrongdoing rather than exposing it. It is ironic but perhaps understandable that calls for reform include calls for greater independence and resolve on the part of in-house staff professionals and outside advisors. So too it is with the executive compensation field. Michael Wilson, chairman of the Canadian Coalition for Good Governance, has said that compensation "is at the heart of many governance problems." Reform groups with the best interests of business at heart are calling for independent compensation committees to have their own compensation consultants beholden only to them and with no divided loyalties. And they are calling for greater skill and independence on the part of in-house compensation professionals who will have direct access and responsibility to the independent committee on matters that come before it. These two trends are not in conflict but can operate in partnership for the long-term benefit of the organization.

There exist now a few pioneer executive compensation professionals in large companies who have been designated as having a dual reporting relationship, responsible to both senior management and to the chair of the compensation committee on executive compensation matters. To be able to handle the potential conflicts in this relationship and to be held in high regard by both is the mark of a true professional. It is something that cannot be granted; it must be earned.

The same holds true for the executive compensation consultant. One point of view, in current vogue, is that the outside consultant or the consulting firm must do no work for management as this is thought to co-opt his or her independence. But, just as we do not want our in-house professionals to be advocates for top management, we do not want our outside consultants to be advocates for the compensation committee, unless untrustworthy top management creates the need for an adversarial relationship.

In the same way that the top of the executive compensation profession on the corporate side is reserved for those select few who work for both management and the board, so too is the top of the executive compensation consulting field reserved for those select few who can work in cooperation with management on behalf of the independent compensation committee, while maintaining the trust and high regard of both, and for the good of the organization as a whole.

FREDERIC W. COOK

PREFACE

WHEN WE BEGAN THIS UNDERTAKING our interest was in serving two purposes; one focused on advancing understanding, the other on facilitating action. By providing a "hub" to forward the knowledge of some of the best and brightest in the profession the publication would serve the former. By imbuing it with templates, samples and practical tools we would serve the latter. But during the long writing period, with the business land-scape awash in compensation and governance-related headlines, we were constantly reminded not only of the need for such a publication but also that the real goal must be to see that professional understanding and action be one and the same.

Executive compensation has historically been something of a hot topic, particularly during the time of year when corporate proxy statements were issued. In the past, the coverage could almost be confused with sports scores; with the news focused on who got the biggest option grant, the biggest raise, the biggest bonus, or the biggest severance package. Today, however, the topic of executive compensation receives more substantive and meaningful attention. On the surface, and for those of us in the profession, this would appear to be very good news. But, as with many things, it is a situation where the good ramifications are not without the company of the bad.

Leading the good ramifications is the fact that there is now greater understanding–within the business, academic, government, legal and corporate governance circles–of what we in the profession have held for some time: that executive compensation programs have the power to guide and motivate behavior. Designed properly, executive compensation programs can help a company focus its energies, develop winning strategies, drive innovation, and lead to operational and financial success. But the bad, and axiomatic, ramification is that, designed improperly, many now believe these programs can lead a management team down a dark path; to consider almost anything to achieve "success"–even activities that are deceptive, fraudulent, or illegal. We have come to see both outcomes in recent years and, as a result, both the spotlight and the bar have been increased for executive compensation and for those involved in its design, administration or oversight.

In this first edition, seventeen key topics have been thoughtfully analyzed and discussed by twenty-four leaders in the executive compensation field. Every chapter is supplemented to provide additional information and, on the accompanying CD, many chapters provide checklists, templates, or project plans for reviewing, auditing or designing one or more elements of an executive compensation program. Depending upon the need, an individual chapter can help a practitioner solve specific issues, or the publication can stand as an overall reference, covering the major components of an integrated executive compensation program.

As shown in the Table of Contents, the seventeen chapters are divided into four overall sections. Part I provides three chapters that are overarching and strategic in nature. The intent of these chapters is to be holistic; looking at executive compensation in totality and in its strategic context. Part II provides four chapters that focus on specific key elements of an executive compensation program: variable pay plans, stock plans, benefits and perquisites, and deferred compensation. Part III provides four additional chapters on advanced topics: corporate governance, compensation committees, performance measures and goals, and business unit incentive plans. Lastly, Part IV provides six chapters on special topics in executive compensation. This includes coverage of employment agreements, regulatory issues, and director compensation. It also covers highly nuanced issues in executive compensation in three distinct groupings of companies: non-public and foreign-owned companies, pre-IPO and high growth companies, and restructurings, spin-offs and divestitures.

We expect there to be significant change in the years ahead and it is our plan that this be an on-going project. New editions will present new topics and featured contributors. Between editions it is our intention to keep the publication updated as executive compensation trends and practices evolve. Readers wishing to receive updates as they are made available may do so either by sending an email to EXECOMPUPDATES@WINDSORPUB.COM or by visiting the Web site ExecutiveCompensationLeadership.com and registering.

ACKNOWLEDGEMENTS

T HIS PUBLICATION HAS OBVIOUSLY INVOLVED the work of many people. We would first like to thank the twelve companies and twenty-four authors for their contributions and thoughtful input to this first edition. The reader will find information on each contributor at the end of their respective chapter(s). Given the technical nature of this work, we also had an extended list of technical reviewers who provided an extra set of eyes for reviewing various materials found in the 17 chapters. They included: Donald Ledbetter of L-3 Communications, Tim Haigh of W.T. Haigh & Associates, Stephen R. Fussell of Abbott Labs, David West, Esq. of Gibson and Dunn, Cathy Kennedy of Eli Lilly, David Eng of American Express, John Hillins of Amgen, Brad Fusco of AT&T, Donna Ng of Avon, Sarah Armstrong of Campbell Soup, Tony Farina of Citigroup, Charles Bell of Dow Chemical, Carl Jacobs of Aon Consulting, Les Jackson of Compensation Consultants, William Caldwell of Caldwell Consulting, and Matt Ward of Aon Consulting. We thank them for this necessary and important help.

Lastly, a heartfelt thanks to our publisher, Rick Hammonds, at Windsor Professional Information. This undertaking was for us both new and sometimes challenging. Rick coached us through the entire process and provided encouragement throughout, including a gentle prod from time-to-time when needed. Rick's strong support and great counsel have led to the completion of this extraordinary new publication.

MLD and JTE
February 2004

1. A Strategic View of Executive Compensation

Our first author takes a strategic look at executive compensation, examining how it fits into the broader executive total rewards umbrella and the company's strategy as a whole. A company expects many things of an executive; financial results, while important, are not the only goal. Likewise, the executive is working for more than just pay, although it is clearly important. Providing a functional structure for understanding how these needs fit together–potentially either synergistically or conflictingly–is the chapter's overall goal.

The executive total rewards model sets the tone for both the framework and context for executive compensation. The traditional elements of executive compensation–base salary, short and long term incentives–are introduced, but the need for income continuity is also discussed, as well as the importance of leadership development and performance, and executive resource planning. The model highlights the importance of executive compensation, but also sets the stage for executive pay in our current business environment. Near the chapter's end, the author makes a final observation that rings particularly true for so many today –"In today's more sober business culture, the how in achieving success takes on greater relevance." Executive compensation may be currently under a microscope, but it is as relevant as ever. –Editors

B USINESS LEADERS ARE UNDER STRONG and unrelenting pressure to perform. Though few top executives are actually fired, the business press reports almost weekly on business leaders who have chosen to resign for failing to meet expectations. We all have read reports such as: The 55-year old executive who became a widely admired star in the late 1990's, and built (the Company) into a Wall Street darling, resigned abruptly for personal reasons, or; The CEO's tarnished credibility with investors has become a major issue of concern for the Board. Eroding support from key board members is expected to lead to (the CEO's) resignation in the next few days. CEO's of the Fortune 500 now have average job tenure of 5.4 years, down almost 20% from 7.0 years at the start of the 1990s.

In addition, executive pay programs and pay levels are under pressure, and not just for abuses. There is a basic demand for a return on the investment by owners. In the early 2nd quarter each year, following the release of proxies and annual reports by most public companies, Forbes magazine addresses this concern by providing its readers with a report on the "Best Bosses and the Worst for the Buck." They are looking to find which executives delivered the greatest return to shareholders and, while doing so, took the most reasonable paycheck.

Is this just "executive bashing?" Not at all. Leadership does make a difference. Companies with outstanding leadership deliver outstanding results, as the late 1990s McKinsey study *War for Talent* found. Fortune magazine annually selects its 100 Best Companies to work for in large part based on the effective operating culture created by the organization's leaders. These same "best-led companies" have consistently outperformed the other S&P 500 companies almost 2 to 1 in shareholder returns. Consistent members of this annual list of Best Companies, such as Southwest Airlines and Johnson and Johnson, are known for top performance and strong leadership cultures built on respect and trust.

Increasingly, companies are expanding the focus of executive compensation to support development of leaders as well as accomplishment of results. They are seeking a dynamic talent pool of executive leaders that can provide a competitive advantage not easily duplicated and create a foundation for long-term financial success. This more integrated approach to executive reward programs–that we will call Executive Total Rewards–is characterized by individual accountability and recognition of the value of investing in human capital, both for the employer and the executive. Executive Total Rewards binds executives and their company in a mutually beneficial deal that is, in general, similar to the broad-based total rewards systems now recognized and used successfully by many large employers.

The following example briefly points out the importance of supporting both leadership development and a high performance culture in an executive total rewards program. A few years ago, I interviewed an executive in a three-horse race to become chief executive officer at a large retail bank in the Midwest. At one point, the discussion came around to potential expansion of executive rewards to add a retention bonus and/or a post-termination income continuance provision to encourage the three CEO candidates to stay through the transition of leadership, whether they were selected or not. The executive told me: "You know, it's not really about the money. I do want the security, it's not unimportant. But the real problem here is that right now we are a mediocre bank, and I'm not growing in terms of my experience or my demonstrated success. If I finish second in the race

2

for CEO and choose to go back out in the market as the number-two executive at a mediocre financial institution, I'm dead. But if we could improve our performance, and if I could be a significant part of that, then I don't care whether I finish first or second, because if I lose I'm still the number-two executive at the leading retail banking institution in the country. I am valuable, whether it is here or somewhere else."

Executive Total Rewards programs are a high-level deal between the Company and the executive contingent on both parties maintaining an acceptable return on their investment at all times. Executives expect direct pay (salary, annual and longer-term incentives), income security (e.g., employment contracts, portable retirement benefits, deferred compensation) and career progression (in responsibilities, power and control, and achievement). The company, in return, expects the executive to achieve specific performance goals, including developing capabilities and exhibiting important leadership qualities that will influence behavior of others in sustaining a successful enterprise.

The "Deal" in Executive Total Rewards

Being capable and possessing the attributes of a leader is great, but leaders must produce results. David Ulrich in his popular book, *Results-Based Leadership*, also says an exclusive focus on results does not work well either. Driving leaders to do whatever it takes can risk the lack of sustainable results. He suggests leaders must strive for excellence in both attributes (e.g., setting direction, mobilizing commitment, engendering organization capability and demonstrating personal character) and results. The outcome is more than cumulative, Ulrich says, it is a multiplier–Effective leadership = Attributes x Results.

The deal in Executive Total Rewards utilizes Ulrich's philosophy and builds on the answers to 4 questions, shown below. These questions are the same ones used in the business planning process by leading public companies and in the not-for-profit environment, as well. We will look briefly at organizations that can provide us concrete examples of these foundation questions and their use:

1. **What results are we seeking?** Executive Total Rewards begins with a focus on results. At HP, under former CEO Lew Platt, the Company's annual planning process started with 1 to 3 overarching strategic goals for the Company, articulated by Mr. Platt. Top operating leaders throughout the Company were then asked to identify what results must be obtained in

your business in order to achieve the strategic goals. The CEO sought unity on the responses to his question as a prerequisite for creating his desired results orientation.

Executive Total Rewards are designed to support achievement of these results. All of the components of the reward program must be evaluated in terms of their ability to contribute to attaining these results. They must be looked at for consistency and thoroughness; that is, creating results across all levels of the organization that lead to attaining the strategic goals. In particular, reward programs should ensure understanding and effective measurement of desired results if they are going to contribute to improvement and goal attainment. Tools such as value driver analysis can help in this evaluation of the rewards program.

2. **Who will provide leadership and deliver these results?** Lucent Technologies has historically used a "personal leadership agenda" as a tool to get at this question. Managers at all levels are asked to respond to 3 questions each year as part of the annual planning and goal setting process. The first is simply "What results do you need to achieve?" The second question is "One a scale of 1 to 100, how ready are you to produce these results today?" Not surprisingly, most scored themselves 60 to 70. Finally, they are asked "What must you learn and do to make these results happen?" The focus in the last question is on the character, knowledge and behaviors they must pursue to achieve the desired results.

In Executive Total Rewards organizations need a leadership framework linked to results. The focus is on actions that create results, as shown in the capability column in the following example. Notice how the various responsibilities, capabilities and results are clearly sorted and defined according to executive level.

Level	Responsibility	Capability*	Results
1	■ Create a framework ■ Identify opportunities ■ Sell the vision ■ Articulate risks ■ Select leaders	■ Create effective strategy/seize opportunities ■ Inspire others ■ Build effective business relations ■ Negotiable effectively	■ Shareholder returns ■ Growth ■ Investment Efficiency ■ Talent pool of current leader
2	■ Set standards ■ Evaluate opportunities ■ Assess risks ■ Develop leaders	■ Apply strategy/identify opportunities ■ Provide direction ■ Build consensus ■ Model behaviors desired ■ Inspire others	■ Operating efficiently ■ New business start-up and implementation ■ Future leaders talent pool
3	■ Develop business plans ■ Staff efficiently ■ Execute opportunities ■ Control risks ■ Identify future leaders	■ Identify value drivers ■ Balance competitinginterests ■ Monitor progress ■ Evaluate behavior ■ Create results	■ Business plan execution ■ Process improvements ■ Develop leaders

*Actions that create results

Notice, too, that the desired capabilities at each level of responsibility are linked closely to the desired resultsæa necessary building block for developing a reward structure linked to performance.

3. ***What will attract these leaders to the organization?*** Most effective leaders are attracted to organizations with the opportunity and resources needed to achieve results. Though the list of what will attract leaders will vary by individual, the following are some of the more common elements needed to attract top leaders:

The potential to create a legacy. This involves some or all of the following:

• Launching a new business, product, concept or facility.
• Turning around a struggling business.
• Some protection from the risks involved with these challenges.

Resources for creating success

• The presence of a high performance culture.
• A willingness of the organization to invest.
• Human capital.

Long-term earnings potential

• Direct pay that provides the opportunity to share in business success.
• Career opportunities that enhance the individual's value to the current or next organization.

The four quadrants of an Executive Total Rewards program mirror the above list. They are shown in the graphic below.

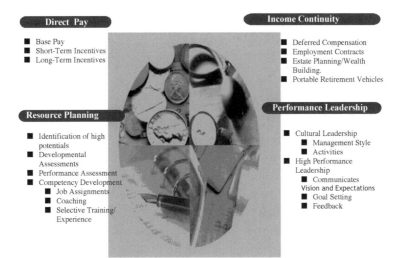

Direct Pay
- Base Pay
- Short-Term Incentives
- Long-Term Incentives

Income Continuity
- Deferred Compensation
- Employment Contracts
- Estate Planning/Wealth Building.
- Portable Retirement Vehicles

Resource Planning
- Identification of high potentials
- Developmental Assessments
- Performance Assessment
- Competency Development
  - Job Assignments
  - Coaching
  - Selective Training/Experience

Performance Leadership
- Cultural Leadership
  - Management Style
  - Activities
- High Performance Leadership
  - Communicates Vision and Expectations
  - Goal Setting
  - Feedback

What will cause these leaders to develop to their full potential?

Business leaders who have achieved at significant levels are internally moti-vated to develop and grow. The challenge for most organizations is to tap into that internal motivation by giving them the opportunities that will allow them to grow. An organization's leadership must:

• Have the freedom to achieve the goals set out in the strategy. John Bachmann, Managing Partner of Edward Jones, a leading private brokerage firm and *Fortune*'s Best Company to Work For in 2002, works with his key leaders to set direction and then gives them the freedom to make decisions consistent with that direction.

• Be given career enhancing opportunities as recognition for their achievement. The Chief Financial Officer of Merck was given the opportunity to run two new joint ventures to provide needed operating experience to advance her career. These opportunities were, among other things, recognition for her unique contributions as CFO and in particular in her contributions in evaluating investments in research and development.

• Be paid for achievement as a form of recognition. Most leaders view the dollars they receive in performance incentives as a statement about their level of accomplishment. This is one reason individual accountability in Executive Total Rewards is so important. This will be discussed in more detail immediately below.

• Be held accountable for actions that yield short-term results at the expense of long-term success. The executive pay programs at companies such as Tyco and Enron were severely criticized in late 2001 and early 2002 for enriching top management just prior to major financial problems for both businesses.

One more point to develop before moving to the individual elements of Executive Total Rewards is the importance of individual accountability.

Rewards that Emphasize the Individual More than the Job Held

General Electric, on the forefront of leadership development for over two decades, was also one of the first companies to adopt broad bands for salary management for its professional workforce. Jack Welch later commented that the broad bands were designed to give the Company greater flexibility to recognize individuals and individual contributions more than paying for the job. He said the role of his leaders was to do more than their job. It was their responsibility to discover what was needed to make a business successful and then do it.

In Executive Total Rewards, there is a primary emphasis on the individual and individual accountability more than just the job held by that individual. This can be seen in the table below where the individual (capability) and individual accountability (results) are reflected in nearly all elements of executive total rewards.

If leaders make a difference and function in "transformational roles," searching for opportunities to change the status quo, inspiring others to excel and fostering collaboration through shared visions of the future, these individuals need to be developed and recognized as individuals, and held accountable, as well.

This emphasis on individual accountability may not be entirely appropriate for leaders who are focused on maintaining a steady state and generally get performance from others by offering rewards, what we typically think of as managers or transactional leaders. These were the types of roles on which job-based pay systems were built and remain valid as tools for supporting these behaviors.

The Elements of Executive Total Rewards

Let us now look at some common designs for each of the key elements of Executive Total Rewards. The programs described herein are examples of actual programs that we know from client experience have been effective. Obviously, each organization should vary these design features and the relative value of each to suit its specific executive pay philosophy and to meet its own market and business needs.

Direct Pay

Base Salary

In Executive Total Rewards, the system of annual base salary increases is often replaced with a system of executive salary plans. The shortcomings of

Typical Determinants of Total Rewards Elements

Base Salary	Annual Incentive	Long-term Incentive	Career Development
Responsibility, Capability, Short-term Success	Short-term Success	Long-term Success	Capability, Short-term Success

annual pay increases are that they utilize a backward look at short-term success and movement in market pay rates to provide a going forward pay increase that represents a career annuity for the executive's tenure with the Company.

Executive salary planning still starts with market pay data, the company's desired competitive position in the market and market-based pay ranges. As we noted in the GE example earlier, these can even be broad bands. Next, the organization charts a base salary path over the next several years for each executive.

Salary plans are built using an assumed level of consistent performance for the executive going forward. At this level of responsibility, uneven performance–and certainly performance below expectations–cannot be tolerated. If the executive performs at levels below what is expected in the salary plan, continued employment is at risk.

Another key element of the salary plan is inputs on the growth in individual responsibility anticipated for the individual executive. Simply, a company may want to move a near term promotable executive over time to a pay level above market median. A simple example is shown below:

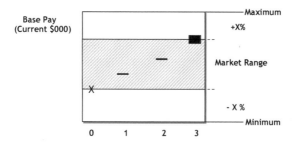

Results:	Meets Expectations
Responsibility and Capability:	Promotable at End of Three Years
Plan:	Move Base Pay to Top of Market Range in Three Years

	Current Year	Year 1	Year 2	Year 3
Annual Base	$200,000	$213,000	$230,000	$260,000
Market Median	$220,000	$226,600	$232,200	$238,000
(% Increase)	N/A	3.0%	2.5%	2.5%
% Base Increase	-	6.5%	8.0%	13.0%
Timing	January	January	April	July
Timing/Interval	12 months	12 months	15 months	15 months
Market Ratio*	.90	.94	.99	1.09
W-2 Salary	$200,000	$213,000	$225,750	$245,000
% Inc. W-2	-	6.5%	6.0%	8.5%

*Ratio of Annualized Base Salary to Median of Market Range

In essence, salary plans provide a context for a pay decision that includes market, performance and career development. The effort required in subsequent years is reduced, though salary plans are adjusted as individual circumstances change.

Annual Incentive

In the context of Executive Total Rewards, annual incentive plans retain many of the characteristics typical of annual incentive plans for executives. Some of the best practices for annual incentive plan design in general can be drawn from *Highlights from the 2003 Towers Perrin Annual Incentive Plan Design Survey.*

In order to insure individual accountability in the annual incentive, an important component of Executive Total Rewards, the following practices differ from majority practice highlighted in the Towers Perrin survey are commonly used:

• Quantitative performance standards are benchmarked to the marketplace to insure that individual pay is aligned with individual levels of results achieved.

• The typical subjective component will be significant, 30% to 50% of the total weighting of factors determining individual bonus amounts, depending on the individual's role. Staff positions, such as a controller, will likely have the largest subjective component. The subjective component will focus on "actions that create results," as noted earlier in this chapter.

This approach does not mean that organizations are creating individual incentive plans for each executive. Quite the contrary. All participants are linked together in the process of creating the funds available to pay bonuses. Total funds available remain linked to the degree of attainment of overall financial objectives. For example, a company that achieves a targeted level on annual EBIT (Earnings Before Interest and Taxes) growth might start with an overall incentive fund equal to the target bonus opportunity of all the participants. Allocation of the total fund to each individual executive will rely on a combination of company, operating unit and individual accomplishments.

Long–Term Incentives

The same principal of individual accountability that applies in annual bonus plans also applies to long-term incentives in an Executive Total Rewards program. The most common long-term incentive element, a stock option, does not recognize individual leadership or provide an opportunity related to individual contributions.

In Executive Total Rewards, additional performance criteria beyond stock price growth will creep into stock option plans. The specific method for introducing performance criteria wills depend in part on the Financial Accounting Standards Boards rules for accounting for stock-based compensation in effect at the time of the stock option award. Under APB-25, the rule in effect through at least 2004, a plan such as the performance truncating options below would have been used. If FAS-123 replaces APB-25 for fiscal years beginning on or after December 15, 2004, as anticipated, plans such as performance contingent options below are much more likely to be used.

Both approaches introduce greater individual accountability in the option program.

Performance truncating option: The option has a typical 10 year term to exercise with the added provision that the option holder achieve a specified objective interim performance goal by the end of the period set for vesting, typically 5 years. If the goal is achieved, the options continue to have a ten year term. If not, the options will vest but expire 31–60 days after vesting.

Performance contingent options: The option has a vesting schedule that is contingent on the degree of attainment of a specified performance objective during the period set for vesting. To the degree performance falls short of the objective, but within a specified range of the objective, a portion of the option will be forfeited. If performance is below the performance range specified for full or partial vesting, the entire option may be forfeited.

Another unique approach to longer-term incentives in Executive Total Rewards comes in stock ownership guidelines. Here the concept is to incorporate anticipated career progression into a standardized set of ownership targets. For example, a company may start with a common set of guidelines as shown below in the first two columns, and then make modifications as shown in the two right hand columns. Additions move the executive forward in anticipation of a promotion to a higher level. Reductions allow some diversification as an executive nears the end of a career.

Level	Standard Ownership Target (Salary Multiple)	Addition, if Promotable in 1-3 years	Reduction, if Career Duration 3 Years or less
CEO	5.0	N/A	N/A
Elected Officers	4.0	.5	1.0–1.5
Senior Vice-Pres.	3.0	.5	1.0–1.5
All Other Partners	2.0	.5	.5–1.0

Income Continuity Programs

For executives today, life with any organization doesn't last very long, even when financial times are good. This is a reality of contemporary corporate culture. Executives know and accept this reality, but they expect to be paid accordingly. Income continuity programs can provide a foundation for both the company and executive to make human capital investments efficiently, even if the period of employment turns out to be relatively short.

Portability is one important element of income security and continuity for the executive. It is also consistent with the concept of individual responsibility in Executive Total Rewards. Portable income security vehicles discussed below, such as nonqualified retirement supplements, provide support for the executive in managing his/her own wealth building opportunities over a career.

The other important element is income protection. Many executives face not only the risk of job loss as a threat to their income, but also non-compete or non-disclosure agreements that limit their near-term opportunities for future employment following termination. The consideration in these agreements is clear for the company. For the executive, consideration typically comes in the form of severance agreements or employment agreements, which guarantee post-termination continuance of salary, annual bonus and benefits, typically for periods of two to three years.

Though still a relatively small portion of the value of most executives' total pay (15% or less), these income continuity programs are growing in absolute value along with the overall levels of executive pay. More organizations are including income continuity programs in the measurement of the competitiveness of their executive pay. An example is Towers Perrin's web-based tool called *Executive Total R* that adds the value of the key income continuity programs to direct pay in assessing the competitiveness of an executive's total pay.

Three key elements of income continuity programs, portable retirement vehicles, severance contracts, and voluntary deferred compensation plans are discussed in more detail below.

Portable Retirement Vehicles

All other things being equal, two pensions each covering 10 years of continuous service in two successive 10-year periods with different organizations, will not provide a benefit equal to one pension covering the same 20 years of continuous service with one company. Job change often significantly reduces the value of defined benefit pension plans.

In defined contribution plans, such as 401(k), or hybrid plans, such as cash balance plans, there is greater portability than in defined benefit pensions, but termination can still cause the loss of unvested benefits.

Portable nonqualified retirement vehicles are an important part of most income continuity programs for executives. To varying degrees, these plans are designed to eliminate the effects of job change on wealth accumulation through the company-sponsored retirement vehicle(s). Three types of nonqualified retirement programs are described below, two fairly common plans and one rather unique plan.

1. **Supplemental pensions:** These plans are most often "make up" plans that are designed to overcome the loss of benefits from a break in service. Recognition of a portion of past service with a prior employer or crediting service at a higher rate (e.g., 1.5 years of service for each 1.0 year of service) with the new employer are common provisions in these supplemental pension plans.

2. **Supplemental defined contribution plans:** These plans may also be "make-up" plans, but often have an element designed to enrich the wealth building for retirement for the executive. As a make-up plan, a lump sum contribution equal to a desired projected supplemental annuity value at retirement could be made. As plan enhancements, executives may receive a contribution rate higher than that offered in the qualified plan. Vesting in these supplemental contributions is often immediate or very short term, 1 to 3 years. These plans are often more popular with younger executives and still leave the executive responsible for managing his/her investments of the funds.

3. **Restricted stock awards:** This less common approach uses restricted company stock awards and subsequent appreciation to fund a portable retirement benefit. The company's contribution in the form of restricted stock functions similar to the supplemental defined contribution plans above, but all of the investment earnings are in company stock appreciation. Unlike the supplemental defined contribution plans, however, the asset appreciation is not a charge to earnings. Benefits typically vest pro rata over 3 to 5 years and penalties occur for sale of stock prior to retirement.

Severance Contracts

At a recent meeting of the compensation committee of the board of a client company, the committee chairman asked, "Why should we give (the executive) a contract that will guarantee two to three years pay when we decide to get rid of him for failing to meet our desired objectives? At the very least, let's leave it to our discretion."

This philosophy toward severance contracts expressed by the director is not uncommon. However, it may also limit a company's ability to attract or retain top executive talent. A survey by Executive Compensation Advisory Services in early 2002 found nearly 90% of CEO's in the largest U.S. companies now have contracts that provide continuance of salary, benefits and annual bonus for periods of typically two to three years following an involuntary severance without cause. Some companies will require the executive to agree to a non-compete or non-disclosure provision as a requirement for receiving these benefits, but in general, few other tangible advantages inure to the company.

Severance contracts are often part of broader contractual arrangements between corporate officers and the company, such as change of control agreements or employment contracts. However, for purposes of Executive Total Rewards, the critical element is the income protection provided in the severance provisions of the agreement.

Voluntary Nonqualified Deferred Compensation

These plans provide an executive the flexibility to manage the timing of receipt of his/her compensation combined with the added benefit of tax deferral. The deferrals can cushion either changes in income or expenditures. For example, in a year when annual bonuses are large, an executive can "squirrel-away" a portion of that money pretax to pay for future one-time expenditures such as college, or as a hedge against below average bonuses in the future. Appreciation credited to the executive in the interim can also accumulate pretax. Payments are taxed as ordinary income when paid.

Though these voluntary elections to defer must be irrevocable and be set for payout at a determinable point in the future to avoid current taxation, this tax standard, in fact, places few limits on the executive. An age 42 executive may simply elect to defer all of his/her current year's bonus for five years and then take principal and interest in a lump sum in the year a child is expected to begin college. Another middle-aged executive with significant cash obligations and a desire to save, might elect to defer any bonus earned in excess of his target bonus for a minimum period of two years, but then payable in the first subsequent year in which the actual bonus is less than the target.

It is important to note that these executives electing deferral are taking a position as general creditors of their employer for payments from these nonqualified plans. Though trust arrangements, such as rabbi trusts, offer a higher level of protection in the event of a change of control, or even a change of heart by the employer, little can be done to protect against bankruptcy of the employer.

Leadership Development

At the levels of direct pay and benefits for today's executives, companies are finding that the marginal return on incremental increases in pay and benefits is small. Studies such as Towers Perrin's 2003 Talent Management Study, *New Realities in Today's Workforce* found that development opportunities and timely and accurate performance feedback are superior ways to get the needed engagement and commitment from leadership necessary to get the desired results.

Executive Total Rewards seeks to balance attainment of critical business results with development of key leadership attributes. This may sometimes mean selecting the candidate for a key executive role based in part on developmental needs and not just that person's ability to deliver results. If necessary, the investment in the selected candidate's development may include securing the team around him/her and providing structure to help insure they deliver results in these "stretch" roles.

I witnessed this process at a large media firm where the CEO and the human resources committee of the board wanted to support the development of the CFO, who was identified in the succession planning process as a top candidate for chief executive, if he could demonstrate operating talent. Following the resignation of the head of its largest business segment, the Company had an easy choice to replace that executive with the top seasoned individual in the same division. However, the company chose the CFO as the business segment head. In doing so, they gave his seasoned competitor for the job the equivalent of a COO job for that business unit. The challenges for the former CFO were to build an effective business relationship with the so-called unit COO, demonstrate his operating skills and identify new business opportunities to grow the business beyond its current scope, all things viewed as necessary for his success later in the potential role of CEO.

There is growing evidence that a company's willingness to invest in this intangible asset, leadership development, is not only a valuable reward to executives, but also key to success in the marketplace and in the company's ability to build value for its owners. Breakthrough research by Towers Perrin and Baruch Lev, the Philip Bardes Professor of Accounting and Finance at New York University's Leonard N. Stern School of Business, shows a strong correlation between a company's investment in human capital and the market value of the firm.

Even if you find it hard to accept some of the tenets of Professor Lev's analysis, you may find the more basic argument offered by Federal Reserve Chairman Alan Greenspan more compelling. The Chairman notes that more value moves over fiber optic cables than over the country's railroads today, and with that a growing recognition of the value that can be created by a company's investment in its human capital as well as its physical capital.

Building an Executive Total Rewards Program

Executive Total Rewards retains many of the elements of what today would be considered a typical executive pay program. What differentiates Executive Total Rewards are the processes used, the expectations for behavior that drives results, and a rewards culture that can be summarized by these five principles:

1. **Manage Leadership Talent.** With Executive Total Rewards, there is a heightened focus on rewards that helps to build the kind of leadership talent the company needs to flourish and stay competitive over the long run. If the organization takes steps outlined in this chapter to build an executive team with the right skills to run the business, using the right reward processes, almost by definition, will be managing talent.

2. **Make the Leaders' Pay More Individualized than Job-Based.** Because the reward system is based on achieved results and the personal characteristics of the individual, pay becomes more individualized and less job-based. Under the old model, a comptroller would be paid for his or her accomplishments in a defined job model, based on execution of a prescribed set of duties that could exist in any of a number of other companies. Under the Executive Total Rewards model, that comptroller is rewarded according to what he or she accomplishes for the organization based on personal performance measures linked to the business strategy.

3. **Recognize Development is a Reward.** Executive Total Rewards recognizes that helping executives advance in their careers, and giving them the opportunities to do so, is part of the reward system. Pay alone, no matter how much, will satisfy the aspirations of creative, energetic people in leadership positions who want a return on their human capital.

4. **Align Performance Expectations with Responsibility and Capability.** This is the flip side to the company's recognition that development is a reward. The executives themselves have a responsibility to meet

performance expectations and grow with the organization in order to meet increasingly demanding performance measures. They have an obligation, based on their level of responsibility, to overcome challenges and achieve at successively higher levels, (for which they receive additional compensation), to help lead the company to greater accomplishments. Companies expect no less.

5. **Pay Decisions Occur in a Longer-Term Context.** With Executive Total Rewards, executive pay is determined according to non-financial measures and other factors that go beyond the traditional short-term criteria for assessing performance, such as annual budget. Budgets, of course, remain important in pay discussions, but the range of factors to evaluate executive performance has widened considerably. High-performing companies have recognized this for some time and have proved that they can thrive using long-term measures (i.e., product innovation, customer satisfaction) in determining executive pay.

At its highest level, Executive Total Rewards is a philosophy of paying people that says, "It's important what you accomplish, but it's also fairly important how you get there." This is an appealing and powerful message today, at a time when executive pay is being challenged in media accounts of abuse at some large corporations and when shareholder demands for leadership accountability are intensifying. If the boom economy of the '80s and '90s proved the extent to which corporations could boost earnings through innovation, increased productivity, global marketing, technology and other areas of accomplishment, perhaps now is a time for corporations to reassess their strategies and what they expect of their executives. Indeed, the rules for achieving profitability may be changing and adding new legal and regulatory constraints. Certainly the ways to measure profits are changing, as demonstrated by the earnings standards issued by Standard & Poor's that exclude pension income and expense stock options. Companies are being bluntly told that there will be more accountability in the perennial quest for profits.

Given these changes in today's more sober business culture, the how in achieving success takes on greater relevance. And that in turn means that successful organizations can help themselves with reward strategies that convey this same message to executives. By contrast, reward systems that lived on off-balance-sheet partnerships and inflated trading have collapsed, as they had to eventually, because they measured success only in the short term and were tied to an unsustainable business model. This is not to say that the pay systems themselves were at fault, but certainly we have seen companies that created executive cultures promoting behavior that was not in the organization's long-term interests.

Executive Total Rewards is not a perfect and all-encompassing solution for designing executive compensation programs. It is relatively new, and because of this organizations that we have worked with have only implemented parts of it. But we have seen these individual elements work well within executive compensation plans, which leads us to believe that a full Executive Total Rewards program can provide an organization with a considerable lift in long-term performance. Executive Total Rewards provides a framework that emphasizes the quality of executive behavior, using some broader measures of performance and a couple of key processes that are grounded in the reality of the market. It can complement and energize traditional incentive designs in executive pay to make sure an organization has the best leaders possible and achieves long-term financial success.

ERIC P. MARQUARDT
Senior Consultant
Towers Perrin

Eric Marquardt specializes in executive and director compensation. He works with leading public and private companies, including many Fortune-ranked companies, on executive pay matters that often focus on effective integration of pay with business strategy, leadership development and operational excellence.

Prior to joining Towers Perrin, Eric was the Director of Executive Compensation for Merck & Co., Inc and also headed the Silicon Valley (Santa Clara, CA), office of another leading consulting firm.

Eric earned a Master of Arts in Labor and Industrial Relations from Michigan State University and a Bachelor of Business Administration from the University of Michigan. He also teaches courses in leadership and in human resources strategy at Washington University, St. Louis, MO.

2. LINKING EXECUTIVE COMPENSATION STRATEGY TO BUSINESS STRATEGY

Defining strategy as "a plan of action intended to accomplish a specific goal" the authors of this chapter present a detailed discussion of both business strategy and compensation strategy; why the two must be in synch and how most successful businesses have particularly clear examples of both. The chapter also provides an interesting overview of five of the major business strategy models, and how each helps the CEO and other senior executives to make informed, strategic decisions about the business.

A model for determining compensation strategy is then presented, with ten specific parameters (design elements) to guide compensation plan design and administration. These parameters cover such topics as pay positioning, pay/performance leverage, comparator group, performance measures and metrics, compensation risk, time horizon, and more.

Business strategy and compensation strategy are interesting, but the magic occurs when the two interrelate and support each other to effectively drive the business. Sensing that many companies may have at least partial misalignment between the two, the authors provide two easy-to-follow models that will be helpful to most compensation practitioners–a five question model for determining whether or not business strategy and compensation strategy are aligned, and a five step process for creating stronger linkage/alignment between the two strategies as needed. –Editors

I N THE 1990s, AN OIL AND GAS Services Company (EnergyCo) was successfully pursuing a strategy of consolidation in a highly fragmented industry. While the company had no defined compensation strategy, its competitive pay positioning and incentives reflected a highly entrepreneurial environment: very low base salaries relative to the market, a performance-oriented, yet subjective, annual bonus program, and a unique and highly leveraged long-term incentive plan. EnergyCo's compensation strategy was not defined, but the lack of structure served EnergyCo well during its initial growth phase, when it acquired many of the smaller players in the industry –most of which had similar entrepreneurial cultures.

However, as EnergyCo matured and grew into a larger organization, the company's strategy shifted to the acquisition of mid-sized and larger players in the industry. Unlike earlier acquisitions, the companies being acquired had the performance and pay structures of larger, more mature organizations. EnergyCo found that it could not successfully integrate employees into its highly leveraged compensation framework. Internal pay equity issues surfaced, leading to morale and retention problems among EnergyCo's employees. In addition, the company began to experience difficulty in attracting executive talent. The lack of alignment of EnergyCo's entrepreneurial compensation strategy with its size and maturity—and the size and maturity of its acquisition targets—presented tremendous challenges for the company. Rather than using compensation strategy as a tool to facilitate execution of business strategy, EnergyCo's compensation strategy became a significant obstacle.

This chapter defines what is meant by business strategy and compensation strategy, and describes the importance of aligning the two. It provides tools to help recognize gaps between business and compensation strategy, and steps for building alignment. These tools and processes will help human resource (HR) professionals avoid situations like EnergyCo's.

Introduction: The Strategic Role of HR Professionals

HR professionals are expected to fulfill many roles: strategist, tactician and administrator. The "strategist" develops principles, policies and action plans to maximize the company's return on human capital (e.g., leadership profile, organization design, talent development, decision-making processes, etc.).

Exhibit 1: Investments in human capital are significant

- Rewards are one of an organization's largest controllable expense items and, despite the size, are often poorly managed
- An organization's *future* success is dependent upon human capital performance more than any other factor

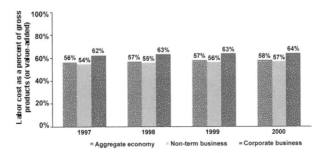

The "tactician" implements these strategies (e.g., communicates new incentive plans, implements new management development programs, etc.). The "administrator" manages HR programs on a day-to-day basis (e.g., internal job postings, employee information, merit increases, incentive payouts, etc.).

Until recently, the strategist role for HR professionals was not explicitly acknowledged. However, recent trends have increased the importance of the strategic role. These trends include: (1) the significant increase in competition for talent; (2) increasing recognition by executives and shareholders of the importance of human capital relative to financial capital; and (3) increasingly larger company investments in human capital through compensation, training and development, and other "people" programs. (See Exhibit 1.)

Due to the increasing importance of human capital, HR is expected to serve as a strategic business partner to all critical internal and external constituencies. This requires a fundamental shift in mindset among HR professionals about how they view themselves and their role.

As the role of HR professionals has become more strategic, so too has the role of compensation evolved. (See Exhibit 2.)

Prior to the 1980s, the primary compensation issues being addressed were how much to pay and how to manage total compensation costs.

In the 1980s, the strategic business environment evolved to focus on achieving a stronger pay-for-performance relationship. Compensation programs began to focus more on tying pay to performance through incentive programs and on emphasizing equity incentives, such as stock options. Unfortunately, while most variable pay programs were (and still are)

Exhibit 2: Today, HR is increasingly viewed as a strategic partner in achieving business success

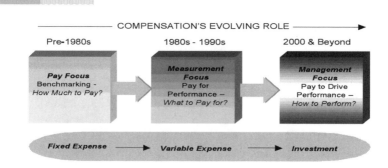

closely tied to performance and business results, many were (and some are still) "bonus" programs rather than "incentive" programs. In other words, program participants earn awards when performance is achieved, even though few participants know what to do differently to affect their pay. Compensation is driven by performance, but performance is not yet driven by pay.

"Many variable pay programs are still *bonus* plans, not *incentive* programs."

Today, shareholders, Boards of Directors and the media are renewing the emphasis on performance and also are beginning to recognize the shortfalls of many of the popular compensation practices of the 1990s. For example, while stock options rewarded executives for increasing stock prices, many executives reaped windfall gains from stock price increases that were a function of overall stock market performance, rather than company operating performance. As a result, stock options provided reward for performance that was largely outside of executives' control.

To address these shortcomings, compensation design is continuing to evolve from the traditional pay-for-performance approach into a strategic tool that, more directly, drives rather than follows business results. (See Exhibit 3.)

The remainder of this chapter discusses how to use compensation strategy as a lever to ensure the successful execution of your business strategy.

Exhibit 3: Pay is increasingly viewed as a management tool to drive business results and create shareholder value

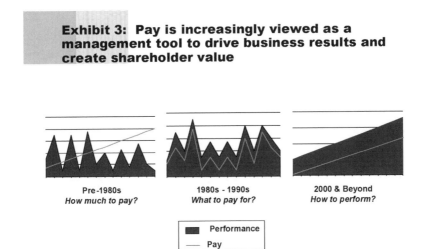

| Pre-1980s | 1980s - 1990s | 2000 & Beyond |
| *How much to pay?* | *What to pay for?* | *How to perform?* |

Performance
Pay

What are Business Strategy and Compensation Strategy?

strat·e·gy \strat-ə-jē\ *n*
"A plan of action...intended to accomplish a specific goal."

"Strategy" is a term that has been defined by many experts in business over the years. Many common definitions include references to competitive position, industry dynamics, products, customers, core competencies, activities, decisions and behaviors. However, strategy can be defined simply as, "a plan of action to accomplish a specific goal."

Southwest Airlines is an example of a company that has a well-articulated and well-executed business strategy. Southwest's strategy is to offer no-frills, on-time, low-cost and friendly air travel. To support its strategy, Southwest's business model maximizes the efficiency of airport turnarounds, keeps operating costs low and provides a fun work environment. The operational decisions that have been made to execute this strategy have included flying a single type of jet, Boeing 737s, to minimize maintenance and pilot training expenses; using smaller, less congested airports; keeping fuel costs down through hedging strategies; maintaining positive relations with its unions; and keeping its employees happy.

Strategy Evaluation Frameworks

Many different strategic frameworks have been developed to help companies understand and evaluate the business environment, and define the right strategy. These strategic frameworks are intended to be used as tools to help HR professionals understand the external industry environment dynamics, a company's competitive position within the industry, and a company's business strategy to maintain and improve its competitive position. HR professionals must be conversant in strategic tools like these to fully realize their value as a strategic business partner. A few of the more well-known strategic frameworks include:

• Market Economics/Competitive Position (ME/CP)

• Growth/Share Matrix

• Five Forces

• Customer Centric Business Design

• Seven Degrees of Freedom for Growth

Let's now look at each of these in more detail.

Market Economics/Competitive Position (ME/CP)

Marakon Associates' ME/CP framework (See Exhibit 4.) helps the strategist understand value creation potential by evaluating a company's position along two key strategic dimensions: (1) the attractiveness of the industry in which the business operates, and (2) the businesses' competitive position within the industry.

The ME/CP can assess the value-creation potential of a company overall or of a company's different business units.

Businesses in the upper right quadrant–those that are in high growth industries with limited competition, and that have differentiated products and unique competitive advantages–offer the greatest value-creation potential. Conversely, companies in the lower left quadrant face the highest probability of destroying value rather than creating it. Companies in the remaining two quadrants can increase their value creation potential by competing in more attractive industry segments or by maintaining a strong competitive position in relatively unattractive industries.

This framework can be developed with qualitative information, or alternatively, businesses can be plotted on the matrix through rigorous analysis of financial and operating data.

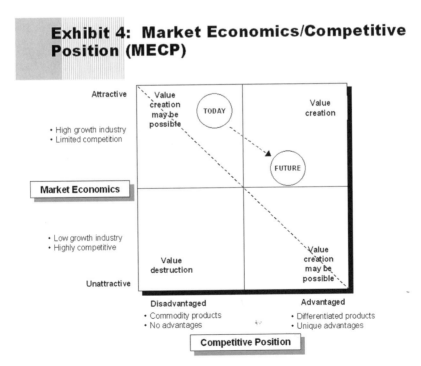

Exhibit 4: Market Economics/Competitive Position (MECP)

Exhibit 5: Growth/Share Matrix

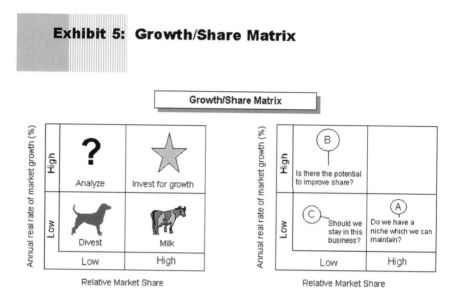

Growth/Share Matrix

Growth/Share Matrix

Boston Consulting Group (BCG) developed a framework to evaluate a company's business portfolio and the implication of each business or product and its cash generation needs (or alternatively, its potential to generate cash). (See Exhibit 5.)

Each business/product's need for cash is a function of the growth rate of its market, and its market share. This framework is based on several key ideas: Profitability and cash generation are a function of share of market; growth requires cash investments to finance additional assets; improvements in market share must be earned or bought; and no market can grow indefinitely—when growth slows and excess cash cannot be reinvested profitably in slower growth markets, excess cash can be returned to shareholders.

Businesses/products with high market share in low growth markets are "cash cows." They generally generate cash in excess of what can be profitably reinvested in the business. Businesses or products that have high share of high growth markets are "stars." If their businesses maintain their leadership position, they will eventually become cash cows. Businesses or products with low share of low growth markets are "dogs" and have little value. Businesses with low share of high growth markets are "question marks." They require more cash to gain market share than they can generate on their own.

Five Forces

Michael Porter of the Harvard Business School developed the Five Forces (see Exhibit 6.) to evaluate the relative attractiveness of an industry. In his book, *Competitive Strategy*, Porter describes the five forces that help to characterize the structural determinants of the intensity of competition in an industry: Threat of new entrants; bargaining power of buyers; threat of substitute products or services; bargaining power of suppliers; and rivalry among existing competitors. Examples of each of these forces can be found in Exhibit 5. Evaluating an industry using the Five Forces can provide numerous insights into the dynamics affecting companies in a given sector of the market. The stronger each force, the less attractive the industry or market segment.

Profit Zone Customer Centric Business Design

Mercer Management Consulting's framework, described by Adrian Slywotsky and David Morrison in *The Profit Zone*, suggests beginning an approach to business design and strategy by understanding where customers will allow profit to be made. Rather than a product-driven approach to business, working backward from the customer allows companies to stay focused on the "profit zone" and understand how the profit zone is shifting. A customer-centric evaluation of your company's strategic value chain (see Exhibit 7.) can identify key strategic priorities for your business.

Exhibit 6: Five Forces

"Threat of Entry"
- Economies of scale
- Proprietary product differences
- Brand identity
- Capital requirements
- Learning curve
- Switching costs
- Access to distribution, key inputs

"Bargaining Power of Suppliers"
- Size and concentration of suppliers to industry buyers
- Presence of substitutes
- Buyer switching costs
- Buyer information
- Differentiation of inputs
- Importance of volume
- Cost relative to total purchases
- Impact on cost/differentiation
- Threat of forward integration

"Intensity of Competition"
- Industry growth
- Number/diversity of competitors
- Product differentiation
- Brand identity
- Customer switching costs
- Industry growth
- Exit barriers
- Capacity utilization

"Bargaining Power of Buyers"
- Size and concentration of buyers
- Differentiation of inputs
- Costs of switching suppliers
- Presence of substitute products
- Buyer volume
- Buyer information
- Ability to backward integrate
- Price as % of total inputs
- Buyer profits

"Threat of Substitutes"
- Relative price/performance of substitutes
- Switching costs
- Growth of substitutes

Exhibit 7: Customer-centric Business Design

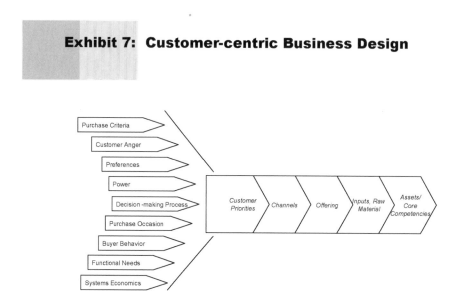

Seven Degrees of Freedom for Growth

McKinsey's Seven Degrees of Freedom (see Exhibit 8.) described in *The Alchemy of Growth*, is a framework that can help systematically identify new growth opportunities. By exploring each "degree of freedom" in turn, a company maintains a broad perspective on potential sources of growth in the business.

Each degree of freedom considers new strategic directions, rather than strategic vehicles (such as mergers and acquisitions or moving to an online sales format). Comparison of strategic alternatives across degrees of freedom is useful in sparking productive discussion of business priorities.

These are just five of numerous different tools that are available to help understand your company's business strategy, industry dynamics, and competitive position. Once business strategy has been articulated and evaluated, human capital strategy implications can be identified and an effective compensation strategy can be developed to support and reinforce your company's business strategy.

Compensation Strategy

Compensation strategy sets the objectives for the compensation programs and describes the general approach for the programs and processes. A well-articulated compensation strategy will define a number of different parameters

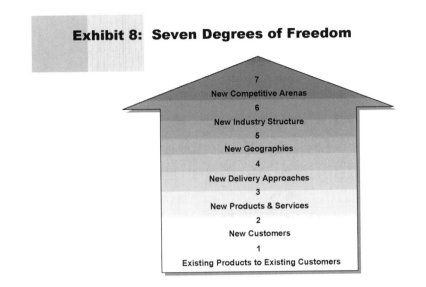

Exhibit 8: Seven Degrees of Freedom

to provide guidance for the design and administration of pay structure and incentive design.

The parameters of an effective compensation strategy include:

• Comparator Group

• Pay positioning

• Pay risk profile

• Participation

• Performance Measures

• Performance Benchmarks and Goals

• Leverage (i.e., relationship between pay and performance)

• Linkage

• Time Horizon

• Vehicles

Exhibit 9 further explains these parameters and shows an example of how each of these parameters can be articulated.

For different companies, industries, and business situations, certain components of compensation strategy are more important than others. For Zeta Manufacturing Company, vehicles (cash rather than equity) and performance measures (operating cash flow) were the most important elements of a new compensation strategy. As Zeta's business strategy evolved from acquisition-oriented growth to a turnaround focused on organic growth

Exhibit 9: Compensation Strategy Elements

Compensation Strategy Components		
Parameter	Description	Example
Comparator Group	Defines the universe of peer companies that will be used to evaluate the competitiveness of specific pay practices (prevalence of vehicles/ programs), pay levels (salaries, incentive opportunities), and to evaluate performance (financial, operating, market performance); Can be a specific set of companies, an industry index/sector, or general industry data	"includes all companies in our industry SIC code, from $5 billion to $20 billion in revenue"
Pay Positioning	Specifies how pay levels are targeted relative to the comparator group	"base salaries are positioned slightly below market median, with total compensation competitive with the median of the comparator group"
Pay Risk Profile	Defines the emphasis on the fixed (salary, benefits, perquisites) and variable components of total rewards, relative to the comparator group	"we intend to provide a pay profile slightly more risky than comparable companies, with at- or below-market base salaries and benefits, but bonus opportunities significantly above market"
Participation	Defines the appropriate participation group for different variable pay programs	"equity incentives are limited to our executive officers who can most directly affect stock price performance"
Performance Measures	Identifies the criteria by which performance will be measured in the annual and long-term incentive programs	"annual bonuses will be based on measures of operating performance, including EBITDA, EPS, ROA, Net Income; long- term incentives will utilize measures of long-term sustainable shareholder value such as Economic Profit and TSR"
Performance Benchmarks and Goals	Defines the level of performance to which the company aspires; Can be relative to comparator group companies, relative to internal budgets/plans, or relative to a standard (e.g., cost of capital)	"we target a level of financial performance equivalent to place our company above the median of our peers, while providing a return on equity over the long term in excess of our 15% cost of equity"
Leverage	Defines the relationship between pay and performance	"in our long-term performance bonus bank, each 1% increase in 3-yr average ROE above our cost of equity will result in a 10% increase in the value of the bonus bank"
Linkage	Defines organizational entity(ies) for which performance will be measured (corporate, business unit, department, team, individual)	"incentive awards for executive officers will be based 100% on corporate performance; all other participants will be 50% corporate and 50% business unit performance"
Time Horizon	Defines the appropriate time periods for measure and evaluating performance for short- and long-term incentive programs	"the short-term incentive program will measure performance on an annual basis; the long-term performance plan will evaluate performance over rolling three-year cycles"
Vehicles	Specifies the use and role of cash and equity vehicles in short and long-term incentive programs	"the short-term incentive will be paid 50% in cash and 50% in stock; LTI awards will be delivered through annual grants of stock options"

and operating profit improvement, it required a new compensation strategy to reflect the change. Zeta abandoned its growth-through-acquisition strategy when performance turned south. Zeta brought in a new management team, which stabilized the business, rationalized assets and prepared the business for a return to profitability.

To facilitate this strategy, Zeta recognized the need for a new compensation strategy that would define a tight linkage between pay and performance. Further, since well over 90% of Zeta's stock options were "under water," options had little to no perceived value among senior managers.

For its performance metric, Zeta decided to focus on growth in operating cash flow (defined as earnings before interest, taxes, depreciation and amortization, or EBITDA). Since the key measure of the company's survival was debt service, EBITDA allowed the company to closely track interest coverage and gauge its ability to maintain the current business. The second key parameter of its compensation strategy was the vehicle used for the long-term incentive. Due to the low perceived value of stock options, Zeta decided to shift its long-term incentive vehicle from stock options to a new long-term cash-based incentive. The long-term cash program enabled the executive team to establish very clear operating cash flow goals, and easily communicate the relationship between pay and performance. Zeta's new compensation strategy is illustrated in Exhibit 10.

Exhibit 10: Example Compensation Strategy – Zeta

Zeta Senior Management Compensation Strategy		
Issue	**Corporate**	**Business Units**
Overall Target Market Pay Positioning	Competitive total cash compensation opportunity, with significant wealth creation opportunity upon achievement of 2005 corporate EBITDA goal	
Market Pay Comparators	General Industry (at similar revenue size); Internal needs-based opportunity	
Pay Risk Profile	More risk-oriented than market; highly leveraged to 2005 EBITDA goal	
Annual Bonus — **Performance Measures**	Corporate EBITDA in 2005	50% Unit EBITDA/ 50% Corporate EBITDA
Long-Term Incentive Strategy — **LTI Mix**	• 100% stock options for CEO, CFO, COO (50% performance-accelerated vesting) • 100% Cash for other participating executives	
Long-Term Incentive Strategy — **LTI - Performance Measures**	• Corporate EBITDA goal in 2005 (with smaller opportunities for achievement of annual performance milestones)	

Linking Compensation Strategy to Business Strategy

To fully understand the link between business strategy and compensation strategy, the HR professional must have an understanding of an organization's overall goal and should help craft the strategies it will deploy to achieve the goal. Every organization's goal is to maximize stakeholder value. In not-for-profit organizations, key stakeholders can include the community (for organizations like colleges, hospitals, and charitable organizations), customers (purchasing cooperatives like TruServe), suppliers (marketing cooperatives like Ocean Spray), employees or other groups. The Value Management Pyramid in Exhibit 11 presents a framework to communicate the alignment of the overall shareholder value goal, the supporting business strategy, and the different organizational processes and decisions. Value Management is the practice of aligning all of these "slices" of the pyramid. For more information on Value Management, visit http://www.mercerhr.com/knowledgecenter/reportsummary.jhtml?id Content=1010655

Shareholder Value Goal

In the framework in Exhibit 11, the Shareholder Value Goal drives the strategy and organizational processes. In public companies, shareholders are the critical stakeholder group, since they are the only group interested in balancing the long-term interests of all other stakeholders (employees, government, customers, suppliers, community, etc.). In public companies, shareholder value is most often expressed as Total Shareholder Return (TSR), a measure of stock price appreciation (including reinvested dividends).

Exhibit 11: Value Management framework for aligning decision-making with shareholder value

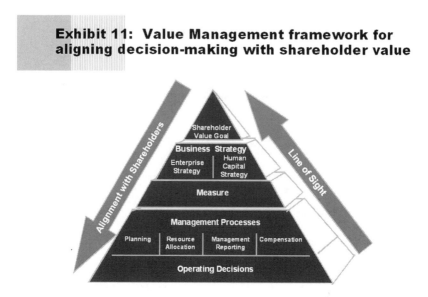

Example goals include: TSR in the top quartile of our peers, or a stock price of $50 in four years.

Strategy

Business strategy answers the following question: "How will our company achieve our goal?" Depending on the business situation, broad answers can range from "low cost provider of products/services" (think Southwest Airlines) to "consistent, quality products and service offered worldwide to the mass market" (think McDonalds) to "one-stop shop for financial services" (think Citigroup) to "best-in-class products/services in each market in which we compete" (think General Electric). In today's world, "business" strategy is comprised of two fundamental components: Enterprise strategy and Human Capital Strategy. The development of one is iterative with the other.

Measure

Measure refers to the organization's performance measurement system. An effective performance measurement system is a critical tool and translation device a company can employ to clarify the link between strategy and decisions. Just as strategy begins to define the plan of action a company will embark upon to create shareholder value, a company's performance measurement system provides critical information for managers to make decisions. Performance measures are used in corporate planning, incentives, management reporting processes, and annual budgeting and resource allocation processes.

"Strategy alone does not create value, decisions do."

For example, a company rewarding executives for year-over-year sales and earnings growth provides very different information and signals than does a company that rewards for return on capital or economic profit performance. For a more in-depth discussion of performance measurement systems and goal-setting, see the chapter entitled: *Selecting Performance Measures and Setting Goals.*

Corporate Processes and Compensation

Compensation strategy (and the accompanying compensation programs) continues this theme of providing managers information and motivation to make optimal decisions. Corporate processes rely on performance metrics from the measurement system to send signals to operating managers and other decision-makers in the form of corporate budgets, long-range strategic plans, financial management reports and compensation programs. Compensation programs focus behavior on the decisions that are required to support the company strategy, and measure and reward execution of the strategy and progress to the organization's overall goal.

Operating Decisions

Operating Decisions are the critical day-to-day decisions that will ultimately create or destroy value for shareholders. All other tiers of the pyramid provide the guidance, information and incentives to ensure the decisions made by operating managers are aligned with the company's strategy and are maximizing shareholder value.

Why is linkage of compensation and business strategy important? Business strategy is the plan of action that guides the achievement of each company's ultimate goal: maximizing shareholder value. Compensation strategy guides the design of compensation programs to effectively focus behaviors and decision-making to drive performance and execute the company's business strategy. Unless compensation strategy and business strategy are aligned, operating decisions will not be optimized, and shareholder value creation will be impaired.

In the EnergyCo example described earlier, the lack of a well-articulated compensation strategy prevented the company from effectively integrating the companies they acquired. Over 50% of mergers and acquisitions fail to achieve the value expected by management and shareholders. EnergyCo is an unfortunate example of how a compensation strategy that is not aligned with the business strategy can prevent a company from achieving its primary objectives and generating value for shareholders.

Alternatively, Southwest Airlines' compensation strategy reinforces its strategic focus on being the low-cost provider of air transportation services, and its shareholder value goal. Southwest's Salary Administration Program is administered "in a manner that promotes the attainment by Southwest of reasonable profits on a consistent basis in order to preserve job protection and security...." And in describing its pay positioning, the Compensation Committee describes that "as a general rule, base salary for the executive officer of Southwest falls below the salaries for comparable positions in comparably sized companies." Stock options are used to "bridge the gap between the lower level of cash compensation for Company officers as compared to their peers and to provide a long-term incentive for future performance that aligns officers' interests with shareholders in general...." Further, Southwest's strong culture, characterized by a friendly atmosphere, is a low-cost, well-defined way to deliver service and attract and retain people in the company that go well beyond compensation. Altogether, Southwest's compensation strategy and pay programs reinforce its shareholder value goal, and business strategy of remaining the low-cost, friendly service provider.

Testing the Alignment of Compensation Strategy and Business Strategy

How does a company begin to know that its compensation strategy supports its business strategy? Exhibit 12 lists a number of common symptoms experienced by companies suffering from misalignment between their business and compensation strategies. If one or more of these symptoms exist, there likely are gaps between your compensation strategy and your business strategy.

For example, several of these symptoms would have raised "red flags" for EnergyCo. The company was experiencing difficulty attracting and retaining talent. Employees had no line-of-sight between compensation and EnergyCo's business strategy. Finally, the compensation programs had not been updated as the company migrated from a growth company to a more mature organization. In fact, in the five years during which the company

Exhibit 12: Symptoms of a misaligned compensation strategy

☐ Executives are unaware of the company's compensation strategy

☐ Company has difficulty attracting and/or retaining high caliber talent

☐ Incentive awards generate little, if any, "bang for the buck" – executive motivation is of concern; appropriate level of performance is not being achieved for the amount of pay being delivered

☐ Employees lack line-of-sight between the compensation program(s) and the strategic direction of the company

☐ Compensation program(s) have not been updated to reflect changes in internal business strategy or external competitive environment

☐ Compensation programs do not reinforce the company's cultural values

had grown from $100 million to over $1 billion in sales, EnergyCo's compensation strategy and programs had never been evaluated or changed.

Key Questions to Help Evaluate the Alignment Between Your Compensation and Business Strategies

Several key questions can help diagnose the underlying causes of these symptoms and test the alignment between compensation and business strategies:

1. **What signals do our compensation programs send?** To recognize and diagnose misalignment between compensation and business strategy, it is critical to understand the signals being sent from a company's compensation programs. Frequently, these signals are sent through the pay structure, and performance measures, and goals in the annual and long-term incentive programs. For example, Zeta's new long-term incentive plan was based entirely on corporate EBITDA growth. This program sent two important signals to participants:

• Corporate, Business Unit and Individual results are valued. However, there is greater emphasis on Corporate results for top executives.

• Survival through generation of EBITDA and payment of debt service is critical.

These important signals from compensation programs indicate which behaviors and decisions the company values. In Zeta's case, all of these signals reinforced the company's goal of organic operating cash flow improvement.

2. **Is our business strategy clearly articulated? Has it been effectively communicated? Do employees understand it?** Understanding your company's business strategy is critical to ensuring compensation programs support decisions that are aligned with your strategy. On the surface, this is a very intuitive and straight-forward notion. However, many executives find it difficult to articulate their company's business strategy, and especially to translate it into terms that are meaningful for employees. Without a clear understanding of the company's strategy, compensation programs will fail to maximize their effect, and at worst, may inhibit the creation of shareholder value.

3. **Are the signals from our compensation systems consistent with our business strategy and our corporate shareholder value goals?** The signals from compensation systems may not be consistent with the company's business strategy and/or corporate goals. After identifying the key signals from compensation systems and understanding and articulating the company's business strategy, an assessment of the alignment between the two will be relatively straightforward. The signals being sent by compensation programs may encourage behavior and decisions that are not properly aligned with the business strategy.

In the EnergyCo example described at the beginning of this chapter, the signals from the company's compensation programs encouraged behaviors that were conflicting with the organization's business strategy of growth through acquisition. EnergyCo's compensation strategy became a barrier to the effective execution of its business strategy. (See Exhibit 13.)

4. **Can executives and senior managers "game the system?" Are compensation programs structured in a way to encourage decisions or behaviors that result in rewards for the individual, even though the decisions/behaviors are not in the best interests of shareholders?** The signals from compensation programs may not be aligned with business strategy–not because of a poorly designed compensation strategy, but because of poorly designed compensation programs, or other poorly designed corporate processes (e.g., the annual budgeting process). A common example: annual incentive programs that reward participants for actual performance relative to budgeted goals can encourage "low-balling" numbers during the annual budget negotiation process.

Another common example is the dysfunctional behavior encouraged when goals for annual incentive programs are built off of historical

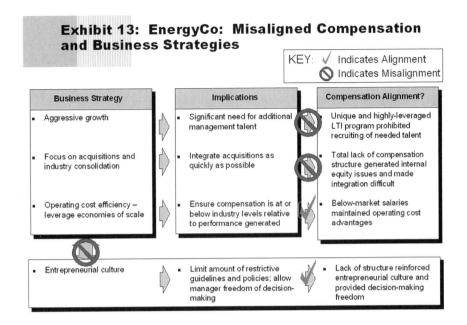

Exhibit 13: EnergyCo: Misaligned Compensation and Business Strategies

KEY: ✓ Indicates Alignment
🚫 Indicates Misalignment

Business Strategy	Implications	Compensation Alignment?
• Aggressive growth	• Significant need for additional management talent	• Unique and highly-leveraged LTI program prohibited recruiting of needed talent
• Focus on acquisitions and industry consolidation	• Integrate acquisitions as quickly as possible	• Total lack of compensation structure generated internal equity issues and made integration difficult
• Operating cost efficiency — leverage economies of scale	• Ensure compensation is at or below industry levels relative to performance generated	• Below-market salaries maintained operating cost advantages
• Entrepreneurial culture	• Limit amount of restrictive guidelines and policies; allow manager freedom of decision-making	• Lack of structure reinforced entrepreneurial culture and provided decision-making freedom

results. When companies use historical results to determine performance goals, performance results for the current year drive next year's goal. Managers who know they are unlikely to make their target for the current year may depress results, in hope of receiving a lower goal in the subsequent year. They can achieve this by pushing off sales into the next year and by bringing forward expenses, such as advertising, training, and other investments. Alternatively, managers who know they can achieve their performance goal this year may "mortgage" next year's award by maximizing this year's award to the fullest extent possible. Neither of these behaviors helps to create value for shareholders. To address this gap, companies should de-emphasize historical performance in setting performance goals for compensation programs. A better approach is to understand the implications of shareholder performance expectations as a basis for establishing performance objectives for compensation programs.

5. **How do I improve the alignment if there is a gap?** Understanding the gap between compensation strategy and business strategy is just the first step in achieving a strong linkage between the two. Bridging the gap involves articulating a compensation strategy that will provide the needed guidance and define the necessary parameters. The real power of alignment between the two comes through the execution of compensation

strategy, i.e., the careful, thoughtful design of the compensation programs and the development of effective processes.

The next section describes the key steps to ensure effective alignment of compensation strategy and business strategy.

Key Steps to Link Compensation Strategy to Business Strategy

Several key steps will help compensation practitioners to ensure that their company's compensation strategy and business strategy are aligned. Exhibit 14 illustrates a process to develop and implement an effective compensation strategy and programs.

Step 1. Evaluate internal business context

Arguably the most important step of the process is a rigorous analysis of your company's business strategy, organizational effectiveness characteristics, and performance and pay issues. This involves careful diagnosis of:

• Stakeholder goals

• Company business strategy

• Competitive positioning in the industry and source of competitive advantage

• Relationships with key customers and suppliers

• Historical performance and management's future performance expectations

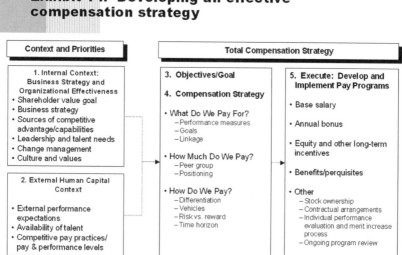

Exhibit 14: Developing an effective compensation strategy

- Current compensation strategy and key signals from current compensation programs
- Current and future needs for talent
- Organizational capabilities and core competencies
- Organizational culture and values

Collection of accurate information is important. Qualitative perspectives collected through executive and Board interviews, employee surveys, and focus groups will add significant context. In addition, fact-based analysis of customer survey data, long-range business plans, historical company and peer performance analysis, and investor expectations for future performance will also inform the process.

This process will enable you to clearly articulate your company's business strategy. In addition, it will help to develop a new compensation strategy or refine an existing one.

Step 2. Review external human capital context

The purpose of this step is to collect and analyze data from the external marketplace to provide context for the new compensation strategy. To complete this step, information should be collected and analyzed, including:

- A review of the competitive marketplace for talent,
- Industry pay practices and prevalence of different pay programs,
- Benchmarking of pay levels among similar companies for similar positions,
- Analysis of historical performance of peer companies, and
- Evaluation of investor's expectations for future performance for your company and other companies in your industry.

An understanding of competitive practices among organizations from which you will recruit talent (or to which you will potentially lose talent) will provide a more informed decision-making process. However, compensation strategies should not be developed by mimicking competitors or industry practices, but should be tailored to internal organization and business strategy requirements. In the EnergyCo example, while the company's highly leveraged stock and stock option purchase programs appeared appropriate for the organization's culture and business strategy, the gap between typical market practice (standard stock option awards) and EnergyCo's long-term incentive approach was large enough to prevent the company from effectively recruiting the top-tier talent it required.

Step 3. Define key objectives of compensation strategy

After understanding business strategy, organizational effectiveness issues and the external marketplace, the next step is to define key objectives of your compensation strategy. Typical objectives that appear often in compensation strategies include:

- Recruit and retain top-tier talent
- Focus on key performance metrics
- Pay for performance–provide above-market pay only for superior performance
- Provide alignment among management and shareholders
- Provide line-of-sight to key corporate objectives
- Deliver compensation in a cost effective manner (cash, accounting and dilution)
- Remain simple and understandable for all employees
- Reinforce the organization's culture

It is important not to have the objectives of your compensation strategy sound like "motherhood and apple pie." Rather, it is critical to define your organization's priorities to fit its business strategy. For instance, an organization with a significant growth objective may require a compensation strategy that facilitates executive recruiting. The importance of the recruiting objective suggests a need for a compensation strategy that is market competitive and that provides new hires with the opportunity to benefit from the expected growth. Alternatively, a company with management talent already in-house has a greater need to focus behaviors and decision-making on driving performance.

Many HR professionals developing new or revised compensation strategies have found it valuable to involve top executives as well as the Compensation Committee to identify and prioritize key objectives of the compensation strategy.

Step 4. Define parameters of compensation strategy

Once objectives of the compensation strategy have been identified, the various parameters of compensation strategy can begin to be defined:

- Comparator group
- Pay positioning
- Pay risk profile
- Participation

- Performance measures
- Performance goals
- Leverage (i.e., relationship between pay and performance)
- Linkage
- Time horizon, and
- Delivery vehicles

Remember that some of these parameters will be more important than others, and some may be unnecessary to define at all. The objective of this step is to provide enough guidance for the company to be able to design effective pay programs and compensation management processes. Before completing this step, ensure that the compensation strategy meets the objectives defined in the prior step, and critically review whether the compensation strategy will effectively support your company's business strategy. Many compensation practitioners find it valuable to seek guidance from the executive team and/or Compensation Committee to help test these parameters.

To illustrate the need for a well-thought out compensation strategy and the importance of Compensation Committee review, take the case of FoodCo, a consumer branded food products company with annual sales around $1 billion. To establish and evaluate the appropriateness of its annual and longer-term performance goals, it evaluated the performance of the various comparator companies. However, to complete the performance evaluation, FoodCo included several of the larger market leaders in the industry to better understand the performance dynamics of the industry. While appropriate for the performance evaluation, these same companies were incorporated into FoodCo's comparator group for compensation bench-marking. However, the Compensation Committee viewed the large company comparator group as inappropriate for a company the size of FoodCo.

Step 5. Execute! Develop programs necessary to execute your compensation strategy

Annual incentives, long-term incentives, and salary administration programs all must be designed and implemented to support the compensation strategy. Different mechanisms can be used to execute different components of your pay strategy. For example, risk profile can be affected through the mix of pay components, or through the pay-performance relationships inherent in the annual and long-term incentive plans. This execution step often is the most time and resource intensive.

In addition to specific compensation programs, two other issues must be aligned with compensation strategy to enable effective execution: compensation management processes and other corporate processes. Compensation management processes such as performance management/individual performance review, salary adjustments/merit increases, stock option distribution and other processes all have the potential to send signals which conflict with the objectives of your company's compensation programs. In addition, other corporate processes such as strategic planning, annual budgeting, resource allocation, and management reporting can also send conflicting signals to managers and employees.

Alignment of pay strategy, program and management processes enables effective execution of company business strategy.

Summary

Today, HR professionals are expected to serve as strategic business partners by being conversant with strategic concepts and helping to craft and execute company strategy. Increasingly, the development of Enterprise strategy and Human Capital strategy is an integrated, iterative, and continuous process. Compensation strategies and programs play a crucial role in the human capital equation.

Effective alignment of compensation strategy and business strategy will change behaviors, focus decisions, and help HR fulfill its role as a strategic business partner.

What finally happened to EnergyCo and its compensation programs? The gap between the company's compensation programs and processes, and external market practices was addressed. EnergyCo developed a transition plan to accomplish two critical objectives: (1) Add more structure to compensation programs by creating broad pay ranges, giving managers flexibility to make pay decisions, but also providing necessary guidance; (2) Develop executive compensation programs more in line with typical industry practices. While EnergyCo did not alter its pay positioning signifi-cantly (still targeted below-market salaries, with significant leverage on the annual and long-term incentive opportunities), the unique highly-leveraged long-term incentive program was replaced with a more traditional stock option program. These two important changes to EnergyCo's compensation strategy and programs filled enough of the gap to provide an effective tool to help execute the company's dynamic business strategy. By re-linking compensation strategy and business strategy, EnergyCo was able to attract and retain talent, integrate acquired companies and better achieve its overall goal of shareholder value creation.

ROBIN A. FERRACONE

Ms. Ferracone is a Worldwide Partner at Mercer Human Resource Consulting. She has over 20 years of consulting experience in the areas of value management, performance measurement, human capital strategy, and compensation design, both on a domestic and international level. She is published widely, has appeared on *NewsHour with Jim Lehrer*, has testified before a U.S. Congressional sub-committee on Presidential pay, and is a frequent presenter for such organizations as The Conference Board, WorldatWork, the CFO Business Week Forum, The National Center for Employee Ownership, and National Association of Stock Plan Professionals. In 2003, WorldatWork honored her with the Distinguished Service Award.

Ms. Ferracone has an MBA from the Harvard Business School, where she was a Baker Scholar, and a BA, *summa cum laude*, in management science and economics from Duke University, where she was elected to Phi Beta Kappa. She serves on a number of corporate and charitable boards.

RYAN COMPAAN

Ryan Compaan is a Senior Consultant in the Performance, Measurement and Rewards practice of Mercer Human Resource Consulting, specializing in Executive Compensation. Based in Chicago, he is an expert in the analysis of financial and compensation data in order to identify the drivers of shareholder value and their relationship to performance management and executive compensation. Mr. Compaan has significant experience in incentive plan design, competitive pay and competitive performance benchmarking and technical advisory work on tax, accounting and SEC regulatory issues.

Mr. Compaan was a Senior Associate with SCA Consulting and joined Mercer through its acquisition of SCA. At SCA he focused on the design and implementation of performance measurement and executive compensation programs. Prior to SCA, he was a consultant with Ernst & Young. Mr. Compaan has worked with public and private companies and not-for-profit organizations across most industry sectors.

Mr. Compaan graduated from the University of Chicago with a B.A. in Political Science.

3. Developing an Executive Total Rewards Strategic Plan

Chapters one and two have painted the context for executive compensation and the critical importance of having its strategic framework tightly aligned with that of the business itself. This chapter follows with the logical next step; delivering specific prescriptive information to put ideas into action. With straightforward guidance it details the elements of an executive total reward strategy, and how to create such a strategy if one does not already exist.

Executive pay strategy and design should be highly contextual and the author begins by describing seven external and five internal context factors that have central importance for understanding or designing an effective strategy. From these twelve factors the reader will gain an understanding of why one company's approach to executive compensation may differ significantly–and justifiably– from another company's approach.

The author devotes time to presenting an executive total rewards strategy model comprised of twelve discrete elements. Each element is described, an explanation is given as to why it is important, and then one or more typical responses are identified. An eleven-step process is then laid out to help guide the reader when developing a strategy, starting with data gathering and ending with a strategy document. The chapter itself concludes with the presentation of a total executive rewards strategy for a hypothetical technology company to illustrate an example of a completed document. –Editors

A N EXPLICIT AND DETAILED executive compensation strategy is an important tool with which to attract, retain, and reward quality executives for your organization. Unfortunately, it is far too easy, and far too common a practice, to jump immediately into plan design before constructing the foundation upon which all of the plans should be built. This generally yields the same results as starting to erect the first floor of a house before its foundation is poured. Sooner or later, and most likely sooner, the structure will fail. The more research and planning that goes into all aspects of the executive compensation package, the better and more efficient that plan can be in addressing the needs of your executives, while remaining true to your overall business strategy. But why spend the resources, time, and money to do this? If you have asked, or are asking this question, think about the following:

1. Is your executive compensation package definitely linked to your business strategy and key objectives?

2. How is the executive total reward strategy impacted by firm financials, industry structure and financials, stage of life, size, etc?

3. Is it balanced between the short-run and the long-term objectives of the company?

4. Have you defined an accurate peer group for comparative purposes using a systematic process including labor market, product market, and capital market competitors as a first screen and then size, financials, location, etc. as a second screen?

5. How does your organization compare to this defined peer group in terms of performance and what impact should that have on the positioning of your executive compensation levels?

6. Is your strategy, and its ultimate impact on package design compelling enough to attract and retain the executive talent you need and flexible enough to meet the needs of a diverse set of demographic and stage of career/life concerns?

7. Are your pay levels too high, too low, or just right given the performance of your organization?

If you cannot answer these questions with certainty in front of the Compensation Committee of the Board of Directors, your first task before doing another analysis or plan recommendation should be to research, develop, and/or revise your executive total reward strategy as soon as possible. The following chapter will examine the best way to add true value and structure to this process.

A Model For Executive Total Rewards Strategy Design

The External Context → **The Components** → **The Strategy** → **Plan Design**
The Internal Context ↗

The Context for Executive Total Reward Strategy Development

Before we can begin to look at each of the components of the total reward strategy, it is critical to understand the major factors (or inputs) that will mold and shape an organization's strategy and begin to show why the strategy must be different for almost each and every organization. These factors can be broken down into two major sub-categories – those of an external nature (External Context), and those of an internal nature (Internal Context).

The External Context

There are seven major external factors that have a significant effect on the ultimate direction executive total rewards take:

1. Industry

2. Overall Industry Financial Position

3. Industry Stage of Development

4. Degree of R&D/Long-Term Orientation of the Industry

5. Executive Supply and Demand

6. Degree of Competition Within the Industry

7. Current and Projected Economic Conditions

Industry

Executive compensation varies significantly from industry to industry in terms of compensation mix, use of long-term incentives, use of supplemental benefits and perquisites, and also overall levels of executive pay. From the 2001 *Wall Street Journal* Special Report on Executive Compensation, we can see some of these differences in looking at the average CEO pay from the following industries:

Industry	Median Salary (000)	Median Bonus (000)	Median Cash Compensation (000)	Median Total Direct Compensation (000)
High Technology	$872	$1,250	$2,100	$3,400
Health Care	$1,077	$1,487	$2,800	$3,200
Financial	$945	$1,500	$2,400	$6,200
Basic Materials	$822	$515	$1,300	$1,600
Utilities	$831	$1,001	$1,900	$2,700

From this table, we can see that the base salary differences are not all that significant, with only a 30 percent difference between these industries. The largest predictor of base salary is revenue within industry, which can often be seen through a calculated regression line. Bonus levels, however, vary by almost 200 percent, due not only to different target bonus opportunities but also to substantial differences in industry performance. Median total direct compensation, which includes base salary, bonus, and long-term incentives, varies by almost 300 percent, almost $4.6M dollars, due to the tremendous differentiation in long-term incentive values–$300M in basic materials and $3.8M in financial services. With these differences in values come significant differences in the overall mix of compensation.

Industry Financials

The growth rate in the industry, the margin levels that are obtained within the industry, and the expected return to shareholders given the degree of inherent risk will all effect executive pay packages. Low margin industries, for example, have to work extremely hard to manage/control costs, so there could be pressure on the levels of cash compensation. The same could be said for the dot-com start-up organizations (which actually were a separate industry–B2B e-commerce, B2C e-commerce, e-commerce consulting firms, e-commerce infrastructure firms, etc.), which have a finite amount of cash from which to operate until the next round of funding. This business model places significant pressure on expense and cash flow management, making it extremely difficult to justify high levels of cash compensation.

Industry Stage of Development

The life cycle of the industry will have a significant effect on both the mix and level of executive compensation. A relatively new industry, genomics for example, will have relatively low cash compensation levels and significant upside opportunities through long-term incentives, mainly stock options, because all or substantially all of the firms in this space are small start-ups. As this industry begins to grow and revenues increase, there will be a greater focus on, and higher levels of, cash compensation, with correspondingly less focus on, and lower levels of, stock option usage. On the flip side, an industry that is mature, and some say even on the decline, is the automotive industry. Industry consolidation has occurred, even global consolidation, and thus the industry is characterized by huge, mature organizations that have been in operation a long-time. Cash compensation levels are high, short-term and long-term vehicles are numerous and diverse, and there are generally significant executive perquisites and supplemental benefits. This level of total rewards could not be supported, financially or culturally, in the genomics firms discussed above.

Degree of R&D/Long-Term Orientation of the Industry

In general, a longer product development or service cycle in an industry corresponds to a longer-term orientation. As a result, success in the industry depends on a long-term focus, leading to a greater use of long-term incentive vehicles. The pharmaceutical industry is a prime example of this model. To make these long-term development cycles yield commercially successful, government approved drugs, short-term deliverables are also extremely important. Therefore, the industry will also use a great deal of short-term incentives as well. If we look at the industries in Exhibit 1, we see that Basic Materials and Health Care have the two lowest levels of long-term incentive usage. It is not coincidental that both of these industries are more short-term focused than most others.

Executive Supply and Demand

Industry growth rates (generally related to industry life cycle) also have a significant impact on the supply and demand for executive talent within the industry. As we saw during the dot-com boom, there simply were not enough seasoned executives to run all of these firms given the tremendous growth rate that was occurring. As a result, many of these organizations ended up being headed by 25–30 year-old founders, most with a technical background. Because of this labor problem of supply and demand, there were simply not enough qualified executives available to run these firms, so prices (pay packages) were bid up to significant and unsustainable levels. When you look at these firms left today, very few are both successful and headed by the founder. Simply put, supply and demand levels, and also salaries, have gotten back into equilibrium.

Degree of Competition Within the Industry

The degree of competition is closely related to the overall industry stage of development. New industries, and the firms within that industry, are initially competing on technical development. Soon, the industry begins to recognize that technical advancement is not the only means of success: quality and customer satisfaction begin to emerge as key strategies. Finally, price will become an important differentiator. This generally does not happen immediately because firms are looking to re-coup the investments they made in the technology, the service, etc. It is clear that the degree of competition within an industry places significant pressure on prices, which in turn place a significant pressure on margins. Compensation expense is generally one of the largest controllable costs, so this will serve to keep executive compensation levels lower.

Current and Projected Economic Conditions

Again, economic condition is not a standalone factor, but its importance, when combined with other factors, becomes significant. For example, in the booming economy of the 1990's, there was substantial growth in new organizations that needed executive talent. As the talent pool shrank due to declining numbers in the work force, there was a serious shortage of labor, driving up prices and wages. In a down economic period, firms are often hesitant to significantly add on to fixed costs, so there will be little base salary movement. A down economy also creates a more plentiful supply of labor (not necessarily with the in-demand skill sets), which keeps wage escalation tempered.

The Internal Context

There are five major internal factors that have a dramatic effect on the ultimate strategic direction executive total rewards take:

1. Organization's Competitive Positioning Within its Industry and its Method of Competing
2. Firm Stage of Development
3. Firm Financial Position
4. Level of Talent Needed to Compete
5. Firm's Ability to Attract and Retain Talent Needed

Organization's Competitive Positioning within its Industry and its Method of Competing

An organization's competitive position within an industry, as defined through firm financials, should have an effect on the levels of executive compensation. All else being equal, higher performing firms should pay more than lower performing firms. Recent studies from Clark Bardes Consulting's total rewards database have found significant pay level and structure of pay differences between high-performing firms and their lower-performing peers across all elements of pay–base salary, short-term incentives, and long-term incentives.

Additionally, the method in which a firm chooses to compete against the other firms in the industry should also have an effect on both the mix and levels of compensation. Again, all else being equal, a firm competing on cost leadership should have lower cash levels than a firm competing on product features. Likewise, a firm competing from a basis of patent protection, pharmaceutical firms for example, make tremendous margins on the drugs during the period of patent protection. This protection allows them to pay aggressive cash compensation levels, while at the same time enjoying significant long-term incentives that allows them to stay focused on all of the drugs in the pipeline.

A different way of looking at the method of competing is as follows: let's assume that all organizations exist essentially for one purpose–to maximize shareholder value for a given level of risk assumed. How the organization goes about accomplishing this objective, whether via price, customer satisfaction, quality, or features/innovation, will determine the type of talent that it needs to execute its strategy. If, for example, a firm adopts a strategy based on price, then it must excel at cost control, execution, efficiency, etc. But a firm competing on features/innovation needs a different type of executive team that knows how to manage creative individuals, does not stifle "outside of the box thinking" and can balance long-term vision with short-term progress. Once the organization has articulated the kind of talent required, it then needs to determine what its total reward strategy will be to attract and retain those individuals.

Firm Stage of Development

Compensation strategies for using the various elements of executive compensation vary by the firm's stage of development. New ventures that need to preserve cash for growth and investment tend to have modest base salaries and significant non-cash stock opportunities in order to offset the modest cash component and to acknowledge the inherent business risks of employment in a start-up venture. High-growth and mature entities tend to rely on providing competitive or more than competitive amounts of each pay element to maintain their firm's growth and financial success. Exhibit 2 highlights some of the compensation strategy issues by stage of company development. These are typical practices/strategies, and it is important to note that variability does exist around the norm due to company and industry-specific factors. Again, you will note that non-cash compensation for executives plays a significant role through the stages of development.

Firm Financial Position

A firm's financial position impacts not only its ability to pay cash compensation, but it also impacts its relationship with shareholders, thus having a role in determining the level of equity that will be available. Shareholders are much more likely to tolerate higher levels of dilution if they are getting significant returns. A poorly performing firm with weak financials, however, may not have access to the same level of stock as higher performing firms as shareholders seek to protect the gains that they have.

Level of Talent Needed to Compete

Most firms state that they need to attract and retain the best and brightest executive talent available, but this goal is both impossible and also

Compensation Characteristics	Entity Development Stage		
	New Venture	**High Growth Entity**	**Mature Entity**
Key Compensation Issues	→ Allocating equity Linking rewards to new venture/shareholder success	→ Attracting employees Establishing internal equity Concerns with dilution Maintaining long-term incentive opportunities Need to begin to focus on line of sight given size increases	Linking short-term rewards to critical success factors Strengthening line of sight given size and complexity of the business
Total Compensation Perspective	→ Less than competitive, but providing tremendous upside potential	→ Must be competitive to ensure the ability to attract and retain employees	Competitive to more than competitive, particularly if benefits are considered
Base Salary	→ Modest	→ Competitive	Competitive to somewhat more than competitive
Short-Term Incentives	→ Modest Awards typically based on discretion Participation typically limited to senior executives and sales positions to preserve cash	→ Competitive target based upon achievement of objectives Participation broadened to mid-managers and professional individual contributors Organization may implement corporate success sharing plan (with universal eligibility and participation	Competitive to somewhat more than competitive target short-term incentives based on financial and non-financial objectives
Long-Term Incentives	→ Very significant opportunities Universal participation Opportunities provided at hire	→ Significant opportunites employing stock options Universal eligibility, less than universal participation Opportunities provided at hire and on an ongoing (typically annual) basis	Significant opportunities employing stock options, restricted stock, and possibly other equity vehicles May begin to employ long-term cash compensation plans (particularly if dilution is very high or stock price growth is flat
Executive Benefits and Supplemental Benefits	→ Benefits are modest Supplemental benefits are generally non-existent	→ Benefits become competitive Supplemental benefits considered and begin to be implemented	Benefits competitive to highly competitive Supplemental benefits are common and diverse in nature/scope
Perquisites and Services	→ Generally not provided	→ Modest	Competitive

Exhibit 2.

unnecessary. Organizations need to be realistic about the level of talent they have or need, and pay appropriately for that level of talent. Over time, it is virtually impossible to attract and retain 90th percentile executives for 50th percentile total rewards, and, likewise, organizations should not target median levels of talent at the 75th percentile of total rewards unless their performance clearly dictates that this is necessary. Overpayment for the level of talent is sure to cause one thing–low levels of voluntary executive turnover. This does not mean that you have to adopt the same targeted percentile of pay for every executive position. If a firm competing on price requires an exceptional CFO and Head of Operations, those positions should be targeted higher than marketing and development, parts of the organization where it may not be necessary to have 75th percentile executives. The caliber and experience of the executives also varies greatly from firm to firm and from industry to industry so again and should be reflected in terms of differences in pay.

Firm's Ability to Attract Talent Needed

It would be far easier, and most likely cheaper, to attract executives into a market-leading, high-growth company with exceptional financials in a high-growth industry than it would be to attract executives into a complete turn-around situation in a low-growth, unattractive industry. It is important for organizations to take a long hard look at their ability to attract and retain the level of executive talent needed. Are executive offers routinely being turned down? Are executive turnover levels high? What do those who really know the market, executive recruiters for instance, honestly think about your organization? As painful as these questions may be to answer, it will provide you with some very clear, compelling data on your overall ability to attract and retain key talent.

The Components of an Executive Total Rewards Strategy

In work completed in this arena over time, there are twelve factors that have a significant influence on the development of an executive compensation strategy. They are as follows:

The Role and Importance of Rewards

There are two main questions that need to be answered here: 1) What role will the executive total rewards system play in the achievement of the HR Strategy/Employee Value Proposition?; and 2) How important of a role will it play in relationship to the other components? When thinking about the former, it is critical not to view the total rewards system in isolation, but rather as part of an integrated system that also includes executive development, performance management, leadership, culture and work environment. All of these components play a role in an individual's attraction to an organization, his or her level of motivation, and the desire to stay with the organization. A decision as to whether total rewards will be a driving system or a supporting system needs to be made based on experience, as well as company and industry specific factors. Total rewards are often best used as a supporting system, helping, along with other systems/components, to influence the appropriate behavior and level of performance as opposed to using this system as a key lever of change. There are companies and industries where executive compensation is a driving system of behavior/change, Mary Kay Cosmetics and the investment banking industry, for example. The importance of total rewards should be considered from two perspectives: 1) importance to the company; and 2) importance to the executive. Generally, the total rewards system is a supporting system, rather than a driving system, in helping to facilitate the accomplishment of key short-term and long-term objectives within the organization. The importance of rewards varies significantly from individual to individual, and even within an individual as he or she moves through various stages of life. That being said, greater flexibility is necessary in the design and construction of executive total reward packages in order to allow individuals to make decisions, within broad philosophical parameters, on the basis of their needs. For example, when it comes to executive new hire packages, our policy is to tailor offers to the specifics of the individual's situation in most cases. However, once the individual has joined the organization, he or she is then treated like every other executive, regardless of how different his or her needs and situations are. Executive compensation is an arena where we can and should think differently. Flexible total rewards packages are not impossible to design; it is just necessary to take a certain level of risk to implement them.

Internal Equity vs. External Competitiveness

To a certain extent, all organizations need to be externally competitive. Whether at the 25th percentile, the 50th percentile, or the 75th percentile, your business needs to pay within 15–20 percent of the market average to attract and retain a reasonably qualified candidate. That being said, the question becomes: how much do we value internal equity at the expense of external competitiveness, or how much will we let external competitiveness drive real or perceived internal inequities? Let's consider the ramifications of choosing one of these over the other. When an organization chooses internal equity over external competitiveness, they generally end up over-paying certain positions and retaining the rest at market because it is extremely difficult to bring the pay of higher worth jobs down to the level of the lower paid jobs. As a result, the pay of the lower value jobs escalates to the level of the higher market value jobs, and the organization ends up over-paying for some positions. An organization may choose to do this primarily because they place a different value on a given role than does the market-place. On the flip side, an organization may run into internal equity issues if it follows the market but actually values its jobs differently than the market. These differences can be minimized through the use of ranges around the market data that will allow for degrees of differentiation in performance, internal job value/criticality, etc.

Team Consistency vs. Individual Customizability

Many organizations want the "look and feel" of the executive total rewards packages, not necessarily the level of pay, to be the same for all executives because there is a strong feeling that this degree of similarity will help the executives think and act more like a team. While this may be true, the reward system then becomes the mechanism that drives behavior rather than making teamwork an integral piece of the executive performance management process by linking incentives to performance. Complete team consistency does not allow for any variance in individual needs, different stages of life and finances, different risk profiles, etc. This sameness may screen out certain candidates that the organization is interest in, or it may discourage the affected executives to such an extent that they leave the organization.

When designing an executive rewards program, there are certain aspects that should be consistent from package to package, including how the overall plans are funded; what overall metrics will be used; what the general philosophy is on compensation mix; and what are the broad ranges of reward levels by component. However, when we get into risk/reward profiles, different stages of life/career, and so forth, there should be a degree of flexibility on how individual packages are tailored in order to respond to these different needs.

Competitive Peer Group Definition

Why a Peer Group?

A Peer Group is a set of carefully selected firms, with a high degree of commonality across a number of characteristics that will provide, to a relatively high degree of certainty, market data that is truly representative of the market. Why do we need one of these Peer Groups? Why isn't using targeted data cuts from available surveys precise enough? Simply put, "averages" over large sets of data are relatively meaningless. Does any firm out there have the same profile as what the average, or median firm, would look like? Perhaps, but in reality, very few organizations would be a close fit. What if you are able to drill down and get more specific cuts of the data? It would be closer, but you would still have to select the firms that are the best fit from those that are available in the survey, not from those that may truly be the best fit.

While most potential comparator firms for a Peer Group will not meet all criteria that make for a best fit, all good comparator firms should meet most of the criteria. Criteria to consider in determining the appropriateness of a firm for inclusion in the comparator peer group include the following macro screens, followed by the more micro-level screens for inclusion or exclusion in the Peer Group:

Macro-level Screens for Peer Group Inclusion/Exclusion

- **Labor Market Similarity:** The most senior executive positions in the largest national or international corporations are generally not sensitive to geographical differences, unless the product or service market happens to be concentrated mostly in a given market–investment banking in NYC, for example. Smaller and more regional or local companies may have differences in pay (particularly cash compensation) based upon the geographical supply and demand for employees and cost-of-living differentials.

- **Product or Service Market Similarity:** Each major industrial and service sector of the economy has its own set of dynamics that influence compensation practices. Some sectors with slow moving stock prices may emphasize cash compensation. Other sectors, such as technology, may emphasize non-cash compensation in the form of stock options for reasons that have been discussed previously.

- **Capital Market Similarity.** It is often very useful to look at what companies the stock analysts consider a given organizations' peers. In many cases, there is a strong correlation with product or service market similarity. When a firm is diversified, is in a small market, or has some other unique quality, however, this uniqueness can often prove a valuable source of information. When making investment decisions and recommendations, the analyst is looking at a firm's projected performance, relative to the defined "peer group," for a given level of risk.

- **Labor Market for Executive Talent.** While both a highly relevant and key variable to the equation, it also represents the opportunity for the greatest "abuse" to the labor market definition. Where executives were previously employed and where they take their next job form the basis for this pool of companies. Typically, they include product/service market competitors, but care needs to be taken to look at the appropriate size of comparator companies and its impact on executive pay. A $500M organization may indeed get its CEO from a $10B competitor, but it is not generally going to attract the CFO of the $10B company. At most, it will perhaps attract someone who reports directly to the CFO. Similarly, a $100M technology firm seeking to acquire world-class product marketing executive talent may see large consumer goods firms as talent providers, but, again, they cannot and should not pay like a $20B firm.

Micro-level Screens for Peer Group Inclusion/Exclusion

Once the macro-level screens have been satisfied, the more micro-level screens for appropriate comparators need to be considered. They are as follows:

- **Development Stage Similarity:** As noted in Exhibit 2, stage of development of a firm has a significant impact on pay strategy and allocation.

- **Size Relevance:** Annual revenue, market capitalization and number of employees are some of the most critical factors in determining the magnitude of pay for any individual executive. Typically, pay (particularly cash compensation) does not increase proportionately as company size increases. Rather, median cash compensation tends to be centered in large ranges over the spectrum of size. Clearly, executive cash compensation is much greater in a multi-billion-dollar firm than in a ten million dollar enterprise. However, there may be similarities in pay practices for companies with revenues within certain ranges, e.g., between one and five billion dollars.

- **Performance Considerations:** Companies enjoying continued financial success, typically (but not always) tend to pay competitively or better. Firms that struggle financially and are more sensitive to compensation expenses may tend to limit cash compensation opportunities or emphasize incentive-based compensation instead of fixed salaries.

- **Ownership Status.** Private versus publicly held or parent versus subsidiary are two of the considerations impacting pay packages. For example, mature private companies generally do not award equity compensation to its executives. Also, subsidiary employees may receive less (or no) equity compensation.

Component Mix

Before exploring the whole area of what the component mix should look like in a total rewards program, it is useful to look at the components of total rewards. Total rewards is a term commonly used for the sum of cash compensation, benefits and the value of stock options and other non-cash equity awards. As shown in Exhibits 3 and 4, executive's non-cash compensation is typically more than 50 percent of total direct compensation.

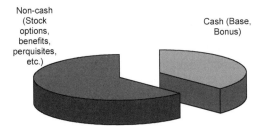

Exhibit 3. Executive Total Rewards

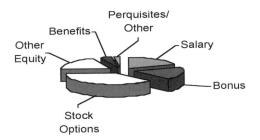

Exhibit 4. Total Rewards: Elements

The mix of total rewards will vary most by the organization's use of short and long-term incentives, which in turn should be linked to the degree of focus necessary on short-term objectives vs. the long-term strategy. It is important to keep an appropriate balance between these two perspectives, but there are times when an organization should be focused on one more than the other, and thus the mix of compensation should change. For example, a company that is in a desperate battle for short-term survival may need to be almost completely focused on the achievement of short-term objectives, and thus, executive rewards should be much more heavily focused on short-term incentives. Likewise, an organization that has historically been too short-term focused may wish to place a greater weight on long-term incentives to facilitate the shift in focus that is necessary.

The components that are or are not available to an organization, most specifically with respect to stock, also have a significant impact on mix. It is far cheaper for an organization to deliver long-term value in stock than it is in cash, so, if stock is not available, there is a very high probability that the level of long-term incentives/incentive opportunity will not be as great due to the cost/cash flow impact. An organization's financial position will also influence the component mix. Are there significant amounts of cash and high levels of profitability to fund high base salaries or bonus levels or are equity components more prevalent (as in small high technology firms) in order to conserve cash? An organization's position in its life cycle (See Exhibit 2.) also has a significant impact on the mix of compensation, although this has changed somewhat in recent years with more well-funded start-ups and the need of larger, more mature organizations to respond to their allure. Finally, industry competitive practice has, justifiably or not, a large impact on what an organization's mix will most likely look like. If high base salaries and bonuses are commonplace, nearly all firms will need to offer this to be competitive and attract and retain the talent they need.

Competitive Positioning

Do we position our compensation at the 50th, 60th, or 75th percentile? Does this level of competitive positioning need to apply equally to all components or can base be positioned at the 50th percentile (for clarity purposes, this means that 50 percent of the organizations in the data set are above this point, and 50 percent of the organizations in the data set are below this point), total cash on target at the 60th and total direct compensation at the 75th? The answer to the first question depends upon four primary factors:

1. At what level must you pay to attract and retain the level of talent needed to execute your goals and strategies? We strongly believe that it is virtually impossible to attract and retain 75th to 90th percentile talent at market median pay levels, especially given the lack of true pay for performance in most organizations.

2. At what levels do your key talent competitors pay, and how does your paying at these same levels impact your financials?

3. What can you afford to pay in cash, and what are acceptable levels of equity usage?

4. Given your level of performance, does your pay roughly match, especially in the variable arenas, these performance levels? Put another way, are your executives sharing in the fruits of the organization's success or, on the flip side, feeling the pain of substandard performance?

In answer to the second question, the components can, and should, be set at potentially differing competitive levels. In far too many firms, there is a strategy that contains a given level of competitive positioning for all components and even to all positions within the organization. This strategy means that the line of reasoning includes the same level of talent being needed at all levels and within all functions, and that your competitors for talent have also adopted the same line of reasoning, which is probably not the case.

In order to prevent this scenario from happening, it is necessary to look at your organization's performance relative to your peer group. The peer group can be stratified into quartiles, and the pay levels and practices of those quartiles analyzed. It is relatively certain that you will find significant differences not only in pay levels, but in how firms pay, with this type of analysis.

Regulatory/External Constraints

Executive compensation has perhaps the largest extent of regulatory constraints as any level within the organization. While it is impossible to go into detail in this chapter, it is critical to pay attention to $1M pay limits, institutional shareholder concerns, public perception and the like.

Linkage to Performance

To what extent will executive pay be linked to performance? How is pay defined? At what level is the performance bar set? Is this performance absolute (against company targets) or relative to the performance of the defined peer group? Sadly, in many organizations, there is little true pay for performance in the purest form. Are shareholders or key stakeholders getting the kind of return they are looking for from the organization? To answer this question, it is necessary to consider, at the end of the day, why organizations exist. In a capitalistic, market-based economy, they exist to satisfy shareholders, public and private alike. Those that do not satisfy shareholders eventually perish. Granted, there are a lot of things along the way that influence this outcome, quality, customer satisfaction, price, value, and features, but those are merely a means to an end, a way to deliver shareholder value.

How we define pay is also critical to how strongly "pay" is correlated to performance. Most studies in this arena have defined pay as base salary and bonus levels in a given year, plus a derived worth of long-term incentives/stock options that are granted during a given year. What is important, however, in the long-term incentive arena is not the derived value of a grant in a given year, but rather the change in the value of an executive's total option/stock holdings, compared to changes in shareholder value. If there is not a strong relationship here, then an organization has a true reward for performance problem.

If more organizations paid their executives based upon relative performance (how did we do versus our peer group?), there would be a far greater level of pay for performance than exists today. We are becoming even stronger believers in this pay for performance concept due to our research and the pay analyses that we conduct based on a performance-stratified methodology. We are consistently finding higher targeted stock values and higher levels of burn-rates and overall dilution in top quartile performing firms. Whether or not this is by design, it clearly seems to be no coincidence, as the relationship holds true through every quartile. Stock/other long-term incentive vehicles are the big differentiator in total rewards, so it is this component to which you should pay significant attention. Although some might say it is impossible to define "appropriate levels of performance," stock analysts and investors make those decisions on a daily basis when they decide to invest based upon the expected levels of return and the anticipated degree of risk.

Team vs. Individual Performance Focus

Once the overall performance parameters have been set, it is then necessary to determine whether corporate (team), group/divisional, and/or individual performance, or a combination thereof, will be factored into the payout levels. We have found that the management committees in organizations (the senior-most executives, generally reporting to the President/CEO, with responsibility for setting the organizational strategy and ensuring its execution,) should have the majority of their short-term incentive based upon overall organizational results (66 percent to 75 percent minimum, with the remainder on group/functional results). This ensures teamwork and sends a message that each executive's role is to help ensure overall organizational success, not just that of their group. Executives below this level should generally be on a mixed corporate, group, and individually based incentive plan, with weights varying between 25 percent and 50 percent on each component, with percentage differences based upon where the level of emphasis most needs to be.

Ownership/Long-term Incentive Orientation

Clearly, the degree of long-term incentive orientation that exists within a given industry, and within organizations, will have a marked effect on the overall reward strategy and resulting design of the programs. If an average industry burn-rate is 1.5 percent in Industry A vs. 7.0 percent in Industry B, it will definitely have an effect on the level of LTI awards executives receive. This may be tempered somewhat in the low burn-rate industries by the fact that far fewer employees participate, but there are still significant differences that exist. Additionally, organizations that are able to incur higher than median burn-rates, because of their exceptional return to shareholders (Microsoft for instance), are in a position to deliver higher levels of options, and significantly higher value in those options, to executives and employees.

Deferral/Tax Advantageousness

As executives are capped in the qualified benefits plans at levels substantially below what they need to maintain their standard of living upon retirement, supplemental executive retirement programs (SERPs) provide a tax advantageous vehicle for solving this problem. There is also the question of tax advantageousness from the company's perspective, as well as different scenarios to consider with respect to income statement considerations. The different vehicles (ISO's, NQSO's, Restricted Stock, Cash) that can be used all have different tax and accounting treatments that organizations need to consider.

Openness and Communication

SEC reporting requirements impose a required amount of openness for the top five executive officers of publicly traded corporations. Outside of this realm, however, you need to determine how much you want and need to share about the overall structure of the executive compensation program with executives, as well as with the general employee population. Again, our experience here is that executives should intimately understand how and why they are paid the way that they are; how the various components of the package work together; and how they are tied to corporate goals and strategies. There is also a strong rationale for communicating throughout the organization, at a high level, how the executives are paid; what the bonus plan is based upon; what the financial targets are; what are key longer-term objectives for the company; and what those are linked to. This openness takes some of the mystery out of executive pay and hopefully shows the organization that the pay of the top executives is linked to performance, while also further communicating key objectives, both short-term and longer-term, to the organization.

Developing the Executive Total Rewards Strategy

Now that we have laid out both the context and the components of the executive total rewards strategy, we can begin to develop it. Clearly, significant research is necessary before implementation. Once all the research and homework is complete (on all contextual elements, as well as on all components of the strategy), the actual drafting of the strategy is quite simple.

Most organizations, however, do not do nearly enough preparatory work before writing the strategy, which is why they often fail to deliver the intended results. Although it entails a great deal of work, it is a highly worthwhile investment of time and energy because it demands that senior executives and the Board clearly articulate the organization's strategy and human capital strategy; think about the design of the program and how all of the components work together; and why the total rewards package is structured the way that it is.

How do you go about structuring an effective process that, in the end, delivers a quality strategy that is linked to the business?

1. Interview Compensation Committee members of the Board of Directors for their thoughts and input.

2. Conduct structured interviews with key members of the executive team.

   a. Business direction

   b. Degree of competition

   c. Their input, from a philosophical perspective, on the 12 areas of the executive reward strategy

3. Obtain the firm strategy and key business objectives. If they do not have this, you simply cannot proceed.

4. Obtain current and projected firm financials from the CFO.

5. Obtain the Human Capital strategy, executive recruitment and turnover information from the VP of HR.

6. Research other relevant information from available sources.

7. Determine, based upon the results of the BOD and executive interviews, if there are any significant philosophical disagreements between:

   a. Management and the BOD

   b. Between BOD members

   c. Between members of the executive team

8. These differences should try to be worked before a draft of the strategy is developed and reviewed, because they often end up being showstoppers.

9. Based on all available information, prepare a draft of the executive total rewards strategy. Present it to the BOD Compensation Committee as a team, and to the executive team or subset thereof.

10. Based on this input, finalize the strategy document.

11. Prepare a thorough review of all current plans against the strategy.

Component	Strategy
Role and Importance of Rewards	Executive total rewards will be used as an important supporting mechanism in the organization, providing a link between executives and shareholders.
Internal Consistency vs. External Competitiveness	Our goal is to be externally competitive at the level we set our executive rewards at, without focusing on internal consistency.
Team Consistency vs. Individual Customizability	In order to be externally market driven, and be able to attract and retain the highest caliber and most diverse executives that we can, our plans will have a high degree of individual customizability, while remaining within the bounds of desired competitive levels.
Competitive Peer Group Definition	After thorough research on our executive labor market, our product market, and our capital market competitors, the set of firms that we will use for comparisons in our executive compensation reviews include 3Com, AOL Time Warner, Applied Materials, Cisco Systems, Peoplesoft, IBM, Intel, Microsoft, SAP, Siebel, Sun, ENC, BEA and EDS.
Component Mix	Our goal is to tightly link our executive compensation system tightly linked to performance, and the best way to accomplish this linkage is through the aggressive use of short and long-term incentives. Thus, we desire our component mix be more highly weighted to the variable components vis-a-vis our competition.
Competitive Positioning	In order to attract and retain the outstanding levels of executive talent that we need, our compensation will be targeted to the following levels, based upon meeting pre-established performance levels; base—60th percentile, Total Cash Compensation at Target—75th percentile, and Long-term Incentives—90th percentile.
Regulatory Constraints	Our programs will be designed to fully comply with all existing regulations factored in.
Linkage to Performance	It is our desire to have one of the highest pay for performance linkages in the country. With the use of heavy incentive levels and relative peformance comparisons vis-a-vis a well performing peer group, we have full confidence that this can be accomplished.
Team vs. Individual Performance	The executive total rewards program will primarily support the accomplishment of broad corporate objectives and strategies—short-term incentive plans will be funded 100 percent based upon corporate measures, and payouts will be at least 75 percent based upon those measures.
Ownership Orientation	We have an aggresive ownership orientation, believing that executives and employees who feel like owners will act like owners. As such, we will aggressively use stock in our executive reward packages, and have stock holding requirements for our key executives equal to 5X salary within a four year period.
Deferral/Tax Advantageousness	It is our desire to have our executives be able to retire at a standard of living to which they are accustomed, so we will provide both voluntary and company contribution-based supplemental executive retirement plans. We will also seek to ensure that our overall plan design is efficient from a tax and accounting perspective.
Openness and Communication	We desire to have full and complete openness (except of individual pay levels and stock awards) in all of our compensation programs.

Exhibit 5.

An example of a completed executive total rewards strategy is shown in Exhibit 5, above. The document should be the product of the company's completed research—such as described in this chapter, and should present a level of specificity that can fully guide the plan design.

Executive Total Rewards Plan Design Linked to Strategy

Once the overall executive total rewards strategy has been developed and approved by the Board, it should be used to fully guide the design of all executive total reward programs. If a current program does not meet the criteria spelled out in the strategy, it should be eliminated or redesigned. Each program being considered should be tested against all of the components listed in the strategy to determine the degree of fit. If substantially all of the components fit, it is a well-designed program that will support overall business goals and objectives. If it does not meet substantially all of the components of the strategy, it should be redesigned, for it will not support the overall needs of the business.

In this chapter, we see that developing an executive total rewards strategy that fits with the overall business strategy is significant work. In order to be effective, it needs to be thoroughly researched and planned. Those organizations that clearly link their executive total rewards strategy to their business strategy will effectively support both their overall business model, while successfully as well as compete effectively for high-quality executive personnel. Those that merely design their plan based on narrow, immediate parameters will continue to struggle, relegated to designing, redesigning, and implementing programs that do not respect the broader, more strategic perspective of their organization. The choice is yours!

JACK DOLMAT-CONNELL
Principal, National Executive Compensation Practice Director
Clark Consulting's Human Capital Group

Jack Dolmat-Connell is a Principal of Clark Consulting. His areas of expertise include executive compensation, performance management, total compensation strategy and competitive analysis, and salary management program design.

Prior to joining Clark Consulting, Mr. Dolmat-Connell had served as the Managing Principal of iQuantic, and the Managing Director of the Wilson Group, where he served as head of all consulting operations and was the firm's Technology Industry and Executive Compensation Practice Leader. Mr. Dolmat-Connell was the Director of Compensation and Benefits at Avid Technology, Inc., and prior to Avid, the founder and Managing Director of Solutions at Work, a consulting firm specializing in all aspects of compensation consulting. Jack has also held executive and managerial positions in Compensation and HR at Stratus Computer, Digital Equipment Corporation, and Data General Corporation.

Mr. Dolmat-Connell holds an M.B.A. in Human Resources and Corporate Strategy and a B.A. in Economics, both from the University of Michigan. His articles have appeared in *Compensation & Benefits Review, WorldatWork Journal, Workspan, Boston Business Journal* and *Mass High Tech.* He has authored chapters in several books on compensation and is a frequent speaker at local and national conferences and forums. He is a Certified Compensation Professional, as well as a WorldatWork instructor and a member.

4. The Design and Use of Short Term Variable Pay Plans

Variable pay plans are an integral part of all executive compensation plans, and are commonly viewed as playing a key role for motivating successful performance. Often linked to the company's annual budgeting and performance management process, and with a typical timeframe for potential payout of one year or less, compensation designers and executives give a great deal of attention to this important element of pay. Its importance notwithstanding, the chapter's author notes that, despite best intentions, many incentive plans ultimately fail, and for reasons that are often readily identifiable and preventable.

The author initially explains there are several types of variable pay plans, but places the focus of the chapter on the most prevalent form of variable pay plan for executives, the annual incentive plan. The chapter covers some of the important issues that must be thought through in designing or revising an executive annual incentive plan; these include determining plan participation, selecting performance measures and standards of performance, determining the pay versus performance schedule, and selecting the timeframe for payout and method for funding the plan payments. The author describes the importance of each issue, and provides examples of common plan design features with an explanation as to the business context that might lead to that particular solution.

The final sections of the chapter detail a number of the most common reasons that incentive plans fail–some are technical in nature, while others relate to how the plan was designed, internally positioned and/or communicated. Sample plan templates and spreadsheets for modeling pay outs are included on the CD. –Editors

Overview of Variable Pay Plans

AS YOU HAVE–AND WILL–SEE echoed throughout other chapters in this publication, an organization's compensation plan should be closely aligned with its business strategy. It should also reflect the market value, expertise, experience and performance of the executives who are needed to carry out the business strategy, and should reflect the management and business culture of the company. Such strategies should include the establishment of the company's long-term value through building its reputation, maintaining longevity in the marketplace, and/or maintaining the stability of business to enhance its competitive position in the global economy.

Short-term goals and operations must also be supported by the compensation plan. This may include such near-term issues as maximum utilization of available capacity, product development cycle time, reduction in overhead cost, or increased cash flow.

For compensation to accomplish this it must be more than an exchange for a fair days work. Compensation is complex and multifaceted. In addition to base pay, it includes a variety of benefits, short-term pay, long-term pay, deferred pay and a variety of other perquisites. This chapter will present and discuss a number of short-term variable pay strategies that have been implemented in the recent past by many companies, as well as a discussion of some common pitfalls.

Definition of Variable Pay

Referred to by many names, the simplest definition of variable pay is any compensation that is not folded into base pay and is awarded for performance achievement over a short period of time, typically one year or less.

There are two main categories of variable pay. The first category is known as bonus payments. A bonus is a payment made after a specific outcome is obtained based solely on management discretion. The second category is incentive payments. Incentives can be any reward of value to the employee (typically monetary), that are predefined, and nondiscretionary i.e., earned when actual performance exceeds pre-set goals based on specific measures. If properly designed and administered, incentive plans can be highly effective and help you to achieve the qualitative results you desire and create a culture of continuous improvement.

The purpose of variable pay in executive pay plans is primarily two fold: to focus the executive on objectives that support the business strategy and to link compensation costs with actual performance results. While bonuses can help reduce the long-term fixed compensation cost, it is most difficult to focus the executive on objectives of any kind through the use of an after-the-fact reward, the actual payment of which is left to the discretion of a higher level of management. For this reason the focus of this chapter will be exclusively on incentive reward plans.

Variable Pay's Role in a Company's Total Compensation Philosophy

Variable or incentive pay must fit with the corporation's compensation philosophy and be an integral part of the total compensation picture. Incentives that cover executive employees are typically designed to recognize and reward the performance results that are under the immediate charge of a given executive. However, incentive pay may also be designed to recognize and reward an entire executive team or group for their collective accomplishment. Since short term incentive pay is only one part of total compensation and is usually expressed as a percent of base pay, we will look at base pay briefly.

Base Pay

Base pay (salary) is initially set at a level that reflects a chosen percentile of the current value of the skill set that is required by the particular position. If the company's compensation philosophy is to pay total compensation at, for example, the 75th percentile of the market, then it will be preferable to keep the base pay level near the median or average of the marketplace. The corporation can then use incentive plans to provide the desired level of total compensation when corporate and individual performance is at the target level. This also provides for upside potential when financial and personal goals are exceeded. An effective incentive plan allows a company to compete for high skills in the market place.

Variable Pay

Variable pay is typically expressed as a percentage of base salary. It may be divided into one or more parts with one part being based on a company measure and one part based on the individual participant's performance. The company portion is only paid out if the Company meets some threshold of performance, which is typically financial. The individual performance is typically defined by agreed upon objectives that support the business plan and enhance the long-term health of the business.

Objectives under the plan, whether reflecting the financial measures of the corporation or tied to individual performance, are reviewed and set each year to reflect the business strategy and to focus the executive on the critical success factors (CSF) of the Company. The objectives are set based on the demand for continuous improvement and using as few measures as possible, but enough to capture all key performance areas (e.g., time, money, quality, customer service). An incentive pay plan must have a sunset clause i.e., a provision that the plan be evaluated and redirected as business strategy dictates, typically at least once every year.

Advantages of using variable pay include that it:

1. Aligns cost with ability to pay;
2. Helps focus the behavior of the executive on meeting defined objectives;
3. Aligns rewards with specific contributions or performance;
4. Is consistent with competitive trends;
5. Builds in a continuous improvement philosophy and;
6. Diminishes the executive's sense of "entitlement."

Some disadvantages are it:

1. Requires careful development of specific performance definitions and measurement;
2. May conflict with the executive's expectation that compensation only goes up;
3. Is difficult to budget accurately;
4. Doesn't encourage long term vision.

Elements of an Effective Variable Pay Plan

Establishing the Criteria to Participate

Once the decision is made to implement a variable pay plan a determination must be made to determine who the plan participants will be. Will it cover just officers? Will it be extended to other levels within the organization? These are questions that must be answered before the design process is started. Although our coverage here of variable pay is focused on only executives, it should be mentioned (in situations involving more than just executives) that it is easier to design a plan when the scope of employee coverage is to be just the senior executives. For example, if only officers are covered, the metrics might conceivably be financial in nature, while additional metrics would be needed if others are going to participate. Employees at different levels within an organization focus on different aspects of the company. For example, if we are designing an incentive plan for plant workers, we would use metrics such as quality of the product, safety, production cost in the plant, etc. If the plan is designed for a group of executives, the metric would be more all encompassing such as Net Income, Return on Sales, Return on Total Capital Employed, etc. With this in mind the metrics chosen should be ones that the participants can see will be directly effected by their contributions.

The criteria to determine appropriate participants for a given plan should include consideration of who is in a position that can directly affect the critical success factors of the company.

Variable pay is also known as "pay at risk" as it is possible for the participant, in situations of poor performance of the organization or the individual, to not receive any pay-out from the plan. With this in mind, the level at which each person to be included in the plan will participate must be decided. Typically, the target payment–the payment that is earned if all metrics are met at the plan level–is expressed as a percent of base pay. When the target incentive is set, the higher a position is in the organization the more pay is at risk, hence the larger the target incentive. Table 1 gives an example of typical target pay levels.

Another organization might use a flat dollar amount for the target payout. For example, the executives as a group might be considered a team and team building might be an objective that the board desires to reinforce. If all of the executives are capable of earning the same amount in absolute dollars, based on the team performance, this might be a more appropriate way to design the target payout levels.

Establishing the Performance Measures

First, establish the foundation by defining what it is that needs to be accomplished. This is done by examining the company's Critical Success Factors

Typical Target Payout Levels

Title	Target as a percent of base pay
President and CEO	75%
Executive Vice President, COO	50%
Chief Legal Counsel	50%
Chief Financial Officer	50%
Vice President Operations	40%
Vice President, International	40%
Vice President New Product Development	40%
Vice President, Sales & Marketing	40%
Vice President Sales	30%
Vice President Marketing	30%
Vice President, Human Resources	30%
Vice President, Quality	30%

Table 1.

(CSFs), the CSFs having been derived from the company objectives and defining what must be done to achieve those objectives. CSFs are important to variable pay design for two reasons:

a. They provide criteria for eligibility—who will participate and at what level. Only those executives who are able to have a direct impact on the CSFs should participate.

b. They indicate what needs to be measured. Look carefully at the critical success factors and, if they were constructed correctly, they should lead to an appropriate measure. For example if improved cash-flow is an objective, and inventories are excessively high and accounts receivable are excessive, one of the measures could be "Return on Net Assets."

These should not be developed in a vacuum. Since most measures are financial in nature, it is important that the Chief Financial Officer or the Controller be closely involved in determining the measures and CSFs.

Establishing the Performance Standards and Goals

This section will discuss several of the most prevalent performance standards and how to adapt them to an organization. It will also look at how to use the criteria to tailor and establish the measure to the unique character and circumstances of an organization. The first performance standard or goal should focus on the core business and which of the CSFs are most fundamental to its on-going success.

The performance standards and goals must capture and directly reflect the organization's business objectives and strategies and those critical success factors necessary to achieve them. The criteria for performance measures typically fall into the following six categories:

1. Financial

There are a large number of well established choices within this category. The focus should be on identifying the few that are most critical for achieving the specific goals that the company has currently targeted. Some of the most common measures include:

- Return on Equity (ROE)
    Net Income available to Common Stockholders
        Common Equity
- Return on Total Assets (ROA)
    Net Income available to Common Stockholders
        Total Assets

- Return on sales
  Net Income
  Net Sales
- Earnings per share
  Net Income Available to Common Stockholders
  Weighted average Common Shares outstanding
- Net income
  Net Income = Revenue - expenses
- Return on Capital employed
  Net Income & Interest on Long Term Debt net of taxes
  Equity & Long Term Debt

2. Time

- Cycle time
  Amount of time it takes to produce a product.
- Time to Market
  Length of time from concept to development to product to market

3. Quality

- Warranty repair
  Total cost of warranty repairs
- Scrap
  Cost of scrapped material
- Service Cost
  Cost of servicing the product
- Cost of recalls
  Cost of recalling the product and repairs or replacement cost

4. Customer Service

- Customer survey information
- Customer Satisfaction

5. Innovation

- Rate of new product development
  How often is a new product introduced into the market?
- Percent of revenue produced by products introduced in past three year

6. Attraction and Retention

- Core Values
  What are the core values by which management lives?
- Line of Sight

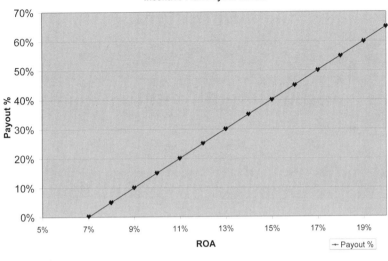

Incentive Plan Payout Levels

Figure 1.

How well can the employee connect their action to the earning of the incentive?

• Desired Behavior
• Skill Enhancement

What is the opportunity for the development of new and needed skills?

Defining the Variable Pay Formulas

Formulas can take on many characteristics, however most can be represented as a straight line as shown in Figure 1.

A straight-line formula simply means that each increase in the measure is associated with a constant increase in the pay out level or a constant increase in the percent of target pay out. The formula for a straight line takes on the mathematical properties of $Y = A + BX$. In this formula, Y is the pay out level; A is the intercept or the value of the pay out when the measure (X) equals zero; and B is the slope of the line or the change in Y as X changes one unit. In our example of Return on Assets (ROA) shown in Table 2, each time the ROA changes 1%, the pay out level (Y) changes 5%. For example, when the ROA reaches 10% the pay out level is 15% of salary and when the ROA reaches 11%, the pay out level is 20% of salary.

(The reader may wish to refer to the Excel spreadsheet and formulas provided on the accompanying CD. The spreadsheet can be used to develop and test your own formulas by inserting the threshold, target and maximum pay out levels that you wish to model for the measure at that level.)

ROA	Payout %
7%	0%
8%	5%
9%	10%
10%	15%
11%	20%
12%	25%
13%	30%
14%	35%
15%	40%
16%	45%
17%	50%
18%	55%
19%	60%
20%	65%

Table 2.

Establishing the Frequency of Plan Pay-Outs

Most companies pay the incentive on an annual basis for executives. This makes sense as most measures are on a fiscal year basis. It is recommended that the incentive measurement and the payment of the earned incentive be based on the fiscal year as well. However, if the measurement period is more frequent, the incentive payout period should be set to correspond.

Techniques for Funding Variable Pay Plans

A question that must be asked when a company moves from an all base pay program to a base pay and incentive program is, "How should the plan be funded?"; where funding refers to the method employed to develop the pool of money from which incentives will be paid. The answer to this question depends upon the cost of the incentive, and the ability of the company to pay additional compensation. If the organization is in excellent financial shape and pay is low in relation to target pay, then it would probably make sense to just add the incentive to current compensation. On the other hand if total compensation is where the organization expects it to be in relation to the market, then it would make sense to add the incentive in place of a merit budget.

When a company first implements variable pay the merit budget is typically reduced until the base pay and the target incentive is at a competitive level in the marketplace. For example if the merit budget would normally be set at 5%, the company would suspend the merit budget for the covered executives and add an incentive of some amount greater than the foregone 5% merit, let's say in this case 10%. If the measure is met at target, the 5% is paid. If it is exceeded, then the greater amount is paid, up to 10%. Note that if no incentive were paid due to performance being below threshold, the participant would end up being paid lower than market. A way to mitigate this is to, for the transition year, guarantee at least the amount that would have been granted under the former merit plan. Other possible alternatives would be to withhold only half of the merit and reduce the amount set aside for the incentive, keep the merit budget, add the incentive program and pay the incentive only if the expected performance is exceeded.

The method that is the best choice for a company will depend upon the compensation philosophy, the comparative position in the market of the current compensation program, and the financial condition of the company.

Once a variable pay program is established there are a number of funding mechanisms that are typically used. The following are three of the most common options and it should be understood that they are not mutually exclusively.

Knockout Trigger Funding

Here the Company stipulates a threshold level of performance on some financial measure (e.g., net income, ROI) before the program is funded.

A knock out trigger is a funding method that only allows the incentive payments to be made if some threshold measure is met. What is typically found is that the Corporation sets a measure such as profit that must be met before any other measure comes into play. For example, let us assume that the Corporation has a number of individuals or business groups that have their own measures. Regardless of how the individual or group performs on their measure there will be no pay out unless the Corporation meets their profit threshold. While this would protect the Corporation since overall performance is below the threshold, it will seen as unfair or de-motivational if one unit exceeds their objectives yet receives no incentive because the remainder of the organization performed below expectations. (See Table 3).

Pool Funding

Pool Funding is based on one or more company wide performance measures, which is used to fund the pool. The size of the pool is based on the actual performance versus pre-determined objectives

Pool funding is a technique that is used to develop an amount of money (a pool) based upon the performance of the company. For example, if the chosen metric is to make $100,000,000 in net profit, taking some percent of all profit above the $100,000,000 develops a pool. This pool is then divided among the participants, typically as a percent of salary. This protects the company in the case of poor company performance and requires management to invest in performance.

Side by Side Funding

Here funds are set up at both the company and the unit level i.e., "side-by-side." Using this approach, either portion might represent anywhere from 10% to 50% of the total incentive award. The performance metric is based on some portion relating to the organization wide measure with the remainder relating to the particular subsidiary or business unit in which the individual works. If the organization wide threshold is met, then that portion pays out regardless of the performance of the units, and vice versa.

Side by side funding is a technique that is considered when an organization has a number of subsidiaries or business units.

This funding method can cause payouts to occur at the unit level even though the company has not performed well.

Administrative Guidelines

The appendix of aids on the accompanying CD includes a sample plan document that can be used as a template. When putting together a variable

Matrix of Selected Funding Method Options

Funding Approach	Pros	Cons
Knockout Trigger Funding	Completely protects the company against funding a large pool in the event that over-all performance is below-threshold	May be perceived as unfair if awards are not funded when specific performance objectives are met
Pool Funding	Protects the company against funding large awards in the event of poor company performance	Requires management to adopt an "investment mentality" Requires management to invest in performance
Side by Side Funding	Increases the prominence of specific CSF performance measures	Significant payouts can occur at the unit level even though the company has lost money

Table 3.

pay plan, there are problems into which the less experienced compensation person typically runs. Let's review and discuss four of those now:

Too many measures

In the performance standards and goals section presented earlier, a number of metrics were mentioned. Since measures have the ability to focus desired attention and quantify actual results, it is easy to fall into the trap of thinking that "the more, the better." However, the goal should be only to include the vital few measures. Go back to the purpose and objectives of the plan. Make sure that the items being measured tightly fit those objectives.

Making the Plan So Complex it Becomes Difficult to Administer

As in any compensation plan, the "KISS" principle is very important. Make it a simple but effective plan. The less administration that is involved the better the plan will be and it will be more easily understood. That is why it is useful to look at current metrics used by the company. The most important ones are already being measured and the system is in place to do so.

Failing to Involve the Finance Department

It is incomprehensible that there are still people in compensation who attempt to design plans without the involvement of other appropriate departments. I was in a workshop a few years ago where an example of a skill-based pay program was discussed. The compensation manager described how it was developed and implemented by the compensation department. He went on to describe how it only lasted for less than a year before it was changed back to the traditional compensation program that preceded it. When asked why it failed, he had no clue. It was easy to see that it was a program thought up and designed entirely by the compensation department and was quickly destroyed because management and those employees covered by it did not understand it or see a need for it.

This shows the importance of getting those who are covered by the plan involved in the design. Regardless of how good we design and implement a plan if it does not have buy-in from the top of the organization, from finance, from those employees covered by the plan and, from those groups involved in administering the plan it will most likely fail.

Losing sight of the purpose of the plan, i.e., approaching it as just a way to deliver more money to the participants instead of directing their behavior

Too often an incentive plan can become an entitlements plan, where the participants assume that each year the payment should be greater than the last one. This defeats the central purpose of variable pay plans. A plan should be designed to payout when the company or business unit is doing well and to not pay out when the company or business unit is not doing well –hence the term variable pay plan.

Developing a "Test" Model of a Variable Pay Plan

Once a plan is designed, perform a cost benefit analysis. Model some "what ifs" such as what if we had this plan in place last year, what would have been the results? What would have been the cost? What would have been the benefit?

Define a set of assumptions concerning who would have been in the plan, and what their target payout would have been. What would have been their total compensation at the target plus their base salary? How does this compare to the marketplace and how does it match up with the company's compensation philosophy?

Make an assumption about the suggested metrics and compare them to the plan. How difficult is it to get the data for the chosen metrics? Is the data already being calculated and used elsewhere in the organization?

What are the standards or goals for the participants and for the company? If there is a personal performance aspect to the variable plan, how is the performance to be measured? Is it measured through setting personal goals, a normal performance appraisal, or is it discretionary? All of these questions need to be answered and applied to the test case to determine how easy it is to administer and to accurately determine estimates of what the proposed program's cost and ease of administration would have been.

Try different formulas for the test plan and look at different payout levels, both below and above the target. Many companies make the upside potential higher than the downside risk. This is a critical concept to consider when designing an incentive plan. For example, if our metric is return on capital employed (ROCE), and we set target ROCE at 15% each percent above the 15% will return more to the bottom line, (net income) than the average return below the target of 15 percent. If designed right and with the right metrics, above plan performance is worth more to the company and thus should be worth more to the participants of the plan. The opposite is true when actual performance is below target performance.

Look at various alternatives to fund the program. Will it be funded out of new earnings, or perhaps out of the budget for salary increases? Model each and look at their projected results.

If this is a proposed variable pay plan for an organization that has never had one, what is the readiness of the organization to put some part of pay at risk? Are there significant barriers to implementing variable pay? For example, has the practice been to give out Christmas bonuses each year. Now as we tie it to performance some employees might see it as a loss of an entitlement. This could lead to opposition to the plan by some key players if not overt at least covert. Set up focus groups and find out what might be the issues against variable pay. What can you do to reduce the opposition to variable pay?

Is variable pay consistent with the company's compensation philosophy? Does the current operating budget support the cost of the plan?

Once all of these questions have been answered for an organization, it is time to present the plan design to management.

In the section of the CD for this chapter is a spreadsheet set up to help facilitate calculating the cost of a contemplated plan. Insert the data into the spreadsheet and run the calculations. Also included in the aids section is a sample power point presentation to assist in putting together a presentation for management's approval.

Developing a Support Infrastructure

Here is a sobering thought for you: approximately two thirds of all incentive programs fail. They typically do so not from bad architecture, but rather because one or more of the following support processes were missing or failed.

Information Infrastructure

1. The information infrastructure must present information that is reliable and valid regarding the performance of the organization and the individual participant (if individual performance is included as one of the metrics). Further, it must be reported in a timely and user-friendly fashion. Likewise, databases must yield timely and user-friendly performance information. The data must be shared with the participants in a format that they can understand and must encourage questions, analysis, and thinking about systems improvement.

2. Develop a transition plan to move from an all base pay to a base pay plus variable pay concept. A careful "no surprises" transition is necessary for a successful program. Following are several suggestions for making the transition:

   a. Take a series of "mini steps." Phase in targets with a bridge program that is funded partially from base pay increases in order to ease into a pay-at-risk concept.

b. Begin with high-level critical success factors and transition to more direct measures in the following year. One might also consider a "risk less" floor for the first several months or year.

c. Consider introducing the variable pay plan by first using it in a pilot situation with assurances given to the participants that they will be guaranteed not less than the amount of money that they would have received under the old pay plan. This is more important where reductions in the normal merit budget is to fund the new variable pay plan

Communications Infrastructure

Effective communication about the program is a necessity. More than one program has failed because management has not properly communicated it to the participants. Developing a communication plan is necessary to ensure that the purpose and goals of the incentive plan are clearly communicated to participants. The communication of the plan must involve accurate information about the design and measures of the plan, the processes used to assess and evaluate performance, as well as the processes used to assess and evaluate the plan itself. The communication process must result in understanding and ownership by the participants.

When developing a communication plan consider the following:

• Who is the audience?

• What is the message?

• What is the best medium?

• Who is delivering the message?

Continuous Improvement Infrastructure

Develop a continuous improvement mentality and process. Develop an effective means for capturing and implementing ideas of continuous improvement. Also make sure that the plan has a "sunset clause" meaning that before the plan is renewed for the following year there will be a review and appropriate changes made to suit the business needs of the company.

A system must be developed to respond to and incorporate the ideas for improvement elicited by the incentive program.

Tracking and Evaluation

Make sure that the program continues to operate as designed and contributes to business improvement. Programs that are tracked and evaluated tend to succeed; those that are not have a tendency to fail. Be prepared to assess the answers to the following questions at least once a year for the life of the program:

1. **Excitement**–Does the program continue to generate attention and interest?

2. **Understanding**–Is the program understood? Can participants give you correct answers about how the program works?

3. **Line of Sight**–As a result of the program have employees developed a better understanding of business priorities (including critical success factors) and how they can personally influence them?

4. **Operations**–Is the program operating as designed? Are any changes necessary?

5. **Business Contribution**–Has the program contributed significantly to improvement on the vital few measures of business success?

Organizational Implications of Variable Pay Plans

When an organization decides to move to a variable pay program, it must assess the impact on the salary structure, and its relationship to the compensation philosophy of the organization. Does it fit the compensation philosophy or does it need to be changed?

How does variable pay fit into the organization's management style, business strategy, culture and risk tolerance? Are there other management systems that need to be changed to fit the new culture putting some portion of pay at risk?

Deferred Compensation

Most companies that have a deferred compensation program allow the executive to elect the deferral of part or all of the incentive earned.

What are the impacts of variable pay on accounting, finance and tax issues?

For the most part, variable pay is treated like base pay. If the plan is designed correctly it is considered pay for performance and is excluded under section 162(m) of the Internal Revenue Code. The Omnibus Budget Reconciliation Act of 1993 added this section. It denies a deduction to any publicly held corporation for compensation paid to a "covered employee" in a taxable year to the extent that the compensation exceeds $1,000,000. There are exceptions for certain amounts payable under written binding contracts in existence on February 27, 1993 that are not materially modified thereafter, such as payments from plans qualified under Code Section 401, payments of commissions, and qualified performance-based compensation. Most executive incentives qualify as performance based provided they are non-discretionary.

Summary

A variable pay program can be an effective tool to focus behavior on objectives that are important to the company's success. However, care should be taken in the process of developing and implementing these programs. This chapter has presented the important areas to be initially considered and acted upon, as well as outlined some possible solutions that will make a variable pay program successful.

Accompanying materials to be found on the CD for this chapter:

• Excel® spreadsheet model: Allowing testing/modeling of payout formulas
• Sample Variable Incentive Plan document template

JERRY T. EDGE, CEBS, CCP
Director Global Compensation
Callaway Golf Company

For more than 30 years, Jerry has specialized in compensation management in a variety of industries, including manufacturing, food and transportation.

At Callaway Jerry is responsible for worldwide compensation, HRIS, and payroll programs. This includes base pay, variable pay, executive compensation, international compensation and sales incentive plan design.

He is a past President and Life Member of the American Compensation Association (now WorldatWork) and has served in several other regional and national roles. Jerry received his B.A. in business from the University of North Carolina, an M.B.A. from Georgia State University and completed his D.B.A course work at George Washington University.

5. Executive Stock Options

Beginning in the 1980s, stock options emerged and ascended to become the foundation of most publicly traded companies' long-term incentive programs. Today, virtually all public U.S. companies use stock options to motivate and reward their employees, and stock options–or their financial equivalent–are also used by a large number of privately held organizations as well.

Because of this prevalence, the recent and anticipated option-related regulatory changes (as well as the often-heated public debate concerning their use) promise to impact the compensation plans of virtually every company. Far from becoming irrelevant, an incisive understanding of options, the aforementioned changes, and the emerging variations on their use is needed if you are to participate effectively in the design, evaluation, or administration of an executive compensation plan. –Editors

Stock Options as the Foundation of Executive Incentives

STOCK OPTIONS HAVE BEEN a powerful tool, enabling the owners of a business to provide an economic incentive to managers to create value, without necessarily requiring the managers to invest their own financial capital. Rather, the managers invest their time and effort (human capital) and become shareholders over time through exercise of the options and retention of the underlying shares.

Reasons for the historic popularity of stock options include:

- Options have enjoyed favorable tax and accounting treatment, which made them a very financially efficient way of delivering employee compensation
- Options establish commonality of interest with shareholders and provide a means for employees to acquire ownership in the Company
    - Options tie employee rewards directly to the creation of shareholder value
    - Options are generally worthless in the absence of share price appreciation
- Options do not require an up-front investment by employees or a cash outlay by the Company
    - Options provide employees with a risk-free opportunity to share in the appreciation of company stock
    - Options provide positive cash flow to the company when exercised

through payment of the exercise price and the tax deduction generally available on the profit realized by recipients

- Options minimize the need to use complex financial measurement in determining the size of incentive plan payouts
  - As a result, options are simple to communicate and easy to understand
  - They also automatically flex with changes in the strategic direction of the business, which reduces the need to subjectively measure long-term performance
- Options are powerful retention devices, since they are usually granted pursuant to a future service commitment (e.g., a vesting schedule)

Environmental Influences and Emerging Trends

For a variety of reasons that will be discussed, the appropriateness and effectiveness of stock options are being reevaluated by many companies. These factors include:

- **Proposed changes in stock option accounting rules**–since 1995, U.S. generally accepted accounting principles have allowed companies to choose whether to determine stock option expense under APB Opinion 25 or FAS Statement 123. Under APB 25, stock option expense is generally determined as the intrinsic value of the award when granted (i.e., zero for standard options), while expense under FAS 123 generally equals the fair value (e.g., Black-Scholes or binomial option model value) of the award at grant. The absence of an expensing requirement has historically made stock options more financially efficient than other incentives, but that is changing. Reasons include:

  1. Companies using APB 25 are required to report the pro forma impact on earnings as if they had expensed options under FAS 123

  2. Investors, securities analysts, and rating agencies are closely examining the FAS 123 footnote disclosure and making investment decisions and buy/sell recommendations based on pro forma rather than only reported results

  3. The Financial Accounting Standards Board (FASB) is working to implement a new accounting standard that would require expensing options under rules similar to those currently in place under FAS 123. While this proposal is contentious, it has strong support in Congress, among investors, and among the general public

  Depending on the final outcome of the FASB's initiative, options may shift from being the most financially efficient form of incentive to being the least. In other words, expensing makes cash and "full-value" equity awards (e.g., restricted stock) less expensive on a relative basis. Accounting rules applicable to options are discussed in greater detail later in this chapter.

- **Shareholder approval requirements**–in 2003, the New York Stock Exchange and Nasdaq implemented rule changes that generally eliminate the ability of listed companies to make ongoing employee equity grants from plans that are not approved by stockholders. The new rules also restrict brokers from voting shares held in street name in favor of management proposals to increase share authorizations without explicit instructions from the shareowner. These rules shift the balance of control over potential dilution to shareholders and impede the ability of companies to replenish the share reserve in employee equity plans when exhausted.

- **Market volatility, operating results, and public sentiment**–since the collapse of the market "bubble" in 2000, many companies have struggled with the negative impact that market volatility has on the ability of stock options to support corporate retention and incentive objectives, as well as long-term shareholder objectives. Market volatility often creates a disconnect between operating performance and share price movement, particularly over the short-term. Critics contend that investors lose either way, since rising markets create windfall gains and declining markets create compensation deficiencies that often result in option repricing or the granting of special awards to retain key executives. There is also public concern that large stock option awards encourage a "quarter by quarter" approach to managing earnings and do not appropriately encourage focus on long-term operating performance and the efficient use of capital. Further, large awards are viewed by many observers as contributing to poor corporate governance, and in worst case situations, may encourage executives to misuse accounting to cover up business failures, artificially sustain high stock prices, and otherwise mislead investors.

As a result of the above, the percentage of total compensation delivered through stock options is declining and participation below the senior executive level is falling. While it is impossible at present to predict exactly what role options will play in the future, it is safe to assume that it will continue to be significant, although likely less so than in the past. Notwithstanding that prediction, anyone who will be involved in the evaluation of an option program, or its potential modification or replacement, needs to have a clear understanding of the information presented here.

Source of Shares

Stock options are generally granted pursuant to formal plans, although grants are sometimes made through individual agreements to key executives in conjunction with special circumstances (e.g., new hire). Formal plans include those designed solely to deliver stock options, as well as "omnibus" plans that allow for the granting of stock options and other stock-based awards (e.g., restricted stock, deferred stock units, stock appreciation rights, etc.).

Omnibus plans have been increasing in popularity over the last decade and have effectively become the standard for new plans being adopted today.

Real Versus Phantom Stock

Options may be granted on a variety of financial instruments, including both real and phantom stock on both publicly-traded and private corporations.

Phantom stock, for the most part, resembles real stock in all ways, except that the value per share is generally determined through some sort of formula that approximates the value that would be determined through the public markets or through non-public sale. The value of phantom stock can also be determined through independent appraisal.

A stock appreciation right (SAR) provides the holder with the right to receive a payment at some point in time equal to the appreciation in stock price above an initial level. SARs and phantom stock options resemble real stock options with one major exception–the gain is often paid in cash and the exercise does not entitle the optionee to any real right of ownership.

Historically, SARs and phantom stock option plans have been used by private companies and subsidiaries of public organizations to accomplish two goals:

• Provide a company-specific stock-based incentive, and
• Protect the balance of control by avoiding sale of real equity and the creation of minority shareholders

Because SARs and phantom stock options do not receive the favorable accounting treatment available to stock options under APB 25, they are relatively uncommon among publicly-traded companies. However, SARs in which the gain is delivered in shares (as opposed to cash) receive the same fixed accounting treatment as stock options under FAS 123, and presumably, under the new standard being developed by the FASB.

This chapter principally addresses options on real stock in publicly-traded companies, although most of the concepts are equally applicable to SARs and phantom stock options.

The Basics of Stock Option Design

Every stock option award includes a variety of basic terms, as described below.

Period of Exercisability

The period during which an option is exercisable is called the option term. Over 90% of all options carry 10-year terms, although a trend toward shorter option terms is developing.

Because optionees typically exercise well before the option is set to expire, the use of terms less than 10 years has little practical effect on most employees. However, shorter terms can be advantageous to companies because most employee stock plans allow options that are not exercised to be returned to the plan and granted again. This enables underwater options (i.e., exercise price is higher than current Fair Market Value (FMV), which are often deemed as valueless by holders, to expire and be granted again without the need to "reprice" the awards.

Cost of the Option to Recipient

The exercise price is the price at which the optionee is permitted to buy the underlying stock over the term of the option. Most options are granted with an exercise price equal to the fair market value of the underlying stock at the date of grant. Variations to the traditional FMV grant include:

- **Premium option**–the exercise price is greater than the FMV of the underlying stock at grant
- **Discount option**–the exercise price is less than the fair market value at grant[1]
- **Indexed option**–the exercise price changes in relation to the performance of the granting company relative to peers or an outside index, such as the S&P 500

Requirements for Exercise

Because one of the primary objectives in granting stock options is to tie the recipient to the company for an extended period (e.g., create a "golden handcuff"), virtually all options require that the recipient remain employed for a specified period (i.e., the vesting period) before the award may be exercised. In some cases, the option also requires that certain performance objectives be met prior to exercise.

Once an option becomes vested, the optionee acquires a non-forfeitable right to exercise the option during the remaining term.[2] The most common vesting schedules are purely time-based, with either 1/3rd of the total stock option grant vesting per year over 3 years or 25% per year over 4 years being the most widely used. However, performance-based schedules in which vesting is based on criteria other than the passage of time (e.g., reaching stock price targets, performance against specified goals) are becoming more common as companies attempt to better link option gains to performance.

In selecting the length and/or appropriateness of performance criteria in a vesting schedule, a company should weigh the retentive and performance benefits of tougher schedules against the reduction in value the recipient may perceive. If the vesting period is too long or the performance criteria too tough, the vesting provisions may actually encourage turnover. When selecting vesting schedules, it is important to consider industry dynamics, and in some cases, the individual circumstances and expectations of the recipient.

Treatment of Unvested Options at Termination of Employment

Because the contributions made by optionees may take several years to reflect itself in share price, it is often appropriate to accelerate vesting upon the occurrence of events that limit an optionee's tenure with the company. To avoid creation of unexpected accounting expense, it is important that the events that result in acceleration be clearly described either in the plan document under which the award was granted or in the grant agreement.

To promote positive employee relations and allow optionees to participate in the shareholder value they help create, companies often accelerate vesting following death, disability, and retirement. Acceleration following retirement (or continuation of vesting, perhaps subject to satisfaction of a non-compete requirement) also helps encourage the orderly succession of management, which enhances a company's ability to retain younger workers by providing greater levels of responsibility.

Treatment of Unvested Options at Change in Control

Upon change in control of the corporation, most companies accelerate the vesting of outstanding stock options. While this practice is widespread, it is coming under intense shareholder scrutiny for the following reasons:

- **Acceleration of vesting eliminates the retentive value of outstanding awards**–this places pressure on the acquiring company to either make new grants or find another way (e.g., stay bonuses) to encourage retention of key staff.[3]

–The cost associated with addressing this issue is likely to be reflected in a lower price that an acquirer is willing to pay for the company

–In other words, single-trigger acceleration of vesting (i.e., acceleration at change in control without a subsequent loss of job) results in a direct transfer of value from shareholders to optionees

- **Acceleration sometimes occurs prematurely**–some companies accelerate vesting before actual consummation of the deal. In the event that the transaction is not closed as a result of regulatory issues or other factors, the company is pressured to make new awards that create additional shareholder dilution even though no reorganization actually occurred

A simple way to avoid premature acceleration is to postpone acceleration until the deal is closed or until all regulatory and other hurdles are cleared. An approach that avoids the windfalls described above and the resulting shareholder costs is to accelerate vesting only if one of the following circumstances occurs:

- **Double-trigger event**–a change in control occurs in conjunction with loss of employment
- **Failure to assume awards**–if the acquirer fails to assume or replace the outstanding grants with awards of equivalent economic value (i.e., same intrinsic value)

The double trigger approach is becoming more widespread and is likely to increase in prevalence over the next several years because certain institutional investors automatically vote against stock plans proposals (i.e., implementation of new plans or increases in authorized shares under existing plans) in which vesting automatically accelerates.

Exercisability of Vested Stock Options after Termination of Employment

For the same reasons companies accelerate vesting following certain termination events (e.g., death, disability, retirement), it is often appropriate to allow post-employment exercisability of vested awards.

The following factors should be considered when addressing post-employment exercisability:

- The nature of the termination event
  –Companies generally allow longer post-employment exercise periods for "good leavers" (e.g., retirement, death, disability, involuntary termination other than for cause) than they do for "bad leavers" (e.g., involuntary termination for cause, voluntary termination)

- The length of time during which an optionee's contribution is likely to continue affecting stock price after employment
    - Individuals setting policy and making high-level, strategic decisions (e.g., CEO) are likely to have a longer post-employment impact than lower level employees
- The organization's tolerance for shareholder dilution and accounting expense
    - The longer the post-employment exercisability of an award, the greater the potential dilution attributable to outstanding options. In addition, accounting expense under FAS 123 is directly related to an option's expected life, which is affected by the length of time an option can be exercised following termination of employment

The longer the time during which a vested option remains exercisable following termination, the greater the level of potential dilution to shareholders (i.e., "overhang") and the more likely the optionee will receive a windfall (i.e., share in appreciation not attributable to their contributions). The following table illustrates reasonable sample post-employment exercisability provisions:

While there is no single approach that works best for all companies and differences often exist among employee levels within a company, the following chart provides illustrative post-employment option exercise provisions and the rationale for each.

Alternative Ways to Pay the Exercise Price

Stock option plans may provide a variety of ways in which an optionee can pay the exercise price. These generally include:

- **Cash**–payment is made in cash or by check
- **Stock-for-stock (stock swap)**–payment is made in the form of company stock already owned by the optionee. To provide maximum flexibility and simplify the exercise process, companies often allow the optionee to formally tender shares or to simply attest to owning the shares. To avoid adverse accounting treatment, it is important that shares used in the exercise be "mature," meaning that they have been held by the employee for a period of at least 6 months
    - For example, assume an employee holds an option on 100 shares that is exercisable at $10 per share (i.e., exercise price of $1,000). If the stock price at exercise is $20, the exercise price can be covered by tendering 50 shares of stock ($20 x 50 shares = $1,000)

Event	Exercisability	Rationale
Death	Lesser of remaining term or 1 year	Provides estate sufficient time to exercise options
Disability	Lesser of remaining term or 1 year	Provides sufficient time for optionee (or representative) to exercise option; note that longer periods sometimes provided to allow optionee to participate in future stock price appreciation resulting from contributions made during active service
Retirement	Lesser of remaining term or 3 years	Mitigates disincentive to retire that would exist under a shorter (e.g.,1-year) provision; enables optionee to participate in future stock price appreciation resulting from contributions made during active service
Involuntary termination w/o cause	Lesser of remaining term or 90 days	Since release is typically due to poor performance, the optionee has little, if any, positive impact on future results and therefore should not profit
Involuntary termination w/ cause	Immediate forfeiture	Employees fired for cause likely destroyed value and should not be permitted to share in success fostered by other employees
Voluntary termination	Immediate forfeiture	While some companies provide a relatively short number of days to exercise (e.g., 30 or 90), many feel little obligation to employees who quit

- **Cashless exercise**–exercise is accomplished through an outside party (e.g., stock broker or third-party plan administrator) and involves no cash or stock outlay by the optionee. Typically, the process involves notification by the optionee to the broker of the intent to exercise. Assuming there are no restrictions on exercise (e.g., vesting, insider restrictions), the broker executes the transaction by requesting that the company deliver the option shares, which are then sold into the public market. The broker then delivers to the company an amount equal to the option exercise price plus applicable tax withholding. The remaining proceeds are delivered to the optionee in cash or stock

Transferability to Other Individuals and Entities

Most companies have historically restricted the ability of an optionee to transfer a stock option to another party, or when permitted, have limited the ability to senior executives. However, companies are beginning to include transferability features in options on a broad basis, primarily as a way to facilitate estate planning objectives and to protect against the negative implications associated with underwater options.

The transfer of stock options is a potentially valuable estate planning tool, since it effectively allows the optionee to transfer appreciating assets out of their estates to family members and reduce Federal estate and gift taxes (note that the transferor retains the tax liability when the option is exercised). To maximize potential tax benefits, it is best to transfer the options when they have their lowest value. However, IRS rules on valuation limit the possible tax benefit associated with the transfer of an option, particularly for optionees in companies whose stock price appreciates rapidly and/or have long vesting schedules. Even when permitted, few executives take advantage of the opportunity to transfer options for estate tax planning purposes. This is likely due to the perceived conflict among executives regarding retention of the tax liability in the absence of financial control over the option. While the optionee retains responsibility for tax liability, control over the timing of the exercise and the use of the proceeds resides with the transferee. In addition, determination of the value of the option is complicated, and few companies provide any formal assistance to executives in this area, which leaves the burden (and risk) of valuation to the executive and external financial advisors.

In 2003, a well-known technology company modified its stock option program to permit the transferability of outstanding options to a third-party financial institution. This program enabled employees to receive value for options that were underwater at the time and were essentially valueless in the absence of an external market into which they could be sold. It is too early at this point to determine if transferability to third-party financial institutions will become common, although there are a variety of factors that will constrain this practice (e.g., cost, perceived shareholder conflicts).

Use and Design of "Clawback" Features

A "clawback" feature is a provision in which the optionee is required to repay to the company all gains attributable to option exercises that occur within a prescribed time period if the optionee engages in certain types of behavior.

Some companies require a clawback of all option profits realized within a prescribed time period in the event the optionee voluntarily terminates employment and engages in direct competition with the company. A reasonable time period is 12 months.

Other companies extend the concept further by imposing a clawback for indirect competitive actions, as well as other activities that can harm the company. In these cases, events triggering a clawback may include soliciting employees, disclosing proprietary information, or publicly disparaging the company. These provisions typically are imposed only on high level executives, and the "no-action" time period is often as long as 2 to 3 years. The use of this feature is subject to state laws and some states prohibit clawback features that are used to enforce "non-compete provisions" as anti-competitive.

While clawback provisions are relatively uncommon, they are increasing in prevalence. However, clawback provisions are less practical for grants made to lower level employees because the cost of enforcement would likely be greater than the amount at stake.

Depending on specific design, a clawback feature serves one or more of the following objectives:

- Prevents an employee who may harm the company (e.g., through direct competition) from simultaneously capturing option gains
- Discourages ex-employees from engaging in actions that may have harmful effect on the company
- Enhances the retention power of the option, even after it is fully vested, since it increases the amount lost upon termination of employment

Clawback provisions also present certain downsides, since they encourage executives to exercise options as soon as possible and can be an obstacle when attempting to recruit new employees.

Stock Option Varieties

There are two basic varieties of employee stock options: nonqualified stock options (NQSOs) and incentive stock options (ISOs). ISOs, which are often referred to as qualified or statutory stock options, provide favorable tax treatment to employees and are subject to certain restrictions that do not apply to NQSOs.

Most large, well-established, companies grant NQSOs, while smaller, less mature companies (e.g., those that have not yet reached profitability) will often grant ISOs. There are several reasons for this bifurcation in practice, which are summarized below and explored in greater detail elsewhere throughout this chapter:

- ISOs result in loss of the employer tax deduction that would otherwise be available upon exercise of NQSOs

–This makes ISOs more expensive than NQSOs to tax paying entities
- Due to the $100,000 restriction on the amount of ISOs that vest in any calendar year, companies with high market valuations (and therefore high stock prices) cannot grant large numbers of ISOs to their top employees
  - –As a result, the tax benefit is relatively more valuable to lower level employees

ISOs are most popular and appropriate among immature technology companies and start-ups (particularly pre-IPO companies) in which large numbers of shares can be granted within the $100,000 per year limit and concern about corporate tax deductions is not high. These companies often grant pre-IPO ISOs at prices as low as $1 or less, which provides a highly leveraged compensation opportunity in the event the company becomes successful. The financial implications associated with ISOs to the granting company are explained in the section entitled "Corporate Tax Deductibility and Cash Flow Considerations."

Incentive Stock Option Requirements

The specific rules attributable to ISOs are outlined under Section 422 of the Internal Revenue Code and are summarized below.[4]

Employer Rules

- The option must be granted under a plan that specified the number of shares to be issued and the employees or class of employees eligible to receive grants
  - –ISOs may not be granted to non-employees
- The plan must be approved by shareholders within 12 months before or after adoption and the options must be granted within 10 years from the earlier of the date the plan is adopted or approved
- The exercise price of the option must be no less than the fair market value (FMV) of the underlying stock on the date of grant
- The option must have a term no greater than 10 years
- The maximum amount of ISO shares that may become exercisable in any calendar year by an employee cannot exceed $100,000
  - –The number of eligible shares is determined by dividing $100,000 by the exercise price of shares vesting in each year
  - –The calculation process can be complicated by a number of factors, such as grants that vest ratably over multiple years (e.g., 25% per year over 4 years) or an event that accelerates vesting (e.g., a change in control)

−Calculation software can be purchased or developed to help track grants

−Options that vest in excess of the $100,000 limit are considered NQSOs

• The option must be nontransferable, except by the laws of descent and distribution

• The employee receiving the option must not own stock representing more than 10% of the voting power of all classes of stock in the company granting the option

   −An exception for 10% owners is available if the exercise price of the option is at least 110% of FMV and the term of the option is 5 years or less

Employee Rules

• The shares acquired upon exercise of an ISO must be held at least two years from the date of grant and one year from the date of exercise

   −In the event of death, the holding period requirement is waived

• The individual exercising the option must be an employee during the entire time from the date of grant until three months before the date of exercise

   −In the event of disability, the 3-month rule is extended to 12 months

   −In the event of death, the ISO is exercisable for the remaining term

Employee Taxation

The following table compares the tax treatment to employees upon exercise of both a NQSO and an ISO and subsequent sale of acquired stock:

	NQSO	ISO
Upon exercise	Gain is taxed as ordinary income in the year received	No tax on gain at exercise as ordinary income, although gain is considered when determining alternative minimum tax (AMT)
At sale	Gain or loss after exercise is considered ordinary income or, if shares held for at least 12 months, as a capital gain or loss	Assuming applicable holding requirements are met, option gain plus subsequent change in share price are taxable as a capital gain or loss

In the event that the holding requirements are not met or the option is exercised more than 3 months after termination of employment (with certain exceptions described earlier), the exercise of the option is considered a disqualifying disposition. In the event of a disqualifying disposition, the option is taxed as a NQSO.

Use of Options in Privately Held Companies

As mentioned in the introduction to the chapter, options are a revolutionary force that enables the owners of a business to provide an economic incentive to managers of a business to create value. While virtually all publicly traded U.S. companies use stock options, they are also common among private companies. The design of stock options in a private company is influenced by whether the company intends to become publicly traded or to remain private.

Use of Stock Options in pre-IPO Companies

Stock options are the most critical element of compensation provided by start-up companies that intend to become publicly traded. This is because start-up companies are often cash poor and unable to pay the higher salaries and cash bonuses typical of more established industry peers. Stock options allow small companies with big ideas to compete with established industry peers by using an equity participation opportunity in lieu of cash.

Because there is often no liquid market for the stock of a start-up company, pre-IPO options are often granted on unregistered stock, meaning that shares acquired through option exercise may not be freely tradable. These "restricted securities" typically bear a legend on the stock certificates that identifies them as restricted. Restricted securities generally cannot be sold or disposed of before they are registered under the Securities Act of 1933 or unless there is an exemption from registration, such as meeting the requirements of SEC Rule 144. Among other things, Rule 144 generally requires that the securities be held for at least one year.

As a result, pre-IPO options are often effectively not exercisable until a liquidity event occurs, such as IPO or sale of the company to a third party. Even after an IPO, liquidity is generally limited by "lock-up" agreements. Lock-up agreements are legally binding contracts between the underwriters (i.e., the investment banks that brought the securities to market) and the insiders of the company. Lock-up periods typically range from 3–24 months.

While the lock-up agreement is intended to support the stock price immediately after an IPO, it can create several concerns for a company. This is because expiration of the lock-up permits insiders to sell their stock, which creates downward pressure on share price as a flood of potential sellers enters the market. This sends conflicting messages to other shareholders about management's confidence in share price, which may be interpreted as a sell signal that creates further downward pressure.

Share price depreciation for a newly public company creates many complex problems with regard to stock options. In particular, the company may look less attractive to potential new hires. In addition, employees hired after the IPO (but before the share price declined) may now be holding "underwater" options. Underwater options create employee retention challenges for an organization, which often results in pressure to either grant new awards earlier than expected or to reprice existing grants. A simple way to protect against lock-up driven share price depreciation is to stagger the required holding periods so that insider sales are smoothed over time.

Use of Stock Options in Ongoing Private Companies

Although less common, many private companies that intend to remain closely held use stock options to compensate key employees. Since a public market in which to sell stock is not anticipated in these circumstances, the ongoing viability of stock options in such an environment is contingent on establishing and maintaining liquidity.

Liquidity is generally provided through creation of an internal market for the stock. The internal market often allows employees and other insiders to buy and sell securities among each other. To protect against illiquidity or transfer of shares to external parties, the following features may be included in private company equity programs:

- **Employee put rights**–this feature allows employees to sell shares back to the company at current fair market value, thus guaranteeing liquidity. It should be noted that the repurchase of shares may create cash flow and accounting complications for the company (discussed in the next section)

- **Company call or rights of first refusal**–this feature allows the company to protect against the possibility of shares being held by or transferred to external entities. For example, upon termination of employment, the company may have a call right that requires the employee to sell the shares back to the company at current fair market value. In addition, prior to selling shares to any external investor, the company might have a right of first refusal that requires the employee to first offer the stock to the company before selling it to someone else

In addition to maintaining liquidity, a successful internal market is contingent on employee confidence in the accuracy and fairness of the share price. Share price can be determined through formulas or through independent appraisal. Factors typically considered in establishing share price include the present value of the company's current and expected future cash flows, the values of similar companies that have been purchased by other organizations or that are actively traded in the public markets, and the values of the fixed, financial, intangible, and other assets relative to the estimated value of all existing and potential liabilities.

Accounting for Stock Options

General History and Background

Accounting implications always play an integral component in the design of a stock option program. The two primary accounting standards that apply to employee stock option plans are:

• Accounting Principles Board Opinion No. 25 (APB Opinion 25)

• Statement of Accounting Standards No. 123 (FAS 123)

APB Opinion 25 was issued in February 1972 and since that time has served as the foundation in accounting for stock-based awards granted to employees. As new types of plans have evolved, continued interpretation and guidance has been required in application of Opinion 25. The frequency of these pronouncements and resulting complexity led the Financial Accounting Standards Board (FASB) to undertake a major project in 1994 to reconsider the accounting rules applicable to stock-based awards granted to employees and nonemployees (e.g., contractors, vendors).

This project culminated with the release of FAS 123 in October 1995. The FASB intended FAS 123 to supercede Opinion 25 in its entirety. However, in response to pressure from a variety of sources, the FASB decided on a compromise position in which employers were allowed a choice of continuing to account for employee stock grants under Opinion 25 (as amended, interpreted and clarified) or adopting FAS 123 in its place.

Under the compromise, companies that elected to continue using Opinion 25 are required to provide expanded "footnote" disclosure in their financial statements that illustrate the pro forma effect on net income and earnings per share that FAS 123 would have had if it were adopted. Most companies have continued to use Opinion 25, since it generally allows companies to avoid recognition of expense for stock option awards. Most employers elected to continue accounting for options using APB 25. However, over the last few years there has been a movement toward voluntary adoption of FAS 123, and as of the date of this writing, approximately 350 public companies are accounting for options under FAS 123.

To address a variety of interpretative issues related to Opinion 25, the FASB released FASB Interpretation 44, Accounting for Certain Transactions Involving Stock Compensation (FIN 44) in March 2000. While the intent of FIN 44 is to interpret, rather than amend, the longstanding provisions of Opinion 25, it adds a considerable amount of complexity to stock option accounting and is filled with exceptions and special rules.

As mentioned earlier, the FASB is currently reconsidering stock option accounting rules and intends to release a new standard that mandates the expensing of options. This standard is expected to become effective for fiscal years beginning after December 15, 2004 (i.e., 1/1/05 for calendar year companies), and to be similar in design to FAS 123. If adopted as expected, the new standard will render APB 25 completely obsolete. However, an understanding of APB 25 will still be important in developing a full appreciation of historic practices and the rationale for decisions made in the past.

The Fundamentals of APB Opinion 25

General

Under Opinion 25, the compensation cost of a stock option award is determined as the intrinsic value of the award on the measurement date. This section provides an overview on how compensation cost is measured under Opinion 25 and how resulting expense is allocated.

Measuring Compensation Cost

For purposes of Opinion 25:

- Intrinsic value is equal to the difference between the option exercise price (i.e., the amount the optionee is required to pay to purchase the stock) and the fair market value (FMV) of the underlying stock, or in other words, the option profit
  - Note that compensation expense can never be less than zero
- A measurement date occurs at the first time when each of two factors are known:
  1. The number of shares that the optionee is entitled to receive
     - A requirement to remain employed for a specified period of time prior to exercising an option (i.e., a time-based vesting schedule) does not preclude a determination regarding the number of shares an optionee is entitled to receive

—However, other contingencies placed on the exercise of the option (e.g., performance targets, approval by shareholders) would delay a determination until satisfied

2. The price that the optionee must pay for the underlying shares

If both of the preceding factors are known at the time the option is granted, the option is deemed to be a "fixed award," meaning that compensation expense is fixed at grant date and equal to the intrinsic value of the award. Assuming that the exercise price equals FMV at grant, compensation cost is zero. If the exercise price is less than FMV (i.e., a discount option), then compensation cost is equal to the intrinsic value at grant, or in other words, the amount of the discount.

If either of these factors is not known at grant, the option is considered to be a "variable award" until a measurement date occurs. When the measurement date occurs, compensation expense is measured and equals the intrinsic value at that point in time. During the interim, the company is required to estimate compensation cost by "marking to market" the value of the award.

The following example illustrates how to measure compensation cost for a fixed and variable award:

- Assume two identical stock option grants are awarded, each with an exercise price equal to FMV at grant
- Assume that a measurement date occurs for Award A at grant (i.e., a fixed grant), but the measurement date is delayed until vested for Grant B (i.e., a variable grant)
- Assume that both awards vest on the same day and are immediately exercised, with the resulting option profit equal to $10,000
  - There is no compensation expense associated with Award A, since the measurement date occurred at grant when the intrinsic value was zero
  - The compensation expense associated with Grant B is $10,000, since the measurement date was delayed until exercise

It should be noted that even if compensation expense is avoided at grant and the award is treated as a fixed grant, this does not necessarily preclude the accrual of compensation expense. There are many issues that could convert an otherwise fixed grant to a variable award or cause a new measurement date, including the following examples:

- Renewal or material modification of the outstanding award

–This is an important concept under Opinion 25, and forms the foundation of many interpretative issues addressed in FIN 44

–Examples of events deemed to be a material modification or a renewal include the repricing of an option and extension of the term or post-employment exercisability

- Settlement of an otherwise fixed grant in cash[5]

   –The amount of cash paid by a company to an optionee in the settlement of an option is the actual, or final measure of compensation expense associated with the grant

   –For example, if the company settled Award A in the preceding example with a direct payment equal to $10,000, then compensation expense would be $10,000[6]

   –It should be noted that the accounting treatment of phantom stock options and SARs is identical to that of an option on real stock that is settled in cash

   –For these awards, compensation cost is equal to the amount of the optionee's gain

- Option pyramiding, or tendering immature shares as payment of the exercise price

   –Pyramiding involves exercise of an option by tendering shares already owned to pay the exercise price on a portion of a grant, and then using the shares received through the exercise to exercise additional options

   –This approach would effectively enable an optionee to exercise an infinite number of options through direct ownership of a single share

   –Pyramiding results in the treatment of the option as a variable plan

   –To avoid pyramiding, tendered shares must generally be "mature," or in other words, owned for a period of at least 6 months

Note that stock options normally contain anti-dilution provisions which provide for adjustments in the event of stock splits, dividends, spinoffs, and recapitalizations. Adjustments for stock splits and stock dividends normally will not result in a new measurement date.

The concept of compensation expense in the design and administration of a stock option program is referenced further in the section on Designer Stock Options. In addition, important interpretive issues addressed in FIN 44 (discussed below) should be clearly understood when making decisions regarding the design of a stock option or any post grant modifications.

Allocating Compensation Expense

Opinion 25 requires that compensation cost associated with stock options be allocated, or recognized as an expense, during one or more periods during which the employee renders services to the company.

In general, the service period is deemed to be the vesting period, as this is the period during which the employee must provide services to "earn" the option. If an award is fixed, the associated compensation expense should be allocated on a straight-line basis over the service period. If the award is variable, the total cost must be estimated during the period from grant to the measurement date, based on the changes to the FMV of the company's stock at the end of each interim measurement period.

The following examples illustrate how expense is typically allocated:

- **Fixed award**–assume an option has an intrinsic value at grant of $10,000 and vests 100% after 4 years (i.e., no interim vesting) based solely on continued service

  –Under these assumptions, each year of service completed by the optionee equals 25% of the service needed to earn the award. Therefore, in each of years 1 through 4, the compensation expense associated with this award would equal $2,500

  –Note that if the award vested 25% per year over 4 years, each separate vesting tranche is generally treated as a separate award for accounting purposes. As a result, compensation expense would be allocated differently to reflect the portion of the award that is earned each year. In this case, expense would be $5,208 in year 1,[7] $2,708 in year 2, $1,458 in year 3, and $625 in year 4

- **Variable award**–allocation of expense on a variable award is more complicated, since cost fluctuates with changes to the price of the underlying shares. Nonetheless, compensation cost equals the intrinsic value of the award at the measurement date, as illustrated in the following example:

  –Assume an option with no intrinsic value at grant vests 100% after 4 years (no interim vesting) if prescribed performance goals are met (which delays the measurement date until the vesting date)

  –The amount of compensation cost accruing each year until the measurement date will vary depending on changes to the intrinsic value of the award, as illustrated in the following table

  –Note that if the award vested ratably (e.g., 25% per year over 4 years), the same mark-to-market approach would apply, but the expense would be front-loaded to reflect the portion of the award being earned in each year

End of Year	Intrinsic Value	Expense	Notes
1	$10,000	$2,500	25% of $10,000
2	$15,000	$5,000	50% of $15,000, minus amount expensed prior year
3	$16,000	$4,500	75% of $16,000, minus amounts expensed in prior years
4	$12,500	$500	100% of $12,500, minus amounts expensed in prior years
Total		$12,500	The total amount equals the intrinsic value at the measurement date

Guidelines Under FIN 44

As mentioned earlier, the FASB released FIN 44 in March 2000 to add interpretative issues under Opinion 25 where questionable application and diversity in practice had developed.[8]

FIN 44 became effective on July 1, 2000 and with several exceptions, applies to all stock option awards granted after this date. The two most significant questions addressed by FIN 44 are:

1. What types of awards can be accounted for under Opinion 25?

   –FIN 44 clarifies that in order for Opinion 25 to apply (1) the stock options granted by the company must be on shares of the granting company, and (2) the options must be granted to employees of the granting company

   –For this purpose employee is as defined by "common law" and U.S. payroll tax rules

   –If an award cannot be accounted for under Opinion 25, it must be accounted for under FAS 123

2. What types of modifications to outstanding stock options trigger a new measurement date or conversion of an otherwise fixed award to a variable award?

   –A new measurement date is generally required if (1) a stock option is modified to extend the maximum contractual life or the post-employment exercise period of an award, (2) vesting is accelerated or continued under conditions not originally contemplated at grant, (3) share withholding on option profits to pay required taxes exceeds the minimum statutory rate, or (4) a nonemployee optionee with unvested options becomes an employee

–Variable award accounting on an otherwise fixed grant may be required under a variety of scenarios, with the most significant being when a stock option is "repriced" or cancelled and replaced with a new grant. A repricing is generally defined as either a direct reduction in the exercise price of an outstanding option, or an indirect reduction that occurs as a result of payment of a cash bonus contingent on exercise. An option is generally treated as cancelled and replaced if an outstanding award is cancelled (or "settled" by the employer) and a new grant with a lower exercise price is awarded 6 months before or after the cancellation date.

Among other things, FIN 44 clarified that Opinion 25 does not apply to options granted to individuals other than employees of the granting company (with the exception of certain leased employees and elected nonemployee members of a company's board of directors). It also created a powerful obstacle to the widely debated practice of stock option repricing.

As with all matters applicable to stock option accounting, practitioners should review specific technical issues with their auditors.

The Fundamentals of FAS 123

Application of FAS 123

As mentioned earlier, the FASB adopted a compromise position regarding FAS 123 in which companies were permitted a choice of adopting FAS 123 or retaining Opinion 25 in accounting for stock option expense.

The choice is binding, meaning that once a company adopts FAS 123, it can never return to Opinion 25. In addition, companies cannot elect different accounting standards for different types of employee equity grants. To date, and as stated earlier, most companies continue to account for employee equity grants under Opinion 25, with only approximately 350 having elected to adopt the recognition provisions of FAS 123 as of the date of this writing.

In addition, FIN 44 clarified that Opinion 25 applies only to grants made to employees using stock of the grantor, meaning that employers that continue to use Opinion 25 may be required to account for certain awards under FAS 123.

The Basics of FAS 123

Unlike Opinion 25, FAS 123 does not employ the concept of fixed versus variable accounting. Rather, it makes a distinction between whether an award is an equity instrument or a liability based on how the award will ultimately be settled (i.e., in shares or cash). Specifically, the cost of an equity instrument is deemed to be its "fair value" as measured at the time of grant (note that the measurement date could be delayed if the award is granted subject to shareholder approval).[9]

The fair value basically represents the amount someone would pay for the right to receive the upside appreciation in the stock option over its expected life. This concept differs considerably from the intrinsic value approach employed under Opinion 25, since it effectively means that an option has value even if it has no intrinsic value (or perhaps negative intrinsic value), and therefore, carries a cost to the company when granted.

Determining Fair Value Under FAS 123

The fair value of a stock option equals a percentage of the FMV of the underlying stock, which can then be expressed as a dollar value. For example, if the fair value of an option equals 33% of the underlying stock, an option on a $100 stock has a fair value of $33.

Fair value is estimated using an option-pricing model, with the resulting compensation cost being recognized over the service period (i.e., vesting schedule) of the award. FAS 123 does not specify which stock option valuation model must be used to determine fair value, although it lists the Black-Scholes and Binomial models as acceptable examples.

There are six factors, or inputs, used in determining fair value using an option-pricing model. These include stock price, exercise price, expected option life, expected stock price volatility, risk free rate, and expected dividend yield. Several of these factors are subject to interpretation and a range of reasonableness can be used to determine the appropriate input value:

- **Expected option life**–FAS 123 allows options to be valued using the expected life of the option, rather than its maximum term. The factors that should be considered in estimating expected life include:
  - –The average period grants have remained outstanding in the past–in determining the average holding period of historical grants, companies are permitted to segregate experiences for different levels of employees (e.g., senior executives versus middle management)
  - –The expected volatility and dividends on the stock–the higher the volatility or dividend yield, the earlier the option is expected to be exercised
  - –The vesting period of the grant–the expected life can be no shorter than the vesting period
- **Expected volatility**–the primary factor in estimating expected volatility is historical volatility over the most recent period that is commensurate with

the expected life of the option. Companies are generally permitted to disregard any periods of extreme or unusual volatility resulting from one-time events, such as a takeover attempt or restructuring

- **Expected dividends**–assumptions about dividends should be based on publicly available data, taking into account historical patterns in increases
- **Expected risk free rate**–the risk free rate must equal that of zero-coupon U.S. Treasury issue with a remaining term commensurate with the expected life of the option
    - –The option grant date should be used to determine the date at which yield is measured

All of the inputs affect the resulting fair value estimate produced by the model, as illustrated in the following table:

Black-Scholes or Binomial Sensitivity	
By increasing:	*Option value:*
Stock price	Increases
Exercise price (relative to price at date of grant)	Decreases
Expected option life	Increases
Expected volatility	Increases
Risk free rate	Increases
Expected dividend yield	Decreases

Determining Annual Expense

Once the fair value of an employee stock option is determined, the annual expense must be amortized over the related service period (i.e., the vesting schedule).

Under FAS 123, stock option cost is generally recognized only for awards that vest. The standard allows for the accrual of compensation cost as if all options are expected to vest. This enables companies to reflect the effect of actual forfeitures as they occur by taking a reversal of previously recognized cost. Alternatively, a company may base the accruals of compensation cost on the estimated number of options that may be forfeited and then revise the estimate, if necessary, to reflect subsequent information as it becomes available. The approach taken affects only the timing of expense, not the amount of expense.

Expected New Accounting Standard

As mentioned earlier, at the time of this writing the FASB was working on a proposed accounting standard that would render both APB 25 and FAS 123 obsolete. A summary of expected features under the new standard is presented below:

- The new standard is expected to follow the basic concepts of fair value expense determination currently in place under FAS 123. However, the new standard is expected to require use of a lattice-based option pricing model in which certain input items (e.g., expected life) are produced by the model based on company-specific history. This presumably will mitigate the ability of companies to manipulate costs by using flawed or inaccurate valuation assumptions

- The expected effective date for the new standard is fiscal years beginning after December 15, 2004, or in other words, January 1, 2005 for companies with calendar fiscal years

- Companies will be required to adopt the new standard using a "modified prospective" method, meaning that fair value cost would be recognized for all awards granted, modified, or settled after the effective date, plus the nonvested portion of awards granted or modified in fiscal years beginning after December 15, 1994

- Award modifications would be treated as the cancellation and exchange of the old award for a new award, and incremental compensation expense would equal the difference between the fair value of the new award and the fair value of new award as of the modification date. Importantly, awards originally accounted for under APB 25 for which no accounting expense was recognized will be accounted for using fair value principles if modified after the effective date

Updates regarding the new proposed standard can be accessed at www.fwcook.com.

Corporate Tax Deductibility and Cash Flow Considerations

The gain realized by the optionee upon exercise of a stock option is generally considered a corporate expense for income tax purposes.

The deductibility of nonqualified stock option gains by a company, when coupled with the favorable accounting treatment provided under APB 25, historically made stock options the most financially efficient way to deliver a given level of compensation. And the higher a corporation's marginal tax rate, the more valuable the deductions become.

For example, if an executive exercises a "plain vanilla" stock option and realizes an option profit equal to $100,000, the gain is a deductible expense for income tax purposes. Assuming the company pays taxes at 35%, the option enabled the company to provide $100,000 in compensation and simultaneously generate a positive cash flow of $35,000. Had the same $100,000 been delivered in cash, it would have generated a negative cash flow equal to $65,000.

A Comparison of Tax Treatment of NQSOs vs. ISOs

Earlier we discussed the differences between NQSOs and ISOs and the tax implications to both the optionee and granting company. In general, the profit realized upon exercise of a NQSO is taxable as ordinary income to the recipient and deductible to the employer in the year realized. Assuming applicable holding requirements are met, gains realized through ISO exercises are not taxable as ordinary income at the time of exercise, but rather are taxed as a capital gain upon disposition of the acquired shares.[10] However, employers cannot deduct employee gains associated with ISOs, which has a cash flow cost to companies.

In the preceding example, the loss of this deduction creates a direct cash flow cost to the company of $35,000. Assuming the employee is taxable at 35% at the Federal level and there is no subsequent change in the stock price after exercise, the benefit of capital gains taxation (i.e., 15%) versus ordinary income provides a marginal after-tax gain of only $20,000. In other words, it costs the company $35,000 to provide an executive with a $20,000 tax benefit.

Depending on individual and corporate tax rates, the value to the individual relative to the cost to a company of the lost tax deduction varies. In general, ISOs are financially sensible only for companies that are paying little or no taxes, such as start-ups (particularly pre-IPO companies) or financially distressed organizations.

Ensuring Deductions on Grants to Named Executive Officers

Section 162(m) of the Internal Revenue Code generally limits the allowable deduction for compensation paid to a public corporation's five most highly paid individuals to $1 million per executive per year.

In determining the five most highly paid, a corporation generally must include its chief executive officer and the four highest paid executive officers other than the CEO who are employed on the last day of the taxable year.

An exception to the $1 million limit is provided for compensation that is deemed to be performance-based. For a stock option grant to be performance-based, it must meet the following requirements:

- It must be granted pursuant to a plan in which the material terms have been disclosed and approved by shareholders
- The size of the award must fall within an individual employee limit specified in the plan
- The plan must be administered by a committee composed solely of two or more outside directors, which means that the committee (rather than the full Board or the CEO) must actually make the grant

While Section 162(m) only affects five employees at any single point in time, it has significant cash-flow consequences for the company if the above requirements have not been met.

For example, assume a CEO with a $1 million salary (which uses up the entire limit for non-performance-based pay) exercises options with total gains of $50 million. Assuming the requirements for performance-based pay are met, the deduction on this award provides an after-tax cash flow of $17.5 million if the corporation pays taxes at marginal rate of 35%. On the other hand, failure to meet the Section 162(m) requirements would cost the company $17.5 million.

To ensure that grants will be performance-based, it is important to:

- Set a limit on the maximum number of option awards any one person can receive in the plan that accommodates special awards as well as typical ongoing grants. The limit should consider the possibility of making special non-recurring grants, such as:

  1. Multi-year awards intended to serve as an acceleration of awards that would otherwise be made in the future
  2. New hire awards in which a large one-time grant is needed to attract a new executive who may be forfeiting unvested awards at his prior employer

The limit should also be large enough to accommodate reload grants, if the company currently includes, or intends to include, such a feature

- Have the Compensation Committee formally authorize and grant all awards to management employees
  - The rules apply to employees at the time the option is exercised, rather than at the time the award is granted. Because most options carry 10-year terms, it is impossible to know with certainty who will be a covered employee in the future
- Request shareholder approval for additional shares before the current share reserve is exhausted
  - If the plan is exhausted and grants are made outside the plan (assuming

such an approach is permitted under the New York Stock Exchange and Nasdaq listing requirements), they will not be tax deductible for covered employees

–If the grants are made contingent on shareholder approval, they will be subject to variable plan accounting until such approval is received

Earnings Per Share Implications

Stock options reduce reported earnings per share to the extent that share price (and intrinsic value) appreciates after the date of grant. This is because the increase in share price results in possible exercise of the outstanding options, which increases common shares outstanding unless the company repurchases shares to offset the dilution.

FASB Statement No. 128 was released in February 1997 and modified the prior rules for measuring the impact of stock options on reported EPS. FAS 128 requires that companies report two versions of EPS:

- **Basic EPS**–reflects net income available to shareholders divided by weighted average common shares outstanding, with no potential dilution attributable to outstanding stock options and other stock-based awards
- **Diluted EPS**–reflects net income available to shareholders after accounting for the dilutive effect of stock options and other stock-based awards

In determining diluted EPS, companies are required to use the "treasury stock method" to determine the increase in common shares outstanding as a result of outstanding stock options (i.e., the increase to the denominator of the EPS fraction). This method assumes that stock-based awards (vested and unvested) are exercised or converted at the later of the beginning of the reporting period or issuance and that the proceeds received by the company are used to repurchase outstanding common stock.

Some important facts about the treasury stock method are outlined below:

- Proceeds include the exercise price tendered to the company by the optionee, as well as (1) the positive cash flow accruing to the company as a result of the tax deduction received upon exercise of the option and (2) any unrecognized compensation cost
- The repurchase of stock is assumed to occur at the average market price during the reporting period
- Awards that are contingent on meeting prescribed performance goals are included in diluted EPS only if the criteria are being satisfied, assuming the

relevant reporting period is the end of the performance measurement period

An example follows:

- Assume a company grants 1,000 options with an exercise price of $10, the average stock price during the reporting period is $25 (option gain of $15,000), and the company has a tax rate of 35%

  - The following table illustrates the net additional shares deemed to be outstanding for purposes of diluted EPS:

Net Shares Deemed Outstanding Under FAS 128		
(a) Shares deemed exercised		1,000

(b) Proceeds from exercise
    Exercise price (1,000 x $10)
    Tax benefit ($15,000 x .35)
    Total proceeds
	$10,000
	$5,250
	$15,250	

(c) Shares deemed repurchased (b/$25)		610
(d) Net shares deemed outstanding (a-c)		390

In considering the dilutive impact of stock options on EPS, it is important to recognize two facts. First, stock options only reduce EPS if the stock price appreciates after grant. Second, actual share dilution will always be less than the number of options granted for purposes of determining diluted EPS. The higher the stock price appreciation rate, the greater the level of diluted EPS dilution as a result of being able to repurchase fewer shares with the exercise proceeds.

Use of Performance-based Stock Options

There are a number of reasons for why companies might consider granting stock option awards that include performance features and other provisions that are beyond that of a traditional plain vanilla award.

While "performance-based" options have historically been somewhat uncommon, there are a number of reasons why they may proliferate in the future, including pressure from institutional investors to better balance employee option gains with relative return to shareholders; the elimination of accounting inefficiencies under the expected new accounting standard; and corporate desires to increase employee ownership, provide flexibility, and enhance the motivation and retentive impact of the awards.

Performance-based Vesting Strategies

Traditional options vest over time irrespective of company or individual performance. As such, they can deliver large gains to participants despite relatively poor performance, especially in rising markets when stock price may appreciate even if performance is relatively poor.

Performance-based vesting requirements condition the exercisability of the option on the achievement of specific goals. The performance requirement can include the achievement of:

• Specific or relative stock price growth objectives or a minimum level of average annual total shareholder return

• Specific or relative earnings per share growth, net income, or other accounting-based performance measures, such as return on equity

• An individually-determined set of goals that varies by participant (e.g., vesting for an executive in charge of the marketing function could be contingent on achieving specific market share objectives)

In designing options with performance-vesting provisions, it is important to note that unless vesting occurs based solely on continued service the option will be accounted for as a variable grant under Opinion 25. This means that it will be marked-to-market and the intrinsic value at the vesting date will be charged against the company's earnings. Because of this, two approaches to performance-based vesting have developed:

• **Performance-contingent options**–these are awards in which vesting is contingent on meeting the performance requirements. These grants receive variable accounting treatment under Opinion 25

• **Performance-accelerated options**–these are awards in which vesting occurs at a delayed date based solely on continued service (e.g., 7 years from grant), but accelerates to an earlier date if performance requirements are met. These awards receive fixed accounting treatment under Opinion 25

Critics of the performance-accelerated approach argue that the automatic vesting feature weakens the linkage to performance goals. Proponents argue that the acceleration feature is necessary to avoid an earnings charge (which would weaken the company's posture in the market) and that continued employment to the vesting date is unlikely if the performance goals are not met.

Under FAS 123 and the proposed new FASB standard, performance vesting requirements decrease the fair value of the award. Further, recognized expense is expected to be reversible under the new standard if the option is forfeited as a result of failure to achieve the threshold goals (unless the goal was stock-price dependent). This will greatly increase the appeal of such awards.

Fewer than 10% of large US companies grant performance-contingent options, while approximately 15% grant performance-accelerated options. Performance-contingent options are expected to increase in prevalence as a result of the proposed FASB accounting standard.

Premium-priced Option Approaches

Traditional options are exercisable at the fair market value (FMV) of the stock at the time of grant, while premium-priced options are exercisable at a price above FMV.

Since option gain is created only after a specified price increase is achieved, premium pricing enhances the incentive for the recipient to work toward increasing the stock price and guarantees a minimum level of return to shareholders before optionees can capture gain.

Premium-priced options are most common in mega-grants and other special grants made to senior executives, but can be used in many situations. In some cases, premium-priced options are granted in several tranches, with the exercise price of each tranche set at a different premium to FMV. This approach provides a continuous incentive for participants to continue reaching for progressively higher price hurdles as the previous one is achieved.

Premium pricing offers the advantage of avoiding the earnings charge associated with many performance-based option innovations under APB 25 and decreasing fair value under FAS 123, but can be more dilutive since they are typically granted in larger amounts than those priced at FMV. The larger grants compensate for reduced value per option share those results from two factors:

- The likelihood of exercise is reduced since the FMV may never exceed the exercise price
- The gain at exercise is reduced by the premium over FMV at the time of grant

Premium-priced options can also lose their motivational impact if stock price performance is poor and the premium prices seem unlikely to be achieved. Approximately 10% of large U.S. corporations grant premium-priced options although, for the same reasons applicable to performance-contingent grants, an increase in prevalence is expected.

Indexed Options

Indexed options are options in which the exercise price rises or falls with a given index. As such, they discriminate between changes in share price due to executive action and those due to the general movement of the financial markets. The index can be market related or internally focused:

- **Market related**–performance is measured against that of a specific peer group or external benchmark, such as peer group average total shareholder return or the S&P 500

- **Internally focused**–performance is measured against peer group return on equity, growth in earnings per share, a fixed appreciation rate (e.g. 6% increase per year) or another performance measure

The exercise price can be structured to change only upwards, but index options can allow for adjustment in both directions. While indexing can take many forms (some of which are very complex), a simple example will illustrate the basic concept:

- Suppose the exercise price is tied to changes in the S&P 500 and the FMV at grant date is $100 per share. If the S&P advances 10% over the next year, the exercise price rises to 110%. If the S&P falls by 15% in the following year, the exercise price would drop to $93.50

Since the exercise price fluctuates based on company performance, this feature can be very effective in equating the value of executive awards to the company's overall performance.

While there is a high degree of interest in indexed stock options, they are very uncommon for several reasons:

- The enhanced performance element requires that more shares be granted to deliver a specific level of economic value

- Because the exercise price is not fixed at the time of grant, indexed options are accounted for under Opinion 25 as variable awards

- The concept of a variable exercise price can be difficult to communicate

Truncating Options

Under this approach, the exercise price is set at fair market value at the time of grant, but the term of the option varies based on the achievement of specified performance goals over the option's vesting period.

To the extent the goals are achieved, the option expires at its normal expiration date, which is typically 10 years. If the performance goals are not achieved, the option's term is reduced considerably (e.g., to the length of the vesting schedule plus one day or month). If the exercise price exceeds the FMV at the truncated expiration date, the options expire valueless. If the options are in the money at the truncated expiration date, the participant is forced to immediately exercise, which penalizes the executive since any gain on potential future appreciation is forfeited.

Truncating options work best when they are coupled with relatively long cliff vesting schedules (e.g., 3 years or longer). Contrary to options where the vesting period is shortened if performance goals are met (e.g., performance-accelerated vesting), which provide a reward for achieving performance objectives, options with truncating terms provide punishment for not achieving goals.

The use of truncating options has been very uncommon. This is primarily because such grants typically receive variable accounting treatment under APB 25. In essence, the possibility of the term being reduced is viewed as tantamount to an increase in the term based on meeting performance goals. Interest in truncating terms may increase under the proposed new FASB expense standard.

Other Stock Option Innovations

Proliferation of Mega-Stock Options

There are many ways in which to define a "mega-stock option grant," with the variations being specific to the individual referencing an award.

Mega-grants became common in the 1990's as a result of rising stock prices, executive confidence in their ability to continually improve operational results, and increased pressure from shareholders to tie greater levels of compensation to the creation of shareholder value. Mega-grants are typically used in the following circumstances:

- To leverage incentive value and equity exposure upon a corporate restructuring or major transaction, such as a merger or initial public offering
- As an attraction device needed to entice a new-hire candidate to leave an existing employer
- To provide additional incentive to work towards an important corporate objective, such as the launching of a new business or introduction of a new product

Because of their size, mega-grants face significant shareholder scrutiny and are often criticized if they do not include special performance requirements. As a result, mega-grants can be somewhat risky to a corporation, particularly if the award is being made as an acceleration of grants that would otherwise be made in the future and the performance requirements are difficult. For example, assume an award intended to serve a 3-year period falls underwater shortly after grant. In this case, the company will be pressured to either make new grants early (which violates the initial promise made to shareholders about the nature of the mega-grant), reprice the award, or face possible loss of key talent to competitors who may offer new awards at current market price.

Reload Stock Options and Enhanced Employee Ownership

A restoration or "reload" stock option is a stock option enhancement that encourages the early exercise of valuable stock options before the end of their term without requiring the optionee to forfeit the benefit of potential future price appreciation during the remainder of the option's term.

When an ordinary option is exercised, an employee must pay the cost of exercise and incur the corresponding tax obligation.[11] As a result, the net profit shares (i.e., shares remaining after paying for the cost of exercise and taxes) is greatly reduced, which discourages exercise until the latest possible moment (particularly if the prospects for future gain are high).

The primary objective of a reload stock option is to create greater executive ownership by encouraging early exercise of valuable options and retention of the option's profit shares.

The basic mechanics of an ordinary reload stock option are simple:

- An employee exercises a stock option by "paying" the exercise price with shares already owned (i.e., a stock-for-stock exercise)
- Upon exercise, a supplemental option (i.e., the reload) is granted for the number of shares used to pay the exercise price
- The exercise price of the resulting reload is the fair market value at the date of the reload grant, and the term is equal to that remaining on the original grant

The concept recognizes that when options are exercised using already owned shares, the optionee has less equity carried interest (i.e., shares directly owned plus those under option) going forward than if the individual had exercised the option for cash. The reduction in carried interest is a disincentive to early exercise if the optionee believes the prospects for continued appreciation are good. By restoring the optionee to the original level of carried interest, the reload eliminates this disincentive.

For example: assume an employee currently owns 50 shares (purchased at $50 per share) and receives an option on 100 shares exercisable at $50 per share (fair market value at grant date) with a 10-year term. Under this scenario, the employee has an initial carried interest of 150 shares. The option is exercised in year 5 when the stock price has reached $100 by tendering the 50 already owned shares. Upon exercise, the employee receives (1) 100 real shares (of which 50, or $5,000, is profit and the remainder is a return of the shares tendered) plus (2) a reload option on 50 shares (the number of shares tendered)

−The reload options restore carried interest to the original 150-share level

−The reload grant is exercisable at $100 and carries a term of 5 years

The early conversion of option profit to owned shares has three effects for the employee:

1. It considerably dampens, but does not eliminate, the effect of a subsequent decline in stock price on the value of the employee's carried interest without increasing the upside potential. This is because real shares always have value (except in the event of bankruptcy), while options become worthless if the share price falls below the exercise price

2. It provides favorable capital gains taxation (as opposed to taxation as ordinary income) on further appreciation on the option profit shares

3. It provides the optionee with dividend and voting rights on the profit shares that did not exist as an option

Adding taxes to the equation complicates the picture, since payment either reduces the carried interest position by the number of shares withheld by the employer or requires the optionee to make payment from other sources.

Assuming a marginal 40% tax rate and the withholding of shares to cover the tax obligation in the above example, the employee is left with 80 shares (30 profit shares plus the return of the 50 used to pay the exercise price) when the original option is exercised at $100. As a result, the employee's carried interest level drops from 150 shares to 130 shares, even after receiving the reload grant on 50 shares.

To counter the effect of taxes on carried interest, some companies provide an additional number of reload shares equal to the number of shares withheld to cover the tax obligation. In our example, the total reload grant would be 70 shares, composed of the 50 normal reload options plus the 20 tax reload options.

Tax reloads are a controversial feature. Proponents argue that it is necessary to fully restore the employee's position in equity appreciation going forward and hence necessary to encourage early exercise. Opponents argue that it is unnecessary and complex, a drain on available pool shares, and has the unseemly perception of being a "gross-up" for taxes.

Both the SEC and the FASB regard reloads as a new stock option grant rather than as a continuation of an existing grant. As a result, reload grants must be disclosed separately in proxy statement stock option grant tables for the five highest-paid executive officers.

Reloads are financially efficient under APB 25 because they do not trigger accounting expense. However, reloads are valued as new grants under FAS 123 for purposes of determining accounting expense, and as a result, are likely to decrease in prevalence if option expensing becomes mandatory.

Deferring Stock Option Gains

An option gain deferral involves the exercise of a valuable option and the deferral of the resulting profit into company stock units that will be paid at a later date. This allows the employee to defer receipt of the option profit and the payment of applicable taxes to a later date.

In addition to the obvious tax benefits of deferral, the approach offers the following benefits:

- Can preserve tax deductions that would otherwise be lost if a proxy-named executive exercises an option that was granted outside of a shareholder-approved plan. This is because the $1 million limit on deductible compensation does not apply to former employees
- Avoids the need to grant tax reloads to maintain pre-exercise carried interest levels under a reload option program. This is because payment of taxes (and the need to withhold shares) is delayed to a future date, which could be even later than the expiration of the original option term

Some general guidelines in the design of an option gain deferral program are outlined below:

- Payment of the exercise price for the underlying option should be made in the form of owned shares delivered through "attestation"[12]
  - Cash and cashless exercises should not be permitted
  - The tendered shares should be mature (i.e., owned at least 6 months)
- To avoid triggering constructive receipt, optionees should be required to make the deferral election in advance of the actual option exercise. The most conservative approach is to require the election to be made at grant, although companies employ a variety of more aggressive rules
- The distribution date should be determined at the same time as the election to defer and subsequent change should be avoided
- The deferred profit should be designated in company stock units and paid

in actual shares. Employees should not be permitted to diversify into other notional investments

Because deferred amounts become unsecured obligations of the company, executives need to assess the risk of forfeiture associated with being a general creditor. Professional guidance is also typically needed regarding the possible impact on current and future taxes, asset allocation, and estate planning.

Paying Dividends on Unexercised Stock Options

Dividend rights can be attached to stock option awards, although the practice has historically been uncommon and, when used, done so mainly by companies that pay high dividends.

While there are many ways a company could provide dividend rights, it is important to avoid tainting the option's linkage to shareholder value creation. A simple approach involves crediting dividends quarterly to individual employee accounts in the form of deferred stock units (i.e., deferred compensation credited in the form of company stock). The accounts would grow based on quarterly credits (i.e., reinvested dividends) plus stock price appreciation. The accounts would be paid out in the form of real shares at the earlier of option exercise or upon vesting. To enhance linkage to shareholder value creation, companies generally make the receipt of the dividend account contingent on meeting prescribed performance criteria, such as relative total shareholder return.

In determining whether dividend rights are appropriate, a company should consider the following factors:

- Dividend equivalents, if not tied to performance, can compromise the basic intention of a stock option award, which is to link the optionee's gain directly to share price appreciation. However, the dividend rights enhance the option by tying value to total shareholder return
- Unless the company is in a high dividend paying industry, use of dividend equivalents could send a poor message to shareholders about management's belief in its ability to grow share price
- The payment of dividend equivalents will increase the present value at grant of each option share
  - Therefore, for purposes of calculating the present value of the award at grant using the Black-Scholes or a similar option pricing model, a zero-dividend yield should be assumed. Alternatively, the present value of the expected dividend stream can be calculated and added to the Black-Scholes value of the underlying option.

- The dividend credits will result in a full earnings charge equal to the value when credited to the optionee

Participation and Grant Sizing

Selecting Participants

Historically, most companies extended participation in stock option programs to employees with salaries of $80,000 or more. The depth of granting practices has increased considerably in recent years. However, as companies have adopted broad-based programs, they have substituted options for cash compensation, and used options as a lure to attract high level talent at all levels.

The trend toward broad participation has been exceptionally widespread among technology companies and start-ups, which use options not only as a leveraged wealth creation device but also as a financially efficient substitute for traditional employee benefits (e.g., pensions). Among these companies, it is not uncommon for virtually all employees to receive periodic option awards.

As participation continues to expand to the lower levels of organizations, the importance of budgeting increases. Like any valuable resource, wise companies carefully plan expected share usage to fit within an affordable budget. A simple way to express a budget is as an annual run rate (discussed below), or in other words, as a percentage of total shares outstanding. For example, a company setting an annual budget of 3% would have a total option pool of three million shares if there were 100 million outstanding shares. From this pool, the company would make its annual grants to existing employees, plus special grants to others. Special grants might include those made to new hires, as well as those to recognize promotions, extraordinary accomplishments, and other non-recurring events.

As a result of a variety of factors discussed earlier, most notably the likelihood of a mandate to expense stock options, companies are beginning to restrict broad-based option participation. In addition, the budgeting process is beginning to focus more on accounting cost, rather than simply share usage.

The Timing of Grants

With the exception of special awards made to new hires and promoted employees, financially mature companies generally make stock option grants annually at approximately the same time each year. However, in response to increasingly volatile stock prices, companies are now beginning to consider more frequent grants in an attempt to avoid unintentionally selecting a "high" exercise price.

Rather than making annual grants, start-ups and development companies (i.e., typically with low stock prices, but high upside) often make a large periodic grant intended to serve a specified period of time (e.g., 3 to 4 years). Depending on whether the company has matured, the company may make another large, multi-year grant or move to more frequent awards upon vesting of the earlier award.

Developing Stock Option Grant Guidelines

As mentioned above, most companies make stock option grants on an annual basis. In determining the size of awards made to each eligible participant, most companies rely on formal or informal guidelines that vary based on level and function within the company.

Practices vary widely among companies, with the key differences attributable to the nature of the business.

Typical Practices Among Large, Mature Companies

In large, mature companies that are financially healthy, one of the following approaches generally forms the foundation for determining target grant levels:

- **Targeted value**–under this approach, the target number of shares varies so that the value of the award remains relatively constant as a percent of salary or target annual cash compensation. As such, the size of annual grants can vary significantly based on changes in the stock price and, if the multiple is expressed as an expected present value, additional factors that impact the option's estimated value (e.g., dividend yield, risk-free rate) For example, assume an employee with a $200,000 annual salary has a target grant guideline equal to 200% of salary (based on face value). If the stock price at the time of grant is $40, this results in a target award of 10,000 options ($200,000 times 200%, divided by $40 stock price). To convert face value guidelines into Black-Scholes guidelines, a company can simply multiply its face value multiple by the Black-Scholes value of its stock

  –In above example, if the company's Black-Scholes ratio is 40%, the guidelines would be reduced to 80% of salary to deliver the same 10,000 share target award

  –$200,000 times 80%, divided by the product of $40 times the 40% Black-Scholes value

• **Fixed number of shares**–under this approach, the target number of shares granted annually is relatively fixed, based on either past practice or the number of shares available under the plan. Since the value of the award can fluctuate widely over time, it is typically necessary to recalibrate award levels more often than under a targeted value approach

The targeted value approach allows greater accuracy in delivering a specific level of total compensation, but carries challenging communication issues since it appears to punish executives for good performance and reward negative results (i.e., the higher the stock price rises, the less the number of options granted). Fixed share guidelines minimize the communication challenges associated with determining annual award levels, but can cause unintended escalation in the value of executive compensation when stock prices rise. The following chart summarizes when either of these approaches is typically most appropriate:

Appropriateness of Alternative Approaches	
The Targeted Value Approach is Best When...	The Fixed Shares Approach is Best When...
1. The company wants the value (and accounting cost) of option grants to remain relatively constant on an annual basis 2. Optionees clearly understand how option values are determined 3. The company is comfortable with wide fluctuations in the total number of shares being used	1. The company wishes to carefully control annual share usage and avoid wide fluctuations due to share price changes 2. Optionees do not clearly understand how option values are determined 3. The company is comfortable in allowing option grant values (and accounting cost) to fluctuate with changes in share price

In general, the targeted value approach is more appropriate in larger companies that have relatively stable stock prices and have invested in specific communication programs intended to educate employees about option values. The fixed share approach is more appropriate in companies with high stock price volatility or less knowledgeable optionees. Some companies combine the two approaches by establishing targets for senior management as targeted value and using a fixed guideline for other participants (i.e., those whose overall compensation package is more weighted to cash-based awards and salary, and therefore less affected by stock price changes).

Irrespective of whether a company uses a targeted value or fixed share guideline, most typically provide a range of opportunity that fluctuates around the target number of shares for individual participants. The high end of the range is often capped (e.g., 120% or 125% of target, except in special situations), and the low end of the range often requires a threshold level of performance to receive a grant. Many companies subjectively evaluate individuals when determining where they fall within the range of opportunity, while others use a formula. In either case, the factors that should be considered include:

• Individual performance over time

• Potential for future contributions

• Difficulty of replacement

• Readiness for promotion into higher level

• Business unit performance

A word of caution is appropriate with regard to setting stock option guidelines in cases where stock price volatility has been high. The sources of competitive data used to set guidelines typically lag the market by a year or more. Last year's competitive data may suggest the need to grant an inordinately high number of shares to deliver comparable value if share price has declined substantially. To test the reasonableness of stock option grant guidelines, companies should do two things:

• CEO and other named executive officer grants–based on comparable numbers at peer companies, the total shares being awarded to this group as a percentage of options granted to all employees should be examined

• Total option eligible population–to ensure that aggregate share usage and cost is reasonable, companies should examine the size of their total annual grant expressed as a percent of total outstanding common shares relative to peers, as well as the value of the total option pool expressed as a percent of the company's total market capitalization

The data needed to perform the two analyses described above is available in the proxy statements and annual reports of peer companies.

Typical Practices Among Start-ups and Turnaround Companies

In other situations, such as start-up companies and turnaround situations, the size of stock option grants is often structured to deliver a targeted level of option profit at an assumed stock price.

For example, a CEO is hired to manage a turnaround of a once well-performing company in which share price has fallen from $35 to $3 per share. If the option grant were sized to deliver a targeted profit of $20 million when the share price recovers to $25, it would require an award of approximately 1.18 million shares (assuming the options are exercisable at current fair market value).

Another way of sizing stock option awards in a start up organization is to express the grant as a percentage of total outstanding shares, using external peer practice as a benchmark for reasonableness. For example, high technology start-ups often offer incoming CEOs an option grant that represents between 2% to 6% of total outstanding shares. For pre-IPO companies, such a strategy reinforces the importance of achieving liquidity (e.g., IPO, sale of company) with minimal amounts of external investment, since each additional round of financing dilutes the CEO's option position and expected profit.

Corporate Governance Issues

Companies face a long list of corporate governance issues in their use of stock options. The primary issues facing companies today are addressed below.

Issues Associated with Potential Share Dilution

Institutional investors are concerned about a company's use of equity in employee stock option plans. Recognition of these concerns is important, because if the potential share dilution attributable to stock awards reaches a level that institutions deem intolerable, the repercussions can be significant. The institutions may simply vote negatively on proposals submitted for additional share authorizations. This can be troublesome, as it may interfere with a company's ability to continue making grants in their ongoing long-term incentive plans. In more extreme cases, investors may decide to liquidate their positions, which will create downward price pressure on the company's shares.

In managing the dilutive impact of their stock option programs, companies should carefully consider the following factors to protect against unexpected EPS and voting power dilution:

- **Average annual share usage**–illustrates the average annual shares granted in employee equity plans as a percent of total shares outstanding (i.e., the Company's annual "run rate")

- **Fully diluted overhang**–illustrates potential dilution attributable to awards already outstanding plus shares reserved for future grants, or in other words, the potential dilution associated with existing stock plans if all shares granted and available were exercised

    –Note that overhang is expressed on a fully diluted basis, meaning that shares potentially issued (i.e., the numerator) are counted in the denominator

A company's annual run rate basically represents the rate at which it intends to dilute shareholders. If the rate is considerably higher than that of similar companies, it is not likely to be sustainable on a long-term basis without raising the ire of investors. On the other hand, if it is substantially lower, it probably means that the company is not fully competitive at all employee levels with traditional peer companies (assuming that the company's capital structure is similar to peers). While average run rate for U.S. companies is approximately 2%, rates vary significantly by industry and have been declining over the last few years after many years of substantial increase. While rates also vary by company within industries, the following table illustrates typical run rates:

Run Rates	Representative Industries
4% and above	Financial services
3% to 4%	Healthcare, Technology
2% to 3%	Banking
1% to 2%	General manufacturing
1% or less	Food, Utilities

Overhang represents aggregate potential dilution attributable to the stock option program. This is the key factor examined by institutions in considering whether a company's stock option program has been overly dilutive. While some institutions have hard and fast rules applicable to tolerable overhang levels, a rough rule of thumb is that 10%–15% is acceptable for asset intensive companies often described as "old economy," while 15%–20% or higher may be acceptable for financial services, high tech, and other "new economy" companies.

To offset shareholder dilution resulting from outstanding option grants, many companies initiate share repurchase programs in which either a specified number or dollar value of shares is repurchased in the market. While these programs offset immediate share dilution and help to support or improve EPS results (share buybacks are not an expense for P&L purposes), they can be harmful to a company's balance sheet. This is because the buybacks reduce cash assets and, if the purchases occur when the stock is relatively overpriced, may not represent a wise use of funds.

Seeking Shareholder Approval of Option Plans

There are several reasons why companies seek shareholder approval of the plans in which they make stock option grants:

- **Basic corporate governance**–many companies generally believe that as a matter of good corporate governance, shareholder approval should be obtained for stock plans

- **Stock exchange rules**–as mentioned earlier, both the New York Stock Exchange and the Nasdaq significantly tightened the shareholder-approval rules applicable to equity compensation plans in 2003. With limited exceptions, both markets now require shareholder approval of virtually all stock option awards. Exceptions include grants made to new hires and those made in conjunction with the acquisition of another company

- **State of incorporation**–depending on the state in which a company is incorporated, shareholder approval of stock plans may be required

- **Tax deductions**–in order to meet the performance-based pay exception for deductibility of compensation in excess of $1 million paid to a company's five highest paid officers, the grants must be made under a plan in which the material terms are approved by shareholders

The "Repricing" of Outstanding Stock Option Awards

The issue generating perhaps the greatest level of attention in the business press in recent years and having the most visible corporate governance issues is stock option repricing.

A repricing is typically defined as either a direct reduction in the exercise price of an outstanding option, or an indirect reduction that occurs as a result of cancellation and replacement of existing options or the payment of some type of cash bonus at exercise. Companies that reprice stock options generally do so when the options fall so far out-of-the money (or underwater) that recovery is believed to be unlikely. The purpose of the repricing, therefore, is to restore the incentive and retention value of the original award.

Advocates of option repricings argue that the practice is necessary to avoid mass loss of talent as a result of significant decline in share price and that repricings restore retention value, particularly among today's mobile workforce that is capable of effectuating independent repricings simply by leaving one employer and joining another (who offers new options priced at current market value).

Before repricing options, however, companies should carefully consider several factors that carry significant consequences:

- Unless expressly permitted in the underlying plan in which the original awards were granted, both the New York Stock Exchange and Nasdaq listing requirements require that shareholder approval be obtained before repricing

- As a result of FIN 44 (discussed earlier), the repricing of an option that is otherwise accounted for as a fixed award under Opinion 25 will generally result in variable accounting treatment until exercise. This means that the option profit captured upon exercise will generate a full charge to earnings, with mark-to-market accounting occurring at each reporting period.[15] Options also result in additional accounting costs under FAS 123

- Repricings that involve an exchange of shares in less than a one-for-one ratio may actually harm employees if share price recovers significantly

- An option repricing may encourage employees to view all incentive pay as an entitlement. In addition, repricings do not generally differentiate between key contributors and marginal performers, but rather treat all employees as if they are equally important

- Repricings increase earnings per share dilution, which forces the company to divert cash from elsewhere to repurchase shares to offset dilution, or alternatively, can result in downward price pressure on the stock as a company's earnings are spread over a larger share base

In some cases, companies may feel they have no choice but to reprice options. However, given the accounting consequences and shareholder considerations, such action is usually appropriate only as a last resort. There are, in fact, many alternatives to restoring incentive and retention value following a substantial stock price decline, two simple approaches include:

- **Acceleration of future awards**–under this approach, option grants that would otherwise be awarded in the future are accelerated. The acceleration could include a single award or multiple years. Assuming the current stock price is artificially low, acceleration enables employees to leverage their upside as the company recovers. Acceleration also sends a positive message to shareholders that management believes share price will not go lower

- **Special restricted stock grants**–under this approach, a select group of key contributors would receive restricted shares on top of their normal annual stock option awards. While this approach generates additional compensation cost, it differentiates between key contributors and marginal employees

Steps for Program Implementation

As mentioned earlier, stock options are usually granted under a stand-alone plan or an omnibus program that enables the granting of options and a variety of other long-term incentives. In developing a new or replacement stock option or omnibus plan, the following issues should be addressed:

- **Administration**–the plan should clearly state the parties responsible for making grants and performing other administrative responsibilities
- **Participants**–the plan should define who is eligible to receive grants (e.g., all employees, officers only) and whether participation will be extended to nonemployee directors, consultants, and contractors
- **Types of awards**–the plan should state the type of options (i.e., ISOs versus NQSOs) permitted, as well as other types of employee equity grants (if any)
- **Individual grant terms**–the plan or the underlying agreements in which awards are granted should address:
  - *Vesting schedule*–the service and/or performance requirements that must be met in order to obtain a right to exercise the option
  - *Term*–the length of time during which the grant can be exercised
  - *Exercise price*–the price at which options may be issued (many plans preclude the granting of discount options)
- **Treatment of awards upon termination of employment**–the plan or award agreements should specify whether unvested awards are forfeited upon various termination events and how long vested options can be exercised after termination
- **Method of exercise**–the plan should clearly describe the methods in which optionees may pay the exercise price
- **Share reserve**–the plan should state the total number of shares available for grant and the source of such shares (e.g., newly issued, direct market purchases, treasury stock)
- **Share counting features**–the plan should clearly describe the rules for determining when a share granted under the plan has been economically used and therefore counted against the share reserve

- **Individual limits**–the plan should clearly state a limit on the maximum number of shares that can be granted to any single individual over a prescribed period of time
- **Change in control provisions**–if special provisions are to apply to outstanding awards in the event of a change in control, either the plan or the grant agreements should identify what constitutes such an event and how outstanding awards will be treated

In designing a new plan that is to be submitted to shareholders for approval, there are a variety of design features that may positively or negatively impact the vote. For example, if a plan does not specify a maximum option term or minimum exercise price, this would negatively impact many investors when considering how to vote on the proposal.

The effectiveness of an option plan is contingent on participants clearly understanding the program, including the tax consequences of exercise. Clear and concise written communication materials increase in importance if option grants are made to a broad base of employees within the organization, since lower level employees are generally less financially sophisticated.

Conclusion

Stock options are powerful and flexible incentive vehicles. By rewarding recipients based on share price appreciation, stock options can provide an effective means to focus the efforts of executives and maintain alignment with shareholder interests.

Unfortunately, specific stock option plans have been implicated as a contributing factor in corporate scandals over the last several years. As a result, public pressure and other factors–most notably the likelihood of mandatory option expensing–are influencing corporations to rethink the appropriateness of past practices and strategies. Nevertheless, options will likely remain at the foundation of senior executive compensation systems. Effective use, however, will require a complex understanding of many issues to avoid fostering an entitlement attitude among employees, losing possible tax deductions, generating unnecessary earnings charges, or damaging shareholder relations.

Endnotes
1. It should be noted that discount options are generally not well received by shareholders, since they compromise the very foundation on which stock options are based. In other words, a discount option not only allows the recipient to share in future appreciation, but also provides

an immediate value that is not contingent on creation of shareholder wealth. For this reason, many stock plans expressly prohibit the granting of discount options.

2. In some cases, exercisability following vesting may be contingent on other conditions, such as continued employment or the existence of a public market for the underlying shares.

3. It should be noted that acceleration of unvested stock options can contribute to receipt of "excess parachute payments," which trigger excise taxes to the recipient and loss of tax deductions for the company. These topics are addressed in Chapter 13.

4. The full text of Section 422 and the proposed regulations are provided on the accompanying CD.

5. Note that if the stock acquired through option exercise is repurchased by the company within 6 months of the exercise, the repurchase results in accounting for the option as if it were a cash settlement. As a result, employee put rights and company call rights and rights of first refusal must have a 6-month holding period requirement to preserve fixed plan accounting treatment.

6. A cash settlement is treated as a conversion of the stock option to a stock appreciation right, or in other words, a cash bonus based on stock price increase. Compensation cost attributable to cash awards equals the amount of the payment when made.

7. In the first year the optionee provides service necessary to earn 100% of the first vesting tranche (i.e., $2,500), plus half of the second tranche (i.e., $1,250), one-third of the third (i.e., $833), and a quarter of the last (i.e. $625), or in other words, approximately 52% of the total award.

8. Interpretation of APB 25 and clarification of FIN 44 has been an ongoing challenge for the FASB. Shortly after the release of FIN 44, the Emerging Issues Task Force of the FASB began a 2-year project known as Issue 00-23, during which the EITF met 9 times to resolve 71 specific issues and sub-issues under APB 25 and FIN 44. A summary of these issues is presented in our Client Alert letter dated 8/2/02, which can be accessed on the accompanying CD or by visiting www.fwcook.com. and clicking on "publications."

9. Note that awards that can be settled in cash (i.e., liabilities of the company, rather than equity instruments) are accounted for under FAS 123 in the same way as variable awards under Opinion 25 (i.e., mark-to-market accounting). Therefore, the measurement date for an award settled in cash is the date of payment.

10. While ISO gains are not taxed as ordinary income upon exercise, they are potentially subject to taxation in the year of exercise under the Alternative Minimum Tax.

11. Except in the case of Incentive Stock Options (ISOs), in which no tax is due until the under-lying shares are sold.

12. In an attestation exercise, the shares are not actually delivered to the company, but rather the employee attests to owning them. Rather than taking receipt of the shares and then returning them to the employee as part of the option proceeds, the company simply delivers the net profit shares.

13. There are various approaches that can be employed to avoid variable accounting under APB 25.

Accompanying materials to be found on the CD for this chapter:

- Full text of IRC Section 422 *Incentive Stock Options and Proposed Regulations*

- FW Cook client letter: EITF Issue No. 00-23 *Issues Related to the Accounting for Stock Compensation under APB Opinion No. 25 and FASB Interpretation No. 44*

- Full text of Proposed Changes for ISOs and ESPPs-IRB 2003-27

- Full text of Title 26 USC Section 422 ISOs

DANIEL J. RYTERBAND
Managing Director
Frederic W. Cook & Co.

Daniel J. Ryterband is a Managing Director and head of the New York office of Frederic W. Cook & Co., where he consults to organizations on all aspects of executive compensation strategy and design including tax, accounting, securities law, and corporate governance issues.

He specializes in the design of cash- and equity-based incentive plans, with a particular focus on compensation issues related to transformative events such as mergers, divestitures, IPOs, spin-offs, and other restructurings.

He has 15 years of direct consulting experience and his clients include U.S. and overseas multinationals in a variety of industries, as well as smaller start-up organizations and private enterprises. Mr. Ryterband has extensive experience in working with Board Compensation Committees and generally attends or participates in 80 or more Committee and/or Board meetings annually.

He is a frequent writer and speaker on emerging issues in the field. He has spoken at numerous conferences including those held by the Conference Board, the American Society of Corporate Secretaries, Northwestern University's Kellogg School, the Harvard Business School, WorldatWork, the Association of Executive Search Consultants, Financial Executives International, and other related trade and educational organizations. He is a member of the teaching faculty at WorldatWork, where he teaches courses on executive compensation to industry professionals.

He is a graduate of Rutgers University (BS, economics and finance) and New York University's Leonard N. Stern School of Business (MBA, finance and management). He is also a certified employee benefit specialist.

6. Executive Benefits and Perquisites: An Overview of Current Trends and Programs

Practitioners tend to speak of executive "compensation" in shorthand. It is a label that covers not only the traditional compensation elements–base salary, annual and long-term incentives–but also the various executive benefits and perquisite programs that are only offered–if they are offered–to the executive group.

This important chapter provides an excellent overview of the currently prevalent executive benefits and perquisites. After first making the case for why executive benefits and perquisites exist and how they fit into an integrated total rewards program, the author then discusses the most common executive benefits currently in use at U.S. companies. These include deferred compensation, financial counseling, executive medical, company cars, club memberships and supplemental life insurance programs and many others. For each, the author describes the benefit, provides prevalence data on usage, gives an overview of design issues, discusses administration, tax or cost issues, and gives a sense of the trend in usage and benefit design.

The chapter concludes with an eight-step process for determining the selection of appropriate executive benefits and perquisites in a company's total executive-rewards program. It explains why different companies arrive at different solutions, and offers one-stop shopping for a reader interested in getting a quick, but thorough overview of what is currently in use. –Editors

Overview of Executive Benefits and Perquisites

LONG VIEWED BY MANY top executives as rights of passage, executive benefits and perquisites are now more than ever coming under the closer scrutiny of boards, shareholders and the media alike. It is important therefore to have an objective basis and system for determining which of the many possible benefits make good business sense, as well as how they may help or hurt an organization's ability to attract and retain the right caliber of executive talent.

First, let's briefly highlight some of the economic and pay strategy shifts that have lead to increased attention on executive benefits and perquisites.

Economic recession across the U.S. has resulted in layoffs, hiring freezes, lower bonuses, lower or no long-term incentive payouts and higher employee contributions to benefits programs. With lower overall rewards being paid through what has become the "typical" executive compensation program, companies are beginning to look at other forms of rewards to potentially "make up" for less than target payments in areas like incentives. Companies and executives are now seeking the right mix of rewards that make sense for the business. This has been seen by some as a push for offering additional or enhanced executive benefits as less emphasis is placed on other compensation elements.

Conversely, these same economic factors can be seen as having resulted in a less competitive market for executive talent. There are certainly more available candidates in the market looking for jobs than there were in the explosive '90s. Although top and key-position talent is still seen as a vital resource for an organization, the difficulty of attracting and retaining these key employees has lessened.[1] Additional pressure for remunerative restraint has been brought to bear from the flurry of related legislation, both enacted and pending, that is maintaining the spotlight on executive compensation. The media, ever anxious to capitalize on a sensational story, has added to the attention by highlighting the details and excesses of some of the largest pay packages including additional executive benefits and perquisites. Stories such as company planes, post-retirement perquisites, lavish parties, personal art collections, vacation homes and the now infamous $17,000 shower curtain have furthered the case to put executive compensation under the microscope. Not surprisingly, these events have lead to an environment of restraint or at least reconsideration of some of the packages and programs already in place.

So how is one to determine what package of benefits and perquisites is best-suited for a given organization, i.e., those that are necessary and in-line with the overall executive compensation philosophy and are likely to add value to the company as a whole?

This chapter will explore the needs of each of the three major constituent groups (employer, employee and shareholder) in a discussion of the most currently prevalent types of executive benefits and perquisites. For each of the following top twelve executive benefit and perquisite programs, a description of the general purpose, objectives, prevalence, structure, tax impacts, cost and cash flow considerations will provide a basis for understanding when, how and how much of each type of program may be appropriate for your organization. These programs include the following:

1. **Supplemental Retirement Programs and Nonqualified Deferred Compensation**–Programs that provide supplemental retirement income or savings opportunities for top executives over and above what is available through broader all-employee pension or other qualified plans; the most popular and costly of executive benefits.

2. **Financial Counseling**–Providing, or more likely, facilitating some form of financial counseling service so that executives can focus more attention on the business while knowing their personal portfolios are in good order.

3. **Personal Loans**–Facilitating the financing of any number of needs (e.g., home purchase, equity purchase, bridge-loans) through direct or indirect company sponsored loans.

4. **Executive Medical**–Highlighting the focus on health and well-being, executive medical programs can provide a system of periodic health examinations as well as supplemental medical insurance.

5. **Long-Term Care**–A growing area of interest in this age of the baby boomer–and generally aging population. Providing the vehicle for executives to obtain or be covered by long-term care insurance.

6. **Supplemental Life Insurance/Survivor Protection**–Providing additional life insurance protection above what is offered in a company's group plan.

7. **Supplemental Disability**–If disabled during their career, most top executives will receive only a fraction of their salary in long-term disability coverage through company sponsored group programs. Supplemental disability coverage looks to increase the level of income replacement so that it is closer to what the average employee would receive.

8. **Severance Arrangements**–What happens when the unforeseen or unexpected change occurs that causes an executive to lose their job? Severance arrangements look to mitigate the risk an executive takes in their role and provide enough security, comfort and income stream to continue focusing on the task at hand–the needs of the business.

9. **Company Cars/Car Allowances**–The extent to which companies provide vehicles or support towards automobile travel for personal and professional use.

10. **Club Memberships**–Company sponsored or facilitated membership into country, city or other types of community or social clubs.

11. **Travel**–As the world becomes smaller and travel demands on executives become greater, these perquisites attempt to make the experience of business travel less onerous and more productive.

12. **Legal**–This benefit could also be listed under Personal Financial Management depending on the needs of the executive. Typically, executive legal counseling services include assistance with will preparation, estate planning or any legal need such as during a divorce or personal liability action.

Executive Benefits and Perquisites in the Context of an Executive Total Compensation Strategy

Where Do They Fit and Why?

Like any component of executive compensation, whether we are looking at base salary, annual incentives, stock options, or retirement programs, benefits and perquisites can be offered for different reasons and structured to accomplish various goals. However, few companies have historically designed these programs in the context of an overall executive total compensation strategy. When considered in this light, it is important to first understand where some of these programs might fall within the spectrum of monetary and non-monetary rewards. Ideally, the executive total rewards strategy supports the human capital strategy of the company which, in turn, supports the business strategy overall. Each of the twelve programs identified above can be seen as fulfilling either a monetary or non-monetary component in that overall strategy.

Further, the twelve programs can be grouped within the four categories shown below. Notice there is some overlap in that programs may have financial costs but be valued differently for different individuals. A company, for instance, that wishes to focus attention on offering a highly competitive benefits package, and feels that health and security are key components, would likely chose to narrow their focus on those benefits that emphasize these components.

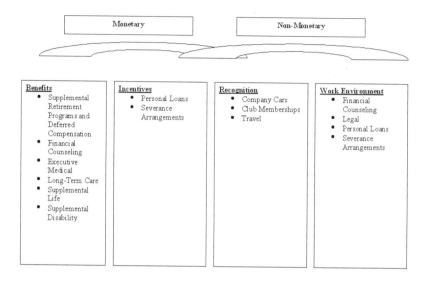

Alternatively, if the desired focus is to provide a convenient work environment with a large focus on productivity, they may want to build their plan offering to focus around those values. This is not to say that a company could not chose to provide each and every one of these programs, simply that it is a useful initial exercise to consider the overall context within which these programs are intended to be aligned and effective.

We can then consider the major objectives that lay behind each of these programs to determine if they again fit within our philosophy. By looking at it in this way, we are able to see that not all programs accomplish every objective, though some may support more than one.

Program Objectives	
Wealth Accumulation and Personal Financial Management • Supplemental Retirement and Nonqualified Deferred Compensation • Financial Counseling • Personal Loans • Supplemental Life Insurance/Survivor Protection • Long-Term Care • Supplemental Disability • Legal	**Security** • Personal Loans • Supplemental Life Insurance/Survivor Protection • Long-Term Care • Supplemental Retirement • Financial Counseling • Supplemental Disability • Legal
Health • Executive Medical • Long-Term Care	**Convenience/Productivity/Quality of Life** • Financial Counseling • Travel • Club Memberships • Personal Loans • Legal • Company Cars

In summary, understanding what the organization's compensation philosophy is attempting to achieve is the first place to start. Next, consider the objectives of the philosophy and the relative weight and importance that should be given to the broad components of total executive pay. Finally, evaluating the objectives behind each of the elements will help determine which programs may be most–or least–important.

The 12 Most Common (and Valued) Benefits and Perquisites–What Are They and How Do They Work?

Supplemental Retirement Programs and Nonqualified Deferred Compensation

Supplemental Retirement Programs and Nonqualified Deferred Compensation plans are two primary vehicles used to provide executives additional retirement income or opportunities to accumulate assets. They are plans that provide deferred compensation or retirement benefits over and above the benefits provided by qualified plans. There are different forms of supplemental retirement programs each with different objectives. To highlight these differences, the following are definitions of each of the primary types of nonqualified plans along with their primary objective(s):

Nonqualified Excess 415 Benefit Plan–A plan that restores executive benefits (also called restoration plans) that are limited by certain IRS provisions, specifically by the IRC Section 415 rules which govern the level of contribution or benefit provided by a qualified retirement plan. The Section 415 limitations were designed to favor lower paid employees, and prevent the highly compensated from receiving greater benefits than the rank and file employees. They are used by companies who recognize that the IRC Section 415 limitations result in executives receiving a substantially lower percentage level of replacement income than rank and file employees, and believe that this should be "made up."

For 2003 the defined benefit plan limit is $160,000 ($165,000 in 2004) and the defined contribution plan limit is $40,000 ($41,000 in 2004). These plans can be in either a defined benefit form, as a supplement to a qualified pension plan, or in a defined contribution form that may, for example, restore benefits contributed into a 401(k) or Money Purchase Plan.

Nonqualified Excess 401(a)(17) Plan–A plan that restores benefits that are limited by the compensation limits (IRC Section 401(a)(17)) imposed on qualified defined benefit and defined contribution plans. In 2003 the compensation limit under this Section is $200,000 ($205,000 in 2004).

This limit could significantly lessen an executive's qualified plan limit, particularly in the top echelon of executives who often earn well in excess of $200,000.

Similar to Nonqualified Excess 415 Benefit Plans, these plans aim to restore benefits that would otherwise be limited due to the IRS rules and achieve an objective of retirement income security. Again, these plans align with a philosophy that emphasizes retirement benefits, tenure and retirement security.

Consider an example of an executive who earns a base salary of $1,000,000 (also her final average pay), works a full career of 30 years and is covered by her company's qualified pension plan that pays 1% of final average compensation per year of service (ignore offsets and distribution options for the moment). Compare her plan benefit in this scenario to a plan that also provides a Supplemental Benefit (Excess 415 and 401(a)(17)) that covers all base salary offset by her qualified plan benefit.

This executive would receive only 6% of her final compensation per year as retirement income under the qualified plan. If she was also covered by the Supplemental Plan, she would receive a much higher income replacement of 30%.

Supplemental Executive Retirement Program (SERP)–SERPs are nonqualified plans that do more than restore excess plan benefits. These plans can provide additional benefits by applying to a different definition of compensation (e.g., includes annual incentives or other compensation types) as well as offer more advantageous provisions than the qualified plan. Some of the typical feature enhancements include an alternative benefit formula, different accrual pattern or different early retirement features.

Here, too, a SERP can be in either a defined contribution or defined benefit form and allows for much flexibility in its design. In addition to the objectives of retirement income security and wealth accumulation, SERPs are often designed to achieve other objectives such as providing an attractive

Element	Qualified Pension Only	Qualified Pension plus Supplemental Restoration Plan
Qualified Pension Benefit ($200,000 x 30 years x 1%)	$60,000 per year	$60,000 per year
Nonqualified 401(a)(17) and 415 Excess Benefit ($1 mil x 30 years x 1% up to $160,000) – qualified benefit	$0	$240,000 per year
Total Retirement Benefit	$60,000 per year	$300,000 per year
Percent of Final Compensation	6%	30%

recruitment tool, rewarding for performance by linking to company performance goals, and replacing benefits given up by executives when they left their prior employer to join the current company. Because of their inherent flexibility, these plans are often considered to be the most effective type of supplemental retirement program and are discussed in greater detail in a separate chapter.

Voluntary Deferred Compensation–Nonqualified programs that allow executives to defer some percentage of their compensation into a tax-advantaged accumulation account. A typical VDC plan allows executives to defer 50% of their base salary and 100% of their annual incentive awards into the plan. The deferrals accumulate and grow at some established rate of interest or at a return established by some form of investment such as a mutual fund. The primary objectives of these programs are to provide an additional vehicle to facilitate wealth accumulation and portfolio management opportunities as well as manage taxes.

Prevalence

Voluntary Deferred Compensation plans are the most prevalent form of nonqualified supplemental program, with nonqualified defined benefit restoration plans being the next most common. Substantially fewer companies take full advantage of the inherent flexibilities of nonqualified deferred compensation in the form of SERPs.

Design Issues and Considerations

Although supplemental nonqualified deferred compensation plans are extremely flexible, there are a number of rules that must be followed. The most important of these are:

Constructive Receipt–A participant cannot have direct control or access

Percentage of Companies (170 participants) who maintain some type of Nonqualified Plan[2]		
DB 415 Excess	52%	55%
DB 401(a)17 Excess	58%	52%
DC 415 Excess	38%	38%
DC 401(a) 17 Excess	36%	36%
DB SERP	40%	18%
DC SERP	13%	14%
Voluntary NQDC	74%	74%

to plan benefits or deferrals. If they do, then the executive is immediately taxed on the value of the benefit, whether received or not. Two issues are key. First, a participant's election as to timing and form of benefits paid must occur prior to when compensation is earned. As an example, all deferral elections into a voluntary deferred compensation plan must be made prior to the calendar year in which the base salary is earned. If deferral of incentives is allowed, then the deferral must also be made in advance of the time the incentive is earned. This may mean electing deferrals significantly in advance of actually receiving the award, depending upon the structure of the incentive plan.

The second key issue is that the participant cannot have control over their benefits. This applies not only to receiving the benefits, but other areas of access such as investing discretion or assigning benefits.

Eligibility–Nonqualified plans can be offered to only a select group of management or highly compensated individuals. There is no specific guidance or rules as to who the IRS or Department of Labor defines as a select group (qualified plan definitions do not apply) although some case rulings do provide some insights and are presented and discussed in the chapter on non qualified deferred compensation. Suffice it to say for our purposes here that it is a good idea to review this criteria with counsel to receive advice on what would be considered a select group based on the facts and circumstances related to your company.

ERISA–Nonqualified Supplemental Retirement Plans must be unfunded Top Hat plans. They are subject to the procedural and enforcement provisions, including claims procedures, of ERISA but exempt from the 410(b) minimum participation, vesting requirements, benefit accrual rules, funding rules and distribution restrictions. There are abbreviated reporting requirements for Unfunded Plans which call for the company to file a statement with the Department of Labor indicating the number of participants, name and number of top hat plans.

Funding–As indicated above, nonqualified plans must be unfunded to take advantage of ERISA exemptions as well as to continue to provide the tax advantage structure for its participants. Although these plans are technically unfunded, a liability accrues in the balance sheet and remains at-risk to the company's general creditors. To manage this liability and the ultimate cash flow requirements of the plan, companies may choose to informally fund or finance their obligations. They may also choose to set assets aside as a sign to participants of the company's good faith and intention to manage and meet the liability.

Selecting the right funding vehicle for a nonqualified plan is a challenge. Unlike qualified plans, any asset set aside to back a nonqualified plan obligation is an asset of the company and does not receive special tax treatment. In other words, the fund's return or gain on any such asset (in most circumstances) creates a taxable event for the company at the time it is earned. Therefore, the company will pay taxes on the return for the taxable asset.

The taxable nature of these corporate-owned investments is only one consideration in the decision of what financing vehicle to choose. In addition to a company's effective tax rate, other factors must be considered in the decision of how to finance the nonqualified plan obligation as well as whether or not it makes sense to set aside assets. These considerations include the demographics of participants, cash flow needs of the plan, taxable nature of the investment (e.g., return, turnover, tax-free), asset liquidity, anticipated liability growth, expected benefit payments, life of the plan and required rate of return of the company. A 2002 Watson Wyatt study revealed that most companies do not set assets aside to back supplemental retirement plan liabilities. Instead, it is more common for companies to finance a voluntary deferral plan.

The fact that a company decides not to set assets aside implies they believe a better return can be achieved by investing in the company itself. Because answering the question "to fund or not to fund" is so complex, it is highly advisable that the Human Resources or Benefits professional work together with the Finance department in analyzing various financing approaches to determine which makes the most sense. A plan with no assets

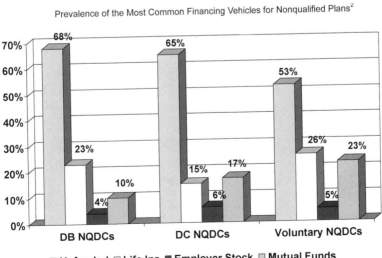

Prevalence of the Most Common Financing Vehicles for Nonqualified Plans[2]

☐ Unfunded ☐ Life Ins ■ Employer Stock ☐ Mutual Funds

set aside has different earnings and cash flow implications than a plan backed by a taxable investment (such as mutual funds or a managed investment portfolio) or a plan financed via insurance products. They also each behave very differently under various time and financial return assumptions.

As a final note on the issue of funding, it is advisable to make the financing decision separately from the design decision. It is not uncommon to see (ill-advised) instances where the use of a funding vehicle drove the design or even the introduction of a plan. A focus on the objectives of the plan and its fit in the total compensation picture is first and foremost.

Accounting and Taxes–All nonqualified or deferred plan obligations are accounted for as a liability on the balance sheet. As the obligation grows, an additional liability is accrued. A corresponding deferred compensation expense is also debited to the income statement.

At the time benefits are paid, the company reduces (debits) the liability and reduces (credits) cash. At this time, the corporate tax deduction is taken. Therefore, the company has a mismatch between the time the expense is booked and when the tax deduction is taken. The tax deduction corresponds to the time the executive recognizes the income and is taxed (constructive receipt).

If the plan has assets set aside backing the liability, there are additional earnings impacts depending upon the type of investment vehicle chosen. Again, here is why the choice of investment vehicles is so important and a thorough analysis should be conducted.

Crediting Rates–Nonqualified deferred compensation plans and nonqualified supplemental defined contribution plans must provide a crediting rate to participant accounts. Companies can choose to offer a fixed crediting rate, a variable investment rate or a rate tied to an index. In recent years, the trend has been to offer some type of variable crediting rate that is tied to a selection of mutual funds (e.g., those offered in the qualified 401(k)) or some other core investment lineup. Offering an alternative that ties to company performance is also an option.

The decision as to what form of crediting rate to offer should be reflective of the objective of the plan. If the goal is to offer a wealth accumulation vehicle, offering a range of choices would be appropriate. If the plan is to provide a more secure type of benefit, possibly a fixed or stable rate would make more sense. If it is purely a vehicle for tax deferred growth and tax management, possibly a rate that reflects the fact that the participants are in reality loaning the company money (by deferring receipt) is in order.

Each of these concepts should be addressed in the design stage and in the process of determining whether or not assets should be set aside to finance the liability. In either case, and regardless of the option chosen, a participant does not actually invest their account in the vehicle that dictates the crediting rate. Any investment used to finance the liability is owned by the company, not the participant. The company directs how investments backing the plan are made. To ensure that the investment returns mirror the returns generated by participant accounts, most companies elect to invest the assets in accordance with what participants have selected. The point is, this is not required and must be structured so the company is actually making the investment decision. Often, the company provides direction to the plan trustee or fund manager to invest in a given manner.

Security–In reality, all supplemental retirement and deferred compensation programs are merely a company's promise to pay. This is because unlike a pension plan a nonqualified plan benefit is not permitted to be secured and the company retains the right to change, modify or cancel the plan.

As mentioned, any asset set aside to support plan liabilities is an asset owned by the employer, and not the plan participants. As such, while these assets are intended to be used to pay benefits, they could also be used for any business purpose. To provide additional security to plan participants that assets set aside will be used to pay plan benefits, many companies place these assets in a Rabbi Trust arrangement. This type of trust provides assurance that any assets in the trust will be used only to satisfy plan obligations. It also protects against what is termed "change of heart" or change of control. In these two situations, the underlying fear of the plan participant is that the company will decide not to pay the benefits (unlikely) or, that an acquiring company will not honor plan promises (a possibility). Many (if not most) companies use these types of trust arrangements if they do in fact decide to set assets aside.

The biggest drawback of a Rabbi Trust (so named because it was first used to protect assets set aside in connection with a Rabbi's deferred compensation benefits) is that it does not protect against the most serious threat to a participant's security–inability to pay! A Rabbi Trust is a form of grantor trust and, therefore, its assets remain assets of the employer and can be attached in the event of bankruptcy or insolvency. All assets are subject to the claims of general creditors. There is no protection mechanism that both retains the tax deferred nature of these plans for participants and also effectively protects against the ultimate failure of a company. Many plan participants do not understand this fact.

Common Designs

There is a great degree of inherent flexibility in designing these programs. The first step in creating an effective design is to determine the program's objective. Next, review the advantages and disadvantages of various design alternatives and what their potential impacts would be on the executive population and on the company. As shown below, there are a number of different outcomes that can be achieved through plan features and decisions in the design of a nonqualified plan or SERP.

While the example above highlights some of the key design features of a SERP there are, of course, other features that can be considered (e.g., disability) as well as a cadre of issues with respect to defined contribution approaches. The essential point is to think the issues through from both the human resources and financial perspectives when considering the design, administration, and financing of the plan. How the program fits with the other elements of the compensation package (e.g., long-term incentives) is also critical in determining whether a nonqualified deferral arrangement is appropriate and likely to be effective in attracting and retaining the right talent, or whether an alternative vehicle is more appropriate.

Design Feature	Typical Design	Executive	Company
Replacement Ratio	50% to 60% of final average pay offset by other employer sponsored programs	**Advantage** – provides secure retirement **Disadvantage** – unsecured promise to pay	**Advantage** – promotes career longevity **Disadvantage** – cost
Vesting*	5 – 10 years of service	**Advantage** – secure retirement **Disadvantage** – Must perform continued service	**Advantage** – some retention **Disadvantage** – time based, no performance requirements
Definition of Full Career	25 years (ranges from 20 to 30 years)	**Advantage** – typically shorter than qualified plan full career definition	**Advantage** – attractive **Disadvantage** – cost
Performance Conditions	Not prevalent	**Advantage** – time based accrual **Disadvantage** – fixed	**Advantage** – simple **Disadvantage** – no performance links
Form of Benefit	Choice of lump sum or 5/10 year installment	**Advantage** – choice **Disadvantage** – taxation, avoid constructive receipt	**Advantage** – simple **Disadvantage** – cash flow
Funding	Life insurance, taxable investments	**Advantage** – assets set aside to pay benefits **Disadvantage** – assets owned by company	**Advantage** – manage liability and earnings **Disadvantage** – monitoring, liability match, earnings impacts, diversion of investment in business
Security	Rabbi Trust arrangement	**Advantage** – secure against change of heart **Disadvantage** – not secure against bankruptcy	**Advantage** – participant positive perception **Disadvantage** – diversion of investment in business

*Note: not typical in the not-for-profit environment where special rules apply. Deferred Compensation for not-for-profit organizations is governed by IRC Section 457 and requires taxation of benefit values at the time there is no longer a substantial risk of forfeiture (typically at vesting).

Cost

It was mentioned earlier that a nonqualified deferral arrangement is likely to be the most costly of all executive benefit programs. The final cost will, of course, depend highly on the type of plan chosen to be offered and the design itself. When considering a SERP or restoration program (whether defined contribution or defined benefit in nature), having actuarial projections of the plan cost (expense) and cash flows are critical for understanding the true impact and value of the program. These programs can run into the millions of dollars in cost each year. For nonqualified deferred compensation programs, the "cost" or expense will track along with the earnings rate attributed to the account. Liabilities will go up and down accordingly. Again, careful consideration should be given to the true cost and cash flow impacts of the plan's design and funding mechanisms.

Administration and Communication

Like qualified retirement programs, most companies (nearly two-to-one) choose to outsource the administration of their SERPs and nonqualified deferred compensation plans rather than to handle in-house. And, like their qualified defined contribution plan counterparts, the choice of administrator is significantly influenced by the type of financing selected.

If a company decides to not set assets aside, it typically will use its pension plan actuary to administer and provide recordkeeping services for a defined benefit form of SERP or restoration plan. However, if the company provides a defined contribution form or voluntary deferred compensation plan (with no assets attached), it is more difficult to find an outside administrator to handle the plan. The 401(k) and defined contribution plan vendor marketplace is not readily eager to accept administration without assets (although this is just beginning to change). If, however, your company has significant clout with a vendor (e.g., significant assets currently held), the vendor may be more inclined to work with you to administer the nonqualified plan. Moreover, if the plan is backed by a selection of mutual funds, the defined contribution provider would likely be very eager to provide administration services, and hopefully at favorable rates (e.g., paid for by investment plan expenses). This assumes, of course, that you have decided to finance your nonqualified plan liability with a taxable/mutual fund investment.

If, however, you decide an insurance product (corporate-owned or trust-owned life insurance) is more appropriate, a broker or administrator experienced in this marketplace would be in a position to provide recordkeeping and administration services. Because there are special attentions and skills required to effectively administer a plan supported by an insurance product it is unlikely that other types of providers would be able to provide an equal level of service.

By the same two-to-one margin that companies outsource administration services, they also outsource their plan's related communications needs. Many brokers and mutual fund providers provide participant communications and enrollment services as part of the administrative service package. These communication packages are usually somewhat customizable. That said, many companies state that communicating the operations and provisions of nonqualified plans is the greatest challenge they face. This is due to the complex nature of these programs and the increased expectations that participants have come to expect as a result of the advances made in the qualified plan marketplace. Those companies that do report high levels of satisfaction with their supplemental retirement plans often note that they have made great efforts to personalize and thoroughly communicate the plans as well as to provide financial counseling services.[2]

As you can see, supplemental retirement programs and deferred compensation are topics of some depth. They are more fully explored in a separate chapter of this publication and the reader may wish to refer to that chapter for more in-depth discussions of several of these topics.

Cautionary Notes and Trends

At the time of this writing, there are a number of proposed legislative bills pending in the Senate and the House that may impact nonqualified deferred compensation arrangements in the future. It is important to check with your counsel or benefits/executive compensation consultant before changing or implementing a nonqualified plan. Much of the pending legislation will affect design provisions such as distribution options, financing and security arrangements. It is this author's opinion that it is likely some regulatory change impacting nonqualified plans will occur in the not distant future.

However, even without these possible changes, the trend is increasingly towards taking a hard look at each element of the supplemental retirement program to ensure that it still meets the needs of the company and the executives. The Sarbanes-Oxley Act of 2002 and other corporate governance reports have focused a microscope on all elements of the executive pay package. Given that, in many cases, nonqualified plans provide such a significant portion of the total executive compensation package, Corporate Boards are becoming much more attentive of the values they create as well as the optics of significant payments. As such, supplemental retirement has become a topic of greater interest even for those organizations that have never wanted to consider these types of plans.

Another trend emerging is in regard to how companies review and monitor their plans. In a recent study, the second highest reported change to current nonqualified deferral arrangements was to take a hard look at the plan's financing arrangements.[2] The single highest reported planned change was to review and strengthen alignment, integration and communications of the program with other programs that make up the total executive compensation package. These indications lead us to believe that nonqualified deferred compensation arrangements will be a hot topic for some time to come.

Financial Counseling

With the ever increasing complexities associated with financial planning and the myriad investments now commonly used by even the average employee, it is no wonder that financial counseling and financial planning services would be a valued benefit to any executive. In fact, roughly one third of companies currently provide some form of such assistance to their executives.[2] The prevalence of organizations providing financial counseling services, like many other executive benefits and perquisites, is chiefly determined by company size, though industry type does show some pattern as well. It is consistently offered more often to CEO's and top level executives than lower level management and is more prominent in large companies. It is more common in the Manufacturing, Retail and Financial Services industries than it is in the Services or in Healthcare as shown below.[3]

Industry Sector	Employee Group	Under 200 Employees	200 to 1,999 Employees	200 to 1,999 Employees
Durable Goods Manufacturing	CEO	26.3%	25.5%	56.5%
	Top Mgmt	21.1%	23.5%	56.5%
Non-Durable Goods Manufacturing	CEO	50%	35.0%	63.6%
	Top Mgmt	50%	30.0%	54.5%
Utilities and Energy	CEO	N/A%	0%	66.7%
	Top Mgmt	N/A%	0%	50.0%
Retail and Wholesale Trade	CEO	20.0%	26.7.1%	35.3%
	Top Mgmt	0%	20.0%	35.3%
Services	CEO	18.2%	35.3%	53.6%
	Top Mgmt	18.2%	32.4%	50.0%
Financial Services	CEO	16.7%	39.3%	69.2%
	Top Mgmt	16.7%	32.1%	69.2%
Healthcare and Not-For-Profit	CEO	8.3%	38.5%	45.0%
	Top Mgmt	8.3%	35.9%	45.0%

But do financial counseling services achieve any other objective other than something valued by the recipient?

Actually, yes. Along with providing access to a program that can be perceived as having value and status, financial counseling services can aid in ensuring that an executive is focusing his/her attention on the company's business, secure with the knowledge that their personal finances are in order. Additionally, as we move into an era where Compensation Committees and company Boards are requiring certain levels of company stock ownership, it is important that an executive sustain personal financial stability so that they are enabled to fulfill their ownership requirements, maintain a balanced and healthy overall portfolio, as well as support other financial needs. Further, the interaction and tax planning complexities associated with stock options, qualified and nonqualified benefits as well as income protection needs are as complicated as ever. Periodic financial examinations can be viewed as keeping the executive's portfolio healthy just as a healthy lifestyle and periodic checkups help keep the executive physically healthy. Financial counseling and planning can also substantially enhance an executive's appreciation and understanding of the value of the total compensation package as offered through company-sponsored benefit programs.

Financial counseling services are typically provided in either of two forms: through a firm or firms retained or selected by the company, or through an organization selected by the executive. The former offers some advantages in that the company has more control over ensuring that the firm selected has the requisite knowledge and qualifications to provide expert counsel to its executives. The company can also work with the firm so that it has a solid understanding of the company's compensation and benefits programs and how they integrate together. With these advantages comes some added risk requiring that the company exercise good judgment when selecting or recommending a financial counseling firm. Most companies do not appear to view the risk as substantial, however, as approximately two-thirds of companies that provide some form of financial counseling services do so through firms retained by the organization. In fact, this percentage increases as financial planning services are extended to the middle manager level.

The other third of companies providing financial counseling services have employees retain a firm of their own choosing. This allows the executive more freedom to select someone they are comfortable working with or a counselor they are working with already. The company then, of course, has less control or assurance that the planner is equipped to understand the company's programs.

Design Issues and Considerations

Selecting the right firm, whether chosen by the company or the executive, is one consideration. There are also many types of other services that can be provided through financial counseling. The most popular form is retirement planning services, with investment planning and estate planning being the next most frequently offered. Tax advisory and tax preparation services are also popular offerings. Full financial planning, although not quite as common, is one of the most valuable.

If the company retains a firm to provide financial planning services, it can often provide these services on site. It is often more comfortable, however, for executives to meet with their planners on their own time.

Administration, Taxation and Cost

The cost of financial counseling services can either be born directly by the company (usually in a retained relationship) or be paid by the executive and reimbursed by the company. Typically, a budget or dollar benefit is established to pay for such services. The range of cost will typically fall between $2,000 and $5,000 per year, range with the lower end of the range reflective of senior management benefits and the upper end reflective of top management benefits. Additionally, the financial planning budget may be substantially greater in the first year (e.g., double) because the foundation of the plan is being created while subsequent year's services are primarily maintenance and annual tax services.

The most common and efficient way of actually handling the service payment is for the company to establish the financial planning services budget and pay the bill directly to the service provider. This is administratively the most expedient and ensures the monies are used for their stated purpose.

All fees paid, whether as a reimbursement or directly to the service provider, are a compensation expense of the company and a taxable event to the executive. The executive is taxed on the full value of services provided as a fringe benefit. The executive may, however, deduct any tax preparation fees on their annual tax return as well as potentially some of the value as investment management expenses under the Other Miscellaneous Expenses Line 22 of Schedule A of an individual's personal tax return.

Trends

There are two trends emerging with respect to the provision of financial counseling. One is a lessening of the amount or budget being used to pay for the annual benefit. The other trend is an increasing use of this benefit. More companies want to ensure that executives have a full understanding of their compensation package, particularly given the current environment of changes impacting various executive compensation programs to which executives have been accustomed.

Personal Loans

Oh, what a difference a year makes! The topic of personal loans would be a chapter unto itself save one little recent Act called The Sarbanes-Oxley Act of 2002 (the Act) also referred to as the Corporate and Auditing Accountability, Responsibility and Transparency Act of 2002. Of the many provisions of this act affecting executive compensation and other areas, Section 402 of the Act amends Section 13 of the Securities and Exchange Act (The Exchange Act) of 1934 to prohibit publicly traded companies and other issuers from making or extending personal loans to directors and executive officers. This section became effective on July 30, 2002 subject to grandfathering provisions and very limited exceptions.

A full discussion of the exact provisions of the Act as it relates to loans is certainly outside the scope of this chapter and is still subject to some clarification even as it relates to all the possible interpretations of what constitutes a loan. For our purposes here, all publicly traded companies in the U.S. as well as any company that files with the SEC (e.g., issues debt) is subject to the provisions of the Act. It applies to directors and executive officers as defined in The Exchange Act and refers to "any director of a corporation or any person performing similar functions with respect to any organization, whether incorporated or unincorporated." This is further defined as the president, any vice president in charge of a principal business unit, division or function, any other officer who performs a policy making function or any other person who performs similar policy making functions.

So what does that mean? Essentially, if the Act applies to you–NO MORE LOANS for directors and officers! This includes any direct or indirect loan for purposes such as purchasing a home, purchasing stock, bridge loans, relocation loans or emergency loans. It also includes such arrangements as premium payments into collateral assignment split-dollar arrangements. Other types of potential loan arrangements are also suspect (which varying law firms have varying opinions as to applicability) include company credit cards, cashless exercise of stock options and even signing bonuses subject to repayment on early termination of employment. That said, it is advisable to discuss any and all potential loan arrangements with legal counsel before making any decisions with respect to issuing any loan-like arrangement to a director or officer. If a loan was already in existence pre-Act, an exemption exists provided there is "no material modification to any term of any such extension of credit or any renewal of any such extension of credit." Again, consult with legal counsel prior to changing ANYTHING with respect to an existing loan arrangement, no matter how minor the change may appear.

But what about organizations not subject to the Act (or have a pre-existing arrangement)? The very first question to ask, now more than ever in this era of heightened governance sensitivity, is **"What is the business purpose and how does this support the company and share-holders/stakeholders?"** Of course, this question should be asked regarding all elements of compensation, but here it is especially important. If no legitimate purpose exits, one that can be clearly seen as directly serving the needs and goals of the organization, than do not grant a loan. Many organizations not subject to The Act have voluntarily adopted many of its provisions in the spirit of good corporate governance. Curtailment of executive loan programs is a popular provision to voluntarily adopt and many organizations (including not-for-profits) have banned the further use of loans.

Prior to the Act, directly or indirectly providing or arranging loans to executives, although not prevalent, was not uncommon. Loans to executives provide no tax advantages, but do make cash available under circumstances where an executive may have more difficulty obtaining financing from a lending institution. Providing a bridge loan, emergency loan, mortgage loan or a loan to purchase stock had been the most common forms of executive loans and these loans were usually provided at favorable interest rates. In fact, many loans have been provided free of interest. Loans are often somewhat hidden because only amounts recognized as income or compensation, or the amount of below-market rates of interest, are required to be reported in a company's annual proxy statement. For those companies with "grandfathered" loans, these amounts are still reportable.

There are no non-discrimination rules for executive loan programs, in fact, loans can be provided to a select group or a single executive. The terms, conditions and amounts can vary by individual. Some key terms to understand concerning loan arrangements include:

Term Loan–loans payable at a specified time in the future.

Demand Loan–a loan payable in full upon demand by the issuer.

Full Recourse Loan–structure where the creditor can seek repayment from the debtor if the collateral is not sufficient to pay off the debt.

Non-Recourse Loan–structure where the creditor can only use the underlying collateral to pay off the debt.

Applicable Federal Rate (AFR)–the rate published monthly by the IRS used to determine a below-market loan. The rates differ for different purposes.

Below-Market Loan–A loan where the interest charged the executive is below the AFR.

Below-Market Interest–The amount of interest that is the difference between the interest charged and the AFR.

Administration, Taxation and Cost

Although The Act effectively discontinued the use of loans for Named Executive Officers (NEOs), many companies may continue to administer grandfathered loans or may offer them to other executives. This section describes some of the administrative issues that are useful for this group.

For most loans, the interest actually paid by the executive is taxable income to the company and is deductible by the executive subject to the normal limitations on interest deductions (e.g., mortgage interest is deductible, personal credit is not). However, if the loan is a below-market loan, the below-market interest is considered additional compensation to the executive and equally deductible for the employer. Depending on whether the loan is a term loan or a demand loan also dictates how and when an executive is taxed. The tax treatment of term loans is unfavorable as the employee generally must declare immediately a substantial portion of the loan as personal income.

Although not very prevalent, some companies have provided loans on a forgivable basis over time–in other words–the interest or loan arrangements are conditioned on the future services of the executive. At the time of forgiveness, the executive has a tax liability in the amount of the loan forgiven. In fact, if it is explicit from the beginning that the loan will be guaranteed and forgiven, the entire amount of the loan is taxed at the time granted. In some extreme cases, companies would gross-up payments to executives to cover the tax liability and make the executive "whole." Unless forgiveness of a loan is tied to the executive achieving some level of performance or objective, the practice of forgiving loans, or even worse, grossing-up the payment to cover taxes, is not likely to be seen as serving the needs of the business or shareholders/owners.

Typically, the best way to arrange executive lending is to indirectly sponsor a loan through a third party (e.g., lending institution). Though many companies have directly provided the funds for a loan the arrangement is rife with risk. Take this example: Company loans Executive $500,000 to enable the executive to exercise stock options and purchase shares. At exercise, the executive paid $20 per share. The Executive does this to satisfy ownership requirements or because she feels she is "encouraged" to own and hold shares. Subsequently, the stock price declines to $1. The Executive now has a $500,000 loan on an asset worth $25,000. The executive may threaten to walk from the loan or demand forgiveness in that he/she was encouraged to purchase stock. The Company is now placed in the undesirable position of having to deal with an angry executive who owes the Company a lot of money and is threatening to default or quit. Not a pleasant situation.

So in the end, for organizations not subject to the Act or for other levels of management, a company should closely scrutinize whether or not a loan makes sense. Does the loan support business objectives (e.g., a third-party loan to assist in relocation needs) and have all contingencies been thought through? Equally as important is the term and structure of the loan. Although the terms of the loan may seem straightforward, there are a number of financial, tax, accounting, SEC and banking regulatory issues that may apply. Special issues are applicable for loans that are performance-based or are used to purchase company stock.

Trends

Not surprisingly, the trend line looks somewhat like a downward sloping hockey stick. The passing of The Sarbanes-Oxley Act of 2002 was the nail in the coffin for executive loan programs. Companies that do continue to offer management loan programs will likely do so through a third party, thereby getting out of the "banking" business itself.

Executive Medical

Companies can provide supplemental executive medical benefits in two different ways. One is to offer executive physicals and the second is through a supplemental medical insurance program.

Executive Physicals

A company can provide executives with physical examination services on a tax-free basis and approximately one-third of companies currently do so. These benefits can be offered to a select group of executives without running afoul of any non-discrimination issues, however, the types of procedures covered are limited under a special section of the tax code. In general, routine types of services can be performed on a tax-free basis such as regular check-ups, blood tests and X-rays. The typical cost runs about $1,000 to $2,000 per year. Additional types of procedures that may be specific to an individual (e.g., from a prior health problem) are usually not permissible on the same tax-advantaged basis.

An executive physical program is an appropriate benefit for any organization that believes strongly in the health and welfare of its employee population. From a business perspective, it adds value by not only keeping the key leadership team healthy and hopefully productive but may also be a way to discover early any potentially serious health issues that could render the executive unable to work. This serves the company not only by saving on any lost work days due to an illness or disease, but can also help in controlling future cost increases in any other group medical programs of the company's that might be incurred as a result of the health history of the executive program.

Supplemental Medical Insurance

Providing additional supplemental medical insurance over and above what is provided to the general employee population is not a common practice. On average, about 15% of companies offer this benefit to its very top management.[3] Within that 15%, most companies are providing supplemental medical insurance that includes medical examinations, as described above. These programs also provide coverage, in whole or in part, for things like out-of-network services, brand name prescriptions, deductibles or co-pays and other services such as medical procedures not covered by the basic group plan. The cost of this type of plan typically runs between $2,500 and $5,000 per year per covered individual.

Trends

Going forward, no change is expected in the prevalence of providing executive physicals. However, it is unlikely we will see any upward trend in providing additional types of supplemental coverage. The latter prediction is based on the assumption that more companies in general will be eliminating unnecessary perquisites, especially those that do not directly link to the performance of the business or are unaffordable by the executive group.

Long-Term Care Insurance

Almost half of Americans over age 65 will be admitted to a nursing facility during their lifetime. Almost half of those will deplete their personal savings in the first year to pay for the care. What many people don't realize is that Medicare does not pay costs associated with long-term care beyond 100 days of need. Medicare supplement policies also generally do not pay for the costs of extended care.

Given this sobering scenario, one might predict that long-term care insurance might be something that begins popping up more often in employee benefit portfolios. This very well may be the outlook.

But in looking at current practices, long-term care is not a particularly popular program to offer to executives. Fewer than one-fifth of companies offer such a program and for those that do, very few supplement the cost in whole or in part. Executives pay the full cost to purchase insurance protection. This may be due to companies' negative experiences with retiree medical programs which have become incredibly costly and associated with unpredictable premiums.

Design Basics

Long-term care policies are flexibly structured in that an insured can choose the type of coverage that suits their needs. Typically, an insured can choose among various home care, nursing home and assisted living plans as well as policies that integrate these various programs together. A participant can choose the daily benefit amount which generally range anywhere from $50 to $250 per day in benefits (a typical nursing home costs about $100 per day) as well as the length of the policy (two to five years or more). Similar to other types of disability policies, an elimination period is also selected.

Other types of features that are similar to those offered in life insurance policies can also be added to the plan. These include features such as deductibles, guaranteed paid up rates, return of premium, survivorship benefits and waiver of premiums upon claim. Further, and more appropriate to a corporate setting, group programs may be available for larger organizations (e.g., over 2,000 employees). These programs can provide a conduit for employees to purchase portable policies that are customizable to their personal needs at a cost favorable rate.

Administration, Taxation and Cost

Long-term care insurance can be offered as part of a group contract or through individual policies. Most organizations that provide this supplemental benefit provide the opportunity to purchase individual policies, typically through payroll deduction. A very small group actually pays for the coverage outright for executives.

If the company pays any portion of the benefit, the value of the premiums would be taxable income to the executive. The premium cost for these policies varies widely depending upon the age and coverage selected. Although few companies pay for the coverage, those that do may be able to contract with a provider for more favorable rates.

Trends

There is some evidence to support the prediction that company sponsored long-term care programs may increase in prevalence over the next few years. Primarily, this prediction is due to the changing demographics of the workforce coupled with the fact that baby boomers are now entering their retirement years. Many of these same baby boomers have either seen or supported their parents in nursing home situations. As such, long-term care may continue to grow in need and ultimately find a place in payroll deduction type supplemental benefit plans at favorable group rates. This doesn't necessarily apply to only the executive ranks but to the broader group of employees as well. Companies should continue to track premium trends before jumping in. Already, the cost of these programs has risen significantly and is predicted to continue to increase.

Supplemental Life Insurance

In connection with sound financial and estate planning, life insurance programs that provide income replacement are not uncommon programs at executive levels. Most basic group plans offer limited opportunity to provide significant levels of death benefit protection. Many group programs, often offered through a flexible benefits or cafeteria program, may allow an individual to purchase two, three or even four times their base salary in life insurance. The basic all-employee group programs provide this coverage using group term products and rates. These programs may not be able to provide enough insurance protection to satisfy the needs of executives. Additionally, any amount of group term coverage selected by an employee that exceeds $50,000 in death benefit is taxed. The employee must claim imputed income for the value of the underlying life insurance protection that is over the $50,000 limit.

As a result, companies who offer a total compensation package that emphasizes security and flexibility will likely consider offering supplemental life insurance protection for its top management. As a company-paid benefit, it is offered on only a slightly more frequent basis than supplemental long term disability programs as you can see below.[5] On the other hand, many

PERCENT OF ORGANIZATIONS THAT PAY (IN WHOLE OR IN PART) FOR SUPPLEMENTAL LIFE INSURANCE

| Position | Organization Size | | | |
	Under 200 Employees	200 - 1,999 Employees	2,000 or More Employees	All Size Groups Combined
CEO	13.1%	18.4%	25.4%	20.1%
Top Management	9.8%	13.2%	20.3%	15.2%
Senior Management	3.3%	5.8%	9.4%	6.7%
Middle Management	0.0%	3.2%	2.9%	2.6%
Professional	0.0%	2.1%	2.2%	1.8%

*Does not include split-dollar arrangements

companies offer executives the option to personally purchase additional life insurance coverage at reduced rates.

Design Considerations

There are two primary ways in which companies today are providing supplemental life insurance coverage: an employer-paid program or a voluntary program that is paid for by the executive. Rather than using group term life products, both of these approaches tend to employ a permanent type of policy such as variable universal life. Use of a permanent policy has the advantage of providing portable protection if the executive should ever leave the company. The executive simply continues making premium payments, if needed, once no longer employed. The second advantage to a portable policy is that if so structured, the policy allows for additional savings opportunities on a tax deferred basis.

Employer-Paid Programs

For employers who believe that paying the cost of supplemental life insurance is a valued benefit, the most common approach is to offer a multiple of base salary. Common multiples are three to four-times salary on a pre-retirement basis. For covered employees, the employer will pay the premium directly to the insurance carrier. Depending upon how many executives are eligible, the carrier may offer favorable group rates on a guarantee-issue or simplified underwriting basis.

The cost of this supplemental coverage varies greatly depending on the type of underwriting, the size and demographics of the group as well as the amount of coverage and features selected. On average, companies who pay some portion of supplemental premiums pay about $3,700 for the CEO and about $3,500 per year for top management.[3] Median costs per year are much lower at $2,500 and $2,000 for the same levels respectively. Premium payments made are tax deductible by the company as a compensation expense. The value of the life insurance protection is fully taxable by the executive. The value is calculated by referring to special tax tables (PS 58 Tables) that compute the value of the underlying death protection. This amount is reported as imputed income on the individual's tax return.

It may also be advantageous to consider a group carve-out program for executives where additional insurance protection over and above that offered in the group plan is appropriate. As mentioned, the value of group term coverage over $50,000 conveys imputed income to the recipient. Carving out the executive's completely from the group plan and transferring the base coverage (e.g., $50,000) to the supplemental plan may reduce the employer's cost and imputed income amounts taxable to the executive. The reason for this is that the supplemental plan uses PS 58 Tax Tables where the imputed income reflected may be at favorable rates to the basic group term plan. If a company decides to pay for supplemental protection, carving out all executives may be a cost-effective approach.

Executive-Paid Programs

When the need for supplemental life insurance exists for some of the executive population, but not all, a supplemental voluntary program may be appropriate. Another purpose in providing a voluntary supplemental program is to complement an executive benefits package by providing flexibility and customization.

In this case, an executive may elect to participate in this voluntary program and pay premiums for permanent, portable policies through payroll deduction. Group plans may still be available depending upon how many executives are eligible for the program as well as how high the participation level is expected to be. It may be advantageous to offer this program to a very broad group of employees to encourage higher participation and therefore secure better rates from the insurance carrier.

For those who do purchase the additional coverage, there are no resulting tax implications to either the company or the executive. The company has essentially provided nothing more than a conduit (though oftentimes with enhanced rates and reduced underwriting requirements) and no additional taxes apply.

In some circumstances, companies will effectively pay for this supplemental benefit by providing additional cash compensation to the executive with the objective of having this added income used towards the purchase of the supplemental coverage. Or course, in this situation, executive's have additional taxable income as part of their base compensation. Some companies also provide gross-ups of this additional income to pay for the resulting additional tax bill. This is certainly an option, but should only be considered in light of the entire executive compensation package so that, in total, the package aligns with the philosophy of the company and is considered in the context of reasonable compensation. These additional forms of payment are coming under much scrutiny and good corporate governance procedures will ensure that these payments are considered in the context of the total package. Another outcome of this type of bonus arrangement is that the additional income also impacts the cost and value of other programs such as retirement and severance. Careful consideration of the full cost of this type of scheme is warranted.

Important Notes to Consider

This discussion does not include a review of the prevalence and design considerations in offering split-dollar arrangements. Although split-dollar has served as another form of providing death benefits, it is primarily offered as a tax advantaged savings program that shifts deferred compensation objectives out of the nonqualified arena. In September 2003, final regulations governing the taxation of split dollar arrangements were published by the IRS and Treasury Department. At a 50,000 foot level, these regulations codify most of what was published under IRS Notice 2002-08. The most significant result is the taxation of collateral assignment forms of split dollar. For collateral assignment forms (the most common), plans must be structured in the form of a loan to participants and thereby taxed under IRC Section 7872 or 1271-1275 (below market loans). For plans in existence prior to final guidance and pre-notice, the Notice and final regulations established a number of transition considerations. If your organization has any split-dollar arrangements in place, it is strongly recommended that competent unbiased advice is sought to understand the various risks, tax implications and options available for continuing, transitioning or implementing any split-dollar arrangement.

To further complicate matters, The Sarbanes-Oxley Act eliminated the use of direct and indirect loans to executives. This applies to split-dollar arrangements given that the new regulations now require collateral assignment forms to be structured as loans. Again, it is advisable to discuss these circumstances with competent professionals including legal counsel as to whether or to whom The Act may impact with regards to split-dollar arrangements and the new regulations regarding taxation.

Supplemental Long-Term Disability

A 40-year-old executive is three times more likely to suffer a long-term disability than die before satisfying a full career. An interesting statistic given that companies are more likely to provide supplemental death protection than they do supplemental disability protection. As you can see in the chart below,[3] most companies do not pay for additional disability protection to executives over and above that which is included in the broad-based group disability plan.

Although the need for some companies may be greater, there actually is a good reason for companies to not pay for supplemental disability coverage, but to instead provide a conduit to purchase additional individual coverage as needed. Let's now see why.

Design Considerations

Many of the considerations one would review in designing an executive supplemental disability plan are the same as those to implement a group plan. The definition of disability, waiting periods, and integration with short-term disability plan decisions are all similar. The level of coverage, however, is the major difference.

Most group plans provide a long-term disability benefit of a percentage of salary (or total compensation). This level typically ranges from 50% to 60%. Some companies allow participants to select the level of coverage as part of their flexible benefits program. The goal here is to provide some percentage of replacement if in fact an employee was rendered disabled and unable to work. The challenge, however, is that there is a limit to the amount of maximum monthly benefit that an insurance carrier will provide regardless of what 50% or 60% of compensation is calculated to be. That limit

PERCENT OF ORGANIZATIONS THAT PAY (IN WHOLE OR IN PART) FOR SUPPLEMENTAL LONG-TERM DISABILITY INSURANCE

Position	Organization Size			
	Under 200 Employees	200 - 1,999 Employees	2,000 or More Employees	All Size Groups Combined
CEO	8.2%	15.8%	27.5%	18.8%
Top Management	4.9%	11.6%	23.9%	14.9%
Senior Management	1.6%	5.3%	11.6%	6.9%
Middle Management	0.0%	2.1%	2.2%	1.8%
Professional	0.0%	1.6%	2.2%	1.5%

limit is typically $10,000 or $15,000 per month. For any executive earning over $200,000 per year, this poses a problem. Consider this example:

Executive Base Salary	$450,000	**Group Plan Replacement**	60%
60% of Salary	$270,000	**Group Plan Cap per Month**	$10,000
Group Plan Replacement %	27%	**Annual Income Replacement**	$120,000
Annual Gap in Coverage	$150,000	**Gap per Month**	$12,500

Therefore, one of the first major design decisions is to consider how many executives have significant gaps in their level of coverage. If in fact there are few who fall in this category, the need for providing supplemental coverage may not be great. Additionally, if other executive compensation programs provide sufficient sources of income or savings (e.g., deferred compensation, other savings programs and accelerated vesting of incentives upon disability), this may also offset the need for providing supplemental coverage.

Taxation

When discussing long-term disability programs, the consideration of taxation implications should precede plan design. When a disability benefit is paid via a company-paid program, all benefits are fully taxable to the recipient. If the executive herself pays the cost (premium) for the coverage, then disability benefits are not taxable. As such, thought should be given to the following:

1. How wide is the gap between company-paid group plan benefits and the same level of income replacement for executives?

2. What is the cost benefit between a company-paid supplemental program and an executive-paid, non-taxable supplemental program?

For most highly paid executives, it will be more advantageous to pay for the additional premium themselves rather than have the company pay for the supplement.

The company, on the other hand, takes an expense and tax deduction for any premium payments it makes to purchase insurance coverage. This applies to both the group and individual coverage. Executives are not taxed on the value of premium payments until the group and individual supplemental disability benefits are received.

Supplemental Coverage and Structure

As mentioned, typical group plans will have a maximum benefit cap (e.g., $10,000 month). Supplemental policies will also have a maximum cap and are often structured to include or offset benefits paid from other programs (e.g., the group plan). This total maximum cap is typically $25,000 in total benefits. It can be as high as $35,000 per month depending upon the type of plan and the carrier. The maximum cap will also be affected by the structure of the plan in terms of plan participant demographics, the level of guaranteed-issue desired, and the amount that the employer pays versus the amount the executive pays. In this regard, employers may decide to pay for:

• Basic group coverage (broad-based plan)

• Supplemental group coverage (e.g., up to a certain replacement value such as 50% or 60%)

• Individual supplemental coverage

All of the benefits ultimately paid under these alternatives would be fully taxed to the recipients at the time benefits are paid.

In addition to these elements, companies can decide to also offer supplemental individual coverage that is 100% paid for by the employee. Again, the advantage to this design is that benefits received would be tax free to the participant.

So what is the right amount of coverage to offer? That of course depends upon the company's compensation philosophy—does the company want to "make-up" what is lost due to external limitations or do they want to provide an enhanced benefit? Most companies who decide to offer supplemental executive disability will target an ultimate replacement percentage that is related to their group plan—usually 60%. In doing so, however, that doesn't mean a company has to pay for coverage that replaces 60%. They can choose to pay for less (50% being most common) and then provide for individually purchased coverage up to 60%. Some may provide 60% company-paid coverage and still allow for additional individually purchased coverage. One note of caution is that there is a behavior element in designing such a plan. Providing for an above-market replacement value (if even possible for the very highly paid) may "encourage" the executive to apply for benefits because the replacement level may be high enough to sustain their standard of living without continued employment. Companies should be careful about the message they send in terms of the value of an executive's time at work versus at home.

Some examples of different structures, and their advantages and disadvantages, are shown in the chart on the next page.

160

Provision	Plan Design A	Plan Design B	Plan Design C
Contribution Basis	Basic Benefit 100% company paid	Basic Benefit 100% company paid; Supplemental Benefit 100% employee paid	Basic Benefit 100% company paid; Supplemental Benefit 100% employee paid
Monthly Benefit Amount	60% of earnings	Basic Benefit - 60% of earnings, Supplemental Benefit - 10% of earnings	Basic Benefit - 50% of earnings, Supplemental Benefit - 10% of earnings
Monthly Benefit Maximums	$25,000	$35,000	$35,000
Advantages	Consistent with basic group benefit (restoration), all company paid	Consistent with basic group benefit (restoration), all company paid and provides supplemental voluntary buy-up. Voluntary portion provides non-taxable benefit for executive	Provides total benefit with tax advantages to executive. Does not encourage executive to apply for benefits unnecessarily
Disadvantages	Fully taxable benefit to executive, cost to employer	Executive pays additional cost, still additional cost to employer	Executive pays for portion

Earnings Definition

Other design considerations include the definition of earnings. Many plans use current base salary earnings as the definition of covered earnings. Other companies may use current base earnings plus some definition of annual bonus. This later definition is appropriate for organizations whose pay philosophy provides a highly leveraged total cash compensation plan (e.g., below-market base salary combined with a high percentage of annual bonus) that is relatively consistent from year-to-year. If including annual bonus is appropriate, it is advisable to develop a formula that considers an average of a number of year's worth of bonus (e.g., 3 years). Otherwise, one might be "encouraged" to apply for disability payments during an extraordinarily high bonus year.

On the other hand, a company's pay philosophy may be highly leveraged, but they also have highly fluctuating annual incentive payouts (e.g., zero in some years, high in others). An example of this type of company could be a high technology software company. In this case, it may be more appropriate to still consider base pay as the earnings definition because the annual bonus is extremely variable.

Other Features

As mentioned, creation of an executive supplemental disability plan must also consider the elements common to any disability program. The following are the most important features along with prominent designs.

Elimination Period–Of course, the elimination period should integrate with the short-term disability plan (and other paid time off programs). The most cost effective and prevalent elimination period is 365 days.

Definition of Disability–The same issues apply here as in a basic group disability plan: should the definition be "own occupation" or "any occupation?" In the ranks of executive supplemental plans, the more common and cost effective approach is an own occupation definition.

Guaranteed Issue vs. Full Underwriting–Most disability programs are guaranteed-issue programs referring to the fact that anyone who fits the eligibility definition is covered or has access to the supplemental policy. Many companies believe that guaranteed issue is best because the executive is not required to undergo an exam and full underwriting procedures. A guaranteed-issue program will generally have to have enough participants to make it viable for the insurance carrier and will use standard rates. Additionally, the guaranteed-issue maximums may be lower than the full employer-paid program. Guaranteed issue may in fact be the appropriate approach, depending on the makeup of your executive population, but full underwriting will generally result in more competitively priced policies. Full underwriting may also be appropriate for any executive paid voluntary supplemental program.

Offsets–It is quite common and appropriate to design the program such that the full benefit comes from all disability programs together. This would include benefits from the employer sponsored short-term disability policy, other supplemental policies and any benefits paid through the social security or worker's compensation system.

Portability–Certainly a desired feature, the executive may have the option to take the policy with them when they leave the company. Individual coverage is the simplest to take with you. Group benefits would have to have a conversion feature to convert from a group to an individual policy to be portable. Unfortunately, conversion features tend to be costly, therefore, if portability is desired, it is wise to consider shifting more of the full benefit to an individual policy in the plan's design.

Cost

Average annual cost for to the organization for providing supplemental long-term disability insurance is about $3,500–$4,000 for the top executives ($2,500 median cost).[3] The average cost declines quickly as you move further down the organization. The cost for the policy also varies greatly depending upon how the program is structured. Sample costs per thousand of coverage can range from $.15 per $100 of covered earnings at younger ages up to $.50 and higher for more coverage and higher ages. Those unfamiliar with insurance premium pricing and disability plan design are well-advised to seek competent advice (consultant or broker) in the design and carrier selection process.

Trends

More and more companies and executives are gaining a better understanding of the need and desire for disability insurance and as such, we can expect to see an increasing trend towards providing this benefit. For those companies who have existing programs, it is clear that many are taking a harder look at the plan design to ensure it is structured in a way that meets the company's and executives needs. Overall, there is a trend towards executive-paid supplemental policies due to the inherent tax advantages. Some companies have provided this option with a corresponding bonus or cash payment to cover these costs and sometimes with a tax gross-up in an effort to offer a no-cost benefit to the executive. It is unlikely that this will continue due to a greater visibility to shareholders and as Compensation Committees take a harder look at rationalizing and balancing all elements of the compensation package.

Severance Arrangements

Severance arrangements have also recently sprung up as a high profile item drawing media attention. We have all read about the special severance and golden parachute deals that executives have reaped, seemingly to only feather their own nests and move on.

But what is (or should be) the real purpose of a severance arrangement? There are four primary objectives that generally are considered when establishing a severance program:

1. **Offset Risk**–how likely is it that an executive may be terminated due to reasons outside his or her control. Economic conditions impact company financial viability, potential for change in control, and marketplace demand for alternative employment opportunities

2. **Attention**–How should a company ensure an executive will give due attention towards the business at hand during times of uncertainty

3. **Competitiveness**–where the goal is to provide a competitive total executive compensation package for attraction and retention purposes

4. **Enhance Executive Relations**–will providing a severance program make an executive feel valued by the company?

Risk and attention are the two objectives that tend to have greater weight in driving the design of severance arrangements. These arrangements can be designed on a blanket basis at a particular executive level (i.e. for all Vice

Presidents) or, can be included in individually negotiated employment agreements. Be aware, however, that blanket severance agreements are subject to ERISA welfare plan requirements (reporting, documentation and communications). In general, these programs should ensure management focuses on company objectives without concern for their personal future employment opportunity. In that same vein, severance arrangements are also often used as a tool to smooth the actualization of a major transaction such as a purchase or sale of an entity. A properly designed severance arrangement will encourage that executive's focus on the transaction, maximizing the transaction value and effective conclusion without regard to the transaction's impact on their own personal future employment. Lastly, severance arrangements can enable a company to recruit critical executive talent at times of economic or industry uncertainty. If two or more of the objectives listed above are critical and looming in your business, it is likely that a severance arrangement is appropriate.

Currently, approximately 80% of companies have some form of severance arrangement in place for their executives. The most common form of severance takes its shape as a change in control agreement. Fewer companies have a formal severance policy without a specific change of control provision. Severance arrangements are also commonly included in an executive's employment agreement. Blanket agreements are more common at lower levels and individualized agreements are more common for top management. In any case, there are a number of design considerations that need to be addressed when crafting a severance policy. Ultimate choices will typically depend on whether the arrangement is to be geared towards a change-in-control trigger or other circumstances. First, let's consider some of these issues and then compare the differences.

Design Considerations

Payment Triggers
The first consideration is the issue of when a severance benefit will be triggered or paid. Severance is most commonly paid upon involuntary or constructive termination of employment. Involuntary termination typically means the executive's position was eliminated and the executive was terminated. The termination was not due to lack of or poor performance and was essentially out of the executive's control. Constructive termination is the term used when an executive's position has changed so significantly that the level of responsibility, pay or even benefits is dramatically decreased. The executive in that case may feel "forced" to leave the company.

Other types of severance benefit activation provisions include some form of event. When it takes only one event to trigger the severance payment, this is called a single trigger. An example of a single trigger is that the benefit is activated upon a change in control. Of course, one would normally only pay the award if the executive voluntarily resigned after such change.

When a severance benefit is activated upon the occurrence of two events it is called a double trigger. Double triggers are more appropriate in a change-in-control situation and could be defined as occurring upon a change in control along with an involuntary or constructive termination within a specified time period after the change in control is complete. Not surprisingly, the use of double triggers is more prevalent than single triggers; approximately three to four times more.

Payment Levels

Severance benefits are commonly paid as a multiple of annual pay. The range of multiples is typically between one to three times annual pay, depending upon level, risk and whether the payment is due to a change-in-control. The chart below represents what has typically been seen in the recent marketplace for severance benefits.

The appropriate placement within the range for your organization can be determined based on the degree of risk the organization faces as well as the level of security the company needs to offer to attract and retain the right talent. Additionally, economic forces also play a role. For instance, currently the war for executive talent has slowed. If severed, an executive will likely face a longer employment search which, from the executive's perspective, suggests a greater need (level) of severance benefits as the security factor is more tenuous. Conversely, from the company's perspective, it is no longer necessary to offer very high severance arrangements to remain competitive in the current market conditions of weaker demand. Each of these factors needs to be considered in determining which level is appropriate. Generally, however, severance levels are decreasing overall and you can expect to see the multiples at the upper end of the ranges shown above begin to decrease.

Level	Basic Severance Multiple of Annual Pay	Change in Control Multiple of Annual Pay
CEO	1 to 2 times	2 to 3 times
Top Management	.5 to 1.5 months	1 to 2 times

Total Pay

As mentioned, the basic severance benefit is paid out as a multiple of total pay. Total pay is typically made up of base salary and annual incentives. The amount of base salary used is typically the most recent fixed annual base salary. The annual incentive amount, however, should not necessarily be the most recent bonus paid. Consider the situation where the company had a superior performing year resulting in significantly above target payouts of annual incentives. If a severance arrangement captured this unusually high bonus as part of the total pay definition, the situation could exist where an executive might be motivated to want the severance arrangement to be triggered. As such, it is more appropriate to consider target bonus levels or the annual bonus paid for an average of some number of previous years (e.g., three years prior). Additionally, if the termination occurs mid year, it is most common (and appropriate) to award, as part of total pay, the amount of the annual incentive that has been earned to date, not the full target award.

Long-Term Incentives

The unanticipated termination of employment can oftentimes have the most significantly negative impact on unvested long-term incentive opportunities. In this case, it is typical to automatically accelerate the vesting of these programs. That way, the executive has not lost out on the current value (if any) of a long-term incentive plan based on the fact that there was no time left to vest.

Most companies automatically accelerate long-term incentive vesting for programs such as stock option grants or restricted shares once a severance benefit is triggered. It is automatic because of negative accounting conse-quences if a discretionary acceleration is given by the Board. In a single trigger situation (e.g., change of control only), this could result in the transfer of potentially significant value to the executive even if he or she were to continue in the position. Consequently, one of the resulting trends has been to move towards a double trigger definition for payment activation or to activate the acceleration provision only if the unvested gains (i.e., those that are in the money) are not replaced by the new company's equity or stock option program.

Benefits

In addition to the payment of an annual pay multiple, there are a number of other benefits programs that are also covered as part of a severance arrangement. The two most common are continuation of health and welfare benefits for a specified period of time and the payment or funding of accrued deferred compensation benefits (e.g., into a Rabbi Trust).

When a severance payment is activated, typical benefit programs such as health coverage, disability coverage, dental and life may be continued at the expense of the company. If the company ceases to exist and the plans are terminated, companies may arrange to pay for extended COBRA coverage that an employee could elect. In addition, an executive may continue to receive years of service credit toward retirement plan benefits. The extension of these benefits can run the "length" of the severance arrangement, i.e. if an executive receives two year's worth of annual pay, then, he or she will also receive two year's coverage in benefits paid by the company. A six month to one year continuation period, however, is becoming more typical.

The payment of a nonqualified benefit (e.g., a SERP or deferred compensation balance) is also a common practice. The simplest approach is to pay the benefit due as soon as practicable after the severance event. There are, however, disadvantages to this in that it creates for the executive another immediately taxable event and the company will have an unanticipated cash outflow. The good news would be that the payout would represent the reduction of a liability and therefore there would be no further concern with the security of a future benefit.

Another related and common approach, particularly in a change in control situation is to require funding of the nonqualified benefit. In this case, funding refers to setting assets aside in a trust (Rabbi Trust) so that the executive participant is "protected" against change of heart/change of management. The amount in the trust will be used to pay trust benefits unless the acquiring organization becomes insolvent.

Another common benefit included in severance arrangements is the provision of outplacement services. These services are provided to assist the terminated executive in finding replacement employment. Some companies also include continuation of other executive perquisites and benefits (e.g., any of the other executive benefits included as a discussion item in this chapter). It is this author's view that the prevalence of this practice will decline.

Special Considerations in a Change in Control
There are certain rules that must be considered when a severance payment is made due to a change-in-control. These special rules are enforced under Section 280g of the Internal Revenue Code. In general, these rules state that

a company may not take a tax deduction on any amount considered to be an "excess parachute payment" that is paid to a "disqualified individual" if such payment is contingent upon a change in control. An employee is a "disqualified individual" if they are an officer, shareholder or highly compensated person as defined in the code. This rule applies if the total parachute payments (the total of all payments received contingent upon the change) have an aggregate present value that exceeds 2.99 times a disqualified individual's base amount. If it applies, the excess is actually the amount over *one* times the base amount. The base amount is calculated by annualizing the individual's includible compensation over the last five years. This includes W-2 earnings reported (e.g., inclusive of option gains, deferred compensation payments and other benefits).

So what happens if an executive is considered to be a disqualified individual and they have an excess parachute payment? If this happens, the company loses its income tax deduction on the excess parachute–the amount over one times the base amount. Additionally, the executive owes an excise tax of 20% of the excess amount. The details of what must be included in calculating the base amount as well as what payments (and how they are valued) are included as part of this regulation. A (very simplified) example of this situation follows to illustrate the impact:

Executive Compensation History		Executive Parachute Payments	
1998	$ 250,000	Severance	$ 700,000
1999	$ 275,000	Gain on Accelerated Options*	$ 1,200,000
2000	$ 290,000	Total Parachute	$ 1,900,000
2001	$ 310,000		
2002	$ 350,000		
Average	$ 295,000		

Base Amount	$ 295,000
Base Amount x 2.99	$ 882,050
Is Total Parachute over 2.99 Base Amount?	Yes
Value over Base Amount (Excess Parachute)	$ 1,017,950
Company Lost Tax Deduction	$ 1,017,950
Executive Excise Tax	$ 203,590

* Note: Under new IRS rules, the value of underwater options must be included in the calculation of parachute payments for purposes of determining the excise tax

Because of the potential costs involved and the affect it may have on consummation of a merger, sale, or consolidation, change-in-control agreements are normally restricted to a small number of executives. Of those companies with change-in-control agreements, about two-thirds provide tax gross-ups to the top five executives. The details involved in calculating each of the factors described above is certainly a chapter within itself and therefore beyond the scope of this chapter. It is highly advisable to ensure that competent experts are available to assist in determining the impacts of regulation 280g in determining who is considered a disqualified individual, as well as to provide the necessary calculations to ensure a full understanding of the impacts, and related costs, in a change of control situation.

Due to the significant impact 280g regulations can have on a change in control situation, many companies consider this up-front in their decision and negotiation of severance arrangements. A cap of 2.99 times the base amount is sometimes included in the executive change-in-control agreement to prevent the loss of tax deduction and avoid the executive excise tax. Also note that a change-in-control agreement must be executed at least one-year in advance of the change-in-control event otherwise all payments will be considered for the excise tax and not deductible by the company.

Administration, Communication and Cost

It is wise to ensure that in-house or external legal counsel is involved in the design and drafting of related documents to ensure all appropriate features are covered. It is also important that these programs are well communicated to participants so that the resulting security they are intended to convey is understood.

Additionally, as outlined in the example above, severance arrangements, particularly in a change in control situation can be extremely expensive. In fact, in a change in control situation, they can represent as much as 1% to 3% of the value of the transaction. Due to the large financial and cash flow impact of these programs, it is recommended that the appropriate team of consultants, accountants and attorneys be involved in their design and costing projections. That way, you can gain comfort that at least the resulting potential impacts of the programs, if triggered, are well known and justifiable.

Trends

The competitive and regulatory landscapes have changed significantly so that high end levels of severance benefits are being trimmed back. In the last 12 to 18 months, many companies have reduced the level of severance benefits for new programs or for newly negotiated employment arrangements.

Company Cars and Car Allowances

The provision of a company paid car is one of the most popular and prevalent of executive benefits. Typically, as seen in the chart below, this benefit is offered to the top group of executives only (CEO and his/her direct reports) as well as senior sales professionals (e.g., sales management) who would use it frequently in the course of their work.[5]

Essentially, any of three objectives are behind the provision of a company car to an executive. The car may be viewed as a necessary business tool to assist the executive in accomplishing their responsibilities. An alternate objective might be to ensure some cost control and financial predictability within a vehicle and travel expense program. Lastly, (and most commonly), company-paid vehicles are provided to upper executives solely as a perquisite.

Design Issues

If a company-paid vehicle has been deemed appropriate within the organization's executive compensation philosophy or business objectives, there are several issues to consider as far as the policy's implementation. Specifically, the method to acquire the vehicle, the annual cost or subsidy, and what expenses will be included or covered. In the last few years a leveling-out of the use of company-paid vehicles (e.g., provided to a smaller, highly select group) has been seen.

The two common approaches for providing company-paid vehicles are the following: Either a company owns or leases the vehicle to the executive or the company provides an allowance towards the cost of owning/leasing. As you can see from the table below,[5] more organizations choose to provide allowances as a simpler approach to providing for the cost of the automobile.

PERCENT OF ORGANIZATIONS PROVIDING COMPANY OWNED OR LEASED CARS OR ALLOWANCE IN LIEU OF CAR

	Organization Size			
Position	Under 200 Employees	200 - 1,999 Employees	2,000 or More Employees	All Size Groups Combined
CEO	72.1%	78.4%	67.4%	73.5%
Top Management	50.8%	67.4%	63.8%	63.5%
Senior Management	27.9%	45.3%	44.2%	42.2%
Middle Management	14.8%	21.6%	15.2%	18.3%
Professional	9.8%	15.8%	8.7%	12.3%

DISTRIBUTION OF ORGANIZATIONS OFFERING COMPANY
OWNED OR LEASED CARS OR ALLOWANCE IN LIEU OF CAR

Position	% Offering Either	% Offering Car Only	% Offering Allowance Only
CEO	24.8%	39.9%	35.3%
Top Management	20.2%	35.2%	44.5%
Senior Management	16.5%	31.1%	52.4%
Middle Management	5.6%	36.6%	57.7%
Professional	4.2%	39.6%	56.3%

The value of the company-owned or leased vehicle tends to vary by position. For example, the current median price range of a vehicle for the CEO is $40,000–$60,000 while the median price for top management and senior management is $35,000–$45,000.

These median prices can be used to understand the investment cost an organization must make for a company-owned or leased vehicle, or as the basis in calculating a competitive monthly car allowance.

Many companies also provide for reimbursement of the primary costs involved in operating the vehicle. These costs typically cover such things as fuel (mileage), insurance, normal service and maintenance. Maintenance expenses are typically paid by the company for a company-owned or leased vehicle, and usually born by the employee if a monthly allowance is provided. Each provision and method has various advantages and disadvantages as indicated in the table on the next page.[4]

Administration, Taxation and Cost

The administration of a company-paid car program can be simplified by providing a monthly allowance that provides a flat dollar amount to cover most ownership costs. This flat amount will typically run in the range of $500 to $750 per month. For top management, the amount ranges between $1,000 to $1,500 per month. A company can instead choose to purchase the vehicle outright and potentially provide for upkeep and maintenance. In this instance, the full cost of the vehicle is born by the company and depreciation charges are taken each year over the useful life of the vehicle. In between these two alternatives are the other approaches including payment for mileage or leasing.

Regardless of the approach used, the executive who benefits from the vehicle perquisite has a fully taxable benefit. If the company makes a flat monthly car allowance, that allowance is fully taxable. If instead a company car is provided to the executive (leased or company-fleet vehicle), the executive has imputed income based on the amount of time they use the vehicle for personal purposes (determined on the basis of mileage for business versus non-business use). Mileage reimbursement is not taxable as long as it does not exceed the IRS standard mileage reimbursement rate for that year (36 cents per mile for 2003).

Travel to and from the primary place of work is not considered business use. The full breadth of IRS rules covering vehicles is quite substantial and

Vehicle Program Type	Advantages	Disadvantages
Monthly Allowance (Flat dollar amount paid each month to cover ownership costs)	**Employee:** • No paperwork/mileage reporting required **Company:** • No mileage padding • Easily administered – no fleet management • No capital requirements • Competitive • Reduced exposure to liability through insurance requirements • Can differentiate as a perquisite for senior management by varying amount	**Employee:** • Payments taxable as compensable income • Flat rate does not recognize geographic differences in gas/insurance/operating costs • Requires FICA/withholding **Company:** • No control over type/age of car driven • Tax gross-ups required to keep executives whole
Monthly allowance plus cents/mile reimbursement (Allowance covers fixed ownership costs such as insurance, title, taxes, depreciation; cents/mile covers operating costs)	**Employee:** • Cents/mile partially recognizes geographic differentials in gas/insurance/operating costs • No IRS paperwork/reporting requirements for allowance portion(does require paperwork for mileage expense reimbursement) **Company:** • No capital requirements • Reduced exposure to liability through insurance requirements • No fleet management • Can differentiate as a perquisite for senior management by varying amount	**Employee:** • Payments taxable as compensable income • Payments for expenses require documentation • Allowance portion requires FICA/withholding **Company:** • Somewhat greater administrative burden for expense reimbursements • No control over type/age of car driven • Tax gross-ups required to keep executives whole on allowance portion • Potential mileage padding • Not competitive
Cents/Mile (Company reimburses employee maximum IRS rate)	**Employee:** • Not taxable if IRS rate not exceeded • Does not require FICA/withholding **Company:** • Limited corporate administration • Reduced exposure to liability through insurance requirements • No tax gross-up required to keep executive whole • Competitive	**Employee:** • Rate does not recognize geographic differences in gas/insurance/operating costs • Requires substantiation of business mileage • Does not recognize competitive perquisite value of vehicles for top management **Company:** • Mileage padding may occur • No control over type/age of car driven
Company-owned fleet (Company purchases and manages own fleet)	**Employee:** • No capital outlay to purchase car • Does not require FICA/withholding **Company:** • Tight control over type/age of car driven • Can differentiate as a perquisite for senior management by varying car type	**Employee:** • Imputed income for personal use is taxable • Personal use benefit calculation method required by IRS **Company:** • Significant capital requirements • High cost • Significant administrative burden • Personal use of company vehicle increases exposure to risk
Company-leased vehicle (Company leases vehicle on employee's behalf – operating lease, not capital lease)	**Employee:** • No capital outlay to purchase car • Does not require FICA/withholding **Company:** • Tight control over type/age of car driven • Reduced capital requirements vs. fleet management • Can differentiate as a perquisite for senior management by varying car type	**Employee:** • Imputed income for personal use is taxable • Personal use benefit calculation method required by IRS **Company:** • Significant administrative burden • High cost • Personal use of company vehicle increases exposure to risk

covers special situations such as luxury automobiles and special valuation methods. It is advisable to review the full tax affects of your chosen design with tax counsel so that the specific tax rules and outcomes are known prior to implementation.

Again, as indicated in the chart above, there are various advantages and disadvantages from a cost, taxation and administration perspective depending upon which approach is chosen. Many companies will choose to outsource the administration of their programs to lessen overall headaches.

Trends

There is a clear trend toward the use of automobile monthly allowances versus actually providing company vehicles. As one of the last bastions of executive prestige, some organizations and industries are reluctant to change their company car policies. As this legacy or entitlement mentality lessens, and as pressure mounts on Compensation Committees to eliminate non-essential pay, there is no supporting evidence for anticipating an upward trend on company-paid vehicles and allowances.

Club Memberships

Once a very prominent perquisite, the use of company-paid club member-ships has decreased dramatically over the last several years, particularly for larger sized companies. This is due to two primary reasons: tax law changes eliminating the deductibility of these perquisites and greater attention on executive compensation governance and the need to ensure perquisites are legitimate business expenses.

However, some companies do still pay for the costs of social club memberships (such as health, athletic, country or luncheon) for their executives. These are usually the types of social clubs that combine pure social enter-tainment with some business use: either through networking possibilities, client entertainment or use of the facilities for functions, meetings, etc. Athletic club memberships are also popular in that they are perceived to support a healthy life style and in turn improved productivity. In deciding whether to offer a club membership as part of the executive compensation package, more and more companies are closely questioning whether there is a legitimate business purpose or, like a company-paid vehicle, the program is solely a perquisite.

As you can see below[3], prevalence of club memberships is most often restricted to the CEO and top management. This does, however, vary dramatically by industry. Industries that rely heavily on client entertainment as a form of marketing (and place a high value on client networking) tend

PERCENT OF ORGANIZATIONS THAT PAY (IN WHOLE OR IN PART) FOR CLUB MEMBERSHIPS

Position	Organization Size			
	Under 200 Employees	200 - 1,999 Employees	2,000 or More Employees	All Size Groups Combined
CEO	29.5%	51.6%	41.3%	44.5%
Top Management	23.0%	38.9%	34.1%	34.7%
Senior Management	14.8%	23.7%	17.4%	20.1%
Middle Management	11.5%	17.9%	8.0%	13.4%
Professional	9.8%	15.3%	5.1%	10.8%

to be heavier users of club memberships (e.g., the Financial Services and Entertainment/Media sector).

Administration, Taxation and Cost

The median cost of one club membership is approximately $3,000 for a CEO and $2,000 for top management. The cost for other eligible levels of management drops dramatically and is more in the $250 to $500 range.

Typically, the cost of the membership is paid directly by the company; however, no tax deduction can be taken for the payment. Executives must pay taxes on the value of the club membership that is used for personal purposes.

Trends

Club memberships are no longer a standard element in the executive compensation package. The earlier tax law changes coupled with the spotlight on company profitability and executive compensation will likely lessen the usage of this benefit in the future. Companies will be pressured to prove there is a good business reason to provide club memberships to its executive team.

Travel

Given the demands and expectations of today's global business environment, most top executives are traveling significantly more than in the past. The major and most common features offered within an executive travel program to lessen the burden of business travel for executives include:

• Business or First Class Air Travel

• Airline Clubs

• Use of Company-Owned Aircraft

• Spouse's Travel Expenses

Primarily, these travel policies are put in place to increase productivity and reduce the stress related to business travel. Beginning with the most common–Business or First Class travel; most companies provide a travel policy that allows business class travel on international flights or on a flight that is greater than a specified length of time (e.g., four or six hours). First class travel benefits are less common and normally restricted to the CEO and senior officers. Other circumstances that a company may consider as criteria for upper class travel is whether the executive is traveling with a customer.

Company-paid airline clubs (or VIP lounge) are more common and more appropriate in companies where more frequent trips are required or where direct flights to frequent destinations (e.g., major customers) can not be accomplished in one stop. When the travel demands are high, and, the company wants to ease the travel burden and decrease unproductive time, a company most often will pay for *one* airline club that is selected by the employee.

The use of company-owned or leased aircraft is not a very common practice primarily because the equipment, liability insurance and maintenance costs are very high and difficult to justify. Company-provided aircraft is more common in large global companies where the business necessitates significant amounts of travel by its executives. If, however, a company does have use of company-owned aircraft its use will be limited to senior management and executives.

Some companies allow personal use of company-owned aircraft for senior officers but most often require the employee to pay for its use. If an executive does not pay for the personal use of the aircraft, that executive is taxed on the value of that service. The tax rules surrounding this issue are both quite formulaic and complex and, as such, are outside the scope of this chapter. It is advisable to discuss the issue with your tax counsel to gain a better understanding of the taxation and resulting administrative requirements.

A company-paid expense for a spouse to accompany the executive is far less common and, in fact, is downright rare. For those companies that do offer it, it is primarily only offered at the very top level (CEO and direct reports) and, presumably, due to the fact that the executive is traveling a significant amount of the time.

Trends

Given the importance of maintaining high productivity levels, it is not likely you will see a significant decline in the number of companies offering business class upgrades or airline club memberships. The benefit itself, however, may be used with less frequency given the decline in business travel as a result of recent economic and global events. The future offerings of the airline industry itself may be the biggest determinant of what trends we see.

Legal Counseling Services

Given the events of the last two years concerning fraudulent, illegal and just plain immoral acts of a few executives at a few now defunct companies, one might think that the provision of executive legal counseling services would be on the rise. But not so.

In fact, legal counseling services are provided by less than 10% of companies overall. Typically, the services are intended to support the executive in ways similar to the objectives of financial planning services–namely, to ensure the executive has his or her legal and financial house in order so attention can be focused on the business.

Plan Design Alternatives

There are three primary types of legal services provided to executives as a benefit: will preparation, estate planning, and legal advice to negotiate employment agreements. Will/trust preparation and estate planning go somewhat hand-in-hand. These are the two more prominent types of legal counseling services and are best offered in conjunction with financial counseling. In this way, an executive can get competent expertise in an integrated way. With the complex and ever-changing laws and tax regulations impacting the creation of wills and estate planning techniques, these services are highly valued by those who receive them.

Legal counseling in the form of contract or employment agreement negotiations is another form of service provided. This, however, is not something that is typically needed on an annual basis and may only be offered in the year the contract term expires. Legal counseling services can include any services the executive requires, although not a prevalent practice. If offered, there is usually a fixed budget amount the employer will pay regardless of type of service.

Administration, Taxation and Cost

Similar to financial counseling services, legal counseling is most often provided via an outside firm that is engaged by the company. There are strengths and weaknesses to this approach. Consider that, when an outside firm is selected by the employer, the employer can provide any necessary guidance and documentation regarding company plans and policies that may be important to the estate planning process (e.g., beneficiary issues and plan documents) in a systematic, efficient and controlled way. Allowing the executive to choose (or, more likely, to continue with an attorney they have been using), allows the executive to gain efficiencies and consistency with prior work performed. The deciding factor is whether the primary objective is for the company to retain control or to provide the executive flexibility through choice.

In either case, the employer will either reimburse the executive for expenses incurred or pay the invoice directly. Companies often allocate a fixed amount each year to pay for legal counseling services and payments are made against that budget. A typical annual average cost for legal counseling is not high, typically around $2,500 for CEO's and $1,000 to $1,500 to top management. The year of initial costs are much higher (up to $10,000) if will, trust, estate planning and employment agreement negotiating services are also needed.

Regardless of how paid, the value of the services is fully taxable to the executive and fully deductible by the company. Essentially, payments made for legal counseling are another direct form of compensation.

Trends

Legal counseling services have never been a highly popular benefit and there are no overwhelming factors or developments that would suggest that there will be a significant change in their prevalence. Nor is it likely that legal counseling services will be viewed going forward as fulfilling a new and different need than what they have done in the past.

The End Result, Summary and Recommendations

So how do we choose the right set of executive benefits and perquisites if we offer any at all? The following steps will help you determine how these programs fit within the total executive compensation package.

1. **Determine your executive total compensation philosophy**–include both monetary and non-monetary rewards
2. **Structure the cash and incentive package to support the philosophy**–base salary, annual and long-term incentives
3. **Identify benefits and perquisites that support the executive total compensation philosophy**–select those that fit within the total package with consideration for all internal and external influences (e.g., shareholder optics)

4. **Add programs to further support the total compensation philosophy**– if needed, engage competent, experienced and non-biased advice in the design and discussion of trends

5. **Calculate the estimated value of the entire package**–and compare to market to determine reasonableness and confirm desired market position

6. Obtain Board of Director's approval and formally reflect the program, its purpose and objective, eligibility, structure and administration/monitoring requirements of each program in the Executive Total Compensation Philosophy

7. **Select vendors and administrators**–if needed, depending upon complexity of programs and products, competent experience and expertise can be invaluable

8. **Communicate, communicate, communicate**–the best made plans can be ignored or undervalued if not communicated properly and frequently

It should be clear that the critical first step in selecting and designing the right executive benefits package is to establish a total executive compensation philosophy that supports the goals and values of the business and provides a compelling employment deal for current and future executives. Once a philosophy is created, the next step is to determine if and how the various executive benefits fit into that entire picture.

Using the framework described in the second section of this chapter, you can begin to identify which of the 12 primary programs presented here best support that overall philosophy. For example, if the executive compensation philosophy provides highly competitive cash compensation along with an opportunity for wealth accumulation, then deferred compensation programs and financial counseling make sense. Other benefits and perquisites may not be necessary or appropriate.

If on the other hand the total compensation philosophy is to pay competitive levels of cash compensation and emphasize security, tenure and longevity, then a focus on providing supplemental benefits at some level might seem appropriate. Programs that might be considered in this vein are long-term disability, supplemental medical and supplemental retirement programs. A final example might be a company that wishes to emphasize performance and cash compensation along with a very flat and egalitarian organization. If that type of company also requires long hours and a lot of travel, then convenience type benefits and perquisites might be most appropriate.

Your company may also want to obtain and analyze the prevalence of programs in your particular marketplace or industry. There are many survey sources that are routinely published by consulting and brokerage firms that can help in the data collecting effort. All in all, determining the right programs and their relationship to achieving the desired market position is an important step in selecting the right programs.

Once the appropriate reward elements are selected, designing the program effectively is the next step. This is often a very challenging undertaking for human resource professionals as it is rare to find one advisory source that understands all of the complicated and intricate rules involved in offering each of these types of programs. The more complicated programs tend to be deferred compensation and supplemental retirement, long-term disability and supplemental life insurance. There are also three in-house constituencies that should be involved in plan design decisions: Finance, Human Resources and Legal. Someone well-versed in tax law is also critical to be included in the process. In general it is wise to ensure that experienced advice is rendered, particularly for programs that require in-depth industry knowledge.

Once the design is completed, or even during the design process, a detailed cost assessment should be conducted to understand the expense and balance sheet impacts of the proposed program. This is particularly important when implementing plans that will have a future value or payment such as a SERP. After any needed refinements to the program are made a product or vendor search can be conducted and cost implications can be further refined with input from the vendors and as part of the overall process.

In regard to administration and vendor selection; the trend continues to be towards outsourcing any administration functions that are not an actual core competency of the company. For executive benefits, that means that most companies try to outsource any and all administration as the most cost effective approach. The current administrators and vendors that a company already uses for its qualified plans or all-employee benefits are natural choices to consider first for possible leveraging opportunities. Benefits such as supplemental life or disability insurance are two examples of where such established relationships can provide further enhancements and/or cost savings to programs.

Other programs provide more of a challenge. The most complex situation is in administering a SERP or nonqualified deferred compensation benefit. The vendors most interested in administering these plans are also interested in having assets or product placed with them—similar to the 401(k) administration marketplace. And, as a result, a vendor's particular product

Program	Possible Administrators	Possible Product Vendors	Challenges/Issues
SERP's	Actuarial Firms, Bank Trust Departments	Bank Trust Departments, Brokerage Houses, Mutual Fund/401(k), COLI Brokers	If plan is unfunded, may only need periodic financial and benefit valuations
Nonqualified Deferred Compensation Programs (Defined Contribution and Voluntary Deferred Compensation Plans)	Third-Party Administrators, Mutual Fund/401(k) Vendors	Bank Trust Departments, Brokerage Houses, Mutual Fund/401(k) Vendors, COLI Brokers	Unfunded plans have limited options for outside administration. Seek opportunities to leverage from current qualified plan providers
Financial Counseling	Financial Planning Firms, Brokerage Houses, Diversified Financial Services Providers	Financial Planning Firms, Brokerage Houses, Diversified Financial Services Providers	Ensure that firm selected has no conflicts of interest
Personal Loans	Banks	Banks	Third-party loans contain less risk than company-provided loans
Executive Medical	Healthcare Providers	Healthcare Providers	May gain synergies with existing healthcare program provider
Long-Term Care	Healthcare/Long-term Care Providers	Healthcare/Long-term Care Providers	May gain synergies with existing healthcare program provider if they also provide long-term care products
Supplemental Life Insurance	Life Insurance Providers	Life Insurance Providers	May gain synergies with existing group life insurance provider
Supplemental Disability Insurance	Healthcare Providers	Healthcare Providers	May gain synergies with existing healthcare program provider if they also provide disability products
Severance	Administer benefits through current providers	Administer benefits through current providers	Lump-sum payments are administratively simple
Company Cars	Third-Party Administrators, Car Leasing Companies	Car Leasing Companies	Volume
Club Memberships	Generally administered in-house	Generally administered in-house	Ensuring policy is written and communicated
Travel	Travel Agency	Travel Agency	Ensuring policy is written and communicated internally and externally
Legal	Law Firms	Law Firms	Ensure that firm selected has no conflicts of interest

specialty often ends up as the funding vehicle. Here is a prime example of why it is important to consider administration requirements in the design stage. Competent professional advice in this arena can be invaluable.

So, as in design, there are a number of alternatives and issues to consider. The chart above provides an overview of some administrator and vendor possibilities for each of the twelve programs, along with related issues in choosing the right outsourcing solution.

And last, but of all things not least, proper communication of any program is the cornerstone to an executive's understanding and appreciation of the benefit and how it supports the total compensation package, the employment deal and the business as a whole. Most companies and executives give the highest marks to programs that are communicated on a personalized basis, providing value and cost estimates for all elements of the package. Many companies provide total compensation statements that include the value of the current compensation and benefits package along with a projection of the potential future values. Increasingly, companies are also looking to provide these statements electronically with modeling capabilities via the company's intranet. Combined with a robust communication program for each individual plan, a personalized tool that can help an executive understand the full value of the program based on various scenarios (service, performance levels) is a very powerful tool. After all, the best designed plans are worthless if they are either not understood or utilized.

Endnotes

1. Watson Wyatt 2002/2003 Strategic Rewards Study
2. Watson Wyatt 2002 Nonqualified Deferred Compensation Study
3. Watson Wyatt Data Services ECS 2003/2004 Survey Report on Non-Qualified Benefits and Perquisite Practices
4. Terri Shuman, Consultant, Watson Wyatt Worldwide, Los Angeles. Special thanks to Terri who provided significant input as to the content and completeness of this chapter.

Ann Costelloe

The Practice leader for Watson Wyatt's San Francisco executive compensation practice, Ann works with clients and their boards aligning executive compensation programs with strategic business objectives, assessing the structure and competitiveness of executive total compensation programs, designing annual incentive and sales incentive plans, understanding the design impacts, financing and implementation of executive benefit plans, creating an effective total rewards philosophy and program as well as due diligence in merger and acquisition situations.

She is a core member of the team that leads Watson Wyatt's research and delivery on nonqualified executive benefits and serves on Watson Wyatt's Total Rewards and Mergers and Acquisitions task forces. Ann has 15 years of consulting experience applying innovative problem solving and strategic planning techniques for clients in the financial services, retail, high-technology, not-for-profit, healthcare and manufacturing industries in the United States, Europe and Asia.

Before joining Watson Wyatt in June 1997 Ann served as regional director of institutional pension services at Metropolitan Life. Prior to that she worked as a management consultant with Diablo Management Group, providing consulting services to financially troubled corporations. Ann also worked as a senior auditor and a controller on the options trading desk at Bear, Stearns & Company. Her career began in the financial services division of Arthur Andersen in New York.

Ann earned a bachelor's degree in accounting and business administration from the State University of New York at Albany. Ann is a frequent public speaker on executive compensation, total rewards, equity arrangements and executive benefits. She has also been quoted in major business and financial journals and is a Chartered Financial Analyst.

7. Deferred Compensation Plans

In the view of many experts, we are likely to see additional regulatory control placed on deferred compensation plans as we go forward, as well as the possibility of additional disclosure requirements. Despite these potential changes, deferred compensation will continue to play an important role in most executive compensation plans and having a strong understanding of their functioning is a must.

Whether specifically stated or not, tax effectiveness is a goal of most executive compensation programs. Deferred compensation plans play an important role in helping companies meet that goal. Simply put, deferred compensation plans create an opportunity for executives to voluntarily defer receipt of taxable income to a later date. Depending on how the plan is designed these opportunities can be applied to salary, short or long term incentive payouts, stock options gains and/or the vesting of restricted stock.

The authors begin their presentation by creating the context for deferred compensation plans, highlighting their growing prevalence, and how they compare to other company sponsored saving opportunities. They then walk us through a number of important ERISA and IRS issues that must be understood and dealt with for the plan to function properly, and for deferred income to remain tax deferred. The authors point out, despite these ERISA and IRS limitations, that there is significant room for design flexibility. They describe in some detail four "best practices" that in their view make for a stronger, more flexible plan design. Lastly, they provide the reader with a very helpful seven-step process for designing a deferred compensation plan.
–Editors

PRACTITIONERS USE THE TERM "deferred compensation" to describe many different types of arrangements that defer compensation or income. But there are really two different types of deferred compensation:

1. Qualified plans
2. Nonqualified plans

Qualified plans (which include the ubiquitous Section 401(k) plans) are plans that satisfy the extensive requirements imposed by the Internal Revenue Code (Code) in exchange for favorable tax treatment. By contrast, nonqualified plans are those that forsake the benefits of qualified plans in order to escape the burdens associated with those plans. Through careful drafting, a nonqualified plan can gain exemption from most of the onerous funding, participation, vesting and disclosure requirements imposed by the Employee Retirement Income Security Act of 1974 (ERISA) on qualified plans.

Of course, neither the qualified plan nor the nonqualified plan is inherently more advantageous–each has its advantages and disadvantages. If an employer is willing to comply with the substantial requirements imposed by the Code and ERISA, it can get a current tax deduction for contributions to a qualified plan, and potentially extend eligibility to most if not the entire employee population. In addition, contributions to a qualified plan will generally be protected from the company's creditors. In contrast, a nonqualified plan offers companies the ability to design and/or fund the plan with considerable freedom, but participation must be limited to a select group of executives, and benefits are not protected in the event of corporate insolvency.

Although the details will be described more fully below, it is important to clarify that a nonqualified plan is nothing more than a contractual agreement between an employer and one or more of its key employees that represents an unsecured promise of the employer to pay benefits at some future date.

There are several types of nonqualified plans, but this chapter is limited to a review of deferred compensation plans (DCPs), sometimes referred to as salary reduction plans.[1] DCPs enable employees to forego a portion or all of their current cash compensation (e.g., salary, bonuses, commissions, long-term incentives) in exchange for the promise to have that compensation paid at a future date certain. Participation in these types of plans is generally voluntary and involves "employee money."

In this chapter, we will discuss the factors that have given rise to DCPs. We will also address the tax, ERISA and legal requirements of such plans and how they work. We will establish the standards for Best Practices in the design of a DCP. Finally, we set forth a simple seven-step process for successful plan design. It is anticipated that human resource executives, once equipped with sound strategies and tools, will be able to more confidently build their own plans.

Factors Driving DCP Adoption

All companies, small and large, share at least one thing in common–the struggle to recruit and retain talented employees. This objective must be achieved at every level of the organization for the company to achieve its strategic goals. In the struggle to recruit and retain executives, the competition for talent is even more fierce. The pool of talented executives is smaller and the stakes are higher. For legal reasons that will be described more fully below, DCPs cannot be used by rank-and-file employees; participation must be limited to a select group of highly compensated or management employees. Consequently, DCPs have been used by many organizations as an important tool for executive recruiting.

The increasing prevalence of DCPs is attributable to several factors which are described below.

The Limitations of Qualified Plans

Qualified retirement plans (e.g., company-sponsored defined benefit plans or 401(k) plans) and Social Security provide little incentive for talented executives to improve returns for shareholders, let alone incentive to remain with the company.[2] Legislation limits the benefits that can be provided by qualified plans, and the qualified plan limits severely restrict the benefits that can be provided to executives. In short, qualified plans cannot provide highly paid executives with retirement benefits that are in line with their pre-retirement pay levels.

For example, the legislative limits on 401(k) plans limit pre-tax elective deferrals to no more than $12,000 in 2003.[3] This absolute restriction permits a decreasing deferral opportunity (on a percentage basis) for highly paid executives. The more one makes, the less one can defer into the 401(k) on a percentage basis. Given the limits on contributions to 401(k) plans, it is easy to understand why companies try to assist executives in providing additional

Prevalence of DCPs

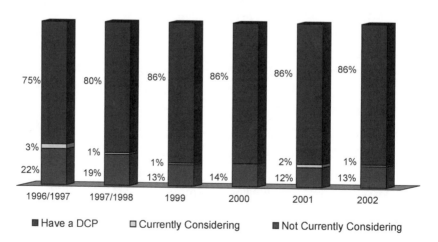

	1996/1997	1997/1998	1999	2000	2001	2002
Not Currently Considering	75%	80%	86%	86%	86%	86%
Currently Considering	3%	1%	1%		2%	1%
Have a DCP	22%	19%	13%	14%	12%	13%

■ Have a DCP □ Currently Considering ■ Not Currently Considering

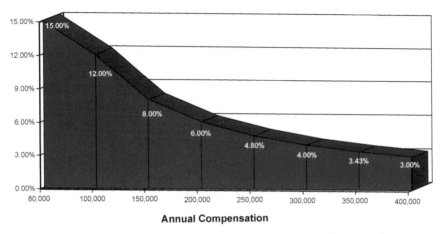

Annual Compensation

401(k) Deferral Limit of $12,000 as a Percentage of Annual Compensation

deferral opportunities through DCPs. Experts estimate that executives will need to replace 70–80 percent of their pre-retirement income in retirement in order to maintain their pre-retirement standard of living. The legislative limits on qualified plans effectively prevent many executives from achieving that replacement level. One could say that qualified plans impose a form of "reverse discrimination," that leads to the need for supplemental benefit plans such as DCPs.

Economic and Corporate Issues Driving the Adoption of DCPs

During the 1990s, and particularly during the technology boom of the late 90s, companies relied heavily on stock options to attract and retain top executives. Virtually every public company lavished executives with substantial grants of stock options, which were welcomed by executives who enjoyed the appreciation of the stock during one of the most intense bull markets in history. These option grants were inexpensive to companies because of favorable accounting rules. In fact, virtually every executive compensation survey reveals that a significant percentage of the total remuneration of executives was represented by the present value of stock options. However, after several well-publicized corporate scandals, significant attention became focused on executive compensation. Moreover, many began to clamor for changes such as the expensing of stock options. Furthermore, as the so-called stock market "bubble" burst, executives had difficulty perceiving value in options that were predicated on a steadily rising stock price. As the retentive value of option grants diminished, companies started looking beyond stock options as a tool to recruit and retain executives. Many companies implemented DCPs to fill that void.

For these reasons, companies are rapidly learning to bring compensation and benefits together into a more unified and powerful package with the type of inventive solutions that effectively address the recruit-reward-retain challenge.

Complying with Tax and ERISA Laws and Regulations

Tax Implications

As stated above, a DCP is an unfunded and unsecured promise by an employer to pay compensation to one or more employees in the future. Perhaps the most important tax aspect of a DCP is that a participating executive can receive a contractual promise for the payment of valuable future benefits without incurring any current income taxation. Since executives are typically at the top of the income tax brackets, the ability of an executive to obtain the promise of future payments without being taxed currently is a significant advantage. It is therefore fundamental to the success of a DCP that the executive not be taxed on the deferred benefits until he actually receives them.

As you develop a DCP for your organization, you must be keenly aware of general tax implications. In a deferral plan arrangement, an individual voluntarily defers receipt of compensation to which he would otherwise be entitled. For the arrangement to achieve the desired income tax results (i.e. that the deferred compensation is not included in the executive's income until actual payment is received), the arrangement must avoid the pitfalls of: (i) the doctrine of "constructive receipt" and (ii) the "economic benefit" doctrine.

1. **The Doctrine of Constructive Receipt**–The general rule of "constructive receipt" states that income becomes taxable when it is "made available" to an individual so that it may be drawn upon during the taxable year. Income is not, however, constructively received if the individual's control of its receipt is subject to substantial limitations or restrictions. DCPs typically avoid constructive receipt because the executive cannot get access to her money immediately or because there are substantial limitations or restrictions on her ability to get the money immediately (e.g., executives can only receive their deferred amounts upon separation from service). To avoid constructive receipt, the election to defer compensation should generally be made before the beginning of the period of service during

which the compensation is earned. The DCP should also provide that participants in the plan are unsecured general creditors and that the plan is a mere promise to pay benefits in the future. The mere promise to pay, not represented by notes or secured in any way, will generally avoid constructive receipt.

2. **The Doctrine of Economic Benefit**–The economic benefit doctrine is sometimes confused with constructive receipt, although they are distinct concepts. The economic benefit doctrine is generally applied to tax anything of value that is bestowed upon an individual. In the deferred compensation context, the economic benefit doctrine is concerned primarily with whether the executive has actually received something of economic value that should be taxed currently. This catch-all doctrine seeks to recognize as ordinary gain "all income from whatever source derived" and all income realized in any form, whether money, property or services. Under the economic benefit doctrine, an individual should be taxed when assets are unconditionally and irrevocably paid into a fund or trust for the sole benefit of an employee and the employee is vested in that fund. However, if contributions are made or amounts are set aside in accordance with the terms of a nonqualified plan, and such amounts are subject to the claims of the employer's general bankruptcy and insolvency creditors, such contributions or amounts should not be immediately taxable under the economic benefit doctrine.

In sum, to avoid current taxation on sums deferred, a DCP participant must make an irrevocable election to defer compensation to some date in the future and must be solely dependent for future payments on the employer's unsecured contractual promise to pay those benefits.

ERISA Implications

The Employee Retirement Income Security Act of 1974 (ERISA) is a comprehensive statutory scheme designed to protect employees by forcing employers to keep their pension promises. In general, ERISA will apply to a plan maintained by an employer to the extent it provides retirement income to employees or results in the deferral of income by employees for periods extending to the termination of employment or beyond. ERISA generally imposes many burdensome requirements on plans that fall into this category such as participation, vesting, funding and fiduciary responsibilities. Consequently, avoiding the substantial requirements of ERISA is critical. The general rule is that ERISA's requirements will apply to any employee benefit plan unless the plan fits within specific exemptions. Therefore, it is absolutely essential that a draftsperson takes care to place the plan squarely within one of the specific exceptions.

The relevant exception for DCPs is the so-called "top-hat" exception, which is defined as "a plan which is unfunded and is maintained by an employer primarily for the purpose of providing deferred compensation for a select group of management or highly compensated employees." Top-hat plans are exempt from the participation, vesting, funding, and fiduciary duty requirements of ERISA, because at least in part, Congress recognized that certain employees did not need the protection of the government, owing to their position or status in the company. While top-hat plans remain subject to the reporting and disclosure requirements of ERISA, a top-hat plan can file a one-time, one page letter with the Department of Labor under an alternative procedure that will satisfy ERISA's reporting and disclosure requirements.

As mentioned above, to qualify for the top-hat exemption, the plan must be (i) "unfunded"; and, (ii) must be maintained by an employer, primarily for the purpose of providing deferred compensation for a select group of management or highly compensated employees.

The First Part of the Top-Hat Plan Test–"Unfunded"

ERISA does not define the term "unfunded" but courts and the Department of Labor (DOL) have considered whether particular arrangements are unfunded. The definition is critical, because it determines whether any assets purchased to support the plan will be treated as plan assets subject to the restrictive prohibited transaction rules of ERISA. The general consensus among courts and the DOL appears to be that a plan is unfunded if it provides benefits solely from the employer's general assets. The determinative question is: can the participant in a plan establish through the plan documents or otherwise a legal right any greater than that of an unsecured creditor to a specific set of funds from which the employer is obligated to pay the deferred compensation. In answering this question, courts seem to focus on whether (i) the participants and beneficiaries can look to separate property for payment and (ii) whether the participants and beneficiaries have rights greater than general unsecured creditors when attempting to recover payments under the plan. As long as the DCP is structured so that all benefits are payable from the general assets of the employer, which are subject to the claims of the employer's general creditors, the plan should be "unfunded" for purposes of qualifying for the top-hat exemption.

A well-drafted plan will contain the following provisions to help ensure that it is "unfunded" for purposes of ERISA.

1. The plan should provide that the parties intend the arrangement to be unfunded.

2. The plan should provide that plan participants and their beneficiaries have no preferred claim on, or any beneficial ownership interest in, any assets of the employer.

3. The plan should provide that any rights to payments under the plan are mere unsecured contractual rights against the employer.

4. The plan should provide that benefits payable to participants and their beneficiaries may not be anticipated, assigned, alienated, pledged, encumbered or subjected to attachment, garnishment, levy, execution or other legal or equitable process or transferred in any other way.

5. The plan should avoid explicit references to any specific assets that will informally finance the benefits provided under the DCP. If assets are mentioned in the plan document, the plan should specifically state that the participants and their beneficiaries have no special rights in those assets and that those assets are general assets of the employer and are subject to the claims of the employer's general creditors.

6. The plan should avoid stating that the employer is required to acquire assets to finance its deferred compensation liabilities.

An Associated Trust Does Not Cause a DCP to Be "Funded"

Frequently, an employer will use a grantor trust arrangement into which it deposits assets to reduce various risks to participants. Under a so-called "rabbi trust" arrangement, the employer contributes assets to a separate trust (usually with a bank or trust company as trustee) with the intent that those assets are to be used to provide the funds to pay the DCP benefits.

Use of a rabbi-trust will not generally cause a deferred compensation plan to be treated as "funded" for purposes of ERISA. However, planners should take care when such a trust holds assets in connection with a DCP. Although use of a properly designed rabbi trust (one not currently taxable for income tax purposes) does not cause the plan to be funded for ERISA purposes, such an arrangement might become funded if it is suggested or communicated to plan participants that they have a beneficial interest in such assets. Generally, a rabbi trust does not cause the DCP to become "funded" for ERISA purposes because the rabbi trust does not address the bankruptcy risk to participants. Specifically, if the employer becomes insolvent, the assets of the rabbi trust will be available to pay creditor claims. Rabbi trusts are discussed more fully below.

The Second Part of the Top-hat Test–Who May Participate?

In addition to being "unfunded," a DCP must be maintained "primarily for the purpose of providing deferred compensation for a select group of management or highly compensated employees." This definition is deceptively short and simple. Determining whether a particular group qualifies for this definition is no easy task. It is helpful to parse through the definition.

"Primarily"

There are two different views on the meaning of the word "primarily" in the top-hat exemption definition. "Primarily" may refer to (i) the type of benefits provided, where, for example, an incidental death benefit is provided along with the deferral benefits; or (ii) the type of employees who can participate, where for example, a small number or percentage of nonmanagement and/or lower-paid employees are allowed to participate. The DOL has, in the past, subscribed to the first view; that the word "primarily" refers to the purpose of the plan (i.e. the benefits provided), not the participant composition of the plan. The DOL's position appears to be that a "top-hat" plan must cover highly paid or management employees exclusively. Many courts, on the other hand, have subscribed to the second view; that a plan could still be a top-hat plan if a small number of participants were neither highly compensated nor management employees. These courts have determined that if a plan were principally intended for management or highly compensated employees, it would not be disqualified from top-hat status simply because a small number of participants did not meet that criteria.

In light of the legislative purpose behind the "top-hat" exemption (e.g., that the group covered by exemption do not need the protections of ERISA by virtue of their stature in the company), it can be argued that the correct interpretation is that "primarily" refers to the type of employees who can participate. If the vast majority of participants in a plan are management or highly compensated employees, the ERISA protections should not be needed under the plan. While a small number or percentage of participants in the plan might not have the influence that management or highly compensated employees have, that fact that the majority of the participants are management or highly compensated should be sufficient to protect the plan benefits (assuming similarly-situated participants are treated similarly). Of course, this is a point on which reasonable minds differ. A prudent human resource professional should consult an expert on this issue.

"Select Group"

One of the major areas of dispute involving top-hat plans centers on the meaning of the phrase "select group." A critical question in designing a DCP frequently is what percentage or number of employees can constitute a select group of management or highly compensated employees. The two extreme cases are easy to resolve. If all employees are eligible to participate, the plan would not qualify because the group was not "selected" in any meaningful sense. By contrast, if there is only one employee eligible, the plan should qualify as a select group (assuming all other conditions are satisfied).

When trying to ascertain whether a group is "select," for purposes of the top-hat exemption, courts have considered what has been described as the "select group fraction" which is calculated by taking the number of employees in the select group into the numerator, and the total employees into the denominator A review of some of the older cases seemed to suggest a few guiding principles: a plan offered to 5 percent or less of the employees can probably be a top-hat plan (assuming all other conditions are satisfied), while a plan offered to about 20% of the employee population probably does not qualify for the exception. However, the Second Circuit Court of Appeals recently determined that a plan that was offered to 15.34% of the workforce was indeed a "top-hat" plan for purposes of ERISA. *Demery v. Extebank Deferred Compensation Plan*, 216 F.3d 283 (2d. Cir. 2000). The court determined that while the 15.34% figure is at or near the upper limit of the acceptable size for a select group, the court was unable to say that it alone made the plan too broad to be a top-hat plan. Despite the fact that the plan was offered to 15.34% of the employee population, the Court found that the covered group was different enough to constitute a select group, noting that the size of the group was less important than its makeup. These findings offer welcome news for many employers and benefits practitioners, as they set clearer standards for eligibility, and will be viewed favorably by employers who want to expand participation in their DCPs.

Once again, given the consequences associated with not complying with the top-hat exemption (e.g., Title I of ERISA applies), it is critically important for individuals to seek the advice of wise and experienced counsel who can opine about the size of the group to which eligibility is extended.

Highly Compensated

Although the term "highly compensated" is defined several times in the Code, ERISA provides no definition for applying the top-hat exception.

Courts use a "facts and circumstances" approach to this definition, and have considered such factors as: (i) the average salary of covered individuals compared to the average salary for all company employees; (ii) the median salary of the covered employees compared to the median salary for all company employees. In general, employees appear to be highly compensated when they earn substantially (often thought to be at least two to four times) more than employees who are not covered by the plan. Courts still have not adopted clear standards for determining how much compensation is enough to make one highly compensated.

Management

Perhaps not surprisingly, there is no definition of "management" under ERISA. Usually this is a factual inquiry that examines the job titles and job duties of the included employees. The extent to which an employee manages, directs or supervises other employees has a direct impact on whether they will be considered "management" for purposes of this section. Other commentators have opined that the extent to which employees are exempt from the Fair Labor Standards Act as administrative, supervisory or professional employees will also have an impact on this analysis.

Summary of ERISA Compliance

It is extremely important that you pay careful attention to determining eligibility for your DCP. If you err, your DCP will fail to qualify for the top-hat exception, and consequently, it will become subject to the onerous requirements of ERISA you sought to avoid. Without the advice of experienced counsel, you should be reluctant to expand the group of participants who will be eligible for DCPs.

Designing Your Deferred Compensation Plan

Assessing Your Corporate Objectives

Like any business tool, benefit plans must be customized to individual corporate profiles. A strategically-sound DCP, one that is well-designed and effectively administered, should directly reflect your corporate culture. Therefore, it is important to take the following factors into account when designing your DCP:

• market position

• business cycle

• long-term strategy and short-term objectives

- human resource policies
- culture, mission and values
- compensation structure
- future business prospects
- availability of executive talent

The Benefits of a DCP

Although there are several types of deferral plans, the most common type of plan, and the one addressed more fully below, is an elective deferral plan that allows executives to voluntarily defer a specified percentage or amount of compensation to a future date such as retirement. Although the compensation is typically limited to base salary and bonus, executives may also defer commissions, long-term incentives, gains on stock options, performance shares, phantom stock and restricted shares. The deferral election, though voluntary, must be irrevocable and must be made at a time before the compensation is earned or before the amount is ascertainable, determinable or known.

Contributions to a DCP provide the distinct advantages of pre-tax deferral and tax-deferred growth.

1. **No current tax.** A deferred compensation plan is similar to a 401(k) plan in that pre-tax deferrals go directly into the plan. This benefit enables executives to reduce current income tax. Without that tax burden, executives can leverage a larger portion of their compensation during the deferral period. By reducing the amount of current taxable income the executive has to pay, executives can avoid the high marginal state and federal income tax rates that can approach 45 to 50 percent. This characteristic is compelling to a current or prospective executive who may be ambivalent about joining or leaving your company. Unlike a 401(k), there are no limits on the amount of the deferral in a DCP.

2. **Tax-deferred growth.** The interest earned on the deferrals into the DCP are not taxable until they are distributed to the participant. Thus, the executive has an opportunity for compounded growth, and can accumulate retirement funds on a tax-deferred basis.

Plan Design

A well-designed DCP brings many advantages to both executive and employer. At the top of the list is flexibility to design the plan in many ways, which can be tailored to individual and corporate needs. Customization is another key advantage. DCPs allow you to custom-design your plan through a wide range and degree of benefits. Best of all, these plans give employers and plan participants welcomed freedom from ERISA and IRS restrictions. But there are ways to design DCPs that will produce optimal advantage.

Best Practices

The widespread use of DCPs stems from the rising demand for low-cost benefit plans that have the power to recruit, retain and reward talented executives. We have noticed an increased acceptance of certain Best Practices; that is, key design features of state-of-the-art DCPs. Companies planning to design DCPs will find it beneficial to adopt Best Practices in plan design. Simply put, Best Practices refer to a standard of planning and implementation that is above average, one that encompasses a wide range of contingencies and strives to offer a level of exceptional quality in benefits planning.

Of course, all DCPs are not equal. To achieve Best Practices, we recommend that you consider at least four key design features in your benefit planning:

1. Build ample flexibility for payout options into the plan
2. Create investment diversity with an unlimited ability to select, move and reallocate funds within the plan
3. Develop appropriate security devices to secure plan benefits
4. Develop appropriate funding vehicles to fund the plan

Best Practice #1–Flexibility of Payout Options

A well-designed DCP should offer participants short-term distribution options, such as the ability to withdraw funds to pay for a child's college education. The prevalence of short-term or in-service distribution provisions has increased in DCPs. This option, which often has a two to five-year minimum deferral period, is especially attractive to younger participants who may face short-term obligations such as college costs.

With the short-term distribution option, plan participants may receive partial payout prior to retirement without the penalty that would be assessed for premature withdrawals from a qualified plan such as a 401(k) plan. Above all, the DCP should provide enough flexibility to allow participants to determine how and when they wish to receive their benefits without penalty.

Best Practice #2–Investment Diversity

A DCP should also provide participants with the unlimited ability to allocate and reallocate their deferrals among a broad menu of investment options representing a wide array of style categories and risk profiles. Participants should be able to select from a variety of investment options to create the wealth-building strategy that is appropriate for their individual circumstances. Some DCPs credit participants with a fixed rate of interest that is often tied to an index such as the Moody's Corporate Bond Index, or the company's cost of borrowing. However, the prevalent practice is for companies to provide DCP participants with a menu of options from which they can choose an asset allocation that is appropriate for their age and risk tolerance.

Best Practice #3–Appropriate Benefit Security

Although DCPs can be attractive from a financial perspective, companies must develop appropriate security devices to secure the benefits in the plan, particularly if executives are concerned about getting paid. In effect, plan participants have exposure as unsecured general creditors of the company to the extent of their DCP balances. In the event of an employer's insolvency or bankruptcy, an executive's promised benefits are at risk. That is why the DCP should provide assurances to participants that their retirement benefits are protected in certain situations.

Risks may include an employer's inability to pay benefits due to cash flow demands, a hostile takeover, an unfriendly change in corporate control or a management change of heart. Employers may have inadequate cash flow to pay benefits at the time the executive retires. Future management may simply decide to eliminate the plan. As a result, consideration of risk management is a key aspect of plan design.

The following chart sets forth some of the areas of concern for DCP participants.

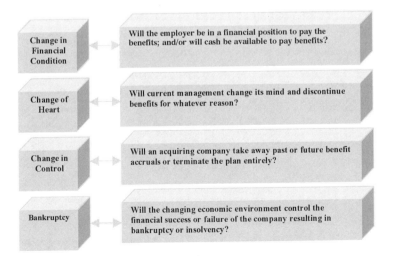

Change in Financial Condition	Will the employer be in a financial position to pay the benefits; and/or will cash be available to pay benefits?
Change of Heart	Will current management change its mind and discontinue benefits for whatever reason?
Change in Control	Will an acquiring company take away past or future benefit accruals or terminate the plan entirely?
Bankruptcy	Will the changing economic environment control the financial success or failure of the company resulting in bankruptcy or insolvency?

Benefit Security Alternatives

There is a wide range of security devices that reduce the participant's risk in a DCP. The most popular is the "funded rabbi trust." Of course, companies should perform a risk/rewards analysis to determine which type of plan benefit security device is right for your participants. The most prevalent security devices are covered below.

Rabbi Trust. A rabbi trust generally (though not always) comes in the form of an irrevocable grantor trust. The trust can be thought of as a bucket into which assets are poured for management and for distribution by a third party (trustee) according to written instructions (the trust document). A "grantor trust" is simply one that results in a flow of income, deductions and losses back to the employer (grantor) for income tax purposes. In the deferred compensation context, a rabbi trust is a receptacle for assets that are set aside to satisfy the employer's obligations to employees under one or more nonqualified plans. The trust simply creates a liquid fund to pay the nonqualified benefits as they come due.

Many, if not most corporations use rabbi trusts to protect DCP benefits. Of course, the skeptic might contend that escrowing or segregating assets against a deferred compensation obligation risks current income taxation to plan participants. But, in 1981, a synagogue created a grantor trust arrangement to hold assets and provide a retirement benefit for its rabbi. In considering this arrangement, the IRS ruled that it did not cause current income taxation to the rabbi (the origin of the term "rabbi trust"). The IRS ruled that because the trust contained a provision that the assets would always remain subject to the claims of the synagogue's general creditors in bankruptcy, the trust arrangement would not cause the rabbi to be taxed on the amounts segregated in the trust for his benefit. With this general tax authority, benefit practitioners pushed the use of this device to protect the benefits provided by DCPs. In 1992, the IRS, responding to the proliferation of such security devices, issued "safe-harbor" model trust language. The model language contains certain provisions that must be adopted "as is," optional provisions that can be changed as long as the substituted language is not inconsistent with the suggested language, and various alternative provisions from which the drafter must pick according to design objectives. Deviations from the model language are not prohibited, but the IRS will generally not issue a ruling on those deviations.

The model rabbi trust language requires an independent trustee, such as a bank or a trust department. The trustee is also required to suspend benefit payments if the company is insolvent. The trustee must also generally have all rights as to the trust's assets, and be given investment direction. Of course, despite the existence of the model trust language, many practitioners have modified the model language to enhance the protection of DCP participants. The drafting of a proper trust document requires the skills of a talented and experienced attorney because of the many drafting issues involved.

The rabbi trust is a significant benefit security enhancement. Proper design of the trust, coupled with placement of sufficient assets into the trust, can largely eliminate the benefit risk of nonpayment for every reason but employer bankruptcy or insolvency. A rabbi trust cannot eliminate the risk of nonpayment in a bankruptcy or insolvency.

Secular Trust. A secular trust goes one step beyond a rabbi trust. A secular trust is set up to formally fund and secure DCP benefits. Funds placed in a secular trust are not subject to the claims of the employer's creditors, but such amounts are usually immediately taxable to the employee. Consequently, a secular trust can protect participants from an employer's unwillingness to pay promised benefits and an employer's financial inability to pay the promised benefits. However, the trade-off is that participants must forgo the advantage of tax deferral in exchange for perfect security.

Rabbi/Secular Trust Combinations. Some practitioners have tried to provide the security of a secular trust while avoiding the immediate taxation of such trusts. They have fashioned a hybrid between a rabbi and a secular trust that would contain triggering provisions that were beyond the control of executives (e.g., a change in control). The rabbi trust would receive and hold contributions and assets currently. Upon the occurrence of a triggering event, however, the assets would automatically be transferred from the rabbi trust to the secular trust. Upon such transfer, immediate taxation would occur, but the assets would be protected from the employer's creditors.

There are some serious questions as to whether this type of arrangement works in the event of corporate insolvency, however. The bankruptcy "lookback" provision is 90 days prior to the date of filing and one year for officers and directors, so the rabbi/secular trust combination may not actually protect participants in a bankruptcy.

Surety Bonds/Indemnity Insurance. An alternate way to provide benefit security is through surety bonds or indemnity insurance. A surety bond is simply an undertaking by a bonding insurance company to pay the promised plan benefits in the event the employer does not pay them. The concept is simple: a plan participant (not the employer)[4] must purchase a bond to protect against the risks of nonpayment for bankruptcy or any other reason.

While the surety bond is a simple and intuitively attractive concept, such bonds are not readily available, and when they are, they are frequently very expensive. Availability and cost are generally a function of the credit-worthiness of the employer. Consequently, employers who are most likely to need the bond, are least likely to get one. Other limitations include the insurers' requirement that corporations with DCPs must disclose detailed financial information that may be inappropriate for smaller or closely held businesses.

Best Practice #4–Appropriate Funding Vehicles

The way in which a company funds its DCP is an important step toward achieving Best Practices. Preferably, you should handle plan funding only after a preliminary design of the plan is determined. Design and funding are both integral to a successful plan.

The funding question can be complicated. For example, to avoid unnecessary charges to a company's income statement, a DCP should be designed to minimize its expenses and impact on cash flow. The informal financing of a DCP has become the standard today as it enables a company to set aside assets in a trust in amounts equal to the plan liabilities, while remaining exempt from ERISA's regulations on vesting, benefit accrual and payment rules.

The best place to begin the funding analysis is to select a number of financial assumptions to be used in the evaluation of various funding alternatives. Those assumptions include: (i) effective corporate tax rate; (ii) cost of corporate capital and (iii) the assumed rate of return. Once you settle on these assumptions, you are ready to evaluate the following alternatives.

"Pay-as-You-Go" Method. Under this method, a company elects not to set aside any assets to pay plan benefits, but instead pays nonqualified benefits out of the company's cash flow when the benefits come due under the plan. In effect, the company is reinvesting executives' deferrals in the company as operating capital.

Some companies are attracted to the pay-as-you-go method, because it does not require extensive financial analysis. To fully evaluate the merits of this alternative, you must determine the corporate return on equity, and measure it against investment options that can be used for funding the nonqualified benefits. In addition, there are qualitative factors that must be considered. For example, contributions to a voluntary deferral plan have all the indicia of "participant money," and funds left in trust with the company ought to have the benefit of earmarked assets.

Managed Portfolio of Taxable Investments. A company can also finance the liability associated with a nonqualified plan with traditional investment choices, such as a taxable managed portfolio (e.g., mutual funds, individual equities, bonds, etc.). In this funding scenario, the company projects the benefits to be paid to an executive at retirement and sets aside a calculated amount into a segregated sinking fund from which benefits will be paid.

The company may use stocks, bonds, mutual funds or any other types of investment to realize an expected return on the portfolio. A disadvantage of this approach is that the income attributable to such funds will be taxable to the corporation, even if they are placed within a rabbi trust.

Companies appear to be moving away from taxable investments as a funding vehicle for DCPs. Part of the reason is certainly the tax liability created by growth in plan earnings. For example, if an executive defers $100,000 into a DCP funded by shares in a taxable mutual fund, earning a 10 percent rate of return, the company would have to book a liability of $110,000 at the end of the year. But the 10 percent return would be taxable to the company, so the company's asset would only be $106,000 after taxes (assuming a 40% effective tax rate) to offset the undiminished liability. The taxability of the assets creates what is known as an asset-liability mismatch. The longer the plan is in place, the greater the disparity between assets and liabilities. As a result of this ever-expanding mismatch, many firms using mutual funds to underpin their DCPs are revisiting their funding strategies, a trend expected to continue.

Corporate-Owned Life Insurance (COLI). The tax advantages of life insurance make it worthy of consideration when deciding whether or how to finance nonqualified plans. Cash values accumulate on a tax-deferred basis, in accordance with Code Section 7702, and death benefits are received income tax free to the owner. Cash value withdrawals by the employer's company are generally income tax free. The tax benefits of COLI make it highly attractive as a funding vehicle for DCPs.

The process of comparing types of COLI products is time-consuming. You will encounter fixed-interest COLI; general account COLI; variable COLI; separate account COLI. Additionally, there is a wide range of ways to determine factors that impact policy performance, as well as short- and long-term performance. We recommend that you consult your insurance advisor or a third-party benefits consultant for assistance.

The Process of Designing Your Plan

It is critically important for you to link your compensation plans to your benefit plans when undertaking the design of a new plan. Compensation and benefits are most effective when woven together as a seamless whole. In this way, you can create the opportunity to drive the type of executive behavior and performance that reflects your commitment to Best Practices, as well as drive your bottom line.

Build a Strategy

As important as it is to tie compensation and benefits together, it is essential to tie the benefits plan to the overall strategic direction of your company. You can create the right strategic framework by developing answers to some key questions below:

- What type of behavior or performance do you want to reward in the company?
- How long is your business horizon? What must happen for the business plan to succeed?
- What is your competitive posture in the marketplace?
- Is your market leadership built on the contributions of a handful of senior managers?
- Are you in an emerging market with an immediate need to attract top talent?
- Are you in a mature market where new generations of leadership are not being cultivated?

Once you gain perspective from this exercise, communicate the information as effectively as possible with all stakeholders and solicit honest feedback. At this point, you can develop a well-reasoned strategy. It is also urged that you to create a clear process before you ever begin to design your plan. Also, strive to incorporate Best Practices in plan design under the guidelines discussed above. By making a commitment to these standards, you will create a powerful solution to the recruit-reward-retain challenge.

Consult the Experts

As you move forward in your benefits project, you will quickly discover that a clear understanding of the tax, legal and financial implications of the plan can minimize potential problems. You may wish to consult key advisors in these areas—early and often. Finally, it is advisable to build in sufficient flexibility to allow your company to adapt to the inevitability of business change.

Build a Team

Before you focus on the specific steps recommended for a DCP, decide who within your company should be involved in the design process. Consider establishing a project study group comprised of representatives from human resources, legal, tax and finance.

Seven Steps to Sound Plan Design

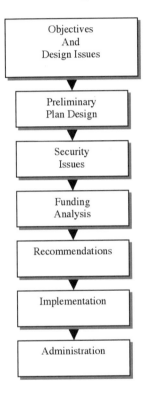

Step 1. Discuss Objectives and Design Issues

It is essential that you begin the process of designing your DCP with a comprehensive understanding of the current objectives for your benefits program, from the perspective of the company and executives. Conduct a series of executive interviews to learn their opinions. Consult your newly-formed project study group to gather and formalize feedback.

We also recommend that you review and discuss the prevalence of data surrounding current trends on benefit plans. It is always helpful to understand how other companies have benefited from sound plan design.

Step 2. Preliminary Plan Design

Determine the structure of your plan by deciding on eligibility, benefit rates, distribution options and benefit security. Set aside ample time to analyze the financial impact of the benefits plan on the corporation, taking into account the impact on other employer-provided benefits.

Step 3. Benefit Security Issues

To secure the benefits of a DCP, you must first determine the type and level of protection that is needed. Then, carefully analyze the wide range of security vehicles available to you and settle on the most appropriate solution.

Step 4. Funding Analysis

The best way to undertake your funding analysis is to analyze a variety of funding approaches. Then, look at the efficiency of each approach by concentrating on a range of rates of return, your company's current tax rate and discount rates. Finally, give careful consideration to the financial impact of your funding analysis. For example, review each approach with an eye towards cash flow, net present value and internal rate of return. Separately, look at the impact of your funding approach of the company's profit and loss statement and balance sheet.

Step 5. Develop and Process Recommendations

It is time to develop specific recommendations on next steps. First, prepare a final report outlining your recommendations. Then, prepare a Board of Directors overview and, if desired, make your Board presentation.

Step 6. Implementation

Once you are comfortable that conditions have been met for the right time for you to implement your plan, you are ready to do some of the more basic work of plan building. Create specimen documents and prepare and provide enrollment materials to participants. Finally, plan to conduct enrollment meetings, either onsite, by teleconference, or in personal phone calls.

Step 7. Administration

Administration is one of the most important aspects in the plan process, and precise record keeping is crucial. It is advisable that you establish account teams, comprised of an account manager, a benefit analyst and a financial analyst.

We also suggest you meticulously monitor legislative and regulatory issues that could eventually affect the plan. Many corporations have found that it is more efficient and cost-effective to outsource plan administration to an expert third-party benefits consultant. Experience has shown that in-house administration of benefits plans, is time-consuming and expensive.

Third-Party Outsourcing

Before you implement your DCP, you should evaluate whether you wish to administer your plan internally or outsource this function to a third party. There are a number of factors to consider. You may already have a plan in place and simply want to evaluate any cost-savings to be derived from outsourcing. Three areas against which to measure the need for outsourcing as an alternative to internal plan administration are economics, complexity, and your department's visibility within the corporation.

Economics

Due to corporate downsizing, many companies have fewer human resources and accounting executives on staff to handle the increased workloads associated with implementing and administering a new benefits plan. Often, an outside consultant will cost less than a full-time employee. Corporations will often realize quick and immediate savings when they outsource plan administration.

Complexity

By their nature, DCPs are highly complex and require special attention. Many companies are relieved to turn the administration function over to outside benefits specialists who are intimately familiar with complex DCPs.

Visibility

Benefits plans are highly visible in corporations, especially with participating executives. They often demand a great deal of attention. Many human resources and finance practitioners have turned to outsourcing to elevate their perception in the company, and to help preserve crucial internal relationships.

Conclusion

From an insider's perspective, we've witnessed all types of benefit plans in our corporate consulting engagements. Some work well, while others do not. Often, the plans that do not "measure up" were not well thought out in the first place. We encourage you to plan ahead and constantly improve. From the outset of plan design, try to create an environment that supports continuous plan improvement.

You can ensure continuous plan improvement by instituting a few straightforward guidelines.

• Develop a sound strategy that supports your overall corporate objectives

- Design a comprehensive and cost-effective benefit plan from the outset
- Always do sound financial modeling in preparing any analyses
- Coordinate with other corporate benefits programs
- Use technology to enhance programs
- Set up an early warning system to track economic cycles

As companies improve their ability to recruit, reward and retain senior talent to lead and manage, everyone benefits. Corporate vision and values are heightened. Best of all, corporate performance and longevity are enhanced. That is why your work as a human resources practitioner contributes significantly to the vitality and future of your company.

Endnotes

1. This chapter does not address supplemental plans, commonly called Supplemental Executive Retirement Plans (SERPs), which are essentially a form of supplemental defined benefit pension plan that is paid for with "employer money."

2. In fact, qualified plans can sometimes have the unintended consequence of encouraging executives to leave. Qualified plans such as 401(k) plans are generally fully-portable following separation from service, and as such, can be rolled over into an Individual Retirement Account (IRA) without adverse tax consequences.

3. The 401(k) anti-discrimination rules may further reduce the amounts that can be contributed to a 401(k) plan by highly compensated individuals.

4. The IRS has made it clear that the executive and not the employer must pay all premiums on the surety bond or indemnity insurance policy. Otherwise the plan would be considered "funded" for purposes of ERISA. To avoid current taxation of the deferred benefits, participants must ensure that: 1) the policy is obtained solely by the executive (the employer should not be involved in the transaction); 2) the executive pays all the premiums; 3) and, premium payments are not deducted by the employee.

Practice aids found on the CD for this chapter*:

- Prototype Plan Document
- Safe Harbor Rabbi Trust

*The sample documents for this chapter are supplied by the Publisher and do not represent work product of either Clark Consulting or Retirement Capital Group. If legal advice or other expert assistance is required, the services of a competent professional should be sought.

WILLIAM L. MACDONALD
President, Chief Executive Officer, and Chairman
Retirement Capital Group
San Diego, California

For nearly two decades, William L. MacDonald has been involved in the design and implementation of a wide range of compensation and executive benefits plans for large, publicly and privately held companies. His professional credentials include founder and director of the Merrill Lynch Executive Compensation Division. In 1978, Bill founded Compensation Resource Group, Inc., an executive compensation and benefits consulting firm. For nearly 20 years, Compensation Resource Group, Inc. consulted with Fortune 1000 and large public and private corporations to provide executive compensation and benefit programs that minimized impact on company profits while providing optimal benefits for key personnel.

Compensation Resource Group grew rapidly from a single office in the Los Angeles area to 10 offices across the money center cities in the United States. In September of 2000, Clark/Bardes Consulting, a New York Stock Exchange company, acquired Compensation Resource Group with Bill serving as Chief Executive Officer and then Chairman of the Executive Benefits Practice of Clark/Bardes Consulting until April 2003. Through his current position with Retirement Capital Group, Bill is leading the company in delivering a Total Retirement Solution using a consultative, unbundled process geared toward best solutions and best practices for plan design, plan funding, communication and administration. In addition to serving the needs of the largest companies in America, Retirement Capital Group also serves small and middle market companies through its many endorsed marketing partnerships with leading professional and trade associations.

KEVIN M. WERNICK
Senior Vice President
Clark Consulting

Kevin M. Wernick is a Senior Vice President of Clark Consulting's Executive Benefits Practice. He works with large public and private corporations to design, fund, implement and administer cutting-edge nonqualified executive benefit plans, which corporations use to attract, retain and motivate executive talent.

Prior to joining Clark Consulting, Mr. Wernick was an attorney with the law firm of O'Melveny & Myers LLP where he specialized in labor, employment and employee benefits law.

Mr. Wernick graduated with honors from Stanford University with a degree in political science. He is also a graduate of the UCLA School of Law where he was a member of the Order of the Coif.

8. THE IMPACT OF RECENT CORPORATE GOVERNANCE CHANGES ON EXECUTIVE COMPENSATION

An executive compensation reference work would be incomplete today without a review and discussion of current and anticipated changes in corporate governance. There is general agreement that too many key governance processes and activities have been handled with insufficient formality in the past–not necessarily causing, but allowing for abuse, and in some cases leading to fraud.

The context for this chapter is drawn largely from three important new sources of regulation and guidance: the Sarbanes-Oxley Act of 2002, and the proposed New York Stock Exchange and NASDAQ listing standards (still largely under review by the SEC). The authors begin by identifying the areas most likely to change in corporate governance, including strengthening the role of the board, redefining what it means to be an independent director, and giving shareholders a more direct say in a larger number of governance activities. These change areas logically impact how directors are selected and how they do their work. The chapter also details a number of suggested and/or mandated changes involving areas such as director qualification criteria, annual performance evaluations, and committee charters.

The reader will see this information as fitting into the executive compensation context in two important ways. First, there are a number of specific executive compensation rule changes or prohibitions including a prohibition on most executive loans and an acceleration in SEC reporting for certain executive compensation actions. Additional changes are possibly forthcoming related to deferred compensation, stock, and certain retirement plans. Second, the executive compensation professional must work together with other professionals from the law, audit, tax and compliance groups to establish a stronger set of processes and cross-checks to minimize or eliminate the potential for possible malfeasance.

Corporate governance will continue to change in the years ahead. The compensation professional must fully embrace and understand these changes if they are to be effective in the design and administration of the company's executive compensation programs.
–Editors

Introduction

MUCH HAS BEEN WRITTEN about the abuse of rogue companies and their executives in the late 1990s and into the new millenium. What this behavior spawned was an encompassing reaction from legislators and regulators aimed at preventing such abuse from re-occurring. The result: new standards for publicly traded companies and how they govern themselves.

The impact of these developments has posed new challenges for the compensation professional. We in the field of executive pay are expected to help ensure that these new standards are upheld and in the process, we must be more familiar with new regulations and reporting requirements in order to do our jobs more effectively. With the passage of The Sarbanes-Oxley Act of 2002 and the changes in the listing standards of The New York Stock Exchange and the NASDAQ Stock Market, we are being asked to share the task for responsible governance with corporate colleagues in other parts of the company; e.g., legal, tax and audit functions.

This chapter is intended to help the compensation professional become more familiar with the salient points of these recent developments and to offer some hopefully useful suggestions on how to respond to them in the workplace. This is by no means the final word on all that is happening. Things will continue to evolve and those taking on a governance role are well advised to stay up to date as regulations unfold. One could not address each major topic and stay within reasonable limits for a reference text. In the appendix are some suggestions for further reading and research among law firms, web sites and other published material.

The reader will find sections devoted to important changes regarding the role and responsibility of the independent director; important elements of corporate governance for directors; the application and practice of principles of good governance; and lastly, an approach that is getting renewed attention among a number of companies that strengthens the link between executive behavior and shareholder interests.

Emergence of Corporate Governance Standards

The three primary sources of minimum corporate governance standards with which we should be familiar are:

- **The Sarbanes-Oxley Act of 2002.** The Act was signed on July 30, 2002 with certain provisions effective on various dates. The Securities and Exchange Commission ("SEC") is to issue regulations over time that will clarify certain parts of the Act in addition to enforcing its provisions.

It includes several governance-related provisions; new corporate disclosure requirements, requirements regarding external auditors and audit committees, and securities law enforcement measures.

- The SEC approved the New York Stock Exchange and NASDAQ listing requirements on November 4, 2003 which create a wide-ranging set of corporate governance standards, supplementing those each already established. For U.S. listed companies, compliance with the rules is generally required by the first annual meeting after January 15, 2004, but not later than October 31, 2004.

Important Changes in Corporate Governance

Those involved in re-shaping the standards of good governance have done so in order to protect the integrity and credibility of our economic system. The logical place to start was with the Board of Directors of publicly traded companies by strengthening their role.

Directors are always expected to be diligent in overseeing management and to act with the highest ethical standards. To be fair, there are already many outside directors who are diligent in their roles of protecting shareholder interests and who are actively and fully-engaged in the work of good governance.

Shareholders should expect to benefit from these changes as well. They should more easily understand financial statements and other performance indicators, enabling them to better monitor the behavior and performance of board members and executives while ensuring adherence to high ethical standards.

That said, we could expect to see some immediate changes in governance while others will evolve over time. The changes address:

Stronger Role and Authority of Outside Directors

The New York Stock Exchange and The NASDAQ Stock Market require that a majority of the board be composed of outside or "independent" directors; meaning that most of those who sit on a company's board are to provide an objective view on all important corporate matters.

To encourage objectivity and to ensure that management acts with the best interests of shareholders in mind, directors are to have *regular executive sessions without the participation of the CEO and other internal high-ranking executives of the company.*

Furthermore, companies are being encouraged to have committees, composed exclusively of outside directors. These might include an audit committee, a nominating committee and a compensation committee. All members of the audit committee are required to have accounting familiarity. The Company must disclose that it has at least one member who is an audit committee financial expert and if it does not have one, to explain why not.

The audit committee (*not management*) must have the sole authority to hire and fire the company's independent auditors and to approve any significant non-audit or consulting work performed by the outside auditors.

Redefining the "Independent Director"

For a director to be truly independent, he/she cannot have *a material relationship* with the company, meaning they will neither gain nor lose anything significant if a company follows a particular course of action.

The idea of a "cooling off" period–a specific period of time which must lapse before a former executive can join the board–has been adopted by both the NYSE and NASDAQ. The same applies to employees of the auditors of the company. For NYSE and NASDAQ listed companies the period is three years.

The *sole source of compensation* for an audit committee member must be director's fees and any committee member having a close association with a major shareholder–defined as someone owning 20% or more of the company's equity–*may not vote* in audit committee proceedings.

Focusing on Good Governance

Although many companies could claim to have practiced good governance before these developments occurred, focusing on good governance today means having in place formal policies and procedures. This includes *adopting corporate governance guidelines; having written charters for the audit, nominating and compensation committees; and adopting a code of business conduct and ethics* and then making these materials available to employees and shareholders.

For companies priding themselves on being entrepreneurial, this may be viewed as creating unnecessary bureaucracy. Constituents, however, will expect nothing less than sensible governing practices from their boards of directors.

Shareholder Participation in Governance

Several requirements are either in place or are being put in place enabling shareholders to have a greater opportunity to participate in good governance. They must be given a chance to vote on all equity-based compensation programs. This will require management to be more judicious in seeking shareholder approval to use company stock and will spell the end of "evergreen plans," whereby a certain percentage of shares outstanding becomes available annually for equity compensation awards.

Stockbrokers lose their discretion to vote on corporate proposals and must now do so in accordance with the *instructions of their customers.*

Codes of conduct and committee charters as mentioned earlier must be published and made available to shareholders and *waivers to such codes of conduct must be promptly disclosed.*

New Mechanisms for Control and Enforcement

CEOs must certify annually that the company has established and complied with procedures that verify the accuracy and completeness of information released to investors. The CEO must further certify that he/she reviewed those procedures with the board.

To impress upon management the seriousness of these measures both the NYSE and the NASDAQ have final recourse in the form of de-listing a company that fails to comply with them.

Implications of Governance for Directors

To ensure that directors are effective and to minimize passivity as cronies of top management, there are several important developments that have significant implications for those desiring to serve on the board.

1. **Qualification Standards**–Board members should embrace practical, sensible standards of independence. Individuals who are qualified, capable people with strong credentials and demonstrated track records of accomplishment should populate boards. In evaluating the number of directors among other things, a company should consider how much time a potential director has by limiting the number of boards on which a director may sit so that he/she is not "spread too thin." Other areas covered by such policies should include director tenure, retirement and succession.

2. **Director Responsibilities**–Board members ought to know up front what will be expected from them, including basic duties and responsibilities with respect to meeting attendance and advance review of meeting materials. Directors should be prepared for discussion of issues and should be fully engaged at these meetings.

3. **Director Compensation**–Guidelines and policies should clearly address the form and amount of director compensation. Compensation should be

"in line" with the pay for directors at peer companies. Shareholders are likely to look askance at pay practices that deviate from the norm for a particular industry. Consulting contracts entered into with a director need to be done very selectively and reviewed by the audit committee. The terms of the contract should be disclosed to shareholders in order to avoid the appearance of any impropriety.

4. **Managerial Succession**–The directors are responsible for succession planning of the CEO and other senior executives in the company. Policies and principles should exist for CEO selection, performance evaluation and succession in the event of an emergency or retirement.

5. **Annual Performance Evaluation**–An evaluation process should be adopted by the board enabling it to effectively evaluate *its own* performance. While self-evaluation is always a challenge, companies who follow such processes are promoting excellence in the companies they serve and militate against tenure based primarily upon personal friendships.

6. **Orientation and Continuing Education**–When a new director comes aboard, companies might consider providing that individual with an *information packet* covering meetings of the board, contact information, committees of the board, compensation for outside directors, regulatory overview and Section 16 of the Securities Exchange Act. It also ought to include director's duties, liability coverage, affiliations and U.S. Tax Requirements. While directors may be responsible for their own continuing education in order to stay current on business developments in the company's industry, under the NYSE Listing Standards, companies would also be expected to assist in on-going educational activities. The NYSE Corporate Accountability and Listing Standards Committee has recommended that the Exchange enhance its support of continuing education programs for directors at Duke, Stanford and New York Universities. Other resources might include the American Bar Association, the Investor Responsibility Research Center and the National Association of Corporate Directors.

7. **Management Access**–Although a balance should be struck between being overly conscientious and too distant from the company's daily operations, directors should have access to management as appropriate. Site visits when planned properly can be a useful way of gaining insight into the company, fostering a deeper understanding and appreciation for the business and the environment in which it operates.

Key Elements of Corporate Governance

Director Qualifications Standards	Embrace standards of independance. Develop policies limiting number of boards on which director may sit, and retirement and succession.
Director Responsibilities	Clearly articulate what is expected from a director, including basic duties and responsibilities with respect to meeting attendance and advance reviews of meeting materials.
Director Compensation	Should address form and amount of compensation. Should be reasonable and customary. Concerns may be raised over substantial charitable contributions to director-affiliated organizations and consulting contracts entered into with a director.
Managerial Succession	Succession planning should include policies and principles for CEO selection, performance evaluation and succession in the event of an emergency or retirement.
Annual Performance Evaluation	Board should conduct annual self-evaluation to determine its effectiveness and that of its committees.
Other	Director access to management and as necessary and appropriate, independent auditors. Director orientation and continuing education.

Application of Good Governance Principles

To keep track of what is required and when, here are a few suggestions enabling you to be prepared for these developments:

Relevant Listing Requirements

Be sure that you as a compensation professional have some basic familiarity with the relevant listing requirements of the exchange on which your stock is listed.

Board Committees

There should be at least three committees composed entirely of independent directors. Those committees are the audit committee, the nomination committee and the compensation committee. This does not apply to controlled companies which are not required to have a nominating committee.

Formal Charters

Each committee is required to have a written charter delineating its roles and responsibilities and key duties.

Annual Performance Evaluation

Each committee is to develop a process that enables the members to evaluate the performance of the committee at least annually, with the results of that evaluation being discussed with full board of directors.

Board Committee Checklist

Committee	Formal Charter	Annual Performance Evaluation	Key Duties
Nomination & Governance	Yes	Yes	Identify qualified candidates to serve on the Board.
			Select or recommend to Board, director nominees for next annual meeting of shareholders.
			Develop and recommend a set of Corporate Governance Principles.
			Maintain oversight of evaluation of the performance of the Board and Management.
			Has the right to retain and terminate any search firm used to identify board candidates including approval of search fees and other terms.
Compensation	Yes	Yes	Discharge responsibility of Board relating to compensation.
			Produce and approve corporate goals relevant to CEO compensation.
			Set CEO compensation in light of performance vs. goals.
			Recommend to Board incentive compensation plans and equity-based plans.
			Has the right to retain, terminate, determine terms of compensation consultant to evaluate director, CEO and executive compensation.
Audit	Yes	Yes	Integrity of company's financial statements.
			Comparing compliance with legal and regulatory requirements.
			Independent auditor qualifications and independence.
			Performance of company's internal audit function and independent auditors.
			Prepare report for annual proxy statement as required by SEC rules.
			Retain and terminate company's internal auditor.
			Annual review of independent auditor report on internal quality control processes.
			Address material issues raised through auditor process or any inquiry or investigation by governmental or professional authorities, within preceding five years and steps taken to deal with such issues.
			Discuss annual and quarterly audited financial statements with management.
			Discuss earnings press releases.
			Discuss policies and procedures pertaining to risk and risk management.
			Meet separately, at least quarterly, with management, internal auditors and independent auditors.
			Set clear hiring policies for employees or former employees of independent auditors.
			Report regularly to the Board.

Plus: new requirements added to enhance independence:
1. Director's fees only compensation audit committee member may receive.
2. If director holds 20% or more of company stock, cannot chair or be voting member of Audit Committee.
3. All audit committee members should have some familiarity with financial management.

Impact on Executive Compensation Administration

Prohibitions on Loans

Under the Sarbanes-Oxley Act of 2002 companies may not make personal loans to their directors or to covered executives, other than certain consumer credit arrangements such as mortgages or credit cards. If such loans under the Act are made, the terms and conditions of the loans must be the same as those offered to the general public.

Stock Option Exercises

This provision has become problematic for executives covered under the act with respect to the exercise of stock options involving a sell-to-cover or same-day-sale. In both transactions, the company acts on behalf of the executive to avoid the executive having to pay out any cash to do the exercise. Under the Act this has been interpreted to be a "loan" by the company to the executive and is therefore, prohibited.

The executive is permitted to arrange financing through a third party, be it a bank or stock broker, and complete the same-day-sale or sell-to-cover with them. The executive compensation unit may not recommend which third party the executive should use but can provide a list of several alternative companies that can provide this service.

While this complies with the Act, it adds a cost to the executive that he/she may not have had to bear in the past. The executive will pay interest on the loan and brokerage fees on the sale of shares. Since executive stock option grants tend to be large, the associated cost can be considerable. It is also more cumbersome to administer, not to mention time-consuming to coordinate given that arrangements must be made in advance. Additionally the executive may be subject to a company policy on personal trading, yet another but understandably valid hurdle in what had been a routine transaction.

Effects on Margin Accounts

Executives covered under the Act who have margin accounts at brokerage firms must ensure that their outstanding balance is not above what it was when the Act was passed on July 30, 2002. Any loans exceeding their margin balance at the time the Act was passed are required to pay down the loan in order to be in compliance with the law.

Exceptions to this provision of the Act are employees of broker-dealers that can make such loans to employees provided that margin loans are not used by employees to carry company stock.

Others types of stock option exercise such as cash purchase, SWAP or reload are permitted under Sarbanes-Oxley.

Accelerated Reporting to SEC

Another provision of the Act requires directors and officers (and owners of

10% or more of a class of company stock) to file a statement (completed on a Form 4) with the Securities and Exchange Commission within two business days of an event in which beneficial ownership changes. Examples include a sale, purchase or gift of company shares. Prior to the passage of Sarbanes-Oxley this report was allowed to be done on a monthly basis.

Sharing Responsibility for Compliance

Companies, particularly large and diverse ones, desiring to comply with applicable regulations dealing with executive compensation will be best served by a "corporate governance team" approach. Those individuals charged with ensuring that their companies adhere to good governance, will find themselves more dependent upon other professionals–Tax, Audit, General Counsel, HR/Compensation–in getting their jobs done.

There needs to be a defined process with clear roles and responsibilities dealing with stock option exercises. Everyone should understand their role in the transaction from the time the executive calls the executive compensation unit, through clearance for the trade with legal and compliance, to the broker or bank involved, to settlement of shares or cash in the executive's brokerage account.

Establish Processes that Support Good Governance

The governance team–and there has to be an accent on the word team–needs to establish *internal processes* that work best for their company and will effectively monitor all insiders (as defined by Section 16 of the Securities and Exchange Act).

THE CORPORATE GOVERNANCE TEAM

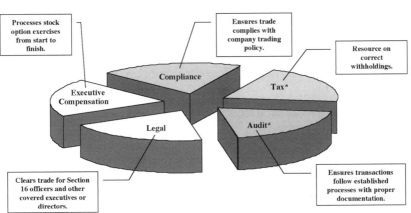

Processes stock option exercises from start to finish.

Ensures trade complies with company trading policy.

Resource on correct withholdings.

Compliance

Tax*

Executive Compensation

Legal

Audit*

Clears trade for Section 16 officers and other covered executives or directors.

Ensures transactions follow established processes with proper documentation.

*Amount of time and involvement will vary with each issue.

This may mean doing a work flow analysis for each type of transaction so that responsibilities are clear.

Some ideas to consider are:

- **Circulate worksheets** on a regular and frequent basis outlining insider transactions and requesting feedback from each team member on its content. This might include stock option exercises, planned sales for balancing one's portfolio or planned giving to an institution or charity.

- Use whatever means of communication is available internally such as e-mail to **keep everyone in the loop.** This should extend to any outsourced activities such as 401(k) plan administrators where such plans involve company shares as an investment alternative. Activities involving company stock in 401(k) accounts are also subject to reporting requirements.

- **Have a game plan in place for major** *vesting events* such as a wide-reaching grant of stock options or restricted stock that affects insiders and covered executives under S-O.

- **Meet periodically with the governance team** to asses and improve upon internal processes, raise issues or to keep each other informed of any important changes among board members, senior executives or regulatory and compliance issues.

- **Develop a regular schedule to prepare for upcoming meetings of the compensation committee.** This can include the committee's meetings for the year and what key items will be covered during those meetings. This will enable sufficient time and attention to be spent anticipating issues and preparing those executives who interact with the chair of the committee and other members.

- **Track share usage for equity compensation plans.** This is a critical activity especially for companies that are large users of equity plans to monitor their "run rate." Such reports should be circulated within the executive compensation unit as well as to other corporate functions as and when appropriate to ensure that share usage is being managed, and minimizing the need to ask shareholders for authorization of additional shares.

Ethical Behavior and Shareholder Interests– An Inseparable Link

Much has been written and debated about the effectiveness of equity-based compensation plans that link the interests of executives with those of their shareholders. In some companies, executive ownership and indeed employee ownership, is ingrained in their culture. They stress the importance of creating shareholder value over time and discourage the mentality of cashing-out their stock at the first opportunity.

We are dealing with the aftermath of a small percentage of irresponsible individuals who falsified financial information about the performance of their companies, inflated the stock price and then cashed out when the price was high by dumping millions of shares on the market through the same-day-sales of stock options. Something was clearly missing in the ethical link between these individuals, their employees and their shareholders not to mention that it also badly tarnished a major executive compensation program.

What would have happened if these individuals were prohibited from dumping their shares? While we'll never know the answer to this question, we do know that for companies who've adopted an ownership commitment prohibiting "cashing out," this could never have happened. In some organizations this commitment is so strong that it is referred to in metaphorical terms!

While not an entirely new idea, stock ownership commitments are getting another look in the wake of Enron, Worldcom and Tyco. The concept of an ownership commitment is very easy.

For as long as someone is in an executive position, they are required to hold a minimum number of shares of their company's stock. Knowing that potentially a substantial portion of their net worth is tied up in the company reinforces a type of behavior that reduces focus on the short run and encourages them to build sustainable shareholder value over time–strengthening the link between the executive and the investor.

Some companies choose to make this ownership requirement a multiple of cash compensation while others simply set a minimum share holding requirement tied to total cash pay. In at least one company, the minimum is actually a moving target where the minimum continues to rise each time an executives receives more shares through an established equity compensation program. Whatever the approach, the importance of establishing such a plan is key.

Establishing such a program can be difficult at first, especially where there has been no commitment to ownership at the top of the company. Over time however, shareholders and interest groups will look favorably upon those companies who recognize the importance of not only talking about linking the interests of the executive with the shareholder but actually using programs like this one to do it.

Practice aids found on the CD for this chapter:

• Directors Form 4 Worksheet
• Officers Form 4 Worksheet

Reference Materials

Web sites:

AICPA: http://www.aicpa.org/info/sarbanes_oxley_summary.htm

American Society of Corporate Secretaries: http://www.ascs.org/

Institutional Shareholder Services: http://www.issproxy.com/

NASDAQ Stock Market: http://www.nasdaq.com/

Skadden, Arps, Slate, Meagher and Flom: http://www.sasmf.com/intro.html

The New York Stock Exchange: http://www.nyse.com/

U.S. Securities and Exchange Commission Homepage: http://www.sec.gov/

Wachtell, Lipton, Rosen and Katz: http://www.wlrk.com/index.cfm

Weil, Gotshal and Manges: http://www.weil.com/weil/index.html

ANTHONY K. FARINA
Director–Executive Compensation
Citigroup, Inc.

Anthony K. Farina is currently Director-Executive Compensation for Citigroup, Inc. His responsibilities include managing compensation for the top 200 executives and for the company's board of directors. He is responsible for Citigroup's Stock Ownership Commitment, and manages the annual incentive and management equity award process company-wide. His unit provides staff support to the Personnel and Compensation Committee of the Board and he serves as a member of an internal governance team including representatives from the law and tax departments.

Previously Mr. Farina was compensation director for Citibank's corporate banking business for North America, Western Europe and Japan.

Prior to joining Citigroup, he was a consultant with Organization Resources Counselors, Inc. and held human resources positions with predecessor companies of JPMorganChase & Co. and with American Express. While primarily based in New York, he has held positions that served Europe, Asia and Latin America. For a time he was based in Singapore covering the Pacific Rim for American Express.

In addition to his corporate experience, he has lectured at several universities including New York University, and has been a guest speaker at WorldatWork.

CYNTHIA LENKIEWICZ
Associate General Counsel and Assistant Secretary
Citigroup, Inc.

Cynthia Lenkiewicz is currently Associate General Counsel for Corporate Governance and Assistant Secretary of Citigroup, Inc. Prior to joining Citigroup in 1985 she held legal positions with Zurich Financial Services Group and Home Insurance Company. She began her legal career as a Corporate Associate at the law firm of Skadden, Arps, Slate, Meagher and Flom.

She received her undergraduate degree in accounting, *magna cum laude*, from Ithaca College and her J.D. from the Law School of State University of New York at Buffalo, also *magna cum laude*. She was admitted to the Bar in New York in 1986 and is a member of the American Society of Corporate Secretaries.

9. The Role and Functioning of the Compensation Committee

Harry Truman's desktop placard "The Buck Stops Here" applies very appropriately to the compensation committee on matters of executive compensation for the CEO and other senior executives. While management and external experts, such as consultants, attorneys and governance groups, play important roles in shaping executive compensation, it is the compensation committee that renders the final judgments and makes the final decisions on all the key items of a company's executive compensation program.

This chapter explores the unique and important role played by compensation committees at most publicly held companies. The chapter first describes the typical responsibilities for the compensation committee, what a committee calendar might look like over a typical year, how meetings are formatted and organized, and the use of an outside consultant. To give readers a good idea of how these structural issues can vary from committee to committee, the author first describes each topic in general and then explains how each might be handled in three different hypothetical company settings– a high growth successful company, a troubled technology company, and a traditional manufacturer.

The chapter then describes a number of areas requiring the committees attention including setting an overall compensation philosophy, making compensation decisions for the CEO and other senior executives, setting stock ownership objectives, determining compensation for the board itself, and monitoring deferred compensation. The author again uses the three companies to show how compensation committees, faced with the same issue but within different settings, reach appropriately different conclusions as a result. Lastly, the chapter focuses on three special issues that may arise for a compensation committee–the need to create one or more employment agreements, the question of repricing (canceling and reissuing) stock options, and the need to determine a compensation package for a new CEO. –Editors

A DISCUSSION OF EXECUTIVE COMPENSATION would be incomplete without also discussing the role of the board compensation committee. Management, outside consultants, and/or other experts all play a key role in developing the executive compensation program. It is, however, the board compensation committee that makes the final judgments and renders the final decisions for virtually all matters related to the compensation of the Chief Executive Officer (CEO) and the company's other senior executives, and it is here where everything comes together for a company's executive compensation program.

While the general functions of the compensation committee are the same today as they've been for years, how the committee operates is in the midst of dramatic change. As a result of new regulations (e.g., NYSE listing requirements), new legislation (e.g., Sarbanes-Oxley), corporate scandals and heightened focus on executive pay, compensation committees are more engaged in the process of managing executive pay than ever before. This engagement is reflected in such areas as how the committee works with management, the hiring of outside advisors, and the frequency of executive sessions. This sea change will have implications for committee-management relations for years to come.

To many observers, the job should be straightforward: Keep fixed elements of pay conservatively competitive, make sure incentive pay is motivating and reasonable in light of company performance, provide equity-based grants large enough to motivate performance but not so big to unjustly enrich, keep a watchful eye on perquisites and other executive benefits, and make sure everything is clearly disclosed in the annual proxy statement. How difficult could that be?

As executive compensation practitioners and compensation committee members know, however, it is rarely that straightforward. To bring the complexities of the committee's work to light, we will examine the role and duties of the compensation committee from the perspective of three very different companies and their respective compensation committees.

A Brief Profile of Our Three Companies

In our first scenario, you are on the compensation committee of HIGROW Corporation. The good news for you and HIGROW shareholders is that everything appears to be going right. The company is growing strongly, profits beat expectations year after year, and the company's stock price has been moving consistently upward. The company is aggressively adding staff and expanding to meet increasing demand for its products. It is clear that this is a success story and that senior management has been integral to that success. Because everything has been going so well, senior management has been well-rewarded through the company's variable pay plans and stock option grants.

In our second scenario, you are on the compensation committee of TECHCO Corporation. There isn't a lot of good news for TECHCO shareholders or employees. In recent years, TECHCO, like other companies in this market segment, has been hammered. While the company has survived and is well positioned for recovery, the company is a shadow of its former self. TECHCO's stock price is 75% below its peak and has 50% fewer employees than it did four years ago. Nevertheless, industry analysts consider this management team to be among the best in the business. But because everything has been so rough, the CEO and others in senior management have seen their company-related wealth all but evaporate and cash compensation levels have been significantly reduced over the last few years.

In our third and final scenario, you are on the compensation committee of MAKEITCO Inc. MAKEITCO is a diversified manufacturer and has grown through a series of targeted acquisitions. The company is conservatively managed, and prides itself on a long history of strong financial performance and growth. MAKEITCO's financial and stock performance has outperformed its peers, but the stock price has been fairly flat over the past few years. The CEO and other senior executives have had good incentive payouts in recent years reflective of company performance, but the flat stock price has kept recent stock option grants valueless.

The Compensation Committee

The Securities and Exchange Commission (SEC) mandates that all New York Stock Exchange (NYSE)-listed companies have a compensation committee (see www.nyse.com for full information on the NYSE's governance standards); as a practical matter, virtually all publicly held companies now have such a committee. The committee, usually comprised of 4–6 independent outside directors, typically has the responsibility for setting and/or approving the company's executive compensation philosophy, approving executive compensation program design, and approving all compensation actions for the Chief Executive Officer and other key senior executives.

Like other board committees, the compensation committee usually meets in conjunction (and just before) the full board meeting so that it can report the results of its meeting to the full board as needed, or gain full board ratification of certain actions if required. The committee usually has a chairman, who runs the committee meetings, works with management to set the agenda for meetings, and reports committee meeting results to the full board.

While those aspects are the norm, it is common to see significant variation from company to company as to the number of times the committee meets, the number of directors on the committee, and the specific duties assigned to the committee. Reflective of that, the compensation committees for our three companies are structured somewhat differently from one another as well.

At HIGROW, the committee is comprised of five board members–two are CEOs of other companies, two are retired executives, and one is a college professor from a well-known university. HIGROW's compensation committee also serves as the nominating committee.

At TECHCO, the committee is comprised of four board members. All four board members are executives at other companies including one, who is the head of human resources at her company. TECHCO's board thought it was important to have an experienced HR executive on the board and on the compensation committee. One director lives and works in Canada where TECHCO has a substantial business presence.

Lastly at MAKEITCO, the company decided long ago to have virtually all of the company's outside directors serve on the compensation committee. This puts eight directors on the committee, which is larger than normal. Four of the directors are employed with other companies, three are retired executives, and one is a retired politician. Two of the directors joined MAKEITCO's board from the board of a recently acquired company.

Responsibilities of the Committee

The NYSE now mandates that all NYSE-listed companies have a written charter that details the committee's purpose and responsibilities. Many believe the compensation committee's most important job is to set or approve the overall executive compensation philosophy. This typically includes setting clear guidance for the mix of executive pay, the key performance measures that will drive annual and longer-term incentive compensation, the performance standards that go along with the measures, and the targeted competitiveness of each component of the program and the program as a whole.

Publicly held companies are also required to publish an annual compensation committee report to shareholders that is included in the company proxy statement. This special report, which is issued over the names of the committee members, spells out the company's executive compensation philosophy, a description of the various elements of executive pay, and a description and rationale for all pay administration actions that impact the CEO. This disclosure also includes a number of tables that must be prepared in a standard format, detailing the compensation for the CEO and the next four most highly paid senior executives.

Section 162(m) of the Internal Revenue Code requires the compensation committee to approve performance goals at the beginning of an incentive period and to certify the performance and resulting incentive payments at the end of an incentive period. The committee typically also has power of approval over all pay actions impacting the CEO and the other four most highly compensated executives. In addition to these executives, the committee usually has approval over pay actions for all officers comprising the company's senior leadership group as well.

Most stock plans require the compensation committee to approve stock or stock option grants, thereby establishing its ongoing role in the administration of those grants. Similarly, compensation committees generally must review and approve material changes to incentive plans, or the introduction of a new plan, as well as any material changes to executive benefit plans, including separation and change-in-control arrangements.

Management typically handles the work associated with administering the executive compensation program. Compensation committees periodically hire independent compensation consulting firms to audit management's administration of the executive compensation program to ensure that it is being administered in a manner consistent with the stated program philosophy.

Depending on the board governance structure, compensation committees sometimes take on certain duties that would otherwise lie in either the nominating or governance committees. These duties might include reviewing and setting board compensation, leading succession planning for the CEO and other senior leadership positions, handling CEO performance assessment, recruiting new board members, and/or making board committee assignments.

As stated earlier, it is typical for a compensation committee to have a written charter or listing of duties and responsibilities. NYSE-listed companies are required to create and disclose their committee charters to shareholders. Compensation committee charters for most large companies can be found in recent proxy statements, which are publicly available through the SEC's EDGAR (see www.sec.gov for EDGAR access and tutorials) or on the company's website.

In the case of our three companies, all have compensation committees. HIGROW's committee also serves as the nominating committee and, as such, has the oversight for selecting new board members and making board committee assignments. MAKEITCO has a practice of having the full board approve all actions related to the CEO's compensation, and also handles succession planning for the six senior-most positions at the full board level.

The Committee Calendar

Compensation committees typically meet in conjunction with board meetings; some every time there is a board meeting, while others meet with lesser frequency.

Not surprisingly, the committee's calendar is closely linked to the business calendar. For example, incentive plan goals are set at the beginning of a fiscal year, and incentive results are reviewed and approved at the end of a fiscal year. These two activities can be handled at two separate meetings, or at a single meeting shortly after the close of a fiscal year.

Other activities, such as merit increases to base salary, stock option grants, competitive reviews and succession planning discussions aren't tied to a specific date in the business calendar, so these can be set at any time during the calendar year. Some committees prefer to have these activities spread out over the year so that they can put real focus on the discussion and review of each issue. Other committees prefer to have many of the pay-related actions take place all at once so that each pay action can be reviewed and made in context with the other pay actions.

In the end, the timing of the company's fiscal year and the company's desired timing for administering pay actions largely drives the timing of the committee calendar. Most compensation committees meet at least two times each year, with the norm being three or four times per year. Obviously, special situations such as a major merger or acquisition, or the hiring of a new CEO, can lead to the need for additional meetings.

Our three companies handle their committee calendars differently. HIGROW meets three times per year. One meeting focuses on base salary and incentive compensation actions, and the assessment of CEO performance. The second meeting focuses on stock-based compensation and, in its dual role as the nominating committee, reviews board committee assignments for the upcoming year. The third meeting focuses on senior management development and succession and board compensation.

TECHCO has been meeting more frequently over the past few years. The committee normally meets three times per year but is now meeting before every board meeting. The company has lost several of its best executives over the past few years and is worried that it cannot continue to keep the senior leadership team intact given the difficult financial condition of the company and depressed levels of executive compensation. The company has retained an outside consultant to help advise the committee and management on options to address this unusual and troubling situation.

MAKEITCO has always met five times per year. The company prefers to have compensation actions spread out over separate meetings so that each can be examined individually. Specifically, one meeting focuses solely on base salary increases for senior executives, another on setting incentive targets for the upcoming year, the third meeting deals with approving incentive results and payouts for the past year, the fourth handles stock grants, and a final meeting reviews the proxy report, board compensation and, in the year of a compensation program audit, also includes a review of the audit.

Committee Meeting Format and Agenda

Compensation committee meetings are usually held before the board meeting and generally take from one to two hours per meeting. All members of the committee attend the meeting, generally in-person but sometimes by telephone. Also attending are one or more members of management, usually the CEO and the senior human resources executive. Depending on the circumstance a compensation consultant or an attorney might be asked to attend all or some of the meeting as well.

Materials to be discussed at the meeting will have been prepared by management or the consultant/lawyer, and, with increasing regularity, are reviewed with the committee chair prior to the meeting. After this review, the materials are sent to all committee members a week or more in advance of the meeting, so that all will have had a chance to review them ahead of time. Generally the materials are prepared in a pre-approved format—usually consistent with prior meetings—to facilitate both year-to-year comparison and to ensure that they are prepared in a manner that is acceptable to the committee.

The committee chair will run the meeting. Most typically the minutes from the prior meeting are reviewed and approved first. Then the committee chair, someone from management or the consultant/lawyer will present and lead a discussion on each agenda item. At the end of the meeting, it is increasingly common to have an executive session that is run by the committee chair and only includes outside committee members. This gives the committee a chance to discuss, in a private setting, any matter including any issue or action pertaining to the CEO. The committee chair reports on the results of the meeting to the full board, and will also report to management on the executive session discussion as warranted.

HIGROW's compensation committee chair meets with management 6–8 weeks before each committee meeting to review the committee agenda and agree upon what will be discussed at the meeting. HIGROW has just changed its practice over the last year to now include an executive session at the end of each committee meeting.

TECHCO has generally had one-hour committee meetings, but has asked management to structure the schedule so that they can have more time for each meeting. Two times over the past year committee members have traveled in early so that the committee could meet for an extended period the evening before the board meeting.

MAKEITCO's system runs like clockwork. The committee chair reviews the agenda and meeting materials in advance of every meeting. Materials are distributed ten days prior to the meeting. The company has a long-standing practice of holding an executive session following each meeting, at which time committee members discuss the meeting format and agenda and provide input to the committee chair for changes if needed.

Use of a Compensation Consultant

Virtually every compensation committee, at some point, will need to retain the services of an independent compensation consultant. Historically, management and the committee have jointly decided on–and then used–the same consultant. But this is an area of major change, as it is now considered a best practice for the committee to independently select a consultant to advise them as needed. The recently revised NYSE listing requirements now mandate that the committee have sole authority to hire a consultant. In some companies the consultant is allowed to also work with management, while in other companies the committee's consultant is prohibited from doing any work for the company except at the committee's direction.

Consultants are frequently retained to perform periodic, independent assessments of actual and targeted pay levels versus predetermined competitive standards. In these assessments, the consultant will compare the pay for the CEO and other benchmark executive positions versus one or more compensation survey sources to confirm the competitiveness of each pay component and the value of the program overall. It is becoming increasingly common to also factor into the analysis the company's relative performance versus the same comparative group. This gives the committee the ability to guage the competitiveness of the company's actual and targeted compensation levels versus relevant peer company practices. While these studies can be conducted annually, most companies engage such studies only every two to three years.

From time-to-time, consultants are asked to conduct broader reviews which commonly include not only a competitive assessment as discussed above, but also a review of overall program philosophy, plan design, payout/performance relationships in incentive plans, stock dilution and overhang, retention strategies, and an assessment of any executive benefit or perquisite plans. Because most executive compensation and benefit programs do not materially change from year to year, a top-to-bottom rigorous review needn't occur with great frequency.

Consultants may also be involved when management brings forward a proposal to make a change to some element(s) of the executive compensation program. It is increasingly common for the committee to receive an independent review and analysis of the proposed change by its own compensation consultant. This might be handled off-line, with the consultant conducting the independent assessment in advance of the meeting and writing the committee a letter detailing his/her opinion. Alternatively, the consultant might either meet with the committee chair in advance of the meeting, or attend the meeting to participate directly in the discussion.

Consultants may also be retained when the company is going through an unusual change such as a major acquisition or divestiture, or when the company is hiring a new CEO or senior executive externally, or when the company is the target of an attempted takeover.

In select situations, the compensation consultant might attend all or most of the committee meetings in a general advisory capacity, or as needed by the committee.

No matter the situation, the compensation committee's direct use of compensation consultants is on the rise. Many groups, including the Conference Board (www.conference-board.org) and Business Roundtable (www.businessroundtable.org), who have recently studied corporate governance, believe it is a best practice for committee's to have their own consultant, and to make appropriate use of that consultant independent of management.

All three of our companies use compensation consultants, but in different ways. HIGROW's committee recently decided it needed a new consultant with specific expertise in working with high growth companies. After selecting such a consultant, the committee chartered the consultant to work jointly with management and the committee to review all elements of its executive compensation and determine how to best implement the company's overarching pay for performance philosophy in a sustained high growth environment.

TECHCO's committee has periodically received consulting advice from consultants also used by management. As mentioned earlier, the committee retained a consultant to help it think through senior management retention issues in light of its sustained industry downturn and poor company performance. This consultant has attended a number of the special meetings of the committee.

MAKEITCO's committee uses a consultant in a more traditional manner. Its committee uses the consultant primarily for its periodic audit, as previously mentioned, and also asks that they review all program changes (which are infrequent) and to provide the committee with their independent, written assessment of the proposed change. This consultant has worked with the company for many years and was originally hired by management. While the committee is very comfortable with the consultant, it has begun a discussion about hiring a new consultant who will be completely independent of management.

Compensation Philosophy

Many consider the committee's most important duty to be developing and/or approving the company's executive compensation philosophy. The SEC requires the disclosure of this information as an integral section of the compensation committee report included in the company proxy statement. A compensation philosophy statement is important for several reasons. First, it provides the link from business strategy to executive compensation program design; serving to explain why each element of the program exists, and providing an overarching rationale for actual compensation levels for the CEO and other senior executives. Second, the committee is not in a position to manage and administer the program; management must do this work. Because management is managing its own compensation program, it is very important that the committee privately and publicly articulate a compensation policy with clear objectives, targets and boundaries. Coupled with periodic audits by independent consultants, the intention is for the stated philosophy to provide sufficient direction and control so that the committee can be comfortable with management handling the detailed aspects of program design and implementation.

Given the importance of having an overarching compensation philosophy statement, we will further examine what is included in a philosophy statement and why it is important for a company to have one.

Just as business strategy sets the direction for a company, a robust executive compensation philosophy statement serves as the compass for the executive compensation program. Most strategists believe the executive compensation philosophy (or strategy) should be a direct extension of business strategy.

The philosophy statement should define key anchor points for the executive compensation program, set the overall direction, and shape the individual pay elements. It usually does not, however, specifically describe how individual elements of the program are designed. While compensation philosophy statements can be many pages in length, most are presented within several paragraphs. Regardless of length, it should answer the question "What are we trying to do with executive compensation?"

So, what is included in a compensation philosophy statement? Usually it will primarily define how targeted pay levels are determined. Often a peer group is established and identified for determining externally competitive pay levels and measuring competitive performance. The philosophy statement will also articulate the intended overall purposes for its incentive plans, both short- and long-term, and possibly include key performance measures and/or standards that will drive each plan. Most importantly, the committee will also explain how performance will drive levels of total compensation, usually articulating one or more clear objectives that link pay and performance. Pay mix is also discussed, with broad direction given to the portion of compensation coming from fixed and variable pay elements, as well as the relationship between short- and long-term incentive compensation. Most committees will also state their position on executive stock ownership and possibly include specific ownership guidelines.

The compensation committees of our three companies have each developed philosophy statements that are disclosed in their company proxy statements. There is much in common between the philosophy statements from the three very different companies. They all recognize the importance of their management teams, so each in their own way describe a desire to attract, retain and motivate their CEO and other senior executives. All three companies have also determined a need for both short- and long-term incentive plans, but the designs of those plans vary noticeably.

HIGROW is clear in its philosophy statement that the company is emphasizing growth. Salaries are kept below competitive norms, but the annual incentive plan will bring cash compensation levels to the 75th percentile if the company's ambitious growth and profit goals are achieved. Long-term incentive compensation is provided solely through stock options. The committee is struggling to determine an appropriate peer group for HIGROW, as most of its competitors are divisions of larger companies. At this point it compares HIGROW to a diversified group of similarly sized companies for purposes of setting compensation targets and comparing performance. HIGROW discloses stock ownership targets that are a multiple of base salary.

TECHCO is clear in its proxy statement that they are in a period of transition. Salaries have been frozen for several years. Annual incentives have been refocused from profit growth to generating a positive cash flow. Long-term incentive compensation has been traditionally all stock options, but has just been shifted to a mix of stock options and restricted stock. The committee has lengthened the time period for vesting of the stock incentives from two to four years. TECHCO operates in a very distinct industry with clear industry competitors; the committee uses this group for purposes of pay and performance comparisons.

MAKEITCO hasn't changed its overall performance goals for many years. It looks for above average top and bottom line growth as compared to a broad industrial peer group. The entire compensation program is targeted to the middle of the market, as defined by a broad group of comparably sized companies. MAKEITCO's compensation committee has purposely developed an annual incentive plan that varies up and down with profit and sales growth performance, but it does not swing inordinately high in good years or very low in difficult years. The committee provides stock compensation to a broad group of managers, and has a separate cash-based long-term incentive plan for top management that emphasizes return on capital and revenue growth over a three-year period. The company also describes stock ownership guidelines that are determined as a multiple of compensation.

CEO Compensation–Overview

While some think the committee's most important role is defining the compensation philosophy, others think it is determining the compensation for the company's CEO. Presently there is a great deal of public cynicism over CEO compensation. This cynicism has been growing for years as levels of CEO compensation have risen higher and higher. Recent years have seen a plateauing of CEO pay levels, but have also seen scandal after scandal, and a growing belief that CEO compensation was at least partially to blame for this corporate malfeasance.

Without a doubt, one of the board's most important roles is the hiring, firing and oversight of the company CEO. There is no other executive that the board gets to know as well. Unless something is going wrong at the company, the CEO operates with the support of most, if not all, board members.

Most compensation committees handle the decisions surrounding CEO compensation and report their actions to the full board; others will handle all other pay decisions in committee and bring recommendations for CEO pay to the full board for approval. No matter which group is involved, the decisions are important and are given significant attention.

Unlike all other positions in the company, getting data on how other CEOs are paid is a relatively straightforward, albeit technical, exercise. Company proxy statements (which can be found through SEC's EDGAR at www.sec.gov) must now disclose CEO compensation in a number of standardized tables. Salary and cash incentive payouts are reasonably transparent. Long-term incentive grants and payouts are the most difficult to value and standardize, but accepted techniques exist for putting this element of pay on a level playing field. Given the technical complexities involved with this work, compensation committees often ask their independent consultant to conduct this analysis. Given the growing importance of understanding compensation relative to performance, the committee should also receive a comparison of company performance relative to the same group of peer companies.

The committee should also conduct a periodic formal performance evaluation for the CEO. This exercise typically has two components. First, the CEO should prepare a written evaluation of his/her performance relative to pre-established company and individual performance goals. This written evaluation should be provided to all board members. Second, each board member should provide written input on his/her view of the CEO's performance. In many companies, the chair of the compensation committee serves as the focal point for collecting this all-important and confidential board input.

CEO Compensation–Base Salary

Armed with the appropriate external and internal data the committee should be prepared to determine the various compensation actions for the CEO. First among these decisions is whether or not to give the CEO an increase to base salary. While salary is often less than 25% of the total value of the CEO's compensation, it is nevertheless viewed as the foundation of the pay program. Most CEOs receive annual increases to base salary at the same time other company employees and executives receive their increases. Committees are mindful of how the company has handled salary increases for all employees and other senior executives and give, as well, due consideration to the external pay data, the CEO's individual performance and overall company performance. The committee may also ask its consultant for his/her opinion on the appropriateness and size of the salary increase. A three-year history of the CEOs annual salary is disclosed in the proxy statement. The committee is also expected to explain in the compensation committee report its rationale for any salary increase as well as the process used for determining the increase.

CEO Compensation–Annual Incentive

The next decision that must be made is the CEO's incentive payout from the annual incentive plan. Most annual incentive plans for CEOs are primarily driven by company financial performance. Goals and specific objectives will usually have been established at the beginning of the fiscal year. The committee's key responsibility is then to assess the company's actual performance versus the pre-established performance targets. In a year in which nothing structural has changed, this is a reasonably straightforward proposition. However the committee has to determine how to handle special situations such as acquisitions and divestitures, corporate restructuring activities, accounting changes, industry factors, and major external events such as war or terrorism that were probably not contemplated at the beginning of the year when goals were established. For most companies, virtually every year has at least one thing that makes this assessment less than totally mechanical. Committees most typically determine how they will handle a specific type of adjustment and will then handle it in the same way each time it arises. For example, for purposes of determining incentive compensation, a committee might choose to ignore the impact of an accounting change that occurs mid-year in the year of the change, and then apply it in all years going forward. Depending on how the company has structured its incentive plans, the committee might be limited, however, in its discretionary decision-making by 162(m) if it wishes to retain tax deductibility of its incentive awards.

Here again, the committee might also ask its consultant for his/her opinion on the appropriateness and size of the incentive payout. A three-year history of the CEOs incentive payouts is also included in the proxy statement. The committee is also expected to provide rationale for the CEO's incentive award and describe the process used for determining the award in the compensation committee report.

As one incentive cycle ends another begins, and so the committee must set incentive compensation targets and performance goals for the upcoming year for the CEO and other senior executives. The performance goals should be a direct extension of the company's longer-range strategic plan and the annual business plan. The most challenging task for the committee is to gauge the difficulty of the performance goals relative to standard and to determine whether the goals are typical, harder, or easier than a normal year; this allows the committee to appropriately align performance goals with incentive compensation payouts at various levels of achievement. An analysis of peer group performance on the same performance measures is often helpful (even though it is usually backward looking), as it gives the committee additional insight into how to best calibrate the forward year's goals.

As to the incentive compensation payout target(s) for the CEO and other senior executives, the peer group compensation competitive analysis will help the committee to understand how the company's incentive opportunities compare to those of the peer group companies. Additionally, the committee should be guided by its own compensation philosophy that will usually indicate the relative importance it puts on short-term incentive pay relative to other elements of pay.

CEO Compensation–Long-Term Incentive Compensation

The committee is also responsible for determining stock option, restricted stock and/or other long-term incentive compensation for the CEO and other senior executives. No area of executive compensation has received more scrutiny in recent years as it is widely acknowledged that large increases in stock-based compensation have fueled increases in executive pay over the last two decades.

The committee must make three key decisions in making these grants.

First, what performance goals are we trying to motivate in making these grants? Second, what compensation device(s) is/are best suited to achieving these goals? Third, how much is appropriate?

Until recently the typical answers to these questions were, respectively: motivate long term performance as measured by total shareholder return, stock options, and however much we need to grant to keep the compensation program competitive.

At the time of this writing, conventional practice in this area is literally being turned on its ear. Recent criticism from shareholder and governance groups, educators, government officials, and other leaders has caused many to suggest that too many stock options led some corporate executives to inappropriate, if not fraudulent behavior. Others are suggesting that committees abandon compensation surveys for determining how much to grant, and to simply "grant what is right," without any clear guidance on what that means. Also, a growing number of institutional shareholders and shareholder advisory groups have developed models or formulas to determine how much dilution they will allow from stock-based compensation and will vote against new stock plans or new share authorizations if practices do not conform with their guidelines. Lastly, it appears as though stock options will generate an accounting charge at grant starting in early 2005. While this will be a change impacting everyone, it is already causing companies to consider the accounting charge for stock options versus other alternative forms of long-term incentive compensation.

So, the committee's work in this area is more difficult than ever as virtually every company in America is simultaneously considering changes to this important and sizeable element of executive compensation. Critics notwithstanding, the committee will undoubtedly want to get as accurate a read as possible as to what changes and practices are being followed by the company's peer companies. Stock grants must be disclosed in company proxy statements, so there is access to high quality data for the CEO and other senior executives, but it is lagged by one fiscal year. Committee's will no doubt also rely on competitive information that management is able to gather on industry practices since the release of the last proxy statement, as well as real time information provided by the committee's consultant.

Most companies will continue to make grants during this several year period of transition, but it is clear that the upcoming years will bring changes to long-term incentive compensation practices at many companies. As with base salary and annual incentive compensation, the company must disclose a three-year history of stock (both stock option and restricted stock) grants, as well as cash long-term incentive compensation payouts for the CEO and the other four most highly compensated executives. The committee report must disclose the rationale for these grants and the process the committee followed in determining the grants.

CEO Compensation at Our Three Companies

Not surprisingly, our three companies are handling this situation in very different ways. HIGROW's compensation committee feels its current incentive design is right, and likes using stock options as the sole basis for long-term incentive compensation. The committee has been providing salary increases to the CEO and other senior executives each year, and has increased its annual incentive targets twice over the last three years due to the explosive growth of the company. The company has plenty of shares approved and reserved for future stock option grants, enough to carry it forward for several more years. However, the company is also aware that it is generating additional stock-based dilution in excess of guideline levels for several of its largest shareholders. The committee has asked its newly retained consultant to help it examine this issue going forward.

TECHCO's compensation committee knew a change was needed. As mentioned earlier, the committee shifted the focus for the annual incentive from profit growth to free cash flow. The committee also shifted from using stock options only to provide a blend of stock options and restricted stock, and also lengthened the vesting period for both grants. The committee is well aware that competitive grant levels in this industry are significantly reduced, and followed suit, although it did provide a round of supplemental restricted stock grants to key contributors who were felt to be "at risk." The committee used its newly retained consultant to help it make these supplemental grants. The committee has not provided any executive salary increases in recent years as the company has had a wage freeze for the same period of time. It has also asked the consultant to look at this issue, although senior management has said that it has no interest in salary increases until the company's fortunes are restored.

MAKEITCO's compensation committee doesn't see the need for any change. They continue to provide annual salary increases to its CEO and other senior executives, and believe the existing incentive plan is providing the proper motivation for generating strong financial performance. The company's use of stock options has been moderate, as they have not provided grants as deeply within the organization as many of its peers. It has also used a cash-based long-term incentive to supplement the stock option grants for its senior most executives, reducing the need for shares. It has enough shares authorized to last for two more years and does not plan any changes at this point. The committee is not bothered that the last few option grants have not generated any short-term value, as they see stock options as longer-term incentives and believe the stock price will rebound as the overall market regains strength. The committee has discussed, if they do hire a new consultant, that this is an area they would like to study in the year ahead.

Executive Stock Ownership

Committees typically provide stock-based compensation to senior management for two reasons. First, the amount of compensation ultimately delivered is in direct proportion to the company's stock price performance. In the case of restricted stock, it is in most cases also linked to the company's dividend performance as well. Second, the hope is that some or all of this stock compensation will be converted to outright share ownership, and that the CEO and other senior executives will become individually, and in the aggregate, stockholders of the company. Recent abuses aside, it is generally believed that these two goals lead to a better run company, with its senior executives thinking like shareholders as they contemplate longer-range strategy and shorter-term business plans.

For many years, it was just assumed that the CEO and other senior executives were accumulating and holding a majority, or at least some, of the shares that were generated from stock option exercises and vesting of stock grants. While this was typically the case, it has become more common for companies, through their compensation committees, to stipulate ownership guidelines for the CEO, other senior executives, and sometimes the board itself.

The most common approach is to develop an outright minimum ownership level, either denominated in a specific number of shares of stock, or a multiple of base salary or cash compensation. So, for example, the company might set a 6X base salary minimum stock ownership guideline for the CEO, and a 3X base salary minimum stock ownership guideline for others in senior management. In this case, the committee might state that it expects all executives to meet these ownership goals in a specific stated period of time, or to see a pattern of improvement until the goals are met. The second most common approach is to set a targeted retention percentage that indicates an expectation that the CEO and other senior executives will hold X% of all shares generated from an option exercise or vesting stock grant, net of taxes and exercise costs. For example, the company might set a 50% ownership expectation for the CEO, that either rises endlessly or until a certain level of ownership, say 10X base salary, is achieved.

This is a topic for committee consideration as it is anchored in the executive compensation philosophy, and its determination is integral to the rationale for providing stock-based compensation to the CEO and senior executives. While not required to do so, companies typically disclose their ownership guidelines in the compensation committee report. Actual ownership levels for the CEO and the other four proxy-disclosed senior executives is required to be stated along with the ownership levels of all members of the board of directors.

Our three compensation committees have all considered and implemented stock ownership guidelines. HIGROW implemented a system several years ago that called for 3X salary as a minimum ownership threshold for the CEO and its other senior executives. Because of the strong stock performance this level was easily achieved, and the committee raised the standard to 5X salary for the CEO and 4X salary for the other senior executives. This was also easily exceeded. The committee is wondering whether a fixed multiple of pay is an appropriate ownership standard for a high growth company and is considering other alternatives. It is also looking to establish stock ownership guidelines for the board of directors.

TECHCO has fixed ownership guidelines as a multiple of salary that were easily met or exceeded when the company and industry was high-flying. Several years ago the committee converted those ownership guidelines to fixed share guidelines, but with the near total collapse of its stock price, it isn't sure how meaningful this system is either. TECHCO, for the first time in years, was silent on the subject of stock ownership guidelines in this year's proxy report.

MAKEITCO has a more traditional stock ownership guideline system that targets 5X salary for the CEO, and 3–4X salary for the remainder of the senior leadership team. It also sets a 5X annual retainer guideline for members of the board of directors. It reviews actual stock ownership levels versus these guidelines at the committee meeting when stock option grants are awarded. While not a hard and fast rule, the committee expects each officer to be at or above the goal, or making incremental progress toward the ownership goal as an expectation for receiving that year's stock option award.

Board of Director Compensation

The compensation committee often has responsibility for monitoring and setting the appropriate level and form for board of director compensation (though, alternatively, some companies manage director compensation through the governance committee). Like CEO compensation, board of director compensation is well disclosed in the company proxy statement, so it is straightforward for a trained practitioner or consultant to determine and assess the board compensation for a company or peer group of companies. Also, like stock compensation for executives, this has been and continues to be an area involving major change.

Director compensation is usually comprised of an annual cash retainer, meeting fees, a stock grant of some kind, and possibly some additional benefits. A decade ago it was very common for large companies to provide director retirement plans; today, it is a shrinking minority practice. Like executive compensation, there has been a substantial rise over the last decade in the value of stock based compensation, as most director compensation plans added and grew the level of stock option awards. This practice has come under the same criticism as it has for executive compensation, with some experts suggesting that directors should receive reduced levels of stock options, or even none at all. Lastly, a number of companies have eliminated meeting fees in favor of an enhanced annual retainer, reflecting the fact that directors contribute throughout the year, not just at formal meetings.

Because of the technical complexities involved in valuing the various elements of director compensation, the committee will periodically have its consultant provide an analysis of director compensation for the company's (or other appropriate) peer group. This gives the committee a clear picture as to the overall magnitude of director compensation and mix of director compensation within the industry.

Unlike executive compensation, which is on an annual review calendar, most companies do not review and/or change director compensation on an annual basis. Hence, it is more common to see the design and level of pay stay constant for three or more years, and then see an increase and/or change in design.

The director compensation programs for our three companies have some similarities but also some significant differences. All three provide annual retainers, although the relative emphasis is different. At HIGROW, directors receive a retainer, no meeting fees, and a sizeable annual stock option grant. The stock option grant has for many years been for a fixed number of shares, adjusted appropriately for stock splits. The value of the stock option grant now provides the majority of the value of the entire package. The company just added a supplemental fee for its audit committee, reflective of the extra time commitment required since Sarbanes-Oxley.

At TECHCO, directors receive a retainer, small meeting fees, and a stock option grant. Like HIGROW, the number of options granted annually has remained constant for a number of years. Most of the outstanding options are underwater, and the value of the options granted today is substantially smaller than it had been previously. The committee is considering making the same switch to a blend of stock options and restricted stock as it did for the executive group.

MAKEITCO has a very traditional director compensation program. It has an annual retainer, meeting fees for board and committee meetings, and a modest annual stock option grant. It recently decided to implement stock ownership guidelines for its directors, and has a formal policy of reviewing director compensation every three years when it reviews the executive compensation program.

Deferred Compensation

Most executive and director compensation programs allow for deferred compensation. In simple terms, a deferred compensation program allows the executive or director to pre-determine that compensation normally earned during the current year will be deferred, free of most taxes, until payment at a later, pre-established date. These obligations must remain general obligations of the company in order to retain favorable tax treatment, and are most commonly "invested" in one or more investments, often similar to those offered in the 401(k). Chapter seven provides a detailed discourse on deferred compensation.

During the past two years, significant public attention was paid to the deferred compensation plans at two major organizations. In one situation, concern was raised by regulators as to how much control executives should be allowed to have over deferred monies; in the other situation, concern was raised over the magnitude of the deferred amounts and the preferential crediting, or interest rates, applied to those monies.

Compensation committees have overall accountability for all elements of the executive and director compensation plans, including deferred compensation. Committees should have a clear understanding of the key mechanics of the plan, the investment alternatives available under the plan (particularly those that provide guaranteed rates of interest at above market rates), and the accrued balances for the CEO and other senior executives.

HIGROW did not have a deferred compensation plan until last year. It now allows executives to defer up to half of their annual incentive awards into a subset of funds that mirror 401(k) investments. It also implemented a stock option deferral plan.

TECHCO has a deferred compensation plan, and the executives are worried about the safety of the plan given the enormous financial strains on the company and the industry. The committee and management have been exploring various ways to secure the value of the deferred balances without causing constructive receipt.

MAKEITCO has had a deferred compensation plan for many years. Executives could defer their incentives and directors could defer their cash compensation. For years, the only investment alternative was a fixed rate of return linked to the prime rate, but in recent years has expanded to offering all the company's 401(k) investment choices; this change was made at the same time the company outsourced the administration of this plan to their 401(k) provider. The company has a rabbi trust covering the plan, but it is minimally funded. The company has explored, but chosen not to implement, a stock option deferral plan.

Employment Agreements

The committee also has the final say as to whether or not the company provides employment and/or change in control agreements to the CEO and other senior executives, as well as the terms and conditions of those agreements. Chapter twelve is dedicated exclusively to this complicated subject and so this chapter will not delve into the form or substance of such agreements.

There are pluses and minuses for using employment agreements. Some companies make liberal use of them, others use them sparingly, and still others refuse to use them at all. To some extent, industry practice and characteristics play an important role. For example, an industry known for mobile talent and frequent job changing will have different usage of employment agreements than one known for stability and career employment. Company culture also plays an important role, as does the overall executive compensation philosophy. It also goes without saying, that the more volatile the situation, the greater likelihood that the senior executives and/or the compensation committee will see value in creating employment agreements.

Committees usually gain and give up something in the creation of an agreement. The company usually gains something it wants (stability, retention incentives, confidentiality, non-solicitation, non-compete agreement), and in return, gives up something the executive wants (stability, severance protection, compensation and employment guarantees). Committee members need to carefully weigh these factors in deciding whether or not to create an employment agreement. Committee members should always seek legal counsel and/or consulting expertise as they create or modify an employment agreement. The company is required to disclose the existence and key provisions of an employment agreement with the CEO or any of the other four named senior executives.

Employment agreements are more common for new senior executives who are hired externally. The executive is usually successful where he/she is currently employed, and the move to an unknown situation increases the likelihood of future termination since a level of personal relationship and trust has yet to be established. In these situations, it is not uncommon for a new, incoming senior executive to look for an employment agreement, possibly only covering the initial couple of years until it is clear that the move has been successful. Employment agreements are also more common in industries or companies that are troubled, or in industries where individual contribution is high and executive talent is highly mobile.

HIGROW does not have employment agreements with any of its senior executives, but is contemplating it as a retention incentive for the CEO and two other members of the senior executive group. The business media has provided extensive coverage of the company and its success story, and the board is concerned that these executives look attractive to many other companies, both inside and outside their industry.

TECHCO has an employment agreement with its CEO that was a condition of employment several years ago. The executive was worried about a downturn in the industry, and wanted severance protection for himself if he were to be terminated as he was leaving what he considered to be a safe job in a safer industry.

MAKITCO has never used employment agreements, and reluctantly agreed to provide them to a few key executives who joined the company from a recent acquisition. These agreements have a three-year sunset and provide a clear description about how severance pay will be handled in case of termination; the company received an explicit two-year non-compete and non-solicitation agreement in return.

Special Situation—Repricing Stock Options

No activity has been more villainized than the repricing of stock options. To many who believe "a deal is a deal," repricing stock options feels like the ultimate "heads I win, tails you lose" proposition. Many companies explicitly forbid stock option repricing as a material term of their stock compensation plan, and support that position philosophically in the compensation committee report. The new NYSE listing requirements now forbid a stock option repricing without shareholder approval. Despite the controversy, a small number of companies each year determine that it is better to cancel and reissue some or all of their outstanding stock options than to leave the situation alone.

The compensation committee is central to a stock option repricing. If the action is allowable, it requires compensation committee (if not full board) approval and extensive external reporting, including a special table that would be included in the company proxy statement for the next ten years. For the committee to consider such an action, it should conclude that it is in shareholder's best interests to cancel and reissue some/all of the company's outstanding stock options, and that the exchange would be done in a manner fair to all constituents. Given the technical, special disclosure, and potential adverse accounting issues associated with a repricing, the committee will surely be advised by its independent consultant and other experts.

None of our three companies have ever done a stock option repricing. HIGROW's plans do not specifically prohibit the practice, but the need has never arisen. MAKEITCO's conservative stance specifically prohibits the action without specific shareholder approval. TECHCO has wondered whether this is a question they will have to consider as they have a sizeable block of stock options outstanding and underwater, generating a sizeable stock overhang that is producing little to no motivation for anyone.

Special Situation—Hiring a New CEO

A board hiring a new CEO from outside the company will usually create a temporary search committee to manage the process. Once a candidate has been identified, that committee, possibly in conjunction with the compensation committee, has a one-time special situation to construct a compensation package and offer that is sufficient to motivate the job change, and reasonably consistent with the company's internal compensation philosophy and practices. The committee will no doubt rely on technical experts to help it understand and value the compensation package from the existing employer. Unless the situation is very unique, the individual will be leaving some value behind and will be looking for the new company to provide some value in return above and beyond the normal compensation arrangement.

The committee, through its technical advisor(s), needs to create a package and communication materials that compare the economic value of the existing and proposed compensation packages, and show how differences and one-time gains/losses will be handled. This usually involves outlining an ongoing compensation package, one or more one-time payments or grants, and (as stated previously) possibly an employment agreement. Time and confidentiality are generally of the essence, as the compensation arrangement is usually not worked out in detail until a final candidate has been identified, but before any public announcement has been made.

TECHCO is the only one of our three companies to have ever faced this situation. Several years ago, when it hired its current CEO from the outside, it needed to determine a compensation package and an employment agreement before the deal was announced publicly. It relied on the internal counsel of the top HR executive, and the external advice of a compensation consultant and an employment attorney to help put the offer and accompanying materials together.

In Summary

This chapter has illuminated the role of the compensation committee in the design and administration of an executive compensation program. Through our three case study companies, we have seen that the job, the demands, and the ultimate decisions can and should be very different company to company—which is why the compensation committee's work does not lend itself to cookie cutter solutions. Every company can benefit immeasurably from a strong, committed, thoughtful compensation committee.

MICHAEL L. DAVIS
Vice President, Compensation, Benefits & Staffing
General Mills, Inc.

Mr. Davis is Vice President, Compensation, Benefits & Staffing for General Mills, Inc. He is responsible for the company's overall compensation and benefit strategy and design, and for the administration of these programs. He is also Vice Chairman of the Board of WorldatWork, and the Chairman of the Board of the National Business Group on Health.

Prior to joining General Mills, Mr. Davis worked for fifteen years as a compensation consultant with Towers Perrin, ultimately as the firm's worldwide practice leader for executive compensation, and was a well-known national-level executive compensation consultant.

Mr. Davis has served on four National Association of Corporate Director Blue Ribbon Commissions on the Compensation Committee, Director and CEO Performance Evaluation, Director Compensation, and Director Professionalism. A frequent speaker and author on executive and director compensation and benefits issues, he has been interviewed or quoted in *Fortune, Business Week, Newsweek, Time, The Wall Street Journal* and *The New York Times* on compensation and benefit matters, and has lectured on these topics at Harvard, University of Chicago, Columbia, Dartmouth, University of Southern California and Cornell business schools.

Mr. Davis has B.S. degrees from Purdue University in Industrial Management as well as Computer Science, and an M.B.A. in accounting and finance from the University of Chicago. He is also a Certified Public Accountant.

10. SELECTING PERFORMANCE MEASURES AND SETTING GOALS

How you "get the [management] power to the ground" via incentive plan design is answered right here. Selecting performance measures and setting appropriate goals around those measures is the heart and soul of an incentive plan. Done well, it can significantly assist a company to achieve its most important goals. Done poorly, the incentive plan can actually become a de-motivator, foster unwanted gamesmanship, and/or cause turnover of key executives.

This chapter helps you to get it right. It first sets the context for performance measurement through incentive systems by discussing the types of performance measures and goals. The author highlights five key questions to ask in selecting a performance measure, all leading to the clear conclusion that the questions themselves are best answered through company-specific analysis, as opposed to generic cross-industry survey prevalence data. Once measures are selected the chapter provides discussion of other important items for subsequent consideration such as determining the appropriate time frame for measurement and the optimal number of measures in an incentive system.

As with the careful selection of the best measures, determining the appropriate goals for each measure is both critical and difficult. The author frames the approach to this decision with a discussion of criteria such as internally vs. externally driven, performance vs. budget or a standard, and achievable vs. stretch.

The chapter concludes with the author's coverage of four pitfalls to avoid when selecting performance measures and metrics. Even the most experienced incentive plan designer would benefit from these final words. –Editors

A Critical Strategic Decision

B ANK CO. WAS AT a turning point in its history. After the foreign bank sustained dramatic losses on several large loans and almost became insolvent, it sold a majority stake to a U.S. investment firm. The investment firm hired a new, expatriate management team to instill U.S. standards in the bank. The investment firm believed that Bank Co. was capable not only of achieving stability and profitability but also of setting a new standard for performance in the country's banking industry.

While Bank Co.'s new executive team had received stock options, no other incentive plans were in place. Therefore, executive rewards were based on a single measure of performance: shareholder value creation. While it was clear that shareholder value creation was a critical measure for this executive team, the Compensation Committee recognized that additional, intermediate measures were needed. The intermediate measures would motivate and reward the achievement of specific financial and strategic goals, and provide line-of-sight for the executives. But what would these intermediate measures be?

Having the right performance measures in place is one of the most powerful ways an organization can support the implementation of its strategy. Performance measures serve as a translation device that clarifies the link between strategy and decisions, and provides feedback to people on results. (See exhibit 1.) When tied to incentive compensation, performance measures provide the information that determines rewards and reinforces behavior.

Selecting the right performance measures is an important strategic decision that merits considerable thought, analysis and input from different sources.

In this chapter, we define key performance measurement concepts and discuss how performance measures are tied to executive compensation

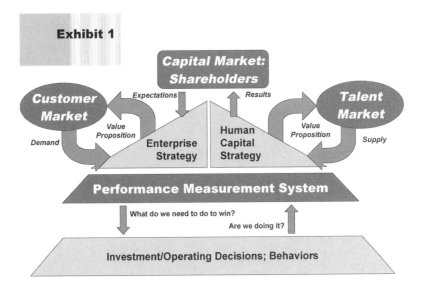

Exhibit 1

strategy. We cover in detail the factors that need to be considered when performance measures are selected and performance goals are set. We conclude with a discussion of the performance measurement and goal-setting pitfalls, and how to avoid them.

The Basics

A performance measurement system is the broad framework that companies use for decision-making and measuring progress toward objectives. Performance measurement systems are used for capital investment decisions, strategic decisions, assessment of operating performance, internal and external communication of progress toward goals, and incentive and reward decisions.

Performance measurement systems have a number of important components:

• Performance measures,

• Performance goals,

• Linkage to corporate, business unit or individual performance,

• The time horizon over which performance is measured,

• Corporate processes, i.e. the rules specifying how performance is assessed (e.g., formula or discretion), communication channels to provide information on progress and results, and education programs to give people the tools the need to understand and use the measurement system.

The first two components, performance measures and goals, are explained in this section. The other components are discussed later in the chapter.

Performance Measures

Performance measures are the criteria that provide feedback on performance. Examples include revenue growth, net income, return on assets (ROA), customer satisfaction, quality and employee satisfaction. Performance measures fall into three general categories: financial measures, operational measures and strategic measures.

a) Financial measures

Financial measures are dominant in executive incentives. The most common financial measures of performance for executive incentives are earnings, returns, earnings per share (EPS) and revenue. (See exhibit 2.)

Financial measures are useful because they provide objective, quantifiable information about performance. However, financial measures cannot

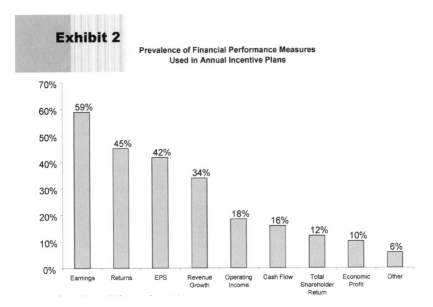

Exhibit 2

**Prevalence of Financial Performance Measures
Used in Annual Incentive Plans**

highlight critical non-financial information, such as customer and employee satisfaction.

Financial measures can be accounting or economic measures. Accounting measures are derived from a company's financial statements. Accounting measures are straightforward to calculate and communicate because they rely on readily available information captured for financial reporting purposes. However, accounting measures may not be appropriate for internal decision-making or incentive and reward decisions, as they do not always reflect the true economics of the business. For example, research and development is a major expense in the pharmaceutical industry that hits the income statement and lowers earnings as incurred. However, the benefits of research-and-development spending are generally realized long after the expense has passed through the income statement. In this example, accounting measures are not equipped to capture the long-term benefits of research and development.

In contrast, economic measures are equipped to capture the long-term benefits of an expense such as research and development. Economic measures typically reflect a firm's profit after incorporating a charge for the cost of capital used in the business. Examples of economic measures include economic value added (EVA[1]), economic profit and cash flow return on investment. While not as common as accounting measures, economic measures are more accurate than accounting measures because they take more information into account and are tailored to include adjustments specific to a company's economics and strategy. To tailor an economic measure to a pharmaceutical company, for instance, research and development costs can be treated like an investment–capitalized and charged to the income statement over time. But, if used "off the shelf" without being properly tailored to a business, economic measures can provide inaccurate information and result in poor decision-making. Because of the added information they take into account, economic measures can be complex to calculate and communicate. However, many companies consider the additional burden of addressing the complexity to be well worth the time and effort because of the clarity that economic measures provide.

b) Operational measures

Operational performance measures are used to assess the effectiveness and efficiency of a company's business operations. Examples include inventory management (e.g., inventory turns), accounts receivable management (e.g., accounts receivable days), equipment utilization, productivity (e.g., revenue or income per employee), product quality and employee safety. Operational measures can be used as "leading indicators" to capture trends before they impact financials or indicate important areas for improvement. Operational measures are typically used to assess the performance of managers or teams of employees who have a direct impact on operations, but are also common in executive incentives.

c) Strategic measures

Strategic measures are used to assess progress toward and achievement of important business objectives. They highlight factors that are not apparent in financial statements but are critical to a firm's success. Strategic measures are common in executive incentives, particularly in start-up or growth companies. Examples of strategic measures include customer satisfaction, market share, achievement of new product development goals, employee satisfaction and employee retention. In using strategic measures, care needs to be taken to clearly define the objectives as well as specify how they will be assessed at the end of the performance period. The assessment of strategic measures may be subjective, and can lead to differences of opinion as to what was agreed upon and what was achieved.

Performance Goals

A performance goal or target is the level of performance for which an organization or individual strives. Some examples of performance goals include:

Performance Measure	Performance Goal
EPS	• $2.46 per share
Revenue Growth	• Revenue growth in top quartile of peer group
New Product Development	• Two new products launched this year
Economic Profit	• $1 million

Performance goals can be either absolute or relative. Absolute goals specify fixed levels of performance. For example, 20% revenue growth is an absolute benchmark. In contrast, a relative benchmark communicates performance expectations through comparison to peer companies or to a market index, such as the S&P 500. An example of a relative benchmark is attaining an operating profit margin in the top quartile of peer companies.

Absolute benchmarks are effective if there is a particular level of performance around which employees need to rally. For example, a high-technology company in a turnaround situation adopted a fixed level of positive cash flow for its annual bonus plan. The company wanted to motivate the whole company toward the achievement of this important goal. In contrast, relative goals are useful in cyclical or volatile industries where targets are difficult to set because they take short-term economic conditions into account. In addition, relative goals are useful in competitive industries to motivate and reward executives for outperforming the competition. For example, an asset management company adopted relative goals to encourage its portfolio managers to provide greater returns than its major competitors, which is the true measure of success in the industry. When using relative goals, peer companies and market indexes for comparison need to be carefully selected if the program is to be effective.

The Critical Link to Compensation

Performance measures are used in many different corporate processes, including resource allocation, planning and financial reporting. One of the most important uses of performance measures is in incentive compensation decisions. The rest of this chapter focuses on selecting performance measures and goals for incentive compensation purposes.

A company's performance measurement system and compensation strategy need to work together in order for either to be fully effective. Both should be driven by the business strategy, industry and culture. Having compensation programs that reward the right performance is a powerful way to motivate employees, influence decision-making and reinforce the desired behavior. Similarly, having the right performance measures and goals lends credibility to compensation programs, and makes people feel motivated and rewarded for their efforts.

Let's revisit our earlier example of Bank Co. Bank Co.'s Compensation Committee identified three important ways that performance measures and compensation strategy needed to work together in the organization:

- To link the interests of executives with those of the investment firm that was the majority shareholder,

- To motivate executives to achieve aggressive growth and return objectives, and,

- To provide competitive compensation for competitive performance and truly superior compensation for standard-setting performance.

The Compensation Committee's primary objective was to ensure that executives made money when the shareholders made money. This meant choosing performance measures for executive incentive plans that were strongly correlated with shareholder value, and that clearly communicated priorities and expectations. With executives financially motivated to make decisions aimed at maximizing company value, a lesser degree of monitoring would be required on the part of the Committee and the Board of Directors.

To motivate executives to achieve aggressive growth and returns objectives, Bank Co.'s Compensation Committee worked with Mercer to develop a performance measurement framework tied to multiple incentive plans. (See exhibit 3.)

Exhibit 3

Bank Co. Performance Measurement Framework

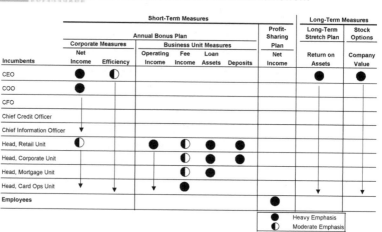

	Short-Term Measures							Long-Term Measures	
	Annual Bonus Plan						Profit-Sharing Plan	Long-Term Stretch Plan	Stock Options
	Corporate Measures		Business Unit Measures						
Incumbents	Net Income	Efficiency	Operating Income	Fee Income	Loan Assets	Deposits	Net Income	Return on Assets	Company Value
CEO	●	◐						●	●
COO	●								
CFO									
Chief Credit Officer									
Chief Information Officer									
Head, Retail Unit	◐		●	◐	●	●			
Head, Corporate Unit				◐	●	●			
Head, Mortgage Unit				◐	●				
Head, Card Ops Unit				●					
Employees							●		

● Heavy Emphasis
◐ Moderate Emphasis

Short-term corporate net income and efficiency measures were used for the annual plans. Aggressive growth goals were built into the net income targets. At the business unit level, short-term measures tracked operating income, fee income, and asset and deposit growth. The long-term measures emphasized returns and shareholder value, and were used to ensure that annual goals were balanced with the long-term success of the business. Bank Co.'s measures and the incentive plans were designed to communicate a consistent message about what would be rewarded in the organization.

For the third and final objective—ensure a direct linkage between pay and performance—Bank Co.'s bonus plan was designed to provide median compensation for target performance and above-median compensation for superior performance. The company's Compensation Committee decided that it wanted the bonus plan to support the company goal of setting the standard for performance in the banking industry with a special incentive plan. The Compensation Committee approved a long-term, cash-based "stretch" plan to provide top-decile compensation for standard-setting performance. Consistent with the plan's intent, performance goals under this plan were calibrated to top the performance of any similarly sized bank in the country.

Five Questions to Consider When Selecting Performance Measures

Selecting the right performance measures is as important as developing the right strategy. Without the right measures to support the strategy, implementation efforts are likely to fail, as executives and key decision-makers look to different targets and measurements to make decisions and assess progress. Because of the critical importance that performance measures play, sufficient time, effort and thought needs to be invested up front to arrive at the best and clearest measures.

While performance measure selection may seem like a quantitative, analytical process, in actuality it involves both art and science. The "science" involves the analytical work – understanding how value is created, what the industry economics and market expectations are, and peer company practices. The "art" involves understanding the culture, leadership style and vision, as well as the ways in which information is communicated within the organization.

We will often suggest the five questions provided next as a means to help practitioners initially navigate the performance measure selection process.

We also caution that judgment must be used, however, as these should not be seen as a "black box" that will alone lead a company to determine the right performance measures. Instead, we recommend that the reader consider each of the questions and, using their answers to each, begin to formulate well-defined performance measures for your company.

1. What are the economics of your business and industry?

Companies need to identify and select performance measures that capture the economics of their businesses and industries. In answering the question, several factors should be considered to help determine which performance measures will be most likely to work best in your particular industry:

• The industry's stage of development,

• Competitiveness within the industry,

• Capital requirements and asset intensity,

• Cyclicality, and

• External economic factors (e.g., interest rates, currency exchange rates, commodity prices).

Using Bank Co. as an example: The banking industry in Bank Co.'s country has been dominated by several large players. While the industry is mature, it was emerging from a severe down period caused by a regional recession. In banks, hard assets are minimal—mainly branch office facilities. However, financial assets, such as loans, are significant. Interest rate risk plays a major role in profits in banking.

In identifying performance measures for Bank Co., Mercer used regression analysis to quantify the strength of the link between different performance measures and bank values. (See exhibit 4.)

Company valuations are based on a complex set of factors, including past performance and future performance expectations. No single performance measure will entirely explain a company's valuation. However, correlation analysis can help identify "the short list" of measures that show a strong link to company value. In Bank Co.'s case, correlation indicated that ROA, ROE and the efficiency ratio (a common measure in the banking industry that tracks operating expenses as a percent of operating income) had the strongest link with value among similarly sized peers. Any approach that relies heavily on peer analysis needs to be balanced with consideration of company strategy, competitive position and capabilities relative to the industry.

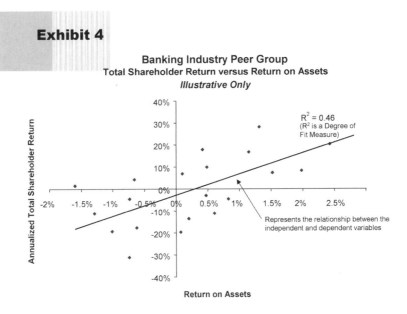

Exhibit 4

Banking Industry Peer Group
Total Shareholder Return versus Return on Assets
Illustrative Only

$R^2 = 0.46$
(R^2 is a Degree of Fit Measure)

Represents the relationship between the independent and dependent variables

Annualized Total Shareholder Return

Return on Assets

Given Bank Co.'s turnaround situation and the need to emphasize year-to-year improvements and growth, Mercer also recommended that Bank Co. use annual net income as an important measure at the corporate level.

Many companies identify performance measures strictly by looking at what other companies in their industry use. While it is important to understand which performance measures peer companies use, we strongly caution against the "me too" approach. Adopting the same measures as industry peers can lead to mediocre support for your strategy at best and a contradiction to the strategy at worst. Just as companies develop business strategies to define and execute a unique customer value proposition to differentiate themselves from competitors, so too should they identify and select appropriate performance measures to support their unique business strategies, rather than "mimicking" what other companies in the industry measure. Many companies also choose performance measures based on Wall Street's preferences (e.g., EPS). While EPS works for certain companies, it can create the wrong incentive in others.

In short, performance measure selection should be driven primarily by consideration of the key economics of your industry and strategy. Consideration of the sub-factors mentioned earlier will help to further refine the selection of the best measures. The *performance goals* set for those measures should be sure to take analyst and Wall Street expectations into account as well.

255

2. Should you focus on growth or returns?

Many people believe that companies need to focus on either growth or returns, but not both at the same time. To test this belief, Mercer analyzed the revenue growth, return on invested capital and total shareholder return (TSR) of the top 200 companies in the S&P 500 Index over the past 10 years. The study found that:

• Companies with the highest rates of revenue growth (more than 13% compound annual growth rate) and returns (more than 22% return on invested capital) generate the greatest return for shareholders. Such companies generate a stellar 29% per year TSR (see Exhibit 5).

• Not surprisingly, companies with low revenue growth and returns produce the lowest returns for shareholders.

While our findings show that companies need to demonstrate both growth *and* returns in order to maximize shareholder value, there are exceptions to this rule. Companies in turnaround situations need to emphasize earnings over growth for survival. Conversely, early start-ups need to invest for growth and market leadership, at least in the short-term, before they can turn their attention to returns. Both types of firms, however, will need to develop both a growth and a return focus over time.

3. What is the right balance between accuracy and complexity?

Performance measures range from very simple (revenue) to very complex (cash flow return on investment). (See Exhibit 6.) Accurate measures–ones that take the most information about the business into account–also tend to

Exhibit 5

10-Year Average Total Shareholder Return
1988-1998
S&P 200 Companies

High

	19%	23%	29%
13%			
Revenue Growth	17%	16%	18%
7%			
	13%	15%	15%

15%   22%

Low ————————————————→ High

Return on Invested Capital

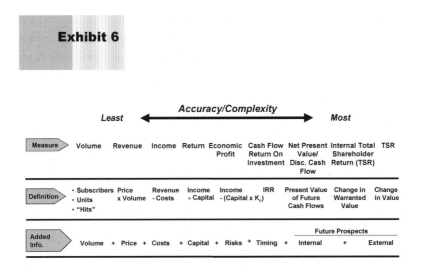

be the most complex measures, and that complexity can create implementation issues, such as training and communication. Before choosing a performance measure, the trade-off between accuracy and complexity needs to be considered.

A real estate company did not fully think through the accuracy/complexity trade-off when it chose a customized economic profit measure for use at the corporate level, in its strategic business units, and in different regions. The company lacked the internal capability to calculate economic profit in a timely manner, and the management team lacked an adequate level of financial sophistication. As a result, information was not calculated reliably or in a timely manner, and management continued to rely on the old measures that they understood and with which they were comfortable. The real estate company was faced with a choice: Either commit resources to appropriately implement the measure, or choose a simpler measure.

To avoid this situation, the tradeoff between accuracy and complexity should be addressed before the measure is selected. The following questions will help you think about the tradeoff.

- Do your information systems have the capability to capture and report the necessary information?
- Are top executives, including the CEO, willing to champion the measure?
- Are well-developed communication channels in place to disseminate information about performance?
- Is the organization willing to devote the necessary resources to training and communications efforts?

257

If the answer to any of the questions is "no," you may want to think twice about implementing an overly complex measure. The best performance measure is not always the most sophisticated. While complex measures such as economic profit can be powerful tools if properly implemented, the ultimate success of a performance measure depends on whether it:

• Is well-understood,

• Provides line-of-sight,

• Enables people to generate insights and evaluate alternatives, and

• Rewards outcomes, not inputs.

4. What performance measures get at the heart of your business strategy?

As many companies have found, this is not an easy question to answer–often because the strategy is not clearly defined or articulated. This question is best addressed through consideration of a company's strategic objectives and internal discussion with members of the executive team. In working through this issue, consider the following questions:

• What is your company's strategy? Is it clearly defined and communicated?

• What is the timeframe for achieving the strategy?

• What key objectives or initiatives support the strategy?

• How is the strategy tailored to different business units?

• If we had to pick only one key measure to use for running the business– one that would most improve business results–what would it be?

A large retail pharmacy chain successfully captured the heart of its business strategy with a single performance measure. The chain's strategy is to be the most convenient health care retailer. In support of its strategy, the chain builds new stores on premium, corner locations at high-traffic inter-sections in densely populated areas. The new stores are open and inviting, and have layouts that facilitate convenient shopping experiences. The chain adopted profit per customer as a performance measure to reflect the strong relationship between convenience and the size of customer purchases. Had the chain focused on profitability at a different level than customer (e.g., per store, per region), the measure would have contradicted its convenience strategy. The measure would have told executives at the chain to maintain existing stores–even if situated in poor locations–to limit capital expenditures.

5. What measures fit your company from a cultural and organizational standpoint?

A final consideration is the fit with your company from a cultural and organizational standpoint. New performance measures can be expected to raise classic change issues:

- Power–How will the new performance measures change who is powerful in the organization and who is not?
- Anxiety–In what ways will the new performance measurement system heighten anxiety levels?
- Control–Does the new performance measurement system alter who has control over what?

The success of a new performance measurement system depends in part on overcoming resistance to the change, and building acceptance and commitment within the company. While addressing the resistance is largely an implementation issue, the challenge can be mitigated by considering important cultural and organizational issues when first determining the key elements of the performance measurement system. These issues would include:

Culture

Culture should always play a role in performance measurement selection. Many companies will use new performance measures to heighten the focus on performance among employees and drive a cultural change. But while performance measures send a strong message about expectations, cultural change can not be driven by new performance measures alone. Instead, cultural change requires leadership support, ongoing communication and time. Without proper support for the new performance measures, they are doomed to fail as a driver of cultural change.

Leadership Support

Leadership support is critical to the success of a new performance measurement system. Company leadership needs to be involved in the process to select and implement new measures so that leaders own and are committed to the process. This means that performance measure selection cannot be driven by a single functional area alone.

To ensure leadership support, Mercer often recommends that companies form a steering committee to oversee the process of developing new performance measures. The steering committee will typically be comprised of key decision-makers who represent multiple functions. The CEO can sit on the steering committee or can provide input and direction at important points during the process. In addition, the Compensation Committee should have an opportunity to review and provide feedback on any performance measures used in executive incentives.

Communications

Internal communications also play an important role in supporting the introduction of new performance measures. Companies with internal communications channels that facilitate frequent updates are more likely to succeed with the implementation of complex performance measures or incentive plans.

Performance Measurement Implementation Considerations

As performance measures are selected, companies need to start thinking about how they will be implemented. Several decisions need to be made regarding implementation:

• Timeframe over which performance is measured

• Number of measures used

• Level of customization of performance measures

• Linkage to different levels in the organization

• Rules to assess performance results

1. Over what timeframe should performance be measured?

A common practice is to use short-term measures of performance (i.e., covering one year or less) in bonus plans and then rely on stock options to provide long-term incentives. Often, the short-term measures are tied to key public disclosures, such as EPS. A number of high-technology and other start-up companies rely on ultra-short-term measures that cover a period of less than a year. This practice has gained prevalence because of the difficulty in forecasting performance and the speed of change in the industry.

While a short-term approach may be appropriate in certain situations, many business decisions require a longer term perspective. Cutting the advertising budget might raise profits in the short-term in a consumer products company, but in the long run it will have a real impact on brand recognition, competitive position and profitability. The timeframe over which performance measures are viewed needs to fit the business just as the measures need to fit the business. Exhibit 7 provides examples of different timeframes for different industries.

Short-term and long-term perspectives can be taken into account by selecting different performance measures for different incentive plans. For example, Bank Co. implemented both annual and long-term incentive plans. The annual incentive plan focused on corporate and business unit operating

Business Type	Measurement Timeframe

Start-up Company	• Milestone driven
	  - Subscribers
	  - New financing
	• Timeframe depends on the urgency of the milestones

Consulting Firm	• Annual emphasis - Cash business

Oil Company	• Long-term emphasis
	  - 3-year rolling cycle for "annual" plan
	  - Heavy emphasis on long-term incentives

Financial Services or a Traditional Manufacturing Company	• Balanced short-term and long-term emphasis

Exhibit 7.

profit, and used a scorecard approach to incorporate other measures and strategic goals.

A long-term cash plan, designed to reward superior financial performance, used ROA. The annual bonus plan rewarded achievement of the business plan each year, while the long-term incentive plan rewarded long-term ROA results, which correlate strongly with shareholder value creation. The dual emphasis on short-term and long-term performance ensures that key annual results are achieved but are balanced with long-term value creation.

2. What is the optimal number of measures to use?

Another important decision is how many measures to use in an incentive compensation plan. A single measure may be used if one compelling, clear measure of success can be identified. However, given the complexity of most organizations, this is rarely the case. Two or three financial measures are common in management incentive plans. The most typical combinations are growth and profit, and profit and returns.

Using multiple measures of performance more accurately captures complex and multi-faceted businesses. However, using too many measures can provide conflicting signals and can cause a lack of focus on any one measure. When Bank Co. initially adopted its new performance measurement framework, participants in the executive bonus plan were assessed on anywhere from two to six performance measures each, plus individual goals. For the second year of the plan, the CEO decided to scale back the number of measures so that executives were rewarded for performance in just two corporate financial measures plus individual goals. Business unit executives had one additional unit-specific measure each. Limiting the number of measures increased executives' focus those that were most critical to Bank Co.'s success.

The Balanced Scorecard

A number of companies use the Balanced Scorecard as a tool to communicate strategy and track performance on specific goals. The Balanced Scorecard approach measures performance from four perspectives: Learning and growth, internal process/innovation, customer/market and financial. (See exhibit 8.)

The Balanced Scorecard can be an effective tool because it acknowledges that companies need to focus on more than bottom-line, financial performance in order to be successful. In addition, the Balanced Scorecard incorporates lagging financial measures, as well as non-financial and operating measures that tend to be leading indicators of company success. A potential drawback however, is that the Balanced Scorecard does not take the relative importance of each perspective into account. For some organizations, an "unbalanced" scorecard can be an effective way to communicate priorities. (See exhibit 9.).

3. To what extent do performance measures need to be customized to correct for accounting distortions?

Unadjusted, accounting-based performance measures do not necessarily lead to the best incentives.

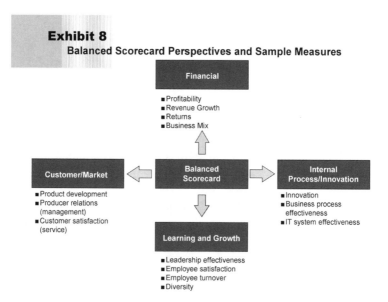

Exhibit 8
Balanced Scorecard Perspectives and Sample Measures

Exhibit 9

Strategic Business Unit Scorecard					
Measure	**Weight**	**Threshold**	**Standard**	**Superior**	**Actual Performance**
		Performance Level			
Financial					
• Growth in Operating Income Before D&A	25%	12%	15%	20%	_____
• Return on Gross Assets	25%	9%	10%	12%	_____

Strategic	Weight	0	1 (Threshold)	2 (Standard)	3 (Superior)	Score
		Performance Level				
Market Leadership / Value Leadership	25%					
• Increase prices across all products				2% increase per product		_____
• Secure long-term supply agreement for key raw material				Yes/No		_____
• Improve capacity utilization; decrease idle plant time				35% decrease		_____
• Complete manufacturing agreement with [ ]				Yes/No By May 1998		_____
Safety (Corporate)	25%					
• OSHA recordable incident rate				≤X.XX		_____
				Average Strategic Score:		_____

Accounting rules can distort performance and result in measures that can be "gamed," are less motivational or lead to the wrong behaviors. Exhibit 10 provides examples of how accounting practices can lead to the wrong behaviors.

To address accounting distortions, many companies decide to adjust the performance measures used for internal decision-making and incentive compensation purposes.

This means that different information is used for internal purposes than is used for public disclosure. Bank Co. adjusted its profit measure for executive incentive purposes to exclude a large reserve for loan losses that stemmed from the prior management team. While the new management team

Accounting Practice	Behavioral Implication
• Expenses are reflected in financial results in the period they are incurred	• Underinvestment in projects with large, up-front costs and long-term positive returns (e.g., research and development, employee training, advertising and marketing)
• Assets under operating lease are not reflected in the asset base	• Assets may be "purchased" through higher cost operating leases to keep assets off of the balance sheet
• Reserves are estimated for such items as sales returns, loan losses and warranty costs	• In good times, estimates may be exaggerated • This creates an "earnings cookie jar" for bad times that can help companies make their numbers

Exhibit 10.

263

can tap the reserves as required by the business, they should not reap the benefits of this reserve to boost their own compensation. However, Bank Co. decided to include the reserves for its broad-based, employee profit-sharing plan. The rationale was that the adjustment would be too complex to communicate, employees have no decision-making authority over the reserves, and employees would feel that they were treated unfairly if the reserves were excluded.

When deciding whether to adjust a performance measure, consider the following questions:

• Is there a compelling reason to make the adjustment?

• Is the adjustment material today or is it expected to be material tomorrow?

• Will the inclusion of an adjustment lead to positive behavioral change that is in line with corporate goals?

• Is the information required to make the adjustment available and easily tracked?

When the decision has been made to adjust performance measures for incentive compensation purposes, care should be taken to communicate the rules of the game to plan participants at the start of the performance cycle. Otherwise, behaviors may not change as intended, and employees become frustrated and demotivated in the process.

4. What is the appropriate measurement linkage?

Clearly, in order for performance measures to be effective in motivating behavior, they need to be within the control of the plan participants. For companies with fairly autonomous business units, tailoring measures to the business unit can help create line of sight and give people more control over the measures on which they are being evaluated. (See exhibit 11.)

An example of a company with a heavy business unit focus is a diversified company in the transportation industry. The company is structured as a holding company with a minimal number of corporate employees and highly autonomous business units. Executives in each business unit are rewarded for unit-specific performance measures communicated through an "unbalanced" scorecard. The corporate executives, including the CEO, are assessed using a roll-up (aggregation) of results for the different business units.

Measures also can be tailored to functional units (e.g., finance, marketing, human resources) and to individuals. Regardless of how deep you go, each level of measurement should support the overall company measures in order to provide consistency of communication.

Exhibit 11

Characteristics Favoring the Use of Corporate Measures	Characteristics Favoring the Use of Business Unit Measures
• Significant corporate management/control of business units	• Business units represent the relevant value-creating platforms
• Business units interdependent because of shared resources/integrative strategies	• Little interdependence between business units
• Need for collaboration across business units	• Little mobility of talent across business units
• Significant mobility of talent across business units	• Desire to support differentiated business unit cultures
• Desire to support strong company culture	

To accomplish this, lower level measures can be cascaded from the corporate measure. (See exhibit 12.) These measures should provide line of sight to the corporate measure and be controllable for the unit, function or individual being measured.

5. To what extent should the assessment of performance results be based on formula vs discretion?

Using a formula to assess performance results involves identifying the incentive

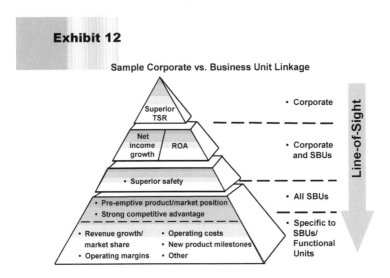

Exhibit 12

Sample Corporate vs. Business Unit Linkage

payouts associated with a range of performance results. (See exhibit 13 for examples of formula-based approaches). In contrast, a discretionary assessment is based on the judgment of an individual or group of individuals.

While formulas and discretion both have benefits and drawbacks (see exhibit 14.), Mercer has found that the most effective executive incentive plans rely on formulas.

Exhibit 13

Bonus Payout Matrix
As a % of Target Opportunity

Return on Invested Capital					
25%	100%	125%	150%	175%	200%
20%	75%	100%	125%	150%	175%
15%	50%	75%	100%	125%	150%
10%	25%	50%	75%	100%	125%
5%	0%	25%	50%	75%	100%
	10%	**15%**	**20%**	**25%**	**30%**

Revenue Growth

Exhibit 13, *continued*

Bonus Payout Calculation
As a % of Target Opportunity

Measures	Targets by Measure			Results by Measure			Final
	Range	Goal	Payout %	Performance	Payout %	Weight	Payout %
Return on Invested Capital	Max	25%	200%	20% ⟹ 150%	X	50% =	75%
Weighted 50%	Target	15%	100%				
	Threshold	5%	25%				+
Revenue Growth	Max	30%	200%	20% ⟹ 100%	X	50% =	50%
Weighted 50%	Target	20%	100%				
	Threshold	10%	25%			TOTAL	125%

	Pros	Cons
Formula	• Enforces accountability for results • Communicates expectations and allows employees to track progress against goals • Provides objective criteria for incentive decisions	• Penalizes strong individual performers for company results • Formulas may fail to take unusual events into account
Discretion	• Effective in companies using strategic goals • Rewards strong individual performers even when company results are poor	• May breed favoritism or perceptions of favoritism • Places a greater burden on superiors for providing meaningful feedback

Exhibit 14.

Formulas enforce performance standards and provide greater motivation to succeed because there is no forgiveness for missed goals.

Setting Meaningful Performance Goals

Executive's pay should vary depending largely on the financial performance of the company. In order to accomplish this, companies need to identify the level of performance they require for specific pay levels:

• What level of performance is required to receive a target payout?

• What level of performance merits a maximum payout?

• What is the minimum acceptable level of performance required for a threshold payout?

Linking performance goals to compensation strategy balances risk with rewards, signals the level of performance required for pay, and motivates desired behaviors.

Different approaches can be taken to linking pay to performance. (See exhibit 15.)

For example, an investment management firm implemented a new incentive plan with the goal of maximizing long-term returns while assuming reasonable risk. One of the selected performance measures was return on equity assets compared to the Russell 3000 Index. The target level of performance was determined to be achieving returns equal to 50 basis points above index. Threshold performance (the performance level required to receive any bonus) required that equity returns outperform the Russell 3000 Index by 10 basis points.

In this competitive industry, outperforming an index by this small amount does not merit a large bonus–in this case, only 25% of the target amount.

Maximum payouts under the plan were paid for returns that outperformed the Russell 3000 Index by 100 basis points (1%). The overall range of performance from threshold to maximum was narrow—only 90 basis points. Maximum payouts were 150% of target, lower than the upside norm of 200% of target in general industry.

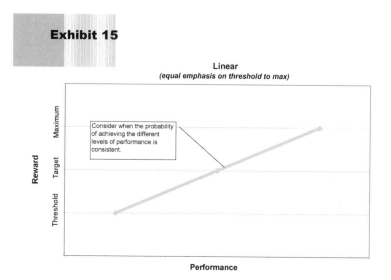

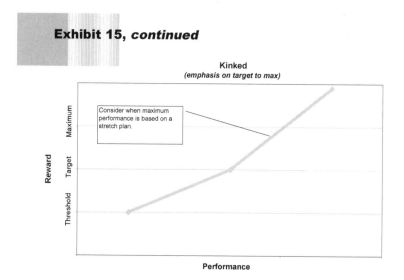

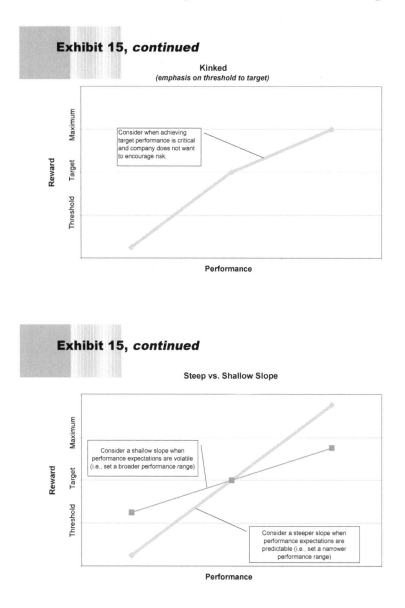

Exhibit 15, *continued*

Kinked
(emphasis on threshold to target)

Consider when achieving target performance is critical and company does not want to encourage risk.

Exhibit 15, *continued*

Steep vs. Shallow Slope

Consider a shallow slope when performance expectations are volatile (i.e., set a broader performance range)

Consider a steeper slope when performance expectations are predictable (i.e., set a narrower performance range)

In line with the plan objective of encouraging long-term returns while assuming reasonable risk, people were intentionally motivated not to try to "hit the ball out of the park" in order to earn a large bonus. Instead, the goal was steady returns that outperform the competition.

A number of questions should be considered when calibrating pay to performance:

• How aggressive is your target?

- How broadly or narrowly have your peers historically performed?
- What performance level constitutes "superior" performance?
- How probable is "superior" performance?
- How probable is "minimal acceptable" performance?
- Could you be motivating participants to game performance?

Setting performance goals

Setting meaningful performance goals is critical to ensuring the success of performance measures and incentive plans. But unfortunately, goal setting is often handled as an afterthought, and companies frequently default to basing goals on the strategic plan or internal budget. While strategic plans and internal budgets are one input to the goal-setting process, a number of inputs should be considered including: historical company performance, historical industry and market performance, ongoing standard (e.g., cost of capital), and projected industry and market performance.

For example, one company wanted to determine its equity growth objectives so that it could translate them into specific financial goals for variable compensation purposes. The company initially decided its forecast of 12% growth was respectable since it exceeded the weighted average cost of capital of 9%. However, the 12% goal fell short of what investors could obtain from other companies with similar market capitalizations and the company's peers (14% and 13% respectively). After taking external factors into account, the company raised its growth goals to 15% per year.

A poorly set target can be very demotivational to employees. A large chemical company had 20 business units, half of which were in developing, high-growth businesses and half of which were in mature chemicals businesses. Business unit performance was assessed using economic profit. The CEO fostered a company culture that emphasized growth, so the economic profit targets across the business units included growth aggressive assumptions. Knowing that the growth assumptions were unattainable for their businesses, executives in the mature chemicals businesses disregarded the performance goals. The disconnect was eventually addressed when the company spun off the main-line chemicals business because the economics were too different from the growth divisions.

Goal-Setting Dilemmas

Because of the different inputs that can play a role in setting performance goals, companies face a number of goal-setting "dilemmas." In this section, we discuss each dilemma and provide insights on best practices.

1. Internally driven vs. externally driven?

Too often, companies over-rely on internal benchmarks such as budget projections and historical comparisons as the basis of goal setting because of the simplicity of comparing year-over-year performance. However, in ignoring external benchmarks, the company may be setting performance targets that are too low. By incorporating external benchmarks such as broader stock indices, the company's cost of equity (which indicates investors' expected return for the level of risk), and analyst forecasts, a company can better establish performance targets that are at or above investor expectations. An external benchmark can be used explicitly in the goal-setting process (e.g., match industry growth rates of 15%) or as one of many factors to consider (including internal benchmarks such as management budgets or historical performance) in establishing targets.

2. Budget vs. standard?

Companies often identify specific standards that reflect long-term expectations for performance for their business. Standards may be used to evaluate investment alternatives (e.g., a cost-of-capital hurdle), or they may be used as long-term performance goals (e.g., 15% annual total shareholder return). While such standards take long-term, external expectations into account, they also have a few drawbacks: Standards do not consider short-term economics, such as a down economic cycle. In addition, standards developed for the company may not be directly applicable to business units, or may need to be tailored to apply to them.

In contrast, budgets are based on internal projections of performance that are developed by seeking input from many areas within the company. Budgets are useful for corporate and business unit target-setting because they take into account specific business information and management's expectations for performance. However, they are political, may encourage gaming and require a reliable budgeting processes and organizational buy-in to provide effective goals. Companies should take both budgets and standards into account when developing performance goals, since the two together provide a more balanced perspective.

3. Long-term vs. short-term?

As in the choice between budgets and standards, the question of whether to use long or short term goals leads to a recognition of the shortcomings of either if used alone. Companies often over-emphasize short-term goals, such as hitting quarterly EPS. This short-term focus leads many managers to make decisions that help the company meet this quarter's profit, rather than

271

maximizing the long-term value of the company. However, setting long-term goals is not always viable given changing market conditions.

It is best for companies to create a balanced (i.e. both short- and long-term) perspective when setting goals. Bank Co. used this approach in its goal-setting process for its annual bonus plan. Under the plan, target performance corresponded to annual business plan objectives. However, maximum performance was based on a "best-in-class" benchmark. This benchmark was determined by looking ahead five years to the level of performance that Bank Co. was aiming to achieve. If Bank Co. hit this level of performance, it would surpass the performance of any similar financial institution in the country. The annual goal corresponded to the level of performance that Bank Co. would need to achieve each year to eventually reach its goal of setting a new performance standard.

4. Achievable vs. stretch?

Companies should incorporate stretch goals into their performance measurement and compensation programs. Mercer studied goal-setting practices in high-performing companies and found that high-performing companies overwhelmingly incorporate stretch goals into their performance measurement and compensation systems. Setting goals that are too low tends to lead to unacceptable returns to shareholders, fosters poor performance and creates a "status quo" mentality among employees. However, companies need to set goals that are aggressive but not unattainable. Setting goals that are too aggressive can be expected to demotivate employees.

5. Top-down vs. bottom-up?

Top-down goals are derived from overall company financial objectives. They are more likely to take external perspectives into account and ideally should reflect investors' expectations for company performance. In contrast, bottom-up goals are built up from business units' perspectives. Bottom-up goals are more likely to reflect achievable levels of performance and to capture future trends, such as changes in customers' preferences. Once again, balancing the two approaches is an effective way to ensure goals that meet investors' expectations and are achievable.

In summary, Mercer has found that an effective goal-setting process:

• Reconciles the internal perspective (e.g., historical company performance and strategic plan) with a external market expectations (e.g., peer benchmarks, investor expectations, analyst expectations)

• Integrates "top down" corporate financial objectives with "bottom-up" business unit perspectives

- Cross checks annual and long-term financial goals against industry and direct peers performance goals
- Balances long-term objectives with short-term business economics
- Sets stretch goals
- Makes sure that the goals are achievable (e.g., check historical performance to target)

Special situation: Setting goals in a cyclical industry

Goal setting is particularly challenging for companies in cyclical industries. Companies in cyclical industries experience volatile earnings from year to year, and have difficulty in forecasting performance and developing budgets. As a result, standard goal-setting approaches, such as basing goals on the annual budget, fail to work reliably.

Unfortunately, many cyclical companies decide to let their bonus payments "ride the cycle." Incentive payouts are generous in years when the industry does well and are minimal or non-existent when the industry does poorly. However, this approach fails to reward executives when the company outperforms during the cycle trough or penalize executives when the company underperforms during the cycle peak.

Though varying with the company and the industry, several approaches can be used to address market cycle risk in goal setting, including indexing performance relative to industry peers or using a multi-year rolling average. Another approach is to develop performance targets that are reflective of the company's expected position in the economic cycle.

As an example, a manufacturing company uses ROA as the company performance measure in its annual incentive plan. The company hit its ROA goals only about half of the time. In contrast, a company in a typical industry achieves its performance targets 80% to 90% of the time. To address the cyclicality, three ROA performance "buckets" were developed, representing the trough, middle and peak of the market cycle. Each of the buckets had distinct threshold, target and maximum ROA requirements. The associated bonus payouts were calibrated to the performance cycle so that cash was conserved during troughs. (Higher payouts are made in a peak cycle than in a trough cycle). At the beginning of each year, the senior executive team recommended which bucket determined the performance goals and payouts for the year. The recommendation was based on the ROA budget for the year, whether ROA was increasing or decreasing, and forecasted changes in economic indicators. While the approach relied on discretion in judging the market cycle (which this company had proven to be adept at doing), it achieved an important benefit: Ensuring that goals would motivate employees even in a down year.

Avoiding Performance Measurement and Goal-Setting Pitfalls

Performance measurement and goal setting are powerful management tools when their implementation is guided by careful consideration, analysis and feedback. But, choosing either the wrong performance measure or goal can lead to unanticipated or suboptimal results, demotivated employees and gaming. In this section, we discuss several performance measurement and goal-setting pitfalls and how to avoid them.

Pitfall #1: The performance measures used in incentive compensation plans are inconsistent with the measures used in other internal processes, such as planning, resource allocation and financial reporting.

When selecting performance measures for executive incentives, strategic planning or resource allocation, using measures that are already used in other processes should be considered. By not doing so, conflicts can arise. As an example, a company uses EPS in its management incentive plan and economic profit in resource allocation decisions. The company is considering an acquisition through a stock swap. Even if the acquisition results in additional economic profit, management will question this value-creating investment if it dilutes EPS and lowers their bonus payments. In this example, the two performance measures send mixed signals, confusing managers and possibly preventing the company from maximizing value.

To avoid this pitfall, performance measures for incentive compensation purposes should be considered within the context of the overall performance measurement system. Any potential conflicts should be considered and addressed by either changing a measure entirely or adjusting its definition. In the EPS vs. economic profit example, the conflict could be addressed by changing EPS to net income, which would alleviate concerns over earnings dilution on a per-share basis.

Pitfall #2: New performance measures are not achieving the desired results because of a lack of organizational buy-in.

Organizational buy-in is critical to the success of new performance measures. Without it, they will be overlooked or ignored, and will fail to achieve the desired results. Buy-in needs to occur at the Board, CEO and executive team level, as well as at the participant level.

If a lack of buy-in is evident at the senior level, the problem likely began during the process to identify the performance measures. The necessary people did not participate in the process or did not consider it to be a priority. To correct this problem, you may need to look at the measures again with the right set of people involved. If the lack of organizational buy-in occurs at the participant level, training and communication efforts need to be ramped up. One common and effective approach is for a team of senior executives involved in the selection process to do an internal "road show" to communicate the new measures directly to plan participants. If the measures are complex, the road show should include or be followed by a training session to promote comfort with how the measures are calculated, why they are effective and how each person can contribute to performance through specific activities and decisions. Ongoing communication of progress and results is also important through internal communication channels, such as an Intranet, videoconferences or employee publications.

Pitfall #3: The incentive plan paid out for the wrong performance.

If your incentive plan pays out for the wrong performance, you are probably using the wrong performance measure. As mentioned earlier, having the wrong performance measure can result in poor resource allocation and lead to decisions that destroy value. A number of companies faced this situation in the late 1990s. In the early 1990s, many companies re-engineered for efficiency and cost savings, and adopted profit measures to support re-engineering efforts. As the high-tech boom of the late 1990s took hold, corporate strategies shifted to emphasize growth. However, a number of incentive plans continued to emphasize profits over growth. While profit measures are not necessarily detrimental to a company with a growth strategy, they can be if growth is not emphasized somewhere in the performance measurement system.

In order to make sure that you are paying for the right performance, incentive plan performance measures should be reviewed periodically to ensure consistency with any strategic shifts. When new performance measures are selected, extensive analysis should be completed to surface any issues. This includes considering several alternatives and evaluating past company performance to determine how the alternatives would have played out in past years. You should also obtain feedback from many different sources when selecting measures. Valuable sources include different functional areas, the Board of Directors, the leadership team and an external resource.

Pitfall #4: The incentive plan paid for inadequate performance or failed to pay out in a good year.

275

If your incentive plan payouts are not appropriately linked to company performance, the performance goals are set too high or too low. This is a very common issue that can lead to shareholder complaints or have a devastating impact on motivation levels.

There are a number of ways to ensure that performance goals are appropriately calibrated. Conducting a "what if" analysis to see what incentive payouts would have been had the goal-setting standards been in place in past years is a useful tool. Calibrating performance goals using multiple sources is another way to reality check performance targets. You should also –once again–obtain feedback from many different sources when setting goals. Finally, periodically review your goal-setting process and standards to ensure that they are still relevant.

Moving Forward

Now that you have new insights on performance measure selection and goal setting, how can you implement some of the ideas discussed in the chapter? The first step is to assess the effectiveness of current performance measures and goals. To assist with this process, we have included a diagnostic test in the Practitioners Tools section of the chapter.

Once the current state has been assessed, the scope and objectives of a performance measurement study should be defined. Are you:

• Developing a new system from the ground up?

• Reviewing existing performance measures for continued relevance?

• Correcting design flaws in a system that is generally working well?

• Developing new performance goals?

• Ramping up communication to increase understanding of the current program?

Once defined, the scope and objectives will drive the process and level of analysis needed.

In summary, performance measures translate your strategy into action and provide feedback on the results. When tied to incentive compensation, performance measures take on a heightened level of importance and drive changes in behavior for the better. If properly defined and implemented, performance measures and goals can be your most powerful tool to support the execution of your company's strategy.

Endnotes
1. EVA is a registered trademark of Stern-Stewart.

Practice aids found on the CD for this chapter:

• Performance Measurement System Assessment Tool
• Performance Goal Checklist

Robin a. Ferracone
Partner
Mercer Human Resource Consulting

Ms. Ferracone is a Worldwide Partner at Mercer Human Resource Consulting. She has over 20 years of consulting experience in the areas of value management, performance measurement, human capital strategy, and compensation design, both on a domestic and international level. She is published widely, has appeared on *NewsHour with Jim Lehrer,* has testified before a U.S. Congressional sub-committee on Presidential pay, and is a frequent presenter for such organizations as The Conference Board, WorldatWork, the CFO Business Week Forum, The National Center for Employee Ownership, and National Association of Stock Plan Professionals. In 2003, WorldatWork honored her with the Distinguished Service Award.

Ms. Ferracone has an MBA from the Harvard Business School, where she was a Baker Scholar, and a BA, *summa cum laude,* in management science and economics from Duke University, where she was elected to Phi Beta Kappa. She serves on a number of corporate and charitable boards.

11. Advanced Topics in Business Unit Incentive Plans: Paying for Value Creation at Its Source

This chapter focuses on how to put an effective business unit incentive plan in place. The author begins this rigorous presentation by making a strong case for the increased use of such plans for business unit executives, rather than corporate plans; arguing that the recent emphasis on corporate plans and measurements is likely due to their relative ease of use and the fear of unfavorable competitive comparison. "Easy and prevalent" are not compelling justifications, the author points out, and are certainly not tantamount to good practice.

In particular, the author presents support for the view that there is too much emphasis on corporate stock compensation for business unit leaders and not enough focus on value creation at the business unit level, where most of the value in a company is in fact created. The chapter discusses a number of ways for creating business unit equity, from phantom stock to subsidiary equity and explains the ins and outs of technical issues such as formula versus market valuation. A number of common problems in designing business unit incentive plans are identified and discussed, with the author providing one or more solutions for handling each type of problem.

The pros and cons of using a more traditional performance-based cash or stock incentive plan to motivate business unit performance are detailed, closing with a review of a number of important design considerations for any type of business unit incentive plan such as setting grant sizes, determining performance targets, capping payout opportunities and determining pay/performance leverage. –Editors

The Case for Business Unit Incentives

EXECUTIVES IN BUSINESS UNITS of companies receive incentive pay in two main forms:

- **Stock options,** which deliver gains based upon stock price gains of the overall company. These are granted like salaries, based mainly upon organizational rank.

• **Annual bonuses.** These typically reflect the financial performance achieved by the business unit and by the overall company in relation to budget-based goals.

This common approach has some very serious flaws. As incentives, stock options offer poor "line of sight" for most of the people receiving them, particularly for executives in key business unit roles. Also, annual bonus plans for business unit executives tend to include flawed metrics, a counter-productive target setting process, short-term bias, risk aversion and, as with options, poor line of sight. Overall, the structure of incentive pay for business unit executives in most companies does not encourage them to maximize long-run results or value. Rather, it encourages them to manage results into a modest, predictable range in the near term.

Clearly, this is an unfortunate problem, given the fact that the bulk of the value of most enterprises is found within their operating units; as are most of their executive decision-makers. This is the organizational level at which incentive plans ought to be making their most important contributions to business performance. But they are not.

This chapter will summarize the main problems with stock options and business unit bonus plans. It will present a range of ways in which the efficacy of incentives can be improved for those critically important executives found in groups, divisions and profit centers—and for the many important decisions they make on the part of shareholders.

Business Unit Equity Plans

Stock options have come under attack recently after their practically universal adoption as incentive devices meant to encourage value creation and produce better results. The trouble with options is that they don't come with instructions on how to do these things. Also, most people who hold stock option grants—particularly those in management of groups, divisions and profit centers—don't have much influence on consolidated results or the company's stock price. The efficacy of options is questionable from an empirical viewpoint as well; companies who make heavy use of stock options do not appear to achieve better performance.[1]

Despite these issues, companies use stock options more heavily than any other kind of incentive. Much of this over-use is driven by the favorable accounting treatment of option grants. Unlike most kinds of incentives, stock options do not require a charge against earnings. Companies fear that if they use other kinds of incentives and are obliged to recognize their book expenses, their financial results will tumble and the stock market will penalize them.

Towers Perrin's standing view is that how companies use incentives, particularly at the executive level, is a strategically pivotal matter and not one that should be prescripted by bookkeeping rules:

- In a January 2002 publication, I noted: "Overall, belief in the book advantages of options–the idea that options accounting keeps stock prices higher than they otherwise would be–appears to be a broadly-held financial illusion. This is unfortunate since the focus on bookkeeping skews incentive design greatly and renders it ineffective for most participants."[2]

- Subsequent events in 2002 proved this assertion in particularly direct terms. In July and August of 2002, over 100 public companies announced they would voluntarily expense their option grants, providing a ready-made test of whether the accounting treatment of incentive plans has consequences to shareholders or not. If option bookkeeping matters, then these companies should have experienced a share price hit when they announced they would be taking on book charges for their options. They took no such hit. Share prices of the companies announcing expenses actually posted better performance than market averages for the July, August and year-to-date periods. And, among the expensers, larger pro forma EPS impacts did not drive large share price hits. We made a closer examination of stock price impacts with data compiled by Towers Perrin in "event study" format for the 60 days preceding and following the announcement date.[3] Results of that study are summarized here:

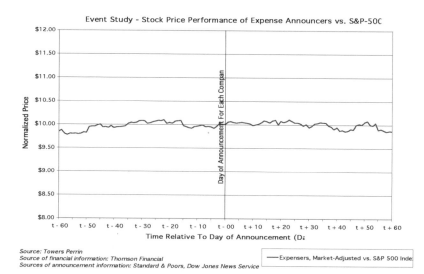

Overall, accounting treatment of stock options is a non-issue to the stock market. This should be a relief to many companies because general changes to accounting rules now appear imminent. FASB and IASB appear to be on course to require stock option expensing by 2005. Since the accounting advantages of options are going away, many companies will be re-focusing on how to provide incentives that do work.

For many of them, this will mean searching for replacements for the stock option grants in such heavy use now. After all, options never did seem to create much focus on the long-term. Rather, focus on short-run stock price movements drove the misguided practice of "next-quarter capitalism," doing whatever it took to dress up current earnings.

Stock Options As Long-Term Incentives for Business Unit Executives

As usual, the view is worst from the trenches. To wit: Business unit executives' own results typically drive 20% or less of incentive pay, with remarkably little effect upon option gains in particular.[4]

Many factors intervene between business unit results and stock option gains. Results of a typical business unit are overwhelmed by results of other business units upon consolidation. Corporate actions have big effects, too, raising concerns about overpriced acquisitions, failed reorganizations, and high levels of expense. A final uncontrollable negative is the stock market volatility that consistently clouds the linkage between business results and share prices.

Thus, thousands of people may receive options but they probably function as an incentive only for a few dozen at best, and imperfectly even for them. Option grants accomplish some important pay-related objectives, but they don't fulfill the goal of encouraging value creation to nearly the extent hoped.

The system can be improved greatly. After all, business unit managers normally are the ones best qualified to run their businesses. They are the ones best suited to take educated risks in their operations and to exploit their close knowledge of relevant markets and operations. Unfortunately, they aren't rewarded for doing so in the present system. If long-term incentives were linked to their own business unit operations, divisional managers would have no trouble finding ways to unleash greater entrepreneurial drive.

Business Unit Bonus Plans Do Not Create "Ownership"

Stock-based incentives tend to reward business unit performance only vaguely. But incentive media are not confined to stock. Operating incentives, like the bonus plans in common use, are the main general alternative to stock-based incentives. Unfortunately, these plans don't create entrepreneurs either.

Bonus targets usually are set by the annual budget process. This can encourage sandbagging of goals, misallocation of corporate resources (like money and management efforts), and it can leave many participants feeling shortchanged. These problems work rather strongly against the usual goals of the process: setting of stretch goals, high-quality resource allocation and overall fairness. As it was put in 2001 in the *Harvard Business Review*, "The corporate budgeting process is a joke, and everyone knows it."

The annual nature of the bonus plan is a shortcoming as well. Each year's bonus opportunity is set in a new budget negotiation, perhaps involving new priorities, standards and metrics for success. The system doesn't encourage management to focus much on the long term, since rewards for any future performance are highly uncertain. Timeframe is a serious problem with business unit incentive structure. Maximizing value requires a long view. The typical bonus plan, on the other hand, encourages management to manage results into a modest, narrow range in the short-term.

Bonus plan metrics are another issue. Most bonus pay continues to be based on achievements denominated in terms like EPS, ROE, and operating income and sales. But they thwart effectiveness because of issues like:

- **Under- or over-weighting of capital usage by the business.** Many business unit incentive plans judge financial success solely based upon operating income, thereby under-emphasizing the important role of capital and risk in determining whether a particular level of operating income creates value or not.

- **The actual complexity of familiar, purportedly simple metrics.** EPS, for example, reflects cumulative effects of many complex accounting deter-minations, each of them distancing pay from the underlying business results that the incentives are said to reward.

- **Poor ability to set goals and benchmark results among business units, against peers and over time.** In one common scenario, a business unit may outperform another one vastly in terms of operating results and value creation, yet report lower return on invested capital. Such a company's bonus metrics might discourage a perfectly good investment depending upon which business unit is looking at it.

The list doesn't end there. Metrics commonly play a part in short-term bias and risk aversion. Excessive emphasis on margins and rates of return can easily bias the company against growth. Sales, volume and even profit measures may encourage uneconomic growth. Financial leverage can skew results and disconnect them from the actions of most managers.

And, of course, much bonus pay isn't even based upon business unit results. For a typical business unit executive, half of bonus potential is driven explicitly by corporate results and the other half is in jeopardy based upon corporate-level "circuit breakers" on overall plan funding.

Analyzing Incentive Structure
from a Business Unit Perspective

The issue really gets down to line of sight–will you get paid better if you increase business unit results, or will you get paid mainly based upon other things? Even in companies with typical, "simple" incentive structures of bonuses and option grants, business unit executives can't tell whether their actions make much difference. The chart below provides an illustration of the overall problem with business unit incentives. It describes the major influences upon incentive pay for a business unit executive.

Incentive pay is largely out of the realm of influence of a typical business unit manager. This isn't pay-for-performance. It is pay driven by actions of other people or of the stock market. It is pay independent of the executive's own decisions, efforts or outcomes. It hardly warrants the label "incentive pay."

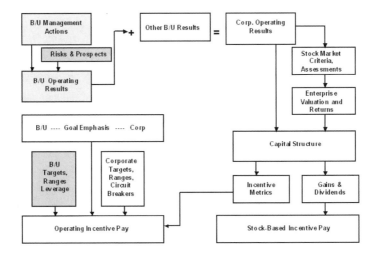

The Corrosive Effects of Current Incentive Practices

These issues aren't purely theoretical ones. Current incentive practices take their toll on business results–and therefore upon overall corporate performance–in a multitude of ways.

- Talented, confident people want to have a stake in their own success, so they leave to find jobs where their contributions are rewarded on a basis closer to one-to-one. Those most comfortable being insulated from the results of their own decisions are those most likely to stay.

- Business unit management teams may set stretch goals, take proper risks and pursue excellence. But sandbagging and income management can be reliable paths to the same pay result, creating an environment of mediocre expectations, internal inequity and general dissonance.

- Management may discount the longer-term. Short-term thinking and risk aversion–encouraged by the system of bonus rewards–work directly against long-run value creation in many businesses.

- The system certainly allows free riding on corporate results; this is the main way one gets paid. Executive incentives are said to encourage participants to "drive" business performance but, where most of the pay dollars are concerned, they encourage a passenger's perspective.

Left to run its course, the incentive system may retain mediocre people, drive down ambitions and create disappointing results.

Three Themes for Structural Redesign

This situation needs fixing. We propose a general shift away from parent company's stock price and budget process as the vehicles for delivering business unit incentive pay. In companies with reasonably separable business units, we propose a re-design of incentive structure in these three directions:

- **Shifting pay opportunities toward explicit goals and measurable results.** This can be done using cash incentives, better-functioning equity incentives, and through hybrid structures that link stock or option awards to measurable goals. Focusing more strongly upon measurable business results, rather than upon the stock market's distant gyrations–greatly increases executive line of sight by clarifying the linkages among business decisions, results and incentive rewards. As part of this shift, we suggest specific improvements in the methods used in setting incentive targets and ranges and in measuring performance.

- **Shifting operating incentive structure toward the longer term.** Short-term bias and risk aversion can be addressed directly by shifting the long-term incentive away from pure options and restricted stock into better long-term performance vehicles. This moves incentive pay dollars directly into line with long-run results and centers it in the executive's field of vision. The issues also can be addressed by introducing more stability into the bonus plan.

- **A general shift of long-term incentive opportunity toward the business unit level.** This is done by weighting business-unit results more heavily within performance plans and hybrid equity arrangements, or by instituting phantom stock plans or subsidiary equity plans tied to business-unit value. This suggestion is sometimes viewed as controversial by some companies but it really should not be; as most have structures of distinct groups and divisions, and profit centers deploying bonus plans that already dis-aggregate results along these lines.

Understanding Phantom Stock and Subsidiary Equity

When evaluating specific proposals for design, phantom stock plans provide a useful starting point, embodying as they do the best and worst of business-unit incentives. If designed well and used in the right setting, phantom stock can create a compelling economic stake in long-run value creation for business units. This can greatly increase the efficacy of management incentives and contribute to success, all in a fiscally prudent and predictable way.

If designed badly or misapplied, a phantom stock plan can be confusing, ineffective and internally controversial. Even worse, badly designed phantom plans can encourage business decisions that destroy shareholder value and subject the company to inappropriate levels of expense.

Handled correctly, phantom stock is quite useful for illuminating key aspects of an incentive plan's design that, in turn, affect other kinds of plans. For example:

- The general structure of overlapping grants and long-run pay-outs used in other types of long-term incentives at the business unit level.
- The potential impact of metrics upon decision-making.
- The approaches to setting goals–and the role of expected performance–in judging success and delivering pay.
- The strength of connection of long-term rewards to actual results, with implications for line of sight and for plan funding.

Some specific plan examples are presented next. Note that though the first few are phantom stock plans, the discussion is applicable to subsidiary equity plans as well. Our initial example of a phantom stock plan design is one that uses a particular form of the performance/valuation measure "total business return" or "TBR."

- **Basic plan mechanism.** A grant under this plan entitles the participant to the TBR generated by a block of stock. TBR is the increase in the value of the business over a period of time plus the cash flows generated by its operations. This two-part measurement approach is much like total shareholder return ("TSR") used to measure capital gains and dividends on a stock investment. A $100,000 TBR phantom stock grant would entitle the participant to the return generated by a $100,000 block of stock, in much the same way that a $100,000 option grant delivers the gains on a $100,000 in shares. In this case the $100,000 is not the corporation's stock. It is enterprise value in the manager's own division.

- **Valuation and TBR computations.** For purposes of the plan, the business unit is valued at ten times income (defined as after-tax operating profit). That is, the business is valued using one of the simplest possible approaches; set equal to a fixed multiple of income. If income is $100 million, it is worth $1 billion in the incentive plan.[5]

In the example, the business increases its income by $25 million so its value rises ten-fold; by $250 million. It also generates $200 million in free cash flows, so its total business return is $450 million. TBR is 45% of beginning value, so the gain on a $100,000 grant is $45,000.

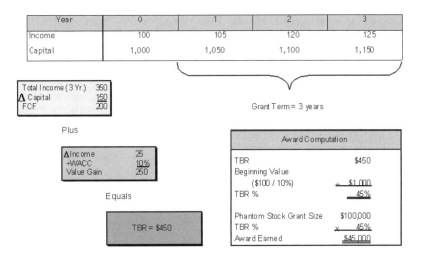

Year	0	1	2	3
Income	100	105	120	125
Capital	1,000	1,050	1,100	1,150

Total Income (3 Yr.)	350
Δ Capital	150
FCF	200

Grant Term = 3 years

Plus

Δ Income	25
÷WACC	10%
Value Gain	250

Equals

TBR = $450

Award Computation	
TBR	$450
Beginning Value ($100 / 10%)	$1,000
TBR %	45%
Phantom Stock Grant Size	$100,000
TBR %	× 45%
Award Earned	$45,000

Thus, participants share in value creation via a format that employs simple measures and a simple valuation approach. This is a straightforward structure offering these benefits:

- **Flexibility and Consistency.** This form of TBR can take businesses with many different levels of risk, growth and capital needs and evaluate their results on a roughly consistent footing. This feature helps in benchmarking pay and performance and addresses many issues that confound traditional performance metrics.

- **Alignment with Value-Creating Business Decisions.** Business investments normally increase the level of capital used by a business unit, so investment outlays by themselves reduce free cash flow. Returns on those investments are expected to increase income over time, causing (under this plans formula) a ten-fold increase in valuation. So, ten dollars of new investment must generate at least a dollar of income—a ten percent return—to break even in TBR terms.[6]

- **Long-Term Orientation.** The way to maximize gains under the plan is to maximize TBR over the long run. By making annual, overlapping grants with maturity dates staggered into the future, these plans do no reward the short-term price bumps that can put standard options temporarily in the money. One-time increases in income or reductions of expense are valuable since they increase TBR dollar for dollar. However, sustainable increases in income increase TBR by a factor of ten. Permanent increases in expense have a tenfold *downside* impact. In this respect, the plan encourages both business growth and cost control, with long-term effects being most important.

Market Valuation of Phantom Stock and Subsidiary Equity Plans

Many companies with phantom stock plans simply have their shares valued by an outside expert in order to determine share valuation and gains. This approach is used even more often when the plan uses actual shares rather than phantom stock. The market-value approach allows companies to have equity-based incentives that work in a way most similar to the option and stock grants used by public companies, aligning gains more closely with actual market value than a formula-based plan would do.

Liquidity is not as great as with public company options or stock, since shares typically are valued at annual intervals. Some companies incorporate quarterly and even daily valuation into their plans by pegging their share prices to those of publicly-traded peers.

Appraisals can add significant administrative costs. However, having shares valued makes sense in a range of settings. The market-value approach often is chosen when the company is already obliged to have shares valued periodically for investor reporting, buy/sell agreements, or to enable use of non-quoted stock in a qualified retirement plan. It can also make sense in private companies that expect to go public within a few years. Some companies are so rapidly growing or have such volatile or uncertain prospects that a formula-based approach is not seen as useful.

Market Valuation Versus Formula Valuation–Accuracy Versus Efficacy

In many other settings, however, market value simply is regarded as a more complete and accurate way of judging management's contribution to value creation and therefore a better basis for delivering incentive gains. Of course, that is the *de facto* stance of so many public companies that use stock options and other stock-based incentives as the centerpiece of their incentive structure.

Serious trade-offs affect the decision of whether to use market valuation or a formula-based method to value shares within a business unit equity plan. The valuation method–the connection between management actions, business results and reward–is, after all, the engine of the incentive plan.

As discussed earlier, gains under many stock-based plans are unconnected to business unit management's actions for two main reasons:

1. Business units often don't have much influence on overall results.

2. Stock prices move around for many reasons unrelated to consolidated performance, particularly during the one- to five-year timeframe that matters so greatly within an incentive plan.

Using a business unit equity plan–whether based upon phantom or actual equity–addresses the first of these issues well by focusing upon performance and value creation at the business unit level. However, if market value is used as the basis for reward, the second issue may remain troublesome. The plan will reflect not only the results produced by the business unit but also the vagaries of market valuation. Valuation formulas, by contrast, link rewards concretely with actual business results, not stock prices.

Reconciling Market Value and Formula Value

When well constructed, such formulas align with market value over time. The difference between market value and a typical formula valuation is greatest when company valuation diverges significantly from a modest multiple of current earnings. If the company expects exceptionally high growth, then current earnings are very low in relation to the future earnings levels reflected by the high multiple. A low multiple usually means earnings are regarded as unsustainable or especially risky. Free cash flow enters into the equation as well. Companies with highly distributable earnings tend to be valued, all else being equal, at higher multiples.

These valuation gaps subside over time as the company's actual performance plays out. For example, when multiples are particularly high, they often reflect hopes for income growth that are expected to be realized over the next few years. The formula-based plan, in such a case, will show a rapid rise in value as income actually grows and will end up tracking value and returns over time in proportions similar to those indicated by market appraisal.

The big difference between the two approaches lies in the timing of value creation and in the standard of proof applied. The formula approach accretes value into the current period based only upon actual performance. The market appraisal, in contrast, also takes into account expected changes in future performance. The latter approach connects pay with timely and accurate market values, while the former connects it with value creating financial performance only as it is earned. The formula based plan effectively says to management, "Show me the money." This is a reasonable demand, considering the senior management's decision-making role and the medium- to long-term timeframe of many of their actions.

Fiscal Prudence and Plan Funding

The distinction between market and formula valuation is important to plan funding as well. Market valuation can increase phantom stock gains beyond a level warranted by current financial results. That means plan costs may become intolerably high in relation to company earnings or may even exceed its ability to pay. And, if financial results are disappointing, market-based plans can pay out big gains based upon hoped-for performance that never does arrive.

Public companies face these same concerns with option and stock plans, since the costs are borne by owners in terms of the cash used to repurchases shares, dilution or both. But for nonpublic companies or business units, gains normally must be paid in cash so funding can be a more acute concern. Formula valuations tend to tie plan expense accruals and pay-outs more closely to company earnings and cash flows, so the funding issue is lessened.

This linkage to actual results is not foolproof, however. Financial results can be volatile, hard to interpret, and subject to manipulation in the short-term. It is clearly risky, therefore, to have a lot of money riding on one year's results, and well-designed plans don't do that. Instead, by including terms like the following, plans can ensure that gains and costs align closely with value creation over time:

• Multi-year grants–typically between three and six years in overall length–so pay is based upon sustained performance. Limiting grants to five or six years at most is prudent as well to prevent liabilities from compounding beyond anticipated levels and preventing large batches of exercisable grants from overhanging some future year's results.

• Annual granting and multi-year vesting, so that exercise or maturity dates are spread over several years.

• Using the ending value each year as the basis for cash-out and also the exercise price for future grants. This has a "ratcheting" effect on goals, requiring that gains in earnings be sustained to deliver high pay-outs on many grants over time.

• Administering grants with close attention to annual share usage. Grants that are within a range 0.5% to 2.0% of annual value tend to keep plan liabilities in reasonable proportion to owner gains while providing competitive grants to management participants.

• Subtraction of plan accruals before calculating earnings and valuation. This procedure smoothes out fluctuations in income, valuation and plan gains, particularly when grant "overhang" is high. In the cases, large increases in income and value would otherwise cause plan accruals to spike to a very high percentage of current income.

So, the important choice between market vs. formula valuation is not simply a question of the cost of annual appraisals. Rather, the choice may also depend upon factors like applicability of valuation formulas, timing of when value creation is recognized, funding and cost concerns as well as the overall effect upon "line of sight" and the efficacy of the plan design.

Market-Indexed and Performance-Based Valuation Formulas

Market indexed valuation provides a kind of compromise between formula valuation and market valuation. In one simple example, the company is valued at a multiple of income determined by an industry peer group. This method reflects the company's actual financial performance as well as the market valuations of similar companies, so it gives management direct credit for improving results and within a scheme that also reflects current industry valuation norms. Under a market-indexed approach, valuation multiples may vary with the market.

Valuation multiples used in incentive plans can also be made to vary based upon performance. Here is one example as used in a captive finance subsidiary of a major automotive manufacturer:

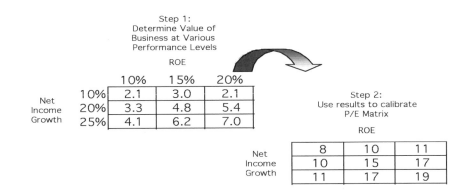

This company's phantom shares are valued as a multiple of earnings. But, the multiple varies based upon net income and return on equity. The multiples were established by:

- Performing multiple regression analysis of peer company valuation multiples and isolating the separate impacts of ROE and earnings growth upon P/E ratios. This analysis provided the target multiple, helped set target performance levels, and guided the general range of valuation multiples to be used.

- Constructing a discounted cash flow ("DCF") model that syncs up with the multiples indicated by the regression analysis. The exact P/E multiples used to populate the matrix were then generated by running scenarios within this DCF model.

This general approach can be applied to many industries and metrics. An example applied in the independent power industry, for example, featured valuation multiples earned based upon operating cash flow and gross capital usage

In each of the foregoing examples, business valuations could expand greatly based upon actual results. So each of these plans delivered potentially strong award leverage and pay-outs. From a cost viewpoint, though, the structure of overlapping, multi-year grants required that high performance be sustained before consistently high rewards could be earned. A pure market valuation-based plan, on the other and, or one simply using a high, fixed valuation multiple may pay out systematically for growth expectations that are never attained.

Companies sometimes wish to create wide "play" in valuations and gains as a way of creating greater plan leverage and motivational power. In such cases, performance-based adjustments can be a more prudent path than writing a blank check based upon either the market's vagaries, the short-run variation in income, or both.

Combining Performance-Valuation and Indexed Valuation

Like other kinds of valuation formulas, the market-indexed variety can be adjusted to emphasize key messages about business priorities. Consider this example used in a wholly owned internet service provider, or ISP.

It shows the extent to which formulas can be tailored to deal with unusual situations, even ones including extremes in terms of valuation levels, volatility and unpredictability:

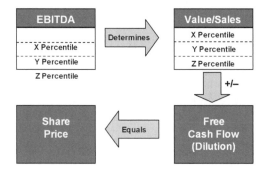

In this case, EBITDA performance determines the market value/revenue multiple used. The indexed approach was chosen because this newly-acquired company wanted employees to continue to participate in market movements. At the same time, the company and its new parent wanted to use a valuation formula to connect pay directly with key goals. The two-stage valuation format is indexed fully with market movement while emphasizing measures like revenue, EBITDA and free cash flow.

The format was also intended to index the stock market's criteria for business results and success. The format effectively placed the company in a race for revenue and EBITDA, with its peers as competitors (this is an example of a flexible target-setting method). The formula was designed to track more subtle market signals as well. EBITDA was expected to become more important in the stock market's valuation of such enterprises (revenue multiples were expected to fall, that is, and EBITDA levels were expected to rise). The formula was designed to track this trade-off as well, assigning higher importance to EBITDA as it emerged as a stronger driver of market value.

This valuation format was intended to last, and it has held up and generated proportionally reasonable results through the course of wild market movements. All the while, it has clearly reflected the company's key financial priorities. For the purposes of this discussion, it serves to illustrate the extent to which market and motivational dynamics can be articulated in a plan's valuation formula.

EBITDA as a Valuation Yardstick

EBITDA is used commonly in some industries as a valuation yardstick. It should be used with care within incentive plans, however. EBITDA is an incomplete measure. It does not take account of the financial claims that taxes and asset replacement can pose on owner income, so it does not provide enough information to judge whether a particular business decision creates value or not. By themselves, EBITDA-based goals encourage the company to make investments with low, value-destroying economic yields. The value/revenue multiple used in the plan presented just above is even less reliable in this regard.

In the ISP example, the valuation format was constructed to provide a continuing, market-based stake, to set out the company's main financial goals, and to reflect drivers in the rewards scheme in proportions indicated roughly by the stock market over time. The company in that example was not using the valuation formula as direct guidance to investment decision making. Rather, that company was well aware of the deficiencies of the

EBITDA metric. It knew it must rely upon thorough procedures in financial analysis in order to keep big-ticket decisions aligned with value creation, since this particular type of plan design would not be adequate to do so by itself.

The issue is an important one at many other companies, as well. Many use TBR-based phantom stock plans in which shares are valued based upon a multiple of EBITDA, often unaware of the fiscal risks that this approach can involve and the extent to which it may harm the quality of business decisions.

Adjusting Valuation Results

Each valuation approach relies heavily upon current earning power, risk, earnings growth and capital requirements as well as other financial drivers of business value. Whether value is determined by appraisal or formula, care must be taken to see that the earnings base being capitalized into value is "representative" of continuing earning power, and not distorted by temporary blips or downturns. In indexed plans, the same needs to be true of the multiple arising from the peer group. (This tends to be less of an issue since peer group multiples are less volatile, often being computed as a peer group's average, median, or inter-quartile mean).

Further smoothing–in the market-indexed plan design as well as many others–may be accomplished through devices like.

• Capitalizing trailing average earnings of the company and its peers.

• Establishing alternative minimum or maximum valuations based on, for example, net assets, equity or sales.

• Establishing a maximum range of price movement per measurement period ("collaring").

These adjustments tend to spread out the timing of price movements, making them depend more fully on sustained financial results while not limiting the valuation ultimately attained. Current earnings or cash flows can be adjusted directly if they contain a large, temporary or one-time element.

In these cases, the "total return" format of many formulas provides guidance on how to adjust. Acquisition outlays, for example, or one-time losses, tend to run through the free cash flow computation only–all at once or over 2 or 3 years–so that management's performance in TBR terms reflects these hits only once. General variation in income, on the other hand, has both a capitalized and multiple impact on valuation since it tends to affect not only the current year but also expectations going forward. As noted earlier, the general architecture of the plan (e.g., overlapping multi-year grants, iterative subtraction of plan accruals from income) does a lot to regularize gains over time.

Financial results may need adjustment to deal with unusual company circumstances. The IPP noted earlier provides an example of this. As an IPP, the company held various percentage interests in many power plant investments. In this situation, typical approaches to consolidation could have resulted in distorted measurements of capital and debt, pulling all the debt of a 51%-owned investee onto the books, for example, while eliminating all the debt of a 49%-owned venture. A "proportional consolidation" approach was devised for the incentive plan, so that its capital levels reflected its share of investee holdings and obligations on stable scale between 0% and 100%.

The captive finance company's incentive plan provided another example of how a particular company's circumstances may require an adjustment. The measures used in their plan–net income and return on equity–are affected by variations in their financial leverage. This factor was a potential source of volatility and bias within their plan, so results were restated pro forma to reflect a targeted, fixed capital structure.

Grant Structure and Leverage

Phantom stock plans normally are designed to compete with equity-based incentive plans used by public companies, mostly stock options. The corresponding form of phantom stock grant is an appreciation-only grant like the alternatives discussed so far.

But phantom stock grants can also be structured like whole shares of stock, so participants receive not only accrued returns at exercise or maturity, but also the beginning value per share. Like restricted stock, full-value phantom shares have a greater per-share value at grant, so a company can grant fewer shares and still offer competitive grant value. As in the public company sector, full-value grants are used more often when retention concerns are particularly important. Appreciation-only grants are used in cases when performance and award leverage dominate the discussion. Discounted grants are possible, too, along with grants that pay out only when returns exceed some hurdle rate (like premium options).

This is an explicit and important design choice. The chart below shows hypothetical payoffs on grant structures that were examined by a wholly-owned realty subsidiary of a diversified company during the design of its incentives. The chart shows equally-valued grants of full-value phantom

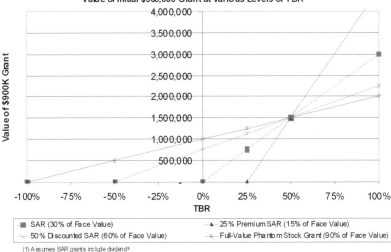

Value of Initial $900,000 Grant at Various Levels of TBR[1]

(1) Assumes SAR grants include dividends

stock (exercise price at zero) and discounted phantom stock (exercise price at 50% of beginning value) as well as grants with exercise prices at current value and at a 25% premium to current value.

The discounted and full-value grants involve gains (and forfeitable grant value) at many different performance levels. The at-the-money and premium grants, in contrast, are more concerned with leverage and home run potential. The exercise price on phantom stock is a variable affecting plan leverage, retention power and dilution. Companies should consider each of these factors when structuring phantom stock grants.

Subsidiary Equity

Of course, some business units of larger companies—as well as closely-held businesses—use their own shares as the award currency within incentive plans. Examples include high-growth start-ups intending to go public, joint ventures, companies recently taken over, and LBOs. Some private companies and business units use real shares rather than phantom ones simply because they regard stock as a superior medium for creating a managerial stake.

Outside such special circumstances, most companies do not wish to use actual stock of a business unit when devising incentives at that level in the organization. The prospect of using stock can engender a range of tax, legal concerns and reporting concerns. Also, some complex corporate structures can make it difficult to figure out which legal entity's stock to use.

Accounting treatment can be an issue as well. Current rules make the book-keeping advantages of stock options harder to achieve for those companies offering non-quoted shares.

Repurchase commitments create a funding issue for companies considering using actual stock, a concern often cited in design discussions. But this is not an issue unique to stock-based plans; equivalently-designed phantom stock tends to create a similar cash commitment.

Typical tax treatment in the U.S. does not encourage using stock options rather than similarly constructed phantom stock. On the other hand, in some countries, tax treatment of stock-based pay is so superior to cash that companies are motivated strongly to figure out ways to deploy it.

Market valuation is used more often as the basis for valuation when actual shares are involved. As detailed earlier, this approach tends to involve the higher accuracy of the market valuation approach, as well as its higher costs and possibly lower degree of line of sight. Valuation formulas can be used as the basis for repurchasing shares in a subsidiary equity plan, thereby creating the financial and motivational effects intended in some phantom stock plans. However, state or country legal issues may limit a company's ability to compel the redemption of actual shares at any price, much less one determined by formula.

Equity-Based Incentive Plans Based Upon Book Value

Small-company phantom stock plans sometimes use book value as the basis for valuation. This is also the method used, in effect, in many professional services firms owned by partners or principals. Book value plans typically reward the participant for increasing stockholders' equity accounts, and therefore for accumulating earnings for shareholders.

A few observations about how these plans function:

• These approaches are based strictly upon actual financial results. However, they do not take into account whether participants have increased the earning power of the business during the measurement period. Rather, they simply reward accumulation of earnings irrespective of whether earnings are rising or falling. Falling earnings tend to mean a falling valuation, so these plans carry the risk of paying out substantial rewards even if performance suggests destruction of value.

• Book value plans don't necessarily attach a complete or consistent cost to the use of capital, so they may reward results that do not create value. Book value plan are driven by book earnings, so they reflect the hodge-podge of capital-related effects normally at issue in computing equity-based metrics like net income, EPS or ROE. But they may omit any cost for the use of equity capital, miss the impact of financial leverage on that cost, or both.

The main advantage of book value plans is their simplicity.

Anti-Dilution Features

Phantom and subsidiary equity plans normally have "anti-dilution" clauses protecting plan participants and sponsors from some serious risks, such as:

• That the business' owners will pay out a lot of money in dividends or otherwise withdraw capital, reducing earning power and value.

• Correspondingly, that an inflow—such as a capital infusion—inadvertently enriches plan participants.

Such clauses can take a range of forms. The "free cash flow" computation involved in TBR is one example. It tracks the investor money going into and out of a business. A $100 million capital infusion by itself simply reduces TBR by $100 million, so management is affected by dilution in proportion to that felt by owners. Capital transactions can also affect share value through issuances or redemptions, whether for real or phantom shares.

Performance Plans

Performance plans comprise the other common category of long-term incentive plans focusing on business-unit level performance. These plans come in two main varieties:

• **Performance unit plans.** These provide cash awards based upon attaining long-term performance goals. Basically like bonus plans in structure, they tend to be based entirely on financial performance in relation to pre-set goals; having award ranges limited on the upside, and dependent mainly upon corporate-level performance. When we cite performance plans and performance shares as a business-unit incentive, we are referring to plans that based at least partly upon business unit results.

• **Performance share plans.** These allow participants to earn shares of the parent company based upon attainment of pre-set goals. This is basically a long-term bonus plan denominated in shares rather than cash. They provide a fairly straightforward means of encouraging long-run success for business units. At the same time, by using stock, they maintain a firm link to parent company success. If subsidiary shares are available for use in an incentive plan, then these may be delivered in a performance-share format as well.

There are many variations on format, but two others warrant particular mention. These may help achieve the key effect of performance share plans –awards that depend jointly upon corporate stock price and performance against predetermined goals:

- **TARSAPs, or time-accelerated restricted stock plans.** Under these, grants vest purely based on continued employment, typically over some period like six or eight years, or sooner depending upon achievement. The fact the grant vests at a certain date, irrespective of performance, has the effect of fixing the number of shares to be issued in the future. This qualifies the grants for fixed accounting under current U.S. GAAP, avoiding the possibly higher charges that attend variable accounting. At the same time, the acceleration feature gives the grant a performance-based look and feel. A TARSAP is like a performance share grant, but without the variable accounting treatment.[7]

- **Performance-based stock options.** These are grants of parent company stock options whose amount, vesting or exercise price depends upon measured business performance. As with performance share plans, the general structure of these grants can allow the company to emphasize corporate stock price performance and, to the extent desired, business-unit performance.

Performance plans have much in common with phantom stock. Their general architecture involves many features of phantom/subsidiary equity plans like overlapping grants, staggered vesting/maturity dates and, when designed well, proper connections between financial performance and executive rewards.

Value-Based Incentives Versus Performance Plans

Performance plans can emphasize value creation in the same terms as a phantom plan with a valuation formula. The TBR-based phantom stock plan presented earlier can be converted into an equivalent performance plan, as one example. This approach would simply involve:

- Making performance plan grants each year, ones with a total term of three to five years and either ratable or cliff vesting.

- Setting up an award schedule involving a 1:1 connection between TBR and cash pay-out, with zero payment at zero TBR and a long interval on the upside.

This approach does what TBR phantom stock and other value-based incentives can do. It creates a one-for-one linkage between value creation over time and pay and it does so across a wide range of performance levels. It reflects the first-level drivers of value–income, capital, and the cost of capital–in reasonable proportion. If a company simply can capture these basic trade-offs and apply them to business unit pay, it will have a better-functioning structure of rewards than most, from a shareholder value perspective.

Economic profit, also known as economic value added, is another well-known value-based metric. Economic profit is computed as after-tax operating profit minus a charge for the use of capital[8], so it takes the main value drivers into reasonable account. A performance plan scaled to reasonable economic profit performance is another way of getting explicit value-based criteria into the workings of a performance plan.

Performance plan designs don't always capture this dynamic. Their traditional metrics and structure often create a range of situations in which management can be paid well for decisions that actually destroy value.

Phantom Stock Versus Performance Plan Format

A great advantage of performance plans, on the other hand, is their relative simplicity; employing familiar metrics and presenting them in familiar, straightforward award schedules. They don't require the company to roll out and communicate a new measurement approach or valuation scheme.

In many cases, the choices available for a business unit's long-term incentives are reduced to two main approaches: A traditional performance plan paying out in either cash or corporate shares, or a business unit phantom stock plan. Companies sometimes believe they face a hard choice in this area:

- They can use simple, familiar plans that people understand, but that may not always align with value creation. In this case, companies are obliged to rely heavily on other governance tools–budgeting, strategic planning, investment and deal evaluation, performance evaluation, moral suasion– to be sure that business decisions consistently favor shareholder interests.[9]
- They can have value-based incentives, ones that align results well with value creation and can be deployed with confidence at the business unit level where line of sight effects are greatest. However, such plans are less familiar and more complex than traditional ones. They pose risks of low comprehension, mistrust, and even some adverse effects on decision-

making (e.g., the "harvest bias" that managers may mistakenly adopt when incentives are changed to reflect capital usage). And, in any event, the company will have to expand its commitment to communication in order to implement such plans.

This is a false dilemma. Companies can offer value-based incentives and they can do so in readily understandable formats. Here is an example of a simple method:

Operating Income

		$ 4.00	$ 4.50	$ 5.00	$ 5.50	$ 6.00
	10.00%	0%	0%	0%	0%	0%
	11.25%	44%	50%	56%	61%	67%
ROIC	12.50%	80%	90%	100%	110%	120%
	13.75%	109%	123%	136%	150%	164%
	15.00%	133%	150%	167%	183%	200%

This incentive plan uses the common, familiar measures of operating income and return on invested capital. It arrays performance and reward schedules in a matrix format; one used in many performance plans. Yet, it is fully a value-based plan since it delivers pay-outs based upon the "value added" implications of the various levels of operating income and ROIC. Performance is rewarded in reasonable proportion to value created over time. Decisions that don't generate value don't increase pay. Note that techniques demonstrated here apply equally to annual incentive plans.

Avoiding Complexity–Minimizing Adjustments

Value-based performance measures can be used to address many matters that trouble the financial integrity of incentive plans. But there is a risk of "mission creep," in which the metrics are used to address too many aspects of company bookkeeping and decision-making. That can lead to high complexity in the pay plans and bring poor comprehension and results. Here is a partial list of measurement issues, simply to sketch out the potential complexity in this area:

• Effects of financing decisions, rather than the operating results that most plan participants are trying to improve, upon common measures like ROE and EPS. Issues include debt usage, leasing policy and repurchase activity.

• Effects of accruals and other accounting determinations on reported earnings. One consulting firm actually boasted over 100 metric adjustments to deal with this sort of thing.

- Inflation and its impact upon the comparability of current-dollar earnings and historic-dollar book value.
- Acquisition effects on the balance sheet presentation of certain assets, throwing off many comparisons of performance among business units or peer or over time.
- The "periodic" format of most metrics, which ignores the effect of value creation on current results.
- Asset composition (depreciating vs. non-depreciating), asset life and their role in determining whether a given amount of cash flow creates value or not.
- Volume measures that ignore profitability, margin measures that ignore volume, profit measures that ignore a portion of costs, and profit measures that ignore the pivotal roles of capital and risk upon value creation.
- The fact that, in the short term, results can be manipulated in such as way as to hype just about any metric.
- General limitations in measuring historical performance when value is based entirely upon expected performance.
- The potential benefits and serious problems associated with non-financial measures including strategic metrics and "value drivers."

Basic measures like TBR, when used within a framework of overlapping incentive long-term incentive grants, actually address many of these issues without any adjustment too the metric. Though adjustments to metrics can be used to mop up the balance of the issues, we rarely recommend doing so. Company experience has shown that doing so can render the incentive system too complex. During the "metric wars" of the mid to late 1990s (covered by *CFO Magazine*), measurements were often advanced as the sole solution. Many value-based metrics proved confusing, posed basic difficulties in plan design and administration, had only short-term effects on results and ultimately were abandoned.

The really compulsory adjustment features needed in a value-based incentive plan are the same ones commonly addressed when administering more traditional plans; how to deal with large outlays like acquisitions, capital expenditures, and costly initiatives in areas like marketing and R & D. In those cases, the goal is to create full accountability for return on such investments in a productive way, normally by spreading out their effects over two to three years.

Other Considerations for Bonus and Performance Plan Design

To this point, we've demonstrated that performance plans can be used to encourage value creation. In this regard, they're about as effective as the formulas used more explicitly in some phantom stock designs.

But performance plans differ in important ways from other forms of long-term business-unit incentives, so let's turn to some of those distinctions. The performance/reward apparatus used in annual bonus plans and long-term performance plans is one that involves first making a set of explicit design choices. We will now proceed through those for the balance of this chapter.

Keep in mind that we haven't really finished with discussing phantom plan design. The design choices we will review now are ones that also warrant examination within a phantom plan as well. In effect, the key dimensions of performance plan design are worth citing as compulsory steps in *any* kind of incentive plan.

Setting Grant/Award Sizes and Performance Targets

Performance plans normally express target award levels as bonus plans do; in dollars or percent of salary to be earned at target. In either format, one is obliged to assess the performance/reward connection to assure that it is competitive for the participant and set appropriately for the company.

And how do companies do that? Well, most set targets based upon long-range plan goals or upon the annual budget process. As noted early on in this chapter, the process may result in sandbagging, income management, bias and dissonance.

We have developed a suite of tools and solutions applicable in response to these issues and others, testing them over the years and implementing them. Here are three examples of such approaches:

• **Setting Targets Based Upon Shareholder Expectations.** Stock prices reflect expectations for future performance of a company and its business units, information that can be particularly helpful in target-setting. To get at it, one needs to consider some basic principles of business valuation. The value of a business—as indicated by its stock price or the price at which it would change hands in a 100% sale—reflects expectations for its future performance. Our proprietary models allow one to study a company's stock price and to deduce from it the levels of expected future performance that underlie the company's valuation. This is very helpful input for the incentive target setting process because it is external and shareholder-oriented, and not the result of a process of internal negotiation.

To apply this information to business unit target-setting, the overall value of the company must be apportioned among its operating units. This is done using valuation guidance from peer company stock prices for each major business unit. The overall exercise reconciles performance expectations for the business units–and their valuations–to those of the overall company. Similar peer-based valuation inferences allow private companies as well to set their incentive targets based upon appropriate market expectations.

- **Mechanical goal-setting procedures and financial algorithms.** A big part of the problem with business unit bonus plans is their very short-term orientation. This year's bonus opportunity, once set, offers fairly clear signals about what management must do to increase pay. Harder to divine are the effects of current actions on future bonuses. The farther into the future one's view extends, the more the platform for bonus rewards is a vague, contingent function of future priorities and negotiations.

This is a problem. Maximizing value creation in a business almost always involves making decisions now, but where the risks and prospects of those decisions will play out over a period of several years. The typical system places the fruits of such actions–the out years' results–in a jeopardized or ineligible status for reward. Companies can fix this issue by lengthening the effective time frame of the annual incentive plan.

To do so, they need to adopt semi-permanent standards–"sticky contracts," as they are sometimes called–so that managers can have some confidence now about the financial claim they will hold against future results. As one example of a solution, a client set targets for each of 10 business units based upon a uniform standard of 18% TBR as a percent of "beginning value." This standard was then translated into the goals used in each plan and could be achieved through strength in one or several of the goal areas. Companies with low ROIC performance were assigned higher growth targets, through the basic device of using their capital levels as the beginning value for purposes of the plan (rather than basing value upon a multiple of current earnings, as in the other cases). The overall effect of this approach was to create for management a predictable, enduring, continuous claim upon current and future results; an "ownership" financial stake.

- **Flexible Target Setting.** A TBR-based example also demonstrates the helpful principle of flexibility. Irrespective of how targets are set, participants in TBR and other value-based incentives often have many paths they can pursue toward a given bonus reward. For example, the TBR standard of 18% noted earlier can be achieved by goals that connote 18% growth in income and zero cash flow yield, zero income growth and very high cash flow at 18% of value, or by innumerable combinations within this range or without. This flexibility makes the setting of targets a lot easier. Since management can earn competitive pay-outs under many different combinations of income growth and cash yield, the company is not under pressure to set hard, precise targets for either measure. The system has a high level of financial integrity, so it provides confidence that the rewards it issues will be strongly connected with shareholder gains over time.

Towers Perrin consultants have developed a range of other methods under which flexible, economically fair results can be pursued. Here are some examples:

- Award sizes can be benchmarked to economic "sharing rates" implied by stock-based incentive plans. TBR is useful here as well, since its capitalized format connects targeted operating results with their implications for valuation and economic dilution.

- Under "choice-based" targeting systems, participants can choose from different award schedules in which higher basic performance at targeted pay levels is accompanied by higher upside.

- The shape of the award schedule itself (the payout curve) has important effects. It determines what range of results is eligible for reward and therefore whether it sometimes pays to defer or accelerate costs or opportunities. It also can drive the urgency associated with any actions affecting business results. Devised well, it can help to create a continuous stake in results, overcoming some of the common temptations to manipulate results.

- Setting income targets based upon beginning capital levels is another example of a target-setting algorithm. Under one version of this approach, goals for income growth might equal a percentage of prior year income plus a fair return on any increase in capital during the preceding year. In place, this procedure works a lot like having an incentive plan based upon the beginning-capital version of the metric economic profit.

As always, a prudent step is to test the plan's system of targets, ranges and metrics under a wide range of scenarios for business decisions and results.

Setting Award Ranges–Limits On Ranges

Like most bonus plans, performance plans involve limited pay-out ranges, with 200% of the target award being typical as the upper limit of pay-out and zero or 50% being common thresholds. Phantom plans, in contrast, tend to offer upside limited only by the valuation of the business unit. Pay-out limitations, in both performance plans as well as bonus plans, are often put in place as a control on the functioning of the plan. Plans with unlimited pay-outs, like many phantom stock plans, are sometimes rejected due to perceived fiscal risk.

Actually, neither form of plan has a monopoly on prudence or risk. Performance plans are imprudent when they use flawed measures, goals or ranges; sometimes giving large pay-outs when performance actually is destroying value. Phantom plans, on the other hand, and other plans with unlimited upside, can be designed with many safeguards and a very strong connection with value creation over time and over a broad range of outcomes.

Finite ranges by themselves don't protect the company from unreasonable pay-outs. Rather, problems with plan design often mean that pay-outs are out of hand even when they are well within range. This can occur for a number of reasons:

- Pay-outs can be too dilutive at target and every other performance level and goals can be too easy to attain.
- Metrics and award schedules allow pay-outs for bad business decisions.
- Granting structures can encourage hyping short-term pay within unsustainable results.
- Narrow ranges can encourage management of income or simply discourage high performance.

And, as noted earlier, finite ranges may simply encourage manipulating the timing of revenues and costs so as to fit widely-ranging business results over time into the narrower interval that is eligible for reward. More effective safeguards than finite ranges include controlling grant/award levels, setting appropriate targets over time, setting award leverage at prudent levels, using value-based or value-calibrated measurement schemes, using overlapping, multi-year grants and subtracting incentive plan costs when arriving at measured financial results. When companies have prudently designed plans, they can expand the upside in their incentives without straying into some fiscal danger zone.

Impact of Performance/Award Ranges Upon Plan Leverage

Award ranges, combined with performance ranges, set the plan's "leverage." Pay upside at 200% of target, for example, when combined with a performance range topping out at 120% implies upside leverage of 5:1 (100 percentage points of award in relation to target is earned based upon twenty percentage points of performance above target). Median leverage of annual incentive plans is around 3.5 to one.[10]

High leverage may be used to create a strong incentive to improve results. It may also fit businesses in which the likely range of business results, along with management's ability to improve them, is unusually narrow. Wider ranges and concomitantly low leverage may fit in cases where results are less predictable or performance gains are easier to effect.

Performance ranges can also be problematic. Some companies, pursuing fairness or perhaps expediency, apply the same performance/pay-out schedules in many different businesses units. Since the actual range of business results tends to vary from one business to another, the one-size-fits all approach can have effects that are at once un-competitive, irrelevant, extremely compelling, or manipulable depending upon which part of the company one works in.

As noted earlier, we suggest that companies increase the fiscal protections in their plan designs since this allows them to offer exciting pay potential across a wide range of outcomes. We also suggest that ranges be set in a consistent and rigorous way. One method allows companies to base their incentive plan ranges upon the measured variability in results, following a process like this one:

- Measure the variability of business unit results around past budgets or, as an approximation, around a regression trend line of past performance. Using these results, sort the company's business units into two to four categories of variability. Peer company analysis and other sources of benchmark data on business uncertainty may be useful to consult as well.

- Use the risk data to construct performance ranges. For the more uncertain businesses, a relatively wide range from threshold to maximum performance–like 70% to 130% of target, may result in reasonably constructed ranges. More stable predictable businesses may warrant a range of 90% to 110% of target in order to move from threshold to maximum payouts. An intermediate risk group may employ the typical 80% to 120% range.

Under this approach, statistical inferences are used to set ranges that all have roughly the same chances of hitting threshold, target and maximum award levels. The company's ranges end up being very consistently derived and at the same time very customized to the characteristics of the particular business unit.

Weightings, Award Leverage and Influence– The Importance of Testing the Plan

Incentive plans may employ metrics that track results at the corporate level, the division level, at intermediate echelons like group or sector, and at sub-divisions like profit centers. So, each of these organizational levels can have different degrees of importance, or weight, in the overall delivery of awards. If awards under a performance plan are weighted equally upon corporate and business goals, then the plan will appear on its face to place equal importance on them.

It isn't that simple, though. The plan's leverage counts as well. Small changes in business unit results might have large incentive pay out effects, while corporate pay-outs may vary much less. In that case, business unit results are featured more heavily than their mere weighting would suggest. In this regard, leverage is a stealth variable in incentive design. Within the overall incentive structure, the *leverage* placed upon business unit results (or upon any goal) can be more important than its *weighting*.

The most important weighting, however, is individual influence. The fact that business unit executives have more influence upon business unit results naturally up-weights those goals within the incentive scheme. In fact, a typical business unit executive's bonus plan may be divided into two parts: a very short-term incentive plan based upon business unit results and a general results-sharing arrangement based upon corporate results.

With all of these design factors moving around, it can be difficult to divine what performance a company is paying for, how strongly, and under what circumstances. The level of expense involved in executive incentives, on the other hand, demands some cost/benefit analysis of incentive policy. And that can't be done without examining closely the inner workings of the plans. For this reason as well as others cited earlier, we recommend using an extensive testing and simulation step in incentive design projects. This is based upon a precise model of the company's plans, upon stock valuation models, and upon a wide range of possible business decisions and results.

Summary

It is well known that placing greater weight upon business unit results will increase line of sight, appeal and efficacy of the incentive structure in many companies. The *extent* to which incentive pay is a corporate-level creature, and the degree to which line of sight effects are degraded, is often startling news to companies when they study the matter. Nonetheless, the demand by business units for a more compelling financial stake is a well-known standing preference.

Current practice, on the other hand, is to deliver incentive pay mainly based upon corporate-level results and to align its themes with company-wide performance and allegiance. More acutely, the high corporate weighting within the pay plan is driven by concerns about:

- **Structure.** Teamwork, sharing of resources like capital, personnel and knowledge and participation of key business unit executives in corporate initiatives.

- **Design.** The administrative difficulty of setting goals well, tracking performance fairly and delivering appropriate pay in many different business units.

- **Rewards Strategy.** Equity and hierarchical concerns, when a successful business unit might earn much more than others and, in some scenarios, more than corporate executives.

This chapter is meant to address these concerns.

- **Structure.** Most companies have business units whose performance can be disentangled fairly well; enough to allow them to deliver incentive pay on that basis effectively. A modest up-weighting of business unit results on the bonus plan, coupled with only partial change in long-term incentive structure, can make business unit incentives far more compelling. This shift is both doable and worthwhile in most companies.

- **Design.** Companies can use business unit incentive plans and systems for performance measurement and target setting that offer clarity, financial integrity and fairness. This may appear more complicated than the corporate result-sharing devices found at the core of incentive systems now. But they are far more compelling in money terms, as well as to partic-ipants at the business unit level, than the current system is. Money has a famously clarifying effect.

- **Rewards Strategy.** Companies wishing to unleash the power of incentives at the business unit level will have to do less of the "leveling" that occurs in the typical structure now. Results won't please everyone at the company, but better business results ought to please shareholders and they are the ones paying the bill.

Endnotes

1. "There is no relationship whatsoever," said Dan R. Dalton, dean of the business school at the University of Indiana, of his 2002 study examining research on linkages between stock option usage and company performance, quoted by David Leonhardt of *The New York Times* (study: Dalton, D.R., Daily, C.M., Trevis, C.S., & Roengpitya, R. 2003. Meta-analyses of financial performance and equity: Fusion or confusion? *Academy of Management Journal*, April 2002).

2. See "Addressing Structural Issues in Executive Incentive Design," *WorldatWork Journal*, First Quarter 2002. Article notes that studies of accounting treatment in areas like mergers, inventories and depreciation consistently indicate that the accounting portrayal of events does not affect company stock prices. Article also cites research indicating that company stock prices are more strongly related to diluted EPS than to basic EPS, making it clear that investors are aware of the dilutive effects of securities like options irrespective of whether they are expensed in the P & L).

3. See Ericson, R. and Grund, M., "Announcement of Option Expensing Has No Impact on Share Price," *The Year in Executive Compensation,* Towers Perrin, 2002).

4. Simulation was used to develop the 20% estimate. The simulation of the incentive structure focused in this case upon a typical participant: a member of top management of a business unit. Movement in business unit financial results was assumed to be largely within the control of business unit management, or at least to represent a tolerable or customary risk. Variation in results of other businesses was assumed to be outside of the control of business unit management, as were market valuation parameters like the cost of capital and very long-run growth expectations. In this example, the overall "line of sight" figure of 20 percent is the amount of variation in incentive pay that is explained by variation in business unit results. The other 80 percent of the variation in incentive rewards was driven by variation in the cost of capital, in long-run growth expectations, in performance of other business units or in the outcome of the annual budget process.

Simulation model specifications: Market-based parameters were assigned to incentive plan terms and financial performance. Typical variation was applied to operating income in the near term (15 % root mean square error around 10-year regression trend line) and this variation drove the 10,000 scenarios examined. Default assumptions about capital usage and capital structure were used to convert each scenario's operating income into the measures used in the annual incentive plan (constant capital structure in market value terms, excess equity cash flows used for share repurchases at ending share price each year). The most common measures were used at the corporate and business unit levels (EPS and operating income). Using this information about financial performance, annual incentive plan payouts were simulated. The annual incentive plan was assumed to comprise modal award ranges and leverage (80-120% performance range, 50-200% payout range). A random error of one percentage point from most likely forecast for growth in operating income was used to determine the target used in the annual incentive (this was done in order to simulate uncertainty, but not bias, in the annual incentive target setting process).

Stock returns (and option gains) were simulated using a 10-year discounted cash flow (DCF) model with separate assumptions applied to near-term, medium-term and longer-term performance. Year one financial results in each scenario were the same ones used in simulating the bonus plan. Medium-term results were based upon adaptive revision of the DCF forecast based upon variation in one-year results. Modest random movement was attached to long-run expectations for business growth and also to the cost of capital (levels of variation resembled the variation in long corporate bond yields). The model's outputs were also validated by market norms; overall, the DCF simulation generated a pattern of stock returns resembling the stock market (continuously compounded shareholder return with a mean around 10 percent, a standard deviation of about 30 percent, and variance driven about one-half by consolidated financial performance over a five-year period. The 50 percent explanatory power attributed to financial performance was higher than typical. This was done in order to give some weight to the stock market's anticipatory nature and to its ability to reward for business decision based upon expected rather than actual results).

5. This valuation example reflects a ten percent cost of capital and accords credit to management only for that portion of enterprise valuation demonstrated by the actual level of operating results. In other words, the business is valued as a no-growth perpetuity based upon the actual current income level.

6. Ten percent is the threshold in this example when the cost of capital is ten percent. This simple version of TBR is an approximation of valuation effects and of the economic threshold for value-creating investment decisions.

7. Note again that relevant accounting rules appear to be on course for change over the next few years.

8. Computed as the company's weighted-average cost of capital multiplied by the amount of capital deployed in the business.

9. To a large extent, public companies have opted out of the "operating incentive" format, relying instead on stock-based incentives that, in effect, outsource the tasks of measurement and reward to the stock market.

10. The structure of the metric can enter into leverage as well. The measure economic profit, being residual in structure, can experience large percentage changes when income levels move only modestly. In that kind of plan, 1:1 leverage in terms of economic profit may be the equivalent of either very high or very low leverage in relation to operating income. .

RICHARD ERICSON
Principal
Towers Perrin

Mr. Ericson specializes in management and reward systems emphasizing principles of shareholder value creation. He is a Principal in Towers Perrin and is one of the firm's leaders in the area of value-based incentive design. He is located in the firm's Minneapolis office and works with many large public and private companies internationally.

Mr. Ericson has twenty years experience in the fields of business valuation and value-based incentive design. He is a frequent speaker to professional and industry audiences on the subject of value-based systems for target setting, performance measurement and executive rewards. He is responsible for Towers Perrin's training efforts regarding the use of financial methods in executive incentive design and has developed a suite of methods and tools used in client projects globally. He has published a range of articles and is the author of the book *Pay to Prosper; Using Value Rules to Reinvent Executive Incentives,* published by WorldatWork.

Mr. Ericson holds holds an M.B.A. in finance and accounting from the University of Chicago. He also holds a B.S. in finance and a B.A. in French literature, each granted *summa cum laude* from Northern Illinois University.

12. Employment Agreements

This chapter provides the reader with a detailed and expert presentation of the executive employment agreements commonly in use today. The authors begin by describing the different kinds of agreements that exist and the pros and cons of their use. The reader is then provided with a tour–clause by clause, element by element–of what might be contained in a typical agreement and their respective effect; from the initial recitals to the description of various forms of compensation and benefits, to the specifics of how various forms of termination will be handled should such a termination arise and, lastly, to other restrictive covenants that may also be included. A complete sample agreement is included on the CD and referred to throughout.

The chapter will provide a useful source of reference for anyone who is involved in either drafting or considering the key terms of an employment agreement, or who is interested in a better understanding of what they commonly contain. –Editors

I<small>N THE</small> U<small>NITED</small> S<small>TATES,</small> employment generally is considered "at-will," meaning that an employer can terminate an employee's employment for any reason, or no reason at all, without incurring any liability. In contrast, the employment contract is intended to define more specifically the relationship between employer and employee and their respective obligations.

Paradoxically, the most significant issue addressed in a typical employment agreement is unemployment–that is, what happens if the contract is breached. The ideal employment agreement anticipates and attempts to resolve, in advance, every significant question or dispute that might arise concerning the employment relationship and its termination.

The use of employment agreements has been fueled by the increased mobility of top executives and the proliferation of tax, securities, accounting and transaction-related issues. Those complex issues will be discussed in detail in later chapters. The increased use of employment contracts also reflects higher levels of involuntary termination of executives. Shareholder intolerance for under-performance has resulted in a very short "proving" period for newly appointed Chief Executive Officers and other leaders. As a result, severance protection serves as a form of insurance for executives, protecting them against the prospect of a career-ending termination.

This chapter is intended to provide an overview of the most salient and common provisions of employment agreements.

Severance and Change in Control Agreements

The term "employment agreement" is often used interchangeably with the terms "severance agreement" and "change in control agreement." All three types of agreements may contain similar provisions. However, an employment agreement typically is a more general document that discusses basic provisions, such as the term of employment, salary and benefits. It may set out the employer's responsibilities if the employee is terminated or there is a change in control of the employer. A severance agreement, in contrast, is characterized by its focus on the employer's obligations in the event that employment is terminated. A change in control agreement centers on payments and benefits the employer is obligated to provide following a change in control.

On the accompanying CD, and provided as an appendix to this chapter, is a thirty-one page sample employment agreement with change in control provisions, including some of the most common provisions found in executive employment agreements. Throughout this chapter, reference will be made to Appendix A in {brackets} to illustrate concepts described in the chapter. The reader may wish to print out the document in advance for easy reference while reading the chapter. We hasten to note that, as with all legal documents, employment contracts should be reviewed by counsel and drafted with great care to appropriately capture the intended relationship between the parties.

Some Advantages and Disadvantages

An employment agreement generally benefits the employee more than the employer, and few senior executives will begin work with a new company without its protections. Among the advantages to both sides, an employment agreement:

- Provides legal protection to employees over their conditions of employment, particularly in regard to termination of employment
- Provides an element of employment stability to an employer
- Reduces the possibility or duration of post-employment litigation, as well as a level of legal protection for an employer through restitution on post-employment actions

Conversely, an employment agreement has the disadvantages of:

- Often limiting an employee's ability to compete and/or disclose certain information following termination of employment in certain circumstances (a restriction that favors the employer)
- Possibly thwarting the employer's entering into certain transactions if the employment agreement contains large payouts in the event of a change in control or other termination of employment
- Limiting the employer's ability to change the duties and responsibilities, place of performance and other terms and conditions of employment
- Requiring public disclosure, under securities laws, of the material terms and conditions of the employment agreements for named executive officers of public companies

Form and Substance

It is essential to understand the language, possible limitations and workings of an employment contract. An employment agreement can be as simple as a one-page offer letter stating the duration of the employment term and, possibly, the compensation. At the other extreme, it may be a lengthy document detailing many extensively negotiated stipulations. As a general rule, the longer the agreement, the more favorable to the employee because a greater number of issues are addressed. It is significant to note, however, that, from a legal perspective, a simple offer letter may or may not be regarded as an employment agreement because it may not contain pertinent provisions, such as term, compensation or severance benefits.

There is a growing trend toward the use of industry-specific employment agreements. While this chapter is limited to discussing general employment agreements, it is important to be aware of provisions that may be specific to a particular industry. For example, hiring agreements for a dot-com company typically would be characterized by a large equity grant, relatively low salary and little severance protection. Alternatively, a hiring contract at a financial services firm usually would avoid post-employment equity vesting, but be likely to include severance protection.

Every employment contract should be reviewed by an attorney before being finalized. Terms and conditions of employment inherently raise a host of complex issues in regard to tax, securities, corporate, labor and benefit laws, as well as accounting implications.

Recitals {page 1}

Recitals are an important and frequent, but not critical, beginning to any employment contract. Recitals are a list of clauses, each beginning with the word "Whereas," that provide background information regarding the contract. Recitals might state that the employee was asked to continue employment after a change in control, or point out that an employee came out of retirement to perform certain services for the employer. This information can help the reader–whether it be a lawyer, judge, accountant or other executive not involved in negotiating the contract–in understanding and interpreting certain terms that otherwise might appear unusual or unjustified.

Term and Duty Provisions

The term is the length of employment, which is usually between three and five years. If the employee continues with the same employer past that term and there is no specific provision in the employment contract for renewal of the term, he or she is legally considered an "at-will" employee. {Section 2(a)}

An "evergreen" provision usually states that after the initial period of employment specified in the contract, the term is automatically renewed for certain periods of time unless the employee or employer is given prior notice by the other party of non-renewal. {Section 2(a)} An evergreen provision typically requires that the employee receive between three and six months notice that the contract will not be renewed. A longer notice period is generally a disadvantage to the employer, since an employee who knows that his or her contract is not being renewed is unlikely to be as productive. Conversely, a very short notice period, or none at all, can leave the employee with neither a certainty of employment nor severance. One solution to this problem is to agree in the contract to provide the employee with severance if the employment contract is not renewed. {Sections 2(a), (b) & (c)}

Regardless of the term of service specified in an employment contract, an employer clearly cannot force an employee to remain in a job (slavery having been abolished), nor can an employee continue in a job after being terminated. Rather, if employment ends before the term of service is up, the contract explains the employer's and the employee's respective liabilities toward each other.

Title {Section 3(a)}

An employment agreement should also clearly define the employee's title or position, which provides a form of protection against reassignment to a new or different title or position with less prestige. To maintain flexibility, however, many companies will simply state in the agreement that an employee will serve as a "senior executive" of the employer. During a change in control, this title can prove of critical importance to higher-level

315

executives because it defines their position in the combined company. Additionally, the employment agreement should specify whether an employee sits on the company's Board of Directors and, if so, whether he or she will be nominated for re-election.

Duties and Authority

A clear statement of the duties and authority of the employee in the employment contract can protect the employee from reassignment to a new job with less responsibility or authority. {Section 3(a)} A clear description of duties and authority is also integral to determining whether an employee was terminated for failure to perform his or her duties. Such failure may constitute grounds for termination "for Cause" and result in the forfeiture of any severance benefits. However, the duties should be defined broadly enough to leave the employer with some flexibility in deciding the level and responsibilities of the job. {Section 3(a)} For high-level executives, agreements typically provide that the executive is employed in a certain capacity (e.g., chief financial officer) and will perform the duties and functions consistent with his or her status and as may be assigned by the Board of Directors. {Section 3(a)}

"Time and efforts" provisions typically state that an employee must devote "substantially all" of his or her attention, time and effort during business hours to the affairs of the employer. Some agreements also require that the employee use his or her "best efforts" on the employer's behalf. However, the term "best efforts" will be open to interpretation if the employee is terminated "for Cause" on the ground that he or she did not devote his or her best efforts to the job. {Section 3(a)}

Service on Behalf of Other Entities: The issue here is the employee's service on other Boards of Directors, not-for-profit activities and management of passive investments should also be clearly delineated. Typically, agreements explicitly list the entities for which the employee currently serves and states whether he or she can serve on another for-profit entity's Board. The agreement may require the employee to obtain permission from the employer before joining another Board. Many agreements also state explicitly that the employee may engage in not-for-profit activities and manage "passive investments" (typically defined as security ownership of less than five percent in a publicly-traded company), as long as those activities do not interfere with performing his or her duties for the employer. {Section 3(b)}

Place of Performance

The agreement should state the city, or the geographic range of a city or metropolitan area, in which the employee's services will be rendered. If two or more company facilities are in one city, the agreement should specify the exact location. The agreement should state whether relocation is required and also may address whether travel is required. Such provisions can prove to be particularly important in determining whether or not an employee terminates "for Good Reason." For this reason and to otherwise maintain flexibility, employers would generally prefer not to insert any statement as to the primary place of employment. {Section 3(c)}

Reporting Relationships

The agreement should specify the individuals or entities to whom the employee must report. The agreement may also identify which organizations or individuals report to the employee. {Section 3(a)} Agreements often state that the employee will report not to a particular person by name, but to a specific position, such as the CEO. In that case, the employee is contractually bound to report to whoever currently holds that position, unless otherwise stated in the agreement. If the contract requires the employee to report either to a certain position or to that individual's "designee"–which could end up being almost anyone in the organization–the employee may have little protection with regard to his or her positioning in the reporting chain.

Compensation and Benefits Provisions

Typically a subject of heavy negotiation, the compensation and benefits section generally discusses the employee's compensation and benefits before, during and after the term of employment. It is essential before starting any negotiations to determine what level of competitive, or "reasonable," compensation the Board of Directors or its compensation committee legally can offer under its fiduciary obligations. A fiduciary determination of "reasonableness" for higher-level executives usually is based on reports and opinions from consultants regarding compensation for employees at similar levels at similar companies. An employee who is negotiating an employment agreement with a public company can find a prime source of comparative data in the proxies of similar public companies and the employment agreements of their senior executives.

Later chapters will discuss in detail the complex legal issues involved in structuring executive compensation arrangements. Generally speaking, the most significant provisions are:

- **Tax Laws:** Section 162(m) of the Internal Revenue Code (referred to as the "Code") states that compensation in excess of $1 million that is paid to particular high-level executives of public companies cannot be deducted for income tax purposes by those companies unless the compensation is deemed "performance-based" as defined by the Code.

- **Securities Laws:** The Securities and Exchange Commission (SEC) requires that compensation paid to certain executives be publicly disclosed and open to public and shareholder scrutiny. That includes the text of their employment agreements and any change in control arrangements, as well as all equity incentive and benefits plans. The SEC also requires that the compensation committee disclose its compensation policies in regard to those executives. Those policies include the specific relationship of corporate performance to executive compensation, the basis for the CEO's reported compensation and a specific discussion of each measure of company performance on which the CEO's compensation was based. Section 16(b) of the Securities Exchange Act, as well as various securities registration rules, will also have an impact on equity awards. [See Chapter 13 for a discussion of Section 16(b).]

- **Benefits Laws:** The Employee Retirement Income Security Act (ERISA) covers participation, vesting and benefit accrual and payment regulations for certain employee benefit plans. Where applicable, ERISA also imposes funding requirements and requires that plan contributions be held in trust (or under annuity contracts) that are secure from the employer's creditors.

- **Accounting:** Employers need to be keenly aware of the accounting consequences of their compensation and benefits programs. Complex rules regarding the accounting treatment of equity-based pay can have a significant impact on the financial statements of a company.

- **Sarbanes-Oxley:** The Sarbanes-Oxley Act of 2002 was enacted on July 30, 2002. The Act creates additional disclosure obligations for public companies, new corporate governance requirements, a new scheme for regulating the accounting industry, and enhanced enforcement powers and criminal penalties to fight corporate malfeasance. Violations of the Act can result in harsh results including imprisonment and fines of up to $25 million. This Act can have a significant impact on the structure and amount of compensation paid pursuant to an employment arrangement.

Annual or Base Salary {Section 4}

The amount and timing of payments of the annual base salary are usually stated in the agreement. In terms of timing, many agreements simply state that the employee will be paid in accordance with the employer's customary payroll practices for senior level executives. Agreements may provide for minimum increases in base salary each year or leave salary increases to the Board's or Compensation Committee's discretion. Guaranteed increases can be described in terms of a fixed dollar amount, a percentage of base salary or an annual cost-of-living adjustment for the term of the contract. Many contracts provide that base salary will be reviewed annually and state that base salary may be increased, but not decreased. Others permit salary reductions if such reductions are consistent with across-the-board reductions.

Many executive employment contracts now limit base salary to $1 million, with the balance of compensation provided through vehicles that either meet the regulation's performance-based criteria for deductibility or are established to defer compensation until the executive is no longer subject to the deduction limitation.

Bonus {Section 5}

The sign-on bonus, in the form of cash or equity such as employer stock or stock options, is a popular means of attracting new talent to an organization. Sign-on bonuses also can be used to compensate new employees for benefits (e.g., unvested stock, stock options or retirement pay) that were forfeited upon leaving their previous job or to provide some reimbursement for the cost of relocation. For a continuing employee, it can serve as a retention device, which is paid only if employment continues for a specified period of time. Employers should specify in the employment agreement that the sign-on bonus is a one-time payment that will have no impact on the amount of the employee's bonus going forward. Additionally, the agreement should specify whether or not the sign-on bonus will be considered for purposes of calculating pension or determining other benefit levels.

The agreement should specify whether the employee will be entitled to an annual bonus and, if so, whether any specific amount is guaranteed or any specific performance is required. The agreement should also specify when the bonus (whether specifically stated in dollars or not) will be determined and paid, as well as whether payment will be pro-rated for partial years of employment.

Frequently, an employment contract will specify a target bonus (often expressed as a percentage of base salary), along with a corresponding maximum bonus. Other issues that may be addressed in the contract are the performance criteria and whether achievement of lower goals will result in any payment. While employees typically prefer that a contract be as specific as possible regarding the amount, or minimum amount, of an annual bonus, employers naturally aim to preserve more discretion. Often, a minimum amount is guaranteed in the first year of employment, after which the annual bonus is based on a formula incorporating revenues, profits and earnings before income tax, or various combinations of financial and/or strategic measures.

In order to meet certain treasury regulation requirements under Section 162(m) regarding deductibility, many companies do not guarantee a minimum bonus in the contract. Instead, the bonus is based on executive performance, as determined by one or more business goals relating to the individual, a business unit or the corporation as a whole ("Performance-Based Compensation"). In order to meet the Performance-Based Compensation exception in Section 162(m), the agreement (or any ancillary incentive plan agreement) cannot give the company discretion to increase the amount of the bonus payable upon achievement of such goals, but the agreement may permit the company to decrease or eliminate the bonus. Many employment agreements simply state that the executive will participate under an annual incentive plan that has been approved by shareholders and qualifies as a "162(m) plan."

The agreement should address the issue of the portion of the bonus, if any, that will be paid if the employee resigns or is terminated before the end of the bonus determination period, or in the event of death or disability. If the bonus is pro-rated and the agreement does not specify a dollar amount, the agreement should specify whether payment will consist of a portion of the target amount, assuming all goals have been met, or based on performance to date. {See Sections 10(a)(ii), 10(b)(iii)(B), 10(c)(iii) & (iv), 10(e)(iii) & (iv) and 10(f)(ii)}

Equity Grants

An employment contract for a new hire often will specify the amount and vesting requirements of any initial equity grants. Some agreements specify the type, amount and timing of subsequent awards, as well as terms and conditions such as vesting, performance goals and options prices. However, the agreement may simply state that the employee is entitled to participate in the company's equity plans at the same level as similar employees. If so, the contract must be sensitive to, and not contradict, the terms of the respective plan and/or equity agreement. {Sections 6(a) & (b)}

A summary is provided below of some of the most common forms of equity awards. Other chapters in this publication present a more comprehensive discussion of equity awards.

- **Stock Awards:** Grants of shares of the employer's common stock.

- **Stock Options:** An agreement under which the employee receives the right to buy a specific number of shares, after vesting, of the employer's stock at a specific price (the exercise price) for a specific period of time (usually not exceeding ten years). There are two basic types of stock options: incentive stock options (commonly called ISOs), which provide for favorable tax treatment in certain circumstances, and non-qualified stock options.

- **Stock Appreciation Rights (SARs):** An agreement giving the employee a contractual right (often granted in combination with an option) to receive cash or stock equal to the appreciation value of the stock from the date of the agreement to the date the SAR is exercised.

- **Dividend Equivalent Rights:** An agreement crediting the employee with cash or the share equivalent, while an option or award is being held, for the value of dividends that the employer otherwise would pay on those shares.

- **Restricted Stock Awards:** Shares of stock that are subject to restriction on their sale and are subject to forfeiture until vested. Vesting usually is contingent on continued employment and typically occurs in increments over several years. During the restricted period, dividends or dividend equivalent rights may be paid, and award holders may receive voting rights.

- **Phantom Stock Awards:** Rather than the employee being issued actual shares of stock, an account is credited with a specified number of hypothetical, or "phantom," shares. The value of the account fluctuates, based on the appreciation or depreciation of the underlying stock price. Final payout of the account may be made in cash or stock. Dividend equivalent rights may also be added.

- **Performance Shares:** Shares of stock, or their cash equivalent, are generally paid only if predetermined performance objectives over a multi-year period are achieved.

- **Performance-accelerated Restricted Stock Awards:** If the employee meets certain performance objectives, some or all of the restrictions on restricted stock awards may lapse early. If, however, the objectives are not met, the restrictions are in force until the employee has remained with the company for the specified time. These are also referred to as PARS (performance-accelerated restricted stock) and as TARSAPs (time-accelerated restricted stock award plans).

Some of the significant advantages of equity-based compensation over cash include the following:

- Most forms of equity-based compensation enable a company to create incentives that link compensation to company performance and align the interests of employees and shareholders.

- Equity-based compensation reduces a company's need for cash to provide the level of compensation needed.

- ISOs generally carry the potential for preferential capital gains tax treatment if the underlying stock is not sold prior to two years after the ISOs were granted and if the underlying stock is held for at least one year after exercise. ISOs are disadvantageous from a company's tax perspective, however, because the company will not receive a tax deduction if the executive satisfies the ISO holding requirements specified above.

- If stock options are granted under a shareholder-approved plan with a fair market value exercise price, their value generally will not be counted toward the Section 162(m) $1 million limit.

Commissions

Commissions are a major performance incentive for sales employees and frequently represent a substantial portion of their pay. The basis on which commissions will be paid for such an individual should be stated in detail in his or her employment contract or related sales commission plan.

Health and Welfare Benefits {Section 7(a)}

While an employee usually is entitled to the same health and welfare benefits provided to other employees at the same level, an employment agreement may include provisions for supplemental medical, life or disability insurance, or other welfare benefits. If no special benefits are offered, the agreement should state that the executive is eligible for benefits generally provided to executives of similar level or position in the company.

Retirement Plans and Deferred Compensation

Typically, an employment agreement simply states that an employee is entitled to participate in the same "tax-qualified plans" maintained by the employer on the same terms as similarly situated employees. Under a tax-qualified plan, amounts contributed to the plan by the employer or employee are not taxed until the employee actually receives the money, while the employer receives an immediate tax deduction for its contributions. In order to receive payments from tax-qualified plans without a penalty, the employee can only begin receiving payments from such plans after retirement or attainment of a certain age. Employees generally prefer to receive such payments after retirement, when they may be in a lower income tax bracket. The income realized by the trust that holds the assets is tax-exempt to the employer. Balances held in an account for individual employees are tax-deferred until distribution, at which point they are taxed as ordinary income. There are certain annual limitations on the amounts that may be contributed to such plans.

The different types of tax qualified pension benefits are covered in detail in a different chapter. But briefly, the two major categories of these benefits include defined contribution plans and defined benefit plans:

- **Defined Contribution Plans:** These plans include a wide array of qualified plans under Section 401(a) of the Code, including profit sharing plans, thrift plans, stock bonus plans, employee stock ownership plans and cash or deferred profit sharing plans. In these types of plans, an individual bookkeeping account is maintained for each participant that records the participant's total interest in the plan assets. One of the most popular plans today is the 401(k) plan, to which an employee may contribute up to $11,000 (in 2002) annually. In some plans, the employer matches the employee's contribution up to a specified percentage.

- **Defined Benefit Plans:** Commonly referred to as pension plans, these programs base participants' benefits on a formula in the plan. The formula usually is based on such factors as age, length of service at retirement and, often, salary or salary plus bonus over a prescribed period of years. Benefits are normally payable as a joint and survivor annuity to a married participant or as a single life annuity to an unmarried participant. Contributions to the plan are usually made only by the employer. However, traditional, broad-based defined benefit plans are becoming less common, and many are being converted to "cash-balance plans" in which benefits are calculated as if contributions were made to the participant's account under a defined contribution plan. However, increments on the account are based on a specified rate of interest, rather than on actual investment experience.

Non-Qualified Deferred Compensation {Section 7(b)}

A nonqualified deferred compensation arrangement allows employees to defer compensation in excess of the limit allowed under tax-qualified retirement plans. In smaller companies, deferred compensation often is specifically designed for an individual employee and described in his or her employment contract. In larger companies, deferred compensation is generally provided through a separate deferred compensation plan in which the employee is eligible to participate.

Nonqualified deferred compensation arrangements can vary in format and substance, but generally the design goal is two-fold:

1. The plan should avoid "constructive receipt," which means that the payment is immediately taxable to the individual regardless of whether he or she took actual receipt of the payment. In order to avoid "constructive receipt," payments under the plan generally must be "unfunded" (i.e., remain subject to the risk of the employer's creditors). In addition, the election to defer such income must be made before the services are rendered or at least far enough in advance of the scheduled payment date.

2. The plan ideally should not be subject to ERISA regulations. In order to avoid most of those requirements, participation in nonqualified deferral plans generally must be limited to what the Code calls "a select group of management or highly compensated employees," which is often referred to as the "top hat" group.

If structured properly, income deferred under a nonqualified deferred compensation plan is not taxable until received, although liability for Medicare and other employment taxes generally is incurred on the vesting date. Payment of deferred income is not guaranteed, but is subject to the risk of other creditors in the event the employer becomes insolvent or otherwise does not meet its obligations. Unlike a qualified retirement plan (in which the employer can take an immediate deduction for contributions), employer contributions to a nonqualified deferred compensation plan are not deductible until the year in which the amount attributable to the contribution is includible in the employee's gross income.

Enhanced Retirement Benefits

Enhanced retirement benefits, or deferred compensation, can be provided through adoption of a separate plan. Alternatively, they may be included in the employment contract if a separate plan does not exist, or the employer wants to increase an employee's benefits beyond those under the existing plan.

If the unfunded deferred compensation arrangement is limited to a select group of management or highly-compensated employees and meets certain other design requirements, it is considered a "top-hat" plan. A "top-hat" plan has the significant advantage to employers of being exempt from most

ERISA requirements. Unlike excess benefit plans (discussed below), contributions to a "top-hat" plan are not restricted to amounts in excess of those allowed under tax qualified retirement programs. Participation must be strictly limited to those who, by virtue of their position or compensation level, have the power to meaningfully negotiate the design and operation of the deferred compensation plan as it affects them. Unfortunately, there is no precise definition of exactly which group of employees may be covered under such plans.

The most common forms of non-qualified deferred compensation arrangements generally fall into two categories:

- **Supplemental Executive Retirement Plans:** A Supplemental Executive Retirement Plan (commonly referred to as a SERP) is designed to provide supplemental benefits specifically for higher-paid executives (e.g., it typically qualifies as a "top-hat" plan). Executive SERP benefits can serve to compensate for benefits lost when an executive leaves one employer to join a new one. An agreement may specify what will happen to the SERP benefit in the event that the executive is terminated. {See Sections 10(c)(xi) & 10(e)(xi)}

- **Excess Benefit Plans or Restoration Plans:** Such plans are expressly limited by law to providing benefits for select employees in excess of the contribution limits imposed by qualified plans.

Fringe Benefits and Perquisites {Section 9}

Specific provisions for fringe benefits and perquisites often are discussed in the employment agreements of high-level executives. Although such benefits may constitute a small part of the total compensation package from a financial standpoint, they can have great symbolic value for the executive. While Chapter 6 deals with different types of fringe benefits in detail, the most common provisions included in an employment agreement include:

- Financial Counseling
- Estate Planning
- Income Tax Preparation
- Spousal Travel
- Airline Clubs
- Company Car or Allowance
- Chauffer Services
- Parking Privileges
- Company Aircraft Use

- Car Phone/Home Fax/PC
- Physical Exams
- Health Club Memberships
- Country Club Memberships
- Supplemental Medical Insurance
- First Class Air Travel
- Home Security Systems
- Corporate Apartments
- Office Size
- Secretarial or Other Assistant Support
- Entertainment Expense Accounts
- Executive Dining Room Privileges
- Flexible Perquisite Allowances

An employee's aggressive request to specify fringe benefits and perquisites in an employment agreement may, however, poison the relationship between an employer and the employee.

Relocation Benefits

Relocation benefits may be incorporated into the sign-on bonus or specifically addressed in a separate section of the employment agreement. Direct expenses, such as moving, packing and closing costs on the sale of the old home and the purchase of a new one, are typically reimbursed. Other expenses that may be covered include temporary storage, house-hunting trips, mortgage prepayment penalties incurred in selling the old home, loss on the sale of the old home, points paid on the purchase of a new home, title insurance, country club initiation fees, temporary housing and miscellaneous, non-itemized costs. The agreement also should state whether the employer will "gross-up" if any of the above reimbursements result in additional taxable income to the executive. In some cases, relocation loans may be provided interest free without imputing taxable income.

Fees Associated with Negotiation of the Employment Agreement
{Section 9(b)}

Many agreements state that the employer will pay any legal or professional advisory fees incurred by the employee in connection with negotiating the agreement, possibly with a cap on the total amount that will be reimbursed. Some contracts include reimbursement for fees as part of the sign-on bonus.

The employment agreement may include a "gross-up" for all or part of the reimbursement that results in taxable income to the employee.

Termination Provisions

Whether, and to what extent, an employee is entitled to severance payments after termination is dictated by the circumstances under which employment ended, as well as the size and type of company.

There are essentially eight categories of termination:

- Termination by the employer for "Cause" {Section 10(b)}
- Termination by the employer without "Cause" {Section 10(c) & (e)}
- Termination by the employee with "Good Reason" {Section 10(c) & (e)}
- Termination by the employee without "Good Reason" (or Voluntary Termination) {Section 10(d)}
- Termination due to death {Section 10(a)}
- Termination due to disability {Section 8}
- Termination due to retirement {Section 10(f)}
- Termination due to expiration of the employment agreement

The most heavily negotiated and most significant portions of an employment agreement often center on either the grounds on which an employer can terminate an employee for "Cause," or the grounds on which an employee can quit for "Good Reason."

Termination for Cause {Section 10(b)}

Generally speaking, an employee terminated for Cause is not entitled to severance from the employer. The exact definition of "Cause" can vary greatly, from a broad set of circumstances, which tends to favor the employer, to a narrow set of circumstances that will tend to be more advantageous to the employee. Terminations initiated by the employer for reasons other than for Cause are usually referred to as "termination without Cause."

Although definitions and standards for the term Cause vary by industry and position, among the typical provisions included in the definition of Cause in employment agreements are:

- **Criminal Acts:** Given the potential negative impact that criminal acts have on a company's public image, as well as on the employee's ability to perform, most employment agreements include such acts under Cause. {Section 10(b)(i)(B)}

  1. **Accusation, Commission, Indictment or Conviction:** The agreement

should state whether Cause is invoked by accusation, formal indictment and/or conviction of the crime. Employers naturally prefer to use accusation, which is the lowest standard, to avoid potential negative publicity if the accused employee returns to work. There could also be a long delay between accusation and conviction. However, the employee could argue that he or she should not be punished until convicted. Most top-level executive employment contracts focus on an actual conviction, or pleading nolo contendere (no contest). Contracts for lower-level employees usually restrict Cause to indictment of an employee for a crime that, in the good-faith judgment of the Board of Directors, materially damages the reputation of the employer or interferes with the employee's ability to perform.

2. **Felony vs. Misdemeanor:** The employment agreement should address what category of crime will trigger the definition of Cause. Extremely broad discretion could lead to employees being terminated without Cause for such things as minor traffic infractions. Often, the definition of Cause is limited to felonies or misdemeanors that involve "dishonesty" or "fraud." Some employment agreements specifically exempt the following criminal acts from termination for Cause: ordinary traffic violations, vicarious liabilities resulting from the employee's corporate position or actions done on the advice of the employer's counsel. Some agreements state that the definition of Cause is triggered only if an employee's crime is related to his or her employment.

- **Dishonesty:** Acts of fraud, embezzlement, theft or other dishonest acts with respect to the employer are typically considered grounds for Cause. However, the employer generally wants to retain discretion over what types of acts constitute dishonest behavior. As with criminal acts, if the definition of dishonesty is too broad, the employer may argue that a termination for Cause could be triggered by relatively minor infractions, such as taking home company pens or pads. To alleviate this problem, some contracts specify only "material" acts of dishonesty will result in a termination for Cause and may also require that the dishonesty be related to company acts. Alternatively, the contract may exclude acts that involve nominal amounts or negligence (as opposed to intentional acts).

- **Abuse of Alcohol and Drugs:** This provision has become less common in employment contracts since passage of the Americans with Disabilities Act in 1990 because, under certain circumstances, the Act protects some addictions as a disability. When used, this definition usually is limited to habitual and continued use and may be further restricted to situations in which the substance abuse affects employment. If defined too broadly, for example, an employer could attempt to invoke Cause because the employee was having a drink at a company party.

- **Willful Misconduct:** Cause usually includes willful acts committed by the employee with the intent of harming the employer. Such provisions should specify whether such conduct must be both intentional and result in harm, and whether such harm must be material or economic or both. This definition often is limited to misconduct that negatively affects the employer, rather than misconduct occurring outside of the workplace that has no effect on the employer. The terms "company" or "employer" should be defined to specify, for example, whether all parents, subsidiaries and affiliates are covered. {Section 10(b)(i)(C)}

  Common exceptions to "willful misconduct" include acts performed in good faith or acts undertaken at the Board of Director's direction or on the advice of company counsel. A contract often will specify that a willful act must be something that is done, or omitted to be done, in bad faith without reasonable belief that it was in the best interest of the company.

- **Negligence:** The term "negligence" generally favors the employer, because it implies that an employee's act or omission need not be egregious, but only a failure to perform one's duties with the "care and skill of a reasonable person of ordinary prudence." Under a broad negligence provision, employment potentially could be terminated for Cause even if the employee acted in good faith and generally performed under the terms of the contract, or if the conduct was immaterial in nature. As a result, Cause termination for negligence is generally limited to "willful negligence" or "gross negligence," or requires that the negligent acts result in material harm to the employer. {Section 10(b)(i)(C)}

- **Gross Misfeasance or Non-feasance:** This definition of Cause is aimed at the employee who fails to show up for work or intentionally and continually does not perform under the terms of the employment contract. The quality of work is not the key issue here—e.g., whether the employee "fails to perform." Instead, the key issue is whether the employee "intentionally refuses to perform." The definition may specify whether "intent" and "material results" are necessary to trigger Cause, or it may exempt limitations on performance that are due to an employee's disability.

- **Insubordination or Failure to Follow Superior Directives:** Termination for Cause generally should include an employee's intentional failure to follow the direction of his or her supervisor or, in the case of senior executives, of the Board of Directors. Many contracts require that such failure be "continual" and that the employee be given written notice of the failure before this element is triggered. The contract should provide that the employee cannot be terminated for refusing to follow an illegal directive. The contract may also state that the employee is required to follow only "reasonable" directives.

- **Breach of Confidentiality:** Contracts typically contain a provision that enables an employer to terminate an employee for Cause if the employee discloses confidential information during the employment period. Some contracts state that the breach must be material and/or intentional or in bad faith. Disclosure of information that is required by law, or information that the employee obtained permission to disclose, should be excluded. {Section 10(b)(i)(A)}

- **Breach of Non-Compete:** In addition to restricting competition with the employer during the post-termination period, many agreements also prohibit competition during the employment period. The term "competition" or "competitor" should be specifically defined in the contract. {Section 10(b)(i)(A)}

- **Industry Regulations:** Because some industries may require an employee to maintain a membership or license, the definition of Cause may include a provision justifying termination if a regulatory body prohibits the employee from holding his or her position, or if the loss of a license limits the employee's ability to perform his or her contractual duties.

- **General Breach of Contract:** In addition to the more specific acts listed above, most contracts state that if the employee breaches any other term of the contract, he or she may be terminated for Cause. Usually this provision is limited to "material" breaches of the contract.

- **Notice and Opportunity to Cure:** The contract should specify whether the employer is required to give notice to the employee of any acts that are considered to be for Cause, and whether the employee will be given the opportunity to cure or correct such acts. {Section 10(b)(ii)}

The employment contract should state how long the employee has to cure the behavior, based on the circumstances. Some agreements provide the employee with only one opportunity to correct the behavior. Some agreements permit the employee to appear with an attorney before the Board of Directors to argue that the actions in question should not constitute for Cause termination. Some agreements require that the final determination of a for Cause termination event be made by the full Board of Directors or with more than a simple majority vote of the full Board. Most agreements require that an employee be given written notice from the employer describing the acts that the Company considers to be for Cause termination events. Sometimes there is a requirement that notice be given within a certain time period (e.g., one month) of the act the employer considers to be for Cause. If the act being cited for Cause is intentional, some contracts do not allow any opportunity to cure.

Termination with Good Reason {Sections 10(c) & (e)}

"Good Reason" means that an employee can resign and collect severance as if he or she was terminated by the employer without Cause. Good Reason is similar to constructive termination, in that the employer commits an action so unpalatable to the employee, or otherwise breaches the employment agreement, that the employee feels his or her employment has effectively been terminated by the employer. Employees prefer a broad definition of Good Reason, while employers typically seek to narrow the definition to just a few sets of circumstances. In any event, it is critical to carefully define the term, as disputes over its meaning (particularly following a change in control) may result in litigation. All terminations initiated by the employee (excepting death, disability or retirement) that are not considered with Good Reason are considered "termination without Good Reason." Typical Good Reason provisions include:

- **Diminution in Position, Responsibility, Authority, Status, Title or Duties:** While any of these factors will usually constitute Good Reason, in many employment agreements, diminution is restricted to a "material" or "substantial" reduction that would be considered important to the employee. For example, termination with Good Reason should not be triggered by a nominal change in title as a result of a restructuring. Such flexibility can be particularly critical at smaller organizations, where reporting relationships are not always completely clear. Generally, before there can be Good Reason termination due to diminution, the employee is required to give notice, and the employer must have an opportunity to cure. {Section 10(c)(A) & (B)}

- **Change in Reporting Relationships:** A termination for Good Reason is triggered by a change from the reporting relationship specified in the earlier part of the agreement, although some contracts state that such a change must adversely affect the employee. Thought should be given to whether the employee will report to one position (or a specific person), or whether the employer will have the flexibility to change the line of command. Reporting relationships often prove to be a particularly sensitive issue in negotiating the employment contract, particularly at senior management levels. {Section 10(c)(A)}

- **Failure to Elect as Board Member:** Failure to grant an employee a seat on the Board of Directors, if stipulated in the titles and duties section of an employment contract, typically triggers Good Reason termination. Since it is ultimately shareholders who have the sole authority to elect Directors, most contracts limit such Good Reason termination to circumstances in which the employer fails to nominate the employee for a Board seat. {Section 10(c)(A)}

- **Change of Principal Place of Employment:** Good Reason often is triggered if the employee's principal place of employment is moved beyond the area specified in the section of the contract addressing "location of employment." The typical distance required varies, but it is usually between 35 to 60 miles from the contractually specified location of employment. Some contracts prohibit Good Reason termination if the employer offers continued employment to the employee in the new location and reimbursement for any relocation costs. {Section 10(c)(E)}

- **Failure to Obtain Assumption of Agreement:** Most employment agreements require that the contract be assumed by the employer's successor following a merger or similar transaction. However, the agreement should specify whether Good Reason termination will be triggered if, after the company is sold or spun off, the employee is slated to run a smaller subsidiary or division of a group of corporations. {Section 10(c)(F)}

- **Failure to Meet Compensation Obligations or Give Raises (including Failure of Grants to Be Made):** Good Reason can be triggered if the employer fails to pay or offer the compensation package specifically stated in the employment agreement, or fails to implement a salary or bonus increase stipulated in the contract. {Section 10(c)(C)}

- **General Breach of Contract:** In addition to the more specific acts listed above, most contracts state generally that if the employer breaches any other term of the contract, the employee may resign with Good Reason. Usually, such breaches are limited to those deemed "material." {Section 10(c)(D)}

- **Change in Control:** Even if a separate change in control agreement does not exist, some agreements treat a change in control as Good Reason for an employee to resign. The subject of change in control is discussed in more detail in Section VIII, but generally there are two types of change in control triggers:

1. Under a "single trigger," just one event–the change in control itself– constitutes Good Reason to resign. Such Good Reason usually is not triggered until six months or one year following the change in control in order to give the buyer necessary transition services.

2. Under the more common "double trigger" provision, the change in control must be followed by a separate Good Reason termination event to be considered Good Reason.

• **Notice and Opportunity to Cure:** Termination due to Good Reason may include requirements for notice and cure periods that are similar to those required for Cause termination. Typically, employers require the employee to make any Good Reason claim within 60 to 90 days after the action or inaction by the employer being cited. Many employment agreements require notice and the opportunity to cure before the employee can terminate for Good Reason. Like termination for Cause, cure may be permitted only if the employer's action is deemed inadvertent or taken in good faith.

Termination Due to Disability {Section 8}

An employment agreement should state that an employee's continuous disability for a particular period of time is grounds for termination. The definition of "disability" depends on the position and company, along with the waiting period and other terms contained in the company's long-term disability policy. A typical provision states that the employee is considered disabled if he or she is "totally or permanently disabled," or unable to perform the material provisions of the job for 90 to 120 consecutive days, or for a total of 120 to 180 days during any one year or 18-month period. Some agreements specify how days should be counted (e.g., whether holidays or weekends will be counted), while others simply refer to the definition of disability in the company's long-term disability plan. Some companies require that any determination of disability must be made by a doctor chosen by the company.

Post-Termination or Severance Payments

Just as the employment agreement should specifically define the types of terminations that may occur, the employment agreement should also specify the types of severance payments that will be paid under each of the different types of terminations. As an overview, the following are some of the types of obligations that are typically found in severance packages, although the inclusion of any of these obligations will, of course, depend on the size and type of company and the level of employee:

If severance pay is triggered by the employment agreement, the agreement should specify how it will be determined. The five main considerations are:

1. **Amount:** The contract should specify the dollar amount to which the employee will be entitled, usually expressed as a multiple of annual salary or of annual salary plus annual bonus. The contract should specify if the salary multiple will be calculated based on the current annual salary or on the highest annual salary earned within a previous period of years. The bonus formula should be very specific as to whether it will be based on the previous year's bonus, the current year's target bonus, the highest bonus earned within the past few years (or an average) or projected performance for the current year. In addition to multiples of annual salary and bonus, the agreement should also state whether a pro rata bonus for the year will be paid if the termination occurs in the middle of a bonus performance period. {See Sections 10(c)(ii), (iii) & (iv); Sections 10(e)(ii), (iii) & (iv)}

2. **Accrued Obligations:** In addition to the amount specified above, most contracts state that the terminated employee is entitled to all salary, bonus and other benefits that were accrued, but not yet paid, as of the date of termination (commonly referred to as "Accrued Obligations"). {See Sections 10(c)(i), (viii) & (xiii); Sections 10(e)(i), (viii) & (xiii)}

3. **The Severance Period and Releases:** The period of time during which severance pay is granted is often referred to as the "Severance Period" or "Severance Pay Period." {Section 10(c)(ii)} The executive receives compensation and/or benefits through the end of the term of the contract. However, as discussed above, more often the employee receives severance pay for a certain numbers of years, or is paid as a specified multiple of his or her annual salary and/or bonus. Typically, the employer's sole obligation in the event of a termination without Cause or with Good Reason is severance pay, with all other obligations under the contract becoming null and void. The employee is generally required to sign a release (discussed in further detail in Section IX(B)) before the employer is obligated to make any severance payments. {Section 10(i)}

4. **Timing of Payments:** The contract should state whether severance will be paid out as if the employee still were working through the end of the

contract or Severance Period {Section 10(c)(ii)}, or whether severance will be in the form of a lump-sum payment within a certain number of days following termination of employment {Section 10(e)(ii)}. Paying install-ments may be advisable if restrictive covenants exist post-termination.

5. **Offsets and Mitigation:** Some agreements state that severance will be reduced by any compensation the employee receives from a new employer within a certain period after termination. Agreements may also require the employee to mitigate the amount of severance pay by using his or her "best efforts" to obtain new employment. Offsets are generally more common when the Severance Period exceeds one year, but often are not applicable in any case. {Section 10(g)}

Most employment contracts that provide for severance also permit the employee to participate in the company's health, life and disability insurance plans through the Severance Period. In cases where severance is paid in a lump-sum, continued coverage would last through the time that the last payment would have been paid under normal payroll practices. In any event, employers should keep in mind that after certain terminations of employment, employees may continue to be entitled to participate in such plans for an additional 18 months, at their own cost, under the terms of the Consolidated Omnibus Budget Reconciliation Act of 1985 ("COBRA"). {Sections 10(c)(x); 10(e)(x); and 10(f)(viii)}

Some agreements entitle the employee to continue to participate in or make contributions under the company's retirement plans through the Severance Period. However, benefits counsel should review this section of the employment agreement, as tax-qualification status may be jeopardized if terminated employees continue to participate in such plans. Some agree-ments will also credit the terminated executive with additional years of service for purposes of a supplemental retirement benefit. {Section 10(c)(xi) and Section 10(e)(xi)}

Employees may be required under the terms of the employment contract to forfeit unvested or unexercised equity upon termination. Alternatively, the contract may allow accelerated vesting and/or extensions of the exercise periods for certain types of terminations. Some contracts merely state that such equity awards will be treated under the terms of the applicable equity award agreement or plan. {Sections 10(a)(iii) & (iv); Sections 10(c)(v), (vi) & (vii); and Sections 10(e)(v), (vi) & (vii)}

Many larger companies provide outplacement services to higher-level executives, which may be capped at a certain dollar amount. The use of outplacement can be an alternative to providing an office and secretarial services to a terminated executive. {Sections 10(c)(xii) and Sections 10(e)(xii)} The employment agreement should describe how any severance that is subject to Section 280G of the Code will be treated.

Because perquisites and benefits can vary widely based on the individual employee and the business, the contract should be very specific about the employee's entitlements in severance-related situations. Some agreements provide the executive with contractual perquisites during the Severance Period, such as continued financial, tax and planning assistance. If the employee had been relocated as part of his or her employment, reimbursement may be made for moving back to the previous location.

The eight categories of terminations described earlier can be grouped into five general categories, with certain types of terminations resulting in similar or identical severance obligations. While such obligations vary greatly depending on the position and business, the following is a summary of typical severance obligations.

Termination by the Company for Cause {Section 10(b)} *and Termination by the Executive without Good Reason (or Voluntary Termination)* {Section 10(d)}

Employees terminated for Cause or who voluntarily quit without Good Reason typically receive the lowest level of severance because they either have done something to harm the company or are terminating the employment arrangement without reason. In most cases, the employee receives only Accrued Obligations, and all other contractual obligations are voided. Employees generally are not entitled to continued coverage, but may elect to continue health coverage at their own cost pursuant to the COBRA laws. Unvested equity awards usually are forfeited, and even vested equity awards may be forfeited if termination is for Cause.

Termination without Cause and Termination with Good Reason {Sections 10(c) and 10(e)}

An employee terminated by the company without Cause or who terminates employment with Good Reason generally receives the highest level of severance benefits, since the company did not have a material and significant reason to discharge the employee, or the company did something to constructively discharge the employee. Typically, the employee is entitled to a multiple of annual salary and bonus, depending on his or her level and whether the termination occurred within a certain time period before or after a Change in Control (See Section VIII). For example, a typical executive severance structure might entitle the CEO to three times his annual salary and bonus, the COO with 2.5 times his annual salary and bonus and the next band of highly paid executive officers with 2 times their salary and bonus.

The size of the company and industry practices will also govern the size of the severance payments. Larger public companies typically provide severance to senior executives without an offset but may subject the executive to a non-compete agreement for a certain period of time following termination. On the other hand, high-tech start-up companies or entities funded with venture capital or private equity are generally less generous with regard to severance than established companies due to cash flow limitations. Typically, employees will continue to receive such benefits for the Severance Period, or while they are receiving severance payments. Some agreements provide for accelerated vesting of the employee's unvested equity awards, along with an extension of the exercise period, whereas some agreements simply refer to the appropriate equity agreement or plan. Generally, unvested equity awards will vest if the termination occurs within a certain period before or after a Change in Control (e.g., within twenty-four to thirty-six months after a Change in Control).

Termination Due to Death {Section 10(a)} *or Disability* {Section 8}

The agreement should address the types of payments or benefits to which the employee (or the designated beneficiary) is entitled in the event of death or disability during the contract period. Arrangements range from payment of full salary and benefits throughout the term of the contract, to no payment at all following death or disability. The agreement should stipulate whether and what portion of the bonus will be paid, including how it will be calculated if termination occurs in the middle of the bonus performance period.

Some agreements provide continued coverage to the employee (or the designated beneficiary.) However, the company should ensure that the applicable insurance carrier will provide such coverage under its contracts. Otherwise, cash equivalent payments to purchase individual policies may be required.

Although vesting requirements may be addressed in the company's plans or the employee's equity award agreement, many employment agreements also specify what will happen in the event of the employee's death or disability. Many companies permit accelerated or continued vesting and award exercises for a stated period after termination.

Termination Due to Retirement

If an employee is at or close to retirement age, the company may stipulate that the contract expires upon retirement. The term "retirement" may be defined, or reference may be made to the definition of "Normal Retirement Age" in other company plans. There is a wide range of post-termination benefits to which a retiring employee may be entitled. At one extreme, the employee may be entitled only to accrued benefits, as if the term of the employment agreement had simply expired. For more senior level executives, the contract may provide for some severance payments along with continued health and welfare benefits and accelerated or continued vesting and exercise of equity awards. {Section 10(f)}

Termination due to Expiration of the Employment Agreement

Once the term of the employment agreement expires, the parties should have no further obligations to each other, other than the employer's obligation to pay the employee any Accrued Obligations and the employee's obligation to observe any non-compete provisions. If the employee continues employment after the expiration of the employment agreement, he or she is then considered an "at-will" employee, and the agreement is no longer in effect. Alternatively, if an evergreen renewal applies, the company's failure to renew may be treated like a termination without Cause, especially if the failure to renew occurs before retirement age.

Restrictive Covenants

Under a "restrictive covenant," the employee agrees that he or she will do or refrain from doing certain things. Because the enforceability of restrictive covenants is generally governed by state law, local counsel should review such provisions.

Most employment agreements contain confidentiality provisions {Sections 12(a), (b) & (c)} in which the employee agrees not to disclose certain information about the company. Often the confidentiality portion of the agreement has no time limit and extends past the contract term. The agreement may include a provision, often highly industry-specific, defining what constitutes "confidential information." Some agreements list what constitutes confidential information, although such a list may be limiting and may fail to cover information obtained by the employee at a later date.

The typical confidentiality provision contains the following exceptions:

• **Public Knowledge:** The employee should be able to disclose matters that are generally known to the public or in the industry (other than information obtained as a result of the employee's improper disclosure).

• **Legal Requirements:** The employee should be able to disclose any information he or she is legally required to disclose, such as in response to a subpoena or deposition.

• **Course of Employment:** If it is within the individual's authority to disclose confidential information in order to perform his or her duties, he or she should be allowed to do so.

Confidentiality provisions usually require that the employee return all company property upon termination. An exception is often made for the executive's rolodex and personal telephone books. {Section 12(g)}

Non-compete

Considered an essential provision by many employers, a non-compete prohibits an employee from engaging in "competitive activities" or working for a "competitor" during the term of the employment agreement or for a specified time thereafter. The agreement must explicitly define the term "competition," which in turn will govern the scope of the non-compete. The definition should indicate the type of business that would be in competition with the employer, the type of activities that would constitute competition, and the geographic area in which the competition cannot occur. Some agreements will specifically list the names of different corporations that are in competition with the employer. The agreement should state whether the competition is limited to direct or indirect activities and should also state whether the employee will be prohibited from working for a company that is in competition with the employer but where the employee does not engage in the type of activity that is competitive with the employer's business. Most non-compete provisions contain an exception for personal investments in public companies, usually permitting ownership of between one percent to five percent of a public company listed on a national exchange or NASDAQ. {Section 13(a)}

The employment contract should address the term of the non-compete. Typically, the employer wants to enforce the non-compete for at least as long as the Severance Period so that if the non-compete is violated, the employer can immediately suspend payments. The agreement may require the employee to return a certain portion of such payments if made in a lump sum, although such a reimbursement may be hard to enforce as a practical matter. In some agreements, the non-compete will apply only to post-termination situations in which the employee was terminated without Cause, or the employee terminated with Good Reason (so-called "pay to park" provisions), although the presence of a non-compete provision in a voluntary quit without Good Reason may be the most likely circumstance in which an employer needs protection. {Section 13(b)}

More than any other provision of a contract, it is imperative that the non-compete provision be reviewed by local counsel, as enforceability varies greatly by state. California, for example, generally does not enforce non-competes on the ground that prohibiting an individual from engaging in a lawful profession violates public policy. Other states will narrow the scope of a non-compete before it is enforced.

Non-solicit

A non-solicit provision prohibits a terminated worker from soliciting or assisting in the solicitation of the former employer's employees, or soliciting the current clients or vendors of the employer, for a certain period. The restriction on soliciting employees may be limited to higher-level employees. The contract also may include a "six-month look back," under which the former employee is prohibited from hiring a current employee of his former company for a six-month period after the current employee's termination. This type of look back would avoid set-ups where there is a quit followed by a hire. {Section 14}

Non-disparagement

An employee may be prohibited in the contract from publicly criticizing the company, its board, its executives, its employees or its services or products. Like a confidentiality provision, non-disparagement typically makes exceptions for complying with the law or courts. {Section 12(f)}

Litigation Cooperation

Some agreements require that the employee cooperate with the employer, both during and after the term of employment, if the company is involved in a lawsuit or other litigious situation. Among other things, the employee may be obligated to be deposed, to testify in court on behalf of the company, or to be interviewed in preparation of litigation. Some agreements limit the obligation to "reasonable requests" and may provide for reimbursement to the employee (or former employee) of any costs incurred in complying with this provision. {Section 12(e)}

Remedies for Breach of Restrictive Covenants {Sections 11 and 15}

The contract should indicate the employer's recourse if any of the above restrictive covenants are breached after termination of employment. If the breach occurs during the period of employment, the obvious remedy is termination for Cause. Courts have been reluctant to enforce what is known as a "liquidated damages" clause, whereby the employee would be required to pay the employer a certain dollar amount. A simpler approach is to cease payment of severance if a former employee commits a breach. Some agreements call for injunctive relief, in which a court orders the terminated employee to perform, or not perform, an obligation under the contract. For example, if the contract so provided, a court may order a former employee to stop bad-mouthing the company or require the former employee to cooperate in a litigation process.

A contract also may require an employee who violates a restrictive covenant to forfeit his or her interest in non-qualified retirement plans, equity plans, incentive plans and deferred compensation arrangements. The plan documents governing such plans also may contain such a forfeiture provision in the event of a breach of the covenant. For example, a company may terminate a former employee's right to exercise stock options if he or she was deemed in competition with the former employer. As equity has become a dominant part of executive pay packages, companies also have used the "clawback," which generally requires an employee who violates a restrictive covenant to pay back to the company any profit on the exercise of options or vesting of restricted stock. The look-back period typically runs from six months to one year from the date of exercise of the option or vesting of the restricted stock. However, because the use of clawbacks may trigger litigation, legal counsel should be consulted in crafting any clawback provision.

Miscellaneous Provisions

The increasing use of non-competes has prompted many employers to include a provision in the employment contract in which the employee states that the agreement does not and will not conflict with, or result in a breach or default under, any employment or confidentiality agreements with previous employers. The employee may also be required to stipulate that he or she does not need the consent of any other party to enter into the new employment contract. Such provisions are a particularly sensitive issue if the employee does not want to disclose (or is prohibited from disclosing) any release, confidentiality or non-competition agreements with prior employers.

Binding Arbitration, Legal Fees and Choice of Law

Many agreements specify that disputes be resolved in arbitration, rather than through the courts. Arbitration, which results in a decision that is final and binding on both sides, offers the advantages of usually being more cost-effective and more efficient, as well as offering a higher level of confidentiality than litigation. Generally, an arbitrator (or a panel of three arbitrators) is likely to be more sympathetic to an executive earning a large sum of money than would a jury, and will often try to strike a compromise between the claims of the employer and the employee. {Section 16}

Under some agreements, the employer must reimburse the employee for the cost of resolving contract disputes through litigation or arbitration. Reimbursement may be required only if the employee prevails or substantially prevails on the merits of the case. Some contracts state that in an arbitration, reimbursement will be determined by the arbitrator. Some contracts also may contain caps on the amount of reimbursable expenses, or simply provide for reimbursement of "reasonable" legal fees. Some contracts are mutual in that whoever loses (employer or employee) reimburses the prevailing party. {Section 16}

Agreements typically specify which state's laws will be used to interpret the contract and where the case will be heard. Usually it is the state in which the company is incorporated, the state where the employee lives or performs services or the company's principal place of business. {Sections 16 & 27}

Indemnification

Most senior-level executives want to be guaranteed reimbursement by the company for any expenses incurred in connection with any action, suit or proceeding resulting from their service as a director, officer or employee of the company. Additionally, the contract may stipulate that the executive is covered by any liability insurance for the directors and officers of the company. The by-laws of most companies contain some form of indemnification protection. {Section 17}

Assignment of Patents and Intellectual Property

When applicable, an employee may be required to assign to the company the rights to any inventions and patents he or she develops during the term of employment. The employee also may be required to promptly disclose, in writing, any inventions or discoveries made during the term. Some contracts additionally obligate the employee to file patent applications as requested by the company, execute the necessary assignments of such applications and/or cooperate with the company in enforcing the patent.

Assignment, Assumption and Successors

An employment contract may allow the employer, but almost never the employee, to transfer the contract to another entity. Such transfers generally are limited to situations in which another entity acquires all, or substantially all, of the assets of the employer or another subsidiary of the company. Most contracts require the company to ensure that the contract is assumed by a successor company in the event of a merger, acquisition or other corporate restructuring. If the employer fails to have the contract assumed under such a provision, it is often considered a "Good Reason" termination event. {Section 20}

Guarantee of Obligations

If an employment agreement is with a company subsidiary that is a start-up or has limited assets, the employee may seek to have the agreement guaranteed by the parent company.

Change in Control Agreements

Change in Control provisions can be part of an employment agreement or contained in a separate Change in Control Agreement. Change in Control provisions are designed to reduce the employee's uncertainty and anxiety and to facilitate a smooth management transition in the event that the employer undergoes new ownership and/or control. These objectives can be achieved by providing employees with enhanced severance if the employee is willing to stay with the employer, both before and for a certain amount of time after a Change in Control, or if the employee is terminated without Cause or terminates for Good Reason within a certain amount of time following the Change in Control. The following summary is intended to provide the reader with a quick reference as to the key elements considered in drafting and reading Change in Control provisions.

Change in Control Definitions {Section 10(c)}

Definitions of Change in Control are complex, varied and should be drafted carefully to ensure that benefits are triggered only under the intended circumstances. Events that typically may be defined as a Change in Control include:

• **Mergers, Consolidations and Corporate Reorganizations:** The consummation of a merger or consolidation of the company with or into another entity or other corporate reorganization. Most definitions require that immediately after such a change, more than a certain percentage (usually

50 percent) of the combined voting power of the acquiring company's outstanding securities must be owned by persons who were not previously stockholders of the acquired company;

- **Certain Stock Accumulations:** The accumulation by an individual or entity of a certain percentage of company stock (usually 20–40 percent). Typically, sales of company stock made directly by the company and acquisitions by employee benefit plans are exempted from consideration;

- **Sale of Assets:** The sale, transfer or other disposition of all or substantially all of the company's assets;

- **Change in the Board of Directors:** A change in the composition of the Board of Directors. Most definitions require that, to constitute a Change in Control, the new Board must be comprised of a certain number (usually at least 50 percent) of members who either:

  1. Were not directors for a certain period (typically 12–24 months) prior to the change in membership or

  2. Were not nominated or elected by at least a majority of members who were directors for a minimum period (again, typically 12–24 months) prior to the change in membership.

It is critical to specifically define the exact events that would constitute a change in control, particularly in the case of single trigger clauses, as discussed below. For example, several years ago Northrop Grumman and Lockheed Martin agreed to merge the companies, and a date of merger was established subject to regulatory approval. Several executives of Northrop Grumman were immediately entitled to certain parachute payments because a change in control was defined in terms of "approval of a merger by the Board," and the parachute payments were triggered solely by the mere execution of a merger agreement. The Justice Department sued to block the acquisition for antitrust reasons, and the merger was abandoned. By that time, however, millions of dollars in stock awards and payments to executives already had been made. In an effort to avoid such complications going forward, many companies now define a change in control in terms of "consummation of a merger" rather than in terms of "approval of the board or shareholders of a merger."

Double Trigger vs. Single Trigger

Benefits paid under a Change in Control can be triggered by the Change in Control event itself, which is commonly referred to as a "single trigger." More commonly, under a "double trigger," such benefits are paid only if there is a Change in Control event and the employee subsequently is terminated without Cause or with Good Reason within a certain period of time following the Change in Control. Some employment agreements contain a "modified single trigger," whereby, for a short period of time (usually the first thirty days following the six-month or one-year anniversary of the Change in Control), the executive can receive Change in Control severance benefits if he or she terminates employment without Good Reason (a so-called "walkaway" provision). The delayed opening of the walkaway window enables the buyer to call upon the employee for necessary transition services and to negotiate a continuing employment relationship if determined to be desirable by both parties. {See Section 10(e) for an example of both a single and a double trigger}

Typical Change in Control Benefits {See Sections 10(e)(i) – (xiii)}

Change in Control benefits typically are similar to, but greater than, the regular severance benefits provided within the employment agreement. For example, if an executive is entitled to twice his or her combined base salary and bonus following a termination without Cause, he or she may be entitled to three times base salary and bonus if the termination occurs within a certain period after a Change in Control. In addition, upon a Change in Control, vesting of equity grants usually is accelerated regardless of whether the employee is terminated. Severance following a Change in Control is usually provided in a cash lump sum to enhance the likelihood that the new employer pays all such benefits in full.

Golden Parachute Tax Issues (Section 280G of the Code)

Change in Control benefits paid to certain employees of some kinds of corporations may constitute "golden parachute payments," which may subject both the employer and the employee to special tax treatment. Parachute payments can include severance plus the increased value of accelerated vesting of equity awards and/or payment of nonqualified pension benefits or other welfare benefits. Because the golden parachute rules are highly complex and contain many exemptions, what follows is only a brief overview.

If the executive's parachute payments equal or exceed three times the "base amount," the executive is subject to a 20 percent non-deductible excise tax on any payment over one times the base amount, and the company also is denied a deduction for the excess. The "base amount" is defined as the executive's average W-2 compensation for the five calendar years preceding the year in which a Change in Control occurs.

Most Change in Control agreements deal with the complex parachute rules in one of the following three ways, listed in order of increasing benefit to the executive:

1. **The "Cap":** The executive's parachute payment is capped at 2.99 times the base amount to avoid tax penalties;

2. **The "Modified Cap":** The executive's parachute payment is cutback to the "cap" if it results in a greater after-tax benefit for the executive; or

3. **The "Gross-Up":** The executive receives a payment (non-deductible to the employer) that is sufficient, after he or she pays income tax and excise tax on the additional payment, to pay the excise tax on the original parachute payment. Although the expense may be significant, this is the most common approach used for CEOs and other top-level executive officers. An alternative is to gross-up if a small cutback (5 percent to 20 percent) will not bring the executive within the 2.99 safe harbor. {Section 18}

Severance Agreements

A separate severance agreement usually is not needed if the employment agreement is complete and includes all the company's obligations in the event of various types of terminations. A separate agreement may be necessary if there is no employment agreement, or both sides want to provide additional severance benefits or to negotiate increased severance benefits upon actual termination of employment. Employers have the option to maintain individual severance agreements or to adopt a "severance pay plan" that covers one or more groups of employees. A group severance pay plan usually provides for different levels of severance pay, depending on employees' seniority and length of service with the company. All the severance arrangements discussed earlier can be provided for in severance agreements or plans.

Releases {See Attachment 1 to Appendix A}

As with employment contracts, a severance agreement may require the employee to sign a release before severance benefits are paid. The release typically protects the employer and its affiliates, officers, directors, employees, agents, fiduciaries and shareholders against any claims that the employee had or has, in exchange for payment of the specified severance benefits. The release should include all claims and potential claims, known or unknown, resulting from employment or termination. It is particularly important that the release cover all discrimination and other civil rights-type claims. Additionally, the release should state that it was entered into voluntarily by the employee with full understanding of its contents, a provision that increases the chances of the release being legally enforceable.

The Age Discrimination in Employment Act of 1967 (commonly referred to as "ADEA") is intended to protect people aged 40 years and older against job discrimination. Because this age group represents a large segment of the workforce, many employers want terminated employees to specifically release the company from any claims that the employee might bring under ADEA. ADEA regulations require that a valid release of ADEA claims include the following five provisions:

1. it must be in writing;

2. it must specifically refer to the waiver of rights under ADEA;

3. it must be conditioned on additional payments above and beyond what the terminated employee would receive without signing the release;

4. the terminated employee must be advised in writing to consult an attorney; and

5. the terminated employee must be given at least 21 days to sign the agreement and be given seven days after signing the agreement to revoke.

Confidentiality {See Attachment 1 to Appendix A}

Many companies require that as a condition of receiving severance, a terminated employee must maintain confidentiality regarding the terms of the severance agreement (or the severance provisions of an employment agreement). Such confidentiality is intended to help avoid a precedent being set for other employees. However, in some cases, public companies may be required by law to disclose severance agreements of high-level executives. Carve outs often exist to permit the executive to discuss such an agreement with his or her attorney, accountant or financial advisor. In addition, it is increasingly common for employers to require new hires to disclose any employment or severance agreements by which they continue to be bound.

Practice aids found on the CD and in the Appendix for this chapter:

• Word® document: Sample executive employment agreement with change in control provisions (page 350)

DEBORAH LIFSHEY

Deborah Lifshey, a Vice President at Pearl Meyer & Partners, is a graduate of the Industrial and Labor Relations School at Cornell University and holds a J.D. from the University of Florida College of Law. Before commencing the practice of law, she served as a federal law clerk to the Honorable Susan H. Black on the 11th Circuit Court of Appeals. Prior to joining Pearl Meyer & Partners, Ms. Lifshey was an executive compensation and benefits associate at Fried, Frank, Harris, Shriver & Jacobson.

CLAUDE E. JOHNSTON

Claude Johnston, a Managing Director at Pearl Meyer & Partners, is a recognized authority on the tax and legal aspects of executive and Board remuneration. Mr. Johnston leads the Firm's services in these areas, advising on the design and implementation of compensation programs, employment contracts, severance agreements, tax-deferral and funding arrangements for major public corporations and private enterprises. Mr. Johnston holds an A.B. from Colgate University, a J.D. from Tulane Law School, where he was Editor-in-Chief of the Law Review, and an LL.M. in Taxation from New York University. Prior to joining the Firm, he was a Partner at Hughes Hubbard & Reed and Chairman of that firm's Executive Compensation Practice Group.

Appendix A.

XYZ CORPORATION

Employment Agreement

<u>EMPLOYMENT AGREEMENT</u>

AGREEMENT, made and entered into as of the _____ day of _____, 2000 by and among XYZ Corporation, a [state] corporation (together with its successors and assigns, the "Company"), and [name] (the "Executive").

W I T N E S S E T H:

WHEREAS, the Company desires to continue to employ Executive pursuant to an agreement embodying the terms of such employment (this "Agreement") and Executive desires to enter into this Agreement and to accept such employment, subject to the terms and provisions of this Agreement.

NOW, THEREFORE, in consideration of the premises and mutual covenants contained herein and for other good and valuable consideration, the receipt of which is mutually acknowledged, the Company and Executive (individually a "Party" and together the "Parties") agree as follows:

1. Definitions.

"Award" shall have the meaning set forth in Section 11 below.

"Base Salary" shall have the meaning set forth in Section 4 below.

"Board" shall have the meaning set forth in Section 3(a) below.

"Cause" shall have the meaning set forth in Section 10(b) below.

"Change in Control" shall have the meaning set forth in Section 10(c) below.

"Committee" shall have the meaning set forth in Section 4 below.

"Competition" shall have the meaning set forth in Section 13(a) below.

"Confidential Information" shall have the meaning set forth in Section 12(c) below.

"Effective Date" shall have the meaning set forth in Section 2(a) below.

"Fair Market Value" shall have the meaning set forth in Section 6(b) below.

"Forfeiture Event" shall have the meaning set forth in Section 11 below.

"Good Reason" shall have the meaning set forth in Section 10(c) below.

"Original Term of Employment" shall have the meaning set forth in Section 2(a) below.

"Renewal Term" shall have the meaning set forth in Section 2(a) below.

"Restriction Period" shall have the meaning set forth in Section 13(b) below.

"Retirement" shall have the meaning set forth in Section 10(f) below.

"Severance Period" shall have the meaning set forth in Section 10(c)(ii) below, except as provided otherwise in Section 2(b) or Section 10(e) below.

"Subsidiary" shall have the meaning set forth in Section 12(d) below.

"Term of Employment" shall have the meaning set forth in Section 2(a) below.

2. Term of Employment.

(a) The term of Executive's employment under this Agreement shall commence immediately upon the date of this Agreement (the "Effective Date") and end on December 31, 2004 (the "Original Term of Employment"), unless terminated earlier in accordance herewith. The Original Term of Employment shall be automatically renewed for successive one-year terms (the "Renewal Terms") unless at least 180 days prior to the expiration of the Original Term of Employment or any Renewal Term, either Party notifies the other Party in writing that he or it is electing to terminate this Agreement at the expiration of the then current Term of Employment. "Term of Employment" shall mean the Original Term of Employment and all Renewal Terms.

(b) In the event that this Agreement is not renewed because the Company has given the 180-day notice prescribed in the preceding paragraph on or before the expiration of the Original Term of Employment or any Renewal Term and, in either case, should such notice result in the expiration of the Term of Employment prior to Executive's 60th birthday, such non-renewal shall be treated as a termination with "Good Reason" pursuant to Section 10(c).

(c) In the event that this Agreement is not renewed because Executive has given the 180-day notice prescribed in Section 2(a) on or before the expiration of the Original Term of Employment or any Renewal Term, such non-renewal shall be treated as a Termination for Cause and Executive shall have the same entitlements as provided in Section 10(b)(iii) below.

(d) Notwithstanding anything in this Agreement to the contrary, at least one year prior to the expiration of the Original Term of Employment, upon the written request of the Company or Executive, the Parties shall meet to discuss this Agreement and may agree in writing to modify any of the terms of this Agreement.

3. Title, Position, Duties and Responsibilities.

(a) Generally. Executive shall serve as President, Chief Executive Officer and Chairman of the Board of Directors (the "Board") of the Company. For so long as he is serving on the Board, Executive agrees to serve as a member of any committee of the Board to which he is elected. In any and all such capacities, Executive shall report only to the Board. Executive shall have and perform such duties, responsibilities, and authorities as are customary for the chairman, president and chief executive officer of corporations of similar size and businesses as the Company as they may exist from time to time and as are consistent with such positions and status. Executive shall devote substantially all of his business time and attention (except for periods of vacation or absence due to illness), and his best efforts, abilities, experience, and talent to the positions of Chairman of the Board, President and Chief Executive Officer and for the Company's businesses.

(b) Other Activities. Anything herein to the contrary notwithstanding, nothing in this Agreement shall preclude Executive from (i) serving on the Boards of Directors of a reasonable number of other corporations or the Boards of a reasonable number of trade associations and/or charitable organizations, (ii) engaging in charitable activities and community affairs, and (iii) managing his personal investments and affairs, provided that such activities do not materially interfere with the proper performance of his duties and responsibilities under this Agreement.

(c) Place of Employment. Executive's principal place of employment shall be the corporate offices of the Company in [city, state].

(d) Rank of Executive Within Company. As Chairman of the Board, President and Chief Executive Officer of the Company, Executive shall be the Company's highest-ranking executive.

4. Base Salary.

Executive shall be paid an annualized salary, payable in accordance with the regular payroll practices of the Company, of not less than $[amount], subject to review for increase at the discretion of the Compensation Committee (the "Committee") of the Board ("Base Salary") provided that in the event that Executive relinquishes his officer positions including President and Chief Executive Officer and continues his employment with the Company as a non-officer employee, Executive shall receive (in lieu of his Base Salary, annual incentive compensation and long-term incentive compensation) remuneration in an amount and form equal to the amount and form of remuneration then paid to the Company's non-employee directors, with cash amounts paid in accordance with the Company's normal payroll practices.

5. Annual Incentive Awards.

Executive shall participate in the Company's annual incentive compensation plan with a target annual incentive award opportunity of no less than 70% of Base Salary and a maximum annual incentive award opportunity of 140% of

Base Salary. Payment of annual incentive awards shall be made no later than 75 days after the Company's fiscal year-end unless Executive agrees otherwise.

6. Long-Term Incentive Programs.

(a) *General.* Executive shall be eligible to participate in the Company's long-term incentive compensation programs including cash and/or stock grants with or without restrictions on a deferred or current basis with a target award opportunity of not less than 35% of Base Salary, and stock option grants.

(b) *Grant of Deferred Stock.* On the Effective Date, Executive shall be granted shares of deferred stock equal to $[amount] at the Fair Market Value on the Effective Date, and which shall vest 25% per annum. Unless otherwise determined by the Committee, for purposes of this Agreement, "Fair Market Value" means as of any given date, the closing sale price per share of the Company's common stock reported on a consolidated basis for securities listed on the principal stock exchange or market on which the common stock is traded on the date as of which such value is being determined or, if there is no sale on that day, then on the last previous day on which a sale was reported.

7. Employee Benefit Programs.

(a) *General Benefits.* During the Term of Employment as President and Chief Executive Officer, Executive shall be entitled to participate in such employee pension and welfare benefit plans and programs of the Company as are made available to the Company's senior level executives or to its employees generally, as such plans or programs may be in effect from time to time, including, without limitation, health, medical, dental, long-term disability, travel accident and life insurance plans. As a non-officer employee, the Executive shall be entitled to participate in the Company's insured welfare benefit plans and programs.

(b) *Deferral of Compensation.* The Company shall implement deferral arrangements, reasonably acceptable to Executive and the Company, permitting Executive to elect to defer receipt, pursuant to written deferral election terms and forms (the "Deferral Election Forms"), of all or a specified portion of (i) his annual Base Salary and annual incentive compensation under Sections 4 and 5, (ii) long term incentive compensation under Section 6 and (iii) shares acquired upon exercise of stock options to purchase Company common stock that are acquired in an exercise in which Executive pays the exercise price by the surrender of previously acquired shares, to the extent of the net additional shares otherwise issuable to Executive in such exercise; provided, however, that such deferrals shall not reduce Executive's total cash compensation in any calendar year below the sum of (i) the FICA maximum taxable wage base plus (ii) the amount needed, on an after-tax basis, to enable Executive to pay the 1.45% Medicare tax imposed on his wages in excess of such FICA maximum taxable wage base.

In accordance with such duly executed Deferral Election Forms, the Company shall credit to a bookkeeping account (the "Deferred Compensation Account") maintained for Executive on the respective payment date or dates, amounts equal to the compensation subject to deferral, such credits to be denominated in cash if the compensation would have been paid in cash but for the deferral or in shares if the compensation would have been paid in shares but for the deferral. An amount of cash equal in value to all cash-denominated amounts credited to Executive's account and a number of shares of Company common stock equal to the number of shares credited to Executive's account pursuant to this Section 7(b) shall be transferred as soon as practicable following such crediting by the Company to, and shall be held and invested by, an independent trustee selected by the Company and reasonably acceptable to Executive (a "Trustee") pursuant to a "rabbi trust" established by the Company in connection with such deferral arrangement and as to which the Trustee shall make investments based on Executive's investment objectives (including possible investment in publicly traded stocks and bonds, mutual funds, and insurance vehicles). Thereafter, Executive's deferral accounts will be valued by reference to the value of the assets of the "rabbi trust." The Company shall pay all costs of administration or maintenance of the deferral arrangement, without deduction or reimbursement from the assets of the "rabbi trust."

Except as otherwise provided under Section 10, in the event of Executive's termination of employment with the Company or as otherwise determined by the Committee in the event of Executive's hardship, upon such date(s) or event(s) set forth in the Deferral Election Forms (including forms filed after deferral but before settlement in which Executive may elect to further defer settlement), the Company shall promptly distribute to Executive any shares of Company common stock credited to Executive's deferred accounts and pay to Executive cash equal to the value of any other assets then credited to Executive's deferral accounts, less applicable withholding taxes, and such distribution shall be deemed to fully settle such accounts; provided, however, that the Company may instead settle such accounts by directing the Trustee to distribute such other assets of the "rabbi trust." The Company and Executive agree that compensation deferred pursuant to this Section 7(b) shall be fully vested and nonforfeitable; however, Executive acknowledges that his rights to the deferred compensation provided for in this Section 7(b) shall be no greater than those of a general unsecured creditor of the Company, and that such rights may not be pledged, collateralized, encumbered, hypothecated, or liable for or subject to any lien, obligation, or liability of Executive, or be assignable or transferable by Executive, otherwise than by will or the laws of descent and distribution, provided that Executive may designate one or more beneficiaries to receive any payment of such amounts in the event of his death.

8. Disability.

(a) During the Term of Employment, as well as during the Severance Period, Executive shall be entitled to disability coverage as described in this Section 8(a). In the event Executive becomes disabled, as that term is defined under the Company's Long-Term Disability Plan, Executive shall be entitled to receive pursuant to the Company's Long-Term Disability Plan or otherwise, and in place of his Base Salary, an amount equal to 60% of his Base Salary, at the annual rate in effect on the commencement date of his eligibility for the Company's long-term disability benefits ("Commencement Date") for a period beginning on the Commencement Date and ending with the earlier to occur of (A) Executive's attainment of age 65 or (B) Executive's commencement of retirement benefits from the Company in accordance with Section 10(f) below. If (i) Executive ceases to be disabled during the Term of Employment (as determined in accordance with the terms of the Long-Term Disability Plan), (ii) the positions set forth in Section 3(a) are then vacant and (iii) the Company requests in writing that he resume such positions, he may elect to resume such positions by written notice to the Company within 15 days after the Company delivers its request. If Executive resumes such positions, he shall thereafter be entitled to his Base Salary at the annual rate in effect on the Commencement Date and, for the year he resumes his positions, a pro rata annual incentive award. If Executive ceases to be disabled during the Term of Employment and does not resume his positions in accordance with the preceding sentence, he shall be treated as if he voluntarily terminated his employment pursuant to Section 10(d) as of the date Executive ceases to be disabled. If Executive is not offered such positions after he ceases to be disabled during the Term of Employment, he shall be treated as if his employment was terminated without Cause pursuant to Section 10(c) as of the date Executive ceases to be disabled.

(b) Executive shall be entitled to a pro rata annual incentive award for the year in which the Commencement Date occurs based on 70% of Base Salary paid to him during such year prior to the Commencement Date, payable in a lump sum not later than 15 days after the Commencement Date. Executive shall not be entitled to any annual incentive award with respect to the period following the Commencement Date. If Executive recommences his positions in accordance with Section 8(a), he shall be entitled to a pro rata annual incentive award for the year he resumes such positions and shall thereafter be entitled to annual incentive awards in accordance with Section 5 hereof.

(c) During the period Executive is receiving disability benefits pursuant to Section 8(a) above, he shall continue to be treated as an employee for purposes of all employee benefits and entitlements in which he was participating on the Commencement Date, including without limitation, the benefits and entitlements referred to in Sections 6 and 7 above, except that Executive shall not be entitled to receive any annual salary increases or any new long-term incentive plan grants following the Commencement Date.

9. Reimbursement of Business and Other Expenses: Perquisites.

(a) Executive is authorized to incur reasonable expenses in carrying out his duties and responsibilities under this Agreement, and the Company shall promptly reimburse him for all such business expenses incurred in connection therewith, subject to documentation in accordance with the Company's policy. During the Term of Employment, the Company shall provide Executive with personal financial and tax planning in accordance with terms adopted by the Company.

(b) The Company shall pay all reasonable legal expenses up to $[amount] incurred by Executive in connection with the negotiation of this Agreement.

(c) Upon commencement of Executive's term as a non-officer employee of the Company, Executive shall be entitled to the use of an office and a full-time secretary. Such entitlement shall cease in the event Executive undertakes full-time employment services to another employer.

10. Termination of Employment.

(a) *Termination Due to Death.* In the event Executive's employment with the Company is terminated due to his death, his estate or his beneficiaries, as the case may be, shall be entitled to and their sole remedies under this Agreement shall be:

(i) Base Salary through the date of death, which shall be paid in a

single lump sum not later than 15 days following Executive's death;
(ii) pro rata annual incentive award for the year in which Executive's death occurs assuming that Executive would have received an award equal to 70% of Base Salary for such year, which shall be payable in a lump sum promptly (but in no event later than 15 days) after his death;

(iii) elimination of all restrictions on any restricted stock or deferred stock awards outstanding at the time of his death;

(iv) immediate vesting of all outstanding stock options and the right to exercise such stock options for a period of one year following death (or such longer period as may be provided in stock options granted to other similarly situated executive officers of the Company) or for the remainder of the exercise period, if less;

(v) immediate vesting of all outstanding long-term incentive awards and a pro rata payment of such awards based on target performance, payable in a lump sum in cash or stock promptly (but in no event later than 15 days) after his death;

(vi) the balance of any incentive awards earned as of December 31 of the prior year (but not yet paid), which shall be paid in a single lump sum not later than 15 days following Executive's death;

(vii) settlement of all deferred compensation arrangements in accordance with Executive's duly executed Deferral Election Forms; and

(viii) other or additional benefits then due or earned in accordance with applicable plans and programs of the Company.

(b) Termination by the Company for Cause.

(i) "Cause" shall mean:

(A) Executive's willful and material breach of Sections 12, 13 or 14 of this Agreement;

(B) Executive is convicted of, or enters a plea of nolo contendere to, a felony; or

(C) Executive engages in conduct that constitutes willful gross neglect or willful gross misconduct in carrying out his duties under this Agreement, resulting, in either case, in material harm to the financial condition or reputation of the Company.

For purposes of this Agreement, an act or failure to act on Executive's part shall be considered "willful" if it was done or omitted to be done by him not in good faith, and shall not include any act or failure to act resulting from any incapacity of Executive.

(ii) A termination for Cause shall not take effect unless the provisions of this paragraph (ii) are complied with. Executive shall be given written notice by the Company of its intention to terminate him for Cause, such notice (A) to state in detail the particular act or acts or failure or failures to act that constitute the grounds on which the proposed termination for Cause is based and (B) to be given within 90 days of the Company's learning of such act or acts or failure or failures to act. Executive shall have 20 days after the date that such written notice has been given to him in which to cure such conduct, to the extent such cure is possible. If he fails to cure such conduct, Executive shall then be entitled to a hearing before the Committee of the Board at which Executive is entitled to appear. Such hearing shall be held within 25 days of such notice to Executive, provided he requests such hearing within 10 days of the written notice from the Company of the intention to terminate him for Cause. If, within five days following such hearing, Executive is furnished written notice by the Board confirming that, in its judgment, grounds for Cause on the basis of the original notice exist, he shall thereupon be terminated for Cause.

(iii) In the event the Company terminates Executive's employment for Cause, he shall be entitled to and his sole remedies under this Agreement shall be:

(A) Base Salary through the date of the termination of his employment for Cause, which shall be paid in a single lump sum not later than 15 days following Executive's termination of employment;

(B) any incentive awards earned as of December 31 of the prior year (but not yet paid), which shall be paid in a single lump sum not later than 15 days following Executive's termination of employment;

(C) settlement of all deferred compensation arrangements in accordance with Executive's duly executed Deferral Election Forms; and

(D) other or additional benefits then due or earned in accordance with applicable plans or programs of the Company.

(c) *Termination Without Cause or Termination With Good Reason Prior to a Change in Control.* In the event Executive's employment with the Company is terminated without Cause (which termination shall be effective as of the date specified by the Company in a written notice to Executive), other than due to death, or in the event there is a termination with Good

Reason (as defined below), in either case prior to a Change in Control (as defined below), Executive shall be entitled to and his sole remedies under this Agreement shall be:

(i) Base Salary through the date of termination of Executive's employment, which shall be paid in a single lump sum not later than 15 days following Executive's termination of employment;

(ii) Base Salary, at the annualized rate in effect on the date of termination of Executive's employment (or in the event a reduction in Base Salary is a basis for a termination with Good Reason, then the Base Salary in effect immediately prior to such reduction), for a period of 30 months following such termination (the "Severance Period");

(iii) pro rata annual incentive award for the year in which termination occurs equal to 70% of Base Salary (determined in accordance with Section 10(c)(ii) above) for such year, payable in a lump sum promptly (but in no event later than 15 days) following termination;

(iv) an amount equal to 70% of Base Salary (determined in accordance with Section 10(c)(ii) above) multiplied by 2.5, payable in equal monthly payments over the Severance Period;

(v) elimination of all restrictions on any restricted stock or deferred stock awards outstanding at the time of termination of employment;

(vi) any outstanding stock options which are unvested shall vest and Executive shall have the right to exercise any vested stock options during the Severance Period in the case of options granted prior to the Effective Date and in the case of options granted after the Effective Date, for 30 months or for the remainder of the exercise period, if less;

(vii) immediate vesting of all outstanding long-term incentive awards and a pro rata payment of such awards based on target performance, payable in a cash lump sum promptly (but in no event later than 15 days) following Executive's termination of employment;

(viii) the balance of any incentive awards earned as of December 31 of the prior year (but not yet paid), which shall be paid in a single lump sum not later than 15 days following Executive's termination of employment;

(ix) settlement of all deferred compensation arrangements in accordance with Executive's duly executed Deferral Election Forms;

(x) continued participation in all medical, health and life insurance plans at the same benefit level at which he was participating on the date of the termination of his employment until the earlier of:

(A) the date upon which Executive attains 65 years of age, provided that the Company shall bear the cost of such insurance only during the 30 months following the date of termination of the Executive's employment; thereafter Executive shall reimburse the Company for the cost of such insurance; or

(B) the date, or dates, Executive receives equivalent coverage and benefits under the plans and programs of a subsequent employer (such coverage and benefits to be determined on a coverage-by-coverage, or benefit-by-benefit, basis); provided that (1) if Executive is precluded from continuing his participation in any employee benefit plan or program as provided in this clause (xi) of this Section 10(c), he shall receive cash payments equal on an after-tax basis to the cost to him of obtaining the benefits provided under the plan or program in which he is unable to participate for the period specified in this clause (xi) of this Section 10(c), (2) such cost shall be deemed to be the lowest reasonable cost that would be incurred by Executive in obtaining such benefit himself on an individual basis, and (3) payment of such amounts shall be made quarterly in advance;

(xi) 30 months of additional age and service credit for purposes of determining the amount Executive's accrued benefits under any supplemental retirement benefit plan ("SERP") maintained by the Company, and immediate vesting of any such benefits;

(xii) outplacement services until the later of the date that Executive obtains subsequent employment or the expiration of the Severance Period; and

(xiii) other or additional benefits then due or earned in accordance with applicable plans and programs of the Company.

A termination without "Cause" shall mean Executive's employment is terminated by the Company for any reason other than Cause (as defined in Section 10(b)) or due to death.

A termination with "Good Reason" shall mean a termination of Executive's employment at his initiative as provided in this Section 10(c) following the occurrence, without Executive's written consent, of one or more of the following events (except as a result of a prior termination):

(A) a material diminution or change, adverse to Executive, in

Executive's positions, titles, or offices as set forth in Section 3(a), status, rank, nature of responsibilities, reporting relationship or authority within the Company, or a removal of Executive from or any failure to elect or re-elect or, as the case may be, nominate Executive to any such positions or offices, including as a member of the Board;

(B) an assignment of any duties to Executive which are inconsistent with his status as President and Chief Executive Officer of the Company and other positions held under Section 3(a);

(C) a decrease in annual Base Salary or target annual incentive award opportunity below 70% of Base Salary;

(D) any other failure by the Company to perform any material obligation under, or breach by the Company of any material provision of, this Agreement that is not cured within 30 days;

(E) a relocation of the corporate offices of the Company outside a 35-mile radius of [city & state of Company headquarters]; or

(F) any failure to secure the agreement of any successor corporation or other entity to the Company to fully assume the Company's obligations under this Agreement.

A "Change in Control" shall be deemed to have occurred if:

(i) any Person (other than the Company, any trustee or other fiduciary holding securities under any employee benefit plan of the Company, or any company owned, directly or indirectly, by the stockholders of the Company immediately prior to the occurrence with respect to which the evaluation is being made in substantially the same proportions as their ownership of the common stock of the Company) becomes the Beneficial Owner (except that a Person shall be deemed to be the Beneficial Owner of all shares that any such Person has the right to acquire pursuant to any agreement or arrangement or upon exercise of conversion rights, warrants or options or otherwise, without regard to the 60 day period referred to in Rule 13d-3 under the Exchange Act), directly or indirectly, of securities of the Company or any Significant Subsidiary (as defined below), representing 25% or more of the combined voting power of the Company's or such subsidiary's then outstanding securities;

(ii) during any period of two consecutive years, individuals who at the beginning of such period constitute the Board, and any new director (other than a director designated by a person who has entered into an agreement with the Company to effect a transaction described in clause (i), (iii), or (iv) of this paragraph) whose election by the Board or nomination for election by the Company's stockholders was approved by a vote of at least two-thirds of the directors then still in office who either were directors at the beginning of the two-year period or whose election or nomination for election was previously so approved but excluding for this purpose any such new director whose initial assumption of office occurs as a result of either an actual or threatened election contest (as such terms are used in Rule 14a-11 of Regulation 14A promulgated under the Exchange Act) or other actual or threatened solicitation of proxies or consents by or on behalf of an individual, corporation, partnership, group, associate or other entity or Person other than the Board, cease for any reason to constitute at least a majority of the Board;

(iii) the consummation of a merger or consolidation of the Company or any subsidiary owning directly or indirectly all or substantially all of the consolidated assets of the Company (a "Significant Subsidiary") with any other entity, other than a merger or consolidation which would result in the voting securities of the Company or a Significant Subsidiary outstanding immediately prior thereto continuing to represent (either by remaining outstanding or by being converted into voting securities of the surviving or resulting entity) more than 50% of the combined voting power of the surviving or resulting entity outstanding immediately after such merger or consolidation;

(iv) the stockholders of the Company approve a plan or agreement for the sale or disposition of all or substantially all of the consolidated assets of the Company (other than such a sale or disposition immediately after which such assets will be owned directly or indirectly by the stockholders of the Company in substantially the same proportions as their ownership of the common stock of the Company immediately prior to such sale or disposition) in which case the Board shall determine the effective date of the Change in Control resulting therefrom; or

(v) any other event occurs which the Board determines, in its discretion, would materially alter the structure of the Company or its ownership.

For purposes of this definition:

    (A) The term "Beneficial Owner" shall have the meaning ascribed to such term in Rule 13d-3 under the Exchange Act (including any successor to such Rule).

(B) The term "Exchange Act" means the Securities Exchange Act of 1934, as amended from time to time, or any successor act thereto.

(C) The term "Person" shall have the meaning ascribed to such term in Section 3(a)(9) of the Exchange Act and used in Sections 13(d) and 14(d) thereof, including "group" as defined in Section 14(d) thereof.

(d) *Voluntary Termination.* In the event of a termination of employment by Executive on his own initiative after delivery of 10 business days advance written notice, other than a termination due to death, a termination with Good Reason, a Retirement pursuant to Section 10(f) below, or a voluntary termination following a Change in Control within the 30-day period described in Section 10(e) below, Executive shall have the same entitlements as provided in Section 10(b)(iii) above for a termination for Cause, provided that at the Company's election, furnished in writing to Executive within 15 days following such notice of termination, the Company shall in addition pay the Executive 170% of his Base Salary for a period of 12 months following such termination in exchange for Executive not engaging in Competition with the Company or any Subsidiary as set forth in Section 13(a) below. Notwithstanding any implication to the contrary, Executive shall not have the right to terminate his employment with the Company during the Term of Employment except in the event of a termination with Good Reason, Retirement, or voluntary termination following a Change in Control within the 30-day period described in Section 10(e) below, and any voluntary termination of employment during the Term of Employment in violation of this Agreement shall be considered a material breach; provided, however, if the Company elects to pay Executive 170% of his Base Salary in accordance with this Section 10(d), the Company shall waive any and all claims it may have against Executive for any breach of this Agreement relating to his voluntary termination of employment unless Executive is found by a court of competent jurisdiction not to be in compliance with Section 13(a) below; provided further, however, that notwithstanding anything contained in the foregoing to the contrary, it is not the intention of the Company to waive any claims it may have against any third parties relating to a voluntary termination by Executive in violation of this Agreement.

(e) *Termination Without Cause and Termination With Good Reason Following a Change in Control.* In the event Executive's employment with the Company is terminated by the Company without Cause (which termination shall be effective as of the date specified by the Company in a written notice to Executive), other than due to death, or in the event there is a termination with Good Reason (as defined above), in either case within two years following a Change in Control (as defined above), or in the event Executive elects within the 30-day period commencing six months following a Change in Control to terminate his employment for any reason, Executive shall be entitled to and his sole remedies under this Agreement shall be:

(i) Base Salary through the date of termination of Executive's employment, which shall be paid in a single lump sum not later than 15 days following Executive's termination of employment;

(ii) an amount equal to 2.99 times Executive's Base Salary, at the annualized rate in effect on the date of termination of Executive's employment (or in the event a reduction in Base Salary is a basis for a termination with Good Reason, then the Base Salary in effect immediately prior to such reduction), payable in a cash lump sum promptly (but in no event later than 15 days) following Executive's termination of employment;

(iii) pro rata annual incentive award for the year in which termination occurs assuming that Executive would have received an award equal to 70% of Base Salary (determined in accordance with Section 10(e)(ii) above) for such year, payable in a cash lump sum promptly (but in no event later than 15 days) following Executive's termination of employment;

(iv) an amount equal to 70% of such Base Salary (determined in accordance with Section 10(e)(ii) above) multiplied by 2.99, payable in a cash lump sum promptly (but in no event later than 15 days) following Executive's termination of employment;

(v) elimination of all restrictions on any restricted stock or deferred stock awards outstanding at the time of termination of employment;

(vi) immediate vesting of all outstanding stock options and the right to exercise vested stock options granted prior to the Effective Date during the Severance Period or for the remainder of the exercise period, if less; options granted after the Effective Date shall be exercisable for the remainder of the exercise period;

(vii) immediate vesting of all outstanding long-term incentive awards and a pro rata payment of such awards based on target performance, payable in a lump sum in cash or stock promptly (but in no event later than 15 days) following Executive's termination of employment;

(viii) the balance of any incentive awards earned as of December 31 of the prior year (but not yet paid), which shall be paid in a single lump sum not later than 15 days following Executive's termination of employment;

(ix) settlement of all deferred compensation arrangements in accordance with Executive's duly executed Deferral Election Forms;

(x) continued participation in all medical, health and life insurance plans at the same benefit level at which he was participating on the date of termination of his employment until the earlier of:

> (A) the date upon which Executive attains 65 years of age, provided that the Company shall bear the cost of such insurance until Executive's 60th birthday only; thereafter Executive shall reimburse the Company for the cost of such insurance; or

> (B) the date, or dates, he receives equivalent coverage and benefits under the plans and programs of a subsequent employer (such coverage and benefits to be determined on a coverage-by-coverage, or benefit-by-benefit, basis); provided that (1) if Executive is precluded from continuing his participation in any employee benefit plan or program as provided in this clause (x) of this Section 10(e), he shall receive cash payments equal on an after-tax basis to the cost to him of obtaining the benefits provided under the plan or program in which he is unable to participate for the period specified in this clause (x) of this Section 10(e), (2) such cost shall be deemed to be the lowest reasonable cost that would be incurred by Executive in obtaining such benefit himself on an individual basis, and (3) payment of such amounts shall be made quarterly in advance;

(xi) 36 months additional age and service credit for purposes of determining the amount Executive's accrued benefits under any SERP maintained by the Company, and immediate vesting of any such benefits;

(xii) outplacement services until the later of the date that Executive obtains subsequent employment or the expiration of the Severance Period; and

(xiii) other or additional benefits then due or earned in accordance with applicable plans and programs of the Company.

For purposes of any termination pursuant to this Section 10(e), the term "Severance Period" shall mean the period of 36 months following the termination of Executive's employment.

(f) *Retirement.* Upon Executive's Retirement (as defined below), Executive shall be entitled to and his sole remedies under this Agreement shall be:

(i) Base Salary through the date of termination of Executive's employment, which shall be paid in a single lump sum not later than 15 days following Executive's termination of employment;

(ii) pro rata annual incentive award for the year in which termination occurs, based on performance valuation at the end of such year and payable in a cash lump sum promptly (but in no event later than 15 days) thereafter;

(iii) continued vesting (as if Executive remained employed by the Company) of any restricted stock or deferred stock awards outstanding at the time of his termination of employment;

(iv) continued vesting (as if Executive remained employed by the Company) of all outstanding stock options granted after the Effective Date and the right to exercise such stock options for the remainder of the exercise period; and all outstanding options granted prior to the Effective Date and the right to exercise such stock options for a period of one year following the later of the date the options are fully vested or Executive's termination of employment (or such longer period as may be provided in stock options granted to other similarly situated executive officers of the Company), or for the remainder of the exercise period, if less;

(v) continued vesting (as if Executive remained employed by the Company) of all outstanding long-term incentive awards and payment of such awards based on valuation at the end of the performance period, payable in lump sum in cash or the Company's common stock (with or without restrictions) promptly (but in no event later than 15 days) thereafter;

(vi) the balance of any incentive awards earned as of December 31 of the prior year (but not yet paid), which shall be paid in a single lump sum not later than 15 days following Executive's termination of employment;

(vii) settlement of all deferred compensation arrangements in accordance with Executive's duly executed Deferral Election Forms;

(viii) continued participation in all medical, health and life insurance plans at the same benefit level at which he was participating on the date of the termination of his employment until the earlier of:

(A) the date upon which Executive attains 65 years of age,

provided that the Company shall bear the cost of such insurance until Executive's 60th birthday only; thereafter Executive shall reimburse the Company for the cost of such insurance; or

(B) the date, or dates, he receives substantially equivalent coverage and benefits under the plans and programs of a subsequent employer (such coverage and benefits to be determined on a coverage-by-coverage, or benefit-by-benefit, basis); provided that (1) if Executive is precluded from continuing his participation in any employee benefit plan or program as provided in this clause (viii) of this Section 10(f), he shall receive cash payments equal on an after-tax basis to the cost to him of obtaining the benefits provided under the plan or program in which he is unable to participate for the period specified in this clause (viii) of this Section 10(f), (2) such cost shall be deemed to be the lowest cost that would be incurred by Executive in obtaining such benefit himself on an individual basis, and (3) payment of such amounts shall be made quarterly in advance; and

(ix) other or additional benefits then due or earned in accordance with applicable plans and programs of the Company.

For purposes of this Agreement, "Retirement" shall mean Executive's voluntary termination of employment with the Company at the earlier of (i) at or after attaining age 55 and 15 years of service with the Company (which shall include all of Executive's years of service with Melville Corporation), and (ii) attaining age 60.

(g) *No Mitigation; No Offset.* In the event of any termination of employment, Executive shall be under no obligation to seek other employment; amounts due Executive under this Agreement shall not be offset by any remuneration attributable to any subsequent employment that he may obtain.

(h) *Nature of Payments.* Any amounts due under this Section 10 are in the nature of severance payments considered to be reasonable by the Company and are not in the nature of a penalty.

(i) *No Further Liability; Release.* In the event of Executive's termination of employment, payment made and performance by the Company in accordance with this Section 10 shall operate to fully discharge and release the Company and its directors, officers, employees, subsidiaries, affiliates, stockholders, successors, assigns, agents and representatives from any further obligation or liability with respect to Executive's rights under this

Agreement. Other than payment and performance under this Section 10, the Company and its directors, officers, employees, subsidiaries, affiliates, stockholders, successors, assigns, agents and representatives shall have no further obligation or liability to Executive or any other person under this Agreement in the event of Executive's termination of employment. The Company conditions the payment of any severance or other amounts pursuant to this Section 10 upon the delivery by Executive to the Company of a release in the form satisfactory to the Company, substantially in the form attached hereto as Attachment 1, releasing any and all claims Executive may have against the Company and its directors, officers, employees, subsidiaries, affiliates, stockholders, successors, assigns, agents and representatives arising out of this Agreement.

11. Forfeiture Provisions.

(a) *Forfeiture of Stock Options and Other Awards and Gains Realized Upon Prior Option Exercises or Award Settlements.* Unless otherwise determined by the Committee, upon a termination of Executive's employment for Cause, the Executive's engaging in competition with the Company or any Subsidiary after a voluntary termination of employment pursuant to Section 10(d), or Executive's violation of any of the other restrictive covenants contained in Section 12, 13 or 14 (each a "Forfeiture Event") during the Term of Employment and for 24 months thereafter, all of the following forfeitures will result:

> (i) The unexercised portion of any stock option, whether or not vested, and any other Award not then settled (except for an Award that has not been settled solely due to an elective deferral by Executive and otherwise is not forfeitable in the event of any termination of Executive's service) will be immediately forfeited and canceled upon the occurrence of the Forfeiture Event; and

> (ii) Executive will be obligated to repay to the Com-pany, in cash, within five business days after demand is made therefor by the Company, the total amount of Award Gain (as defined here-in) realized by Executive upon each exercise of a stock option or settlement of an Award (regardless of any elective deferral) that occurred (A) during the period commencing with the date that is 24 months prior to the occur-rence of the Forfeiture Event and the date 24 months after the Forfeiture Date, if the Forfeiture Event occurred while Executive was employed by the Company or a Subsidiary or affiliate, or (B) during the period commencing 24 months prior to

the date Executive's employment by the Company terminated and ending 24 months after the date of such termination, if the Forfeiture Event occurred after Executive ceased to be so employed. For purposes of this Section, the term "Award Gain" shall mean (i), in respect of a given stock option exercise, the product of (X) the Fair Market Value per share of common stock at the date of such exercise (without regard to any subsequent change in the market price of shares) minus the exercise price times (Y) the number of shares as to which the stock option was exercised at that date, and (ii), in respect of any other settlement of an Award granted to Executive, the Fair Market Value of the cash or stock paid or payable to Executive (regardless of any elective deferral) less any cash or the Fair Market Value of any stock or property (other than an Award or award which would have itself then been forfeitable hereunder and excluding any payment of tax withholding) paid by Executive to the Company as a condition of or in connection such settlement.

"Award" shall mean any cash award, stock option, stock appreciation right, restricted stock, deferred stock, bonus stock, dividend equivalent, or other stock-based or performance-based award or similar award, together with any related right or interest, granted to or held by Executive.

(b) *Committee Discretion.* The Committee may, in its discretion, waive in whole or in part the Company's right to forfeiture under this Section, but no such waiver shall be effective unless evidenced by a writing signed by a duly authorized officer of the Company. In addition, the Committee may impose additional conditions on Awards, by inclusion of appropriate provisions in the document evidencing or governing any such Award.

12. *Confidentiality: Cooperation with Regard to Litigation; Non-Disparagement; Return of Company Materials.*

(a) During the Term of Employment and thereafter, Executive shall not, without the prior written consent of the Company, disclose to anyone (except in good faith in the ordinary course of business to a person who will be advised by Executive to keep such information confidential) or make use of any Confidential Information, except in the performance of his duties hereunder or when required to do so by legal process, by any governmental agency having supervisory authority over the business of the Company or by any administrative or legislative body (including a committee thereof) that requires him to divulge, disclose or make accessible such information. In the event that Executive is so ordered, he shall give prompt written notice to the Company in order to allow the Company the opportunity to object to or otherwise resist such order.

(b) During the Term of Employment and thereafter, Executive shall not disclose the existence or contents of this Agreement beyond what is disclosed in the proxy statement or documents filed with the government unless and to the extent such disclosure is required by law, by a governmental agency, or in a document required by law to be filed with a governmental agency or in connection with enforcement of his rights under this Agreement. In the event that disclosure is so required, Executive shall give prompt written notice to the Company in order to allow the Company the opportunity to object to or otherwise resist such requirement. This restriction shall not apply to such disclosure by him to members of his immediate family, his tax, legal or financial advisors, any lender, or tax authorities, or to potential future employers to the extent necessary, each of whom shall be advised not to disclose such information.

(c) "Confidential Information" shall mean (i) all information concerning the business of the Company or any Subsidiary including information relating to any of their products, product development, trade secrets, customers, suppliers, finances, and business plans and strategies, and (ii) information regarding the organization structure and the names, titles, status, compensation, benefits and other proprietary employment-related aspects of the employees of the Company and the Company's employment practices. Excluded from the definition of Confidential Information is information (A) that is or becomes part of the public domain, other than through the breach of this Agreement by Executive or (B) regarding the Company's business or industry properly acquired by Executive in the course of his career as an executive in the Company's industry and independent of Executive's employment by the Company. For this purpose, information known or available generally within the trade or industry of the Company or any Subsidiary shall be deemed to be known or available to the public.

(d) "Subsidiary" shall mean any corporation controlled directly or indirectly by the Company.

(e) Executive agrees to cooperate with the Company, during the Term of Employment and thereafter (including following Executive's termination of employment for any reason), by making himself reasonably available to testify on behalf of the Company or any Subsidiary in any action, suit, or proceeding, whether civil, criminal, administrative, or investigative, and to assist the Company, or any Subsidiary, in any such action, suit, or proceeding, by providing information and meeting and consulting with the

Board or its representatives or counsel, or representatives or counsel to the Company, or any Subsidiary as requested; provided, however that the same does not materially interfere with his then current professional activities. The Company agrees to reimburse Executive, on an after-tax basis, for all expenses actually incurred in connection with his provision of testimony or assistance.

(f) Executive agrees that, during the Term of Employment and thereafter (including following Executive's termination of employment for any reason), he will not make statements or representations, or otherwise communicate, directly or indirectly, in writing, orally, or otherwise, or take any action which may, directly or indirectly, disparage the Company or any Subsidiary or their respective officers, directors, employees, advisors, businesses or reputations. The Company agrees that, during the Term of Employment and thereafter (including following Executive's termination of employment for any reason), the Company will not make statements or representations, or otherwise communicate, directly or indirectly, in writing, orally, or otherwise, or take any action which may directly or indirectly, disparage Executive or his business or reputation. Notwithstanding the foregoing, nothing in this Agreement shall preclude either Executive or the Company from making truthful statements or disclosures that are required by applicable law, regulation, or legal process.

(g) Upon any termination of employment, Executive agrees to deliver any Company property and any documents, notes, drawings, specifications, computer software, data and other materials of any nature pertaining to any Confidential Information that are held by Executive and will not take any of the foregoing, or any reproduction of any of the foregoing, that is embodied an any tangible medium of expression, provided that the foregoing shall not prohibit Executive from retaining his personal phone directories and rolodexes.

13. Non-competition/Prior Employment Covenants.

(a) During the Restriction Period (as defined in Section 13(b) below), Executive shall not engage in Competition with the Company or any Subsidiary. "Competition" shall mean engaging in any activity, except as provided below, for a Competitor of the Company or any Subsidiary, whether as an employee, consultant, principal, agent, officer, director, partner, shareholder (except as a less than one percent shareholder of a publicly-traded company) or otherwise. A "Competitor" shall mean (i) [insert names of specific competitors]; (ii) any [insert type of industry/products] store, specialty store or other retailer if either $25 million or 40% or more of its annual gross sales revenues (in either case, based on the most recent quarterly or annual financial statements available) are derived from the sale of [insert type of industry/products] or other goods or merchandise of the types sold in the Company's (or any Subsidiary's) stores; (iii) any corporation or other entity whether independent or owned, funded or controlled by any other entity, engaged or organized for the purpose of engaging, in whole or in part, in the sale of [insert type of industry/products] or other goods or merchandise of the types sold in the Company's (or any Subsidiary's) stores; (iv) any business that provides buying office services to any business or group of businesses referred to above; or (v) any business (in the U.S. or any country in which the Company or any Subsidiary operates a store or stores) which is in material competition with the Company or any Subsidiary or division thereof and in which Executive's functions would be substantially similar to Executive's functions with the Company. If Executive commences employment or becomes a consultant, principal, agent, officer, director, partner, or shareholder of any entity that is not a Competitor at the time Executive initially becomes employed or becomes a consultant, principal, agent, officer, director, partner, or shareholder of the entity, future activities of such entity shall not result in a violation of this provision unless (x) such activities were contemplated by Executive at the time Executive initially became employed or becomes a consultant, principal, agent, officer, director, partner, or shareholder of the entity or (y) Executive commences directly or indirectly to advise, plan, oversee or manage the activities of an entity which becomes a Competitor during the Restriction Period, that activities are competitive with the activities of the Company or any Subsidiary.

(b) For the purposes of this Section 13, "Restriction Period" shall mean the period beginning with the Effective Date and ending with:

(i) in the case of a termination of Executive's employment without Cause or a termination with Good Reason, the Restriction Period shall terminate immediately upon Executive's termination of employment;

(ii) in the case of a termination of Executive's employment as an officer or non-officer employee for Cause, 24 months from the date of such termination;

(iii) in the case of a voluntary termination of Executive's employment pursuant to Section 10(d) above followed by the Company's election to pay Executive (and subject to the payment of)

170% of his Base Salary, as provided in Section 10(d) above, the first anniversary of such termination;

(iv) in the case of a voluntary termination of Executive's employment pursuant to Section 10(d) above which is not followed by the Company's election to pay Executive such 170% of Base Salary, the date of such termination; or

(v) in the case of a Retirement pursuant to Section 10(f) above, the remainder of the Term of Employment.

(c) Executive represents and warrants to the Company that performance of Executive's duties pursuant to this Agreement will not violate any agreements with or trade secrets of any other person or entity or previous employers, including without limitation agreements containing provisions against solicitation or competition. Executive has provided the Company with copies of the employment agreement dated [date] between [name of immediate preceding employer] and any other agreements that could restrict Executive's activities in the course of Executive's employment hereunder, and a violation of this Section 13(c) shall be grounds for termination for Cause.

14. Non-solicitation of Employees and Customers.

During the period beginning with the Effective Date and ending 24 months following the termination of Executive's employment, Executive shall not induce: (i) employees of the Company or any Subsidiary to terminate their employment (provided, however, that the foregoing shall not be construed to prevent Executive from engaging in generic non-targeted advertising for employees generally), or (ii) customers of the Company or any Subsidiary to terminate their relationship with the Company. During such period, Executive shall not hire, either directly or through any employee, agent or representative, any employee of the Company or any Subsidiary or any person who was employed by the Company or any Subsidiary within 180 days of such hiring.

15. Remedies.

In addition to whatever other rights and remedies the Company may have at equity or in law, if Executive breaches any of the provisions contained in Sections 12, 13 or 14 above, the Company (a) shall have its rights under Section 11 of this Agreement, (b) shall have the right to immediately terminate all payments and benefits due under this Agreement and (c) shall have the right to seek injunctive relief. Executive acknowledges that such a breach of Sections 12, 13 or 14 would cause irreparable injury and that money damages would not provide an adequate remedy for the Company; provided, however, the foregoing shall not prevent Executive from contesting the issuance of any such injunction on the ground that no violation or threatened violation of Sections 12, 13 or 14 has occurred.

16. Resolution of Disputes.

Any controversy or claim arising out of or relating to this Agreement or any breach or asserted breach hereof or questioning the validity and binding effect hereof arising under or in connection with this Agreement, other than seeking injunctive relief under Section 15, shall be resolved by binding arbitration, to be held at an office closest to the Company's principal offices in accordance with the rules and procedures of the American Arbitration Association, except that disputes arising under or in connection with Sections 12, 13 and 14 above shall be submitted to the federal or state courts in the State of [state]. Judgment upon the award rendered by the arbitrator(s) may be entered in any court having jurisdiction thereof. Pending the resolution of any arbitration or court proceeding, the Company shall continue payment of all amounts and benefits due Executive under this Agreement. All reasonable costs and expenses (including fees and disbursements of counsel) incurred by Executive pursuant to this Section 16 shall be paid on behalf of or reimbursed to Executive promptly by the Company; provided, however, that in the event the arbitrator(s) determine(s) that any of Executive's litigation assertions or defenses are determined to be in bad faith or frivolous, no such reimbursements shall be due Executive, and any such expenses already paid to Executive shall be immediately returned by Executive to the Company.

17. Indemnification.

(a) Company Indemnity. The Company agrees that if Executive is made a party, or is threatened to be made a party, to any action, suit or proceeding, whether civil, criminal, administrative or investigative (a "Proceeding"), by reason of the fact that he is or was a director, officer or employee of the Company or any Subsidiary or is or was serving at the request of the Company or any Subsidiary as a director, officer, member, employee or agent of another corporation, partnership, joint venture, trust or other enterprise, including service with respect to employee benefit plans, whether or not the basis of such Proceeding is Executive's alleged action in an official capacity while serving as a director, officer, member, employee or agent, Executive shall be indemnified and held harmless by the Company to the fullest extent legally permitted or authorized by the Company's certificate of incorporation or bylaws or resolutions of the Company's Board or, if greater, by the laws of the State of [state] against all cost, expense, liability and loss (including, without limitation, attorney's fees, judgments, fines, ERISA excise taxes or penalties and amounts paid or to be paid in settlement) reasonably incurred or suffered by Executive in connection therewith, and such indemnification shall continue as to Executive even if he has ceased to be a director, member, officer, employee or agent of the Company or other entity and shall inure to the benefit of Executive's heirs, executors and administrators. The Company shall advance to Executive all reasonable costs and expenses to be incurred by him in connection with a Proceeding within 20 days after receipt by the Company of a written request for such advance. Such request shall include an undertaking by Executive to repay the amount of such advance if it shall ultimately be determined that he is not entitled to be indemnified against such costs and expenses. The provisions of this Section 17(a) shall not be deemed exclusive of any other rights of indemnification to which Executive may be entitled or which may be granted to him, and it shall be in addition to any rights of indemnification to which he may be entitled under any policy of insurance.

(b) *No Presumption Regarding Standard of Conduct.* Neither the failure of the Company (including its Board, independent legal counsel or stock-holders) to have made a determination prior to the commencement of any proceeding concerning payment of amounts claimed by Executive under Section 17(a) above that indemnification of Executive is proper because he has met the applicable standard of conduct, nor a determination by the Company (including its Board, independent legal counsel or stockholders) that Executive has not met such applicable standard of conduct, shall create a presumption that Executive has not met the applicable standard of conduct.

(c) *Liability Insurance.* The Company agrees to continue and maintain a directors and officers' liability insurance policy covering Executive to the extent the Company provides such coverage for its other executive officers.

18. Excise Tax Gross-Up.

If Executive becomes entitled to one or more payments (with a "payment" including, without limitation, the vesting of an option or other non-cash benefit or property), whether pursuant to the terms of this Agreement or any other plan, arrangement, or agreement with the Company or any affiliated company (the "Total Payments"), which are or become subject to the tax imposed by Section 4999 of the Internal Revenue Code of 1986, as amended (the "Code") (or any similar tax that may hereafter be imposed) (the "Excise Tax"), the Company shall pay to Executive at the time specified below an additional amount (the "Gross-up Payment") (which shall include, without limitation, reimbursement for any penalties and interest that may accrue in respect of such Excise Tax) such that the net amount retained by Executive, after reduction for any Excise Tax (including any penalties or interest thereon) on the Total Payments and any federal, state and local income or employment tax and Excise Tax on the Gross-up Payment provided for by this Section 18, but before reduction for any federal, state, or local income or employment tax on the Total Payments, shall be equal to the sum of (a) the Total Payments, and (b) an amount equal to the product of any deductions disallowed for federal, state, or local income tax purposes because of the inclusion of the Gross-up Payment in Executive's adjusted gross income multiplied by the highest applicable marginal rate of federal, state, or local income taxation, respectively, for the calendar year in which the Gross-up Payment is to be made. For purposes of determining whether any of the Total Payments will be subject to the Excise Tax and the amount of such Excise Tax:

(i) The Total Payments shall be treated as "parachute payments" within the meaning of Section 280G(b)(2) of the Code, and all "excess parachute payments" within the meaning of Section 280G(b)(1) of the Code shall be treated as subject to the Excise Tax, unless, and except to the extent that, in the written opinion of independent compensation consultants, counsel or auditors of nationally recognized standing ("Independent Advisors") selected by the Company and reasonably acceptable to Executive, the Total Payments (in whole or in part) do not constitute parachute payments, or such excess parachute payments (in whole or in part) represent reasonable compensation for services actually rendered within the meaning of Section 280G(b)(4) of the Code in excess of the base amount within the meaning of Section 280G(b)(3) of the Code or are otherwise not subject to the Excise Tax;

(ii) The amount of the Total Payments which shall be treated as subject to the Excise Tax shall be equal to the lesser of (A) the total amount of the Total Payments or (B) the total amount of excess parachute payments within the meaning of Section 280G(b)(1) of the Code (after applying clause (i) above); and

(iii) The value of any non-cash benefits or any deferred payment or benefit shall be determined by the Independent Advisors in accordance with the principles of Sections 280G(d)(3) and (4) of the Code.

For purposes of determining the amount of the Gross-up Payment, Executive shall be deemed (A) to pay federal income taxes at the highest marginal rate of federal income taxation for the calendar year in which the Gross-up Payment is to be made; (B) to pay any applicable state and local income taxes at the highest marginal rate of taxation for the calendar year in which the Gross-up Payment is to be made, net of the maximum reduction in federal income taxes which could be obtained from deduction of such state and local taxes if paid in such year (determined without regard to limitations on deductions based upon the amount of Executive's adjusted gross income); and (C) to have otherwise allowable deductions for federal, state, and local income tax purposes at least equal to those disallowed because of the inclusion of the Gross-up Payment in Executive's adjusted gross income. In the event that the Excise Tax is subsequently determined to be less than the amount taken into account hereunder at the time the Gross-up Payment is made, Executive shall repay to the Company at the time that the amount of such reduction in Excise Tax is finally determined (but, if previously paid to the taxing authorities, not prior to the time the amount of such reduction is refunded to Executive or otherwise realized as a benefit by Executive) the portion of the Gross-up Payment that would not have been paid if such Excise Tax had been applied in initially calculating the Gross-up Payment, plus interest on the amount of such repayment at the rate provided in Section 1274(b)(2)(B) of the Code. In the event that the Excise Tax is determined to exceed the amount taken into account hereunder at the time the Gross-up Payment is made (including by reason of any payment the existence or amount of which cannot be determined at the time of the Gross-up Payment), the Company shall make an additional Gross-up Payment in respect of such excess (plus any interest and penalties payable with respect to such excess) at the time that the amount of such excess is finally determined.

The Gross-up Payment provided for above shall be paid on the 30th day (or such earlier date as the Excise Tax becomes due and payable to the taxing authorities) after it has been determined that the Total Payments (or any portion thereof) are subject to the Excise Tax; provided, however, that if the amount of such Gross-up Payment or portion thereof cannot be finally determined on or before such day, the Company shall pay to Executive on such day an estimate, as determined by the Independent Advisors, of the minimum amount of such payments and shall pay the remainder of such payments (together with interest at the rate provided in Section 1274(b)(2)(B) of the Code), as soon as the amount thereof can be determined. In the event that the amount of the estimated payments exceeds the amount subsequently determined to have been due, such excess shall constitute a loan by the Company to Executive, payable on the fifth day after demand by the Company (together with interest at the rate provided in Section 1274(b)(2)(B) of the Code). If more than one Gross-up Payment is made, the amount of each Gross-up Payment shall be computed so as not to duplicate any prior Gross-up Payment. The Company shall have the right to control all proceedings with the Internal Revenue Service that may arise in connection with the determination and assessment of any Excise Tax and, at its sole option, the Company may pursue or forego any and all adminis-trative appeals, proceedings, hearings, and conferences with any taxing authority in respect of such Excise Tax (including any interest or penalties thereon); provided, however, that the Company's control over any such proceedings shall be limited to issues with respect to which a Gross-up Payment would be payable hereunder, and Executive shall be entitled to settle or contest any other issue raised by the Internal Revenue Service or any other taxing authority. Executive shall cooperate with the Company in any proceedings relating to the determination and assessment of any Excise Tax and shall not take any position or action that would materially increase the amount of any Gross-Up Payment hereunder.

19. Effect of Agreement on Other Benefits.

Except as specifically provided in this Agreement, the existence of this Agreement shall not be interpreted to preclude, prohibit or restrict Executive's participation in any other employee benefit or other plans or programs in which he currently participates.

20. Assignability: Binding Nature.

This Agreement shall be binding upon and inure to the benefit of the Parties and their respective successors, heirs (in the case of Executive) and permitted assigns. No rights or obligations of the Company under this Agreement may be assigned or transferred by the Company except that such rights or obligations may be assigned or transferred in connection with the sale or transfer of all or substantially all of the assets of the Company, provided that the assignee or transferee is the successor to all or substan-tially all of the assets of the Company and such assignee or transferee assumes the liabilities, obligations and duties of the Company, as contained in this Agreement, either contractually or as a matter of law. The Company further agrees that, in the event of a sale or transfer of assets as described in the preceding sentence, it shall take whatever action it legally can in order to cause such assignee or transferee to expressly assume the liabilities, obligations and duties of the Company hereunder. No rights or obligations of Executive under this Agreement may be assigned or transferred by Executive other than his rights to compensation and benefits, which may be transferred only by will or operation of law, except as provided in Section 26 below.

21. Representation.

The Company represents and warrants that it is fully authorized and empowered to enter into this Agreement and that the performance of its obligations under this Agreement will not violate any agreement between it and any other person, firm or organization.

22. Entire Agreement.

This Agreement contains the entire understanding and agreement between the Parties concerning the subject matter hereof and, as of the Effective Date, supersedes all prior agreements, understandings, discussions, negotiations and undertakings, whether written or oral, between the Parties with respect thereto, including, without limitation any prior change in control agreement between the Parties.

23. Amendment or Waiver.

No provision in this Agreement may be amended unless such amendment is agreed to in writing and signed by Executive and an authorized officer of the Company. Except as set forth herein, no delay or omission to exercise any right, power or remedy accruing to any Party shall impair any such right, power or remedy or shall be construed to be a waiver of or an acquiescence to any breach hereof. No waiver by either Party of any breach by the other Party of any condition or provision contained in this Agreement to be performed by such other Party shall be deemed a waiver of a similar or dissimilar condition or provision at the same or any prior or subsequent time. Any waiver must be in writing and signed by Executive or an authorized officer of the Company, as the case may be.

24. Severability.

In the event that any provision or portion of this Agreement shall be determined to be invalid or unenforceable for any reason, in whole or in part, the remaining provisions of this Agreement shall be unaffected thereby and shall remain in full force and effect to the fullest extent permitted by law.

25. Survivorship.

The respective rights and obligations of the Parties hereunder shall survive any termination of Executive's employment to the extent necessary to the intended preservation of such rights and obligations.

26. Beneficiaries/References.

Executive shall be entitled, to the extent permitted under any applicable law, to select and change a beneficiary or beneficiaries to receive any compensation or benefit payable hereunder following Executive's death by giving the Company written notice thereof. In the event of Executive's death or a judicial determination of his incompetence, reference in this Agreement to Executive shall be deemed, where appropriate, to refer to his beneficiary, estate or other legal representative.

27. Governing Law/Jurisdiction.

This Agreement shall be governed by and construed and interpreted in accordance with the laws of [state] without reference to principles of conflict of laws. Subject to Section 16, the Company and Executive hereby consent to the jurisdiction of any or all of the following courts for purposes of resolving any dispute under this Agreement: (i) the United States District Court for [state] or (ii) any of the courts of the State of [name of state]. The Company and Executive further agree that any service of process or notice requirements in any such proceeding shall be satisfied if the rules of such court relating thereto have been substantially satisfied. The Company and Executive hereby waive, to the fullest extent permitted by applicable law, any objection which it or he may now or hereafter have to such jurisdiction and any defense of inconvenient forum.

28. Notices.

Any notice given to a Party shall be in writing and shall be deemed to have been given when delivered personally or sent by certified or registered mail, postage prepaid, return receipt requested, duly addressed to the Party concerned at the address indicated below or to such changed address as such Party may subsequently give such notice of:

If to the Company: XYZ Corporation
[address]
Attention: Secretary

If to Executive: Mr. Executive

[address]

29. Headings.

The headings of the sections contained in this Agreement are for convenience only and shall not be deemed to control or affect the meaning or construction of any provision of this Agreement.

30. Counterparts.

This Agreement may be executed in two or more counterparts.

IN WITNESS WHEREOF, the undersigned have executed this Agreement as of the date first written above.

XYZ CORPORATION

By:_____
Name:
Title:

EXECUTIVE

_____

[Name]

ATTACHMENT 1
RELEASE

In exchange for certain termination payments, benefits and promises to which _____("Employee") would not otherwise be entitled, Employee, knowingly and voluntarily releases XYZ Corporation, its subsidiaries, affiliates or related corporations, together with its/their officers, directors, agents, employees and representatives (collectively, the "Company"), of and from any and all claims, demands, obligations, liabilities and causes of action, of whatsoever kind in law or equity, whether known or unknown, which Employee has or ever had against the Company on or before the date of the execution of this Release, including but not limited to claims in common law, whether in contract or in tort, and causes of action under the Age Discrimination in Employment Act, 29 U.S.C. Sections 621 et seq., Title VII of the Civil Rights Act of 1964, 42 U.S.C. Sections 2000e et seq., the Employee Retirement Income Security Act, 29 U.S.C. Sections 1001 et seq., the Americans with Disabilities Act, 29 U.S.C. Section 12101 et seq., and all other federal, state or local laws, ordinances or regulations, for any losses, injuries or damages (including compensatory or punitive damages), attorney's fees and costs arising out of employment or termination from employment with the Company.

Employee acknowledges that he has had a period of twenty-one (21) days from the date of receipt of this Release to consider it. Employee acknowledges that he has been given the opportunity to consult an attorney prior to executing this Release. This Release shall not become effective or enforceable until seven (7) days following its execution by Employee. Prior to the expiration of the seven-(7) day period, Employee may revoke Employee's consent to this Release.

Employee acknowledges by executing this Release that Employee has returned to the Company all Company property in Employee's possession.

Employee acknowledges that the terms of this Release and Employee's separation of employment are confidential and, unless otherwise required by law or for the purposes of enforcing the Release or when needed to consult with Employee's immediate family or tax or legal advisors, neither Employee nor Employee's agents shall divulge, publish or publicize any such confidential information to any third parties or the media, or to any current or former employee, customer or client of XYZ Corporation or its businesses or any of its affiliates.

EMPLOYEE ACKNOWLEDGES HE FULLY UNDERSTANDS THE CONTENTS OF THIS RELEASE AND EXECUTES IT FREELY AND VOLUNTARILY, WITHOUT DURESS, COERCION OR UNDUE INFLUENCE.

[NAME OF EXECUTIVE]

Signed: _____

Date: _____

13. CURRENT REGULATORY ISSUES IMPACTING COMPENSATION DESIGN

It is impossible to work effectively in the executive compensation area without a good understanding of the related tax, accounting, securities and other regulatory issues. Sometimes these technical issues are enabling, allowing you to more easily achieve an important design goal. More often, however, the opposite is the case and a successful path is only achievable with a sound understanding of the pertinent regulatory facts and forces. As the authors point out, many common design features of contemporary executive compensation plans are a direct result of regulation.

The authors label the United States as a "laboratory for complicated plan design." And given that U.S. executive compensation plans tend to serve as an important benchmark for most other countries, understanding the rules of the road in the U.S. is key. The chapter, which could easily have been dryly factual and literal, is actually quite colorful and easy to follow. The authors discuss all of the major accounting, tax and securities issues that are in place or under consideration, and then offer a myriad of examples of how these various issues come to life in contemporary executive compensation plan design.

The authors conclude by noting that "the influence of regulation on compensation strategy is immeasurable" and that "the most disquieting aspect of regulation is that it is constantly in flux; what applies in one era is overturned in the next." This is what makes both this chapter and topic very interesting and highly relevant. —Editors

Pay for Performance–An Elusive Goal?

"PAY FOR PERFORMANCE" is supposed to be the rationale behind corporate incentive plans. It implies accountability, an appropriate balance between effort and reward, and prudent use of corporate assets. Who can argue with such high-minded goals? Yet upon closer examination, many incentive plans will reveal the opposite: incentives that reward tenure rather than effort, have no connection to individual effort at all, or that actually appear to encourage adverse behavior.

At its simplest level, incentive compensation ought to operate roughly along the lines of that most basic of human motivators, the pleasure-pain principle. That is, good behavior is rewarded with pleasure–in this case with more money–and bad behavior with pain in the form of less money. But regulations and legislation often subject this straightforward proposition to hoops that must be jumped through and roadblocks that need to be detoured around. By the end of the day, the relationship between pleasure-and-more-money vs. pain-and-less-money is anything but straightforward.

Regulation and other external influences come from many sources and in various forms, such as shareholder pressure or the effect of country-specific tax, accounting, or securities law legislation. While well-meaning on their own, these forces often combine to contradict the principles of pay for performance, or at least fail to support them in any meaningful way.

How contradictory are these elements? On a national level, they tend to produce conformity within each country because regulatory policies lead to fairly consistent design decisions for all companies that are subject to them. Tax codes, accounting conventions, and securities laws impose arbitrary constraints that plan designers need to consider. By the time these are satisfied, there may be very little leeway for each company to make the most of its individual strengths. "One size fits all" doesn't work in the case of incentive compensation.

The problems are compounded as companies operate across national borders, as is increasingly the case in the global economy. Since regulatory environments vary from one country to the next, companies may have very different incentive plans for similar personnel. For example, U.S.-headquartered companies may want to offer a U.S.-style stock purchase plan or incentive stock option plan globally, so all of its employees around the world will have a common tie to the company's stock. But non-U.S. participants in a plan designed to address the specific requirements of IRC Sec. 423 (for employee stock purchase plans) or IRC Sec. 422 (for incentive stock options) won't enjoy the same tax benefits as their U.S. counterparts, and may actually be worse off than with some other design. So companies have to weigh tradeoffs between having a one-design approach, or tailoring programs to various regulatory systems.

There is a movement underway to harmonize accounting standards around the world, via the activities of the International Accounting Standards Board (IASB). An early test-case of how this might work involves accounting rules for stock-based compensation. After issuing an exposure draft in November 2002, the IASB made revisions to its proposed treatment of stock-based compensation that essentially brings it more in line with

FASB Statement 123 (FAS 123). Meanwhile, the Financial Accounting Standards Board (FASB) was having second thoughts about FAS 123 and undertook a project of its own to reconsider the accounting issues of stock-based compensation. While the end of this process may well be a convergence of international standards, the jury is out on whether in fact that objective will be fully attained. The IASB intends to issue a revised statement in 2004, and the revised or clarified FAS 123 will pertain to all U.S. accounting statements for fiscal years starting after December 15, 2004.

This means that, for the moment, U.S.-based companies must plan around at least two different accounting systems–the current Accounting Principles Board Opinion 25 (APB 25) or FAS 123, and the final regulations, with the possibility that even these final rules may be subject to further clarification as the IASB continues its own study. Clearly, the accounting system is currently in a transitory phase. While companies can be fairly confident with respect to some design elements and how they fit in the new paradigm, other issues are still up in the air–a state of affairs that's likely to make near-term design decisions quite challenging.

Furthermore, corporate governance mandates–although not regulation per se–sometimes steer companies either toward particular plan designs that they otherwise would not choose, or away from other designs that could make sense. For example, the plan voting guidelines of many institutional shareholders rule out plan features allowing so-called "discount options" (options that are granted with an exercise price below 100% of the stock's value on the date of grant). Yet the same shareholders may willingly allow the granting of restricted shares (for which participants typically pay no purchase price at all). So companies are precluded from using a hybrid of two acceptable approaches–at-the-money options and restricted stock–even in instances in which the hybrid may make more sense.

Within each area of regulation, whether taxation, securities law, accounting rules, corporate governance mandates, and the rest, there are anomalies that pull companies in different directions simultaneously. When faced with conflicting design issues, companies must choose the ones that are most in accord with (or rather, least disruptive to) the purpose of the incentive plan.

The United States–Laboratory for Complicated Plan Design

For fully appreciating the complications that corporations around the world face in designing incentives, there can be no better–or should we say worse –model than the United States. The United States' highly evolved securities markets, history of shareholder activism, and complex tax and accounting protocols make it a particularly interesting case study. The U.S. experience shows clearly the contradictory logic that seems to pervade compensation plans because of the welter of technical requirements that must be considered in their design. The plans that result may be compliant, but do they really accomplish the goal?

Some common conditions, such as the need to obtain shareholder approval for incentive plans, appear to be consistent with principles of pay for performance. However, they don't necessarily guarantee that this objective always will be attained because of weaknesses in the methodologies for measuring performance, and because, as recent history makes clear, outcomes can be manipulated.

In other cases, incentive terms are dictated entirely by technical considerations, and are totally at odds with the incentive's stated objective. Indeed, the plan design landscape is littered with such non-sequiturs. Yet these provisions retain their hold, suggesting that companies are ill-disposed to give up tax deductions or sacrifice favorable accounting treatment for better alignment of pay and performance.

Accounting for Stock-Based Compensation

The effect of accounting regulations on plan design is strong and obvious. APB 25, issued in 1972, causes companies to favor stock options, time-vesting restricted stock and other so-called "fixed" awards over other possible designs. Now in its twilight–APB 25 will cease to be a generally accepted accounting principle when the FASB enacts its new rules–the current accounting method contains several examples of how incentive plans have been encumbered by technical considerations that run contrary to real incentives.

APB 25 created a two-tiered system in which some awards receive favorable "fixed" accounting treatment and others receive less favorable "variable" treatment. A grant is "fixed" if two criteria–(1) the number of shares an employee is going to receive or be allowed to purchase, and (2) the purchase price, if any, the employee is going to pay for the shares–are both known on the grant or award date. Otherwise, a grant is "variable," and subject to mark-to-market accounting until such time as these criteria are satisfied. Time-based vesting conditions do not preclude "fixed" accounting treatment; however, performance-based vesting conditions require "variable" accounting, since the number of shares to be issued is not known until they are earned.

Stock options that vest on the basis of the holder's service (and nothing else) are the classic example of a type of award eligible for favorable "fixed" accounting under APB 25. The expense for such an award is based on its "spread" on the grant date (amount by which the stock's fair market value exceeds the exercise price). Since these two amounts are usually set to be equal, there would be no expense for such an award.

Likewise, restricted stock that vests on the basis of time qualifies for "fixed" treatment under APB 25 since it is presumed there is reasonable certainty that the vesting condition–continued employment–will be satisfied. Accordingly, the number of shares awarded on the date of grant, multiplied by the value of the shares on that date, represents the expense that the granting company must recognize on its financial statements over the vesting period.

If stock option or restricted stock vesting depends on satisfying certain conditions that are not based on tenure–attaining a three-year cumulative growth in EPS, for example–the award's cost needs to be recognized on a variable basis, since the number of shares to be earned is unknown. Accordingly, until performance conditions are achieved, the company must reflect the value of the grant on a variable basis.

As a rule, companies prefer fixed charges to variable ones, since they can determine the full extent of the expense at the time the award is made. And, of course, the best type of "fixed" accounting involves no expense at all, which explains much of the popularity of traditional stock options (with a fixed exercise price set at the stock's fair market value at grant).

Under APB 25, this preference for fixed accounting treatment over variable led companies to dismiss alternative plan designs that would require variable accounting treatment, such as:

• Performance-vesting options or shares.

• Indexed options, or any other type of options with a "floating" exercise price.

• Stock appreciation rights and other cash-based awards.

By omitting everything that requires mark-to-market accounting under APB 25, companies gave up a range of incentive vehicles that might produce better pay-for-performance. It is as if a football coach gave up the running game entirely because he got paid only for the passing yardage his team accumulated. Touchdowns, interceptions, and, above all, winning and losing became irrelevant.

What if a company under APB 25 wanted to make stock options or restricted shares more sensitive to performance than with service-based vesting, but didn't want to undermine the benefits of fixed accounting? One solution involved a somewhat convoluted design using an accelerated vesting feature commonly known as a TARSAP (Time Accelerated Restricted Stock Award Plan)–a term that gradually came to include stock options as well as restricted shares. This feature permitted vesting to occur on a designated date, usually several years in the future, or upon the satisfaction of performance-based vesting conditions, whichever was earlier.

TARSAPs are highly artificial constructs; except for the accounting treatment, there was little logical reason for them to exist. Yet, because they preserved fixed accounting treatment, they were much more prevalent than performance-vesting awards that had no time-based vesting provision. We believe that TARSAPs will become dinosaurs under the FASB's proposed accounting treatment and anticipate that their prevalence will decline sharply.

Stock plans outside of the United States often depart from these characteristics. Part of the reason for this disparity is attributable to a shorter history with such plans and a different corporate governance environment. But much of the answer can be attributed directly to the accounting treatment. The effect of APB 25 on plan design is felt mainly in the U.S. and countries with similar accounting standards, such as Canada. Elsewhere, such as in Europe, the pressure for fixed plan designs is less powerful because there are no accounting reasons for them.

In 2000, the FASB issued FIN 44, which was intended to resolve some of APB 25's ambiguity. It has been a target of criticism from the start and probably was the single most influential consideration for companies switching voluntarily from APB 25 to FAS 123 over the past few years. Under FAS 123, companies recognize a fixed charge for all types of equity awards–no free lunches here–but avoid the application of variable treatment in the event of repricings or other modifications. Since many such modifications trigger variable accounting under APB 25, FAS 123 responds well to companies' preference for a certain fixed charge over an uncertain variable one. For companies that stayed with APB 25, the introduction of FIN 44 led to some interesting developments in plan design, particularly with respect to option repricing.

It will be interesting to see if some common design conventions in stock plans survive the transition from APB 25 to a different accounting policy. If all award forms become expensed in some manner, it is likely that companies will begin to incorporate performance-based vesting. Furthermore, TARSAP features would probably disappear entirely.

The result would be a more targeted incentive for recipients who should own stock, but don't necessarily have a direct line of sight to stock price growth. In fact, such awards might conceivably become more attractive to companies than time-vesting awards, since the additional performance conditions might well decrease the amount of compensation expense that needs to be recognized. In that respect, we can anticipate that the successor to APB 25 will have an influence on the design of stock compensation at those companies that adopt it.

Plan Designs and Arbitrary Limits

Astute readers of proxy statements and other documents containing compensation-related information may be struck by the recurrence of certain numbers—a 15% discount, for example, or a "2.99 cap" placed on compensation in the event of a change in control. There are also similarities that appear to pop up in various different contexts—six months, for example (or more recently, six months and a day). Such seemingly arbitrary limits have their basis in legislation, and plan designers need to be sensitive to these "inflection points."

Further, in a country where the complexities of the tax code have given rise to loopholes, taxation also exerts a heavy influence on incentive planning. Specific provisions of the tax code—IRC Sec. 422, IRC Sec. 162(m), and IRC Sec. 280G, among others—figure prominently in the deferral or avoidance of taxation, which is possible only if certain conditions are met.

A. IRC Sec. 423 and the "15% Discount Rule"

When is compensation not compensation? The answer: When the government or the accounting authorities say so. IRC Sec. 423 allows favorable tax treatment for employee stock purchase plans meeting certain requirements. And plans that satisfy these tax requirements also get to be treated as "non compensatory" for accounting purposes under APB 25. Even though employee stock purchase plans offer shares at a discount (of up to 15% in most instances), no part of the discount needs to be reflected as an expense on the income statement. In this sense, accounting and tax regulations "hard-code" a specific number—i.e., a fifteen percent discount—into plan design.

The "15% Discount Rule" is likely to be revised, given the current direction of the FASB. Under FAS 123, the qualification for "non-compensatory" treatment is stricter than under APB 25, making it necessary to recognize expense for IRC Sec. 423 plans for the first time. In particular, the allowable

15% discount for a plan to be considered non-compensatory under FAS 123 was cut to 5%. The FASB has proposed to further cut this allowable amount to zero, so non-compensatory treatment would apply only for purchase arrangements available to all shareholders. What's more, so-called "look-back" features–the opportunity to buy the shares at the lower of the grant-date market price or the fair value on the date the shares are delivered–will be cut back significantly, to control the size of the fair value expense arising from this feature.

In a sense, this accounting change may hasten the demise of IRC Sec. 423 plans altogether. Alternatively, the tighter parameters may simply end up replacing the old ones. Design will no longer gravitate to the allowable limits under IRC Sec. 423 in terms of allowable purchase amounts, discounts and look-backs. Instead, companies will weight the benefits perceived by participants against the cost of the program. If that happens, we will have witnessed yet another example of how legislation influences design. The numbers may change, but the pattern of cause-and-effect continues, with plan design taking its cue from arbitrarily imposed limits in accounting and tax protocol.

B. Incentive Stock Options (ISOs) and the Cost of a Tax Break

Under IRC Sec. 422, companies may grant employees options that have special tax advantages. Like traditional stock options, ISOs provide recipients with an opportunity to purchase shares of company stock at a fixed price during a specified period of time. Unlike nonqualified stock options (NQSOs), on which ordinary income tax is due upon exercise, ISOs delay taxation until the acquired stock is sold.

The benefit of this deferral is twofold. Under many circumstances, grantees exercising NQSOs are forced to sell some of their shares right away in order to pay their taxes. By contrast, employees exercising ISOs increase their financial leverage by retaining their shares.

A second significant advantage exists when capital gains rates are lower than ordinary income rates, since all of the gain on an ISO is taxed as a capital gain, assuming that the stock is held for at least one year after exercise and two years after the option was granted. With NQSOs, only the post-exercise gain receives capital gains treatment.

Sounds like a slam-dunk, but it isn't, at least to the companies. ISO regulations impose requirements on plan administrators that simply don't exist for NQSOs. The need to distinguish ISOs from NQSOs and to track disqualifying dispositions is not necessarily burdensome, but it is avoided altogether at companies that grant only NQSOs.

A more significant detriment is that companies receive no tax deduction when an ISO is exercised (except ex-post in cases of disqualifying dispositions, which usually happens because the mandatory holding period isn't met). With NQSOs (and disqualified ISOs that are taxed in a similar manner as NQSOs), companies can claim a tax deduction on the spread at exercise, which can result in substantial tax savings. Under most circumstances, companies would be better off financially by granting NQSOs and keeping executives "whole" in other ways such as giving them either more or discounted NQSOs.

But–and there's always a *but*–each of these solutions comes with a custom-made set of issues that are attributable to accounting costs or shareholder concerns about dilution, so granting ISOs often is the preferable choice after all. Participants encounter disadvantages as well, including a potential for alternative minimum tax liability, mandatory stock holding periods, and a current vesting limit of $100,000 per year–none of which would be applicable to NQSO awards.

In order to qualify for ISO treatment, the exercise price cannot be paid through the sale of the securities at the time of exercise. If the participant's broker sells the stock in order to cover the exercise price, the ISOs automatically convert to NQSOs and taxes are payable on the spread. Accordingly, recipients must choose between deferring taxes or finding alternative sources of financing. In that respect, the fine print that governs ISO qualification (specifically, the holding period) may undermine the vehicle's most attractive aspect (the tax deferral).

When weighing the choice between awarding ISOs instead of NQSOs there is no clear winner. On the plus side, employees obtain a tax deferral, and the potential that eventual capital gains taxes will be applicable at a lower rate than the prevailing ordinary income tax rates. This benefit should be compared with the opportunity cost of losing the tax deduction and having to accept certain restrictions, as well as the additional administrative burden of tracking stock sales.

C. Tax Deductions, Plan Administration, and Corporate Governance

Tax legislation has two purposes: first, to raise revenue and second, to raise the cost of what Congress deems undesirable behavior. For consumers, levies on alcohol and tobacco are obvious examples of taxation as social policy, in which individual consumers pay the added cost or kick the habit. For companies, the process is less direct: a disallowance of the tax deduction on compensation. But the issues related to compensation policy are not as black and white as smoking. In this case, the cure can create pathology of its own, and has.

Responding to rapidly rising compensation packages for senior executives in the early 1990s, the IRS enacted IRC Sec. 162(m), which denies a deduction to publicly held corporations for compensation to its "covered employees" above $1,000,000. The purpose of this regulation was threefold:

• Encourage companies to seek shareholder approval for their incentive plans.

• Encourage adoption of more structured and performance-oriented plans.

• Control pay.

This legislation effectively capped base salaries at many companies and gave rise to now-typical highly "performance-leveraged" (or at least "variable") compensation packages.

One distinction that sprang from IRC Sec. 162(m) was the designation of a rarified class of "covered employees" who can receive incentive awards: the proxy-named executives who hold office at the end of the fiscal year. While there may be no other special difference between the fifth highest-paid individual and, say, the sixth in terms of role or responsibility, the fact that one is "covered" and the other is not has profound implications for incentives.

"Performance-based compensation" is not subject to the $1-million deduction limitation under IRC Sec. 162(m). It is remuneration payable solely for attaining one or more performance goals that satisfy the following criteria:

• The goals are determined by a compensation committee of the board of directors consisting solely of two or more outside directors.

• The material terms under which the compensation is to be paid are disclosed to the shareholders and approved by a majority in a separate vote before payment is made.

• Before any payment is made, the compensation committee certifies that the performance goals and any other material terms have been satisfied.

In the case of options, continued employment alone does not qualify as a performance-based goal (nor does a TARSAP feature make it so). Furthermore, discounted options are not considered performance-based. However, all other options are considered performance-based by virtue of the fact that their value ultimately depends on stock price appreciation (which is a performance-based goal). The terms of the payment formula or standard must not allow any discretionary increases, although there can be a discretionary reduction.

The performance-based exemption in IRC Sec. 162(m) led to changes in corporate governance after 1993. For instance, most companies restricted membership on the compensation committee to "outside" directors as defined in IRC Sec. 162(m), and the compensation committee's function expanded as described above. Furthermore, IRC Sec. 162(m) encouraged many companies to bring their incentive plans to shareholder vote; consequently, public access to plan texts increased substantially.

In addition to designating the decision-makers, IRC Sec. 162(m) determined the timing of decisions. The compensation committee must establish performance goals in writing not later than 90 days after the start of the period to which the performance goal relates or 25 percent of that period, whichever is shorter. The outcome must be substantially uncertain when the goal is set—a condition that imposes some rigor on the compensation committee's deliberations, though it doesn't ensure that the targets themselves are necessarily appropriate.

Qualification for the performance exemption under IRC Sec. 162(m) is determined on a grant by grant basis. Consequently, some companies maintain as much flexibility as they can by splitting their awards into two separate grants, one of which qualifies under the statute's provisions and the other of which does not. In this regard, IRC Sec. 162(m) has increased the cost and/or administrative burden on companies that grant discretionary awards; however, it hasn't entirely eradicated the practice of granting them.

Disclosure of the compensation payable under a performance goal must be specific enough so shareholders can determine the maximum compensation that could be paid to any employee. If the terms of the goal do not provide for a maximum dollar amount, the disclosure must include the formula under which the compensation would be calculated.

In incentive plan texts, this provision requires companies to set a maximum number of shares for stock-based awards or a dollar maximum for cash-based awards. Setting the appropriate level has occasionally posed challenges because the self-imposed limits defined under this provision may be insufficient to provide a competitive level of compensation. Companies have thus occasionally been forced to use alternative sources of shares to supplement arbitrary limits imposed in their qualified plans.

Under recently-enacted stock exchange rules, however, these sources have been cut back significantly. Whereas companies used to be able to create non-shareholder approved pools of shares that could be drawn from at any time, the New York Stock Exchange and the NASDAQ have both enacted stringent new shareholder approval policies that forbid the unauthorized use of treasury stock to supplement qualified plan reserves and may put an end to some broad-based incentive plans.

IRC Sec. 162(m) created a paradigm shift in the process and form of incentive compensation delivery. Proxy-named executives, already an elite class, became more so, while companies that wanted to preserve their tax deduction had to observe limitations of several kinds. And while some aspects of the legislation have encouraged constructive changes in corporate governance, others have placed arbitrary restrictions on companies' ability to grant awards–restrictions that prevent incentives from being used to their full economic potential.

D. Deferred Taxation: Doctrines of Constructive Receipt and Economic Benefit

Finding the optimal moment for companies to pay their employees on the one hand, and for employees to receive their compensation on the other, and for both to attain the maximum benefits under tax law, is a continuing challenge to tax specialists. The tradeoffs include matters such as liquidity needs, benefit security, and diversification of risk–considerations that are not necessarily tax-driven.

A deferral election should be made prior to the time that the compensation is due–in some circumstances, even before the start of the performance period to which the payoff applies, though in some instances it is made after the performance period has commenced. The deferral agreement must indicate the timing or conditions under which payments will be made–usually a long period of time or milestones like a specified age, retirement, death, disability, or termination of employment.

In addition to constructive receipt, tax legislation is built on the economic benefit doctrine, which mandates the inclusion in the employee's taxable income of "any economic or financial benefit conferred on the employee as compensation, whatever the form or mode by which it is effected." Hence, even if an employee doesn't receive the property or it is not in the form of cash, it may be taxable as income.

For their part, employers who defer compensation on behalf of their employees may avoid receipt to those employees under the economic benefit doctrine by recording the compensation in a non-funded form, such as book-entry credits. IRS Rev. Rule 60-31 determined that "a mere promise to pay not represented by notes or securities in any way, is not regarded as a receipt of income within the intent of the cash receipts and disbursements method."

Under IRS Rev. Rule 60-31 and IRS Rev. Rule 71-19, the deferred amount must not be placed unconditionally in a trust or in escrow for the executive's benefit. The promise to pay the deferred amount must be merely a contractual obligation, not evidenced by notes or secured in any way. Thus restricted shares are converted into stock units rather than kept as actual shares, and deferred cash balances are maintained in book-entry form only. In this respect, the need to satisfy the mandated conditions give rise to some compensation devices that otherwise would have no need to exist.

To further complicate matters, while the IRS's position expressed in Rev. Rule 60-31 is quite strict, the courts have sometimes taken more liberal positions, especially about the timing of the deferral election. Consequently, many companies permit deferral elections to occur after the period of service has begun, as long as the award amount is not yet determinable.

Tax rules force a choice between avoiding current taxation and ensuring the receipt of a benefit, since the employee must take the risk of losing it if it is either not funded or not vested. The company may renege on payment in the event of a change of control, say, or bankruptcy. While there is no way to protect a benefit completely—for example, by funding or insuring it on a particular executive's behalf—without adverse tax or cost implications, several approaches can enhance benefit security as long as Rev. Rule 60-31 is in effect. These approaches include:

- **"Rabbi" trusts:** Arrangements under which the employer sets aside funds for the payment of a SERP or other benefit, but such funds would be made available to the company's general creditors in the event of the company's bankruptcy. Regardless of whether employees are vested, they are not taxed until actual receipt because assets can be used to pay general creditors if the company defaults on other debts.

- **"Secular" trusts:** Like rabbi trusts without any strings attached in the case of bankruptcy. Under such agreements, the employer irrevocably places assets in a trust for the payment of supplemental/nonqualified benefits. Such funds can be used exclusively to pay benefits and cannot be attached by a company's creditors in the event of bankruptcy. This arrangement affords security to executives but no tax deferral.

- **Third-party guarantees:** Surety bonds and letters of credit give an employee a second line of defense from which to collect if the employer is unwilling or unable to pay a promised benefit. However, to avoid current taxation on the benefit, the employee—and not the employer—must arrange and pay for the third-party protection.

Some of these strategies are the subject of current congressional debate that may render them ineffective as tax deferral mechanisms. Thus the tactics that apply today may have no bearing on compensation design in the future. But what is significant about all three of these methods is that, in the absence of rules governing constructive receipt and the doctrine of economic benefit, there would be no reason for a company or their employees to create any of them.

E. IRC Sec. 83(b) and "Irrevocable" Elections for Early Taxation

A principal tenet of deferred compensation is that executives have made a voluntary decision to postpone the fruits of their labor, and this decision is supposedly not subject to subsequent revision. For all practical purposes, the terms of the contract are set in stone when the deferral election is made.

Irrevocability is also an important concept in so-called Sec. 83(b) elections, governing taxation of non-cash compensation. Specifically, executives can elect to pay taxes on unvested equity-based grants and accelerate, for tax purposes, recognition of ordinary income arising from the assets. A timely election causes later appreciation in the value of the property to be treated as capital gains, which under JGTRRA are taxed at less than half the rate of ordinary income taxes.

Why would one willingly choose to pay taxes early, rather than when they come due? Since capital gains tax rates typically are lower than ordinary income tax rates, appreciation after the date of transfer is taxed at a preferential rate. Furthermore, such tax liability is deferred until the property is sold or otherwise disposed.

Electing to pay taxes now rather than later can be risky, however. Specifically, taxes paid on any part of the property that subsequently is forfeited cannot be recouped directly; rather, the difference between the amount reported and the amount received upon vesting is treated as a capital gain or loss. Furthermore, the value of the property—even if it vests—may decline substantially after transfer, in which case the executive pays taxes on a higher value than would otherwise be the case (as happened frequently in the aftermath of the dot-com bust).

In some instances, the advantages outweigh these considerations—particularly if the executive can lock in, for ordinary tax purposes, a fairly low taxable basis and he or she has no intention of selling the assets once they vest. Because the Sec. 83(b) election is irrevocable, however, executives who find themselves on the losing end of the proposition have no recourse to switch their tax strategy from Plan A to Plan B.

F. IRC Sec. 280G and the "Three Times" Rule

The tax code imposes an arbitrary limit on parachute benefits that are payable to "disqualified individuals" as a result of a change in corporate control. IRC Sec. 280G permits parachute payments without penalty for up to, but not including, three times an executive's average annual compensation over the executive's past five tax years. For purposes of this calculation, a parachute payment equals the present value of any compensatory cash or property payments for the benefit of an executive that are made on account of a change in control.

Some or all of the value resulting from the settlement or accelerated vesting of stock options or other long-term incentives at the time that control changes may also be counted toward the parachute amount. Included as well are any property transfers, or payments pursuant to contracts made within one year before control changes, unless clear and convincing evidence shows that such payments are not contingent upon the change in control.

If total parachute payments are determined to equal or exceed three times the base amount (i.e., the executive's average annual compensation over the preceding five years), penalties may be imposed on all such payments that exceed one times the base amount. In particular:

- Executives are charged a 20% excise tax on all excess amounts above one times the base amount, which is owed in addition to the ordinary income tax on the entire parachute payment.
- Companies are denied a tax deduction for all parachute payments that exceed one times the base amount.

These tax sanctions create an artificial boundary that encourages companies to cap benefits at the statutory limit (or more typically, at 2.99 times the limit) to preserve their tax deduction. However, the cap can result in considerably lower severance benefits than the company intended, especially due to the treatment of gains from options or nonqualified retirement benefits where vesting is accelerated.

That being said, however, the cap may prove to be a boon. Recall that the 20% excise tax is owed on all payments that exceed one times the base amount, if the value of the total parachute exceeds three times the base amount. Thus it is possible–and surprisingly common–for executives to be better off after tax if they voluntarily cap their payments at the statutory three-time limit and thereby avoid the excise tax.

Accordingly, many companies offer a "best-net" alternative to executives with excess parachutes, the purpose of which is to provide disqualified individuals with the largest after-tax proceeds. The choice–to cap or not to cap–is determined on the basis of a comparison of after-tax capped benefits with the impact of paying the excise tax on an unreduced parachute value.

Another strategy–particularly common for very senior executives–is to make a special gross-up payment that spares participants the impact of the excise tax. The gross-up payment raises the company's cost, since it is itself subject to the 20% excise tax in addition to ordinary income taxes. In order to protect an executive's payments entirely from the effect of the tax, it may be necessary to pay substantially more than the excise tax itself.

G. Stock Holding Periods and Black-Out Periods

Today, executives are faced with a patchwork of requirements and suggestions about what they can do with company stock that they own. Some requirements are imposed by plans themselves–e.g., by the terms of the award, holders of restricted stock aren't allowed to sell the shares until the restrictions lapse. In most instances, even though the executive is the owner of record for such shares, the physical certificates are retained by the company and have a legend on them noting the terms of the restriction.

Other holding requirements are conditions for getting favorable tax treatment, but not absolute requirements. For example, to qualify for treatment as an ISO under IRC Sec. 422, stock that is received upon exercise must be held for at least two years from the date of grant and one year from the date of exercise.

Still other requirements are imposed by federal securities laws. For example, the SEC's Rule 144 governs the resale by an executive of stock not registered with the SEC. While some aspects of Rule 144 have changed over the years–a two-year holding period requirement was reduced to one year in 1997–the fact that the restriction exists at all continues to influence design, at least for executives who are subject to Rule 144.

Beyond these formal requirements, there may be other factors that affect an executive's ability to freely dispose of shares. Section 16 insiders are required publicly to report their company stock trades within two days of when they occur on a Form 4 filed with the SEC. The investing public monitors such filings routinely for signals about the company's prospects for stock appreciation. And many companies have formal or informal stock ownership guidelines or requirements that often dictate how much stock executives must hold and the circumstances under which they can sell.

H. "Blackout" Periods

Many companies establish routine black-out or "quiet" periods–often lasting for days or weeks–during which some or all employees are prohibited from exercising options or otherwise buying and selling company stock. These periods routinely occur before the company's public release of financial data, to lessen suspicion that employees or executives are engaging in stock transactions based on inside information. Further, companies may impose additional trading black-outs on some or all employees when they are engaging in merger or other transactions for which there is concern that corporate insiders may have specific information not available to the general public.

As a result of several highly-publicized circumstances involving potential abuses of inside information by senior corporate executives, many companies are tightening their policies regarding such trades. The Sarbanes-Oxley Act of 2002 imposed trading bans for executives when other employees are subject to trading black-outs under employee benefit plans. Other legislation or regulation in this regard may be forthcoming.

Trading programs set up under Rule 10b5-1 allow individuals to trade a company's securities during a closed trading window, provided the plan was set up prior to the closing. As such, they provide the mechanism for executives to avoid charges of insider trading at a time when they possess material, nonpublic information. The operative word in Rule 10b5-1 plans is "mechanism," since they require several conditions to be satisfied. Furthermore, these conditions–once set–are subject to modification only when the insider is not in possession of material, nonpublic information. In this regard, Rule 10b5-1 plans impose somewhat rigid constraints of their own.

I. "Six Months and a Day" Repricings

For companies following APB 25 accounting for their stock plans, FIN 44 imposes adverse, variable accounting on underwater options that are "repriced" if the option is cancelled and reissued (or vice versa) within a six month period. To get around this accounting treatment, companies began canceling underwater options with a promise to grant new ones, at the then-current fair market value, more than six months later. This so-called "six and one" practice became a common end-run around the accounting rules after FIN 44 came into existence, even though it had no incentive design merit. We anticipate that companies subject to the new accounting rules quickly will abandon the practice of six-months-and-a-day repricing of underwater options, since many repricings will have a relatively benign impact on the accounting statements (no additional compensation expense required for substitutions that result in no additional incremental economic value).

J. Award Modifications under APB 25

The designation of an award as "fixed" or "variable" under APB 25 is not necessarily set in stone. Under FIN 44, events subsequent to an award's grant can alter the auditor's perception that the grant's initial terms–specifically the number of shares awarded or the value of those shares–were determinable at the time of grant. The hazard that a formerly fixed grant can be re-categorized as variable encourages companies to hardwire as many aspects of their granting provisions as possible.

The strategy of "truncating" an option's term may avoid variable accounting treatment under APB 25 if a company wishes to minimize any stock overhang that is attributable to underwater options. Specifically, the option contract states that the term of the option–typically 10 years–reduces to a very short term in the event that a pre-established performance standard is not achieved. The alternative–simply canceling underwater options–may taint the accounting treatment of any other options granted within a six-month period. This roadblock will be lifted under the FASB's new protocol, and it remains to be seen if the benefit of reducing stock overhang is strong enough to perpetuate the truncating option design feature in the absence of any real accounting benefit.

Likewise, the treatment of options or other stock-based awards in the event of retirement, death, disability, or change in control is likely to be articulated in the original award certificate. This foresight is attributable primarily to accounting conventions; under APB 25, changes to the original provisions required the company either to account for the award on a variable rather than a fixed basis, or to recognize a new measurement date.

K. Stock Option Exercises

There are several different ways to exercise option contracts. If one has a sufficient amount of cash on hand, one can exercise the options and pay the exercise price in cash. Alternatively, one can borrow the cash from a broker. If the employee lacks the cash and cannot obtain a loan, however, there are other choices.

A stock-for-stock exercise requires that the participant tender "mature" shares (stock that has been held for at least six months), receiving newly minted shares in return. Six months appears to be a critical and defining period of time. It is likely that the six-month tenure originated with Sec. 16(b) insider trading rules, which prohibited 16(b) officers from selling stock within six months of a purchase. In this regard, six months–like the 15% discount on securities obtained through qualified employee stock purchase plans, which influenced both tax legislation and APB 25 accounting rules–serves as a basis that, originating in one context, has continued its life in another.

L. APB 16, IRC Sec. 280G, and Stock Incentives

With the issuance of APB 16 in 1970, companies gained two generally accepted ways of accounting for business combinations: as a "pooling of interest," or as a "purchase." Until it was disallowed in 2002, "pooling of interest" was clearly the favorite, and companies structured their deals to comply with its requirements.

You may wonder why we're mentioning an accounting rule that no longer is allowed. It's because the rule had both a profound effect on shaping plan designs during the 30-plus years it was in effect, and because those design features continue to be prevalent today. Many plans explicitly prevent the cash-out of stock options upon a change in control, under a so-called limited stock appreciation right (LSAR) feature. This was because such a cash-out would make a merger ineligible for pooling accounting treatment.

But now that pooling treatment is not longer available, it may be time to rethink LSARs, especially in light of new IRS guidance about how stock options will be valued under IRC Sec. 280G. Specifically, the parachute value of cashed-out equity is based on the value of the cash itself, whereas the parachute value of options must be determined on the basis of the Black Scholes model or its equivalent. In all but a few instances, the Black Scholes model attributes a higher cost than the actual cash spread.

The higher attributed cost systematically raises the possibility that executives will exceed statutory limits and be subject to excise taxes, thereby requiring either a gross-up or a cutback in the value of goods received. Thus, the very thing that companies seemed so anxious to avoid when pooling of interests accounting was allowed–namely, a cash-out of equity–may become a desirable and prevalent design characteristic.

Regulatory Catalysts

Regulations of corporate business practices tend to arise from calls for reform from influential constituents. Shareholders became an increasingly vocal, organized voting block during the 1990s, and the messages they conveyed were consistent: pay for performance, make executives more accountable for corporate performance, and curb corporate waste.

The outcome of this discontent was IRC Sec. 162(m), increased proxy disclosure rules, and an examination of accounting rules that led to the enactment of FAS 123. But solutions reached in the middle of a crisis are usually counterproductive in the long run, and recent clamor for change grew from the seeds sown during earlier attempts at reform. Specifically, we see five areas of shareholder dissatisfaction:

• Traditional options allow executives to receive outsized returns, even if the stock's performance is lackluster.

• Dilution from stock plans should not exceed a set level, irrespective of individual company circumstances.

• Cancellation and reissuing of stock options lets option holders off the hook while shareholders have to live with significant losses.

• Absent significant performance-based conditions, restricted stock and discounted options are giveaways, allowing executives to make money even if the stock price declines.

• Mega-grants of options are manifestations of runaway pay.

In the short term, we are unlikely to see any significant decrease in the use of at-the-money, time-vesting options–at least among the senior executive group. Such grants require expenditure of more shares than would be necessary to make restricted stock or discounted option awards of an equivalent economic value. However, deductibility limits under IRC Sec. 162(m) continue to influence companies' use of time-vesting restricted shares and discount options, even if such devices are more efficient in terms of share utilization than at-the-money options..

Despite shareholders' perceptions, restricted shares, discounted options, and mega-grants are not intrinsically bad. But they need to be structured with a sense of the compensation package as a whole and how each piece reinforces the principles of pay for performance, accountability, and the responsible stewardship of corporate assets. In this regard, it would be unwise to mandate any legislation regarding these pay vehicles, but rather to consider the circumstances that best suit their use.

Ultimately, shareholders are primarily interested in having a voice in corporate affairs. The Internal Revenue Service, the SEC, and the various public exchanges all have supported this objective. In order to satisfy the performance-based exemption under IRC Sec. 162(m), for example, incentive compensation must be awarded from plans that have been approved by shareholders. This condition is also necessary for ISOs. The New York Stock Exchange and Nasdaq now require most grants to come from plans that shareholders have approved, eliminating former exemptions for broad-based plans and those using treasury stock. Furthermore, new proxy rules give investors comprehensive information about plans that have not heretofore been put to a shareholder vote.

Via their approval rights for stock compensation plans, shareholders' preferences are reflected in plan design. Voting guidelines of influential and vocal shareholders and shareholder advisory services, such as Institutional Shareholder Services, have an impact on plan design similar to legally-mandated regulations.

The influence of regulation on compensation strategy is immeasurable. It is difficult to imagine any viable compensation program being created in a regulatory vacuum, unencumbered by any consideration of the regulatory environment in which the system would operate, and based entirely on considerations that would motivate employees to produce exactly the results that shareholders desire. Technical rules governing most aspects of compensation would sooner or later need to be addressed.

Ultimately, companies need to make tradeoffs among different design alternatives and live with the outcome of their decisions. Before one can evaluate those alternatives, however, it is crucial that one understands their origin. In many instances, design features derive from accounting, tax, and securities laws, and a firm grasp on the intricacies of these regulations is a crucial competency for the plan designer.

Perhaps the most disquieting aspect of regulation is that it is constantly in flux; what applies in one era is overturned in the next. Witness the new strategy of cashing out or imposing "double triggers" on equity awards in the event of a change in control. The strategy makes more sense now, with the recent clarification of the parachute rules; it made no sense at all while pooling of interest accounting was allowed. And the transition from APB 25 to FAS 123 and its successor is certain to leave many companies with plan designs that no longer suit their original purpose—may, in fact, be the worst things possible in an altered regulatory universe. Thus evolving regulation forces us to reconsider our choices, and there is but one thing of which we can be completely confident, namely: Things Will Change.

Things will change, and plans hopefully will better reflect some virtues that appear immutable: Pay for performance. Hold executives accountable for their actions. Use corporate assets wisely. If regulation and technical considerations cannot ensure that the first two virtues will be met, a prudent regard for evolutions in tax, securities law, and accounting rules may nonetheless at the very least prevent the squandering of corporate assets. And this is progress.

But we clearly can and must do better than simply tailor our plan design to the latest regulatory fashions. Hewing rigidly to the terms of a regulation merely in order to avoid taxes or other penalties is to disregard the forest for the trees. The forest in every case should be strategies for bona fide excellence and the behavior that supports it, not just accounting or tax gymnastics. Recognizing an accounting expense, say, to reward good management will pale beside the operating gains that might come of it.

We hope that in advance of major regulatory reform, companies examine what it is that they want to accomplish by compensating their executives and design their plans accordingly. Who knows? If enough such sensible, company-sponsored reform is undertaken, it might be the best road to reforming a Byzantine regulatory structure, both at home and abroad.

Paula H. Todd
Towers Perrin

Paula Todd is a Principal of Towers Perrin specializing in executive, outside director and stock-based compensation. She serves as a firm-wide technical resource, consulting on executive compensation issues related to corporate governance, mergers and acquisitions, employment contracts and retention or severance arrangements. She also oversees Towers Perrin's Executive Compensation Resources (ECR) business, which is the data collection, analysis, research and information services unit of the firm's Executive Compensation consulting practice.

Ms. Todd is based in Stamford, Connecticut. She has been with Towers Perrin for over 20 years, first working in the firm's Washington, D.C. office. Prior to joining Towers Perrin, she was the Manager of Tax Analysis for the National Corporation for Housing Partnerships and served as the Administrator of the Bureau of Naval Personnel Non-Appropriated Fund Activities Retirement Plan.

Ms. Todd has a B.A. in Economics from the University of Maryland and an M.B.A. degree from Stanford University. She is a Certified Public Accountant and a member of the American Institute of CPAs and WorldatWork. She served on the FASB Advisory Task Force for the Stock Compensation Project and serves as a member of the Advisory Board for the National Association of Stock Plan Professionals.

Edward Jarvis
Towers Perrin

Ted Jarvis is a San Francisco-based Consultant affiliated with Towers Perrin's Executive Compensation Research and Development Unit. Mr. Jarvis oversees the development of templates, processes, and methodologies for a broad range of executive compensation-related financial and quantitative applications at Towers Perrin. In this capacity, he serves as a liaison between field practitioners, database developers, and Towers Perrin's Executive Compensation Resources (ECR) division. He serves as an internal resource on accounting, tax and securities law, and contributes to many of the Executive Compensation practice's intellectual capital development initiatives.

With Paula Todd, he collaborated on chapters for Executive Compensation Advisory Service's *Guide to Management Stock Incentive Plans* (2000) and *Guide to Board Compensation* (2002), as well as articles for the *Journal of Compensation and Benefits* and *WorkSpan.* He also wrote several articles for Towers Perrin's annual anthology on executive compensation-related issues *The Year in Executive Compensation,* (2002 and 2003 editions).

Mr. Jarvis joined Towers Perrin in 1994 after two years at McKinsey & Company. A Fulbright scholar at the University of Vienna, he graduated *cum laude* from New York University and obtained an M.B.A. from the University of Chicago.

14. DIRECTOR COMPENSATION

The prevailing views concerning board compensation have been changing since the mid-1990s and continue to change today. This has led to a corresponding change in how these programs have been structured. This chapter identifies and discusses these change areas, including a decline in the use of many benefit and perquisite programs, and a surge in the amount and use of stock and stock options in board compensation packages.

The authors begin by providing a road map for analyzing and designing director compensation plans. Inside (employee) directors typically do not receive additional compensation for their board duties, and so the programs covered here generally apply only to the company's outside (non-employee) directors. The role of a director differs from that of an executive and, therefore, while the compensation elements might be similar, the mix and structure of a director compensation program will most likely differ noticeably from the company's executive compensation program.

After setting the internal and external context for the board and reviewing a board's key duties and responsibilities, the most common elements of the board compensation package are identified and discussed.

The authors then focus their discussion on several interesting special topics related to director compensation including how to compensate a director who conducts a special assignment for the company, how to compensate a non-CEO board chair and/or lead director, and how to handle board compensation at a pre-IPO company. Lastly, the authors make a series of forecasts for where director compensation is likely to head in the years ahead, and provide a number of useful practice aids for the reader's use. –Editors

Overview

IN THIS CHAPTER, we discuss compensation design for the "outside" (non-employee) members of the Board of Directors. What is competitive practice for Board pay? What types of compensation programs will effectively attract and retain the right talent for your organization's board? What types of compensation will support the Board's role in corporate governance? What kinds of special situations arise in the area of Board pay? These are the questions we address in this chapter.

We are writing this chapter not long after the Enron debacle and in the midst of a healthy and active debate in the press and the business community about corporate governance and the role of the Board. These recent events have highlighted and reinforced to most Americans the importance of the Board and the need for a Board that objectively and carefully represents the interests of the shareholders. In the current environment, it is more important than ever to consider the corporate governance implications of Board compensation and we have paid special attention to this topic throughout this chapter.

The Role of the Board Is Different

As with executive compensation programs, it is critical to align the Board compensation program with the business objectives for the role. Since the role of the Board is different than the role of executives, certain compensation programs that make sense for executives/employees are not appropriate for Board members. Since the role of the Board is not always well understood and is often perceived to take place "behind closed doors," we thought it would be helpful to begin this chapter with a review of the role and the activities/time requirements of the Board.

Board Role

One good summary of the key roles of a Board is provided in a September 1997 Business Roundtable Statement on Corporate Governance which we have paraphrased below.

"The business of a corporation is managed under the direction of the board of directors, but the board delegates to management the authority for managing the everyday affairs of the corporation. The extent of this delegation varies depending on the size and circumstances of the corporation.

In addition to reviewing and approving specific corporate actions as required by law (e.g., declaration of dividends), the principal functions of the board are to:

- Select, regularly evaluate, and if necessary, replace the chief executive officer; determine management compensation; and review succession planning;
- Review and, where appropriate, approve the major strategies and financial and other objectives and plans of the corporation;
- Advise management on significant issues facing the corporation;
- Oversee processes for evaluating the adequacy of internal controls, risk

management, financial reporting and compliance, and satisfy itself as to the adequacy of such processes; and

• Nominate directors and ensure that the structure and practices of the board provide for sound corporate governance."

Board Activities/Time Requirements

Generally, Boards meet several times (usually 7 to 12 times) per year as a full Board; they also delegate certain responsibilities to Committees who are responsible for in-depth review of specific subjects. The Committees approve certain actions and recommend other actions to the full Board for approval. A subset of the Board members will sit on each of the Committees. Most Boards have Compensation and Audit Committees in order to comply with regulatory and stock exchange rules (see Regulatory section). Other possible committees are Nominating, Public Policy, and Governance Committees.

Given the role of the Board and the activities of the full Board and its Committees, a significant amount of time and effort is necessary to do the job properly. A Board member needs to review the reports in advance of Board meetings, consider key questions that need to be discussed during the meeting, and manage projects that are taking place in the Committees. And when the company is facing big challenges, the Board needs to be involved in making very difficult decisions that affect the shareholders. The increased scrutiny of the Boards, the increased levels of regulation, especially for the Audit and Compensation Committee roles, has increased the demands of the job.

Ideally the board members should bring a wide range of related business experience and should have the objectivity and independence to be able to make difficult decisions and the future of the corporation.

Given that the role is quite different than an executive role, the compensation package needs to be different as well. While the dynamics between the Board role and executive role vary, here are a few of the comparisons that need to be reflected in the compensation package.

In considering the differences, a few basic principles apply to the formulation of a compensation package for a Board member:

• **Pay is for experience.** While pay is lower than for full-time executives because of the reduced time requirements, the package nevertheless needs to be sufficient to attract talented people, most of whom have other interesting opportunities that they can pursue.

	Board	Executive Team
Accountable to	Shareholders	Board
Key Responsibilities	Oversight of the business including selection of the CEO	Developing and executing business plans
Time Period of the Job	Elected for a term; can be re-elected for subsequent terms	May have a contract with a specific term, but employment can change at any time at the choice of the executive or the corporation
Hours Required	Two to four days per month, could be more	Full time
Experience Required	Both braod and deep expertise spanning many different types of companies and situations	Particularly below CEO level, deep experience may be sufficient
Liability	Greater	Yes

- **Golden handcuffs are less important.** Board members are expected to stay for their term and generally only leave for personal reasons–not because they are recruited to work on other boards. Therefore, there is less need to hinge compensation to continued employment as is common in executive compensation plans. While vesting is sometimes used for stock plans, the need for handcuffs is not as relevant as for executives.

- **Pay is for quality of advice rather than for operating results.** The Board's role is to make sure the right strategy and right executive team is in place to achieve operating results–not to achieve them themselves. While there are some proponents of performance-based Board pay (such as incentives or stock tied to operating results), many are concerned about the conflict-of-interests in tying compensation to operating goals that the Board must approve. We believe in this post-Enron era, those concerns will increase.

- **Rewards should not run the risk of creating a real or perceived conflict of interest.** Independence of the Board is critical. Over the years, the general trend has been to move away from programs that could cause the Board members to be reluctant to challenge the CEO. Those programs include pensions, perquisites, and charitable trust arrangements.

Elements of the Board Pay Package

We have already discussed the fact that a different type of pay program is needed to reflect the different role of the Directors. In this section, we will discuss the commonly used elements of Board compensation. Design considerations involved in putting all of these elements together is covered in the Design section later in the chapter.

Six elements of pay are most common (see also table on page 414).

1. Annual Retainer

The retainer is similar in concept to a base salary–it is a level denominated that is considered necessary to attract and retain the right caliber of Board member. Retainers are usually denominated in annual terms (e.g., $25,000 per annum) but may be paid on a monthly, quarterly or other schedule.

Retainers historically were paid entirely in cash. Over the past decade, an increasing number of companies have moved towards paying a portion or the entire retainer in stock, as a means of increasing the stock-based emphasis of the package.

Various forms of stock are used for stock-based retainers:

• Companies may use restricted stock which vests over a time period, such as over a three-to-five year period.

• Companies may issue outright shares of stock.

• Alternatively, many companies use deferred stock units. Deferred stock units are immediately vested, but in order to facilitate tax deferrals, the Directors may elect to defer receipt of the shares until a future date, such as their retirement or the end of their term.

2. Meeting Fees

Deciding whether to use meeting fees is a fundamental design consideration. The majority of companies continue to pay a per-meeting fee for each full Board and Committee meeting that a director attends. The fees are a means of paying the director for their specific time requirements and a way to tacitly encourage attendance. When meeting fees are paid, they are almost always paid in cash, although the company may offer an elective deferred compensation plan. Some companies vary the size of the meeting fee based on the timing and type of meeting. For example, they may pay a full meeting fee for an in-person meeting, 50% of that amount for a telephonic meeting, and some companies do not pay a separate Committee meeting fee if the Committee meets on the same day as the full Board.

3. Committee Retainers

Another majority practice, but not used by every company, is to pay a separate retainer to those Directors who chair a Committee. Doing so is another way to recognize those directors who take on additional responsibility and companies who do, generally pay the same Chair retainer for all Committees although some vary the retainer based on the nature of the Committee. When the retainer varies, higher retainers are usually paid to the Chairs of the Audit and Compensation Committees. Most retainers are paid in cash although some companies use stock or stock options instead.

4. Stock Awards

Many different types of stock-awards are used and increasingly companies are using more than one form of stock as part of the Board pay package. The most common forms of stock grants are as follows:

• Stock options as a separate element of the Board package. Stock options are most commonly granted annually and denominated as a first number of options rather than a present value. Over the past decade, particularly since the NACD report in 1995, the number of companies granting options and the size of the option grants has increased.

• The frequency of stock option grants varies, with the majority of companies making annual grants. Other choices are to make grants at the election and reelection of the director. That would translate to one grant every three years, as that is the common term length. A small number of companies make one-time awards at the initial election, generally larger awards intending to cover a period of ten years or more.

• Stock retainers are the second most common stock-based element. Using a stock retainer allows for the stock element to be integrated into the retainer rather than using another vehicle. In the Design section, which follows later in the chapter, we discuss the pros and cons of using stock options versus stock-based retainers.

• Elective stock is another very common form of stock award, which we will cover under Deferred Compensation.

• Since the relaxation of Section 16(b) rules (described in the Regulatory Section), some companies have moved to performance-based awards, with grants tied to achievement of operating goals such as Earnings Per Share Growth. It is our belief that the use of operating goals raises conflict-of-interest questions, however, since the role of the Board is to objectively monitor company performance rather than participating in operating performance results. Also, operating results may not correlate to good stock performance and the ultimate goal of the Board is to create value for shareholders.

5. Deferred Compensation

The majority of companies allow the Director to defer all or part of earnings. In our experience, deferred compensation is particularly attractive to Directors since this compensation is generally not their primary source of income and they are typically very interested in tax-advantaged savings. With the growing emphasis on stock-based compensation, an increasing number of companies allow Directors to defer retainers and meeting fees into deferred stock units. In addition, many companies offer deferral into other types of investments or rates of return, often mirroring the choices provided under their executive deferred compensation programs.

Deferred compensation programs are generally administered similarly to the plans offered to executives. See chapter on Deferred Compensation for more details on deferral elections, investment choices and funding.

6. Reimbursement of Travel Expenses

Since travel is usually required for attendance at Board meetings, the majority of companies reimburse Directors for their travel expenses. From a corporate governance standpoint, it is advisable to establish a clear policy for allowable expenses, such as using the company's executive/employee expense reimbursement policies for Directors. A minority of companies pay for spouse travel expenses as well. We believe this would be considered a perquisite and would be cause to raise corporate governance concerns associated with other Director benefit and perquisite plans.

Other Forms of Compensation Sometimes Used In Board Packages

Other compensation programs do exist but are less prevalent. These would include:

7. Retirement Plans

In the 1970s and 1980s, Director retirement plans grew in popularity. They created a method for recognizing long-service Directors and providing income security when their Board service was over. In the 1990s, there were several studies that explored how to best link Director compensation to shareholder value creation. One of the best known studies was the NACD Blue Ribbon Commission Report on Board Compensation, referenced in the next section. These studies harshly criticized Director retirement plans because they were not linked to shareholder value creation and created a potential conflict-of-interest in that participation in benefit programs could cause Directors to be biased in favor of the executive team who had created these benefit plans. During the 1990s, most corporations terminated their pension plans. Today, most studies show no more than 10% to 20% of companies still have Director retirement plans.

8. Insurance Plans

Another practice from the 1970s and 1980s was to have insurance coverage for Directors for things such as life insurance, medical insurance, etc. These benefit coverages fell under the same criticism as retirement plans and for the same reason—they are benefits that are unrelated to shareholder value creation and also can create too much allegiance to the incumbent executive team.

9. Perquisites

Like retirement plans, the use of Director perquisites has declined and for the same reasons as the decline in Director retirement plans. Among the perquisites still in place at some companies are spouse travel reimbursement, corporate legacy plans providing for charitable contributions in the Director's name at his/her death, matching gift programs, and financial counseling.

10. Liability Insurance

The majority of companies indemnify Directors from financial losses arising from a legal suit. Given the status of the Enron, and other similar situations, it will be interesting to see if Directors become more aware of the risks of litigation and demand higher levels of indemnification protection or, conversely, if there is pressure from shareholders to remove protections from litigation in order to ensure that Directors are not shielded from litigation and their related accountability.

Trends/Best Practices In Board Pay

In 1995, in the wake of increased focus on corporate governance in the early 1990s, the National Association for Corporate Directors (NACD) formed a Blue Ribbon Commission which issued a report on Director Compensation. This report described five "Principles" and six "Best Practices" for setting Director compensation.

Principles

1. Director compensation should be determined by the board and disclosed completely to shareholders.
2. Director compensation should be aligned with the long-term interests of shareholders.
3. Compensation should be used to motivate director behavior.
4. Directors should be adequately compensated for their time and effort.
5. Director compensation should be approached on an overall basis, rather than as an array of separate elements.

Best Practices

Boards should:

Market Prevalence Table

Program	Covered in the Following Item Number in Preceding Section	% of Companies Offering
Annual Retainer	1	95.4%
Mandatory Stock-Based Retainer Element	1	23.3%
Meeting Fees	2	81.2%
Additional Compensation for Committee Service (either retainer or meeting fees)	2/3	89.4%
Additional Compensation for Committee Chair Versus Other Committee members	3	65%
Long-Term Incentive	4	88.8%
Elective Deferred Compensation	5	81.2%
Reimbursement of Travel Expenses	6	91.3%
Retirement Programs	7	13.2%
Life, Medical, Dental, AD&D Insurance	8	3% to 13%
Group Travel Insurance	8	23.4%
Corporate Legacy Plans	9	24%
Reimbursement of Spouse Travel Expenses	9	19.5%
Indemnification of Directors	10	78.9%

Source: 2003/2004 Watson Wyatt Data Services (WWDS) Report on Board of Directors Compensation, Policies and Practices

1. Establish a process by which directors can determine the compensation program in a deliberative and objective way.

2. Set a substantial target for stock ownership by each director and a time period during which this target is to be met.

3. Define the desirable total value of all forms of director compensation.

4. Pay directors solely in the form of equity and cash—with equity representing a substantial portion of the total up to 100 percent; dismantle existing benefit programs and avoid creating new ones.

5. Adopt a policy stating that a company should not hire a director or a director's firm to provide professional or financial services to the corporation.

6. Disclose fully in the proxy statement the philosophy and process used in determining director compensation and the value of all elements of compensation.

These guidelines brought about significant changes in Board compensation during the remainder of the 1990s. The particular areas of change:

• Greater emphasis on total compensation, rather than the pieces

• More use of stock as part of the total package

• Elimination of most benefit programs, particularly director retirement plans

• Better disclosure

• Increased articulation of the philosophy for board pay

In addition, there has been an increase in total pay, partly we believe as a result of heightened recognition of the importance and value of the Board role and increased time requirements to do the job properly.

It is open to debate whether any real improvement has been made on Director stock ownership (Best Practices #2) and Board independence with respect to not using the firms of Board members for professional services (Best Practices #5).

Tracking the Trends Through Data

To illustrate some trends since the NACD report, we have looked at the WWDS Board Report for the years 1996 versus 2003. Here are some of the differences:

	1996	2003/2004
Average retainer (all companies with $1-2B revenues)	$20,000	$26,364
% of companies reporting at least one LTI plan	86%	88.8%
Median value of annual stock option grant	$50,715	$99,125
Median value of an annual restricted stock grant	$12,000	$29,300
% of companies with Director retirement plans	61%	13%
% of companies with corporate legacy plans	30%	24%
% of companies with Director medical insurance	24%	3%

Designing a Board Compensation Package

In designing a compensation package for the Board, as with the executives, it is best to start by articulating the philosophy and then designing a package that fits that philosophy.

Board Pay Philosophy

The Board pay philosophy should address the following:

• Competitive positioning

• Against what market is board pay being compared

• How competitive should the total package be against this market and what is the rationale (at median, above/below median)?

• Compensation mix

- What portion should be delivered in cash and stock and why?
- What forms of compensation should be used and why (cash retainer, stock retainer, meeting fees, committee retainers, stock options, other stock, benefits, perquisites)?
- Recognition of time spent
- Should meeting fees and Committee Chair retainers be used to ensure that Directors who spend greater amounts of time on the Board receive higher levels of compensation?
- Compensation timing/cycles
- Should compensation be delivered entirely on an annual/monthly basis or should some portions of compensation (such as the stock grants) be tied to term elections or other events?

Selected Plan Design Issues

In designing the total package, while the philosophy will serve as the guide, there are generally a few specific elements that are often subject to classic debates.

Meeting Fees

While the majority of companies continue to have a cash payment per meeting for Board and Committee meetings, the number of companies without meeting fees has increased to approximately 25% to 30% of large companies. The pros and cons commonly cited for using (or not using) meeting fees are outlined in the table below.

Forms of Stock

The two most common choices for stock-based compensation are stock-based retainers and stock option grants. Each has pros and cons and the common reasons for selecting one or the other are outlined in the table below.

Although it is too soon to say with certainty, we are expecting some shifting away from stock options and towards stock grants in 2004 and later

Using Meeting Fees	Not Using Meeting Fees (using a retainer only, potentially a higher retainer to offset the lack of meeting fees)
• Recognizes variations in time requirements (for example, when comparing a Director serving on two Committees to a Director not serving on any Committees)	• Does not differentiate for meeting time differences which appeals to Boards who believe all Directors contribute equally whether through formal meeting time or other contributions
• Reinforces the value of attendance as part of the duties of the Director	• May be preferred where there are other, stronger mechanisms within the Board for addressing attendance problems

Stock Retainer	Stock Option Grants
• Integrates the stock element with the main piece of board pay—the retainer	• Better matches the way executives are paid in many companies and sectors
• Uses real stock which can be perceived as closer to real ownership than options	• Had superior accounting historically (although as of this writing, FASB is proposing stock option expensing beginning in 2005)
• Conserves shares, which can be attractive if the company has limited share availability or high overhang	• May be preferred where the corporation wants a balance of cash and stock—so the retainer is cash and the options are a separate element
	• May be perceived to be more simple or offer more tax flexibility

(either restricted or outright grants) given the current compensation environment and as companies reduce their emphasis on executive stock options and try to better manage dilution.

Common Plan Design Models

Depending on the Board pay philosophy, any number of Board pay models may be used. Below, we have mapped out some common models and outlined the typical underlying philosophies behind each approach.

Pay Model	Typical Underlying Philosophy
All Stock Model Competitive retainer delivered entirely in the form of stock (restricted stock or deferred stock units) with no meeting fees, no Committee retainers or fees. No benefits.	• Real stock ownership is the overriding priority • The Board does not want to pay for attendance or time, usually based on the assumption that each Board member overall puts in the same amount of effort irrespective of the Committees he/she serves on.
High Stock Model Competitive retainer delivered 50% in cash and 50% in stock. Also annual stock option grants. Meeting fees for board and committee meetings. No benefits.	• Focus on stock via combination of stock retainer and stock options • Meeting fees to reinforce time spent and attendance
Typical Pay Model (as of year 2002) Combination of cash retainer, meeting fees for Board and committee meetings, Committee Chair retainer, stock option grants either annually or at election/reelection, voluntary deferred compensation program for retainer into deferred stock units. No benefits or very limited benefits.	• Focus is on matching the competitive market (this has been the most common pay mix). • Balances cash and stock, and allows Board members to increase stock component at their choice (via voluntary deferred compensation program) • Lower stock emphasis may also reflect already high levels of existing ownership • Recognizes extra time requirements via Committee Chair retainer and meeting fees • Meeting fees also reinforce attendance
"Legacy" Pay Model Cash retainer, meeting fees for Board and Committee meetings, annual stock option grants, and more than one of the following: retirement plan, charitable award plan, life insurance, medical insurance.	• Representative of a company that is slow/resistance to change and/or where there is a strong paternalistic philosophy that is oriented towards providing security

Conducting a Competitive Analysis of Board Pay

Since one of the important factors in developing a board pay package is to be competitive, it is important to be aware of the various ways to compare a board package to the market.

Defining the Peer Groups for Comparison

As with executive pay, board pay levels tend to correlate with the size and the industry sector of the corporation. Depending on the data sources being used, the peer group should represent an appropriately large sample size that reflects some combination of revenue size and industry sector. Sometimes, the Board believes the labor market for Board talent is broader, such that they could recruit from different size and different sector companies. In this case, it may be useful to do a secondary analysis looking a other samples. However, ultimately, for governance reasons, it is important to arrive at a peer group that can be supported on an objective and analytical basis.

Choosing a Data Source

There are two approaches to comparing Board pay to the market. One choice is to use published surveys. Published surveys generally organize the data by size and industry sector. Published surveys have several advantages. They provide a relatively quick way to collect market information. Most surveys also collect useful trend information about the prevalence of various programs so that you can see the direction the market is moving. There are also some disadvantages to published surveys. Despite the NACD best practice guidelines, most surveys still collect pay information separately for each piece–for retainer, for meeting fees, for stock. It is then necessary to add up the medians/averages for each piece and hope that the sum of the medians reflects median company practice. Another disadvantage of surveys is that you cannot tell exactly which companies are in the sample and cannot array the data by company.

The other alternative is to analyze proxy data to conduct a market analysis. Here, again, there are advantages and disadvantages. The primary advantage is that a proxy analysis allows for a customized selection of companies in the comparison and data can be reported on a company-by-company basis. Also, it is easier to determine the value of the total package by company because each element can be added together on a company-specific basis. Some of the disadvantages of using proxy data are that it is more time-consuming, and there is a higher chance of making an error in trying to interpret the disclosure. Also, unlike published surveys, it may be difficult to identify market trends when using proxy samples.

Dealing with the Unique (Sometimes Quirky) Issues of Board Pay

There are a few issues that are unique to Board pay market analyses.[1]

- The need to develop a "prototype" Director for comparisons. To calculate the total pay package, the package will usually vary for each Director depending on whether he/she is a Committee Chair, and based on how many Committees he/she attends (which impacts meeting fees). Therefore, the common approach is to develop a set of assumptions for comparison across companies–that the Director sits on the Audit Committee and is a non-Chair, for example. If this is not done, market comparisons will be flawed because total pay is different depending on the Committee representation of each Director.

- Addressing unusual numbers of meetings. Sometimes, in a year of major activity such as a major acquisition or the replacement of a CEO, the Board of a corporation will meet an unusually large number of times. If a total pay analysis is conducted using the actual number of meetings and meeting fees, it can appear that the Board package is way above market norms. However, the Board may have simply been paid a competitive level of per-meeting fee and it was necessary for them to spend more time than the usual Board in that given year. In years when this situation occurs, it would be necessary to normalize the data for the meeting fees.

- Factoring in the timing of stock grants. As with executive compensation, not every package involves an annual grant. While annual grants are the most common, some Boards grant "one-time" grants intended to cover a ten year period. Other companies grant at election/reelection. In these cases, a standard methodology needs to be developed to spread the stock value over the relevant time period.

Special Topics In Board Pay

In our experience, the most important decisions, with respect to corporate governance, come when a corporation needs to address special situations that arise. In the balance of this chapter, we address some of the most common special situations.

Special Fees & Consulting Arrangements

Sometimes, one or more Directors are asked to take on a special activity that is beyond their role as a Board member. They may be asked to take on a special activity to address a short-term gap in the existing management structure or they may be asked to bring some particular expertise to help the corporation with a special project. In these cases, the Board member is, all of a sudden, being asked to spend a lot of additional time with the company. Should the Director be compensated for this extra time? Will the extra time demands negatively impact the Director's other sources of income? (For example, if the Director is self-employed)

While the extra time requirements can create a logical argument for special fees, there are also opposing arguments for not paying special fees and it is important to answer the following questions:

- At what point are these activities truly beyond the Director's job as a Director?
- Is there a reduction in independence caused by using a Director for advisory services? Would the Board be more independent if other resources were used...even if those resources might be more expensive?

This topic clearly warrants Board discussion. Despite the concerns about special fees, there are some situations where a Director is in the best position to provide help (based on his/her knowledge of the company and outside expertise) and the time demands are clearly beyond board service. In those situations, there is a basis for providing the Director with special fees.

The Executive Compensation Advisory Services Guide to Board Compensation is one of the few surveys which covers the subject of special fees in depth. In their 2002 report, they found:

- 11% of companies paid consulting fees to outside directors or their firms in 2000, with a median amount paid of $144,000.
- 17 of the 250 survey companies (roughly 7%) paid a fee for special services or assignments that directors were asked to undertake with a median amount of $1,000 per day.
- In addition, other companies paid special fees for other special situations.

With respect to consulting arrangements with the Director and/or his/her firm, it is important to keep in mind that these special compensation arrangements may cause that Director to fail to meet the definition of "outside" or "independent" director under the various regulations relating to Audit and Compensation Committee membership (see Regulatory section).

Non-CEO Chair of the Board & Lead Directors

In the United States, the CEO is also the Chairman of the Board at a majority of companies. However about 25% of companies have a separate (non-CEO) Chairman at any given time. For some companies, a separate Chair is part of the corporate governance policy. For example, Campbell's Soup has a long-standing history of a maintaining the Chair position as separate.

At other companies, a separate Chair is the response to a transitional situation:

- There is a new CEO in place and the separate Chair is in place until that new CEO has matured into the role.

- There is a difficult issue facing the company and a separate Chair is considered important to help the company manage through current challenges.

- The company is in the process of replacing the CEO and needs stable leadership until a CEO succession can be achieved.

- The ex-CEO has just retired and is offered the separate Chair position either for transition reasons or as a reward for past service.

When the CEO is the Chair, there is no explicit compensation for the Chair role—it is simply part of the CEO pay package.

However, if a company is going to move to a separate Chair position, it obviously becomes necessary to figure out how much that separate Chair should be paid. Most studies of this subject "group" separate Chairs into two categories:

- An "inside" Chair who is reported as an employee in the proxy statement of the company. Often, these Chairs had a previous relationship with the company—either as the former CEO or founder.

- An "outside" Chair who is reported as a Director in the proxy statement of the company. Often, these Chairs are outside board members who have assumed additional responsibilities, or represent significant investors of the company, or are brought in strictly to serve as Chairman with no previous employment relationship with the company.

While there is a tremendous amount of variation, there are a few patterns that can be observed from proxy analyses:

- Inside chairs are paid more than outside chairs.

- Insider chairs, on average, earn about 30% to 50% of the CEO's pay package.

- Outside chairs, on average, earn some multiple of a regular Board Director's package—ranging from 2X to 10X the regular package.

  1. For outside Chairs, their extra role is typically recognized via a higher cash retainer. This would follow a philosophy of using a cash retainer to compensate for a Director's time and value provided to the Board. A cash retainer might also be viewed as a more direct offset to reduced cash pay that the Director might be receiving at his/her full-time job or business.

  2. Sometimes, the additional compensation is delivered via stock—either through a larger stock-based retainer or through a special stock option

grant. This can be particularly effective in a turnaround situation because it increases the Chair's linkage between pay and shareholder performance.

There are situations where there is an inside Chair who is paid very similarly to the CEO in both the form of pay and the amount of pay. Sometimes, this is due to a very active role in the company. Other times it may be due to a temporary transition period during which the Chair is turning responsibilities over to the CEO. However, there are situations where these large packages appear to be for retiring long-service CEOs and we hypothesize that this separate Chair package is being used as a retirement gift. Suffice it to say that in this age of increased corporate governance scrutiny, we would expect that this practice will diminish.

A relatively new variation on the board role is a "lead independent director." A lead director might be responsible for organizing the Board agendas and/or coordinating Board performance evaluations in a company with a CEO Chairman. While this is a relatively new role, early patterns show that most lead directors earn a premium over regular Board members but less of a premium than a separate Chair.

Pre-IPO Companies

Start-up, pre-IPO companies have very different dynamics which affect the nature of their Board compensation packages. It is useful to understand these dynamics not just for pure start-up situations but also in the event that your corporation is planning to spin-off a start-up business and form a Board for that operation.

For a pure start-up business, there are a few unique dynamics that affect the nature of the Board package:

• The companies are generally extremely cash constrained and therefore would rather to avoid cash payments whenever possible.

• The entire value of the enterprise is tied to stock results and the ability to bring the company public–therefore, all of the executive pay is very skewed towards stock-based compensation.

• The members of the Board often are representatives of the financiers of the business–for example, employees of a venture capital firm, or a corporate partner. For them, their role on the Board is to "mind the store" for their employer's investment.

Given all of these dynamics, the Board compensation package tends to be comprised of the following elements:

- Reimbursement of travel expenses.
- An up-front stock option grant made at the time of joining the board (usually denominated as a percent of outstanding).
- For venture capitalist and other investor Board members, the stock grants will either be forgone or they will turn their individual grants over to their employers.

Finding Competitive Board Pay Data For pre-IPOs

The best method for finding data on pre-IPO board packages is to read the prospectus published at the time of the IPO. Although the information is not necessarily perfect, it usually provides some description of the method in which board members were compensated during the pre-IPO period. A prospectus analyses will also provide information on the changes being made to the package as the company moves into the post-IPO period.

Underwater Options

Let us begin this section with our (admittedly blunt) editorial viewpoint–*we cannot think of any situation where a repricing (a cancel and exchange) of director stock options is appropriate.*

As discussed in another chapter, the repricing of stock options for any employee is a controversial action. Because in any repricing, the employee's incentive position is being restored at a time that the shareholders have lost money.

The argument for employee restoration is the need to retain the employee, the need for a motivational incentive and perhaps that these employees (when executives are excluded) did not directly contribute to the stock price decline.

Unlike the average employee, the Directors are directly responsible for representing shareholder interests and, in fact, need to be able to objectively decide whether to approve a repricing. Given their role, we believe it is a clear conflict-of-interest for them to approve a repricing for themselves. One can certainly argue that repricing the Director's options leaves them in a position where they may be indifferent to stock price declines.

Most surveys do not cover the topic of Director repricings and we hope that the reason is that the prevalence is very low. A 2001 Unifi Survey of Board of Directors Compensation reports that two companies repriced in 1998 and 1999 and no director options were repriced in 2000.

Regulatory Considerations

While there are many regulations that have impact on the role of the Board, the composition of various Committees, and the elements of the executive compensation packages, there are fewer regulatory considerations that directly affect Director compensation. In general, Director compensation is more heavily influenced by corporate governance policy and by investor sentiment.

However, there are a few regulations that affect Director pay.

SEC Rule 16(b)(3)

In the SEC Exchange Act of 1934, there were a number of rules under Section 16 designed to address the treatment of "insiders." Among the groups falling under the "insider" rules are members of the corporation's Board of Directors.

In Rule 16(b)(3), there was a provision requiring that directors who administered employee or director stock plans be "disinterested." In order to meet the requirements of the "disinterested" test, the directors either had to be non-participants in the stock plan or they had to adopt shareholder-approved formulaic plans that involved no discretion whatsoever on the part of the Directors. As a result, the majority of companies have formulaic Board stock plans where the number of shares/options and the timing of the grant is set by a formula. For example, a formula plan might provide that 2,000 options will be granted every year on March 1.

In 1996, as part of an overall liberalization of the rules under 16(b)(3), the "disinterested" requirement was dropped, which allowed for other types of stock granting practices. For example, a company can include the director stock grant provisions under the employee omnibus plan (assuming a specific total number of shares is allocated for directors), performance-based stock grants can be used, and the method for determining stock grant sizes can be varied.

Despite the changes in 1996, most companies have maintained a formulaic grant practice. According to the Executive Compensation Advisory Services 2002 Guide to Board Compensation, 28% of companies use non-formulaic approaches to granting stock. While this has increased significantly from 12% in 1999, the vast majority have maintained a formulaic approach.

Proxy Reporting Requirements

Under the SEC's 1992 proxy reporting rules, publicly traded companies have to report their board compensation package in the proxy. This disclosure includes reporting on the regular components of the Board pay package as well as any separate arrangements such as consulting arrangements, special fees, charitable contributions on behalf of a director, etc.

While this reporting requirement has not, in and of itself, changed the nature of Board pay, it does promote the needed discipline to make sure the package is competitive and contains elements that fit with the company's philosophy.

Committee Composition

While not under the topic of Board compensation, there are SEC, IRS and stock exchanges rules which guide the composition of the Committees, specifically the Audit and the Compensation Committees. These Committees need to have independent directors who are not only non-employees of the company but also meet certain other independence tests regarding the amount of compensation they or their employers receive from the company. For Compensation Committees, if the Committee does not meet the independence test, executive compensation cannot qualify as "performance-based" compensation under Section 162(m).

Current Regulatory Activity

In response to Enron's collapse and the associated corporate governance concerns, the SEC, NYSE and NASDAQ have recently approved new rules for Board membership as part of the exchange listing requirements. Among the changes:

- Require that members of the Compensation and Audit Committees meet a more stringent definition of "independent."
- Require that a majority of the Board members be from outside the company.
- Broaden the role of Audit Committee to include responsibility for hiring and firing the outside auditors.

Forecasts for the Moment

With compensation design in so much flux at the moment, it is difficult to precisely predict the changes that we will see in board pay over the next few years. Our sense, however, of what some of the current trends are is:

- Board pay levels are moving up by 10% to 15% in recognition of added scrutiny and added time requirements.
- Meeting fees are moving up for the first time in many years; meeting fees are a flexible way to recognize additional time demands that, for example, one Committee may require to do their jobs.
- There is a lot of discussion about raising compensation for the Audit Committee members due to additional regulatory responsibilities and

some companies have created some kind of premium for Audit Committee service; other companies are concerned about having a two-tier Committee pay systems when other committees could be faced with equally challenging issues.

- Stock ownership guidelines for Directors have gained new popularity; our most recent Watson Wyatt Data Services board survey reports over 51% of companies have formal director stock ownership guidelines in place; this is in keeping with the resurgence of stock ownership guidelines for executives in response to the recent scandals.

- From an attraction perspective, we continue to believe that Board members are more interested in making sure that the company has both appropriate controls and corporate governance practices, and that there is sufficient liability insurance–in other word, reducing exposure to litigation is more important than a small incremental increase in the Board pay package.

Conclusion

The compensation for Board directors continues to evolve and change as perspectives on the best way to enhance corporate governance are reviewed. As practitioners, we believe that by understanding the corporate governance implications, the competitive market and the key objectives for the Board role, you will have all the tools you need to develop an effective Board compensation program.

1. See Appendix and CD for sample competitive analyses templates.

Practice aids found on the CD and within the appendix for this chapter:

- Sample of Published Survey Sources (page 428)
- Selected Links to Regulatory Information Pertinent to Board Compensation (page 429)
- Sample Job Descriptions for the Board (5) (page 429)

  Exhibit A: Responsibilities of the Board of Directors. Source: A Large Pharmaceutical Firm (page 434)

  Exhibit B: Responsibilities of the Board of Directors. Source: A Machinery Manufacturer (page 436)

Exhibit C: Responsibilities of a Corporate Director. Source: A Manufacturing Company (page 437)

Exhibit D: Responsibilities of the Chairman of the Board (page 438)

Exhibit E: Responsibilities of the Chief Executive Officer (page 439)

• Sample Competitive Analysis Formats (page 441)

IRA T. KAY
Director
Watson Wyatt Worldwide

Mr. Kay is the Practice Director in charge of Watson Wyatt's Compensation Practice. His primary objective is to help Watson Wyatt's clients to use compensation programs to drive business, organizational and cultural change.

Mr. Kay has worked closely with U.S. public, international and private companies, helping them to develop annual and long-term incentive plans to increase shareholder value. He is also experienced in specialized situations such as mergers, initial public offerings, turnaround and bankruptcy situations. Mr. Kay conducts research on stock option overhang, executive pay and performance, and CEO stock ownership.

Mr. Kay has a B.S. in Industrial and Labor Relations from Cornell University and a Ph.D. in economics from Wayne State University. He has written and spoken broadly on executive compensation issues. He is a co-author (with Dr. Bruce Pfau) of the book *The Human Capital Edge,* from McGraw-Hill. He is also the author of *CEO Pay and Shareholder Value: Helping the U.S. Win the Global Economic War,* published by St. Lucie Press, and *Value at the Top: Solutions to the Executive Compensation Crisis,* published by HarperCollins, and numerous other research studies. He has been published in the *Harvard Business Review* and the *McKinsey Quarterly.* Mr. Kay has presented analysis of executive compensation issues before the Federal Reserve Board, the S.E.C., the F.A.S.B. and a U.S. Senate subcommittee.

DIANE LERNER
Senior Consultant
Watson Wyatt Worldwide

Diane Lerner is a Senior Consultant in Watson Wyatt Worldwide's New York office specializing in the Executive Compensation Practice area. In this capacity, she works with companies to help them develop effective short- and long-term incentive programs that align pay with performance and long-term shareholder value creation.

Assignments have included the design of stock based compensation plans for public and IPO companies, the design of phantom long-term incentive plans for private companies and subsidiaries, recommendations on Board compensation, and the development of executive and broad-based variable compensation programs.

Prior to joining Watson Wyatt Worldwide, Ms. Lerner served as a Senior Consultant in the Executive Compensation Practice for the Hay Group, and was Vice President, Human Resources, of Kidder Peabody, specializing in designing executive, incentive, and sales compensation plans.

Ms. Lerner has a B.S. in Industrial & Labor Relations from Cornell University and an MBA degree from New York University's Stern School of Business. She speaks widely on compensation-related subjects at industry forums such as the Global Equity Organization, National Association of Stock Plan Professionals, and Institutional Investor.

1. Sample of Published Survey Sources

There are numerous published surveys covering board pay practices. While the largest number of surveys are those covering larger public companies (the Fortune 1000, the S&P 1,500 type companies), there are specialty surveys for almost every sector. A sample of some (but definitely not all) of the survey sources published in the past year are listed in alphabetical order below:

- Buck Consultants Board of Directors Compensation
- Buck Consultants Board of Directors Compensation Planning Survey Summary Report
- Executive Compensation Advisory Services (ECAS) Guide to Board Compensation
- Frederic W. Cook & Co., Inc. Board of Directors Profile and Compensation at NASDAQ-100 Companies
- Grant Thornton LLP/The Segal Company Annual Study of Small-To-Midsize and Large Public Company Boards
- Investor Responsibility Research Center (IRRC) Board Practices/Board Pay: The Structure and Compensation of Boards of Directors at S&P Super 1,500 Companies
- Mercer Human Resource Consulting Emerging Trends in Board of Director Compensation: SnapShot Survey Results
- Mercer Human Resource Consulting Outside Directors' Compensation and Benefits Among 350 Major Industrial and Service Companies
- National Association of Corporate Directors (NACD) Director Compensation Survey
- Pearl Meyer & Partners Director Compensation
- Spencer Stuart Board Index (SSBI)

• Watson Wyatt Data Services Survey Report on Board of Directors Compensation, Policies and Practices

2. Selected Links to Regulatory Information Pertinent to Board Compensation

The following are links that readers may find useful for regulatory information (note: all links were current and functioning at the date of publication but are subject to change):

The University of Cincinnati link covers securities laws:

http://www.law.uc.edu/CCL/intro.html

Proxy disclosure rules:

http://www.law.uc.edu/CCL/regS-K/SK402.html

Rule 16b-3:

http://www.law.uc.edu/CCL/34ActRls/rule16b-3.html

SEC site covering recent stock exchange listing rules:

http://www.sec.gov/news/press/2003-150.htm

http://www.sec.gov/rules/sro/34-48745.htm

3. Sample Job Descriptions for the Board

Information on the Role of Board members excerpted from the *Survey Report on Board of Directors Compensation, Policies and Practices* from Watson Wyatt Data Services

Introduction

This section describes the legal framework, role, and responsibilities of the Board and individual directors. In addition, typical responsibilities are listed for the Chairman of the Board as well as other top management positions where incumbents are typically elected officers of the company. At the end of this section, exhibits from participants are included as examples of Board and director responsibilities. The actual sources used are not identified in order to protect company confidentiality.

Legal Framework

A corporation is defined as an association of investors who have joined together to conduct a business enterprise for profit. The stockholders, as the owners of the capital stock of the corporation, are the owners of its assets. Within the limits of the rights granted to them by the State where incorporated, the stockholders establish the rules that govern their own relations and regulate the conduct of the directors to whom they entrust management of the corporation. The stockholders elect the members of the Board of Directors who manage, control and direct the affairs of the corporate enterprise. The Board, in turn, delegates actual operations of the corporation to the top management of the company. Some of the directors also may be officers of the corporation.

The rules established by the stockholders to guide themselves, the directors and officers, are found in the Certificate of Incorporation and By-Laws. Under these rules, certain fundamental requirements are prescribed. Typically, the stockholders meet annually to elect all or a specified number of directors. The directors serve for a prescribed term, usually one to three years, but may remain beyond the prescribed term until their successors are elected.

Overall Responsibilities of the Board of Directors

Within the framework controlling state laws and accountability to the stock-holders, the Board of Directors typically functions in 11 principal areas of responsibility.

- Stockholder Relations
- General Board Functions
- Short- and Long-Range Planning
- Major Policies and Business Decisions
- Financial Responsibilities
- Responsibilities with Respect to the CEO
- Top Management/Officers of the Corporation
- Human Resources
- External Relations
- Audit Functions
- Compliance Functions

Within the principal areas of responsibility, actual Board duties vary widely from one company to another. The following list is derived from participants' written statements of Board responsibilities and includes representative Board duties.

Stockholder Relations

- Represent the interests of the stockholders.
- Approve reports to stockholders.

- Determine the amount and manner of the payment of any dividends paid by the company.
- Approve proposals and contracts to be submitted to stockholder meetings.
- Submit annually to the stockholders, proposals regarding the size and make-up of the Board.

General Board Functions

- Recruit and nominate new members of the Board.
- Set the compensation and retirement age for directors.
- Establish and terminate committees of the Board and appoint committee chairs.
- Approve contracts for professional services required by the Board.

Short- and Long-Range Planning

- Establish short- and long-range strategic planning objectives and evaluate the progress of the plans.
- Approve long-range objectives as to profitability, growth, technology, etc.
- Review company performance against policies, objectives and plans.
- Propose changes in company direction.

Major Policies and Business Decisions

- In coordination with the CEO, establish and/or approve corporate policies.
- Approve major contracts, reorganizations, broad price changes and changes in distribution methods.
- Suggest new lines of business.
- Suggest and approve acquisitions, mergers and divestitures, with stockholder authorization.
- Identify roadblocks to company progress.
- Inquire into causes of major deficiencies in performance.

Financial Responsibilities

- Approve annual operating and capital budgets.
- Approve major capital investments.
- Authorize the building of major new facilities and the disposal of any major capital investments and assets.
- Approve major research investments.
- Appoint officers to carry out financing programs. Approve these programs, seeking stockholder authorization as required.

- Establish policies concerning the issuance, transfer and registration of company securities.
- Approve major short-term and all long-term loans.
- Evaluate and advise on the establishment and maintenance of favorable banking and financial relationships.
- Review annually all lease liabilities, pension plans, insurance coverage and loan guarantees.

Responsibilities with Respect to the CEO

- Provide for orderly succession to the post of CEO.
- Elect the CEO and define the limits of authority.
- Appraise the performance of the CEO and establish compensation.

Top Management/Officers of the Corporation

- Elect the officers of the company.
- Review the performance of officers and establish their compensation.
- Authorize officers to sign various written instruments and to take financial actions.
- Provide advice and counsel to officers/top management on matters within the scope of the Board's responsibilities.

Human Resources

- Evaluate and advise on the establishment and maintenance of favorable employee relations.
- Approve compensation and benefits plans, pensions, insurance, stock options and other related long-term incentive programs.
- Approve broad programs for management development.
- Fix broad boundaries for union relations and collective bargaining.

External Relations

- Approve broad plans of relations with the government, labor, distributors, and consumers.
- Evaluate and advise officers and top management on the establishment and maintenance of favorable trade and public relations.

Audit Functions

- Subject to stockholder approval, propose outside auditing firm.
- Provide for independent review of performance reports.

Compliance Functions

- Monitor the conduct of the CEO, directors, officers and employees to ensure that their conduct is in keeping with prevailing ethical and professional standards.
- Make certain that the company complies with all national, international, foreign, state and local laws affecting the company.

Responsibilities of Individual Board Members

Members of the Board of Directors have the same responsibilities on an individual basis as those described in the preceding section. In exercising these responsibilities, Board members:

- Attend Board meetings and participate constructively in the decision-making process.
- Actively participate in assigned Board committee(s).
- Develop and maintain familiarity with the functions and activities of the top management of the company as well as external developments and trends that affect the business.
- Represent company and stockholder interests.
- Comply with all laws, regulations, By-Laws, and codes of ethics to ensure that there is no conflict of interest or personal gain resulting from Board membership.

In considering the qualifications of directors, it may be noted that some states require that a director be a stockholder. This requirement is generally satisfied by the director qualifying through ownership of a nominal number of shares called qualifying shares. Beyond the statutory provisions, the By-Laws of the company stipulate additional requirements.

Directors from outside the corporation ("outside directors") apply their pertinent experience to furthering the interests of the corporation, providing advice to the Chief Executive Officer, acting as the group to which the officers are accountable for their actions, and aiding in gaining new business for the corporation.

Directors from within the corporation ("inside directors") apply their in-depth knowledge of the company's activities, and serve as communication links between the Board and employees.

Exhibit A
Responsibilities of the Board of Directors
Source: A Large Pharmaceutical Firm

Objective and Philosophy

The primary responsibility of the Board of Directors, as defined by state law, is to manage the business of the Company. To carry out this responsibility, the Board membership provides a balance between directors who are also officers of the Company and so-called external or "outside" directors, who represent general fields of interest to the Company, especially the scientific field. The present number of "outside" directors is eight, compared with four directors who are also operation officers, reflecting the philosophy that "outside" directors comprise the majority on the Board.

Four Board committees have been established to facilitate the operation of the Board. The Executive Committee, the committee of the Board with the broadest field of interest, consists of three "outside" directors and three directors who are also officers, including the Chief Executive Officer of the Company as Chairman. The Finance Committee membership is independent of operating management and consists solely of "outside" directors, although Company financial officers are invited to attend meetings regularly. The Scientific Committee consists of two "outside" directors and two directors who are also officers, one of whom, the Chief Executive Officer of the Company, serves as an ex officio member. The Stock Option Committee consists of three "outside" directors, plus two directors who are also officers, all of whom are ineligible to participate in the Stock Option Plan.

General Responsibility

The Board of Directors is responsible for determining policies, goals, and philosophies of the Company and for seeing that they are carried out by the officers; for electing and appointing the Chairman of the Board and the officers of the Company and the fixing of their responsibilities; for authorizing the President and other Company officers to act for or on behalf of the Company in performing delegated responsibilities as prescribed in the Corporate Resolutions of the Board; for establishing committees of the Board and defining their responsibilities; and in general for directing the management and control of the business, finances, property, and concerns of the Company.

Functions

The functions of the Board are as follows:

1. **Objectives.** Determines the general objectives, goals, and philosophies of the Company; and guides the development and operation of the business toward their accomplishment.

2. **Policies and Programs.** Formulates or approves broad policies for execution by the Chief Executive Officer and other officers; and approves programs proposed by Company officers.

3. **Organization.** Elects the Chairman of the Board and other officers specified in the By-Laws; appoints, upon recommendation of the Executive Committee, other officers of the Company; establishes committees of the Board; and fixes the responsibilities and authority of Board committees, the President, and other Company officers to act for or on behalf of the Company in the operation of the business.

4. **Stockholders.** Considers and approves for submission to the stockholders all proposals which are recommended for stockholder action; and gives final approval of the periodic reports to stockholders.

5. **Capital Investment.** Authorizes directly or through appropriate delegations the making of new capital investments and the sale and exchange of assets.

6. **Profit Distribution.** Determines the distribution of profits; and authorizes dividend actions.

7. **Appraisal.** Reviews and appraises the results of Company activities and performance of management to insure the protection of the rights and interests of stockholders.

8. **Auditing.** Appoints outside auditors upon the recommendation of the Finance Committee; and provides direct access at all times for reports and recommendations from the outside auditors and the Controller of the Company on any matters they may wish to bring to the attention of the Board.

9. **Executive Compensation.** Approves compensation to be paid all officers and directors, as well as to all other employees in cases involving annual compensation of $_____ or more.

10. **Advice to Management.** Provides advice and consultation to the Company's officers on general matters affecting the management of the business.

Meetings

The fourth Tuesday of the month. Meetings are attended by the Directors, the

Secretary of the Board, and a representative of the Company's outside legal counsel. The Board will also from time to time request other officers and employees to attend the meetings, and in particular the Controller and Treasurer will be available for all Board meetings.

Exhibit B
Responsibilities of the Board of Directors
Source: A Machinery Manufacturer

THE BOARD OF DIRECTORS, AS TRUSTEES OF THE OWNERS OF THE BUSINESS, have the responsibility of keeping a proper balance among the interests of the stockholders, employees, customers, and the public; and, because of their experience and past accumulated administrative know-how, have the additional responsibility of seeing that management gets things done in accordance with the broad overall objective of operating the Company on a profitable basis.

Its principal functions are as follows:

1. To secure competent executives to operate the Company and to insure the continuation of able management.

2. To consider and approve broad policies, such as the manufacture of new products, acquisition of new manufacturing facilities, changes in distribution methods, price changes, and relations with consumers, distributors, labor, and government.

3. To monitor management and the results they have secured by analyzing financial results, such as increase in sales volume, profits, and overall competitive position.

4. To supervise, control, and act on important matters, such as capital structure changes, large loans, and dividend payments.

5. To review and approve capital and operating budgets.

6. To approve the selection of general counsel and formal action required by law.

7. To establish the salaries of senior executives, approve bonus, stock and pension plans, and control all other policies relating to compensation of executives.

8. To make discerning inquiries of members of management at Board meetings.

9. To present an outside, detached point of view.

10. To inspect properties and review actual operations.

11. To request inside and outside audits and secure professional services, such as management consultants and public accountants.

12. To see that the Company is legally operated.

Exhibit C
Responsibilities of a Corporate Director
Source: A Manufacturing Company

Basic Function:

As a trustee of the stockholders of the company, the director is responsible for formulating and approving company policies, establishing goals and objectives, and reviewing and appraising all other matters which affect the overall aspects of company operations; also establishing By-Laws, electing the officers of the company, and affecting all other regulation necessary to control the company's operations.

Duties:

1. Perform the functions of a director as delineated by the By-Laws.

2. Regularly attend meetings of the board.

3. In conjunction with the other board members, consider the plans and performance of management and approve or revise them to suggest any specific actions which management should take upon orders from the board.

4. Jointly with the other board members and with final responsibility to the stockholders, exercise total authority over all aspects of the company's operations.

Performance Appraisal:

Effective performance is determined by the extent to which the director aids board members in guiding company affairs and the satisfaction of the stockholders with activities.

Exhibit D
Responsibilities of the Chairman of the Board

Position Summary:

Presides at all meetings of Board of Directors. Provides leadership to the Board in reviewing and deciding upon matters which exert major influence on the manner in which the corporation's business is conducted. Acts in a general advisory capacity to the Chief Executive Officer and other officers in all matters concerning the interests and management of the corporation. Performs such duties as may be conferred by law or assigned by the CEO or the Board.

Position Responsibilities:

Prepares agendas for and convenes and conducts regular and special meetings of the Board of Directors.

Advises and gives counsel to the CEO and other officers of the corporation. Reviews major activities and plans with the CEO to insure conformity with the Board's views on corporate policy.

Possesses the same powers as the CEO to sign all certificates, contracts, and other instruments of the corporation, which may be authorized by the Board.

Exercises all powers and discharges all of the duties of the CEO in that individual's absence.

Participates in outside activities which will enhance corporate prestige and fulfill the corporation's public obligations as a member of industry and the community.

Carries out special assignments in collaboration with the CEO or Board of Directors.

Counsels collectively and individually with members of the Board, utilizing their capacities to the fullest extent necessary to secure optimum benefits for the corporation.

Presides at all meetings of stockholders and shall be an ex officio member of all standing committees.

Nominates officers of the corporation for election by the Board of Directors.

Appoints all members of the committees of the Board of Directors, subject to approval by the Board. Presents any proposed changes in major policies of the corporation for Board action.

Exhibit E
Responsibilities of the Chief Executive Officer

Position Summary:

May serve as the presiding officer of the Board of Directors, and in that capacity, guides the deliberations and activities of that group. Responsible for directing the organization with the objective of providing maximum profit and return on invested capital; establishing short-term and long-range objectives, plans, and policies subject to the approval of the Board of Directors; and representing the organization with its major customers, the financial community and the public.

Position Responsibilities:

Develops the basic objectives, policies, and operating plans of the business; submits these to the Board of Directors for approval.

Ensures that organization policies are uniformly understood and properly interpreted and administered by subordinates; reviews and approves proposed internal policies of subordinate units.

Ensures that adequate plans for future development and growth of the business are prepared, and participates in their preparation; periodically presents such plans for general review and approval by the Board of Directors.

Presents proposed operating and capital expenditure budgets for review and approval by the Board of Directors.

Plans and directs all investigations and negotiations pertaining to mergers, joint ventures, the acquisition of businesses, or the sale of major assets.

Takes necessary actions to protect and enhance the organization's investments in subsidiaries and affiliates.

Represents the organization as appropriate in its relationships with major customers, suppliers, competitors, commercial and investment bankers, government agencies, professional societies and similar groups.

Analyzes operating results of the organization and its principal components relative to established objectives and ensures that appropriate steps are taken to correct unsatisfactory conditions.

Ensures the adequacy and soundness of the organization's financial structure and, reviews projections of working capital requirements. Negotiates and otherwise arranges for any outside financing that may be indicated.

Prescribes the specific limitations of the authority of subordinates regarding policies, contractual commitments, expenditures, and personnel actions. Reviews and approves the appointment, employment, transfer or termination of all key executives. Resolves any conflicts arising between operating groups, staff units and other elements under immediate supervision.

4. Sample Competitive Analysis Formats

There are many ways to present competitive pay data for Board pay. We have attached two formats that Watson Wyatt has used: one is for proxy analyses and one is for survey reporting.

Published Survey Outside Directors' Compensation Summary

Survey	Industry	Revenues	Annual Retainer	Committee Retainer	Meeting Fees	Total Retainer & Meet. Fees	Stock Awards	Total Comp.[1]
Survey 1	All Organizations [2]	$200-$500M	$16,000		$1,000	$24,000	$31,250 [4]	N/D
	All Organizations [2]	Less than $500M		$1,000 [3]				N/D
	Retail & Wholesale	Less than $2 B	$20,000		$1,500	$32,197	$30,274 [4]	N/D
	Retail & Wholesale	Less than $5B		N/D [3]				N/D
Survey 2	All Org (excl Fin Serv)	$150-$399.9M	$15,000	$3,250	$1,000	$31,344	N/D	$45,933
	Other Non-Manufacturing	$150-$399.9M	$15,000	N/D	$1,500	$32,857	N/D	$51,000
Survey 3	All Organizations	$200-$600M	$13,183	N/D	$1,595	N/D	$17,583	$43,784
	Gen Merch/Spec Retail	$200-$600M	$13,087	N/D	$1,055	N/D	$18,186	$38,661
Survey 4	All Organizations	Less than $3B	N/A	N/D	$1,040	$36,552	N/D	N/D
	Retailers	All	N/A	N/D	$955	$38,431	N/D	N/D
Survey 5	Retail Trade	All				$32,500		
	Wholesale Trade	All				$29,250		
Survey 6	All Organizations	Less than $1B	N/D	N/D	N/D	$35,773	N/D	$48,271
Our Company		$269 M	$20,862	$0	$1,200	$36,222	$5,553	$41,775

[1] *Includes total cash plus expected value of stock awards*
[2] *Excludes Banking and Finance, Insurance, Health Care and Not-For-Profit*
[3] *Based on Compensation Committee average*
[4] *Stock options valued at 50% of face value*
[5] *Average not median amounts. Includes all stock awards valued at date of annual meeting, stock options valued at 33% of grant value*

Board and Committee Meeting Frequency and Fees

| Company | Board Meeting Fees | | | Number of Meetings | | | | Committee Meeting Fees | | | | |
	No. of Meetings	Fees Per Meeting	Total Fees	Audit	Comp	Exec	Other[1]	Average Committee No. of Meetings	Member-ships	Meetings Per Director[2]	Fees Per Meeting	Total Fees
ABC	4	$1,000	$4,000	6	1			3.5	1.3	4.7	$1,000	$4,700
BCD	11	$0	$0	4	0	7	12	5.8	2.6	15.1	$0	$0
DEF	6	$2,000	$12,000	6	4	4	1	3.8	1.1	4.2	$1,000	$4,200
FGH	4	$2,500	$10,000	4	1			4.0	2.5	10.0	$2,500	$25,000
HIJ	4	$1,000	$4,000	2	1		0	1.0	1.0	1.0	$1,000	$1,000
JKL	10	$0	$0	1			0	0.5	1.8	1.0	$0	$0
LMN	5	$0	$0	3	4			3.5	1.0	3.5	$0	$0
NOP	8	$1,000	$8,000	5	2	0	0	1.8	1.5	2.6	$750	$1,950
PQR	8	$1,000	$8,000	5	7		1	4.3	1.6	7.0	$1,000	$7,000
RST	4			5	3	4		4.0	1.0	4.0		
TUV	4	$1,000	$4,000	4	2	4		3.0	1.0	3.0	$800	$2,400
Peer Statistics												
75th Percentile	*8*	*$1,000*	*$8,000*	*5*	*4*	*5*	*1*	*4.0*	*1.7*	*5.9*	*$1,000*	*$4,575*
Median	*5*	*$1,000*	*$4,000*	*4*	*2*	*4*	*1*	*3.5*	*1.3*	*4.0*	*$900*	*$2,175*
Average	*6*	*$950*	*$5,000*	*4*	*3*	*4*	*2*	*3.2*	*1.5*	*5.1*	*$805*	*$4,625*
25th Percentile	*4*	*$250*	*$1,000*	*4*	*1*	*3*	*0*	*2.4*	*1.0*	*2.8*	*$188*	*$250*
Our Company	**8**	**$1,200**	**$9,600**	**3**	**5**	**0**	**3**	**2.8**	**2.6**	**7.2**	**$800**	**$5,760**

[1] *Average of other committees*
[2] *Average number of committee meetings attended by each non-employee director*
[3] *All remuneration received as undisclosed stock awards*
[4] *Number of Board meetings includes the a special meeting held in 2001, in addition to the seven regular meetings*

Stock Award Summary

Company	Type	No. of Shares	Grant Price	Face Amount[1]	Award Frequency	# Yrs. to Avg.	Annualized Award — Face Amount[2]	B-S % of Face	Real Value[3]	Vesting Schedule[4]	Option Term
ABC	Options	5,000	$14.00	$70,000	One-time	6	$11,667	60%	$7,000	50% 1st yr/25% per yr.	10
	Options	3,000	$14.00	$42,000	Annually	1	$42,000	60%	$25,200	50% 1st yr/25% per yr.	10
									$32,200		
BCD	Options	50,000	$0.20	$10,000	One-time	6	$1,667	60%	$1,000	33% per year	10
	Options	10,000	$0.20	$2,000	Annually	1	$2,000	60%	$1,200	33% per year	10
									$2,200		
DEF					-- No Stock Based Awards --						
FGH	Options	10,000	$11.25	$112,500	One-time	6	$18,750	60%	$11,250	det at time of grant	10
	Options	8,000	$11.25	$90,000	Annually	1	$90,000	60%	$54,000	det at time of grant	10
									$65,250		
HIJ	Options[5]	3,000	$20.75	$62,250	Annually	1	$62,250	35%	$21,788	1 year	10
JKL	Options	37,500	$8.25	$309,375	One-time	6	$51,563	60%	$30,938	N/A	10
	Options	9,375	$8.25	$77,344	Annually	1	$77,344	60%	$46,406	N/A	10
									$77,344		
LMN	Options[6]	20,000	$2.35	$47,000	One-time	6	$7,833	60%	$4,700	33% per year	5
	Options	10,000	$2.35	$23,500	Annually	1	$23,500	60%	$14,100	Immediate	5
									$18,800		
NOP	Options	5,000	$8.15	$40,750	Annually	1	$40,750	60%	$24,450	50% per year	N/A
PQR	Shares			$12,000	-- Included in Retainer --						
	Options[5]	5,000	$6.11	$30,550	One-time	6	$5,092	35%	$1,782	20% per year	10
	Options[5]	2,000	$6.11	$12,220	Annually	1	$12,220	35%	$4,277	50% per year	10
									$6,059		
RST	Options			-- All Remuneration Received as Undisclosed Stock Award --							
TUV	Options	4,000	$5.90	$23,600	Annually	1	$23,600	60%	$14,160	N/A	10
Median – All companies									*$18,800*		
Median – Excluding companies with no awards									*$21,788*		
Our Company	Shares	950	$6.17	$5,862	-- Included in Retainer --						
	Shares[7]			$15,000	-- Included in Retainer --						
	Options	1,500	$6.17	$9,255	Annually	1	$9,255	60%	$5,553	100% in 8 years	10
									$5,553		

[1] Grant price is taken as the price at the end of the annual meeting month, unless otherwise stated in proxy
[2] Assumes six-year annualization period for one-time awards
[3] Based on Black-Scholes option valuation model. Unless noted otherwise, a Black-Scholes value of 60% is used.
[4] If vesting schedule is not given then awards are assumed to vest in the same manner as executive awards
[5] Russ Berrie & Co and Hunt Corp both paid dividends, giving them an approximate Black-Scholes value of 35%
[6] The Chairman of the Board is granted 30,000 options at time of commencement
[7] Only non-Chairmen members of the Board receive this grant of common stock shares valued at $15,000

Directors' Remuneration Summary

| Company | Retainers and Meeting Fees | | | | Stock Awards | Total Remuneration[3] |
	Board	Board Fees	Committee Fees[1]	Total[2]		
ABC	$15,000	$4,000	$4,700	$23,700	$32,200	$55,900
BCD	$40,000	$0	$0	$40,000	$2,200	$42,200
DEF	$16,000	$12,000	$4,200	$32,200	$0	$32,200
FGH	$0	$10,000	$25,000	$35,000	$65,250	$100,250
HIJ	$8,000	$4,000	$1,000	$13,000	$21,788	$34,788
JKL	$10,000	$0	$0	$10,000	$77,344	$87,344
LMN	$25,000	$0	$0	$25,000	$18,800	$43,800
NOP	$15,000	$8,000	$1,950	$24,950	$24,450	$49,400
PQR	$17,000	$8,000	$7,000	$32,000	$6,059	$38,059
RST	-- All Remuneration Received as Undisclosed Stock Award --					
TUV	$15,000	$4,000	$2,400	$21,400	$14,160	$35,560
Peer Statistics						
75th Percentile	*$16,750*	*$8,000*	*$4,575*	*$32,150*	*$30,263*	*$54,275*
Median	*$15,000*	*$4,000*	*$2,175*	*$24,975*	*$20,294*	*$43,000*
Average	*$16,100*	*$5,000*	*$4,625*	*$25,725*	*$26,225*	*$51,950*
25th Percentile	*$11,250*	*$1,000*	*$250*	*$21,975*	*$8,084*	*$36,185*
Our Company	**$20,862**	**$9,600**	**$5,760**	**$36,222**	**$5,553**	**$41,775**

[1] Average committee membership times average disclosed committee meetings times per committee meeting fees

[2] Total is the sum of Board retainer, Board fees, and Committee fees

[3] Total Remuneration is the sum of annual compensation and stock awards

15. Designing Compensation for Non-Public and Foreign-Owned Companies

There are a host of intriguing executive compensation design issues that arise when dealing with a non-public or foreign owned company. Chief among these is the frequent lack of stock-based compensation, or stock compensation that is offered at a significantly reduced level as compared to the typical U.S. publicly-owned company. In the case of foreign-owned companies, they must also factor in cultural differences that can necessitate significant alteration to how certain compensation and benefit programs are offered. Family-owned businesses have their own intricacies, and often depend on how active the family is in the business, and what the family's goals are for the company. Pre-IPO companies are often run with very specific financial goals, as are post-LBO companies.

The authors caution against the error of drawing generalized conclusions across the varied types of non-public companies, and provide separate discussion of the different types of non-public or foreign-owned entities, detailing the interesting issues to be addressed in each. —Editors

IN EARLIER CHAPTERS of this book, many of the aspects that deal with Executive Compensation, in general, have been covered. These discussions have focused largely on issues relevance and importance to publicly held companies. This chapter now provides guidance on non-public organizations and on some of the unique issues that these organizations face.

Some readers might believe that, with the exception of some technical and legal issues, there should be little difference in executive compensation solely due to the nature of ownership of the organization. In reality, however, there are many areas in which the world of executive compensation within non-public companies is very different. For the executive or HR professional who is involved with a non-public entity, it is important to not only understand what these differences are, but also why they exist and how to address them.

In this chapter we will provide some background; a description and delineation of the different forms of non-public companies. We will then take a closer look at each; providing comparison and discussion of the issues involved when dealing with executive compensation design and strategy.

Why Non-Public/Private?

But first, let's begin with an answer to why companies choose to be privately-held. There are many reasons but, in the end, the decision is that there was never a choice; the shareholder(s) or parent organization chose to own the entity privately and fully.

Why would a shareholder or parent company make this choice? Perhaps more telling than the reasons why a company remains private are the reasons why a company would seek public ownership. The answer, simply, is to gain access to capital. There is a period of time when a privately held company can exist, grow and flourish via internally generated funds, equity that exists in the business, and debt. But many entities reach a point in their life cycle where they need access to more equity capital. The eventuality of selling shares to the public may be known or anticipated from the time a company is formed, or it may be a later reality given certain changes in business structure and financing.

Companies may choose not to become publicly traded, or may delay this decision, in order to avoid certain "costs" (financial and non financial). These costs of public ownership include:

- Real cash and opportunity costs associated with securities registration, conducting a public offering, and servicing the public market;
- Non-cash costs of loss of control (formal governance procedures, independent Board of Directors, changes to the decision making process); and
- Cash costs and labor costs to produce and manage the mountain of public disclosure (not to mention the competitive and personal "costs" associated with the sudden lack of privacy surrounding performance, business plans, compensation practices, etc.).

The cost of public ownership can be quite high. In response, many companies (both foreign and domestic) choose private ownership as the best means to control synergistic business units. Private investors and family groups choose private ownership to continue dynasties, maximize personal flexibility/benefit, streamline decision making, and maintain privacy.

Description of Non-Public Companies

There are a wide variety of "non-public companies." It is therefore important to first define what we mean by the term For the purposes of this chapter, a non-public company is one whose stock/ownership is not traded on a recognized exchange*. Within this definition there can be included a relatively wide variety of different structures, such as:

- "C" Corporations;
- Sub-chapter "S" Corporations;
- Personal Service Corporations;
- Limited Liability Companies;
- Limited Liability Partnerships;
- Partnerships;
- U.S. Subsidiaries of Foreign Parents;
- U.S. Subsidiaries of U.S. Parents;
- Joint Ventures;
- Divisions;
- Groups; and
- Others.

The variety of names needn't be confusing. Consider first the issue legal structure (Corporation, LLC, LLP, Partnership, etc.), then turn your attention to where the ownership/control lies. We will return to the latter issue in a moment.

It is important to have at least a general understanding of some of the key distinctions among these different types of legal structures. Of the various "corporate" structures, all are essentially trying to achieve the same central purpose: shielding the shareholders from any liabilities of the organization. But there the similarities end, and the tax differences begin. Consider:

- A "C" Corporation is one where the net income is taxed at the corporate level, and then any distributions (other than compensation) are usually taxed again as dividends. The "C" Corporation has the greatest flexibility from an ownership standpoint.
- Closely following the "C" Corporation is the "Personal Service" Corporation. Once again, the key difference revolves around taxation. Rather than having a graduated tax rate like the "C" Corporation, the "Personal Service" Corporation is taxed at a flat rate of 35%, and the owners do not enjoy the same employee benefit treatment as in a "C" Corporation.
- Finally, there is the "S" Corporation. This is almost a hybrid structure, where the taxation is more like that of a partnership than a corporation. At the end of each year, any net income left is taxed directly at the individual shareholder level (regardless of whether it is distributed), rather than

being double-taxed as it is in a "C" Corporation. But, with this tax advantage go many restrictions that reduce flexibility. In addition, there are limits on employee benefits to owners.

• Limited Liability Companies (LLCs) and Limited Liability Partnerships (LLPs) are both relatively new. Each attempts to limit the liability of the owners, while providing partnership-type taxation. Like the "S" Corporation, LLCs and LLPs limit the employee benefits that can be provided to owners.

• Partnerships provide for flow-through taxation, like that of an "S" Corporation; however, the liabilities of the partnership flow through to the individual partners as well. Employee benefits for partners are limited in a manner similar to "S" Corporations, LLCs, and LLPs.

You will notice as well that many other proper-sounding designations may go with a non-public organization. These include words like "Joint Venture," "Subsidiary," "Group," and "Division." None of these, however, necessarily reveal anything about the legal structure. For example, you can have a "Joint Venture" that is a partnership, an LLP, an LLC, an "S" Corporation, or even a regular "C" Corporation.

A central question in this regard might be "Why do we care what the legal structure is?" We do because it can end up dictating some of the vehicles available for use within the executive compensation program. For example, only corporations can have shares of stock. But an additional reason is to better understand some of the motivations behind the owners themselves.

Executive Compensation Issues Unique to the Privately Held

The purpose of this section is to begin exploring some of the issues that are unique to the privately held organization, especially as contrasted to their publicly held counterparts. This becomes important when attempting to compare executive compensation between the two and, as we will see, very significant differences would be found even if variables such as size, performance, and complexity were to be held constant. These differences in compensation can generally be summarized within the following three categories (all of which are interrelated):

Amount

The amount of total compensation paid at the executive level in privately held companies is often substantially less than that paid to publicly held companies of similar size. Part of this is caused by differences in the "form" and the "mix" of pay as described in greater detail below. But, even when adjusting for form and mix differences, compensation is still lower in a privately held company in an absolute sense. Differences in job complexity is part of the answer. The CEO of a privately held company reports to the board of directors, just like in a public company. But, unlike a public company, the CEO of the privately held company is not likely to have to deal with securities law issues. Assuming further that there is no publicly held debt, there are oftentimes significantly fewer legal and shareholder issues facing a private company CEO, as there are no proxy or 10K statements to file, and annual reports are likely to be far less complex.

Another reason for the difference may be associated with job risk. Executives of privately held companies are not having to operate under the same level of intense scrutiny that their peers are in publicly held organizations. Without the constant focus of institutional and private investors on quarterly earnings, executives in privately held entities are typically in the job for a longer period of time. Some would suggest that this reduced level of personal risk may be an explanatory variable for the relatively lower level of compensation within these organizations.

A final reason for this difference is the impact of a more active shareholder/owner or group of shareholders/owners in the case of the non-public company. In a publicly held company, with shareholders numbering in the tens of thousands, the impact of the shareholder is greatly reduced and is felt largely through the board of directors. While the Board has the same influence in privately held companies, it is common for a major shareholder/owner to serve on the Board. This more direct involvement from the owners in matters affecting executive compensation can directly impact the amount of pay that is delivered (as well as the form that it may ultimately take), as the result of the shareholder/owner of the privately held organization feeling that the compensation paid is coming directly from his/her own pocket.

Form

A second significant difference between publicly and privately held organizations relates to the "form" of executive compensation that is paid. This is seen principally rooted in the lack of equity opportunities within privately held organizations versus their publicly held counterparts.

Over the past two decades, the role of equity within the total compensation package for a senior-level executive of a publicly held company has grown immensely. The value of long-term incentives has reached the point where it is not uncommon for it to well exceed that of salary and bonus combined (based on a comparison done at the time of grant using valuation models to put equity onto equal footing with cash). When you further factor in the phenomenal growth in publicly traded equity values during this same time period, "delivered" compensation can be in the millions, if not tens of millions of dollars, over a multi-year period.

Many privately held organizations, for a wide variety of reasons, want to keep the ownership closely held; thus, it is not unusual to see employee executives having no equity holdings in the organization. This is an immediate and significant difference between publicly and privately held companies in terms of the form of pay. When this is further coupled with the inability of private companies to even come close to being able to provide a cash-based plan that could match the growth in equity markets, the compounding of this gap can become quite extreme. As a result, the difference in form is a factor that drives, and leverages upward, the difference in amount.

Mix

Finally, privately held companies will tend to be different than their publicly held counterparts in terms of the component "mix" within the compensation package. This can be seen in a number of different ways. Target bonus opportunities will tend to be lower in privately held organizations. One of the factors causing the growth in target bonuses in the public sector has been the impact of Internal Revenue Code ("IRC") Section 162(m), dealing with the $1 million limit on the deductibility of compensation. One of the exclusions from this limit is payments made under certain performance-based plans, such as bonus programs. Thus, many publicly held companies have been delivering compensation increases through the bonus plan in order to ensure the continued deductibility of these amounts.

Privately held companies are not subject to IRC Section 162(m) and, therefore, have not felt the same pressure to deliver compensation that meets the tax deductibility requirements. As a result, target bonus percentages have not grown at the same rate as within publicly held organizations.

The overall impact of this is that fixed pay (i.e., base salary) is typically a greater percentage of total compensation within privately held companies. Further, the reduced role for equity-based vehicles in private companies results in a dramatic difference in the mix of pay, with salary being a greater proportion and bonus and long-term incentives being smaller proportions of total compensation.

However, "mix" also impacts "amount." Since target bonus percentages will tend to be lower, so too will the dollar payouts when performance is very strong and payments are at or near maximum.

Other Differences

Of course, there are other areas that differ between public and private companies. One of the most interesting of these is in regard to the focus on financial statements. Executives within publicly held companies tend to be heavily focused on reported earnings, either in the form of net income or, more frequently, earnings-per-share ("EPS"). Further, this focus is often on very short term (typically quarterly) results, as there is a perception that this helps to drive equity values.

In comparison, within privately held organizations the focus tends to be that "cash is king." Executives and owners alike are more focused on cash flow than they are on net income. A focus on EPS is, for the same reason, very uncommon, as shares outstanding will typically be very constant and repurchases are rare. This focus on cash flow carries over to incentive plans as well; financial statements within private companies will often focus on measures such as EBIT (Earnings Before Interest and Taxes) or even EBITDA (EBIT less Depreciation and Amortization). Further, not only do you see differences in the performance measures used, you will also more likely to see a longer-term focus within private companies. Without the scrutiny of the financial press, privately held organizations appear more willing to be patient as new markets/products/services develop.

Types of Private Companies to be Discussed

As mentioned earlier, there are many situations and circumstances that give rise to a private rather than a publicly held organization. Depending on these reasons, many of which have to do with the nature of the parents/owners, views and strategies for executive pay practices can differ widely. The next several sections of this chapter will deal with the most common of these parenting/ownership situations and the typical influences they bring to bear on executive compensation. Specifically, the following pages will address:

• Non-U.S. based parents;

• Family-owned companies;

• Professional investors as owners; and

• U.S. subsidiaries of U.S. based parents.

Non-U.S. Based Parents

During the decade of the nineties, many companies that were domiciled outside the United States began or acquired U.S. based operations. Most often, the source of these U.S. units or subsidiaries was acquisition, either by purchasing a captive business unit from another organization or as a result of the acquisition of an entire stand-alone company. The formation of a new U.S. based unit or subsidiary from the "ground up," where all employees are new to the company, was not a common approach for a non-U.S. based parent to undertake.

Given the implicit nature of acquisition, typical integration issues exist. These issues include transition of pay packages–both cash and stock, conversion of plan metrics and design elements, and the constructs of the underlying philosophy and approach to pay. However, beyond the specific issues presented in any sale or acquisition, a non-U.S. based parent and its U.S. business unit will encounter many of the same executive compensation issues as other non public entities. Even in the case of a "ground up" formation of a U.S. business by a non U.S. parent, executive pay issues can eventually present themselves as a result of the influence of the U.S. business environment.

Consider the fact that the highest common denominator in terms of global executive pay is the United States. Over the past 15-20 years, executive pay in the U.S. has grown at rates far in excess of the experience in other countries, with the single most obvious explanation being the growth in both value and use of stock-based vehicles, further amplified by the buoyant U.S. equity markets, particularly during the 1980s and 1990s.

Further consider the frustration of the new, non-U.S. based, parent/owner who has to manage expectations set by the previous U.S. parent's pay package. Alternatively, in the case of a newly formed business unit, the non-U.S. parent may be forced to deal with the pressure of the U.S. pay markets in order to attract or retain the desired caliber of individual. Regardless of the catalyst or the eventuality of timing, non-U.S. based parents will, at some point, be put in the position of having to reconcile their relatively lesser executive pay practices to those available in the U.S.

Beyond the issue of sheer quantity of pay, there are issues regarding the U.S. vs non-U.S. design and construction of pay plans. This is true in several regards:

• The basis for extracting market data and setting pay can be subject to debate;

- Non-U.S. parents/owners are accustomed to different norms regarding the relationship between pay and performance within the context of an incentive plan;
- Outside the U.S. the use of equity. is more reserved and fewer vehicles commonly exist;
- The design elements surrounding options differ by country and often do not match the U.S. "typical market;" and
- Knowledge of limits on U.S. retirement benefits is often marginal, and the need for either supplemental plans or deferral opportunities is not understood.

Let's explore the significance of each of these "mismatches" further.

Market Data selection and analysis

To be quite frank (and many U.S. companies miss this point); non-U.S. parents/owners view executives within a captive U.S. business group as being direct-reports, not as executives of a stand-alone company, regardless of their former structure or reporting level. They are now members of a larger, global organization and the parent often feels that pay for the business unit executives must fit within the parent/owner's global compensation structure. The parent/owner's approach and attitude toward pay for their non-domestic business units (particularly those in the U.S.) is highly dependent on the size and sophistication of the parent and the length and depth of their global exposure to human resources issues.

These influencing factors make the issue of market data selection (i.e., which comparison companies to use and at what level jobs should be benchmarked) a critical one and another source of difference. Polar extremes can exist as seen in the following three scenarios:

- The parent may be globally savvy in all aspects of executive compensation and may have a global pay philosophy that acknowledges pay levels within the U.S. and accepts some or all elements of pay at those competitive market levels. Even where this is the case, the U.S. business group must be cautious to understand how their positions are viewed within the marketplace: Are they business unit level executives (either at the "Subsidiary," "Group," or "Division" level in similar U.S. benchmarking terms)? Are they, or should they be, a mix between those business unit level benchmarks and the next higher level because their level of guidance from the parent/owner is distant-to-non-existent and, therefore, the executives recruited are acknowledged as being "larger" in order to fulfill the needs of the job? (This hybrid benchmarking philosophy must be carefully and logically broached with the parent, as it will not likely be their first inclination. While it may be logical, it may produce market data that is untenable in the parent/owner's pay scheme. This approach might also not be acceptable to the parent on conceptual grounds. As a result, this method should never be assumed and undertaken without careful seed-planting with the parent/owner in advance.)

• The non-U.S. parent may be experienced but, despite their exposure to international markets, still relies on domestic processes for setting the boundaries and ranges within which their U.S. businesses' pay levels are reviewed. We all know the drill from experience here in the U.S.: "select peer companies, determine benchmarks, pull market data, slot actual data versus market, perform a gap analysis...Now what about the international jobs?..." In the mind of the non-U.S. parent/owner, U.S. executives' pay may first (and inevitably) be compared to the market data gathered domestically by the non-U.S. parent. Whether or not the analysis drills down further to review pay versus U.S. market standards, the issue of sticker shock and relative internal inequity arises here. Where the non-U.S. parent uses home country data as either a portion of the analysis or, worse yet, as the means by which to slot their international executives, market data can present a huge issue that often cannot be easily resolved.

• The non-U.S. parent/owner who either relies on their U.S. business unit to supply data, because of their own lack of experience in the U.S. market, or prefers to allow their U.S. businesses to provide the information as part of their semi-independence. The largest error this U.S. business unit can commit is to jump to the conclusion that they can select peers and benchmark positions without first discussing the appropriate philosophy and approach with the parent. More than once, large knowledgeable U.S. business units have performed this analysis comparing themselves to stand-alone U.S. companies. And, more than once, these situations have resulted in negative, bristling reactions from the non-U.S. parent/owner when they discover this assumption has been made without their input to the process.

Market data processing is an art, not a science. Data can be prepared and analyzed in any mutation desired, and many variations in outcome can be produced. The basis for sourcing market data information should be explained and agreed upon prior to the presentation of any results or recommendations. If this is not possible, multiple "views" of the data should be produced so that a range of results can be explained and considered.

Without this level of preparation, trust can be broken and will be difficult, if not impossible, to repair in the short term.

Pay for Performance Structures

The relationship between pay and performance within an incentive plan varies company by company, but generalizations can be made. The median practice in a short- or long-term performance incentive plan follows a pattern something like this:

Level of Results Delivered	Actual Performance Versus "Plan"	Payout as a Percent of the "Target" Opportunity
Maximum	130% of "Plan"	200% of Target
Target	100% of "Plan"	100% of Target
Threshold	70% of "Plan"	50% of Target
Below Threshold	<70% of "Plan"	Zero

Further to this table, payment for performance between Threshold and Target, and Target and Maximum, are interpolated between 50–100% and 100–200%, respectively.

This pay-performance relationship is a curiosity (or even an outrage) to many non-U.S. based parents/owners. Practices vary by country, but design norms such as these listed below can prevail, thereby making the U.S. approaches seem out of step.

• There may be no payment for missing Target (e.g., zero for performance below 100%).

• Where a perception of paying for "missed" goals is imbedded in a non-U.S. plan, it may be much less forgiving (perhaps paying 50% of Target opportunities for performance at 85–90% of Plan, and zero below that).

• "Plan" will often incorporate top-down expectations regarding performance, or the use of a standard ("we expect our divisions to achieve a 10% ROIC level"), and no forgiveness for performance levels at units that may be "transitioning" toward those goals.

• Performance in excess of Plan is not heavily rewarded, with upward payments generally maximized at 130% of Target opportunity.

Attitudes regarding incentive pay, particularly short-term incentives, are often very different between other countries and the U.S. While "incentive" pay has gained much stronger acceptance outside the U.S., it is still a bit new or untested in certain countries. The most common chasm to broach can be whether or not an executive's salary implicitly is paid for them to deliver performance; therefore, short-term incentives are simply a "bonus" for good effort and not a substantial leverage point. Paying executives a salary for "attendance" and a separate "incentive" for delivering short-term performance can, when pushed, make certain non-U.S. executives feel they are being held hostage. While this is not meant to paint non-U.S. based parents/owners as opponents of incentive pay, the system in which U.S. incentives are established and earned can leave many outside the U.S. less than enthusiastic.

Equity-Based Long-Term Incentive Usage

Equity-based compensation has been raised to an elite art form in the U.S. Having potentially ingested a majority of this tome, by now you have no doubt been able to appreciate the wide variety of forms in which "equity" is available as an executive compensation element in the U.S.

• Incentive stock options;

• Nonqualified stock options;

• Extended term options;

• Collapsing term options;

• Discounted options;

• Premium options;

• Indexed options;

• Reload options;

• Performance accelerated vesting options;

• Stock appreciation rights;

• Performance shares;

• Junior stock (outmoded but enjoying a little dust-off in the new millennium);

• Restricted stock;

• Performance accelerated vesting restricted stock;

• Deferred shares;

• Phantom stock;

• Phantom stock appreciation rights;

• Tracking stock; and

• Outright stock.

Enough? Most of these twists and hybrids are specific to the U.S. and have come about in an effort either to create a more tax-effective compensation vehicle, to further incorporate performance in equity-based pay, or to be responsive to certain equity available (or not available) to the organization for use as a compensation tool.

But consider for a moment countries who have just recently been permitted to use stock options, countries who do not (culturally) share equity, or even those who still do not believe in incentive pay in general. How do they internalize, comprehend, and opine on the use of these U.S. specific creations? Can they find someone in their own country who can explain the whys and wherefores of some of these more elaborate vehicles, not to mention outline the securities laws registration and disclosure treatment within their own country should they decide to inherit, continue, or adopt one of these gems?

Suffice it to say that the use of equity in a business unit of a non-U.S. based parent/owner will not be as complex, sizeable, or varied as it potentially would be; were the parent or owner to be a U.S. entity. Typically, it is limited to options (in the parent/owner's country) and perhaps performance or restricted shares. Even where equity is used, it may not be available in enough quantity (due to internal equity considerations and overall dilution concerns) to be used as the sole or main long-term incentive instrument. Therefore, long-term incentives will be comprised, to a large extent, of cash, perhaps in the form of phantom stock, but most likely framed as a three-year performance plan measured and paid in cash. Cash will either supply the entire long-term incentive instrument, or it will serve as the bridge between the parent's home country program and some level of competitiveness with U.S. pay practices.

Stock Option Design

Staying on the topic of equity, another possible area of missed expectations can exist within the design of stock options (the most commonly used form of equity within non-U.S. parents). As in the U.S., those companies outside the U.S. often design their option plans in ways to make them as tax-effective as possible within the parameters of their own country's taxation scheme. A lack of understanding of the differences between typical U.S. design and that of the parent/owner's home country can lead to misunderstandings.

For example, in one client situation, the U.S. executives wanted vesting to occur in installments over the four years following the date of grant; the European parent's option plan called for five-year vesting. While the difference may not, in the end, be material, this became a point of question and frustration for both sides. When the U.S. executives came to understand that this was not some intentional effort to postpone vesting beyond what were then U.S. market norms, and instead was a domestic tax effectiveness element for the company, their level of acceptance was higher. Likewise, when the European parent came to understand this issue as a gap between their practices and typical stock option program designs in the U.S., they found a simple way to modify their plan to permit flexible, country-specific vesting.

While this situation may seem simple on its face, it was one of several executive compensation gaps between the U.S. subsidiary and the European parent's perspectives. A lack of understanding for "typical practices" and country-specific norms (as highlighted by this small option vesting example) initially prevented the two sides from understanding the philosophy and approach to pay within this subsidiary. In the final analysis, this gap in understanding (as with all communication gaps) became temporary fuel for other discomforts in overall business dealings between the parent/owner and the U.S. subsidiary.

Retirement Benefits

Retirement benefits, while undergoing change in some countries outside the U.S. (particularly the U.K.), are still a well developed and sizeable portion of pay for non-U.S. executives. While total retirement benefits are still a large portion of total compensation for U.S. executives (often 30% of total pay in a "target" year for both short-term and long-term incentives), the tax-qualified portion of U.S. executives' retirement is miniscule due to limitations imposed by ERISA and the Internal Revenue Code. (A discussion of those limits is beyond the scope of this Chapter.)

Given that the subject of retirement limits has warranted chapters, even entire books, dedicated to it as the sole subject, the reader hopefully can appreciate the breadth and complexity of these limitations. Unfortunately, non-U.S. parents do not typically have the resources to fully understand these limitations and the impact on U.S. executives' retirement pay. Frankly, the number of their executives who are impacted by these regulations and limits are relatively few in number; and spending time on this issue may not therefore be at the forefront of their minds.

Often, non-U.S. parents will dismiss the subject of retirement benefits for their U.S. executives, presuming that U.S. retirement benefits are economically on-par with their own. When the regulations and limits are explained and the retirement benefit realities are laid out, the non-U.S. parent/owner's reaction may be to say that the size of U.S. incentives more than offsets the lack of a retirement program, which is comparable to that of the parent/owner.

Non-U.S. parents typically will not understand the need for a nonqualified retirement plan (as seen in more than 60% of U.S. companies). If they do not understand the inadequate level of retirement benefit provided through tax-qualified plans in the U.S., they have no grounding to understand, or be supportive of, the need for a nonqualified or supplemental retirement arrangement.

This is not a particularly easy subject between the non-U.S. parent/owner and the U.S. business unit executives. It can go unaddressed permanently because of its complexity. In the case of most non-U.S. owned business units, executive retirements are sorely lacking in terms of the level of benefit they provide.

In Summary

Many factors influence a foreign-owned, U.S.-based business in its approach to pay. These include:

• Cultural attitudes and experience regarding pay;

• Home-country market practices;

• Domestic equity market opportunities;

• Opinions about the sufficiency of performance levels;

• Breadth of exposure to global human resource issues; and

• Knowledge of international compensation markets and regulations.

It is important to keep in mind that pay is a touchy subject for nearly everyone around the globe–it is personal; it is a measure of self-worth and success; it is a statement about value and fairness. Additionally, cultural differences should be consciously observed.

U.S. executives are used to open conversations about compensation; it is a subject that is actively "managed" between management, the board of directors, and private company owners. However, within a majority of cultures outside the U.S., pay is a top-down process, and conversations initiated by the recipients of pay are not always welcome, particularly when done in a way in which the parent feels "put on the spot." Pay change in these situations is often not immediate, but requires many conversations, "seed-plantings," and analysis. Oftentimes, the U.S. approach to pay can be overwhelming and a bit affronting to a non-U.S. parent. These dynamics need to be considered carefully and respected in order to ensure desired outcomes have the best possible chance of success.

Whatever the perspective, virtually no one is "neutral" when it comes to pay. In a situation where two countries meet on the playing ground of executive pay–this value-laden concept–experience, and communication are key to understanding differences and negotiating to a middle ground that is acceptable to all parties.

Family-Owned Companies

Family-owned companies represent one of the most challenging areas in terms of executive compensation from almost every perspective. This section discusses some of these challenges and the reasons behind them.

Organizational Structure

The organizational structure in family-owned companies can take a wide variety of different forms, from a regular "C" corporation, to a sub-chapter "S" corporation, to an LLC, even to a partnership. To complicate things further, there can be family-owned companies which have to file their financial statements with the SEC due to having more than 500 share-holders (even though there may be no publicly traded equity). Even further to the point are family-owned companies with minority interests that are publicly traded.

Amount

Family-owned companies can be quite conservative in terms of the "amount" of compensation provided, especially when compared with publicly held organizations. Many of the reasons for this conservative posture were outlined earlier in the chapter, but there are additional reasons that are more unique to the family-owned structure.

Active Family Members

Often, members of the family are still active in the management of the business. This can act as a form of compression on the pay of other, non-family members in the company. The compensation of family members is often a "tense" issue, especially to the extent that there are other family members who are not employees of the company. The non-employee family members can become resentful of the compensation being received by those within management, believing that their dividends are effectively being reduced by the compensation received by those employed. To avoid the potential for conflict, oftentimes the employed family member takes a more conservative compensation package than might be otherwise paid in an arms-length and independent transaction. This more conservative compensation level can, therefore, act as a "lid" on the amounts paid to non-family members within the organization.

In family-owned organizations where no family members are active within management the compression issue can be less severe, yet we still find these types of companies having a more conservative pay philosophy. Sometimes the reason can be traced back to the time when family members were active in the business. They tend to have good memories about how they were compensated, and this can influence their view of appropriate levels of compensation.

Job Security

The employee turnover rates within family-owned companies, especially at the senior levels of management, tend to be quite low, despite a conservative philosophy towards pay. In addition to lower turnover rates, family-owned companies will tend to be more generous with severance packages and, furthermore, usually more patient with employees who are not performing at desired levels. This suggests that family-owned companies attract a different type of individual than publicly held companies, one who is motivated by job security, commitment, and, perhaps, a more personal job relationship.

Volatility

Then, there is the issue of the volatility of pay, which can also influence the amount of pay. Family-owned companies tend to have significantly less volatility in terms of compensation than in publicly held organizations. However, with this reduced level of volatility goes a reduction in the number of large incentive payouts when results are extraordinary. Family-owned companies will tend to view performance that is far in excess of expectations as windfall and, therefore, more to the benefit of the owners than the employees. Thus, there are often lower maximums on incentive plans and far fewer "uncapped" incentive pools than in public companies.

Form

Family companies, for the most part, use different "forms" of compensation than do the publicly held organizations. This is, perhaps, most evident in the long-term incentive area; equity-based, long-term incentive programs are relatively rare in family-owned entities. Indeed, the existence of long-term incentives is lower in these types of organizations than in any other type of non-public company. Long-term incentives, when used, are usually cash based, either taking the form of a performance unit plan or a deferred compensation program. This area is discussed in more depth below.

Performance-Based Plans

Performance-based plans are the most prevalent of the long-term incentive plans in family-owned companies. Most of these take the form of a three-year performance plan, with a new performance period beginning every year. A performance goal is established at the beginning of the performance period and serves as the basis for determining what the ultimate payout will be at the end of the three-year period. In concept, these plans are identical to the programs in place at publicly held companies.

The key difference in family-owned organizations is in the performance measure used within the plan. Many publicly held companies will use EPS, net income, return on equity, or return on capital. Although some of these measures apply in family-owned companies, they are not commonly used in long-term, performance-based plans. There are several reasons why these measures are not more common, including:

- **Lack of focus on per-share amounts.** Many times, family-owned companies do not focus on outstanding shares, especially in cases where a single family may own 100% of the shares outstanding. Even in cases where the ownership may be spread beyond a single family, there may be share redemptions from time-to-time that could have a material impact on any per-share calculations, and it would not be fair to hold non-family members of management responsible for the impact of such decisions.

- **Unusual capital structure.** In order to use measures such as return on equity or return on capital, it is necessary to have a stable and traditional structure to the balance sheet, as well as the income statement. In family-owned companies, the capital structure can often be quite unusual and may reflect estate-tax planning, individual financial circumstances, etc. Indeed, the structure can change from time-to-time irrespective of what is going on in the business, driven more off the needs and objectives of the family itself. In addition, family-owned businesses often own assets that are more for use by the family than are required by the business. Thus, measures such as return on assets may be inappropriate to use for management compensation purposes, since they would hold management responsible for assets not under their control.

- **Inability to drive the business.** The effectiveness of any incentive plan is driven by the extent to which it is reflective of the needs and objectives of the business. Performance measures in publicly held companies are typically driven off the perceptions of the board or the "hot buttons" of the security analyst. In family-owned organizations, the performance measures are usually driven directly toward the needs of the business and the shareholders/owners.

It is interesting, though, to explore the types of performance measures that are in use in family-owned companies. These include measures such as:

- **Cash Flow.** This is usually the number one most critical measure in a family-owned business. Whether the cash flow is needed for the continued payment of dividends, for servicing bank credit and loans, or for rein-vestment back into the business, it is a critical element and is, therefore, often used as the performance driver.

- **EBIT/EBITDA.** This performance measure allows a family-owned business to exclude the costs that may be more a function of certain family needs than true business needs. In the case of EBITDA, the measure begins to resemble a true cash flow measure.

- **Net Income.** This measure is also used within long-term performance plans, especially on a cumulative basis. However, care must be taken to make sure that various family needs do not have an undue influence on the ability of management to reach the goals established.

Deferred Compensation Plans

Sometimes family-run companies feel uncomfortable with the concept of a long-term incentive plan, especially in those situations where the family's needs may cause significant variations in performance from year to year, despite the best efforts of management. In those cases, companies may consider a deferred compensation arrangement in lieu of the traditional long-term performance plan. Where used, these deferred compensation plans typically involve placing funds into an account (usually held by a rabbi trust), on behalf of the participant, and allowing the individual to have some discretion in terms of how these funds are invested. In concept, this would be similar to a qualified profit sharing plan; but, in this case, the partici-pation would be quite discretionary, and the amounts contributed on behalf of each individual would be as well. Such a concept allows a company to respond, at least in part, to the competitive pressures of not having a long-term incentive plan.

Phantom Stock Plan

In some situations, although a minority of cases, the family is willing to offer a phantom stock plan to the non-family members of management.

The objective behind this type of program is to offer individuals some of the benefits of equity ownership, without actually transferring ownership. Phantom stock is not a single type of vehicle. In fact, there are many different directions that phantom stock can take, including the following:

- **Comparable to restricted stock.** Phantom stock can look like, and act like, restricted stock, giving the individual all of the benefits of ownership, including the right to receive dividend equivalents but not the right to vote. At the end of the holding period, the participant has the right to receive the then current value of the shares, but be paid in cash rather than shares of stock.

- **Similar to a stock option/stock appreciation right.** Phantom stock can also look like a stock option or stock appreciation right. Within this context the phantom stock offers the participant no rights to receive dividends; however the executive does have the right to share in the increase in the value of the shares since the date of grant. When the individual desires (following the vesting period), the participant can elect to exercise the phantom shares and receive the appreciation in the value of the shares (but not the initial value).

- **As a dividend equivalent.** There are some family-owned companies where the primary objective of shareholders is the ability to receive the dividends on their shareholdings. In these types of situations, phantom stock can be used as the vehicle through which the executives are aligned with the interests of the owners, by allowing them to receive dividend equivalents on a given number of phantom shares. In this arrangement, the participant has no rights to the underlying stock or any change in value, only to the dividends that may be paid out.

Of course in any of these phantom plans, one of the most important elements is the valuation of the shares. Once again, there are a number of different ways that companies may approach this very sensitive issue. Some of these methods include:

- **Appraisal.** Some family-owned companies get a regular (at least annual) appraisal of the fair market value of the company. This valuation can be done by a number of different firms, from the large investment banking houses, to members of the large public accounting firms, to specialized appraisal companies. In some situations, the family may actually employ more than one firm and take the average of the two appraisals for purposes of establishing the fair market value. The biggest single issue that companies appear to wrestle with in these valuations is the volatility in the appraisal. Often the owners will instruct the appraisal firm to do some smoothing to the results so that this can be minimized. When used, the appraisal usually applies to not only the phantom stock plan, but also the price used for trades between family members or for estate tax purposes.

• **Formula Value.** Another approach is to employ a formula value process for purposes of the plan. Under this alternative, the company would develop, or have developed, a formula for determining the value that would be used for the phantom stock plan. The formula could be a stated multiple of earnings or book value. It could either have a multiple fixed or one that varies based on the multiple found in publicly traded companies in the same industry. Sometimes this formula value is used solely for purposes of the phantom stock plan. In other cases, it may also be used for trades between family members.

Mix

Family-owned companies will tend to use a very different "mix" of pay within the total compensation package for executives. There are a wide variety of ways in which companies may do this, and much of it depends on the objectives of the individual company. But, to generalize, base salary and retirement benefits will typically comprise a greater proportion of total compensation in family-owned companies than in publicly held ones. Conversely, variable pay, both short-term as well as long-term incentives, will commonly be a smaller percentage of the total. Further, within variable pay, long-term incentives would typically be significantly smaller, mirroring the more restrictive approach taken to equity among family-owned companies.

Summary

In summary, executive compensation in family-owned companies can be very different from that in almost any other type of organization, especially from a comparison with publicly held companies. It is important, though, to consider some of the unique, non-compensation factors that allow family-owned companies to retain quality people and to flourish in terms of their performance. Family-owned companies clearly present credible evidence that it is not how much you pay your people, but the total employment environment, that ends up being key to the attraction and retention of employees.

Professional Investors as Owners

This section will explore executive compensation practices within one of the most interesting areas of non-public companies, those owned by the professional investor. This area is interesting because, unlike any of the other types of non-public companies, it is one that typically has a relatively short life span. Professional investors will have little interest in being long-term owners of a non-public company. The lack of market liquidity inherent in a non-public company is typically a significant negative to the professional investor. Thus, this type of company is in a state of transition. The objective of the professional investor is not to hold on to the non-public company for any longer than is necessary to achieve their desired return on investment. This type of non-public company is one that is preparing for some type of "event."

To be sure, the exact nature of this "event" may not be known immediately, nor is the timing for the "event." However, at the time that the professional investor becomes involved in the ownership of the company, they are conscious of, and focused on, this ultimate "event."

It is important to recognize that there may be many different ways that the professional investor takes ownership of this non-public company. This becomes important because the process by which this ownership comes about can have an impact on the executive compensation program. For that reason, some of the more prevalent paths to ownership are reviewed below:

• **Leveraged/Management Buyouts.** These became quite popular in the 1980s. They describe a situation where a company is purchased with large amounts of debt by a group of professional investors, oftentimes with participation by management. But, the company involved is an active organization with a management group that is used to being rewarded in certain ways. Indeed, if the organization used to be publicly held, this represents a transition from a public to a private company.

• **Start-up.** In the decade of the 1990s, these became quite popular, especially in the technology area. In this type of situation the company is truly new, as are all of its employees. In the early years, there is no "business"–it is being developed; it is a "work in process." These early years may be marked by periods of further equity investment on the part of the professional investor in order to facilitate the building of the business model.

• **Bankruptcy/Turnarounds.** Unfortunately, there are also times when a business fails, and it must go through bankruptcy (or a near bankruptcy turnaround). The equity of these businesses often becomes worthless in this process, and the debt holders end up becoming the owners. It is then up to them to figure out how to turn the business around, so they can ultimately realize a return on their investment.

The critical thing to understand is that much of what may drive the executive compensation program is a function of how the organization got into the hands of the professional investor. Similarly, the process by which the professional investor plans to turn their investment into cash has a bearing on the ultimate design of the executive compensation program. The list below outlines some of the different "events" through which a cashout may take place:

- **Initial Public Offering (IPO).** This was the desired "event" that non-public companies would go through during most of the nineties. Regardless of the process by which the professional investor acquired the stock, the successful IPO represented "hitting a home run" in terms of their return on investment.

- **Sale to another organization.** In this type of "event," the non-public company is sold to another organization, who will then take over the business. In most cases, this does not represent as large of a "home run" to the professional investor as the IPO. However, depending on the conditions of the IPO marketplace, it may represent the only near-term way that the professional investor can exit the investment.

- **Liquidation.** Sometimes, it becomes clear that the business cannot be "saved," and, in these cases, the best way to maximize the return on investment for the professional investor is to liquidate/sell the business in parts. In these cases, the "sum of the parts may be worth more than the whole."

Amount

Let us first review the "amount" of compensation that is typically paid in these professional-owned organizations. Most likely, the reader will quickly observe that, to an extent, the ultimate "amount" may indeed be a function of both how the professional investor acquired the company in the first place, and how the investor hopes to exit the investment.

Leveraged/Management Buyouts

We might expect to see at least two different types of LBOs: one in which management is retained, and one in which a new leadership group is brought on board. Assuming that the current management team continues as part of the buyout, there will be relatively little change in the amount of compensation paid by this non-public company compared with the publicly held counterpart. A buyout of this type usually leads to a reduction in head-count and cutbacks in a number of areas, particularly employee benefits.

There is no question that there may be changes in the form and mix of pay (these will be described later); but, for the most part, compensation remains unchanged.

Indeed, in certain circumstances, such as where the professional investors believe a new management team needs to be brought in, the packages may actually increase as compared to the levels that used to be paid. This increase occurs due to the relatively greater degree of risk, borne by the executive, that is inherent in these organizations. The professional investor's objective is to turn the business around as quickly as possible, to prepare it for the "event" and their exit. Given the returns possible for the professional investor, the amount of compensation paid to the executives is relatively immaterial—the focus is on the "event."

As we look at these two cases (where management is retained vs. where management is replaced), there are classic changes in pay that occur post-LBO.

• **In the case of retained management:** salary tends to be unchanged; benefits (to the extent there are across the board cutbacks to reduce costs) might decline; perquisites may also decrease (to the extent there were generous entitlements in the previous pay program); long-term incentives are often eliminated and replaced by real equity ownership; and short-term incentive design may change somewhat (to emphasize different performance measures and metrics, require increased performance levels, and less certainty of payment). These changes may continue in place for several years as the company works to pay off debt. Therefore, the impact on executive compensation will be a decrease in pay received in the short-term, and the potential for increased total compensation in the long-term IF the company survives and its value (stock price) increases.

• **Where new management has been brought in:** salaries reflect a premium over what they received from former employers (and likely a premium over typical market levels); benefits and perquisites will be a least equivalent to what those individuals were receiving elsewhere (unless this element of pay is offset through another piece of the total compensation offer, such as stock); long-term incentives will be tied to equity appreciation (via grant size, vesting, amount "paid," etc.); and short-term incentives will be structured around highly negotiated goals that are viewed as "realistic" and achievable by the new management team.

Start-up

The only way the executives of the start-up get paid is if there is an IPO and their equity holdings experience significant run-ups. To explain:

- Compensation within start-ups is a subject worthy of its own book, and you will find an extended discussion of this topic in chapter 16. For the moment, it will suffice to say that the amounts are quite low, at least in terms of any measurement that can be applied by an outsider.
- Base salary is low, as compared with levels in publicly held organizations.
- Bonuses, too, are quite different. If paid at all, they are sometimes set with a very short near-term horizon; quarterly, or even monthly, as a means of motivating employees and executives to focus on business creation quickly. Moreover, the amounts paid are quite conservative by publicly held standards, and for good reason; in all likelihood, the organization is still using cash at an alarming rate, and it is coming out of the pockets of the professional investor.
- Employee benefits are almost nonexistent, with the exception of medical benefits. Even if equity is provided, by any valuation process used for publicly held companies, this too is low.

Bankruptcy/Turnarounds

The amount of pay in these situations can vary widely depending on where the executives came from initially. To the extent that they were part of the current management team, we might expect to see a continuation of the existing levels of compensation. However, if the professional investor brings in outsiders to replace all or part of the management team, the amount of compensation could be substantially higher, once again to reflect the risk that is inherent in this type of situation. But, unlike some of the other scenarios, the professional investor owning a business out of bankruptcy may not have the patience to wait for an IPO. The exit strategy in this case may be to clean up the organization for sale to another company, which may have an influence on the form and mix of pay provided to the executives.

Form

In terms of the form of compensation there may be substantial differences depending on the nature of the company, as shown next. For instance, in the cases of buyout and bankruptcy, the levels of salary, bonus, and employee benefits may remain quite similar, if not exactly the same, as the company had previously, while the start-up, in the case of salary, bonus, and benefits, is quite different. The most interesting issues can come in the form of long-term incentives. More specifically:

Leveraged/Management Buyouts

The buyout organization presents some interesting challenges. In many cases, most members of management will not have any equity in the new organization. The outside investors are typically quite careful about keeping the number of equity partners small. Thus, only a handful of executives may have equity, and the equity they do have is purchased by them at the same price as the investor. However, this is not to say that the buyout organization has no long-term incentives, as indeed they do. Most often, the form that these take is three-year performance plans which are typically paid out in the form of cash.

Startup

For the start-up, the form is easy–it is the stock option and only the stock option (and, by the way, lots of stock options). There is very little concern around the valuation process, since the strike price of the initial options granted is set at (or near) the same level as the stock price attributed to capital that is put in by the professional investor when they fund the company. No one worries about interim valuation, as the focus is only on the "event," in this case the IPO.

Bankruptcy/Turnarounds

Then, there is the firm acquired out of bankruptcy or in a near bankruptcy turnaround. The focus of these organizations is typically on improving the business so that it will become an attractive acquisition candidate by another company. Equity is not often used in these circumstances, and, like the buyout situation, three-year performance plans paid in cash are the most common form of long-term incentive.

Mix

That leaves mix as the final area to address in these types of non-public companies. Using traditional valuation methods, one would conclude that the executive compensation mix within the buyout and bankruptcy acquired organizations are quite similar to their publicly held counterparts. Indeed, because of the continuing nature of most members of the management team, there is little motivation to make significant changes to the overall mix of the program.

The same cannot be said in the case of the start-up. As pointed out earlier, the mix in the start-up is heavily weighted in favor of the long-term incentive, more specifically, the stock option; but, this conclusion can only be reached if one uses a process for valuation that is different than that used for stock options in publicly held companies. This occurs because valuation models, like Black-Scholes, derive their value from the price of the underlying stock; and, if the underlying stock has a value that is measured in pennies per share, even very large grants of options will result in very small valuations using Black-Scholes. Rather, the conclusion that the mix is heavily weighted toward options is reached only by looking at the expected price of an IPO. Then, regardless of whether the price is $10 or $20, the return to the executive is almost infinite, and the amounts delivered measure in seven, eight, and even nine digits!

Summary

In summary, executive compensation in non-public companies owned by the professional investor can be, in some situations, quite different from their publicly held counterparts; in other situations quite similar. The difference is in the details of the acquisition and the expected exit strategy.

U.S. Subsidiaries of U.S. Parents

This chapter would be incomplete if it were to ignore this last classification. U.S. subsidiaries of U.S. companies appear to be a more straightforward situation than those discussed so far, but many can be much more complex than they would seem initially.

Not to be confused, you will note that most issues involving a U.S. subsidiary that is owned by a U.S.-based private company have already been addressed the preceding sections of this chapter. Therefore, this section will focus on the situation of a U.S. subsidiary, maintained as a private entity, but owned by a publicly held U.S. company.

The situation of a closely aligned subsidiary, whose business operations are completely within the business stream of the parent and are entirely symbiotic with the core business, is not part of this discussion. (This includes situations where the subsidiary status was chosen simply for some financing, legal, or other more transparent reasons; but for those reasons, the subsidiary could have even more easily remained an internal business unit of the parent company.) These businesses would have a compensation program that is reflective (or closely mirrors) that of their parent.

Instead, this discussion specifically centers around the U.S. subsidiary whose business is distinctly differentiated from the core functions of the parent and the subsidiary status that was chosen either because the group was acquired or because the business was different enough that some organizational distance from the parent was deemed strategic. As an example, this might include a financing subsidiary owned by a manufacturing parent or an e-business company owned by a "bricks and mortar" company. Both of these situations would imply the business of the subsidiary is significantly-to-substantially different from the core business of the parent.

In these examples, the human resource needs and compensation markets may be completely different from those with which the parent company regularly works. Specifically, the following topics may become issues over the course of time and will require resolution (arguably, these may start to sound familiar, based on previous issues discussed in this chapter):

- What is the appropriate market for talent? If different from the parent's market, how will this be addressed?
- How will compensation packages fit within the parent's overall compensation structure? Is the pay philosophy the same or different as that of the parent's?
- What are the appropriate incentive vehicles? Are they different from the parent's?
- Will other components of the overall pay package differ from those of the parent company?

It is very common in such a diverse business for the compensation program (specifically salary and bonus) to be reflective of the industry practices specific to the subsidiary (rather than the parent). However, in this type of situation, benefit practices are often split. Many companies will strive to simplify programs and costs by holding to one structure for the entire organization; while others may craft a subsidiary-specific benefit program that is different from that of the parent's, and is responsive to the needs of the subsidiary in the industry in which it operates. (This last approach is NOT the norm, but it does exist). Up to this point in corporate history, long-term incentives have been corporate (not subsidiary) driven mainly because the "vehicle of choice" has been stock options. Relatively few companies have, so far, been so bold as to design a long-term incentive that is specifically reflective of their subsidiary's own industry. This approach may become more prevalent in the future as companies rethink their strategy with respect to options in the face of new options–expensing guidelines and norms.

Market for Talent

At the executive level, the business-specific markets for talent and experience can be vastly different. The experience and skills necessary to run multiple profit centers in a manufacturing environment vary from those needed in a financing subsidiary, an e-business company, or a distribution company. While executive pay levels may be, in some cases or for some jobs, comparable in total, the composition of pay may be entirely different.

In order to successfully find and keep the right people to make the business succeed, it is important to have a pay package that is somewhat "customary" for the industry in question, and, just as critical, to align pay and performance properly for that business in order to drive the desired behaviors and accomplishments. Perhaps, more importantly, in order to build trust and credibility in the working relationship, it is necessary for both sides to understand the parameters of their different pay markets and to work together to find an effective answer for both parties.

Approach to Pay

It would be wrong (naïve) to assume that, based on "typical market practices," the parent will immediately support and target pay packages at what the subsidiary considers to be the "appropriate" percentile level, and that the packages will be comprised of the "necessary" components of pay. Consider a diversified energy company which, during the boom of the e-business start-ups, was persuaded to form an e-business technology subsidiary. The subsidiary approached conversations with the parent presuming the parent would embrace the typical pay approach then present in e-business companies. The issues that arose might appear, from the reader's perspective, to be predictable, but from both the parent and subsidiary's perspectives, they were blindsiding. Let's first look at a sampling of the issues that can arise, and then how to address them. For example:

- **Titling.** Would the CEO of the parent be the COB (and perhaps CEO) of the subsidiary? Would the head of the subsidiary business be the President? The CEO? The COB and CEO?

- **Salary.** Would the assumption of roles in the subsidiary impact salary at all? Would it slide the incumbents upward in the parent's existing salary structure? Would it cause salaries to be reset within the market ranges established by the subsidiary's own industry (which, in this case, would have reduced salaries and the subsidiary argued against this idea)?

- **Short-term incentive opportunities.** Would these remain within the parent's opportunity ranges, or would they, as with most start-up companies, be suspended until revenues and/or profitability was established?

- **Long-term incentive opportunities.** Would the parent be willing to contribute a percentage of their ownership for management's grants? Would the amount shared be on par with e-business practices, or would it stay within the grant norms of the energy industry and/or the parent's practices? The parent, in this case, was shocked to learn of the typical sharing percentages and what this might mean in terms of the potential gain to be realized by the subsidiary executives. Beyond sticker shock, they were concerned with the imbalance this might cause internally with employee-peers who would immediately become "have-nots" unless the e-business successfully translated substantial value to the parent's own stock (not likely).

More issues could be listed, but these examples offer some insight into the perspective and the disparate expectations that can come to the table in the formation of a less closely aligned subsidiary. Education, as with the preceding examples, will go a long way to allowing the parent to make critical decisions that will benefit the subsidiary in appropriate, symbiotic ways. Planning, and diplomatic sensibility, on the part of the subsidiary will prevent them from approaching these conversations in ways that might close the conversation down before it even begins.

Incentive Vehicles

For all the reasons previously discussed in this chapter, it may not make sense to replicate and extend parent company incentive programs down to the subsidiary. This is particularly true if the subsidiary's business is, indeed, substantially different than that of the parent.

- Different business objectives and economic factors should be considered. It may not make sense to extend cash-based incentive schemes to businesses that are using, not generating, cash flow.

- Where the use of cash is appropriate, paying based on parent company-appropriate performance measures and objectives may not drive the desired results from the subsidiary. Due to financing structures, return on equity may make no sense as a measure of performance; absolute levels of EPS may be meaningless. As with the design of any incentive plan, it is important to look for the right measures of success for the business in question. Some tolerance of differences is important in order to maximize the results of the subsidiary's business, and, while focus on subsidiary results is appropriate, overarching business needs or philosophical approaches to pay may still cause the parent to overlay some measure of corporate performance. The key is balance in how these measures mesh together in creating opportunity and outcome.

• Equity may be the right incentive tool, but parent equity programs may not be the right mechanism. Whose stock should be used, parent or subsidiary? Is there a market for the subsidiary's stock? If not, will the parent, in essence, create an artificial market for it? Will use of subsidiary equity be limited to subsidiary executives? What about higher ranking executives within the parent? What about individuals within the parent who may provide supporting services to the subsidiary or may have increased responsibilities due to its creation? Conversely, the parent needs to consider whether use of parent stock will create the right incentive for the subsidiary executives. If parent stock is shared at the subsidiary level, to what degree should it be used, and will it be in conjunction with subsidiary equity grants? What impact will creating a tandem equity plan have on the parent company employees?

• What form of equity makes the most sense? If subsidiary stock is to be used, is it real or phantom? (Recall the previous question regarding the existence of a market to allow executives to realize potential gains on their stock holdings.) Indeed, options are the classic instrument for sharing value created and may be an obvious choice; however, if there is a need for retention, will options do the job? For that matter, will subsidiary stock suffice, or is it time to resort to a more solid, overarching parent company restricted stock grant? This question begins to challenge the degree to which the subsidiary executives will be allowed to completely succeed or fail on the back of the value of their own business. The more the answer becomes "yes," the more emphasis should be placed on subsidiary-specific programs and industry-specific approaches. The more the answer leans toward "no," and the more that parent safety nets are allowed to exist, the solution would argue for less "subsidiary-specific" compensation plans.

A Starting Point

It is not possible to pose and answer all of the possible questions surrounding the decision to/not to design subsidiary-specific compensation plans. Each subsidiary-parent relationship is situation-specific; the reasons why the subsidiary exists, its differences from the parent, and the compensation differences being considered are all fairly unique. Generalization in this regard can only lead to frustration on the part of the individuals charged with reaching these compensation decisions. However, the following comments offer a starting point for companies faced with these types of decisions; a place from which to begin—and to ask or evaluate WHY these "typical" conclusions are not in the best interests of the parent and the subsidiary.

- Salary and short-term incentives (both design and opportunity) should be reflective of the subsidiary's own industry and market for talent in order to prevent these pieces of pay from being non-starters in the "attraction/retention" effort.

- Benefit practices within the parent's and the subsidiary's industries should be compared and considered. The purpose of this analysis should be to determine whether industry-specific benefits provide a substantially better offering than those of the parent, and whether this added value, balanced against its costs, makes this separate program worth having. If the answer is "no," then the parent might choose to communicate and reinforce the value of simplicity in the benefit programs, and of being part of a bigger entity's buying power.

- Long-term incentives should be driven by the anticipated "end-state" of the subsidiary. If it will be a completely synergistic entity with the parent, then long-term incentives should emphasize the overall, corporate good (e.g., be tied to the long-term incentives of the parent). If the entity has very little synergy with the parent and the industries/talents/resources differ greatly between the two, then the case for subsidiary-specific long-term incentives should be considered. Situations that fall in between (somewhat synergistic with the parent, yet not insignificantly different as a business) may argue for answers from both alternatives (e.g., some overall, parent-related element such as options; and some portion tied to long-term business results of the subsidiary, such as a multi-year performance plan).

- Depending on the direction taken regarding benefits, and more substantially, long-term incentives, total compensation amounts may or may not be internally equitable with comparable employees within the parent organization. Industry-specific salaries and short-term incentives may create one difference from the parent's pay structures; however, the addition of subsidiary-specific long-term incentives will create a completely different total compensation target. This will create potential communication and cultural issues within the parent's broader organization, especially if these differences exist only on behalf of one subsidiary. While the parent cannot ignore this fact, it should not become the primary driver for the decisions made regarding pay philosophy and program design for that subsidiary. Approach to pay needs to be a business decision first; implementation hurdles should be considered and conquered once the primary decisions are reached.

Other Elements of Pay

The remaining pieces of pay, notably health and welfare benefits and perquisites, depend upon a question that was teed up in the preceding paragraph. How independent and disconnected from the parent will this subsidiary actually be? If programs are to be highly tailored for the subsidiary, then total compensation should be subject to this tailoring. It is difficult to argue for the highest pay dictated between the two entities' compensation markets: bonuses in a non-bonus paying environment, parent company retention equity, subsidiary options, and parent company benefits and perquisites. Subsidiaries pay packages will, predictably, be smaller than those of the total parent company. Some of the changes potentially involved in setting the subsidiary afloat (if that is even a planned eventuality) may result in large opportunities if the business succeeds, but these may result in risks and discomforts as some elements of security (more reliable bonus plans, reliable equity grants, pension plans, and perquisites) are grand-fathered and/or removed.

Disparate subsidiaries present a double-edged sword for both the subsidiary executives and the parent. Tough, sometimes uncomfortable, decisions must be made regarding how independent the subsidiary will be in its treatment by the parent. Focus must be maintained on exactly why the subsidiary was created, what it is intended to deliver to the parent, and how that can be maximized. Honest answers to these questions will lead to conclusions about pay and, inevitably, to conversations regarding how those pay decisions may impact the greater good of the parent. To some extent, this becomes a circular equation searching for the balancing point of the maximum outcome for both entities.

Summary

Non-public companies are a unique world. They struggle with issues on the executive pay front that are specialized and potentially limiting. In some cases, given the pure nature of privately held status and the complexities of ownership, it is difficult to create compensation packages that are comparable to those within publicly held companies.

Information and education is important for both sides–not only information and education about competitive market practices and pressures, but also information about existing attitudes surrounding executive pay. Paying competitively can mean many different things. Creating "typical market" programs can be obvious or obscured in the minds of the parties involved. Underlying business objectives and other existing entities' best interests will inevitably influence all outcomes.

Perhaps more than any other compensation design situation, non-public companies epitomize the saying that "there are no cookie-cutter solutions." This chapter was created with specific sensitivity for the uniqueness of the situations that give rise to non-public entities. As a result, the approach advocated here, and the information/processes that have been presented, are ones that will allow companies to form a basis and a structure with which to better analyze their specific situation. Through this thoughtful analysis they can hope to reach a truly useful solution that can be successfully implemented in their own organization, and can avoid the pitfalls associated with trying to fit their business and circumstances into either another organization's "best practices" or some broadly and badly defined surrogate for "typical market practice."

Practice aids found on the CD for this chapter:

- Design question checklist for situations involving Non-U.S. Parents/Owners
- Design question checklist for situations involving Family-Owned Companies
- Design question checklist for situations involving Professional Investors
- Design question checklist for situations involving U.S. Subsidiaries of U.S. Parents

E. WEBB BASSICK IV
Chief Executive Officer
Compensation Strategies, Inc.

Webb works with the company's largest clients on total compensation strategy development, technical aspects of executive pay, design and communication of all components of total pay, and competitive measurement of total compensation (including fixed pay, short- and long-term incentives, supplemental executive benefits, and perquisites). Webb also works at the Board of Director level on executive compensation as well as Board compensation issues. Webb has consulted in executive compensation for more than 30 years. Prior to forming Compensation Strategies, he served as the Managing Director and Global Practice Leader for Hay Group's Executive Compensation Practice. Before Hay, he was a senior owner and leader in Hewitt Associates' global executive compensation practice. A frequent speaker to The Conference Board, WorldatWork, and The National Association of Stock Plan Professionals, Webb has also been quoted widely in business periodicals such as *The Wall Street Journal, Business Week, Fortune, Forbes, Newsweek,* and *Time.*

ANNA-MARIA B. TAPLING
Executive Vice President
Compensation Strategies, Inc.

Anna consults with top executives, senior management, and outside directors on all aspects of executive pay, including base salary, short- and long-term incentives, supplemental executive benefits, and perquisites. Anna has extensive knowledge of the technical aspects of executive compensation and assists clients with issues involving securities requirements, tax implications, and accounting practice. She has equally extensive knowledge and experience working with Board of Director compensation. Anna has more than 15 years experience addressing executive compensation issues. Prior to forming Compensation Strategies, she served for six years as a Vice President with Hay Group's Executive Compensation Practice. Before Hay, Anna was a Unit Manager with Hewitt Associates' global executive compensation practice. A frequent speaker to The Conference Board and WorldatWork, Anna has been quoted widely in business periodicals such as *The San Jose Mercury News, Business Week Online,* and *Telefony Magazine.*

Contact Information: Compensation Strategies, Inc., 3000 Lakeside Drive, Suite 115N, Bannockburn, IL 60015, 847.295.0657 or visit www.compstratinc.com

16. Equity Compensation Design in pre-IPO and Growth Companies

Entrepreneurs start companies in all economies, with down economies often seeing the most start-up activity. Designing effective employee compensation plans for these companies is a critically important issue, with equity-based pay receiving the most focus, rather than cash. Equity is the most effective means to align business success and compensation, while conserving precious cash, which can be used to grow the business. This emphasis on equity compensation is a big part of what differentiates growth company compensation design from that of mature companies and will be the focus of this chapter.

Compensation professionals working with growth companies must have a detailed understanding of their unique equity compensation design issues. Though pre-IPO and growth companies may be viewed as "immature" compared to a Fortune 200 company, this does not make designing and administering their equity plans comparatively easier. In fact, plan design and administration in growth companies is often more difficult, due to the number of unique considerations, practices, techniques and metrics that may seem foreign to professionals accustomed to typical mature-company compensation methodologies and reasoning.

The goal of this chapter is to provide the needed background education for pre-IPO and growth company compensation professionals, as well as to provide a new framework for developing option grant guidelines. The chapter is presented in three sections addressing:

1. The types of equity commonly used, why they are used, and their advantages and disadvantages.

2. How private placement financing and market illiquidity cause pre-IPO design and measurement to differ from mature companies. This will include guidance on how to incorporate expected private placement dilution into stock planning models, as well issues related to option pricing and grant timing.

3. A novel approach for developing option grant guidelines in pre-IPO and growth companies using annual option usage as a guide, rather than "traditional" value-based metrics (which the reader will see are subject to distortion from pre-IPO stock prices and post-IPO price volatility). This section is applicable to compensation professionals in public growth companies (e.g., high-tech or biotech), as well as late-stage pre-IPO companies.

Types of Equity

MOST COMMONLY, PRE-IPO companies utilize stock options (both tax-qualified and non-qualified), as well as other full-value stock vehicles like restricted or deferred shares.

Stock Options

Stock options are the most common equity incentive in pre-IPO companies, since they cause no P&L expense at grant under current accounting standards and they are only valuable to the employee in the event that the Company's value increases after grant (as opposed to fully owned shares, which have value as long as the company continues to exist). Even as accounting rules change to require option expensing, pre-IPO option expense will be low as a result of low pre-IPO corporate valuations. Further, the P&L expense from options does not affect cash flow, which is where early investors tend to focus their financial attention. Of course, most pre-IPO and growth companies are not yet as valuable as their investors expect them to eventually be, which represents options significant future "upside." It is this potential for growth that employees bet on when they take pre-IPO positions. The potential for option value increases is also a central rationale for pre-IPO companies to provide reduced cash compensation (relative to similar positions at more mature companies).

Incentive Stock Options (ISOs)

There are 2 types of options: (1) tax-qualified incentive stock options (ISOs), and (2) non-qualified stock options. Of the two, ISOs are more advantageous for employees because they provide an opportunity for future option gains to be taxed at lower capital gains rates (as opposed to ordinary income rates) as long as the employee holds the shares acquired from exercise for at least one year. The incentive to continue holding ISO shares after option exercise is one of the reasons companies provide ISOs. However, providing employees the potential for lower taxes comes at a "price" for the company, which loses a tax deduction on the employees' future option gains. In contrast, non-qualified options result in option gain taxation at higher ordinary income rates upon exercise, but allow the company to recognize a tax deduction for the employee's option gain.

ISOs also have other regulatory requirements, including that their exercise price equals fair market value on the date of grant (see discussion of determining fair market value of a pre-IPO company in section II of this chapter), a $100,000 per-year limit on the value that may vest, and other limits for anyone owning 10% or more of the company's shares. Once option expensing becomes mandatory, the P&L cost of ISOs will not be tax-effected, while the expense associated with non-qualified options will be reduced by the Company's tax rate.

Although ISOs appear to provide advantageous tax rates for employees, companies should be aware that under certain (relatively common) circumstances, employees' option gains will be subject to the Alternative Minimum Tax (AMT). Though a complete discussion of the AMT is outside the scope of this chapter, companies that grant ISOs should be aware that it could effectively cancel most of the tax advantages employees receive from ISOs. More importantly, the AMT is fairly complicated and often overlooked, even by sophisticated employees.

The AMT provides an element of risk for employees who hold ISOs, since AMT tax is due in the year of ISO exercise, regardless of future stock prices. This risk was illustrated in the late 1990's and early 2000's when employees exercised valuable ISO options and then held the underlying shares in order to meet the one-year holding requirement for capital gains taxation. During the one-year holding period, their company's stock price collapsed quickly with the result that their ISO shares were suddenly less valuable than the amount paid to exercise the original ISO option. On top of this, these employees sometimes found, unexpectedly, that they owed AMT taxes for the year of exercise. In the case of companies whose price dropped precipitously, this AMT tax could be higher than the exercised share's market value. The result was that employees could not recoup their exercise funds and had to find additional cash to pay their AMT taxes. Although similar circumstances occurred with non-qualified option exercises, it was less frequent because non-qualified options do not present a similar disincentive to sell shares after option exercise.

Non-qualified stock options (NQSOs)

Non-qualified stock options (NQSOs) are more flexible than ISOs, with no special tax-related requirements. However, NQSOs do not provide tax incentives to hold shares after exercise. As such, employees are more likely to sell their shares immediately after NQSO exercise than they are after ISO exercise. Companies often prefer NQSOs because the tax deduction on employee's exercise gains saves cash that would otherwise have to have been paid to the IRS. Also, though NQSOs are taxable to the employee at exercise, they do not have the associated risk of incurring AMT taxes that accompanies tax qualified ISOs. Most employees pay taxes due upon non-qualified option exercise by selling shares, but companies that want to limit open-market sales may also withhold shares for a portion of the taxes (with-holding more than the minimum statutory rate has negative accounting consequences).

Considerations in Choosing an Option Type

Pre-IPO companies often consider different facts than mature companies when determining which type of option to grant. For example, the fair market value of a pre-IPO company's stock may be quite low, particularly at an early-stage company. Therefore, while many mature companies do not grant ISOs because they are limited to $100,000 per year, low pre-IPO company valuations allow them to provide more ISOs than most mature companies. For example, if the per-share value of a pre-IPO company is $0.25 per-share, it can vest 400,000 at-the-money options in any given year without crossing the $100,000 per year ISO limit (whereas a mature company with a $25 price could only provide a grant that vests 4,000 ISOs per year).

Other Equity

Full-value shares (e.g., restricted stock) are rarely used in pre-IPO companies as a long-term incentive because they are taxable when vested. Therefore, an unrestricted share grant would be immediately taxable as income, like salary. This is a problem with pre-IPO shares, which do not have market liquidity, so it may be impossible to sell shares as a means of raising cash for taxes. It is rare that an employee has cash available (or is willing to risk personal savings) to pay taxes on pre-IPO shares, which may never be valuable (remember that early stage companies may either never IPO or be sold, and are more likely to go out of business than mature companies).

Even restricted shares, which are not taxable during the restriction period, carry some of the same risk, since taxes will eventually be owed when the restrictions lapse. If the restrictions lapse prior to an IPO, the same tax-related liquidity problem exists, since there is no market to sell shares and pay taxes. However, in rare instances some pre-IPO companies grant restricted shares with unusually long restriction periods (e.g., restricted shares which vest 100% only after 5 years), under the assumption that by the time the shares vest, an IPO or capitalization event will have occurred. Of course, the downside of this tax strategy results if the employee terminates prior to the cliff vesting date and forfeits all of his or her shares, even after substantial service.

Deferred share units (DSUs) can be used to delay taxation until pre-IPO shares are liquid. DSUs are not actually shares; rather, they are a "promise to pay" shares in the future. Until the actual shares are provided, deferred units are pegged to the company's stock price in tax-deferred compensation accounts. The deferral account is usually designed to disburse the units as full shares at some point in the future (to preserve the "fixed" accounting treatment common to other equity incentives, units must be paid in shares). This is a different use of deferred share units than is usually seen in mature companies, which often utilize deferred stock to augment retirement accounts.

However, this deferred share structure is rarely used in pre-IPO companies because of complications if employees terminate. Usually, deferred units are disbursed upon termination if they are vested. However, disbursement creates taxable income, which is a problem if the company is not yet public. Some companies pay out account balances in cash or buy back the shares so former employees can pay taxes, but these strategies can create accounting issues if not structured properly and use precious cash in an unproductive manner.

Founder's Shares

Founder's shares are shares owned by the people who started the Company. Often, they were literally the shares created at its inception, but sometimes the term is also used to describe low-priced shares granted to early hires, who are not technically the founders. It is common for the founding employees to have "founder's shares" instead of options, but after the company begins to operate few founders' shares are granted.

Founder's shares do not usually create the tax problems associated with other full-value share types because they are nearly valueless at grant (when their tax basis is calculated). Of course, the shareholder still owes taxes in the value of the vested shares. Many make IRC 83(b) elections to pay tax at grant while the pre-IPO share price is very low. As soon as the per-share value is above a certain level (e.g., $0.25 per-share), further share grants are usually precluded by the taxes employees would owe on illiquid shares, and options become the primary equity vehicle. For those in a position to accumulate them, founder's shares are tax-advantaged because they are eligible for the lower long-term capital gains tax rate when sold. Of course, founding a growth company carries plenty of risk to offset the potentially enormous reward.

Equity Financing

To understand stock options in pre-IPO companies, it is first necessary to understand the effects of equity financing. Adding financing events into a compensation model is one of the primary differences in pre-IPO pay design compared to more mature companies. Even companies that do not expect to raise cash with equity will still find some points in this section that will assist with option plan administration or with making valid market comparisons to other pre-IPO companies.

Private Placement Dilution

It is common for pre-IPO companies to issue new shares to outside investors in "private placements" as a means of raising the cash needed to grow the business. In contrast, mature companies are more likely to raise cash using debt (e.g., bond issues or lines of credit) and their own cash flow for growth.

In a typical private placement (as well as in an IPO or follow-on public financing round for an already-public growth company), the company sells new shares to outsiders (typically venture capital investors, but there are many variations and exceptions). This dilutes the ownership of the original shareholders, including employees with stock options. The example below illustrates the effect of financing-related dilution on a company's value and on an employee's option stake.

Step 1: Company raises $20,000,000 in additional cash by issuing 5,000,000 additional shares to private investors at $4.00 per share.

Company Before Private Placement Financing

A. Common Shares Equivalents Outstanding		25,000,000

The Private Placement Financing

B. Raise $20M at $4.00 per share ($20M ÷ $4.00	+	5,000,000

Company After Private Placement Financing

C. Post-Money Shares Outstanding (A + B)	=	30,000,000

Step 2: A hypothetical senior executive who owned 4% of the company before the financing round finds that ownership is diluted to 3.33% after the new shares are sold.

Executive Before Private Placement Financing

A.	Shares Owned Before Private Placement	1,000,000
B.	Shares Outstanding Before Private Placement	25,000,000
C.	% of Company Owned Before Financing (A ÷ B)	4.00%

Executive After Private Placement Financing

D.	Shares Owned After Private Placement	1,000,000
E.	Shares Outstanding After Private Placement	30,000,000
F.	% of Company Owned After Financing (D ÷ E)	3.33%

The higher a company's market value, the fewer shares it must issue to raise a fixed amount of cash (minimizes dilution), or alternatively, the more cash it can raise for a fixed number of shares (maximizes the efficiency of financing-related dilution). For example, a company with a $2.00 share price would have to issue 1,000,000 new shares to raise $2,000,000. If investors suddenly determined that they were willing to pay $4.00 instead of $2.00 per share, the company could either issue half-as-many shares (i.e., 500,000) to raise the $2,000,000 or it could raise $4,000,000 in cash by issuing the same 1,000,000 shares. It is important that the compensation professional is aware of these dynamics because they directly affect option plan design.

Determining Option Exercise Price

It is most common to grant options with exercise price equal to the fair market value of the stock on the date of grant. In a publicly traded company determining fair market value is a relatively easy exercise. In contrast, pre-IPO companies are not traded, so determining the fair market value of a share is not always obvious. Further complication arises from the tendency of pre-IPO companies to capitalize themselves with more than one class of shares (common and preferred), which must also be included in equity design.

Preferred shares are created to reduce the investment risk of early stage pre-IPO investors. Prior to IPO, a typical start-up is unproven and may never make a profit or meet any other measure of "success," such as providing existing shareholders with an "exit" opportunity (through IPO or company sale). To lessen their risk, pre-IPO investors usually purchase preferred shares, which give them advantages over other common shareholders. Typical preferences may include annual cash dividends, advantaged conversion rights (e.g., each share of preferred converts to 2 common shares at IPO), advanced liquidation rights (i.e., other shareholders are subordinated), additional voting rights, etc. Often, these preferences are structured to disappear at the time of an IPO, with preferred shares converting to common at that time.

While the company usually sells investors preferred shares, it usually issues common stock and common stock options to employees. These are less valuable than the preferred shares issued to investors. For example, while investors buy preferred shares at $4.00 per share, employees may be granted fair market value options on common shares with exercise prices of $1.00 per share. The amount of the discount from the preferred share value depends on the specific preferences added to the preferred.

The differences between employee's common shares and investor's preferred shares are important for compensation design for three reasons: (1) any P&L expense for options will depend on the exercise price, with a lower fair market value price for common shares resulting in a smaller expense on common options; (2) lower exercise prices allow optionholders greater opportunity to benefit from future price increases (e.g., assuming a company is worth $10 per share, a rational employee would prefer to own an already-granted option with exercise price of $1.00 rather than one worth $8.00, since the gain is greater); and (3) the discount serves the interests of both prior investors, who want the market value of the company to go as high as possible after they invest, and also key employees, who initially want a low valuation until IPO/exit (so their option gain is as high as possible).

Professional venture investors are savvy at determining the price they will pay for preferred shares, but since they rarely buy common shares, it is not always so easy to determine the market value of common shares. In practice, the discount applied to common is often estimated internally by the company based on two factors: (1) the number of advantages inherent to the preferred shares, and (2) the amount of time until an exit is expected (e.g., time until IPO).

The more exclusive the preferences provided to the preferred investors are, the greater will be the discount provided to common. For example, if the issued shares are "highly preferenced," then the value of common shares may be 30%-to-50% lower than the preferred share value. Of course, the actual discount will depend on factors individual to every company. Of note, the SEC requires multiple factors to be considered, such as business growth, investment, liquidity, etc. when estimating the common stock value. The SEC's official stance is that it will not accept undocumented "rules of thumb" in estimating the value of common shares.

Still, in practice, if a pre-IPO company knows that an IPO (or other exit) is not going to occur for a long time, it can discount its common value more aggressively, reasoning that many events could occur that result in a failed exit. Here, the following reasoning supports the common stock discount: "The longer the expected time until IPO, the more likely it is that investors will actually utilize the preferences on their preferred shares (for example in a liquidation)." As the company grows more successful, and an IPO becomes more likely, the common share discount from preferred is reduced. For example, a company with $8.00 preferred shares two years away from an IPO could conceivably estimate its common share value at $2.00. Two years later, when an IPO is near, if the preferred price is $20.00, the common stock value may be $16.00.

To avoid mis-pricing common shares (and having to recognize additional P&L expense for "discounted" option grants) consider hiring professionals who are experienced with estimating corporate valuations. Ultimately, the Board is responsible for setting fair market value of common shares, but many Boards utilize the opinion of outside experts.

There is an exhibit on the next page that will help illustrate how most companies modify their estimate of common stock price as they mature towards an IPO.

How Often to Reconsider Option Exercise Price

A publicly traded company can determine the fair value of its stock at any time; a pre-IPO company cannot. This does not release the pre-IPO company from the burden of accurately estimating the fair market value of its common shares. A common question concerns when to restate fair market value of common shares. In general, pre-IPO companies simply reset the fair market value of their common shares when there is good reason to believe that its value has changed.

By definition, a share-based transaction establishes market value. The most prevalent example is private placement financing by outside investors; however, other kinds of share buybacks (e.g., from early investors) or other sorts of development deals could also set a new common share value. During the time between such transactions, pre-IPO companies typically keep their share price constant, with the difference between the common and preferred price, as stated earlier, getting smaller as the company nears its IPO (see next exhibit).

Cheap Stock

If the discount provided to common options is too great, a P&L expense for "cheap stock" may be incurred as the result of a retroactive SEC determination that the common option grants had too great a discount relative to the actual fair market value of the common shares. For most companies (with preferred share financing) this results from discounting the preferred share price too aggressively when estimating the value of its common stock. The charge must be recognized under the current accounting rules because the option exercise price was actually below the fair market value at grant. The greatest risk of a cheap stock charge occurs during the year prior to IPO, since comparison of the IPO price to the price of prior option grants can be clearly made.

To illustrate the cheap stock expense, consider a pre-IPO company that sold preferred shares to its investors at $5.00, while at the same time also granting its employees an aggregate of 2,000,000 common options with a $0.50 exercise price (i.e., a 90% discount from the preferred price). If, one year later, the company registered its securities in anticipation of a public offering at $15.00 per share, the SEC could claim that the 90% discount was too great and did not reflect fair market value at that time. For example, the SEC could rule that the fair market value of a common share was really $3.50. This would mean that the options had an in-the-money gain of $3.00 at grant ($3.50 - $0.50). Under the current APB 25 accounting rules (which may be obsolete shortly), if 2,000,000 options were granted with $3.00 of intrinsic gain, the company must recognize an expense of $6,000,000 ($3.00 x 2,000,000). Once FAS123 option expensing becomes mandatory, there will be a smaller additional expense for the marginal fair value provided by the discounted exercise price. The problem is that pricing the common shares of a private growth company is more art than science and it is difficult to predict how the price will be viewed after-the-fact.

For strategic reasons, many pre-IPO companies do not pay heed to the possibility of a cheap stock P&L charge from employee options. Instead, they choose to discount their common options aggressively, as an attraction and retention tool. Then, if the company succeeds in going public, they "accept" the resulting charge for granting discounted options. This strategy is usually justified using either or both of the following two reasons:

(1) *The cheap stock expense does not affect company cash flow (i.e., it is a*

non-cash P&L expense), which is what most early stage companies are most concerned about. Many about-to-IPO companies have such great losses that the addition of another non-cash charge would likely do little to change investors' perception. This removes the urgency to report profitable earnings (and makes the company less concerned with option-related P&L expense).

(2) *Cheap stock charges are only relevant if the company is successful enough to file for an IPO.* The charge is levied by the SEC, which typically only becomes involved with pre-IPO companies at the time they register their securities for an offering. Therefore, recognition of an option related cheap stock expense is a sign that "success" is near.

But, while the company may not be overly concerned about the potential for a "cheap stock" finding, since ISOs are required to be granted at fair market value, it is possible to accidentally disqualify shares from ISO treatment if they are ruled to have been granted with an exercise price below fair value. This mistake could have significant tax consequences at exercise for employees who were provided the now-disqualified ISO shares.

Setting Option Grant Guidelines

This section identifies the shortcomings of the traditional value-based option valuation models for setting pre-IPO and growth company grant guidelines. It provides two alternative frameworks for determining grant guidelines: (1) a carried-interest ownership approach and (2) a dilution-based method. Please note that the two methods are not mutually exclusive; in fact, they complement each other to provide a full picture of a company's option situation.

Determining the proper number of options to grant is a difficult proposition in most pre-IPO companies. The source of this difficulty often stems from the inability to accurately estimate the value of an option in terms that are meaningful to employees. Mature companies typically estimate the present value of their option grants using option valuation methodologies such as the Black-Scholes formula, the binomial method, or the minimum option value model (also called "growth model"). These models will also be used to determine the cost of options after expensing becomes mandatory. Most pre-IPO companies do not consider this cost to represent the value provided to employees, however, and the non-cash cost will not factor heavily into their business decision-making.

Value-Based Shortcomings

All of these option valuation models suffer from various shortcomings, which are amplified in pre-IPO companies. The Black-Scholes and binomial models both depend on using a stock price's past volatility to predict the future. Also, both models were really created to value fully tradeable options, with short lives (e.g., 6 months), that are not subject to forfeiture. Yet, many companies use the models to value employee options that cannot be sold and have 10-year lives. Further, the Black-Scholes model and minimum value model do not allow for the possibility of early exercise prior to the expiration of the term (the binomial model does account for this possibility).

Yet, the biggest problem with all three models for pre-IPO and volatile growth companies is their dependence on the company's stock price to determine the present value of an option grant. This is problematic in pre-IPO companies where common stock prices are often low and are usually estimated by discounting the value of preferred shares. High growth companies that are public find price-based option valuation methodologies are distorted by their stock's volatility.

How Stock Price Affects the Present Value of an Option

No matter which of the traditional valuation models are used (Black-Scholes, binomial, or growth), the output can be stated as a present value modifier, which is multiplied by the stock price (exercise price) to determine the fair market value of an option. For example, if a company has a present value modifier of 50% and has a share price of $10 the present value of an at-the-money option grant would be 50% x $10 = $5.

This relationship is clearly linear. That is, if the price of the company above doubled (to $20), its option present value would be roughly 50% x $20 = $10. Or, conversely, if the price of the stock fell by half to $5, the present value of an option would be roughly 50% x $5 = $2.50. Because growth companies tend to have highly uncertain stock prices, their option values are more likely to fluctuate as just described. If present value models were used to set grant guidelines it would result in uneven grant amounts depending on the timing of the grant.

To further illustrate the inherent shortcomings of using price-based option valuation models in these situations, consider which option is more valuable to an employee: the option with a high exercise price or the one with a low price? Clearly, employees would prefer the option with a low price because it provides more potential upside opportunity. Yet, the option valuation models would indicate that the high-priced option is more valuable. This is contrary to logic, and to one of the fundamental allures of working at a pre-IPO company, which is the opportunity to get options priced while the stock price is very low.

In practice, there is an emerging body of thought that believes the use of option "values" for setting grant guidelines creates illogical results in pre-IPO companies and public growth companies (e.g., some high-tech companies). This is because compensation practitioners are trained to look up the option "value" for a given position in a pay survey (or using available SEC proxy data) and then grant enough options to equal the desired value. For example, if a company was trying to target a senior executive's option grant at the median, it would determine the median value for the executive's position using a pay survey. If the survey indicated that the median option value was $500,000, and the company had a stock price of $10 and a 50% present value modifier (i.e., the present value of each option is 50% x $10 = $5), then it would grant 100,000 options with $5 present value to provide the median option value of $500,000.

Imagine that the stock price of the company in this example increased to $20 per share the next year. Again, the company wants to provide the executive with a median option value of $500,000. The present value method would say that each option is now worth $10 per share (50% x $20). Therefore, to provide this executive with $500,000 in option value, the company would grant 50,000 options (50,000 x $10 present value per option). The model's failure becomes apparent when the grant is viewed from the executive's perspective. The executive would ask, "Why did my option grant get cut in half from last year after the shareholders benefited from the company doubling its share value?" Further, if asked, the executive would probably tell you that his or her preference is to get options with a lower exercise price ("they are more likely to become valuable") than the higher exercise price options. Here, the present value approach provided the executive fewer options at the same time that the likelihood of future stock price increases went down.

In other words, using price-based models, option grant amounts do not vary logically with company price increases, providing the greatest number of shares when executives feel that they are most valuable and the least when they are least valued by recipients. The illogical relationship is illustrated as follows:

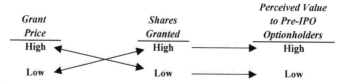

When the share price drops, this backwards present-value relationship enriches executives at the price of shareholders. Using the earlier example (i.e., $500,000 median pay value for the executive and present value modifier of 50%), if the company's price were to fall in half the present value of an option would be 50% x $5.00 = $2.50. To provide $500,000 in options, the company would grant 200,000 options, which is double what it granted the year earlier. Now, the shareholder perspective illustrates the disconnect, as they ask: "why are we rewarding the executive with a larger grant after our loss of value? Are we paying for performance effectively?" Assuming all employees were granted options at the median, a 50% price decline would cause the company to double its annual option usage from the previous year, thereby diluting shareholders' ownership interest at twice the rate. These examples illustrate the reason that value-based option grant programs do not work well in companies with volatile stock prices.

Value-Based Method Inappropriate Prior to IPO

The option present value method may not be appropriate for public growth companies, but it is even less so for pre-IPO companies, where the true fair market value of the stock is estimated and often quite low. Further, pre-IPO companies do not have historical volatility information, so volatility must be assumed to use the Black-Scholes model. Even after assuming enough data to calculate a hypothetical present value modifier (say 50% in this example), is it really accurate to say that the present value of a pre-IPO option with exercise price of $0.50 is $0.25? Would one-quarter of a dollar realistically estimate the probable risk-adjusted gain opportunity for an option that will likely either have an enormous gain (e.g., if the company is successful and has an IPO) or go out of business (gain of zero)? Even if the present value estimate were accurate, there is no comparative pre-IPO pay data, since the price of common shares at other pre-IPO companies are probably only hypothetical estimations of value based on the price of their preferred shares. And, it would be inappropriate to tie pre-IPO option values to public company values because public companies usually have higher valuations by virtue of their market liquidity. Continuing the example from the previous section, a pre-IPO company with option value of $0.25 must provide too many options to provide a given position a median grant value of $500,000 to make it feasible.

Carried-Interest Ownership Comparisons are Better

To avoid the present value model shortcomings, pre-IPO companies should focus on the ownership stake of employees. The most common measure of ownership is carried-interest ownership, which is the sum of fully owned shares and options (i.e., options + owned shares = carried interest). This ownership is usually expressed as a percentage of common shares (or common share equivalents, after allowing for preferred shares to convert to common). For example, if an executive in a company with 10 million common share equivalents held 50,000 options and owned 50,000 shares, total carried interest would be 1% of the company (100,000 shares ÷ 10 million shares outstanding). As a practical matter, this measure shows the amount of the company's future growth that will be shared with the executive.

Since carried-interest ownership is not subject to price fluctuations or to future assumptions about volatility or interest rates, it provides the most meaningful comparison of pre-IPO option grant amounts to the market. For example, it is meaningful to compare a position with 0.5% ownership to a median level of 0.6%, but not to compare two pre-IPO estimates of option value.

Measures of carried-interest are relatively easy for compensation practitioners to obtain. Ownership stake data for pre-IPO companies is available from some compensation survey sources. In addition, public data, such as prospectuses (the final statement a company files before IPO) and proxies from recent IPO companies can be used to estimate the market carried interest value. Carried-interest need not be complicated to compare.

The following hypothetical competitive analysis for a company with 15 million common share equivalents outstanding illustrates how to use carried-interest ownership data as a market comparison tool:

	a + b = c			$d = c ÷ 15m\ shrs$	e Hypothetical Median Carried-	$f = e - d$	$f\ x\ 15m\ shrs$
	Pre-IPO Co. Current Carried-Interest Ownership					Competitive Shortfall	
Position	Shares +	Options =	Total	as % of Shrs	Interest	% Shrs. Out.	Co. Shares
CEO (non-founder)	100,000 +	400,000 =	500,000	3.3%	3.5%	0.2%	23,500
COO	0	250,000	250,000	1.7%	2.0%	0.3%	50,000
CFO	10,000	100,000	110,000	0.7%	0.8%	0.1%	15,400
General Counsel	12,500	110,000	122,500	0.8%	0.9%	0.0%	6,700
Hd. of Reserach	10,000	85,000	95,000	0.6%	0.9%	0.3%	37,600
Etc.							

Shares Oustanding: 15,000,000

Ownership info. can be found in prospectuses of recent IPO companies for top-5 named executive officers

Another advantage of using carried-interest to determine pre-IPO equity is that investors accept its results. From an investor's point of view, employee option grants simply take away from the eventual value of their ownership.

The rationale for providing options is that giving employees an interest in a successful outcome makes the odds of the outcome much more likely. However, most professional investors keep a close watch on how much they have "given away" to employees. Though an experienced investor in mature companies may care about the present value of an executive's grant (hence the FAS 123 accounting rules for expensing options), a venture- or growth-company investor is unlikely to ask about the present value of the CEO's grant.

Designing an Option Grant Program Using Carried-Interest

The example provided in the previous section assumed that the competitive carried-interest was a valid point of comparison. This is not always the case in pre-IPO companies, however, because financing increases the number of shares outstanding. Some pre-IPO companies prefer to lead the market with the expectation that ownership will be diluted from financing (e.g., executive carried-interest is 3% with the expectation that private placement financing will reduce it to 1% over time).

As a result, it is advisable to model the company's expected equity needs using its business plan. Recognize that such a model is subject to change as the business plan develops and as the business environment changes. Following a grant plan will assist with equity administration, hiring, and performance management. It will also assist with structuring a meaningful discussion about compensation with the company's investors (e.g., the board or board compensation committee).

To design a grant program you need the following company data: (1) the current number of shares outstanding, (2) an assumption concerning future financing needs (the number of future private placements and their expected value), (3) an employee census, (4) an estimate of the number of employees that the company expects to hire in the near term. Using this data, designing an option strategy can be accomplished in six steps, as follows:

1. **Calculate the number of shares that will be outstanding at IPO or exit.** This depends on the share dilution calculation, which was already explained in the "Equity Financing Section." Determine how many additional shares will be issued for financing (use the number of expected financing events and the expected price per share in each round). Add the additional expected shares to the current number of shares outstanding to calculate the number of shares that are expected at IPO.

2. **Use competitive data to determine desired ownership levels.** Since carried-interest adjusts shares to reflect estimates at IPO (see step 1),

apples-to-apples comparisons with public companies allow compensation practitioners to use readily available public company data. Most companies target their positions at a given carried-interest market level for individual employees and use this to estimate how much ownership will be shared across the entire organization. This "roll-up" of all employee ownership is dilution, which is what pre-IPO and public company investors ultimately care about (see step 4).

3. **Establish how many shares must be provided for each position to attain its desired ownership level.** For example, if you know that the median ownership level is 1%, simply figure out how many shares will represent that amount at IPO (competitive carried interest x expected shares outstanding = number of shares that must be granted). For administration purposes, targeted ownership levels are usually set up as a range with low, mid and high. This allows adjustment for considerations such as the actual employee's experience, tenure, performance, cash compensation level, etc. A typical range for actual grant guidelines may allow for + or – 50% of each position's final guideline ownership.

4. **Estimate expected aggregate overall dilution by adding each position's targeted carried-interest to the competitive overall dilution levels of other companies.** Adjust your company's individual grant guidelines, as needed, to manage overall dilution to the target. (Note: competitive dilution data is available from 10-k disclosures).

5. **Adjust individual grants so that the total dilution is in a reasonable range.** For example, if the estimated aggregate usage is 25% of fully diluted shares outstanding when all employees are provided target ownership, but your company's shareholders are only willing to share 20% of the company using options, then individual grant levels would have to be adjusted accordingly.

6. **Develop a strategy for distributing the shares.** Typically, larger hiring inducement grants are followed by regular (e.g., annual) refresher grants of a smaller size. However, there are many different ways to break-up delivery of shares to build ownership to target levels. For example, some companies may "front-load" 50% of the target grants and reserve the remaining 50% for refresher grants. Then they would adjust refresher grants for each employee's performance and for an evolving business plan. Others may provide the entire amount at hire as an attractive way to provide employees with a low exercise price.

Design the Option Grant Program Using Carried-Interest (Use 6 Steps Above)

The following table illustrates the output of an equity strategy created using competitive carried-interest ownership. The hypothetical company in the example expects to have 75 employees by IPO:

Level	Estimate of Empls. w/in 2 Yrs	Competitive Carried-Interest [1]			Estimated Aggreggate Equity Usage		
		Low	Mid	High	Min	Mid	High
CEO (Non Founder)	1	1.75%	3.50%	5.25%	1.75%	3.50%	5.25%
COO (Non Founder)	1	1.00%	2.00%	3.00%	1.00%	2.00%	3.00%
Top Mgt (EVP/SVP)	3	0.50%	1.00%	1.50%	1.50%	3.00%	4.50%
Other VPs	5	0.25%	0.50%	0.75%	1.25%	2.50%	3.75%
Directors	10	0.13%	0.25%	0.38%	1.25%	2.50%	3.75%
Managers	15	0.08%	0.15%	0.23%	1.13%	2.25%	3.38%
Other Professionals	25	0.04%	0.08%	0.12%	1.00%	2.00%	3.00%
Admin	15	0.00%	0.005%	0.01%	0.00%	0.08%	0.11%
Total:	**75**				**Total: 8.88%**	**17.83%**	**26.74%**

The "number" investors care about is the total usage.

Individual executives would be positioned in range based on factors such as experience, performance, and cash compensation levels.

If the company estimated that it should have 25 million shares outstanding after IPO (based on its financing assumptions), it could convert its carried-interest guidelines (see previous table) into a specific number of shares for each level.

Level	Estimate of Empls. w/in 2 Yrs	Competitive Carried-Interest [1]			Estmated Number of Options Necessary Assuming 25m shares at IPO		
		Low	Mid	High	Min	Mid	High
CEO (Non Founder)	1	1.75%	3.50%	5.25%	440,000	880,000	1,310,000
COO (Non Founder)	1	1.00%	2.00%	3.00%	250,000	500,000	750,000
Top Mgt (EVP/SVP)	3	0.50%	1.00%	1.50%	125,000	250,000	375,000
Other VPs	5	0.25%	0.50%	0.75%	63,000	125,000	188,000
Directors	10	0.13%	0.25%	0.38%	31,000	63,000	94,000
Managers	15	0.08%	0.15%	0.23%	19,000	38,000	56,000
Other Professionals	25	0.04%	0.08%	0.12%	10,000	20,000	30,000
Admin	15	0.00%	0.005%	0.01%	0	1,000	2,000
Total:	**75**						

[1] Hypothetical. Data should not be used.

Individual executives would be positioned in range based on factors such as experience, performance, and cash compensation levels.

Grant Strategy

The previous tables provide an estimate of an appropriate amount of equity at IPO; they do not, however, provide insight into how to grant the desired equity. This is where having a grant strategy becomes important. A grant strategy should fit a company's overall business strategy and essentially provides a blueprint for how the Company intends to provide options to participants. Considerations include the timing of their grants, their corresponding size, vesting, etc. The grant strategy should allow for considerations such as the intended competitive positioning of option ownership (e.g., above or below median), how much of this stake will be provided at hire, and how often the company expects to provide refresher grants. Typically, it would also account for individual performance and cash compensation levels. The example below shows a hypothetical grant plan that provides 50% of options at hire and then 2 additional refresher grants prior to IPO.

A grant plan like the one above can assist a rapidly growing organization with hiring new employees by providing HR with an easy-to-access guide for making employment offers, while at the same time communicating future pay-for-performance expectations to employees. Since the schedule comes from competitive data and "rolls-up" into a known aggregate dilution level, the company knows that following its guidelines will not result in uncompetitive grants or excessive dilution levels.

Option Grants in Late-Stage pre-IPO & Public Companies

As a pre-IPO company matures towards IPO, it usually is appropriate to start making direct comparisons to small-cap public companies. Typically, this means managing the option grant program like a public company, so that grants are competitive and dilution is kept reasonable. At this later stage, option grant amounts become similar to public companies and the increased likelihood of public market liquidity reduces option risk.

Level	*Hypothetical Hiring Grant Guideline*			*Hypothetical Refresher Grant Guidelines Assuming 2 Refresher Grants Before IPO*		
	Min	*Mid*	*High*	*Min*	*Mid*	*High*
CEO (Non Founder)	220,000	440,000	655,000	110,000	220,000	327,500
COO (Non Founder)	125,000	250,000	375,000	62,500	125,000	187,500
Top Mgt (EVP/SVP)	62,500	125,000	187,500	31,250	62,500	93,750
Other VPs	31,500	62,500	94,000	15,750	31,250	47,000
Directors	15,500	31,500	47,000	7,750	15,750	23,500
Managers	9,500	19,000	28,000	4,750	9,500	14,000
Other Professionals	5,000	10,000	15,000	2,500	5,000	7,500
Admin	0	500	1,000	0	250	500

Most public companies struggle with how to set appropriate grant guidelines. Many use an option present value methodology as previously described, but this subjects them to the same illogical results already illustrated. The solution for many has been to design annual grant guidelines that target option usage to a desired level (usually a competitive level) and "work backwards" to allocate the annual options to employees appropriately.

Dilution-Based Grant Guidelines

Dilution-based grant guidelines allow growth companies to design fully competitive annual option grants without regard to their stock price. The dilution-based method is a "top-down" approach, which sets aside an annual option share pool based on a reasonable or competitive annual share usage rate. This pool is then allocated to individual employees using competitive data on annual option allocations. The dilution-based method does not consider stock price, preferring to focus on the use of company equity rather than the value of employees' options.

The following statement best illustrates the dilution-based guideline concept: "A median allocation of a median-sized annual option pool provides a given position with a median-sized annual grant."

Besides its simplicity, this methodology is also useful because readily available public company data can be used to (1) set an appropriate company-wide option pool using option usage rates ("run rates") and (2) to figure out how to distribute the pool.

The following example illustrates how a company might use this information. Please note that the percentages are not reflective of actual competitive data:

A company with 15,000,000 shares outstanding has determined that an appropriate annual option grant rate would be 4% for all employees and new hires (ideally this determination would be made through competitive analysis and through discussions with the company's board). Once the 4% target usage rate is established, this company would set aside an annual option pool of 600,000 options for all grants during the year (4% x 15 million shares outstanding), and then develop company-wide grant guidelines using competitive allocation data. So, if competitive allocation analysis shows that a competitive annual grant to the CEO is 5% of a company's annual option pool, then a competitive annual CEO grant would be 5% x 600,000 = 30,000 options. This process could be repeated for every position and/or level through the organization, with the sum of all the projected grants totaled to see whether individual grant amounts exceed the company's internal 4% run-rate target. If so, individual grant amounts could be adjusted.

The methodology is relatively easy to employ and is easy to communicate, as it does not depend on complex or arcane "black-box" equations. Also, investors tend to embrace the concept because the grant guidelines answer their primary question: "how much of the equity are we giving away?"

Mechanics for Setting Dilution-Based Grant Guidelines

Assuming the company already has a peer group of public comparison companies, compensation practitioners should take the following steps when using the dilution-based grant guidelines methodology (illustrated first with a checklist and supporting diagram with additional detail provided in the text):

Steps for Setting Dilution Based Option Guidelines

1. Target a desired annual option usage rate (analyze peer company SEC disclosure data or base on internal considerations), and set aside an appropriate share pool for Company-wide grants

2. Determine a competitive allocation for executives (use proxy disclosure data)

3. Determine a competitive allocation for other employees (use survey data measured as a % of the CEO's grant)

4. Calculate total annual share usage, by level

5. Add in expected hiring grants (data available in surveys as multiple of annual grant) & outside directors grants

6. Check resulting run rate for the whole company and compare to the target (step 1)

7. Make proportionate adjustments to each level until overall usage is at the target level

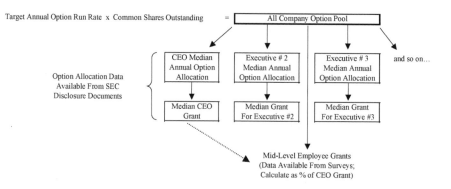

1. **Determine a Target Level of Option Usage and Set Aside a Corresponding Number of Shares for Company-wide Grants:** Most companies target a competitive usage rate, but internal concerns are also worth considering, such as if significant hiring is expected (which might justify usage above-competitive levels for a year-or-so). Competitive analysis of similar companies can be completed using information

available in the stock option disclosure of public company 10-Ks and the prospectuses of recent IPO companies.

Also, since the goal of this analysis is to determine the amount of annual option usage exhibited by similar companies, many practitioners average three years' worth of data in order to smooth out inconsistent year-to-year grant practices.

Regression analysis (run rate versus market cap) can also be used to size-adjust the competitive usage data. This is not necessary if all peer companies are fairly similar in market capitalization, but it can be helpful if there is a wide range of size differences in the sample data. In general, option usage has an inverse relationship with market cap, so estimating a median market cap by plotting a best-fit regression line will usually result in a higher regression-estimated median usage rate for a small cap company than for a large cap company.

The following exhibit provides a hypothetical example of a competitive option usage analysis. Here, the median annual option usage is 5.0% of common shares:

Peers	3-Year Average Option Grants	÷	3-Year Average Common Shrs. Outstanding	=	3-Year Avg. Annual Option Usage
Company A	2,500,000	÷	45,000,000	=	5.56%
Company B	1,500,000		30,000,000		5.00%
Company C	360,500		8,500,000		4.24%
Company D	1,250,000		19,500,000		6.41%
Company E	3,250,000		66,500,000		4.89%
Company F	9,000,000		84,000,500		10.71%
Company G	900,000		18,000,000		5.00%
Company H	1,200,000		27,000,000		4.44%
Company I	3,650,000		115,000,000		3.17%
Company J	900,000		14,500,000		6.21%
Company K	850,000		19,500,000		4.36%
Company L	3,500,000		96,500,000		3.63%
Company M	1,200,000		15,000,000		8.00%
Company N	2,875,000		72,500,000		3.97%
Company O	1,425,000		28,500,000		5.00%
Company P	750,000		18,000,000		4.17%
Company Q	3,600,000		43,000,000		8.37%
75th Percentile					*6.21%*
Median					*5.00%*
25th Percentile					*4.24%*

To set aside a median-sized pool for company-wide grants, simply multiply the 5% peer median above by your company's total shares outstanding to calculate the annual pool size.

2. **Determine How to Allocate the Desired Annual Option Pool for Executive Positions, Followed by Lower-Level Positions:** First, competitive senior executive allocation data are available in the annual grant table provided in public company proxy disclosures. To calculate competitive allocations, divide the annual grant provided by each comparison executive by the total shares granted during the year. For example if a peer CEO was provided 100,000 options in a peer company that granted 1,000,000 options, the CEO's allocation would be 10% of the overall option pool in that year. If enough samples are taken, it develops into a custom survey. Again, it is best to research three years' worth of grant data to average irregular annual grant patterns. It is also good practice to "annualize" or eliminate front-loaded hiring inducement grants, since they do not reflect the market for a typical annual grant amount. A competitive analysis of executive option allocations once completed may look as follows:

| | 3-Year Average Option Allocation (% of Co.-Wide Annual Option Grants) | | | | |
Peers	*CEO*	*COO*	*CFO*	*Executive #4*	*Executive #5*
Company A	9.74%	N/A	4.09%	1.59%	1.27%
Company B	11.23%	8.20%	2.81%	2.19%	1.75%
Company C	14.12%	10.30%	8.89%	5.90%	4.72%
Company D	6.23%	3.68%	2.27%	2.93%	2.35%
Company E	4.35%	N/A	1.83%	3.21%	2.57%
Company F	12.32%	7.27%	3.08%	6.57%	5.26%
Company G	7.42%	4.82%	1.86%	1.52%	1.22%
Company H	9.30%	5.49%	5.86%	3.67%	2.94%
Company I	4.01%	2.37%	1.46%	1.00%	0.80%
Company J	2.13%	1.55%	1.55%	3.49%	2.79%
Company K	11.71%	6.91%	4.92%	2.00%	1.60%
Company L	7.35%	4.34%	3.09%	1.69%	1.36%
Company M	10.30%	6.08%	6.49%	1.19%	0.95%
Company N	8.16%	5.30%	3.43%	1.38%	1.10%
Company O	5.76%	N/A	2.98%	3.18%	2.54%
Company P	3.65%	2.15%	2.30%	3.24%	2.59%
Company Q	9.29%	6.04%	3.90%	2.29%	1.83%
75th Percentile	10.30%	6.08%	4.09%	3.24%	2.59%
Median	8.16%	4.82%	3.08%	2.29%	1.83%
25th Percentile	5.76%	2.15%	2.27%	1.59%	1.27%

To determine competitive annual option grant amounts, the executive allocation analysis should be applied to the company-wide share pool determined in step 1. The next exhibit illustrates a median grant calculation continuing to assume a hypothetical company with 25,000,000 outstanding shares:

Median Annual Share Usage	x	Company Common Shrs. Outst'g.	=	Co.-Wide Annual Option Pool
5.00%	x	25,000,000	=	1,250,000

Title	Median Option Allocation	x	All Employee Share Pool		Median Annual Option Grant
Chairman & CEO	8.16%	x	1,250,000	=	102,000
COO	4.82%	x	1,250,000	=	62,000
CFO	3.08%	x	1,250,000	=	40,000
General Counsel	2.29%	x	1,250,000	=	30,000
CTO	1.83%	x	1,250,000	=	22,000
			Total Executives:		**256,000**

3. **Determine Ongoing Allocation for Other Employees:** Proxy disclosure data only provides information for the top-5 officer positions (because SEC rules only require disclosure for the CEO and the four other most highly compensated officers). Below that level, it is possible to utilize survey data to determine lower-level option grant guidelines. However, most surveys report option data using a present value approach. To convert present value data into option pool allocation data, simply "tier" the lower level positions as a percent of the CEOs value. For example, if a survey shows that a CEO is provided a median annual option value of $1,500,000 and a Director of Marketing is provided a $100,000 value, then one can surmise that the Director of Marketing is provided about 6.67% of the CEO's grant ($100,000 ÷ $1,500,000). The example exhibit indicated that that a median CEO annual option grant is 102,000 options. Based on this we can use the relationship of option values found in the survey data to calculate that a median annual grant for a Director of Marketing grant would be 6.67% of the CEO grant, which is about 6,800 annual options (6.67% x 102,000).

4. **Calculate New-Hire Grant Levels:** The dilution-based methodology for determining competitive option grants depends on the idea that company-wide option grants should target a specific run-rate. Therefore, it is

necessary to consider how many options are needed for hiring new employees. Hiring grants usually are larger than ongoing grants because they contain a hiring inducement. One good method for calculating competitive hiring grant levels is to use survey data to measure hiring grants as a multiple of annual grants. This multiple can be applied to the annual grant guidelines developed in step 3. For example, if survey data shows that median annual option grant value for a given position is $10,000 and its hiring grant value is $20,000, then a competitive hiring grant is a 2x multiple of its annual grant. We calculate hiring grants as a multiple of ongoing grants because the guidelines developed in steps 1–3 are based on annual grant levels.

5. **Determine Total Share Usage if All Positions at the Company Receive Competitive Guideline Ongoing and/or Hiring Grants:** This requires a current census of employees as well as a set of hiring expectations for the upcoming year. Multiply the competitive annual grant amounts by the number of incumbents at each level (include outside director grants) to determine the number of shares needed for competitive ongoing employee grants. Similarly, multiply the hiring guidelines by the expected number of new hires to determine how many aggregate shares must be set aside for hire grants. Add the aggregate ongoing grants to the expected new hire grants to see how great overall company usage would be using the grant guidelines. If overall usage is greater than the run-rate targeted by the company, it may be necessary to make adjustments. Grant guideline adjustments should reflect the competitive situation of the company and may be made proportionally throughout the organization (e.g., all guidelines adjusted –20%), or may reduce some levels more than others depending on the importance of their function within the organization (e.g., lower-level guidelines adjusted –35%, while senior positions are not adjusted).

The following exhibit provides an illustration for the final output of the dilution-based grant guideline steps listed above. It shows how to project ongoing usage, how to calculate hiring grants as a multiple of ongoing grants, how to project hiring grant usage and finally how it all adds up to the targeted usage rate of 5% of shares.

Shortcomings of the Dilution-Based Method

We believe that the dilution-based method for setting option grant guidelines is best for public growth companies and late-stage pre-IPO companies

(a) Position	(a) No. Empls.	(b) Median Annual Option Grant	(a)×(b)=(c) Ongoing Projected Ongoing Option Grants	(d) Projected New Hires	(e) Median Hire Grant as Multiple Annual Grant	(e)×(b)=(f) Median Hiring Option Grant	(f)×(d)=(g) Projected Total New Hire Grants	(c)+(g) Total Projected Option Grants (Ongoing + Hiring)
CEO	1	102,000	102,000	0	4.5	460,000	0	102,000
COO	1	62,000	62,000	0	3.2	200,000	0	62,000
CFO	1	40,000	40,000	0	3.2	130,000	0	40,000
General Counsel	1	30,000	30,000	0	3.2	95,000	0	30,000
CTO	1	22,000	22,000	0	3.2	70,000	0	22,000
Other VPs	5	20,000	100,000	2	2.8x	56,000	112,000	212,000
Directors	15	12,500	187,500	7	2.5x	31,500	220,500	408,000
Managers	25	6,500	162,500	11	2.0x	13,000	143,000	305,500
Professionals	15	2,500	37,500	11	1.5x	4,000	44,000	81,500
Admin & Staff	19	500	9,500	10	1.0x	500	5,000	14,500
Outside Directors	5	20,000	100,000	1	3.0x	60,000	60,000	160,000
Total:	**89**		**853,000**	**42**			**584,500**	**1,437,500**

Shares Outstanding: 25,000,000

Less Expected Forfeitures: (187,500)
Net Option Grants: 1,250,000
Net Grants a % Shrs Outstanding: *5.0%*

because it is not subject to distortion from volatile or estimated stock prices. However, it is not appropriate to use in all situations and does require the compensation professional to view pay levels a little differently than is traditional.

First, this methodology is designed to determine option grants only; it is subject to distortion if the competitive data makes significant use of full-value grants, such as restricted stock or performance shares. This is because full-value incentives are more valuable than options, but are measured in the methodology as being the same. For example, a competitive run-rate of 2% of shares outstanding, using only options, is a lot less valuable than the same 2% if only full-value shares are used.

Second, it is not possible to calculate a "total compensation" value, since the entire purpose of the methodology is to measure options without giving consideration to their "present value." Some organizations are accustomed to measuring "total pay" consisting of base salary, bonuses and the present value of options. Here, it is possible to measure only total annual cash compensation and discreet option grant levels. They do not combine to form a total compensation value. However, it is still possible to estimate an organization's total compensation level. For example, a company that provides median total cash compensation and median option grants is probably pretty close to median "total compensation." Or, a company providing total cash compensation at the 75th percentile and option grants at the 75th percentile is probably approaching the 90th percentile in total compensation, since percentiles do not usually "add" evenly except at the median.

Accompanying materials to be found on the CD for this chapter:

• Design Checklist for Developing a pre-IPO Equity Program

MICHAEL REZNICK
Consultant
Frederic W. Cook & Co.

Michael Reznick is a consultant in the Los Angeles Office of Frederic W. Cook & Co. He has experience designing total compensation strategies, including short- and long-term incentive plans, as well guidelines for initial public offering and, M&A activity. He has consulted for a wide variety of industries, including high technology, biotechnology and pharmaceuticals, manufacturing, oil & gas, healthcare, and professional/financial services. Michael has also provided assistance to companies in many business phases, from early stage start-ups and IPO/spin-offs to mid-level growth companies and mature Fortune 200 clients.

17. Executive Compensation Issues in Spin-Offs, Divestitures and IPOs

This final chapter focuses on another important special topic in executive compensation; anticipating and addressing the executive compensation issues that arise when a company is either spun-off, divested, or goes public.

The authors begin with important background explaining some of the intricacies of the different kinds of corporate restructurings and also briefly examining the accounting, tax and securities law issues that are relevant in such transactions.

The core of the chapter is devoted to a discussion of the variety of compensation issues, and implications, that arise as a result of these organizational changes. Because the effects of these changes are so far-reaching, the authors make a clear case for the need for a fundamental and systematic reexamination of just about everything; from total rewards philosophy, to pay levels and mix, to plan design, and to a number of special one-time issues.

There is considerable attention paid to both severance plans and retention incentives, as both can become very important in a major corporate restructuring. The authors also discuss the variety of issues surrounding the treatment of outstanding equity, and how to think about initial-year equity grants in a new entity. Divestiture incentives are also discussed in regard to situations where it is in the parent company's best interest to make certain that executives' interests remain clearly aligned with the goal of achieving a timely and successful divestiture.

This chapter is important for all compensation professionals as it highlights not only the key issues that need to be anticipated and addressed at the time of a corporate restructuring, but also plan design and philosophical issues that should be set well in advance of such a change. –Editors

Overview

D ESPITE THEIR GREAT FINANCIAL and strategic significance, the human resources issues associated with a corporate restructuring are frequently overlooked (or paid very little attention) by those responsible for structuring the transaction. In fact, the human resources costs are often viewed as "inconsequential" and play only a minor role in analyzing the deal economics. Because of this, human resource professionals in the organization must get involved in any anticipated restructuring transaction as early in the process as possible. This will allow human resource leaders to understand the transaction, how it is to be structured, and the intended outcomes. Early involvement also will help to ensure that adequate focus and attention is given to the very important employee issues surrounding such a transaction.

Corporate capital structure changes are an important and significant part of a company's business evolution. Whether it is an IPO, a spin-off, or a divestiture, and regardless of stock market conditions, some form of restructuring is sure to be in vogue. Restructuring can create and/or unlock value, or act to return a company to its core business. Thus, periodic updating of corporate strategy can be counted on to cause capital structure changes to continue to occur.

At the top of the restructuring food chain are the key executives of the respective entity. And it should be recognized that these executives can find themselves with situations of potentially opposing interests in these transactions–that is, they must act in the best interests of shareholders to maximize value, while simultaneously protecting their own personal interests, families, and fortunes. If this potential misalignment of executive interests is not prevented (or corrected early) in the restructuring process and maintained throughout, the success of the transaction will be in imme-diate jeopardy. Success of the transaction is at the mercy of your executives.

Appropriate incentive design, pay clarity, and severance protection is essential to allow your executives to focus on the business goals and strategies, and not on their own self-interests. Note, compliance with tax, accounting, and securities laws, while maintaining an internally and externally competitive posture, can complicate achievement of business goals and vision. Further, replacement of human resources shared services (such as payroll and performance management), along with administration and delivery of all HR plans and programs, further complicates matters.

Creating a holistic HR approach for executives, one that maximizes the odds of fulfilling the business strategies, requires retooling and achieving a smooth transition with various constituencies who each may have competing demands. Couple this with the many variations that exist for changing a company's capital structure, and it should be evident why early involvement and proper planning by the HR professional is critical. We believe that the information in this chapter will provide the reader with the information and guidance needed to anticipate and plan for capital structure change situations.

Although some similarities exist with the many capital change variations, the specific structure of a particular transaction must be understood, along with the strategic objectives of the change, in order to appropriately prioritize efforts and to design and align a forward-looking executive compensation plan and program. The following section provides a short summary of the most common forms of restructuring used by businesses.

Types of Restructurings

Spin-Offs

In a spin-off, a company distributes to its shareholders, on a pro rata basis, stock of a subsidiary company. If structured properly, the transaction is treated as a tax-free stock dividend, resulting in no cash to the distributing company. As a result, two independent, publicly traded companies now exist, each owned in the same proportion by the existing stockholders. The original company effectively distributes complete control of the subsidiary to its shareholders.

Initial Public Offering

In an initial public offering (IPO), some percentage of the shares of a private company is sold to the public. Typically, anywhere from 10 to 25 percent of a company's shares are initially sold. As a result, the company's stock becomes publicly traded on an exchange and the company receives cash for the shares sold.

Equity Carve-Outs

In an equity carve-out, a company sells a portion (generally 15% to 20%) of the stock held in a subsidiary corporation, typically through an IPO. The important thing to note is that the selling company receives cash for the shares sold and retains some ownership interest in the subsidiary company. In many instances, an equity carve-out will be followed by a spin-off (to the existing shareholders) of the remaining interest in the subsidiary.

Split-Ups and Split-Offs

In a split-up, a large company is split into two or more new companies. The original company then ceases to exist. Split-offs occur when the shares of a subsidiary are given to some (but not all) of the parent company shareholders in exchange for the parent company stock they hold.

Divestitures

Divestitures occur when a portion of a business is sold to a third party. Companies may sell a division, a product line, or a subsidiary. In such a case, a group of assets and/or employees will become owned by the buyer.

Summary

There are numerous forms of corporate restructuring, not all of which are mentioned here. The form ultimately chosen in a given situation will be a function of the objectives to be achieved, including shareholder value creation, along with the compliance requirements of the applicable tax, accounting, and securities laws. The important point here is to make certain that the form of the transaction is completely understood by those charged with the task of establishing and/or maintaining the executive compensation and overall human resources programs. Rather than trying to cover every specific executive compensation issue related to each type of corporate restructuring, this chapter will focus on the numerous executive compensation issues commonly arising in these specific types of transactions: IPOs, spin-offs, and divestitures.

Technical Requirements

This section provides an overview of the most pertinent executive-compensation-related technical rules to consider in capital structure change transactions. These rules have broad application and, therefore, should be kept in mind in all steps of formulating the executive compensation program.

Accounting

The accounting treatment afforded to the various forms of compensation can vary. Of particular importance is the accounting for long-term incentives such as stock options and restricted stock. "Variable plan" accounting requires a charge to earnings each reporting period based on fluctuations in the market price of the underlying stock. On the other hand, "fixed" accounting allows the grant price of the underlying stock to be expensed ratably over the vesting period, without considering price fluctuations (i.e., future stock price appreciation escapes an earnings charge). Under current accounting rules, the two primary forms of equity compensation that can receive fixed accounting treatment are time vesting stock options and restricted stock (assuming certain additional requirements are met). For example, stock option grants, in an "IPO'd" subsidiary, to parent company executives may generate an ongoing variable accounting charge, since the option recipients are not employees of the issuing entity.

In a restructuring transaction, it is common for outstanding equity compensation to undergo some modification (e.g., cashed out, exchanged for equity of a different entity, etc.). Without proper planning and an understanding of these accounting rules, the treatment of compensatory equity in a restructuring transaction could inadvertently trigger a full accounting charge where an otherwise lower or nonexistent accounting charge would lie.

Tax

Constructive Receipt

For a cash basis taxpayer, such as individuals, income is generally considered earned in the year in which it is received. However, even if income is not actually reduced to a taxpayer's possession, the income can be deemed "constructively received," and thereby taxable, if the income was otherwise made available to the taxpayer and the taxpayer had control over when the income is to be received. Given this constructive receipt doctrine, care needs to be used in offering executives involved in a capital structure change transaction the ability to choose or select between taxable and nontaxable forms of compensation. For example, giving an executive the choice of immediately cashing out or maintaining nonqualified bonus deferral accounts upon a spin-off or divestiture may result in taxation to the executive regardless of the executive's actual choice.

Internal Revenue Code Section 162(m)

Section 162(m) of the Internal Revenue Code ("IRC") provides for limits on the amount of nonperformance-based compensation paid to the top five executives that can be deductible by publicly held corporations. Generally, nonperformance-based compensation in excess of $1 million paid to the CEO and the four highest paid officers during the year cannot be deductible by the company. However, certain actions can be taken to help minimize the impact of Section 162(m) and allow certain types of compensation in excess of $1 million to be deductible. Further, care must be exercised to ensure that forms of compensation otherwise thought to be exempt from Section 162(m) (as being performance-based), do not lose their preferential treatment based on part of the transition plan of the capital structure change.

IRC Section 280G

Sections 280G and 4999 of the Internal Revenue Code are the sections that apply to payments, commonly known as "golden parachutes," made to the top paid "disqualified" executives in the context of a change in control of the company, such as a merger or acquisition. If these payments exceed an individual-by-individual statutorily defined level, then an excise tax (equal to 20%) is applied to the individual to a significant portion of the payments, and the company loses its tax deduction on a similarly significant amount of the payments. Certain capital structure changes may be deemed to be a change in control, and can inadvertently trigger the applicability of these onerous and arbitrary tax rules. Planning around these excise tax rules is possible if the rules are understood.

Securities

In addition to the accounting and tax issues, designers of executive compensation programs need to be aware of the securities laws and how they affect executive compensation. Some of the more common securities compliance issues include:

- **Section 16**–The insider trading rule requirements of Section 16 of the Securities Exchange Act of 1934 impose restrictions on when and how a corporate "insider" may buy and sell shares of company stock and/or company stock derivatives (e.g., stock options, phantom stock, deferred stock units, restricted stock). Governmental and public reporting requirements and profit disgorgement issues can arise particularly due to the strict liability nature of these rules.

- **Proxy Disclosure**–Each year public companies are required to disclose a summary of executive compensation using tables, an executive compensation report written by the compensation committee, and a graph which compares the company total shareholder return (TSR) to the TSR of a select group of companies. All compensation earned and/or delivered to top company executives needs to be reported.

- **Securities Registration Requirements Under the Securities Act of 1933**–Pursuant to Section 5 of the Securities Act of 1933 (the "1933 Act"), all securities that are sold in the United States, absent an exemption, must be registered with the SEC.

1. Registration under the 1933 Act can be burdensome for private companies due to the requirement of a full-blown registration.

2. Companies filing for an IPO must meet the 1933 Act registration requirements through the filing of a detailed and lengthy prospectus.

3. Public companies (which have already filed a full-blown securities registration statement) can generally rely on the streamlined procedure of filing a Form S-8 for the registration of securities to be issued in an employee benefit plan such as through a stock option, a restricted stock, or an omnibus long-term incentive plan.

• **Long-Term Incentive Plan**–The long-term incentive plan document provides for the terms and conditions under which various forms of equity compensation may be granted. Many companies implement an "omnibus" long-term incentive plan that allows for the grant of many forms of cash/performance-based compensation and equity-based compensation (e.g., stock options, restricted stock, performance shares, etc.). For companies that are already publicly traded, the long-term incentive plan is typically registered using a condensed Form S-8 registration statement, and submitted to shareholders for approval and disclosed in the proxy statement. Companies that are going public for the first time typically implement an omnibus plan just prior to the public offering, or do so as part of the offering. In such case, registration of the stock plan is "piggybacked" into the full-blown offering prospectus. A summary of the key SEC forms can be found at www.sec.gov/info/edgar/forms.htm.

The HR Implications of a Corporate Restructuring

A corporate restructuring will result in a significant change event that is sure to have an impact on the HR programs and systems of the "restructured" entity. Some of the most successful companies today understand that their people are their most valuable asset. Therefore, a successful restructuring event will require getting everyone aligned, informed, and excited about the new organization and its direction, including executives.

This section begins with a discussion of the executive compensation issues specific to IPOs and spin-off transactions and is followed by a discussion of issues specific to divestitures. This section concludes by summarizing some of the executive compensation implications generally applicable to all three transaction types.

IPOs and Spin-Offs

IPOs and spin-off transactions produce many of the same executive compensation issues due to the fact that, in either case, the company is becoming a public, stand-alone entity with new shareholders. The following discussion of key issues (which is not intended to be all-inclusive) pertains to both IPOs and spin-offs, unless otherwise noted.

Appropriate Executive Positions

Being an executive of a newly public company brings additional reporting and other responsibilities as compared to being an executive of simply a subsidiary. For example, a top executive of a public company may have responsibilities for multiple profit centers and the financial results of which, in the aggregate, are reported each period in publicly filed and audited financial statements for the world to see. Also, as compared to subsidiary executives, a company may need to hire executives for positions that may not have existed prior to the reorganization. For instance, executives may be needed for such functions as shareholder relations, media relations, and regulatory compliance.

Types of Pay

Generally speaking, privately owned companies do not deliver equity-based compensation to the extent publicly owned companies do. For example, a post-IPO company will typically experience a significant shift in the percentage of total compensation delivered through equity-based, long-term incentives. Private companies use base pay and annual bonus as the primary pay components. When long-term incentives are used, they typically take the form of cash/performance-based vehicles or phantom stock. Moving from a private to a public company will require a transition in the type of long-term incentive vehicles utilized, and in the overall mix of pay (between base, bonus, and long-term incentives).

Treatment of Outstanding Equity

In some situations, a subsidiary of a publicly traded company either undergoes an IPO or is spun off to shareholders. In many of these cases, the executives of the subsidiary company will hold stock options (or other equity-based awards) of the parent company. The company must determine whether these outstanding equity awards will be converted into equity of the (now public) subsidiary, cashed out, or forfeited. However, before any action is taken, the securities, tax, and accounting ramifications must be fully reviewed and understood.

First-Year Equity Grants

Many companies make a "special" restructuring grant to certain senior executives (possibly to executives of both the parent and the "to-be-spun" company) to celebrate the new company and to properly align interests. These grants can be competitively sized grants with the intention of making a normal-sized, first-year grant that reflects annual grant practices.

However, some companies opt for a front-loaded grant that is intended to cover an extended period (e.g., three years), and skip one or two annual grant cycles thereafter. In an IPO, this method has the advantage to recipients of providing a greater number of options at the initial IPO price.

Board of Director/Corporate Governance

As a public entity, more attention will be required on establishing and compensating a qualified board of directors. This may entail recruiting directors with appropriate skill sets. Also, director compensation will need to be reviewed to ensure that the type and amount of compensation is market-competitive.

In addition, becoming publicly owned throws a company into the highly scrutinized corporate governance arena. Due to the recent corporate mishaps, much focus has been placed on how the board of directors (and audit and compensation committees) operate.

The New York Stock Exchange (NYSE), the NASDAQ, and the AMEX have put forth new rules (which have not been adopted by the SEC as of the date of publication) aimed at improving corporate governance and alleviating the concerns of shareholders and the public. These rules, if and when they become effective, will impact such things as the membership of the board and its committees, the duties and responsibilities of the board and committees, the requirement of written charters, a code of ethics and governance guidelines, and the requirement for annual performance reviews of board and committee members.

Divestitures

In a divestiture, the seller must maintain the value of the entity (to be divested) at least until the close of the transaction. As a result, much more of the executive compensation focus is on retention of key individuals. The next two sections focus on the implications and rationale involved specifically in divestitures, followed by a discussion of retention as it applies generally to all types of restructurings.

Employment Uncertainty

When a divestiture is announced, executives may become uneasy about their future with the company due to the upcoming change in ownership. Many current executive positions may become redundant if the purchaser organization already has a qualified and tenured executive holding the position. Headhunting also proactively focuses on key executives in these corporate change situations. The implications of this disruption are: (i) a number of key executives may leave to join a more stable work environment; and (ii) executives scrambling to leave do not focus their attention on the ongoing business.

Retention/Severance Protection

Typically, the announcement of a divestiture requires a company to implement a retention program to help executives maintain objectivity in performing their duties. The four basic considerations of retention awards (i.e., the length of the retention period, the level of benefits, the form of benefits, and the timing of benefits) are discussed in the next section. However, for key executives whose jobs are clearly jeopardized, a retention award by itself may not be sufficient. In these situations, in addition to a retention award (which is paid for staying), severance protection may be necessary to assure these individuals that they will be protected in the event they are involuntarily terminated. Some coordination would be required between these benefits if both are to be paid. The advantage to severance protection is that retention benefits can be obtained while no actual company costs are incurred unless covered executives are actually terminated.

Divestiture Incentives

Although retention benefits and severance protections can be effective to retain senior management, these vehicles provide little direct incentive to improve the successful completion of the divestiture itself. For this reason, some companies will provide divestiture incentives or sale bonuses. In these situations, incentives are generally provided to a very limited group of individuals who will be actively involved in the marketing and the close of the divestiture, and to those who otherwise have the ability to directly influence the divestiture's success.

If used, divestiture incentives can take a number of different forms. Some incentives are structured as a straight percentage of the sale proceeds over some threshold level. For example, the individual would be eligible for a percent of sale proceeds over $100 million. This method may also include a cap on the potential incentive.

Another method provides a specified multiple of pay at various threshold levels. For example, a human resources vice president may be eligible for a divestiture incentive of one times annual base pay at the targeted sales point, and two times annual base pay at 120 percent of the targeted sales point. Transaction timing goals also may play a part in the size of the bonus.

A third method involves the use of stock options in the subsidiary entity to be divested. While this method clearly ties the incentive to the price obtained in the divestiture, it requires that a valuation be done to establish the exercise price.

HR Issues Common in All Restructurings

Many executive compensation issues arise regardless of the type of restructuring. This section addresses the most pressing executive compensation issues common to all transactions, including the following:

• Compensation philosophy;

• Severance protection;

• Retention; and

• Communication.

Each of these four areas is discussed in more detail below.

Compensation Philosophy

Following a corporate restructuring transaction, a company's compensation philosophy will need to be examined and modified to reflect the company's post-restructuring posture. The compensation philosophy will help to define how competitively the company desires to compensate executives against a peer group of similarly situated companies. Within the overarching compensation philosophy, there is a well-defined purpose and role for each pay component. Each pay component should be analyzed to ensure that it is: (i) delivering the value intended, (ii) satisfying its intended role while not negating the desired impact of other pay components, and (iii) consistent with the new compensation philosophy.

Base Salary

An executive's base salary represents an integral component of the overall compensation opportunity. Base salary is not an entitlement but, rather, remuneration for services provided. Payment of base salary is typically offered to:

• Position compensation at the intended competitive market position;

• Recognize an executive's immediate contribution to the organization; and

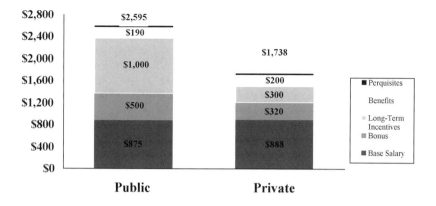

- Establish an appropriate level of incentive and welfare benefits (as many components of the executive compensation package are tied to base salary).

Following a restructuring, base pay levels often remain unchanged in the short-term. However, the comparator group used for competitive pay studies will likely change to reflect the new company's size, structure, and newly-public nature. This change in the corporate comparator group will likely result in the need to alter pay levels over time. The following chart shows the potential difference in pay levels for a CEO at a public versus private company (each with $2 billion in revenues).

In addition, position-matching changes may be necessary given the changes in job responsibilities and reporting relationships. This is particularly true for the executive population. Most importantly, due to the high correlation of executive pay levels with annual revenue size of the entity, if a company is being spun off from a much larger concern, chances are that competitive pay levels will decrease. This will cause significant transition issues and may require one-time special equity grants to make up for a decreasing or frozen base pay and annual bonus program.

Annual Incentives

One way to provide payment of compensation based on the achievement of preestablished performance criteria is through an annual incentive plan. This type of pay program is essential for new stand-alone entities. It encourages executives to meet certain short-term milestones and/or performance measures selected by the board of directors or the compensation committee. The performance measures to be selected should reflect the business strategy and goals of the new organization. Short-term incentives are typically offered to communicate critical success factors and to motivate executives to seek higher levels of success. Some design decisions to be considered include:

- **Eligibility**–How will executives be selected to participate in the annual plan?
- **Size of Opportunity**–What will be the minimum, target, and maximum bonus opportunity for each executive?
- **Performance Measures**–What performance measure(s) and levels will be selected to align executive actions/behaviors with the strategic direction of the company?
- **Shareholder Approval of Plan (for Tax Purposes)**–Will shareholders be asked to approve the annual bonus plan? If shareholders approve the plan (and if certain other conditions are met), payouts under the plan may be considered performance-based and will not be impacted by the IRC Section 162(m) deductibility limitation (as previously discussed).

If the executive was recruited from a parent entity (pre-restructuring), an issue exists as to how the annual bonus from the original entity will be paid to the executive who leaves during the year to accept a position at the new stand-alone company. Alternatives include:

- Pay out the entire annual bonus at either the target amount or based on actual results; or
- Pay out the annual bonus on a pro-rata basis based on the number of months employed by the parent.

Long-Term Incentives

As mentioned earlier, any restructuring event will have some impact on long-term incentives. First, the organization will need to determine how to treat any outstanding awards (granted prior to the restructuring). Second, it must be determined when and how future grants of the new company will be made. Other considerations affecting the use of equity compensation include:

- **Dilution**–Dilution measures the potential value-reducing effect of equity-based compensation plans on the ownership of current shareholders. As a result, shareholders (especially any institutional shareholders) will pay close attention to the grants made to employees, particularly to executives. Thus, care must be exercised in determining the pool of shares to be utilized for executive long-term incentive grants.
- **Global Impact**–Granting stock options to executives outside of the United States poses additional concerns. First, the attractiveness of receiving stock

options as part of the overall compensation package may differ from country to country. Second, there are technical issues (accounting, taxation, and securities) that may affect the grants on a country-by-country basis. In addition, the value of long-term incentive grants may vary based on the compensation philosophy (e.g., will long-term incentive values be based on a global or local basis?).

Retirement Benefits

Retirement benefits are an important component of the total compensation package offered to executives. Retirement benefits can be delivered to executives through qualified plans, nonqualified plans, or both. If the executives have retirement benefits provided through plans that will remain in existence (e.g., a corporation initiates an IPO), then there may not be an immediate need for adjustment. However, if the executives are provided retirement benefits through plans that will remain available only to employees of the former parent organization (e.g., in the case of an IPO followed by a spin-off of the remaining shares or in a divestiture), then the new company will need to implement new retirement programs. Oftentimes these may be modeled after the parent company programs but, in others, that may not be feasible due to cost concerns, employee demographics, etc. The following are some of the issues to consider in developing retirement programs.

Qualified Plans

Qualified plans are those retirement plans that are intended to meet the funding and other requirements dictated by the Employee Retirement Income Security Act of 1974 (ERISA). Qualified plans can be designed in several ways including defined benefit plans, defined contribution plans, or cash-balance plans. The type of qualified plan chosen by a company, if any, will be based on what objectives must be met. There are numerous design issues that must be considered when implementing a qualified plan including, but not limited to:

• Will the plan be a defined contribution, defined benefit, or cash-balance type plan?

• Will the executives get age, service, and vesting credit for past service at the parent company?

• If a defined benefit plan, what will be the targeted pay replacement?

• If a defined contribution plan, will the company provide any contributions and, if so, how much (e.g., through company match, profit sharing, discretionary, etc.)?

Nonqualified Plans

In contrast with qualified plans, nonqualified plans are designed to be exempt from most of the requirements of ERISA. Therefore, although funds may be set aside to pay benefits in the future, nonqualified plans must be "unfunded." Any such funds set aside remain subject to the company's creditors in the event of bankruptcy. This characteristic of nonqualified plans helps to maintain the nontaxable nature of the plans. Any of the following can be considered nonqualified retirement plans:

• Defined benefit restoration plans;

• Defined contribution restoration plans;

• Supplemental executive retirement plans (SERPs); and

• Voluntary nonqualified deferred compensation plans (VNDCs).

Severance Protection

Change in Control ("CIC") Protection

A restructuring transaction that results in the company becoming a stand-alone entity increases the likelihood that a CIC of the company may occur. Therefore, many companies often review the desirability and need for a CIC program to protect the senior management team on a prospective basis, including the following:

• **Rationale for CIC Protection**–The most significant factors underlying the decision to adopt a CIC program include the following:

• **Executive Security**–The destabilizing impact of a potential CIC on employees can create a significant disruption to operations. Employees often perceive a CIC as a direct threat to their continued employment, due to the job redundancies that often result. CIC severance protection can help neutralize the negative impact stemming from this perception by offering the prospect of some form of financial bridging in the event of a CIC-related termination. CIC arrangements can be critical to minimizing the workforce disruptions to productivity and morale that result from pending CIC activity. It is also important to promote job stability and retention even if the transaction is not consummated and the company remains independent.

Due to the potentially high levels of merger and acquisition activity, companies of all sizes and within all industries experience challenges stemming from employee insecurity even when no deal is currently pending. Accordingly, CIC severance protection has become a more visible and important component of the overall compensation program of these employees, often impacting the company's ability to attract and retain top talent.

• **Executive Retention During CIC**–CIC transactions frequently result in the elimination of many top executive positions. Those employees who remain often face a dramatically altered work environment, with a new–potentially hostile–management structure.

The knowledge of these impending changes can cause wholesale turnover among executives whose continued employment is critical to consummating the transaction. This is especially true where there is a significant amount of time between public knowledge and completion of the deal. CIC severance agreements can operate as a retention incentive, since participants typically will not receive the heightened level of severance unless they are terminated after the transaction is completed (severance typically is not paid for voluntary terminations after the close of the deal, or for any form of termination prior to the CIC).

• **Maintenance of Executive Objectivity**–The risks and insecurities described above can result in executives taking a less open view toward potential business combinations and may even result in executives opposing the CIC. One of the primary objectives in adopting a CIC program is to counterbalance these hurdles to transactions which would benefit shareholders–the protection presented by the CIC arrangement can offset the downside risk the potential deal presents.

Similarly, in the event of competing CIC offers, executives may be prone to favor the organization which promises the most favorable post-CIC working environment. A CIC arrangement can serve to focus executives on maximizing shareholder value through the transaction, regardless of the employment risks faced by the executives.

• **Compensation for Career Dislocation**–Another goal of most severance programs is to help terminated employees financially bridge the period of unemployment. In the case of top executives, equivalent jobs are often difficult to obtain quickly, making the cost of termination more significant. In addition, late-service executives stand to lose some of the most significant buildup in a number of components of their compensation arrangements–most notably, supplemental retirement income plans, where values typically rise most substantially after age 55.

- **Potential Participation**–Actual participation in a CIC program should be based on the facts and circumstances of each situation. Typically, CIC severance protection is extended to executives that are critical to effectively consummating the transaction and to those who are at the greatest risk of being terminated.

  Delivery of CIC protection is typically provided in one of two ways:

- Providing for different levels or "tiers" of participation related to the organizational structure; or

- One level of protection for all executives covered.

  Factors considered in determining participation would include reporting level, duties and responsibilities, susceptibility to termination, and participation in "key employee" plans and programs.

- **General Severance**–Even if companies opt to not implement a CIC program, the top executives should be provided some level of general severance in the event of an involuntary termination without cause. This will provide some of the protections described above, but will differ significantly in the level of benefits provided (general severance typically provides for lower benefits) and the types of terminations that result in benefits.

Retention

The announcement of a contemplated restructuring (e.g., a divestiture) can lead to a considerable amount of uncertainty, particularly among members of senior management whose positions may be jeopardized by the transaction. This uncertainty can lead to the departure of key members of senior management just at the time when the retention of those individuals is critical. For these reasons, many companies implement retention programs in connection with the announcement of a contemplated divestiture.

Retention arrangements involve four basic considerations: the length of the retention period, the level of benefits, the form of the benefits, and the timing of the payment of the benefits. The following discusses each of these considerations in the context of a divestiture.

Length of Retention Period

The length of the retention period needs to cover the entire period of uncertainty. If the retention period is not long enough, there is a risk that a company will incur retention expenses without accomplishing the intended retention objectives. Further, an unintended cliff may occur immediately following payout of the retention award, during which executives may actually be enticed to leave if the retention plan is designed with an inappropriately short retention period.

With divestitures, the length of the retention period is often tied to the anticipated time to complete the divestiture, with the actual closing date triggering at least a partial payout. The principal objective is to retain senior management through consummation of the transaction. In some instances, the retention period extends for a period of time following consummation of the transaction. This design is intended to provide assurances to potential investors of the stability of management through a transition period following consummation.

Level of Benefits

The level of benefits provided depends on the individual's current pay, the importance of the individual to the organization, and the likelihood the individual may leave. The greater the individual's pay, the more benefits that will be required to create a meaningful retention incentive. The more important the individual is to the organization, the more an organization may be willing to provide to retain that individual. Finally, the likelihood that an individual will leave may bear on the amount of retention benefits provided. An individual with numerous other opportunities may warrant more retention benefits than one with limited opportunities.

Another factor that bears on the level of retention benefits are existing levels of unvested long-term incentives (the same applies to unvested retirement benefits). To the extent an individual has significant value in unvested long-term incentives that would be lost on resignation, the need for significant retention benefits may be reduced. Absent significant long-term incentive values, the level of retention benefits becomes more important.

Form of Benefits

Retention benefits are usually provided through cash or restricted stock. Restricted stock may make less sense in a divestiture situation where the individual will no longer be employed by the entity issuing the stock. Performance-based retention incentives tend to be more effective where the retention period is long enough to permit the individuals to impact performance. Note, however, that the most common practice (to obtain the most direct retention result) is to pay out on the mere passage of time—without also requiring the achievement of a preestablished performance goal.

Timing of Benefits

The timing of benefits can have a significant impact on the overall effectiveness of a retention program. If significant amounts of the benefits are paid too early in the retention period, the organization risks paying for retention never received. Further, paying benefits in two payments may act to extend the retention value of a program without adding additional company cost.

Communication

Any changes to an organization's mission or goals, such as those encountered when undergoing a restructuring, can shock both the organization's structure and culture. By recognizing the potential effects, planning carefully, and executing a thorough communication effort, an organization can minimize any potentially risky effects of the restructuring and provide a smooth transition. A well-defined communication plan is crucial not only for the executive population, but to keep all employees informed throughout the transition process.

Communication Should Be an Ongoing Process—Not an Event

Communication during any restructuring is an ongoing process—not an event. Unlike the announcement of a new product, service, or facility, the announcement of a new organization evokes emotions and concerns that must be addressed over the span of weeks or months.

The most challenging questions are not raised immediately. They emerge after people have had a chance to reflect on the implications of the restructuring. New directions take time to smooth out. For these reasons, a communication strategy should take into consideration a time frame of a year or more.

Establish Communication Principles

Every communication should be able to satisfy the following key criteria: what you want people to know, what you want people to do, and how do you want people to feel. Therefore, communications should be organized and crafted around the following principles:

- **Honesty**—Possible bad news such as layoffs (if applicable), lower job titles, and reduced responsibilities will be faced squarely and communicated promptly, without sugarcoating. Good news such as enhanced career opportunities in the new organization will be communicated with equal candor.

- **Integrated Messages**—In an organization undergoing such a change, it's important to integrate the messages; to communicate both the big picture and the detail for each individual ("what does this mean to me?").

- **Consistent Messages**—Messages should be consistent across the organization. A key to achieving consistency is the in-depth involvement of leadership in the communication process. Public presentations, memos and letters, and e-mail responses from the appropriate spokesperson to questions allow stakeholders to check rumors and possible misinformation against an authoritative source.

- **Upward Communication**—Employees have good ideas, including ideas about improved productivity, better customer service, and more effective management. To capture these ideas, leadership should incorporate upward feedback mechanisms, including upward appraisals of management.

- **Evaluation of Communication Effectiveness**—The communications process should be subject to continuous improvement. Build ongoing feedback mechanisms to measure communication effectiveness and to help management structure ongoing communications.

Know Your Stakeholders

Identify and define stakeholder groups and assess the effectiveness of current communications. To identify the strategic challenges surrounding the restructuring transaction, conduct interviews, focus groups, and/or surveys. During these sessions, assess the current willingness to accept the change, how each group prefers to receive information, what feedback mechanisms currently exist so that progresses can be tracked and measured, and gain a snapshot of the current state of attitudes, concerns, and perceptions.

Develop a Targeted Communications Strategy

Through the development of the communication strategy, you will answer key questions that will allow the organization to deliver relevant and timely communications. The communication strategy will include the identification of stakeholders and their information needs as well as how and when to deliver the relevant messages. It is intended to be a living document to define and manage the communication needs of the organization as it undergoes transformation. The communication team will continue to define information needs and messages as the restructuring progresses

Cascade From Level to Level

The best method for unveiling an organizational restructuring is to "cascade" it from level to level. The formation of a new business organization will affect everyone. Employees prefer receiving the message from their direct supervisors, rather than from an HR manager or executive with whom they have no regular contact.

Focus on Personal Impact–Identify the Change Influencers

"Change influencers" are groups or individuals that are able to impact how the change is accepted by the rest of the organization and/or are responsible for implementing the change. Many times a change influencer could be a manager.

When communicating to a change influencer, keep in mind that he or she will focus first on how the restructuring will affect them personally; their future, their status, and their compensation. Before you expect the change influencer to deal confidently with the concerns and questions of their employees (audience group) you need to build both their understanding and acceptance.

Use CEO as Spokesperson

Typically, the most credible spokesperson for a restructuring is the chief executive. Employees want to hear the CEO's thinking and understand his or her vision regarding the outcome of this transition. Since the CEO is the principal agent of this major change event, his or her time will be required at major communication events.

Address Change Influencer/Managers' Communication Needs

Though change influencers and top managers usually provide strong support for a restructuring, they are not always effective spokespersons for getting the story across. They have special communication needs. To ensure these individuals present the background and issues with a consistent rationale, they need to receive periodic briefings and scripted presentation outlines.

State What Is Known When It's Known

Communicate what is known without waiting until everything is known. Silence provides the perfect grist for the rumor mill to operate at full speed. Rather than waiting for all names to be put into the new organizational chart, it's best to communicate where the restructuring stands on a semifinal basis–even though positions still may be unfilled. Of course, the full organizational chart should be distributed as soon as it is finalized.

Set Up a Rumor Control Mechanism

Establish a way to deal with rumors. Even with fast-moving cascade communication, the grapevine will pass information faster. Rumors should be forwarded to a central source who can create a response to them, and send both the rumor and the response to all managers. Some contingency communication media, such as telephone hotlines, electronic mail, or posted bulletins should be available for use if needed.

Manager Preparation Is Key

Despite divestiture activities and the seemingly constant changes presented, business must carry on as usual and everyone must continue to meet customer, client, and business needs.

Repeat Mission and Vision

You need to repeat the organization's mission and vision statement constantly. An understanding of both will put the restructuring into perspective and will provide a framework for adapting. While employees may read and hear about the organization's strategic plan, they may not experience direct results until the transition is completed.

Day-to-Day Issues are Important

Employees care about day-to-day logistics issues. As mundane as these may seem and to minimize disruption, the operational details need to be communicated early in the process.

Communication Needs to Extend Beyond Announcement

Consider other communication needs. Recognize that the divestiture will affect all communication elements now used in each work unit. The communication plan should acknowledge that other materials need to be adapted and updated as quickly as possible.

Tap Internal Resources

Wherever possible, internal resources should be utilized. Because the audience for transition communication goes beyond the employee population, the role of public relations will be important. The messages for outside audiences should agree with messages to employees.

Summary

Corporate restructuring transactions play a major role in the ongoing evolution of companies. These types of transactions produce human resources issues that in some cases may "make or break" the deal. Therefore, it is important for the human resources team to understand the specific type of transaction being proposed, as each will have its own set of issues. The human resources team must also understand the technical (tax, accounting, and securities laws) ramifications of the various compensation and benefit plan designs and actions.

Many issues such as compensation philosophy, severance, and retention are important regardless of the type of transaction and should be thoroughly understood. Finally, communication is vital to the success of any restructuring campaign. A well-developed communication strategy should help minimize potential risk factors while encouraging actions necessary for a smooth transition.

Human resource professionals should feel an obligation to bring executive compensation considerations to the forefront of any capital change transaction. The planning aids provided on the CD for this chapter can assist you in anticipating and preparing for many of the compensation issues that arise in conjunction with a restructuring.

Practice aids found on the CD for this chapter:
Appendix A: IPOs–A Checklist for HR Professionals

• Workforce Strategy

• Executive Equity

• Broad-Based Equity

• Retirement Redesign

• Health and Welfare Benefits

• Communication/Change Management

• HR Delivery/Technology

• Leadership Assessment

• Organizational/Cultural Considerations

Appendix B: Divestitures–A Checklist for Executive Protections

• Executive Protections to Be Considered

• Why Executive Protections are Important

• Executive Protections–Action Plan

ROBERT A. ROMANCHEK

Robert A. Romanchek, J.D., CPA, leads Hewitt's Midwest Market Group Executive Compensation Practice and is a manager of Hewitt Associates LLC with more than 18 years of experience providing guidance on a broad range of executive compensation-related matters, both domestic and global.

Bob has consulted with hundreds of public companies, and his expertise includes all forms of long-term incentives, executive supplemental retirement and deferral programs and their related funding mechanisms, change-in-control and general severance programs, employment contracts, retention plans, and executive pay levels. He also has specialized executive compensation knowledge in global merger and acquisition transactions, in initial public offering/spin-off/divestiture situations, as well as in turnarounds and bankruptcy proceedings. Bob also has authored numerous articles and publications in the executive compensation area, and is a frequent speaker at industry and trade group events. His recent work has included considerable time spent consulting directly with the Compensation Committees of various Boards on issues pertaining to corporate governance, executive compensation, and outside director pay.

Bob is a graduate of the DePaul University College of Law, and also holds an M.B.A., *cum laude*, from the DePaul University College of Commerce. His undergraduate degree is in accounting and economics.

THOMAS W. RAMAGNANO

Thomas A. Ramagnano is a consultant in the Talent & Organization consulting practice at Hewitt Associates LLC. He consults on a broad range of executive compensation matters, including mergers and acquisitions, short- and long-term incentives, executive pay levels, employment agreements, executive retirement and deferral programs, change in control, and severance.

Prior to joining Hewitt, Tom worked for a global manufacturing company as Tax and General Counsel. His responsibilities covered a wide range of tax, legal, and corporate governance issues. Tom is the co-author of *U.S. Companies Buying in Europe: HR Issues of EU Directives*, published in the *International HR Journal* Fall 2000 issue. In addition, he co-authored a chapter titled "Executive Compensation Plans" in *The Handbook of Employee Benefits, Fifth Edition*.

Tom holds an M.B.A. from the Kellogg Graduate School of Management (Northwestern University), a J.D. from Loyola University of Chicago School of Law, and a bachelor's degree in accounting from Indiana University.

INDEX

CD-ROM Contents

The CD-ROM included with this publication contains checklists, sample documents, templates, and other practice aids pertaining to specific chapters throughout the book.

Subject to the conditions of the license agreement and limited warranty, presented below, you may duplicate or modify the files as needed for your personal use.

The files on the CD-ROM are intended to be used in conjunction with Microsoft Word® and Adobe Acrobat® (or Acrobat® Reader®) software.

Accessing the Files

The CD-ROM contains an auto-run feature which will automatically open and present the user with the main menu upon inserting the CD. If the settings on your computer prevent this, simply open your preferred Internet browser (e.g., Internet Explorer), select "Open," browse to your CD drive and choose the file named "index.htm" on the CD. This will open the file in a new window.

6. TERMINATION: This license is effective until terminated. This license will terminate automatically without notice from the Company and become null and void if you fail to comply with any provisions or limitations of this license. Upon termination, you shall destroy the Documentation and all copies of the SOFTWARE. All provisions of this Agreement as to warranties, limitation of liability, remedies or damages, and our ownership rights shall survive termination.

7. MISCELLANEOUS: This Agreement shall be construed in accordance with the laws of the United States of America and the State of California and shall benefit the Company, its affiliates, and assignees.

8. LIMITED WARRANTY AND DISCLAIMER OF WARRANTY: The Company warrants that the SOFTWARE, when properly used in accordance with the Documentation, will operate in substantial conformity with the description of the SOFTWARE set forth in the Documentation. The Company does not warrant that the SOFTWARE will meet your requirements or that the operation of the SOFTWARE will be uninterrupted or error-free. The Company warrants that the media on which the SOFTWARE is delivered shall be free from defects in materials and workmanship under normal use for a period of thirty (30) days from the date of your purchase. Your only remedy and the Company's only obligation under these limited warranties is, at the Company's option, return of the warranted item for a refund of any amounts paid by you or replacement of the item. Any replacement of SOFTWARE or media under the warranties shall not extend the original warranty period. The limited warranty set forth above shall not apply to any SOFTWARE which the Company determines in good faith has been subject to misuse, neglect, improper installation, repair, alteration, or damage by you. EXCEPT FOR THE EXPRESSED WARRANTIES SET FORTH ABOVE, THE COMPANY DISCLAIMS ALL WARRANTIES, EXPRESS OR IMPLIED, INCLUDING WITHOUT LIMITATION, THE IMPLIED WARRANTIES OF MERCHANTABILITY AND FITNESS FOR A PARTICULAR PURPOSE. EXCEPT FOR THE EXPRESS WARRANTY SET FORTH ABOVE, THE COMPANY DOES NOT WARRANT, GUARANTEE, OR MAKE ANY REPRESENTATION REGARDING THE USE OR THE RESULTS OF THE USE OF THE SOFTWARE IN TERMS OF ITS CORRECTNESS, ACCURACY, RELIABILITY, CURRENTNESS, OR OTHERWISE.

IN NO EVENT, SHALL THE COMPANY OR ITS EMPLOYEES, AGENTS, SUPPLIERS, OR CONTRACTORS BE LIABLE FOR ANY INCIDENTAL, INDIRECT, SPECIAL, OR CONSEQUENTIAL DAMAGES ARISING OUT OF OR IN CONNECTION WITH THE LICENSE GRANTED UNDER THIS AGREEMENT, OR FOR LOSS OF USE, LOSS OF DATA, LOSS OF INCOME OR PROFIT, OR OTHER LOSSES, SUSTAINED AS A RESULT OF INJURY TO ANY PERSON, OR LOSS OF OR DAMAGE TO PROPERTY, OR CLAIMS OF THIRD PARTIES, EVEN IF THE COMPANY OR AN AUTHORIZED REPRESENTATIVE OF THE COMPANY HAS BEEN ADVISED OF THE POSSIBILITY OF SUCH DAMAGES. IN NO EVENT SHALL LIABILITY OF THE COMPANY FOR DAMAGES WITH RESPECT TO THE SOFTWARE EXCEED THE AMOUNTS ACTUALLY PAID BY YOU, IF ANY, FOR THE SOFTWARE.

SOME JURISDICTIONS DO NOT ALLOW THE LIMITATION OF IMPLIED WARRANTIES OR LIABILITY FOR INCIDENTAL, INDIRECT, SPECIAL, OR CONSEQUENTIAL DAMAGES, SO THE ABOVE LIMITATIONS MAY NOT ALWAYS APPLY. THE WARRANTIES IN THIS AGREEMENT GIVE YOU SPECIFIC LEGAL RIGHTS, AND YOU MAY ALSO HAVE OTHER RIGHTS WHICH VARY IN ACCORDANCE WITH LOCAL LAW.

ACKNOWLEDGMENT

YOU ACKNOWLEDGE THAT YOU HAVE READ THIS AGREEMENT, UNDERSTAND IT, AND AGREE TO BE BOUND BY ITS TERMS AND CONDITIONS. YOU ALSO AGREE THAT THIS AGREEMENT IS THE COMPLETE AND EXCLUSIVE STATEMENT OF THE AGREEMENT BETWEEN YOU AND THE COMPANY AND SUPERSEDES ALL PROPOSALS OR PRIOR AGREEMENTS, ORAL, OR WRITTEN, AND ANY OTHER COMMUNICATIONS BETWEEN YOU AND THE COMPANY OR ANY REPRESENTATIVE OF THE COMPANY RELATING TO THE SUBJECT MATTER OF THE AGREEMENT.